HISTORY'S SPOILED CHILDREN

KOSTAS KOSTIS

History's Spoiled Children

The Story of Modern Greece

Translated by

JACOB MOE

OXFORD
UNIVERSITY PRESS

Oxford University Press is a department of the
University of Oxford. It furthers the University's objective
of excellence in research, scholarship, and education
by publishing worldwide.

Oxford New York
Auckland Cape Town Dar es Salaam Hong Kong Karachi
Kuala Lumpur Madrid Melbourne Mexico City Nairobi
New Delhi Shanghai Taipei Toronto

With offices in
Argentina Austria Brazil Chile Czech Republic France Greece
Guatemala Hungary Italy Japan Poland Portugal Singapore
South Korea Switzerland Thailand Turkey Ukraine Vietnam

Oxford is a registered trade mark of Oxford University Press
in the UK and certain other countries.

Published in the United States of America by
Oxford University Press
198 Madison Avenue, New York, NY 10016

Library of Congress Cataloging-in-Publication Data is available
Kostas Kostis.
History's Spoiled Children: The Story of Modern Greece.
ISBN: 9780190846411

Printed in the USA on acid-free paper

CONTENTS

List of Tables and Graphs vii
List of Maps ix

Introduction 1
1. The Empire Transforms (1700–1821) 11
2. The War of Independence (1821–32) 47
3. The Bavarians in Greece (1833–43) 77
4. King Otto and the Greeks (1844–62) 109
5. The Greeks Among Themselves (1863–80) 147
6. The Flight Forward (1881–97) 189
7. Unexpected Developments (1898–1913) 217
8. A New Greece (1914–23) 247
9. Parliament and Dictatorship (1924–40) 267
10. Wars (1941–9) 293
11. The Anti-communist State (1950–74) 331
12. In Europe (1974–2010) 365
13. Crisis (2007–) 397

History's Spoiled Children: In Lieu of an Epilogue 423

Notes 431
Bibliography 443
Index 447

LIST OF TABLES AND GRAPHS

2.1: Places of Origin and Catechism for Members of the Etaireia 49
4.1: Greek State Public Spending 1833–62 123
4.2: Adjusted Public Expenditure by Category, 1833–62 125
4.3: Taxation Rate in Greece, 1834–62, in Drachmas Per Capita as a Percentage of GDP 128
4.4: Estimates of the National Estates by Leading Contemporaries and Historians 131
5.1: Population and Extent of Greece, 1828–79 162
5.2: Distribution (%) of the Population of Greece by Geographic Regions, 1839–79 166
5.3: Change (%) in the Population within the Greek Kingdom's Geographical Regions, 1828–1907 167
5.4: Per Capita Gross Domestic Product at Constant Prices, 1834–1912 170
5.5: Real GDP Per Capita in International Dollars with 1990 Purchasing Power Parity 171
5.6: Settlements with More Than 5,000 Inhabitants in Greece, 1856–79 176
5.7: Distribution of Cities by Geographic Region, 1856–79 177
5.8: Estimates of Infant Mortality in Greece, 1860–1910 181
6.1: Debt Servicing as a Percentage of Regular Income, 1833, 1912 208
6.2: Public Debt of Greece, 1869–93 (in drachmas) 208
6.3: Tax Burden in Greece, 1833–1912, in Drachmas Per Capita and as a Percentage of GDP 212
7.1: Relation of Indirect to Direct Taxes, 1879–1991 223
7.2: Total Taxes as a Percentage (%) of GDP, 1879–1911 224

7.3: Settlements with More Than 5,000 Inhabitants in Greece, 1879–1907 226
7.4: Distribution of Cities per Geographical Region, 1889–1907 226
7.5: Public Expenditure of the Greek State, 1862–1912 231
7.6: Adjusted Public Spending by Category (%), 1863–1912 232
9.1: Gross Domestic Product Per Capita in Constant Prices, 1912–38 (in 1914 Drachmas) 279
9.2: Ratio of Public Expenditure to GDP, 1912–38 (%) 285
10.1: Population Shift in Greece, 1930–46 301
10.2: Monetary Indicators, 1941–4 302
10.3: Industrial Production in Western Europe, 1947–51 326
11.1: Annual Percentage Change in Gross Fixed Capital Investments, 1950–73 347
11.2: Annual Percentage Change in Gross Domestic Product and Secondary Sector Production, 1950–74 349
11.3: Public Expenditure by Category as a Percentage of GDP, 1962–73 361
12.1: Public Sector Hires as % of Total Growth in Employment from 1975 to 2003 375
12.2: Average Annual Rates of Change for Basic Economic Indicators from 1982 to 2004 378
12.3: Employment and Educational Level of PASOK and New Democracy Voters 1993–2004 384

LIST OF MAPS

Map A: National Network of Roadways in 1892 201
Map B: The Greek Railway Network, 1912 228
Map C: The Balkan Peninsula, 1913 250

Greece Today

INTRODUCTION

The first edition of *History's Spoiled Children* was published in Greece in May 2013. The book is now in its seventeenth reprinting. It is not for me to judge the reasons for this success. I believe this book belongs to a class of scholarship that seeks to escape from stereotypical *Metapolitefsi* accounts of current-day Greece—that is, accounts examining the period following the fall of the seven-year military dictatorship (1967–74)—all of which have experienced a greater or lesser degree of success in the Greek publishing market. Though a concerted national effort has been made to revisit the country's past and present through a more contemporary perspective, outdated stereotypes—such as those just mentioned above—prevail internationally. With this in mind, an explanation of what I attempted to accomplish in this book may be useful for the international reader; that is to say, an elaboration of the ways in which I moved against the current of existing attempts to interpret Greek history.

First of all, I must insist that I did not seek to write a general history of Greece—in fact, I am not even sure exactly what this would mean. The subheading of the book, 'The Formation of the Modern Greek State from the Eighteenth to the Twenty-First Century', clearly defines my focus.

I was mainly interested in studying the ways in which the state forms as a human community, one that, as Max Weber states, claims a monopoly on the legitimate use of violence. The term 'formation' refers to a particular methodological approach, and to specific theories of the state, which thus impose constraints on the way the subject is analysed. Thus the book contains elements related to the study of state-formation as a field of research, a field that has been much enriched since the 1960s.

The starting point for such an approach is the rather obvious idea that it is impossible to understand a state outside its environment; in other words, that the concept of an 'individual state' cannot exist. We are only able to understand the process of state-formation as one linked to the relationships developed in an inter-state system, regardless of whether state sovereignty takes a ruler, a nation or a people as its point of reference.

We must therefore understand Greece, and other nations, as states invested in their own geopolitical power, exercising policies serving their own interests in an environment of relentless international competition. In this context, Greece, like all states, has sought to strengthen its military and diplomatic power in every which way so as to achieve its objectives. Through such an approach, I believe we can better understand the position of the Greek state, both avoiding a moralising treatment of various problems and understanding political practices themselves much more effectively.

The entire process of 'modernising' the Greek state, and other states, can be explained in this manner, without recourse to a bourgeois class (which in this case was non-existent or had extremely limited influence). Bismarck, for example, was the creator of modern Germany, though I doubt anyone ever described him as a 'bourgeois moderniser'. He remained forever a representative of Prussia's big landowners.

In the same manner, a realistic approach to the state helps to avoid various moralistic approaches that are all too common in Greek historiography, such as the assumption that military weaponry is a terrible thing, because, whether we speak of Greece, Prussia or any other state, in the end everything begins with the army. That is where the core of the state is found. A modern army is much more than an aggregate of people: it is also public administration, technology, transportation, education and economy. And the proof of Greece's need to create an army capable of fighting—capable of more than eliminating banditry or solely protecting the king's throne—arose when the Crimean War brought upheavals to the international economic and political environment that completely upset pre-existing approaches to international relations. In other words, King Otto's Greece was a country that did not have the ability to claim all that its ruler thought it rightfully could. Contrarily, under the rule of George I and Charilaos Trikoupis (who served as prime minister of Greece seven times between 1875 until 1895), Greece was obliged to change completely in order to survive on the inter-state playing field, since the balances and constraints of the Concert of Europe were no longer in place. The Great Powers no longer decided on behalf of the smaller states, or, at least, not to the extent that they did before the Crimean War. Each country would have to cope with international circumstances, making the most of its capabilities in various sectors. The situation worsened in 1878, when the time constraints for resolving the Eastern Question proved exceedingly restrictive. This was during the transition from the 'Great Idea' to the 'Model Kingdom', a race Greece ran to ensure its geopolitical survival.

The importance of this approach is evident in every historical period, and, naturally, at every latitude and longitude. Indeed, in previous periods, the emergence of a transnational system under the Treaty of Westphalia enabled a better understanding of the transformations experienced in the Ottoman Empire, and how, through these transformations, Orthodox Christian subjects of the empire became Greeks, gaining such stature within the empire that a certain group of them was motivated to claim their autonomous political status.

Finally, this approach allows us to escape from our excessive ethnocentrism. For example, post-war Greece is often characterised as a 'stunted democracy' or described in other similar terms that suggest an incomplete political system in comparison with the ideal systems represented, naturally, by Western nations. The reason for this is the existence of the so-called 'Para-Constitution'—the extra-constitutional regulations enforced mostly from the period of the Civil War onwards.

But I could never understand why this para-constitutional Greece was a more stunted democracy than the United States of the same period, with its limitations on the political rights of African Americans or the effects of McCarthyism; the same goes for Italy and its parastatal organisations, or France with its flagrant violations of constitutional legality during the decolonisation period. In fact, Greece was just as democratic as the remaining Western nations, and an anti-communist state like the rest of the Western world. If we uphold this rationale of stunted democracy, we avoid recognising the entire international environment determining the existence of the Greek state, an environment that shaped each and every country, Greece included. We fashion ourselves as a particularity, overlooking our similarities with the other populations of the Western world.

The social foundations of the international restrictions upon which the state functions consist of societies, or, more correctly, societies of peasants with unique economic practices, social codes and political cultures. It would be inconceivable to trace the history of a country such as Greece without taking into account the analytical tools to study these societies, crafted with great care by sociologists, historians and anthropologists. Above all, such a view mitigates the rigidity of the polarising traditionalist–modernist opposition, one that, in my opinion, offers little instrumental use.

I must add here that this rationale based on peasant societies does not exclude the existence of cities, merchants or even factories; quite the contrary, in fact, since it presupposes the existence of a surrounding society. It enables us to better track significant changes taking place in Greece, and especially to realise that the country's great social transformation did not take place until after the Second World War. It also offers all the tools necessary for understanding certain critical moments in Greek history—the War of Independence, the occupation and the Civil War, for example—without resorting to political refrains or simplified solutions that ignore the nature of the populations informing the societal status quo. Certainly, in these cases, the results may prove relatively mundane and debunk models we hoped might exist, but they are clearly more accurate with respect to lived experience and expectations.

In so using the tools of this 'society of peasants', social dynamics retain all their significance and are integrated into a wider framework, which—in my opinion—provides the historical dimension needed to render it realistic.

This then allows us to make use of certain variables that link the international environment to local reality. One such variable is the institutionalisation of political power, which allows us to survey the degree to which political machinations are embedded in certain state institutions, or, in another reading, the extent to which state authority can impose its own rules on the political scene. From this perspective, we may observe transitions in mechanisms of governance employed by the modern state, and the setbacks in this process.

In the Ottoman Empire, this process began in the eighteenth century and was upset by the Greek War of Independence. The same process reappeared as a major concern for the nineteenth-century Greek state: it tempered the power of political oligarchies and rendered the nation a democracy. The situation changed with the Balkan Wars, and even more so during the Second World War—at which point the impact was felt all around Europe. The period of European civil war, which in the Greek case lasted until at least 1974, demonstrated both the upheavals that occur in the process of state-formation and the non-linear nature of historical evolution. What remains to be seen is whether the *Metapolitefsi* is a temporary phase, or whether the process of its political institutionalisation, currently under extreme pressure, is in a position to survive.

A second and equally important variable is the penetration of state mechanisms in a national territory and population. Though indirect mechanisms of governance had previously prevailed, modern states now sought direct control over their populations.

The simplest way to estimate the degree of state penetration in an area and population is, naturally, through statistics: police stations per square kilometre, policemen per thousand residents, schools, public warehouses per unit of space and so on. But, in fact, for the most part these are secondary effects of a developed transportation network. From the latter, we may estimate the degree of state cohesion, the existence of a national territory and—some might even say—a national market.

Such a network only came into existence relatively late in Greece. At least until 1870, connective links between the state's various territories were lacking. This was a logical consequence of the lack of transportation networks at the national level—with the exception perhaps of sea routes, which in fact conformed to regional and even international standards. The result was simple: the Greek state may have been legally established in 1830, but networks of settlements—and certainly urban concentrations—continued to follow the pre-revolutionary model. Some urban centres were oriented to the west and others to the east. Certainly, no hierarchy had formed on a national level—that is, a hierarchy rooted in domestic forces.

This situation changed with public works in the Trikoupis era, even though the aims they served were other than those we are normally led to believe. It was only after this period that urban concentrations began to settle into a hierarchy, and only then that a clearer concept of national space emerged. But the big leap came during the interwar period, and, naturally, even more so after 1945. This was the period in which the available statistics reveal a hierarchically organised network of urban settlements.

This penetration into national territory had consequences for the population's governance. The initial model, one that Otto inherited from the Ottoman Empire, was nothing more than governance of a population by the political elite, a process of continuous negotiations between the king and groups of notables. The model of political organisation did not automatically shift with the passage from Ottoman hegemony to Otto's reign; nor did the reactions of the populace to their rulers. Indeed, any line of reasoning arguing that the state was created *ex niliho*, just because some laws were published in the government gazette at the time, is simply too bold and too naïve to be true.

This is why I decided to begin this study of the modern Greek state's formation with a chapter on the Ottoman Empire, which, theoretically, is not necessary. Through the transformation of the empire into a modern state, the institutionalisation of political power and the diffusion of mechanisms of power into the populace, conditions arose that drove the marginal elite—a fundamental variable in all revolutions—to initiate the War of Independence. It was the empire's transformation, and not its decline, that led to the creation of the Greek state. In any case, as much as the Bavarians sought to impose Western institutional models, the Greek state continued to be marked by hierarchies and power relations that had already existed during the Ottoman period, which the Bavarians in turn sought to incorporate into their new framework.

Practices of this type finally changed towards the end of the nineteenth century. But again, these changes mainly concerned regions that had acquired transportation infrastructure—something that did not occur on a broader scale. Indeed, in some instances it had even come to a halt. In this respect, the Greek state's annexation of new territories, with their inferior structures and infrastructure in comparison with the prevailing conditions in Old Greece, was a setback. It was only during the post-war period that the Greek state acquired all the elements necessary for direct governance of its population, despite the obvious fact that negotiations between local communities and the central government would never cease.

This penetration into state territory had other effects, the first being the gradual elimination of robbery, expressed to a large degree by banditry. Pacification of society is a key feature of modern nations, and the state under Otto had not been able to achieve such peace. All it achieved, at times, was the assimilation of its opponents, or, in other cases, the solution of 'exporting' them beyond state borders. The process of pacification only seemed to come to completion in the late nineteenth century, when the state gradually penetrated the countryside and limited the scope of freedom for various groups seeking to use coercion and violence for their own benefit. Only after the Second World War were these incidents completely eliminated.

The changing nature of state borders constitutes a similar case: in an admirable study, historian John Koliopoulos has identified and described the Greek kingdom's boundaries with the Ottoman Empire as completely permeable, crossed by various groups that used this phenomenon to their advantage. This was the border as frontier, and the Civil War would have to end to before the modern conception of a border was established, a border that determined (and was determined by) the modern state.

All these elements are fundamental to the process of state-formation, as well as the process of transitioning from one model of state organisation to another. It was during the transition from Otto's Greece (and indirect governance of the population) to the Greece of the twentieth century that the state penetrated into both territory and the population, asserting direct control over them.

We can understand exactly what this diffusion into territory means if we take the example of public health. A study of health in nineteenth-century Greece reveals that it did not constitute a problem the state confronted on behalf of its subjects; rather, it was seen as potential threat to the state itself. The individual did not exist, nor did society. The state was paramount. As a result of this conception, the state did not venture far into its territory and population, and efforts and exchanges occurred among elites with regard to disease—namely concerning empirical doctors—with the aim of incorporating the latter group into state mechanisms. In short, the health sector is an exemplary case for demonstrating what state-formation meant in nineteenth-century Greece.

Finally, all these variables must be complemented by a study of both the state and the range of activities it develops. To calculate the size of a state is straightforward; but before making this calculation, we must take into account the context in which these numbers are formed. In any case, the Greek state certainly was far from being the oversize state, or even the 'state-employer' we have all become accustomed to hearing about. Data at our disposal does not justify these claims. Thus we must put aside all reasoning that has been developed based on such logic, and abandon the possible consequences of this issue, which often take on a life of their own unrelated to the original issue. If the state is not so large, it then becomes hard to justify the existence of a clientelistic state, even if we decide—in yet another exception to prevailing international trends adopted by the Greek historiographical community—to use this 'clientelist logic' to speak of politics in Greece. In fact, we need not resort to any of this. Indeed, on a macro-scale, the use of clientelism as an explanatory variable was abandoned internationally, if not by 1970 then surely by 1980. Of course, in Greece it continues to be used, whether by habit, or as the guilty symptom of a certain corruption that we have decided is a national trait—though it is more often a political pretext. But this line of thinking contributes nothing to efforts at understanding the formation of the modern Greek state.

I could keep listing such variables enabling study of the Greek state in accordance these previous models, but that seems unnecessary. According to Max Weber, a political community can be considered a modern state if it possesses certain characteristics: for example, an administrative and legal system that can be changed by legislation, and, regarding the latter, an administrative mechanism that manages affairs in accordance with legal regulations. The modern state possesses power that can be exercised over all individuals living within its territory and most of the activities taking place within its jurisdiction. Another characteristic is the legitimate use of force within this territory, insofar as it is allowed for or provided by the legitimate government. Therefore, all the variables I have previously mentioned—and many others I have omitted but will refer to later on, such as property rights and the marginal elites—directly or indirectly address characteristics of the state and underline potential divergences or convergences. These approaches enable us to discern the nature and features of state-formation itself.

There are two remaining points I would like to make: first, my choice not to overlook political history. In fact, I sought to speak in terms of political history, because I cannot imagine the processes of state-formation divorced from political fact. It would be like someone trying, in the name of some historiographical fundamentalism, to speak about a war without taking military operations or diplomacy into account. Because it is daily political practice that forms institutions, but also state mechanisms, which otherwise remain legal bodies with no content. Conversely, these same political practices effect change within—or outside—the institutional framework.

Though it may not always be possible to achieve the level of insight that such an approach necessitates, this is no reason to ignore it. Besides, it is important to recognise the difference between two different efforts at understanding post-war Greece: the first of which analyses political figures' actions in terms of a dependency that subjugates personal choices to foreign influence, and the second that grants individuals and groups the freedom to operate in a specific context. Here, I would like to reference a particularly indicative example. Post-war political policies may be understood one way if we concede that the Sacred Bond of Greek Officers (IDEA)-led coup was simply an attempt by officers to control the system in place and strengthen their place in the Papagos government, and another if, as is often wrongly assumed, we suppose that they continued to be active and led to the dictatorship. The National Union of Youth Officers (EENA), which leaders of the subsequent military coup participated in, had a completely different social and ideological makeup and orientation from IDEA, and it was this unique character that led to the coup on 21 April. These were two diverging ways of understanding processes of consolidating power mechanisms and, by extension, the formation of the state—unless we believe that the seizure of power does not concern the state. In one case, we have parties acting voluntarily within the Cold War environment of the time, while in the other they are subservient to foreign forces. These scenarios are entirely different from one another. Thus, I maintain that political history cannot and should not be absent from a history of state-formation.

The second point concerns documentation. Bibliographic references are selective, and I did not attempt a completely comprehensive approach, which would have been impossible for both personal and objective reasons. This selectiveness is based on my own preferences, something I have stated openly from the outset. In any case, I avoided adopting opinions, which, even if they seemed plausible, did not have any empirical basis. Thus, for example, I did not speak about the post-war bourgeois class born from the black market in the years of the occupation. There is no research that can support such a conception—in fact, evidence points to the contrary—and I consequently ignored it, even though it is such a widespread opinion that it is often considered a given. In fact, it expressed nothing more than a political faction's efforts to morally compensate for its political and military defeat in the wake of the Civil War. So, this category of opinions—those that are indeed widespread but lack even basic documentation—are ignored.

I would like to conclude by insisting on a rather obvious point. I sought to interpret the history of the formation of the modern Greek state differently, in a way that takes into account both the current situation and the changes that have come to Greek and international historiography. I do not know if I have succeeded or not, but the interest shown in the book gives me reason to believe that there is a corresponding openness to hearing something different.

The 'Spoiled Children of History' are clearly the Greeks that consider themselves entitled to special treatment because their ancestors laid the foundations of Western civilisation. Yet those who established Greek historiography over the course of the nineteenth century, and who defined themselves as those very same 'spoiled children of history', did so with their gaze towards the future, hoping for the creation of a new Greece.

Unfortunately, Greece today continues on a similar path, citing its past so as to avoid its future. Its leaders make arguments based on the nation's relationship to history, without having convinced anyone that they are in a position to safeguard the historical achievements of previous decades. More than ever, the country seems to be clinging to its past, refusing to look towards its future. To this end, I believe (perhaps naively) that a different reading of its history may help.

Before invoking the past, the Greeks must respect the present. To do this, they must think about their history in a different way. This, at least, is what

History's Spoiled Children has attempted: a study of the ways in which, over two centuries, a small province of the Ottoman Empire became (and continues to be) a prosperous state in the heart of Europe. But at this moment, the Greeks find themselves facing a challenge, and their response to it will determine Greece's future: the way forward seems difficult, and regression is not out of the question. In any case, 'History's Spoiled Children'—the Greeks, that is—now face one of the greatest challenges in their history, and nothing guarantees an auspicious future.

Athens, October 2016

1

THE EMPIRE TRANSFORMS

(1700–1821)

The Orthodox Christian aristocracy

In 1683, the last minute arrival of Polish King John Sobieski's military support rescued Vienna from the Ottomans and defined a critical period in the Ottoman Empire's history. One year later, the establishment of the Holy League by the Habsburgs, Poles and Venetians (with the Russians joining soon after) forced the Ottoman Empire into a military conflict that lasted nearly fifteen years and resulted in the Treaty of Karlowitz. Despite their impressive record at the negotiation table, Ottoman representatives were forced to concede the loss of essential European territories for the first time, to their opponents' great surprise.

Alexandros Mavrokordatos (1641–1709), an Orthodox Christian subject of the sultan who held the rank of chief dragoman, played an important role in negotiating the treaty. Born in Constantinople but originally from the island of Chios, he studied at the Greek College of St Athanasios in Rome and continued his studies in literature and theology at the university there. He later went to Padua to study medicine, eventually defending his doctoral thesis in Bologna in 1664. Returning to his birthplace, Mavrokordatos taught first at the school led by Manolakis Kastorianos and then at the Patriarchal School. As secretary of the first Orthodox Christian Chief Dragoman Panagiotis Nikousios (1613–73), Mavrokordatos was incorporated into the empire's administrative system. He assumed his position, which provided power, money and prestige in addition to its fair share of perils, after Nikousios's death in 1673. Indeed, in 1683, after the failed Ottoman siege on Vienna and the dominance of his protector's rival, Grand Vizier Kara Mustafa, Mavrokordatos fell into disgrace: his fortunes were confiscated, and his mother and wife were imprisoned. He was allowed to leave Constantinople a year later, though he would subsequently return in 1685. After paying a large compensatory sum, he was able to re-establish himself and regain his assets. As previously noted, his position was strengthened considerably during the negotiations that led to the Treaty of Karlowitz, after which he emerged as a leading expert on European diplomacy.

Mavrokordatos was not the first Orthodox Christian chief dragoman of the Sublime Porte. As previously mentioned, Panagiotis Nikousios had held this title: as a confidant of Köprülü Fazıl Ahmed Pasha, he assumed the position of dragoman to the Imperial Council in 1661, a position previously held by Jews and Western European proselytes. This rendered him an intermediary between foreign forces and the Ottoman administration. Mavrokordatos is considered the first who can be described as a 'Phanariot', a term that was later used to characterise the Orthodox Christian aristocracy of the Ottoman Empire.[1]

The term Phanariot has its origins in the Phanari district of Constantinople, where the Ecumenical Patriarchate had been established in 1601 and remains to this day. But it is more difficult to clarify exactly which elements classify an individual as a member of the Phanariot aristocracy. First of all, their creation had to do with political, not national or ethnic criteria. Phanariot families came from many places; from the Black Sea region, from Karamania, Albania, Bulgaria, Moldavia, Ragusa and Chios. But they did have something in common: they were all Orthodox, and according to Konstantinos Koumas, writing at the dawn of the nineteenth century, all were careful to self-determine as 'the prestigious Orthodox Christian race ... they considered being called Hellenes or Greeks blasphemy'.[2] Yet their orthodoxy and close relations with the Ecumenical Patriarchate rendered cultivation of Greek education a common characteristic. A Greek education constituted one of the essential preconditions for a career in the upper echelons of Ottoman bureaucracy, which necessitated passing through the mechanisms of the Greek-speaking Patriarchate.

Secondly, a precarious foothold in Phanari, or perhaps economic or familial bonds with its residents, was a minimum precondition for acquiring the title of Phanariot. From another angle, if we were to define Phanariots as members of a group holding high ranks in the Ottoman administration, certain

Timetable 1683–1820

1683	The Ottomans besiege Vienna for a second time, and fail.
1683–99	War between the Ottomans and the Habsburgs, in which the latter ally with Poland, Venice and Russia.
1684	Venetian occupation of Lefkada and Preveza.
1685	Military campaigns in the Peloponnese. Venetian occupation of Koroni.
1686	The Habsburgs occupy Buda/the Venetians occupy Nafplion.
1686–15	The Peloponnese placed under Venetian rule.
1687	Suleiman II
1691	Ahmet I
1695	Mustafa II
1699	Treaty of Karlowitz.
1703	Ahmet III
1710–11	Russo-Ottoman War, in which the Russian army miraculously avoids annihilation.
1715	The Peloponnese again placed under Ottoman rule.
1718	Treaty of Passarowitz/the Ottomans lose Belgrade, to the Habsburgs' benefit.
1721–9	The first printing house to use Arabic characters operates in Constantinople.
1724	Ottoman invasion of the crumbling Safavid Empire.
1725–9	The Ottomans conquer Tabriz.
1730	Mahmud I
1736	Austrian and Russian war against the Ottomans.
1739	The Ottomans conquer Belgrade again.
1754	Osman III
1757	Mustafa III
1768–74	Russo-Turkish War.
1770	The Orlov Revolt.
1774	Treaty of Küçük Kaynarca/the Ottomans are forced to accept Crimea's independence, under Russian influence by this point/ Abdul Hamid I.
1783	The Russians annex Crimea.
1787–92	War against Russia and Austria.
1788–90	Lambros Katsonis active in the Aegean.
1789	Selim III
1793	Selim III attempts military reforms.
1797	Bonaparte's French troops occupy the Ionian Islands/Treaty of Campo Formio.
1798	Napoleon occupies Egypt/Rigas Feraios executed.
1800	Treaty of Constantinople in which the Ionian State is created.
1801	Mehmet Ali restores Ottoman sovereignty in Egypt.

1803	The Wahhabis occupy Mecca.
1804–13, 1815	Serbian revolts.
1805	Mehmet Ali becomes pasha of Egypt.
1807	Deposition of Selim III; his execution the following year.
1808–39	Sultan Mahmoud II.
1812	Treaty of Bucharest.
1814	Ionian Islands subject to British protection under the Treaty of Paris/Philike Etaireia founded.
1820	Alexandros Ypsilantis assumes leadership of the Philike Etaireia.

Orthodox families holding ruling positions in the Danubian regions during the Phanariot period (such as the Doukas, Kandakouzinos and Stourzas clans) would be excluded. An exception to this was the Gikas family, which had already acquired its title in the pre-Phanariotic period, and would therefore be considered Phanariot.

Generally, inclusion in the Patriarchate's networks was another common feature. Through this inclusion, they acquired the administrative experience and political contacts within the Ottoman administration that were necessary for their political development. Unsurprisingly, the most coveted official title in the patriarchal system was none other than that of the chief dragoman, the intermediary between the Patriarchate and the Ottoman administration. At the same time, this group's professional specialisations, whether as fabric and fur merchants or doctors, offered them further opportunities to reach powerful Ottoman families and integrate with the empire's political establishment so as to profit from the latter in the race for more money and power.

Indeed, the development of the Phanariot aristocracy can hardly be understood without accounting for the transfer of power from the house of the sultan to the 'political houses' of viziers and pashas, a transition marked by the rise to power of the Köprülü family in the mid-seventeenth century. In these houses, personnel were trained and recruited for the empire's administration, and it was these individuals that then staffed the state bureaucracy. Marriages to Ottoman princesses also offered members of these families opportunities to ally with the Imperial Council. In contrast to the earlier system, the new administration looked to strengthen its position by controlling religious institutions or by farming tax revenues. Alliances with other political houses and even a wider array of groups and interests—chiefly the Janissary Corps—were an essential prerequisite to young political leaders' developing careers, and the same held true for Phanariots. The latter group's rise and fall kept pace with the respective fates of their patrons, that is to say, the leaders of the house they were allied with.

Phanariots not only held the position of chief dragoman of the Porte but also other corresponding ranks such as dragoman of the fleet: the latter accompanied the *kapudan pasha* (commander-in-chief of the Ottoman navy) during the Ottoman fleet's expedition to the Aegean islands with the mission of collecting taxes and recruiting crews. In addition to these positions, many lesser hierarchical stations were often held by members of families that happened to control individual posts. But the most important position a Phanariot could hold, the one with the greatest prestige and power, was to be ruler of the Danubian Principalities.

Phanariot hegemony in the Danubian regions was the product of several long-term, convergent processes. Since the Ottoman conquest of Constantinople, close relationships had been forged between the Ecumenical Patriarch and these regions. After all, it was from these regions that the church derived a significant portion of its income, while local leaders often had a say in the election of patriarchs. These principalities were also major grain- and meat-supply centres for Constantinople, and many Orthodox merchants benefited from the commerce resulting from these two basic staples, enriching themselves as they developed close relationships with the Janissary Corps, which controlled the distribution of these goods within the city. Beginning in the sixteenth century, various Greek-speaking Orthodox merchants had succeeded in controlling a large part of this regional trade, while many others were employed as scribes or teachers by local rulers. In this context, one should not be surprised at the impressive ease with which Phanariots infiltrated these Danubian Principalities, nor at the intermixing of Phanariot families with families of local boyars. Rather, this explains the Phanariots' orientation towards these regions and the ease with which they adapted to these new environments, when such a thing was possible.

Wallachia and Moldavia were both autonomous principalities under Ottoman control, ruled by local leaders until around 1713, when their alliance with Peter the Great during the Pruth campaign forced the Porte to reconsider their status. Phanariots stood to benefit from these new conditions: their location near decision-making centres and their rapidly expanding takeovers of official posts offered them an unparalleled advantage, which they maximised. In 1709, Alexandros Mavrokordatos came out on top again, managing to obtain the title of prince of Wallachia on behalf of his son Nikolaos.

The Phanariots' presence in the Danubian Principalities widened the international scope of their political activities. As the site of confrontation between

Ottomans, Habsburgs and Romanovs, these territories formally accepted the Russians as their Orthodox patrons with the Treaty of Küçük Kaynarca in 1774. This treaty offered the Phanariots greater potential for political manoeuvring and gave rise to hopes for their independence from the empire. In the meantime, Russian and Anglo-French political parties had already been founded in Constantinople, driven by Phanariot families identifying with one nation or the other, and siding with the nation from which they often received support for their claims.

Nothing stood in the way of Phanariot aspirations of autonomy and exemption from Ottoman rule. To the contrary, the entire web of relationships determining the existence of the Danubian Principalities reinforced these aspirations. Indeed, certain families had identified so completely with the Russians, the main opponents of the Ottomans, that the Porte discredited them. The ambivalent attitudes of these Phanariot families towards their Ottoman rulers led to a *kanunname* in 1819, according to which the right to pursue ruling positions could only be held by four families in the Phanariot system, families judged most reliable by the Porte. Thus this network of Christian aristocratic dominance became insular and precluded any possibility of third-party competition.

Over a short period of time, the Phanariots benefited from changes taking place in the Ottoman Empire: they supplanted or marginalised the upper strata of Orthodox Christian populations, and exclusively staked their claim as the aristocracy of the Orthodox peoples, fully embedded in Ottoman administrative institutions. But this aristocracy would be unable to exist and function without controlling the basic mechanism of political sovereignty for Christian populations: the Patriarchate.

A new ecclesiastical hierarchy

In 1766–7, the Ecumenical Patriarchate successfully incorporated the archbishoprics of Ohrid and Ipek, thus gaining a monopoly over the ecclesiastical jurisdiction of the Ottoman Empire's Orthodox populations. It is no coincidence that the absorption of these two autocephalous Balkan churches occurred under the Phanariot Patriarch Samuel Chatzeres, and that consolidation of this new arrangement (which met with opposition from local notables) was attributed to another Phanariot, Ioannis Ypsilantis. Meanwhile, the fact that the Patriarchate of Constantinople was a component of the central Ottoman administration allowed it to supervise other ancient patriarchates of eastern Orthodoxy such as Jerusalem, Alexandria and Antioch. Even though these patriarchates were considered equal to the Ecumenical Patriarchate, they were economically dependent on it, as their congregations were numerically small.[3] As a result, shortly after the mid-eighteenth century, the Ecumenical Patriarchate achieved something unprecedented: it extended its geographic jurisdiction to include all Orthodox Christian populations of the Ottoman Empire.

As the church broadened its geographic scope, its juridical responsibilities also increased. While the church's authority was initially limited to questions of canonical law, its legal jurisdiction gradually extended to include issues of civil law, chiefly involving property relations and financial transactions. Evidence of the church's jurisdiction when resolving differences between Christians was first noted in the eighteenth century. As legal historian Konstantinos Pitsakis points out, this led to 'the nearly undeniable jurisdiction of the church in private affairs'.[4] As an extension of these developments, the church established civil courts during the eighteenth century in both Constantinople and the provinces. In the latter case, representatives from local populations would often participate. Though the church naturally made every effort to monopolise juridical jurisdiction, in many cases it did not manage to do so, as Christian populations always had the option of resorting to Ottoman court systems. Excommunication, threatened or real, was a weapon the church wielded all too frequently to deter practices that undermined its power: 'And do not expose yourselves to foreign criticism and betray yourselves to the censure of Turks. For this, such traitors shall not receive Holy Communion for twelve years,' declared Cosmas of Aetolia, perhaps the most important priest in the period of Ottoman rule.[5]

This expansion of the Patriarchate's juridical jurisdiction corresponded to a tendency towards the homogenisation of legal practices. Legal codes and texts from the first centuries of Ottoman rule progressively gave way to a code capable of handling the requirements of a new era and the problems faced by the church's judicial authorities. The private codification of secular rights, known as the *Hexabiblos*—attributed to Constantine Harmenopoulos, guardian of the law and a judge in Thessaloniki during the fourteenth century—constituted the Patriarchate's basic legal code, and an attempt was made to enforce it as the only applicable tool for regulating juridical differences. Its translation into the Greek vernacular and publication by the Venetian printing house owned by Nikolaos Glikis in 1744 finally contributed to its wide dissemination in areas under the Patriarchate's control.

The geographical and judicial expansion of the Patriarchate's jurisdiction was linked to the progressive transformation of the Patriarchate itself: its personal dimension shrank as it turned into a collective institution. Prelates of regions near Constantinople, who in most cases resided within the city, became permanent members of the 'Resident Synod', exercising decisive influence in the management of ecclesiastical affairs. In 1741, the system of so-called gerontism was institutionalised, in which the patriarch was chosen with the approval of elders—the aforementioned prelates from nearby regions. This institutionalisation of ecclesiastical power advanced even further, so that by 1757, and even more so by 1763, the synod was recognised as a co-governing body in the Patriarchate's affairs, thus putting an end to patriarchal autocracy. Later, the role of these 'notables of the nation' was institutionally recognised, and as a result the elders, the Phanariots, and the leaders of Constantinople's guilds were the ones who gained the power to defrock and proclaim patriarchs. They consequently had a decisive say in managing the church's resources.

But there was another, equally important aspect to the institutionalisation of ecclesiastical power. By 1525 at the very latest, when the first written testimony emerged, the patriarchal title was included in the venal office system. According to the Ottoman administrative system, until 1714 the patriarchal title was offered through the auctioning of empire incomes to a bidder without recognising its lifelong validity. Yet beginning in 1714 and up until the mid-nineteenth century, the patriarchal title was assigned as a lifelong lease of the sultan's incomes. Thus its lifelong character was recognised for the first time, and the Ottomans began attributing a more collective dimension to the position.

In other words, during the period in question, the patriarchal rank and other ecclesiastical titles were positions that were obtainable through the system of public-revenue leasing. The overthrow of a patriarch required, first, presentation of proof that he had failed to meet the obligations of his title. In special cases, this meant his inability to pay public treasury debts inherited upon accession to the throne. A successor would then be selected by auctioning the rank. The frequent alternation of patriarchs, in which the same individuals were often returned to the patriarchal throne, can only be understood in light of the competition existing within the Patriarchate for the collection of ecclesiastical incomes; this competition was also related to disputes arising between factions of secularists and clergy members, Muslims and Christians.

Indeed, it is no coincidence that from early on the Patriarchate, and more specifically individual patriarchs, found themselves under the influence of secular groups. In most cases, these groups played a decisive role in electing a new patriarch, as they were in a position to influence decision-making among the most powerful members of the empire. The various payments the patriarch was obliged to pay to the sultan or other officers, both in order to ascend to the patriarchal throne, and in the form of annual obligations (and, finally, other contributions paid to secure various graces and favours), decisively influenced relations between religious and secular prelates. In order to fulfil these obligations the patriarch often resorted to lending, ending up at the mercy of his creditors. As a result, patriarchal debt and its consequences often became a catalyst for developments in the patriarchal institution. Lending relations within the Patriarchate thus shaped bonds with Christian—and other—rulers who undertook to fulfil these obligations, managing and benefiting from the Patriarchate's income in return. Koumas writes:

> Both notables, through their tax collectors, as well as the chief dragoman, became the protectors or (to put it more accurately) usurpers of ecclesiastical law, and the provinces were distributed, by their agencies, to those who paid the most. Patriarchs were appointed and replaced as they pleased. And soon, since the patriarch had been granted license to convey to the government what pertained to his subjects, they undertook control of affairs in the provinces and, looking after matters on behalf of the patriarch, enjoyed vast sums of money as reward for their efforts.[6]

On a local scale, prelates under the control of the Patriarchate performed similar functions and actions.

The patriarchal title was of course granted to a specific individual by the sultan himself in return for the effective fulfilment of certain obligations. The patriarch's obligations to the sultan could include the settling of tax debts, or in other cases the enlisting of crew members for the Ottoman fleet. But one such fundamental obligation was the supervision of his subjects, 'both as pertaining to the priestly calling, and as befitting the overseer appointed by the mighty Ottoman realm for protection of its Orthodox Christian people'.[7] This obligation to supervise the Orthodox populations arose both from the archpriest's own duties and the fact that the patriarch had been called on to represent the sultan. For this reason, the political philosophy of the patriarchal institution was necessarily composed of these two components of patriarchal office, and certainly mandated respect for the political system:

> When ingratitude is accompanied by a malign and apostate spirit, undermining our mutually beneficent, caring, mighty and indefatigable realm, it implies also a godless disposition: for, one can say, there is no such thing as kingdom and power unless directed by God, and all who fight against this mighty realm that has been given to us from God are fighting against the decree of God.[8]

The transformations of the Patriarchate of Constantinople over the course of the eighteenth century constitute nothing more or less than a process of institutionalising political power within the Ottoman Empire. On the eve of the Greek War of Independence, state mechanisms had formed through which the Patriarchate governed the Christian populations of South Eastern Europe. While Paschalis Kitromilidis has argued that this constituted the creation of an Orthodox commonwealth, it was in fact much more than that and was not limited to a religious context: it was one component of the Ottoman Empire's adaptation to new international and domestic realities, with the final aim of consolidating central control over local communities and power centers.

It is no coincidence that the concept of the *millet* first made its appearance at the end of the eighteenth century,[9] despite the fact that it was only officially established in the Ottoman Empire after the mid-nineteenth century. By the early nineteenth century, the Patriarchate had become a central administrative mechanism, controlling populations both in terms of its geographic scope and through its ability to penetrate into local communities. Its administration through secular groups—the Phanariots doubtless the most distinguished among them—intensified the sense that a central Christian governing power existed within the Ottoman Empire. This further stoked the political ambitions of the groups governing the Patriarchate.

These transformations did not take place without eliciting reactions, which reverberated from the centre, as for example with Patriarch Cyril V (1748–51 and 1752–7) who relied on the guilds of Constantinople to compel local prelates in power to give up their seats. Yet his attempts would only be successful in the short term. The Phanariots reacted, managing to claim control of the Patriarchate once again. In fact, certain patriarchs in the second half of the eighteenth century such as Joannicius III (1761–3) and Samuel Chatzeres (1763–8 and 1773–4) were descendants of Phanariot families, while many more members of Phanariot families had managed to claim and occupy ecclesiastical offices of lesser importance.

Reactions to these transformations were also evident in the provinces. In the monastic realm, it appears that the opposition was even more intense, judging from the disputes of the Kollyvades and Anabaptism movements. It would not be an exaggeration to argue that the greatest opposition to the Patriarchate's efforts at extending power came from the monasteries—but there is not enough research on the topic to allow for anything more than a hypothesis. In the early nineteenth century, we may recall the efforts to impose patriarchal power on Mount Athos—a rich source of income—by creating a metropolis of the same name. This venture was supported, as expected, by the Phanariots, but it failed after being met with strong opposition. Besides these monastic reactions to the extension of patriarchal power, we must not overlook the role played by local elites.

Local leaders

Both the ecclesiastical and Phanariot Orthodox elite, who from the end of the seventeenth century permanently strengthened their position in the greater Ottoman governing apparatus, functioned at the level of the empire's central administration and profited from the institutionalisation of political power, mainly via patriarchal networks. In this way, they were progressively recognised as leaders and representatives of the Orthodox Christian populations. But their rise would not have any significance (and would not even have been conceivable) without the simultaneous aid of local elites—that is, dominant groups of notables. It is mainly the relations between two social strata—the elite within the central administration and the local elite—that created the preconditions for the formation of a real, not imagined, 'community' of Orthodox Christians spanning the entire empire.

The extended period of war during the latter half of the seventeenth and early eighteenth century created a major fiscal problem for the empire, which sought to address the issue by reforming the system of collecting tax revenues. To this end, timariot relationships were gradually abolished and a more generalised system of tax farming was established. Initially, this farming was practised on a short-term basis, but it was abused extensively by a large portion of the taxed populations, and the arrangement of lifelong tax farming (*malikane*) was adopted soon after in 1695. From then on, this system constituted the link between central and provincial powers: the political houses of Constantinople were in a position to supervise the auctioning of lifelong leasings, which they managed through local elite groups, as only the latter were able to enforce the collection of taxes. In this manner, mutual interests were established that help shed light on the behaviour of local notable groups, regardless of their religion—and most of all the legal compliance they demonstrated with respect to central power.

Yet, at the same time, tax reforms were an extension of the *maktu* system—taxes not collected separately by household, but via a total sum for an entire community. In this system, the community undertook collective responsibility for the fulfilment of its tax obligations, distributing the tax burden among its members as necessary. With these changes, social and religious differentiations between the populations weakened, as did the differences between urban and provincial populations. Relations between the state and taxed citizen also became more fluid. Another consequence of these reforms, certainly no less important, had to do with the fact that land titles could be transferred with greater ease.

The farming and collection of taxes was a complex procedure that Christians participated in as well, whether as collectors or sub-letters. The close relations they developed with powerful individuals in their respective regions or in Constantinople allowed them to insert themselves into the empire's administrative system and render themselves essential to the smooth collection of taxes. The same is also true of more 'autonomous' communities, where the process of organising and fulfilling tax obligations gave more affluent residents the opportunity to take up a leading role in community administration.

The emergence of notable groups was linked to these tax-farming arrangements and to the development of trade in the eighteenth century. Most of these notables participated in the farming or sub-letting of tax revenues. In other cases, they represented their communities, provided that the community farmed taxes on its own behalf, taking on the obligation of repaying them via distribution of tax burdens to the indebted. "They were also in charge of disbursing loans, enabling the community to meet its obligations in a timely manner, in addition to providing loans for individual members of the community who were unable to fulfill their obligations."

These same notable groups, which functioned on a local or provincial scale, were the ones to profit most from the growth of trade. Most of the notables were reputable owners of property, without a doubt the more affluent members of the community, even if the extent of the land they possessed was insignificant compared with the territories held by Muslim landowners. In the case of the Peloponnese, we know that Christian populations possessed around a third of all arable land, mostly found in semi-mountainous and mountainous regions. Despite the smaller scale of the Christian notables' operations, it appears that the practices they pursued for the extension of their lands were identical to those of the Muslims, with whom they were often at odds.

Although noble Christian groups were uniformly involved in the administration of various regions, each area nevertheless maintained its individual particularities. In areas with a large Muslim presence, noble Christian groups were less influential. But in regions belonging to members of the imperial family, or to church institutions, their presence was much more prominent. It is precisely here that the most well-known and powerful notable families appeared. Examples in the Peloponnese included the Deliyannis family in Karytainia, the Papatsonidis family in Emlakika and the Papalexis family in Phanari.

In certain cases, these notables were determined by the Ottoman administration, while in others they were elected by the community. In this context, relations with the ecclesiastical authorities were critical, because they were capable of influencing relationships with both central powers and local representatives. And this held true in an era where the church, representing central power, tried all the more to penetrate into Balkan societies and intervene in the administration of local populations—often in a manner that would antagonise the local leadership. Sources cite the notables of Chios and Livadia as examples that managed to prevent Muslim intervention in community affairs. Yet such examples are infrequent, and in most cases community administration was characterised by acute disputes and opposition. This is why, at the beginning of the nineteenth century, doctor and man of letters Michael Perdikaris maintained that the Greeks were not ready to be liberated from Ottoman despotism because they were not mature enough to manage their own affairs.

These notable groups were not unified; rather, they were composed of rival factions battling for dominance in each region. The ability to win over the Ottoman authorities played a decisive role in the outcome of these rivalries. In the end, a group's survival depended on its ability to maintain power for the longest period of time, and this could only happen with the support of the Ottoman authorities. In many cases, the opposition became violent. In the Peloponnese, the opportunity to manage an income of Beyhan Sultan—an Ottoman princess—resulted in two mixed factions of Muslims and Christians with rival claims to power. One included notables from Corinth, Kalavryta, Vostitsa, Ileia and Patras, while the other included notables from the southern regions, led on the Christian side by the Deliyannis family from Karytainia. These factions were split

> down to the level of towns and villages. To increase their number of voters and supporters, they all tirelessly endeavoured to make matches, engagements, become godparents, that is, by baptising children in the holy font, or making bridesmaids at weddings soon to be newlyweds, and effecting fraternal bonds between armatoles ...[10]

In 1812, opposition within these two factions led to the decapitation of Sotiris Lontos, a Bostitsa notable and member of a provincial council; three years later, the leader of the rival party, Ioannis Deliyannis, met the same fate.

These notable groups jointly participated in the administration of each region with the Ottomans. Decisions on various issues were made via consultation between Ottoman officers and the notables, who were then responsible for carrying out the orders in their own regions. In the Peloponnese, a council was convened in which representatives of the regions were present and questions about the peninsula were decided. The notables were also responsible for maintaining peace and order in their regions. To cite just one example, in 1806 Christian notables joined with Muslims in the Peloponnese and played a central role in reducing robbery, coordinating the armed militias of their regions to hunt down and kill Christian bandits.

The local Christian elites' ability to gain partial or complete hegemony depended on maintaining good relations with local *ayans*,[11] representatives of the Porte, and the central Ottoman administration. This, after all, is why notables sought to secure representatives in Constantinople: namely to support their interests and defend them from potential abuses by local Ottoman officials. To this end, Peloponnesian notables retained vekils in Constantinople, as did groups of provincial notables, especially when they sought specific objectives. Specifically, so as to achieve their objectives, they made sure to use either Phanariots or the Patriarchate as mediators. This system proved effective, since neither the pashas—emissaries of the central authorities—nor the *ayans* or tax-collectors could ignore these notable groups. Apart from this, positions held by the notable groups were important enough so as to play a decisive role in the outcome of oppositions within Muslim communities. In 1762, for example, Orthodox vekils supported the pasha of Morea, Topal Osman, in his conflict with Muslim *ayans*, and managed to uphold his position and ensure the execution of Muslims that had gone to Constantinople demanding the pasha's removal. Nevertheless, when Topal Osman was replaced, all five vekils involved lost their lives.

In the conditions of widespread violence common to rural communities, the Ottoman state often used armed auxiliary groups to ensure the safety of local communities. These *armatoles*, or warlords, were used to protect populations and trade from bandits and were paid by the communities they protected, within which they often gained considerable power. This phenomenon mainly occurred in Central and Northern Greece. But in the region of Morea, evidence indicates that armed groups were dependent on the notables of each region and did not retain the autonomy and power they exercised elsewhere. Often, these *armatoles* covered large tracts of land and were exploited by armed dynasties with huge economic and political power. While they derived their political power from arms, in the economic sector, they were active as tax farmers in addition to offering services of safety and protection. Available information also suggests that they owned much livestock and, often, geographically important land. Similar to the quest for gaining local and regional power among notable groups, competition for the ability to wield arms was fierce, and challenges to families in command would often occur through armed attempts by opponents. Throughout the eighteenth century, the Ottomans preferred Albanian Muslims over Christians for these *armatoles*—a tendency that only increased towards the end of the eighteenth and beginning of the nineteenth century in the regions controlled by Ali Pasha.

Although rural revolts did not occur in the Ottoman Empire in the way they did in Western Europe—Suraiya Faroqhi has claimed that this is due to the ability of villagers to abandon their lands—uprisings sparked by notables, armed or unarmed, certainly took place. The most exemplary case, one that certainly influenced relations between Christians and Muslims and later the attitudes of local elites towards the Philike Etaireia, was the revolt of 1770 that wreaked havoc in the Peloponnese in addition to other regions of Central Greece, Epirus, Thessaly and Macedonia.

This revolt was also indicative of the first phase of Russian influence in Ottoman territory. During the Russo-Turkish war of 1768–74, Russian agents came into contact with notables from Morea in order to organise a revolt against the Ottomans. The local leaders agreed to do so, though they kept a few avenues of communication open with the Ottomans, as they had always done. But the revolt that followed proved impossible to suppress, all the more so since the Russians were unable to send significant support to the Peloponnese. It ended tragically for a large share of the notables and the general population, as the Porte allowed armed Albanian groups to invade the Peloponnese. In the end, Turkish–Albanian groups prevailed, exploiting the population and pillaging the countryside, hoping to extract the most they could from the land under the pretext of the Porte's inability to remunerate them. The solution offered was typical of the period: the Kapudan pasha and his dragoman, Mavrogenis, asked Christian notables and the armed forces to collaborate in eliminating the Turkish–Albanian terror. In this way, they were able to eradicate the gangs that pillaged Morea.

On the eve of the Greek War of Independence, local elites, both armed and unarmed, found themselves under tremendous pressure. On the one hand, the context in which armed groups would act was shaped by the pursuit of bandits by Ottoman authorities, checks on *armatole* power, restrictions on the possibilities of promotion for chieftains following the end of the Napoleonic Wars, and finally the consequences of the conflict between the Porte and Ali Pasha. On the other hand, political elites were subject to similar pressures: in the Peloponnese, specifically after Ali Pasha's son Veli gained power from 1808 to 1812, relations among Muslim *ayans* and Christian notables soured. All this took place while the Russo-Turkish wars at the end of the eighteenth century (1768–74 and 1787–92) and the beginning of the next century (1806–12) upset—if only temporarily—the reciprocity of interests between the central administration and the provinces. The upheavals that resulted, with an exceptionally high human and economic cost, led to a weakened relationship between centre and province, while the system of lifelong leases lost the importance it once had. It is no coincidence that the first Serbian uprising took place (1804–13) at the beginning of the nineteenth century, at the same time as a large spike in bandit activity in the Peloponnese (1804–6). Similar events occurred on the mainland, in addition to Efthimios Vlachavas's revolt against Ali Pasha.

It was in these circumstances that the powerful and quasi-autonomous rulers of the late eighteenth and early nineteenth century emerged. Examples include the Karaosmanoğlu clan in Asia Minor, Osman Pazvantoğlu in Vidin, Mehmet Ali in Egypt and naturally Ali Pasha in Epirus and Albania. In certain cases, these rulers originated from the places they administered, managing to acquire the rank of pasha from the Porte thanks to their abilities. Such is the case of Ali Pasha. In other cases, they were sent by the Porte to fulfil an administrative position, after which they acquired a local foothold and eventually established their own dynasty, as with Mehmet Ali. However, such separatist tendencies were rather short-lived, a product of the circumstances of the late eighteenth century, as previously discussed. The Ottoman government was able to counteract and finally exterminate most of them, with the exception of Mehmet Ali, who nevertheless failed to gain formal autonomy from the Porte.

Thus, in the beginning of the nineteenth century, the processes of transformation within the empire that began in the seventeenth century took shape in such a way that new hierarchies became established: local elites, Muslim or not, administered the empire's provinces through the continuous renegotiation of their relations with the Porte. In other words, in the seventeenth century the Ottoman Empire began a process of increasing its revenues in accordance with its military needs, a process that led to changes in the ways in which it governed its populations. Local Muslim and Christian elites took the place of Muslim military officers such as *timariots* and began to administer the

Ottoman population. In fact, the empire had incorporated these local dominant groups of elites into its administrative mechanisms regardless of religion so as to increase its administrative effectiveness—and these groups made sure to make the most of this opportunity.

Merchant elites

It must be remembered that these transformations took place in a social and economic environment that remained traditional in nature for the entirety of the period in question. Thus the role of trade transactions remained limited, though not unimportant.

The first factor characterising trade transactions in the Ottoman Empire during these years—and much more so after the signing of the 1740 capitulations between France and the Ottomans—was that Western and especially French trade now gravitated towards the western Ottoman territories. This acted as a catalyst for the empire's urban hierarchies; Smyrna, for example, developed rapidly and took on a leading role in trade with Western Europe. Constantinople, the most important centre of consumer goods in the West, occupied second place. In the same period, and in the same context, Thessaloniki became an important trade centre in the Balkans. Thus in the period from 1688 to 1700, Smyrna accounted for 30 per cent of all exports to Marseille, Egypt accounted for 29 per cent, Syria 25 per cent, Constantinople 11 per cent, and the regions included in the current-day Greek state a mere 5 per cent. A century later, in 1784, the distribution of exports had changed considerably. Smyrna constituted 32 per cent, Syria 23 per cent, Egypt 13 per cent, Constantinople 4 per cent and the 'Greek' regions 24 per cent.

As these relationships changed, the empire's commercial partners shifted. Beginning at the end of the seventeenth century, British supremacy in Eastern Mediterranean trade diminished to the benefit of the French, while the Dutch and Venetians maintained roles of lesser importance. In 1686, British trade accounted for 39 per cent of Ottoman exports, while the Dutch accounted for 21 per cent, the French 19 per cent and the Venetians 12 per cent. By 1784, however, the British represented only 9 per cent of Ottoman exports, the Dutch 18 per cent and the Venetians 12 per cent, while the French share had risen to 37 per cent.

The French dominance of Levant trade is open to multiple interpretations. First, from a political standpoint, the close diplomatic relations the country fostered with the Porte facilitated the development of commercial trade between the two states. Equally important was the role played by the quality of fabrics made by Languedoc manufacturers, which successfully competed with corresponding British products. The French also established an extensive network of consulates and representatives, even in small ports, in order to facilitate their commercial dominance. Finally, England's shifting of trade interests towards the Indian and Atlantic oceans proved equally consequential. Regardless of which factors affected the re-composition of the empire's external trade, the bottom line is that the French imposed their sovereignty on Eastern trade from 1730 onwards and managed to maintain it until the last decade of the century.

The above description of the empire's trade with the West does not account for the importance of land trade with Central Europe. The latter became all the more important beginning in the eighteenth century. In 1718, the Treaty of Passarowitz created new possibilities for non-Muslim tradesmen traversing the paths and marine commercial trade routes of the Eastern Mediterranean; now, non-Muslim traders could benefit from paths across the Danubian Basin and the southern valleys of Vardar and Morava. It was these same trade routes that led to the emergence of significant concentrations of Orthodox populations in the regions of Central Europe.

These developments in trade had significant consequences for Eastern Mediterranean societies. First of all, the capitulations of 1740 between France and the Porte established a new group of non-Muslim traders that enjoyed *beratli*—protected status. Initially, this group included dragomans of ambassadors and consuls, whose rights were equivalent to those of the Western Europeans. In addition, by the second half of the eighteenth century, a considerable number of tradesmen had paid large sums to embassies and consulates to acquire *beratli* status. This led to the emergence of a non-Muslim merchant elite, which, as Edhem Eldem has claimed, had very few reasons to express solidarity with the Ottoman Empire, despite owing its privileged existence and prosperity to Ottoman institutions.

As was to be expected, *beratli* status was claimed mainly by members of the local elite who played an important role in external trade, facilitating the reorientation of productive needs in accordance with Western European demand. They supported commercial agriculture, organised the transport of goods towards their respective ports and final land destinations, and negotiated with European traders in their capacity as regional representatives. Additionally, the role of local elites was reinforced due to the inability of European traders to insinuate themselves into local societies—the French being a likely exception during the peak of their trade in the Levant. In most cases, Western Europeans found themselves limited to a few harbours, compelled to live in a separate, and for the most part, isolated region. The purchase of products for export depended on local traders that had the access and networks necessary to buy products for export from producers, then channelling the products they imported from the West to their markets, most of which were luxury goods. Within the empire, Western traders found themselves compelled to depend on local traders, and they supported the latter's positions—at least within the context of local communities.

Western economic sovereignty was not yet fully in force during the eighteenth century. Overall trade volume remained comparatively limited, while it should be noted that total export-oriented Ottoman trade continued to fluctuate at levels similar to the previous hundred years. But even in terms of unequal 'exchange', we cannot make a case for Western dominance. Though the empire exported raw materials, which the West had begun to demand in ever greater quantities, the latter's imports were not tied to industrial products or to the re-importation of raw materials exported in processed form. On the contrary, the empire imported either luxury goods intended for its wealthy residents—in this case mostly fabrics—or other raw materials and consumables such as coffee, while its exports included manufactured products such as textiles. In terms of internal trade, local manufacture—especially in rural areas—took the helm until the beginning of the nineteenth century, accounting for significant exports to neighbouring countries. One would have to wait until the next century to see radical changes in the nature of the empire's external trade.

These dynamics of economic change were also evident in the agricultural industry. During this period, agriculture entered a more productive phase, internationally deemed 'proto-industrialisation', in which rural populations were employed, activating their seasonal labour power and providing them with an additional income. The system of distributing goods manufactured in this way was supported by tradesmen, who were frequently notables themselves. Relationships between trader and producer varied; what is important is that the traders distributed goods on a transregional or international scale. Cloaks were exported to Italy from the mountains of Epirus; wools, cottons and mixed fabrics were sent from Pelion to the empire's cities and the islands of the Aegean; and red threads were sent from Ampelakia to Central Europe. This trend was particularly widespread on the Balkan Peninsula in the late eighteenth and early nineteenth centuries and only declined when British manufactured goods established themselves in markets that had previously been the preferred fields of operations for Orthodox traders. Moreover, guild regulations and a strong janissary presence in large urban centres led industrial production to decline in cities, leaving considerable room for corresponding growth in rural areas. In Thessaloniki, for example, where manufacture of woollen textiles had already been established in the sixteenth century with the arrival of Spanish Jews, this decline was in full swing by the nineteenth century. By then, taxes-in-kind that had to be paid were not extracted from domestic production, but largely from the purchase of imported textiles.

In this setting, it also proved possible for shipping trade to develop. Beginning in the seventeenth century, Cephalonians, Zakynthians and Corfiots maintained close relations with Venice, Trieste and the Italian coasts in general. Boosted by these dynamics, Missolonghi became a powerful maritime centre reaching all the way to Malta and Trieste, utilising resources from the Ionian Islands. After 1780, Aegean fleets extended into the Western Mediterranean. Until then, they had mostly conducted coastal commercial activities, progressively managing to gain notable profits with the transport of grains from Alexandria, Volos and Thessaloniki to Constantinople. They had also benefited substantially from a lack of French trade during the Seven Years' War (1756–63). This allowed Orthodox Christian ship-owners and traders to enforce their presence, affecting the French merchants' caravan system. Soon after, in 1780, initiation of trade on the Black Sea granted new opportunities for wealth to Orthodox Christian captains rushing to meet Western European needs for grain.

In 1774, the Treaty of Küçük Kaynarca offered a boost to the development of Christian shipping operations. The necessity of Russian and Austrian communication channels with the Porte as a result of the treaty facilitated the development of certain island communities at the expense of the French. Orthodox Christian subjects of the Ottoman Empire and other Balkan traders profited from the use of routes where the French were barely present, such as the Adriatic—where in 1719 Trieste had become a free harbour—and the Black Sea. Other difficulties faced by French traders, and finally their complete collapse during the French Revolution, gave Christian sea captains further momentum. Furthermore, France's need for imported grain from the ports of the Black Sea and the Balkans constituted a main reason for the development of the Orthodox Christian fleet, which ended up controlling Eastern Mediterranean trade. The fleets of Hydra, Psara and Spetses, which would soon support the War of Greek Independence, developed during this period. But the nature of their growth led to an acute crisis after the end of the Napoleonic Wars and to intense social tensions, at least on a local scale.

Reformers

A major turning point in the history of the Ecumenical Patriarchate took place under Patriarch Cyril Loukaris (1572–1638). Loukaris, who sought to confront the Jesuits' aggressive educational and proselytising campaigns in Constantinople, sought to strengthen the Patriarchal School and the education of Orthodox Christians in the empire more generally. For this reason, he invited the neo-Aristotelian philosopher Theophilus Corydalleus to become director of the school, and he also established the first Greek printing house in the Eastern Mediterranean, though this was destroyed by janissaries shortly thereafter at the instigation of the French ambassador and the Jesuits. Loukaris's tenure came at a critical period, during the Thirty Years' War, where he found himself in a dangerous balancing act between Catholics and Protestants, siding decidedly with the latter over the supporters of the pope that threatened both him and the Patriarchate. His project failed and he was strangled; accused of atheism and Calvinism, Corydalleus was forced to leave the school.

Loukaris's efforts had a substantial impact in later years. For example, Corydalleus's comments on Aristotle soon became the 'absolute rule' of educational practice when the Patriarchate suggested that any deviation from it be considered reprehensible; he himself later became metropolitan of Athens. Led by I. Karoifillis, a group of Loukaris–Corydalleus followers secured shelter in the Danubian regions and obtained significant support from their rulers, Basarab and Kantakouzenos. They maintained close relations with the Patriarchate, and Kariofillis even became the Great Logothete, evidence of his political power. He was also close to Alexandros Mavrokordatos—he had taught his mother—though they did clash at one point. On a different trajectory, another student of Corydalleus, Evgenios Giannoulis of Aetolia, created the foundations upon which the School of Agrapha would develop.

Regardless of the recorded instances of persecution, which were largely linked with political issues and personal or factional disputes over control of the Patriarchate, a first group of reformist intellectuals of the patriarchal system formed around Cyril Loukaris. The Phanariots could hardly be absent from this newly forming environment, and indeed their relation to it manifested itself in Mavrokordatos's project. His achievement—and the achievement of his son Nikolaos—was to create the preconditions for the systematic unification of Christian Orthodox, Western European and Greek education. Linguists, well educated and informed about what was happening in the West, took interest in the new currents of moral and political thought of the time. Mavrokordatos's project saw Greek education as an element of the Christian faction of Ottoman reality, rather than being independent or manipulated by it. This issue is further underlined in the work of Nikolaos Mavrokordatos, *Filotheou Parerga*, which remained unpublished until 1800.

In practical terms, a form of hegemonic cosmopolitanism took hold that sought social recognition from the West. As conservative as this cosmopolitanism was, it soon came into conflict with established conceptions and reversed the intellectual status quo—even if this happened among a closed circle of individuals. Meanwhile, the Phanariots led the way, making sure their future generations were acquainted with Europe and could travel there for their studies. Learning foreign languages was an essential precondition for advancement in their careers, while a large portion of them studied medicine, a science that granted its practitioners easier access to power. The limitations of a closed society thus began to loosen and the Phanariots' social position furthered their cause all the more.

Along with this momentum that rendered education a fundamental component of the intellectual capital of this rising group, the Phanariots created infrastructure in the Danubian region that was necessary for its further development—schools, academies, printing presses. That many important scholars who comprised the so-called modern Greek Enlightenment spent some time in these territories is telling. Grigorios Konstantas, Daniel Filippidis, Rigas Velestinlis and Konstantinos Stamatis (to name but a few of the more renowned individuals) developed their ideas under the influence of two important intellectuals: Iosipos Moisiodax and Dimitrios Katartzis. But the Phanariots also sought to improve education more broadly through the creation of schools and libraries in various regions of the Ottoman Empire.

If we abandon prevailing historiographical stereotypes, the importance of Phanariots in Greek letters can also be understood through the process of ecclesiastical reform—to be precise, the Ecumenical Patriarchate's reforms. As we have seen, this was a process that originated in the patriarchal tenure of Loukaris and in the opposition between Catholics and reformers. Phanariot political influence was such that the group could often overcome the opposition it faced, even though opponents of these pro-reform currents can be found in the same group.

The Phanariots best demonstrate the first traces of this shift in the collective interest of elites within the empire's Orthodox populations towards the West and Western letters; but we must turn to two Corfiots—Evgenios Voulgaris and Nikiforos Theotokis, descendants of aristocratic families—to identify an intensification and clarification of the reform process and its limitations. Voulgaris was a typical representative of the period together with Iosipos Moisiodax, a Hellenised Vlach scholar who could be considered a student of Voulgaris. During this period, Voltaire's work was highly influential and widely admired. Voulgaris had translated Voltaire's work and adopted a stance of intellectual liberalism, showing a special interest in the natural sciences. His teaching over what were most likely short intervals at various schools in Ioannina (1742–5 and then again in 1748–52), in Kozani (1745–8) at the Athonias Academy (1753–9) and finally at the Patriarchal School (1759–62) injected something completely new into the world of Greek letters and undoubtedly established modern scientific and philosophical thought within them. Understandably, his influence reflected this fact, rendering him the spiritual father of the second, plentiful generation of scholars of the so-called Greek Enlightenment and beyond. Along with Cosmas of Aetolia, Athanasios Parios was another energetic scholar fighting against reforms, and another student of Voulgaris.

In general, many were largely tolerant of Voulgaris's actions. If in 1723 Methodius Anthrakitis, a typical representative of religious humanism, was condemned by the church under the category of Korydalism for his assertion that it is a right of man to philosophise freely and study any philosophy he may like, Voulgaris went much further two to three decades later, arguing that the philosopher should be 'a detector of the exact truth, an impartial judge of all discourses, and a wise arbitrator of each concept' without coming to any harm. In addition, in 1767 he dared to translate Voltaire's work *Historical and Critical Essay on the Dissent of the Churches of Poland* barely a year after it was published. Annotated so as to support the Orthodox Church in response to the pressures it had experienced from Rome, it was accompanied by *Notes on Religious Tolerance*, in which he sought to supply an Orthodox foundation for the idea of religious tolerance and rescue it from what he thought to be Voltaire's exaggerations. This very focus helps shed light on the nature of the reformist phenomenon.

In Voulgaris's case, the reformist dimension of this so-called Enlightenment of the church is explicit, and is perhaps confirmed most by the severe reactions within the Patriarchate against Voulgaris's teachings in Athonias and at the

Patriarchal School. On the other hand, precisely because Voulgaris's teachings operated within the bounds of the Orthodox Church, their influence was long-lasting, and his instructional textbooks continued to be taught until the beginning of the nineteenth century, circulating in book form fifty years after he himself stopped teaching. Let us not forget that both Voulgaris and an overwhelming majority of reformers did not dispute the foundations of Christian faith and knowledge—the truth of Revelation.

Nikiforos Theotokis's project developed in a similar way to that of Voulgaris, with whom he shared a specific trait: their visits to Russia and subsequent stays turned them towards more conservative positions. He demonstrated innovative thinking early on, publishing *Elements of Physics* in 1766–7, while he also gained great renown as a preacher. But his career was interrupted abruptly: first, he entered into conflict with the Patriarchate and Patriarch Samuel Chatzeres, and later, with the princely academies of Iasi, where he left 'overnight, as a fugitive'. At the end of the century, Voulgaris offered him his support, resulting in his succession to the episcopal throne in Russia. By then, both condemned Voltaire, while Theotokis's linguistic preferences, initially tending towards the vernacular, turned increasingly conservative.

Phanariots continued to make their presence known in the developments of the period, as was to be expected, in which Dimitrios Katartzis (1730–1807) emerged as a preeminent figure of the group. The Phanariot conception of government was clear in his thought, while his pedagogical proposals, linguistic concepts and reformist utilitarianism made him an outstanding presence in the reformist community. Based on his perceptions, a particular view of 'what Greeks were' came to be: the historical descendants of ancient Greece now constituted a distinct group in the same way that the ancient Greek language was a historical ancestor of modern Greek, though the latter was grammatically autonomous and would be exclusively used in teaching and writing.

Efforts to assimilate European thought provoked other outcomes as well. The first was the abandonment—by some scholars, at least—of the traditional conception of historical time as expressed through religious chronicles. In its place came a different, modern historical consciousness that supported an understanding of the ancient Greeks as their ancestors. Secondly, and of equal importance, this same modern historical consciousness led to an increased understanding of contemporary international realities and the possibilities they offered Orthodox Christians for an existence separate from Ottoman despotism. Finally, local historical particularities, as expressed in local histories, shaped common denominators in the differentiation of the Greeks from

Christian populations: a shared national–historical past took the place of a shared Christian past. But to remain only with this view of reformist thought would only allow access to one perspective on this process of intellectual transformation among the Orthodox elite. A second and equally important view was linked to the instrumentalisation of millenarian prophecies and explanations of the Revelation. These texts were highly influential, even among elites, who found themselves adapting to the demands of a new political climate in the second half of the eighteenth century. Russia's growing political influence provided an answer to the search for a Christian leader who could restore order among the Orthodox populations, an order that had been disrupted by Ottoman conquest.

The reformist movement remained politically conservative. Neither the church nor the Ottoman establishment were contested in any way. On the contrary, the Russian example gave scholars such as Moisiodax hope that the Ottomans could be tamed. Moreover, the element that constituted a basic attribute of the European Enlightenment, or at least a large part of it, was missing from the reformist movement: the 'demystification of the world'. In other words, abandoning the function of religion in determining human thought and action. This is evident in the relationship scholars shared with science: as K. Gavroglou and M. Patiniotis have remarked, development of the sciences in the West for Orthodox Christian scholars in the Ottoman Empire was above all 'a triumph of the stated declarations in ancient Greek philosophy, and not a break with traditional ways of thought or legitimation of an alternative model to study nature'. In such an environment, Greek scholars could not, and probably did not even try to, oppose traditional philosophic reason.

It would not be out of line to include individuals in the ranks of this reformist effort that would normally be hastily excluded due to their political tendencies. Perdikaris, a declared supporter of the Greek cause under Ottoman sovereignty, ceaselessly fought for the need to develop schools, blaming the Patriarchate for its stupidity in this regard. He also defined himself as Greek without hesitation, worry or doubt and occupied himself with whether he should send his written work, *Rigas, or against False Philhellenes*,[12] to Adamantios Korais for his opinion. For Perdikaris, as for Korais and many other reformers, their political project focused on the moral renewal of Orthodox Christian subjects of the empire. This could happen only through education, which in turn required the Patriarchate's support to properly flourish.

To a great extent, the political radicalisation of the Ottoman Empire took place at the same time as the French Revolution and its calls for freedom and equality. The presence of French democrats on the Ionian Islands, the experience of wars and the revolution's consequences for the Orthodox populations living in the urban centres of Western and Central Europe affected the Orthodox political and intellectual elite in different manners depending on their situation. Louis XVI's execution in 1793 provoked a first divide among the Orthodox political and intellectual elite, as some turned against the revolution. Progressively, the Patriarchate began to react to the growing number of 'iconoclastic' texts attempting to spread a new political philosophy. The works of Rigas Feraios were the first to be subject to prosecution, condemned along with the French Revolution and other new ideas not conforming to traditional standards. Moreover, hostile relations between the French and the Ottoman Empires during these same years intensified changes within the Patriarchate: after Gregory V's ascent to the throne, policies combating these new ideas occupied the centre stage of its political project.

The French Revolution imprinted a radical legacy on South Eastern Europe at the very moment when radicalism in France seemed most lost. Political conditions were ripe for this development, and Feraios was by all accounts a distinguished representative of this current of thought and political practice. As Kitromilidis has argued, we can make the case for a radical movement led by Feraios, extending both to the interior of the Balkan Peninsula and to Western and Central Europe. Feraios's own demise in 1798 after his arrest by Austrian police and subsequent surrender to the Ottomans (who then strangled him in Belgrade) confirmed the radical movement's Balkan front, of which we know very little. On the other hand, according to *Hellenic Nomarchy*,[13] a text written by an anonymous author that severely criticised the Orthodox elite, this very same phenomenon of Balkan radicalism highlighted the movement's unwavering elements: though prelates could be judged severely, the church was not to be disputed. As reformers, Feraios and the radicals addressed the ecumenicity of the church, replacing it with a system dominated by the principles of freedom and equality. It is worth noting that, for the writer of *Hellenic Nomarchy*, the terms 'Greek' and 'Christian' could be used interchangeably. In this instance, the effects of the Phanariot–ecumenical tradition were evident.

Yet radicalism was a political phenomenon of limited dimensions, and Feraios's heroic death made him seem much more powerful than he really was. Most reformers continued their much more moderate and focused efforts in the area of education. The course charted by Adamantios Korais, a distinguished figure of the modern Greek Enlightenment by any standard, is indicative. Education remained a central issue for him in these years, as it also progressively became a point of conflict between the different groups involved in Orthodox education. Living in Paris, he capably summarised the thrust of the so-called modern Greek Enlightenment, defining its limits in the process. At the time, he was mostly dealing with pedagogical methods and was a proponent of the peer-tutoring method. He also embarked on a massive project to publish ancient Greek writers: the fight against superstition, the securing of individual liberties, the promotion of critique and dialogue all served to link contemporary reality and ancient Greece. A prerequisite for doing so was the creation of a living linguistic corpus purged of archaic or 'vulgar' elements, with consolidated rules.

The individuals comprising this group of reformers belonged to the elite strata of the Orthodox population. This movement's centre focused on the great trading axes of South Eastern Europe, where young men dashed off to their studies, published their works and then served as teachers. We are speaking of a very small number of individuals, who in reality lived and acted in limited areas; their influence over the broader population was non-existent or insignificant. Most of them were clergy, who could thus escape from the miserable reality of traditional society through the channels of the church, pursuing the education they desired, but also continuing their educational work. The Patriarchate was their only stable reference point, and for most people also the only institution that could ensure their survival; criticism was directed at the duties, customs and behaviour of clerics and monks, and much less so at an institutional level. Generally, it was the Greeks' ethical catharsis that would deliver them, with the passage of time, their political freedom.

Yet by absorbing and adapting to the West European intellectual community's needs, the same reformist movement allowed for the possibility of fashioning a religious construct that in turn acquired the elementary political foundations of a community. The movement thus managed to think in national terms and to equate Orthodox Christian with Greek, even if the relationship between the two was not absolutely clear at the beginning of the nineteenth century.

Reforms

The study of the modern Greek Enlightenment illustrates the innovative perceptions shaped in the wings of the reform movement, and the genesis of a national movement—an inevitable consequence of defining the field of research as such, and of an approach based exclusively on the history of ideas.

What we have ignored so far—which distorts our understanding of the overall picture—is a complete approach to this momentum in sociological terms, and the significance these new ideas had for the Ottoman Empire.

The limits of the reformist phenomenon known as the modern Greek Enlightenment first appeared in the educational realm; its viability in societies where oral means of communication predominated determined limitations on its development. In earlier years, the church had been the only institution invested in education. Sources confirm these observations, but they also point to another element: acute disparities in the educational process between common schools and Greek schools. Education in the arts and letters—or, more formally, in the 'common school of holy ecclesiastical letters'—was mostly aimed at those destined to don the priestly robe. The objectives of this type of education were clear, since attaining them determined a priest's ability to fulfil his duties with respect to his clergy. In contrast, the Greek school—the 'school of grammar, curricula and secular philosophy'—concerned itself, initially at least, with the small number of individuals that aimed to occupy higher positions in the ecclesiastical hierarchy.

This dichotomy between the two educational camps was maintained and solidified by the church itself. At the beginning of the eighteenth century, when the ruler of Wallachia, Constantin Basarab, requested a translation of the *Interpretation of the Four Gospels* by Theophylact, archbishop of Bulgaria, into the vernacular, the patriarchal synod categorically replied:

> Not everything is for everyone ..., so, too, in the church there is a need for those who teach and those who are taught; not everyone can be a teacher. Ordinary folk are capable of one thing, teachers another: wise things for the wise, holy things for the holy. Not everything is appropriate for all.

And thus the translation was rejected.[14]

The situation changed over the course of the eighteenth century, when common letters, Romaic, ceased to concern priests partially if not exclusively, and began to reach a wider public: chiefly traders, notable families, and in general all those travelling along major road, land or sea routes connecting South Eastern Europe with Western or Central Europe. As the language of the church, Romaic was an essential tool and vehicle for populations wishing to engage in trading activities. This was especially true of certain national groups such as the Vlachs or Albanians who did not have a written language. Thus, from 1750 onwards, Romaic became the preeminent language of commerce in the Balkans, and a significant percentage of Balkan traders—regardless of their national origin—generally spoke common Greek. For affluent traders in the Balkans, Orthodox Albanians, Serbian Vlachs and Bulgarians, it was a mark of success and recognition to be considered Greek, to speak Greek and support Greek education. From the church's point of view, the language acquired another dimension: that of educating its populations. It is no accident that Cosmas of Aetolia, preaching in regions where significant conversions to Islam were noted, unequivocally supported the founding of schools. At the time, he stated: 'And if fathers be not learned, let your sons study and learn Greek, because our Church is also Greek.'[15]

As conditions became ripe for the emergence of common schools, Greek schools also began to grow in number. As they developed, the Patriarchate and the church in general found themselves in need of more and more literate individuals to support their bureaucratic and intellectual activities. The Phanariot bureaucracy had similar needs in order to staff various activities related to its actions in the Danubian Principalities, Constantinople and elsewhere. At the same time, the high-level of sophistication of the upper social classes—most of them Phanariots—led to the development of an educational model that was not based on common letters but on Greek. This inadvertently linked Orthodox reality with Greek education. Despite the group's ethnic heterogeneity, its proximity to the Patriarchate made knowledge of the Greek language a basic tool for social advancement and success, extending its circle of influence out to the Danubian Principalities. As such, the consolidation of the Phanariots as a group was related, if only symbolically, to the idea of progress through education and the thirst for knowledge as an end in itself. As a result, education became an inherent part of the group's existence.

Beyond the quantitative development of both common and Greek schools, the era's great innovative leap, aptly noted by Nikos Sigalas, was in linking the two—an association that provided the opportunity to identify the experience of Orthodox Christian subjects of the empire with Greek lineage. It is precisely this link that led to confrontations between reformists and their opponents and produced the educational foundations for the creation of a national movement. As a result, use of everyday language in education, historical elements offered by Greek education undertaken in Romaic, and pedagogical methods all became explicitly political, upending previously existing educational practices.

The extension of this educational momentum over the course of the eighteenth century must be understood in relation to attempts at reforming the church and the consolidation of patriarchal authority. This shift was not exclusively Christian: as Faroqhi has shown, there were also developments in Muslim education during the eighteenth century, championed in particular by leaders within the empire's theological and legal hierarchies. Though it remains impossible to study Christian Orthodox populations as a disparate element within the empire, it would be worth entertaining the hypothesis that this reform movement was nothing more than a component of a larger movement taking place on an empire-wide scale. Evidence for this is not in short supply.

As these schools gained practical support from a developing trade network, the burgeoning trade that resulted determined the geographical extent of this educational innovation. A rise in education could be seen in regions feeding the waves of immigration towards Central and Eastern Europe, whose populations, often Vlachs or Albanians, made up the majority of Orthodox Balkan trading networks. Another axis of development was Smyrna, the most important trade centre of the Eastern Mediterranean. It is no coincidence that the triangle formed by Chios, Kidonies and Smyrna had become the centre of educational growth by the eve of the War of Independence. Greek schools were also created in the hubs of Central European and Venetian Orthodox communities, since Orthodox populations had migrated to these areas. Venice, neighbouring Padua, Vienna, Livorno and Trieste—even Mariupol and Odessa—also acquired Greek schools.

The only way to understand what this eighteenth-century educational movement represented, or rather grasp what transformations it caused, is to trace the publishing activity resulting from these reformist efforts. The number of Greek book titles proliferated, largely after the mid-eighteenth century, while the makeup of books in circulation altered correspondingly: by the mid- to late eighteenth century, the proportion of popular or secular books grew in relation to overall production. Books used for teaching in schools were increasingly printed by Greek publishers, along with popular fiction and publications of a more practical nature. In this way, epistolaries, accounting textbooks, books for learning foreign languages and more were all made available to a Greek-speaking readership. But there were also differences in terms of the content itself: old epistolaries, which contained examples of epistles for clergymen, were replaced by others with examples from commercial or personal correspondence. These changes can be measured statistically: in the five years leading up to the War of Independence, religious books represented one-third of the total production, of which 40.6 per cent were ceremonial. Secular books comprised two-thirds of this production, while re-issued editions accounted for 42.5 per cent. The change is particularly noticeable when compared with the corresponding data for Greek books in the period from the fifteenth century to 1821—in which 75 per cent of books contained religious content (ceremonial books accounting for 51.7 per cent of the total), 25 per cent were secular books, and re-issued editions represented 66 per cent of all publications.

However, it would be wrong to link this data with an impressive rise in literacy, or to make a case for radical transformations in education within the Greek regions of the Ottoman Empire. In the period from 1749 to 1821, the people who subscribed to these books, who paid in advance for their copies, mostly resided in Vienna, Bucharest, Constantinople and Iasi. In contrast, there were few people who subscribed to these publications in the regions of the current-day Greek state, with the possible exception of Mount Athos. In other words, the diffusion of scholarly books in Greek regions—and, indeed, books published with the explicit support of these subscribers—was minimal. The importance of scholarly books was also limited in terms of their circulation, as printing runs for these editions were smaller than those for religious books. Korais may have printed 1,000 to 1,500 copies of his books, but upon his death half of them were found to still be in storage warehouses. Thus, as has already been stated, scholarly (and thus reformist) books were read mainly beyond the territorial boundaries of settled Greek-speaking populations. Most of the books read in the latter regions, such as the *Oktoichos* and *Psalter*, were mainly used for educational purposes—that is, for the purpose of religious education. Examples that deviated from this, such as basic language-learning books, which also appeared at this time, were few and far between.

These eighteenth-century educational developments are too broad to be understood solely in terms of the so-called modern Greek Enlightenment. The tensions and opposition manifest in the educational realm could hardly be represented by two opposing terms: on the one hand, a conservatism represented by the church, and on the other the 'modernity' championed by an undifferentiated group of intellectuals. Essentially, this opposition reflected conflicts within the church and the contest for its control, a subject about which little is known. The establishment, for example, of the Athonias School in the mid-eighteenth century came into conflict with the function of the Patriarchal School in Constantinople, under Phanariot control and more precisely, under the supervision of the future Patriarch Samuel Chantzeres. With Voulgaris invited to teach, the Athonias School was placed at the vanguard of Orthodox education. Yet Voulgaris's short stay at Athonias and the reactions he received demonstrated the limits to operating within a monastic context at the exact moment when clashes with the Patriarchate become most severe. Even so, Voulgaris's next step was to teach at the Patriarchal Academy, a move that hardly made sense in the context of the modern Greek Enlightenment. Hence we should not think of the Phanariots as a group with a unified position on educational and ecclesiastic matters. There is every indication that the group's internal opposition was first reflected in the church, and consequently in the educational realm.

It has been argued that reactions within the Patriarchate to the reformist movement in the late eighteenth and early nineteenth century were products of its own weakness. In fact, the opposite is true. The official church reacted precisely because it was more powerful than ever and in a position to impose its will. By then, a large part of the educational system for the Ottoman Empire's Orthodox subjects and the Ecumenical Patriarchate's political power had become institutionalised and increasingly adapted to the demands of the official church. Thus, while church supervision of educational matters was nearly non-existent at first, after an initiative taken by Nicodemus the Hagiorite, an influential figure and monk, oversight of religious books began. By the beginning of the nineteenth century, as conflicts increased, this supervision was expanded to include control over pedagogical content and books taught in schools. It comes as no surprise that the committee established to review books published by the patriarchal press was headed by the Patriarch Gregory V. He was aided by the chief dragoman, two notable city subjects and two Phanariot officials—an example, if nothing else, of the powerful positions that Phanariots held in official Patriarchate circles and their interest in supervising the production and distribution of knowledge.

The French Revolution undoubtedly affected the situation, in the sense that many reformists turned more conservative. Understandably, the Patriarchate faced the new French threat first with suspicion and then hostility. This same context goes a long way in explaining both the persecution of radicals and the shifts in many reformers' initial views. Progressively, the realm of education began to experience a convergence: reformists within the empire's territory could only survive by integrating themselves into ecclesiastical circles, diminishing the reformist educational spirit in the process. The church, in turn, was in a position to accept these developments to the extent that they did not encroach on its power, and, by extension, the reach of Ottoman sovereignty.

Convergences

In the early nineteenth century, Adamantios Korais, a permanent resident of Paris, gave a lecture at the Society of Observers of Man in which he discussed the state of culture in Greece. He presented a simple explanation, which was to be repeated many times thereafter as a standard interpretation of the Greek War of Independence. In the early eighteenth century, Greece was an impoverished country, repressed by a terrible yoke. Few schools and students resulted in incomplete knowledge of the Greek language, and the rest of the population lived in a state of ignorance. But this was also the era of the European Enlightenment, of which Diderot's *Encyclopaedia* was one of the causes, which had specific consequences for Greece. Certain rays of the Enlightenment reached the country, and it, in turn, was aware of them; yet the country was impoverished. Then, flourishing trade and the Russo-Turkish War changed the situation. The former enabled material conditions for the development of education, while the latter—during which the Russians abandoned the Greeks, and Ottoman vulnerability was exposed—led this subjugated nation to believe that freedom was an attainable goal, one that they themselves could achieve. Schools multiplied, intellectuals rebelled and books were published in vast quantities. The moral revolution—for this is what Korais named it—had begun, and it accelerated as the French Revolution added one more impulse to this quest for freedom.[16] It was an era where 'national vanity gave way to a population ostensibly preparing to become a nation'.[17] The Greeks returned to their past to discover their future.

Korais's view of the developments leading to this Greek revival saw the Ottoman Empire as a given, unchanging form of savagery and despotism. This was the context in which the empire's Orthodox Christians found strength to be reborn and become Hellenes. Thus the impetus to change the situation arose exclusively from the subjugated peoples themselves; a natural position for a scholar influenced by the principles of the French Enlightenment. But this same approach can still be detected in modern Greek historiography, which overlooks the fact that all transformations in the realm of Orthodox existence were linked with the Ottoman state's adaptation to new international realities—that is, with Ottoman attempts to survive international competition. Let us not forget that Selim III and Mahmud II, the last two sultans to occupy the throne before the fight for Greek independence, were associated first and foremost with reformist attempts during the pre-Tanzimat period.

In fact, it was the Ottoman state itself that motivated these transformations, as it sought to secure more resources and enact more administrative and political reforms, rearranging the balance of power in the empire's political administration. Though this process has been associated with the decline of the Ottoman Empire, in reality it was simply the Ottoman state mechanism's process of adapting to new international balances of power. Though some considered the existence of quasi-autonomous rulers within Ottoman territory (such as Ali Pasha in Epirus and Albania, or Osman Pazvantoğlu of Vidin) proof of the empire's disintegration, it must be remembered that the empire was always capable of subduing these figures (with varying degrees of difficulty, to be sure).

Within this context, the Patriarchate played a key role, becoming a fundamental mechanism for the empire's political sovereignty, spreading over large expanses of territory and assuming command over the Orthodox populations. This allowed the Ottoman state to infiltrate local communities and institutionalise political control of these populations—something that would have been unthinkable previously.

The Orthodox group known as the Phanariots benefited from this extension of patriarchal mechanisms. Included in the empire's political houses, the Phanariots were able to occupy high-ranking positions, making use of new systems of administration to assume leadership of the Danubian regions and claim their transformation into a Greek Orthodox aristocracy, whom they were able to dominate and profit from through religious mechanisms, but also directly via their positions in the Ottoman administration. As such, above all else, the Phanariots were members of the Ottoman administrative elite. This is from where they derived their power.

As a result, administrative mechanisms emerged within the empire that specifically, if not exclusively, addressed Orthodox populations; that is to say, they addressed an Orthodox Christian assemblage. Although under Ottoman rule, this assemblage was also keenly aware of its position, at least from a bird's-eye view. Along with them, local elites equally essential to the administration of Christian populations strengthened their positions for many of the same reasons. Conflict between the church and Phanariots existed, but so did certain mutual arrangements necessary for the existence of both. As mentioned earlier, the expansion of tax-farming mechanisms had brought the group closer than ever before to the Ottoman administration.

These new circumstances gave rise to new Orthodox needs. It became clear that an increasing number of educated Phanariots and local elites were now able to fill church positions. Though this process had already begun during the patriarchal tenure of Loukaris, it accelerated year by year, further boosted by the rise of traders and other elites that relied on those educational mechanisms for their own advancement. But these very same mechanisms, supported and promoted by the church, also led to confrontations and tension. The church's reformist tendencies found their complete expression in the scholars said to belong to the Enlightenment school—despite the fact that they never confronted the ecclesiastic environment to which they all owed their existence as monks or priests.

The manner in which the educational process itself developed—especially after being subjected to influences from Western Europe—led to the formation of a new perspective on the nature of the Orthodox population. A new Greek national identity made its appearance in Western European thought, gradually giving many Orthodox Christian subjects of the empire the opportunity to extract themselves from the ecumenical fold and turn towards a national understanding of their destiny.

However, it would be premature to make an argument for nationalism at this point. In reality, all of the opposition movements within the Orthodox political community were mainly concerned with the way they were ruled, rather than establishing an independent Greek state. It is worth noting that Korais did not believe in the necessity of revolt, because he did not think the Greeks were ready for such an event. Similarly, though in different terms, Perdikaris believed that Greeks had to remain under the Ottoman yoke. The only exceptions were Feraios and Balkan radicalism, but by the nature of the views they advocated they were far removed from any nationalist or proto-nationalist positions, as their political views were expressed in universal terms.

Even by the beginning of the nineteenth century, the Orthodox population did not dispute Ottoman sovereignty. Rather, it negotiated with it. Koumas, a notable representative of the reformist movement, asserted in 1832:

> The Greek nation, despite all the misfortunes which it has suffered at the hands of its rulers, remained ever tranquil, and attributed its present plight to the inexplicable designs of divine providence ... No trace of revolutionary ideas can be found in any sane individual's head. Indeed, the sound of mind denounced those responsible for the tragic scene that unfolded in the Peloponnese in 1769. There were many of religious disposition who out of pious zeal preached that divine providence subjected us to the Ottoman sceptre in order, by this means, to protect us from heresies and from the growing indifference for divine matters that has been noted in various Christian countries.[18]

Internal opposition existed; anything else would have been paradoxical. On the one hand, there were those that believed in maintaining the political status quo, which granted Greeks a chance at economic and social progress. On the other, there were those that saw the Ottomans as despots and savages, but who also believed that the moment was not right for change, or that change had to be accompanied by a complete educational rebirth of the nation.

New balances in international relations were largely responsible for upsetting the situation. Russia, disputing Ottoman integrity and hoping to win over the empire's Orthodox Christian political, religious and trade elite, found itself in a position to exert influence previously deemed unthinkable. While Anastasios Gordios, another distinguished representative of the Loukaris–Koridalefs circle, had previously believed the apocalyptic interpretations foretelling Orthodox Christian liberation from the Ottoman yoke were wrong and that his people would remain endlessly under Muslim rule, Russian influence was enough to convince him that things might turn out differently. In fact, the Orlov Revolts showed the true nature and limits of this potential reversal. It was certain political elites, chiefly local ones, that sought to establish more favourable positions in a system that would be free of Muslim domination. Elites from the central powers resisted these changes, as they diminished their authority, their position and their income.

But influences were not exclusively Russian and did not only concern local elites. It is no coincidence that within the Orthodox Christian pockets of Constantinople—Phanariot and ecclesiastical—both French and Russian parties formed. Those allied to England were less influential. The solution would come from outside, about that there was no doubt; but it was clear that foreign influences could also have an impact on the empire's politics in the meantime. Depending on their positions and political choices, the Phanariots could hope for their own autonomous hegemony, supported by a member of the Great Powers. The arrival of the French within striking distance of the empire's territories rendered these prospects all the more attractive for its Orthodox Christian subjects, as did the founding of the Ionian State, the first independent political government at the time.

2

THE WAR OF INDEPENDENCE

(1821–32)

The Greek territories are those that took up—or will take up—arms against the Ottoman dynasty.[1]

The 'Philike Etaireia'

In 1814, three little-known traders of Odessa—Nikolaos Skoufas, Athanassios Tsakalof and Emmanouil Xanthos—undertook an initiative that would later prove decisive for the future of the Balkan Peninsula's Christian populations. They founded a secret organisation called the Philike Etaireia, with the objective of liberating their 'homeland'. With no educational background to speak of—save for Tsakalof, who was certainly more educated than the others—the three founders of the Philike Etaireia were not distinguished by their professional achievements. All three were small traders, and one of them, Skoufas, went bankrupt after the Etaireia's founding. It appears that all three already had experience participating in secret societies and Masonic lodges, and they based the establishment of their organisation on these experiences. The example of a secret society founded by Rigas Velestinlis also played a role.

As agreed upon by its founders, the Etaireia was led by an 'Invisible Authority' that guided its actions and could not be revealed, for obvious reasons. The Authority most likely had links with Russia, home to many important Orthodox Christian families, and with the tsar himself. In practice, until

1820, the Etaireia was led by a small group of largely unknown individuals (Sekeris being a possible exception), which hid its actions behind the ambiguity and non-existence of this Invisible Authority.

In 1816, two years after its creation, the Etaireia was made up of only thirty members, all Greek immigrants from the lower and middle classes. That very same year, the Etaireia changed its strategy. In 1817, it moved its headquarters to Constantinople, the heart of the Ottoman Empire, a relocation that thoroughly altered its future and makeup: it is indicative that almost one in five members was catechised in Constantinople, though this figure did not include any senior clerics or members of key Phanariot families. Meanwhile, its leadership grew, adding members who compensated for a basic organisational weakness: the Etaireia's limited access to previously inaccessible groups, such as chieftains or seamen.

Timetable 1821–32

1821	Outbreak of the War of Independence. Kalteza Assembly (June). Tripoli is occupied by the rebels (September).
1822	Defeat and death of Ali Pasha. Destruction of Chios. First Ottoman attempt to occupy Missolonghi. Dramalis's defeat in the Peloponnese. Provisional Constitution of Epidaurus.
1823	The government is established in Nafplion. Second National Assembly (30 March–11 April). Constitution of Astros. Civil war begins.
1824	First foreign loan. Mahmud II enlists the help of Egyptian Pasha Mehmet Ali. The Turkish fleet suppresses the revolt in Crete and ravages Kasos and Psara. Ibrahim lands in the Peloponnese.
1825	Kolokotronis is imprisoned. Second foreign loan. Second siege of Missolonghi.
1826	Third National Assembly. Exodus of Missolonghi.
1827	Death of Karaiskakis. Athens surrenders to Reşid Mehmet Pasha. Ioannis Kapodistrias elected by the Third National Assembly. Political Constitution of Greece. Treaty of London. Sea battle of Navarino.
1828	Kapodistrias visits Nafplion. Following the recommendation of Kapodistrias, Parliament suspends validity of the political Constitution of Greece. Protocol of London.
1829	Fourth National Assembly. Battle of Petra. Treaty of Adrianople.
1830	London Protocol. Leopold of Saxonburg elected king of Greece.
1831	Murder of Kapodistrias. Istanbul Convention. Election of Otto.
1832	Fifth National Assembly. Treaty of London: the Greek state declared a hereditary monarchy with its first king, Otto, second son of King Ludwig I of Bavaria. Treaty of Constantinople: Greece's borders are defined from the Pagasetic to the Ambracian Gulf.

Membership in the Philike Etaireia increased gradually, without any spectacular increases in recruitment. In 1820, it amounted to a few hundred members in total. Internal frictions and conflicts between members—some of whom sought to use it as a means of financial enrichment—rendered the process of recruiting new members all the more difficult. The Etaireia's central leadership reacted by attempting to impose stricter criteria for selecting members and did not hesitate to kill at least one of its antagonists so as to avoid leaking information.

2.1: Places of Origin and Catechism for Members of the Etaireia

Place	*Member Place of Origin (% of total)*	*Member Place of Catechism (% of total)*
The Peloponnese	37.2	21.1
Mainland Greece	3.9	1.6
Epirus	10.5	–
Thessaly	6.2	–
Ionian Islands	12.3	7.8
Macedonia	2.3	1.8
Aegean Islands	14.6	5.2
Asia Minor	2.9	1.8
Constantinople	5.4	18.2
Wallachia	–	5.5
Southern Russia	–	15.6
Moldova	–	19.1
Europe	–	2.1

Source: G.D. Frangos, 'The Philike Etaireia, 1814–1821: A Social and Historical Analysis', PhD dissertation, New York: Columbia University, 1971, pp. 251, 318.

The issue of leadership remained important, especially with regard to the establishment of the Invisible Authority. Many of its members and some new recruits faced the ambiguity surrounding leadership with a certain suspicion and asked for more than the assurances of catechists. For this reason, the Etaireia's leaders turned to the Corfiot Ioannis Kapodistrias, the tsar's deputy minister of external affairs, asking him to take on the leadership. His refusal led to the assignment of his position to Alexandros Ypsilantis, son of Konstantinos Ypsilantis, former ruler of the Danubian regions who was forced to escape to Russia in 1806 when his communications with the Russians had been revealed to the Porte. Alexandros Ypsilantis was an adjutant of the tsar and had participated in the Napoleonic Wars at a young age, where he had lost his hand.

Ypsilantis's nomination as leader completely changed the way Etaireia operated. As it pivoted from its existence as an organisation supported by small traders, professionals and military members, it began recruiting members of the upper classes, undermining its very roots. Power shifted away from those who had played a primary role in its development thus far towards Ypsilantis's circle, which was in the midst of feverish preparations for war. Naturally, this group, which came to lead the fight for independence, substantially influenced the strategy that was to follow. In fact, from the moment Ypsilantis came to power, the Etaireia's battle preparations were increasingly influenced by Phanariot perceptions of the political governance of Christian populations. To a large extent, this was the Etaireia's main weakness and inconsistency: though it was undoubtedly aimed at the Greeks, the ambitions and geographical spread of the movement far exceeded the regions in which a majority of the population was Greek or Greek-speaking. By electing Ypsilantis as their leader, the Etaireia showed that it also hoped to win over leading groups from other non-Greek Christian populations. Contact had also been confirmed with Serbs and Vlachs.

The Etaireia was never a large organisation. Until 1820, it could not have exceeded 600 or 700 total members and it is only from this year onwards that certain sources make a case for large-scale recruitment. On the contrary, based on available evidence that contradicts testimonies claiming mass catechisms of Etaireia members in the immediate pre-war period, this number began to decrease after 1819. Yet the statistics available after this year must be fabricated, as the Authority's new leadership under Ypsilantis in 1820 created entirely different organisational conditions for which we do not have substantial information. However, the existing estimate of 1,093 individuals still indicates a fairly closed organisation even if the figure is doubled or tripled. For all intents and purposes, the Etaireia's goal was the recruitment of a political, religious and military elite. This is evidenced by the organisation's makeup: farmers, who represented the majority of the overall population, made up an insignificant 0.7 per cent of the Etaireia.

A typical example of participation in the Etaireia can be seen in Petrobey Mavromichalis of Mani's accession following hard-won negotiations and the anticipation of short-term and long-term favours. Mavromichalis secured his family's sovereignty in Mani following the creation of the state whose founding was portended by the Etaireia, and he also secured the region's relative autonomy. Similarly, the organisation's actions in the Peloponnese were aimed at local notables. On a regional level, this resulted in a certain degree of autonomy from the Authority—maintained with fierce dedication—and decidedly oligarchic characteristics that manifested themselves both before and directly after the beginning of the war. Each more or less discrete group created in the Etaireia's embrace attempted to shape its future and the Etaireia's own strategy based on its own interests and prospects, respectively honing its tactics for the beckoning war.

The Etaireia's social composition is more or less known and yields no surprises. Of the 910 members with known professions, more than half (53.7 per cent) were traders, 13.1 per cent were 'professionals' (including doctors, teachers and professors), 11.7 per cent were landowners (most of them from the Peloponnese), 9.5 per cent were clerics, and 8.7 per cent were military men serving as mercenaries for foreign armies in Russia or the Ionian Islands. The disproportionate influence of traders in the Etaireia is considered by many to be representative of the nature of the War of Independence itself. It should also be noted that this group also included large numbers of secretaries, messengers and other low-ranking workers in trading enterprises, as well as craftsmen or independent merchants. The large percentage of traders that participated in the Etaireia expresses nothing more than the ease with which groups living outside the Ottoman Empire were able to join, since they could participate in the Etaireia with minimal personal risk. Additionally, precisely because of their status, they often took on a subversive attitude towards the Ottoman Empire. But the major characteristic of Etaireia members, perhaps the most important of all, was that many of them were Greek merchants, professionals or soldiers who identified with the experience of the immigrant. This group shared many similarities, including average age, date of accession and even the manner in which they carried out proselytising activities. This held true even for those who were converted in Constantinople itself, where their large numbers were justified by their short stay. Notables and clerics who joined the Etaireia constituted another equally distinct group: they were converted in their own countries of origin, were consistently older than the other groups, and joined the Etaireia later (although they stopped joining as a group earlier than the rest).

More generally, it should be noted that both the great trading centres of the West and the nuclei of the reform movement in Central Europe were notably absent from the Etaireia. Vienna, the chief locus of the modern Greek Enlightenment and host to a significant Greek population at the time, was represented by only one member. The only areas outside the Ottoman Empire with high accession rates were the Danubian regions and Russia. Similarly, regions in Asia Minor and Macedonia (especially the large trade and educational centres of Thessaloniki, Ioannina and Smyrna) showed extremely low rates of participation. In contrast, the Ionian Islands, beyond the reach of Ottoman sovereignty, exhibited high rates of participation. As George Frangos has plausibly argued, the existence of both a homogeneous Christian population and strong political oligarchy rendered the Etaireia's endeavour successful. Such were the cases found in the Peloponnese and certain Ionian Islands.

The Philike Etaireia was the group that organised the War of Independence. But with the outbreak of war it ceased to exist, its political importance annihilated. There are many reasons for this. First of all, it was a secret organisation that could not play a wartime role, as it would de facto lose its importance. Secondly, it would act, as became evident, in opposition to leading local groups that took on the cost and organisation of battle and consequently wanted to control the resulting power themselves. D. Ypsilantis's (brother of Alexandros) conflict with leading groups in the Peloponnese is just one example of this; a poorly organised battle in Moldavia also served to discredit their work. Then, the early death of notable players in the Etaireia's establishment and expansion—N. Skoufas, A. Papas, G. Dikaios and Anagnostaras—deprived the organisation of key individuals. Alexandros Mavrokordatos's diplomatic efforts (which aimed to weaken D. Ypsilantis's position, shake allegations of Carbonarism, and secure recognition for the Greek struggle from the Great Powers) also served to discredit and marginalise the Etaireia's project.

By the eve of the War of Independence, the Etaireia may not have been a massive organisation, but rumours of its existence and activities circulated and seem to have reached the ears of the Ottoman authorities in one form or another. Time was running out. Hoursit Pasha's allocation to the Peloponnese in 1820 shows that the Porte's unease had spread—the new pasha was particularly known for his rebellion-quelling abilities. At that very moment, Alexandros Ypsilantis and other leading members of the Etaireia were obliged to step up organisational preparations for an armed uprising, as well as the recruiting effort necessary to support it.

Wars

In late February 1821, Alexandros Ypsilantis, uniformed as a Russian general, crossed the border of Moldova with Russia and initiated the war. He was accompanied by just 200 infantrymen. Ypsilantis's move seemed to be a reversal of the original 'master plan', which had him passing through the

Peloponnese. But the death of Alexandros Soutzos, ruler of Wallachia, had created a power vacuum that was judged to be beneficial for the rebellion.

In very little time, all the hopes upon which Ypsilantis's plans rested collapsed. Alexander, the Russian tsar—in Ljubljana at the time, meeting with the other leaders of the Holy Alliance—condemned the movement and denounced Ypsilantis, removing him from his position in the Russian army and granting the Ottomans permission to invade the Danubian Principalities. Then, the support Ypsilantis counted on from local rulers and boyars turned to hostility and opposition against a possible victory for the Etaireia, which soon manifested itself as open confrontation. Expectations of Serbian support proved to be in vain, while the tsar's renunciation and the patriarch's excommunication of Ypsilantis further weakened his position. In the end, a complete lack of military organisation, rampant defections, and the limited potential for recruitment on the ground doomed the undertaking from the outset.

By late August 1821, virtually all sources resisting the Ottoman Empire in the Danubian regions had been eliminated. This desperate war was marked by a few heroic acts, and Ypsilantis was soon forced to cross the Austrian border, hoping to continue the battle in mainland Greece. But he was arrested by the Austrians and imprisoned for an extended period of time. He died in 1828, soon after he had been released.

The battle developed more favourably for rebels in the Peloponnese, despite the fact that the Ottomans were very suspicious of the Christians: they had asked the local leaders of Morea to move to Tripoli, the capital, to establish direct control over them. Many complied and were imprisoned at the outbreak of the war. Others with more foresight anticipated the outbreak and avoided the fatal consequences in store for those held hostage in Tripoli.

As planned, the war was to begin on 25 March, the day of Annunciation. However, trouble stirred several days earlier, and Muslims, mainly tax farmers, were attacked by Christians. Other such attacks soon followed on individual Muslims, and in some cases even on Christians. This created panic among the Muslim populations of the Peloponnese, who sought refuge in fortified positions. Some of them were able to protect fugitives, while others quickly fell into Christian hands. Certainly, nowhere was prepared for a long-lasting siege.

The Muslim exodus to fortified positions and towns sparked looting of properties left behind but also the massacring of individual families that sought refuge too late. Despite all this, the Greeks had not yet begun any significant offensives; this was due to the groups of notables and their reluctance to wage a war in which there were no guarantees—or even any information—about what the Invisible Authority of the Philike Etaireia represented or what assistance it could provide. The already noticeable violence, especially in Patras, accelerated this decision-making process out of fear that the situation would escalate beyond their control.

And so the notables of the northern Peloponnese, most of whom had avoided moving to Tripoli, went to Patras to limit the looting and massacres. Here, the war took on a more organised form. Though the Greeks were scattered by a small Ottoman force that had arrived in Patras from mainland Greece to support those besieged in the city's castle, the war had begun, and notables had now entered the fray. A few days later, upon hearing news of the events in Patras, the Maniots, led by Petrobey Mavromichalis, attacked and quickly conquered Kalamata.

With the Muslim population holed up in castles and cities, the Greeks' objectives were clear. They needed to lay siege and capture them. This was a difficult task, which would only be made easier if the fortresses were rendered incapable of restocking supplies from the sea. The besiegers had neither the weapons nor the knowledge necessary to take over fortified settlements.

For their part, the Ottomans incorrectly assessed the Greek effort, believing the Russians were behind it, or that it was motivated by Ali Pasha of Ioannina, who was already in conflict with the Porte at the time. For this reason, most of their available troops remained in the Danubian territories or were involved in the siege of Ioannina, thus facilitating Greek control of the Peloponnese and Central Greece. Simultaneously, a brief war with Persia engaged significant military forces, and the subsequent fire in Constantinople on 17 February 1823 destroyed storehouses holding supplies for the Greek campaign. A war against Ali Pasha had also used up significant resources.

Tripoli, the capital of the Peloponnese, is situated in the centre of Morea and was a strategically important position for controlling the peninsula. The Greeks had hoped to capture the city since the outbreak of the war, and it was here that they tested their wartime forces, mainly against the Ottoman Empire's cavalry. Initial failures turned to successes, and a combination of hunger and unrewarded hope of reinforcements led to the fall of the city with unprecedented massacres and pillaging. This was an important victory for the Greeks, and if nothing else, it strengthened morale.

The rebels had earlier secured another important success by occupying the castle of Monemvasia. They also occupied the fortress of Neokastro in the western Peloponnese. Yet these initial successes were accompanied by comparable failures. The siege of Corinth, for example, was abandoned at first sight of Ottoman reinforcements arriving from Ioannina; Nafplion, with its extremely strong fortifications, did not fall into Greek hands until 1822. Methoni, Koroni and Patras remained Ottoman possessions, and constituted the only Ottoman-held territories in the Peloponnese.

In Central Greece, the conditions were quite different. Here, leaders of the armed elite played a primary role. Their familiarity with mountainous territories had rendered them masters of the political playing field, and they managed to limit the dominance of local leaders. The Porte's war against Ali Pasha had already upset the region's political balance as some local chieftains rallied behind Ali while others joined the sultan's troops, hoping for a better fate in the event of the Pasha's defeat in Ioannina. The area's proximity to centres that were of fundamental importance for the Ottoman military, such as Larissa, Ioannina (after the Pasha's fall), Trikala and Thessaloniki, made all attempts against the empire risky.

This was clearly evident from the ease with which the uprisings were suppressed in Northern Greece. In Macedonia, Thessaly and Epirus, the Ottomans had no difficulty facing down their opponents' military efforts. Yet in Central Greece, the shift in local balances ultimately proved favourable to the Greek struggle. Despite the fact that the region tallied, by no accident, the least amount of Etaireia members, local leaders' claims to controlling *armatoles* played an essential role in determining which side they would take in the war against the empire. Some allied with the sultan's troops, others waited on the side-lines, and still others who sought to claim their rivals' *armatoles* took up arms and joined the battle. As a result, many of the undecided parties—waiting to see which side would be victorious, but in danger of losing their position in the process—made up their minds. This indecision and the maintenance of open channels of communication with the Ottomans so as to back out in case of Greek defeat continued until the war's end.

Thanks to their naval strength, the islands came to play a decisive role in the war. But their inhabitants viewed the initial conflicts of mainland Greece with scepticism. Spetses, with a large number of notables and Etaireia members, first joined the battle in early April. The inhabitants of Psara, upon hearing significantly delayed news of the war's outbreak in the Peloponnese and Central Greece, took care to immediately begin preparations and contact Spetses. The situation was not so straightforward in Hydra, where hesitation and reservations among the notables greatly delayed them joining the battle. Ultimately, it took a mutiny led by Antonios Economou, a second-class captain, together with Peloponnesians and seamen from Hydra, to force the island's notables to join the war. It was no coincidence that Economou—who had challenged the local oligarchy's authority in the process—was assassinated shortly thereafter.

Of the remaining islands, some with Catholic populations, or those protected by the French king, remained neutral. This often proved convenient for the warring Greeks, who managed to use the islands as refuge or for the development of trading activities without risking Ottoman intervention. Ultimately, the remaining islands were incorporated into military operations with various degrees of eagerness from local leaders.

The Greek fleet in particular benefited from initial Ottoman inaction; despite the Ottoman fleet's superiority in relation to Greek grain-carrying vessels, the former did not pursue aggressive tactics at sea, limiting itself to supporting the empire's fortresses. As a result, Greek ships succeeded in maintaining their superiority over the Ottoman fleet and securing control of the Aegean.

In these conditions, the Greeks were quickly able to consolidate their struggle against the Ottomans—even if this was only the case in the territories of the Peloponnese, mainland Greece and the islands. In all other areas that sought to overthrow the Ottoman regime, repression was swift and brutal. This situation prevailed until 1825. Only in 1822 did the Ottomans manage to rally together a significant army numbering 25,000 men under the leadership of Mahmud Pasha Dramali in an attempt to crush the revolution. Yet, plagued by the issues involved in supplying such a large army, they were eventually defeated by the Peloponnesian General Theodoros Kolokotronis in Dervenakia, in the northern Peloponnese. From this point onwards, the Ottomans failed to re-establish an organised and sizeable army. The Greeks, for their part, lacked the military power and organisation necessary to achieve complete victory. Thus the war continued without an obvious conclusion. Sultan Mahmud II then attempted to put an end to the stalemate in 1825, inviting Mehmet Ali, ruler of Egypt, to crush the Greek rebellion in exchange for Crete and the Peloponnese.

Mehmet Ali dispatched an army led by his son Ibrahim Pasha—a regular army, organised by French officers. It landed in the south-western Peloponnese in February 1825, surprising the Greeks, who did not expect such a move in wintertime. The Egyptian army's regimented organisation completely changed the terms of war, and the Greeks were in no position to rise to the occasion. Ibrahim began suppressing outbreaks of Greek resistance, while offering the opportunity for those who had betrayed the revolution's cause to peacefully settle in their own villages. The Greek war effort seemed about to flounder, and only the reactions of the greatest Peloponnesian general, Kolokotronis, ensured the resistance's survival. The combined Egyptian and Ottoman forces succeeded in occupying Missolonghi in 1826, which constituted one of the two main fronts of the war in mainland Greece. In 1827, they occupied Athens, the resistance's last remaining military stronghold beyond the Corinth Canal.

The situation at sea also changed with Egypt's involvement in 1825, after which the united Turkish–Egyptian fleet gained key bases in regions of open conflict, as well as Souda in Crete, Navarino in the Peloponnese, and Kos. They also caused significant damage on islands such as Psara and Kasos, succeeding in limiting the operational effectiveness of the Greek fleet.

Yet just at the moment when the Greek struggle seemed doomed, the Great Powers altered the course of battle. In 1826, Britain, France and Russia agreed to the creation of an autonomous Greek state, though it was not yet clear exactly what form it would take. To this end, they dispatched fleets preventing Ibrahim Pasha from continuing his devastating operations. A huge battle, most probably sparked by chance, took place between the two fleets at Navarino and resulted in the annihilation of the Turkish fleet. Soon after, France sent an expeditionary force to the Egyptians, compelling them to leave.

Army and fleet

As previously noted, the Greek War of Independence was conducted by the rebels' military and political elite. No organised army existed, and these Christian units were initially composed of *klephts*—bandits—and *armatoles* with extensive wartime experience, as well as military groups secured by notables and chieftains through a system of remuneration. Anyone with economic power organised and maintained their own military forces, without which it would have been difficult to fight the Ottomans while simultaneously maintaining control of their provinces. It is telling that in the beginnings of war, in the Karytainia province where the Deliyannis and Kolokotronis families comprised the two poles of opposing political power, an agreement existed between the two such that recruitment and encampment was undertaken separately by each group without one imposing on the other. Under these conditions, implementation of centrally administered operations was incredibly difficult, if not impossible.

Acquiring economic power was an essential precondition for maintaining military (and by extension political) force. This necessity to gather economic resources by any means necessary often explained the behaviour of these leading groups and the logic of their military manoeuvres. It even explained the rebels' often ruthless and relentless exploitation of Christian populations—this, of course, in cases when the latter were far removed from their native lands. This army of Greeks was made up of fighters that became more and more professional as the war progressed, without the organisation of a regular army.

Though this problem was widely acknowledged, all attempts at organising the forces fighting for independence—attempts already manifest in preparations by local polities at the beginnings of the war—failed. First, in Central Greece, chieftains were the ones with military power, and they were intent on keeping it. Secondly, confrontations in the Peloponnese between notables and chieftains, led by Ypsilantis and Kolokotronis, inevitably resulted in a lack of military coordination. In fact, notables made repeated efforts to expel this army from their lands. The first timid attempts at organised military action came about only after the arrival of money via foreign loans. These loans also led to the temporary ascendance of a central government, as we will see below.

The compensation offered by leaders, as well as loot and the hope for social and economic gains offered incentives to many villagers to take part in the War of Independence. The concentration of a considerable number of villagers outside Tripoli during its siege does not express so much a militant disposition as much as the hope of plundering it after its occupation, which indeed happened. From the moment that this looting was no longer widespread (by the time the fortresses had been occupied, which is to say, at the beginning of the war), the potential for recruitment was limited. This resulted in the frequent use of violence to mobilise villagers. Towards the end of the war, new individuals were selected for military and political leadership as others lost their importance and power. Particularly in the Peloponnese, the war strengthened the power of chieftains—as was to be expected—who in the years leading up to the war had depended on notables to varying degrees. In Roumeli, to the contrary, efforts were made to restrict these chieftains' powers.

The basic problem within these Greek armed units was their lack of coordination, and for a long time no central command existed. Even when it was created, it was not easily imposed on the respective chieftains. Apart from two or three exceptions, the Greek army never managed to assemble in large numbers to fight the Ottomans. The one time it attempted to do so—under the command of foreign officers that had been recruited despite opposition from local chieftains—the result was catastrophic. This was the case in the 1827 Battle of Phaliron, where the Greek army reached 10,000 in number for the first time but was trounced by clearly inferior forces led by Reşid Mehmed Paşa in the siege of the Acropolis. So, inevitably, guerrilla tactics became the dominant way of fighting the Ottomans. There were no decisive battles and many simultaneous fronts, in which a victory or defeat for one side or the other would not decide the outcome of the entire war. This also explains why the war lasted for an extended period of time.

Moreover, Greek fighters would seldom agree to fight in places that were far from their own provinces. Experienced fighters in the Mani Mountains repeatedly refused to move far from their region, as did other Peloponnesians. Only the fighters from Central Greece moved to the Peloponnese for the duration of this civil war so as to obey the wishes of the central government, which paid them for this very reason. But even on expeditions involving a minimum of cooperation, the army's leadership remained divided. As the Athenian campaign was being prepared, the Souliotes agreed to participate only under terms that granted them their own leader, while the Peloponnesians had their own ruler, Nikitas, and the Roumeliots, Karaiskakis.

The conditions of war were such that casualties caused from military operations were rather limited. But civilian casualties must have been very high, both due to the conditions caused by long-term military campaigns and the violence they were subjected to by both sides whenever the opportunity arose. In many cases, the slaughter of Muslim populations was conducted on a mass scale; wartime military and political leaders resorted to this measure to exclude any possibility of retaliation from the local populations. Inevitably, familiarisation with violence over time rendered it a means of resolving political differences, even among Greeks. As a consequence, population estimates for the regions constituting the Greek state (the Peloponnese, Central Greece and the Cyclades) decreased by 20 per cent between 1821 and 1828.

Capturing and taking the Ottomans hostage with the possibility of their eventual return or exchange for Christian hostages did occur, but it was obviously the case for more prosperous and important individuals—that is to say, a relatively small number overall. Agreements often existed between Greek leaders and their opponents, especially with the Albanians with whom they shared a certain familiarity, as they originated in the same provinces. This was often the case in Central Greece. For example, when the Souliotes refused to participate in military campaigns in November 1821, the reason was none other than an agreement they had made with the *aghas* from Roumeli: one party would not proceed with any action without consulting and agreeing with the other first. Especially in Central Greece, this salvaged the potential for compromise with Ottoman authorities in instances when the wartime developments demanded it, as both a tactical decision and a decision to maintain control of a certain province.

The Greek navy was similarly disorganised. Ships used in battle campaigns were private trading vessels until the final years of the war, when fleets were finally purchased by the central government. These ships were adapted to the needs of war, but the basic problem—one that was never really solved for the entirety of the war—was the financing of military operations. The cost was huge, and seamen demanded a secure wage in order to continue offering their services. In the early stages of the war, captains and local island leaders themselves took on a large part of the costs of these military operations. Each island maintained its own fleet, commanded by its own admiral. The lack of coordination mentioned previously was also evident on the seas, and ships were frequently withdrawn during operations because of disagreements, personal conflicts or even an inability to pay the crew.

These weaknesses in the ranks of the Greek army and navy also existed in the Ottoman armed forces. The latter was not a regular army; it was composed of groups of chieftains invited by their respective pashas to participate in annual campaigns to suppress the rebellion with the promise of payment and plunder. The Ottoman troops were mainly Albanian, though some troops from Asia also played a part. The nature of this army determined the limits and nature of the military conflict itself. As the summer months ended, many wished to return home; delays in payment could also lead to the army's dissolution, a situation similar to that of the Greek army at the time. Furthermore, a lack of logistical support made the task of assembling a large army impossible and rendered its survival dependent on exploitation of the lands it was occupying at the time.

The Ottoman fleet was plagued by similar problems. Ill-maintained, it faced a serious problem of staffing its ships after the outbreak of war as until then its crew had been largely composed of residents from Hydra, Spetses and Psara. In any case, it was more suited for supporting army operations on land than it was for undertaking independent maritime operations.

This balance shifted only after the arrival of regular Egyptian troops, who, organised by French officers, were much better trained than Ottoman troops. From this point onwards, Greece's inability to confront an organised military enemy became obvious. All attempts at establishing a regular army—mostly focusing on recruitment of philhellenes—failed, as they were continually opposed by leaders of the irregular troops, for whom a regular army always posed a potential threat to political power.

Alliances between Christians and Ottomans certainly existed at every stage of the War of Independence. Anything to the contrary would be paradoxical, as from its very beginnings the Greek rebellion contained all the elements of a civil war, to the extent that inhabitants of the same regions were fighting each other. From early on in the war, the besieged Ottomans of Patras were aided, certainly not selflessly, by Missolonghites. A. Vakalopoulos has raised this issue from a different perspective, downplaying the phenomenon's significance. Over time, one opponent or another prevailed within a certain territory, determining whom the local populations would side with. The same was true of captains from Roumeli, who according to both the composition of their *armatoles* and the balance of power, sided with either the Ottomans or the rebels.

Indeed, in the last years of the war, the number of Christians participating in Ottoman military campaigns grew. The case of Nenekos, a minor chieftain from Kalavryta, who not only joined Ibrahim's army but managed to influence other leaders of the north-western Peloponnese, is the most well known. Overall, Christian participation in the Ottoman army seems to have been a more common phenomenon than we are led to believe. Before the Battle of Agrafa, for example, Mahmud Pasha of Shkodra called on Georgios Karaiskakis to surrender to his army, telling him among other things that the bulk of his army consisted of Christians.

Politics

With the outbreak of war, each region hastened to create its own administrative system. Immediately after Kalamata was occupied, the Messinian Senate was founded there. Two months later, in May 1821, the Peloponnesian Senate assembled in Kaltezes. Despite claiming to represent the entire Peloponnesian region, in truth it represented a faction of the Ottoman Peloponnese headed by the Deliyannis and the Mavromichalis clans, excluding powerful notables of the northern Peloponnese who disputed the Senate's legality and the extent to which it was properly representative. Likewise, military leaders who had progressively gained power and prestige through their leading roles in the war effort also found themselves excluded from the Senate.

In November 1821, the provisional administration of Western Greece was founded, while, around the same time, the 'Legal Arrangement of Eastern Greece' was ratified in Salona. This defined the autonomous state's scope. In turn, Crete established an autonomous administrative system, while the islands functioned under yet another independent arrangement.

Dimitris Ypsilantis's (brother of Alexandros) arrival in the Peloponnese momentarily gave rise to expectations of unified leadership. He had arrived in Greece as 'Attorney to the Authority's Delegate', that is to say, as his brother's representative, with orders to assume power, and he immediately showed his paternalistic and monarchic intentions.

But Ypsilantis was opposed by local leaders, and his role was quickly marginalised. A lack of local support rendered his ambitions of leadership futile, especially after the revelation that the Etaireia's Authority had no relationship with Russia and the tsar—which further weakened his position. All Ypsilantis managed to do was to rally those dissatisfied by how events had developed up until that point. He turned to them, denouncing the 'tyranny of those who, echoing Turkish sentiments, seek to harm or oppress the people'.[2] In this way, he was able to win over Maniot opponents of Mavromichalis, local leaders excluded from the Peloponnesian Senate, and Etaireia members such as Anagnostopoulos, Anagnostaras and Papaflessas. Though Kolokotronis initially allied with Ypsilantis, he also kept channels of communication open with notables.

The first political balances were established, or at least began taking shape, with the convocation of the First National Assembly in Epidaurus at the end of 1821. Though representatives of various regions were rather arbitrarily selected from among local leaders, the legality of the assembly itself was never called into question. Alexandros Mavrokordatos, descendant of a Phanariot family, was named president of the assembly. Mavrokordatos, in Italy when the fighting broke out, was a member of the Etaireia and had rushed to Greece, bringing supplies and accompanying philhellenes on their way to join the battle. He first entered in Western Greece, specifically in Missolonghi, where he managed to establish himself and act as a leading force in defining new balances of power in Western Greece. He also inspired *Organismos*, a text which defined new power balances in Western Greece. Meanwhile, another Phanariot, Thodoris Negris, the Porte's vice-ambassador in Paris who had also returned to fight in Greece, sought to accomplish the same in Eastern Greece. Both these figures and Ioannis Kolettis—Ali Pasha's doctor and someone who would play a significant role in the years to follow—profited from divisions between local chieftains and notables. They used their expertise, which was most useful for contacting representatives of Western powers, and their political experience, taking on a leading role in shaping the War of Independence.

With the convocation of the National Assembly, the divisions among the rebels became visible for the first time. Notables from the Peloponnese, the islands, archpriests and representatives of the western and eastern mainland united against military leaders capable of challenging their power. Mavrokordatos was the individual capable of reaching compromises between these separate interests, which often clashed, and of removing these military leaders—who were incapable of collaborating among themselves—from the political playing field. On 1 January 1822, the assembly declared the political existence and independence of the Greek nation. The ideological and political principles announced at this time were grounded in political liberalism.

This liberalism was hardly relevant to the political reality Greeks experienced during these years of battle; it was directed more to the Western Europeans, while on a local level it simply expressed the fragmentation of power and the inability to establish a strong central government. Under this plan, all parties were satisfied, as they could all potentially claim a share of power. But it harmed Ypsilantis, who continued to use the title of prince and stated his intentions to reinstate pre-war social norms. A. Mavrogordatos, a fierce opponent of his, had understood the contradiction in this move and had renounced use of a similar title.

The provisional Greek Constitution provided for a representative government and separation of powers, establishing a civil administration consisting of an executive and parliamentary branch, with one-year terms. These two institutions were complementary, but in reality they cancelled each other out, as laws drafted by the executive branch had to be passed in Parliament. On the other hand, laws passed in Parliament had to be approved by the executive. The latter was made up of five members and had the right to appoint ministers.

The provisional Constitution of Epidaurus was based on the French constitutions of 1793 and 1795 and was a triumph for Mavrokordatos, who was elected president of the executive branch on 15 January 1822. It also ensured the continued dominance of notable groups. D. Ypsilantis was elected president of Parliament, which actually constituted a demotion from his previous position in the political hierarchy. The Etaireia had been completely marginalised; this was evident not only from the fact that its name was not mentioned anywhere but also thanks to the National Assembly's adoption of the symbol of Athena instead of the Etaireia's symbol, the Phoenix.

Yet the First National Assembly could not, and in reality did not even attempt to, face the issue of how to deal with local polities and whether to abolish them, despite the fact that the islanders had raised the matter out of their own interest. The solution offered provided a compromise at best, recognising and maintaining local administrations that would be subject to the jurisdiction of the central administration from which they would receive commands, and upon which the validity of their decisions would depend. The obvious dysfunctionality of this administrative arrangement led to its elimination in the Second National Assembly—though this reversal was not met without oppositions.

As might be imagined, the process of configuring the nascent Greek state's institutional functionality was hardly relevant to wartime political opposition. Military successes in the first year of conflict strengthened the prestige of military leaders, led by Kolokotronis in the Peloponnese and Odysseas Androutsos on the mainland. As the Second National Assembly at Astros convened in March 1823, the political situation was becoming increasingly tense.

The second National Assembly elected Petrobey Mavromichalis president, Bishop Vresthenis Theodoritos vice-president and Theodoris Negris head secretary. Initially, it was decided that the basic principles of the constitution of Epidaurus were not to be altered. Notable modifications made to the constitution included protection of individual rights to property, honour and safety, as well as the freedom of press and the prohibition of slavery and the slave trade. The Second National Assembly also tended towards centralising power; various individual sources of power such as the Peloponnesian Senate, the Senate of Western Greece and the Supreme Court of Eastern Central Greece were all abolished. Only in Crete and Samos were analogous organisations retained. These islands were far removed from the military centre, and their autonomy—even if only apparent—was essential. Finally, a decision was taken in the Second National Assembly according to which the title of commander-in-chief, then held by Kolokotronis, was abolished, save for times of war. At the war's end, the commander-in-chief would assume his previous rank. Meanwhile, the decision to eliminate local polities weakened many of the more important local leaders.

The creation of the executive and parliamentary branches—the latter of which gained power and strength over the course of the National Assembly—led to confrontation. Petrobey Mavromichalis was elected president of the executive and Andreas Metaxas vice president. Sotiris Charalambis and Andreas Lontos, both Peloponnesian notables, were among the other members of the executive branch. Notable families continued to hold a large degree of power in the Peloponnese, to the displeasure of the military, which showed a willingness to ally with other unsatisfied individuals as long as they agreed to oppose these notable leaders together. Kolokotronis's alliance with the Deliyannis clan, which had been excluded from positions of power, was indicative of imminent polarisation. In an attempt at resolution, Kolokotronis was offered the position of vice president of the executive branch, which he accepted. But his decision proved detrimental for his faction, as it provoked a rift in military alliances.

Kolokotronis sought to restore the balance by demanding that his ally, Anagnostis Deliyannis, be appointed president of Parliament, which forced the resignation of Spetses native I. Orlandos, who had previously occupied the post. However, Mavrokordatos was voted in by an overwhelming majority. The reaction of the executive branch, led by Kolokotronis, was violent, and Mavrokordatos was forced to resign immediately and take refuge on Hydra island. Yet the parliamentary branch never accepted his resignation and continued to function without a president.

In this manner, two camps formed. The first identified with the executive branch, primarily attracting Peloponnesian notables, and the other was represented by Parliament, supported by islanders and local chieftains from Roumeli, joined by Mavrokordatos and certain Peloponnesians including Andreas Lodos and Andreas Zaimis. Soon, the parliamentary branch called for the dissolution of the executive, arguing that it had acted illegally. It then moved to create a new executive branch led by Georgios Koundouriotis in Kranidi, where other supporters of the parliamentary camp had settled. Their opponents established themselves in Tripoli.

The tensions and conflicts between these groups were mostly manifestations of the struggle to control the configuration of a developing central power, and a battle to preserve their assets on a local level. Indeed, for islanders, and certainly for residents of Hydra who were the most powerful of the group, stronger central authority meant the ability to successfully fund naval operations and realise aspirations for land in Argolis. It was only natural for fighters arriving from territories in which the fight for independence had been suppressed to quickly support the same cause, joined by others aspiring for positions occupied by rivals. It was also no coincidence that Kolokotronis, for example, insisted on the local nature of political power, fighting off all attempts at introducing non-Peloponnesian intervention in Morea.

In early 1824, the parliamentary branch sought to capture all castles occupied by the former executive branch. Proceeds from the first loan secured after independence arrived in Greece and were used to fund the 'Kivernitikon', as the new government was called. It easily occupied Acrocorinth and Tripoli, while Nafplion surrendered after a two-month siege. Up until that point, Nafplion had been controlled by Kolokotronis's son, Panos. Though Kolokotronis sought to reach some sort of a compromise upon accepting Nafplion's surrender, this soon proved to be impossible.

Thus despite the amnesty declared after the Koundouriotis government established itself in Nafplion, the extent of the political conflict took on a new dimension, even within the victorious camp. Peloponnesian notables felt excluded from the coalition of citizens from Hydra, Spetses and Roumeli, and they joined forces with Kolokotronis. This polarisation became evident in its entirety in October 1824 when the Koundouriotis faction took up most of the positions as a result of elections held for the government's newly established judicial branch. In the clash that followed, which took a violent turn when Roumeliot troops descended on the Peloponnese, the Peloponnesians were soundly defeated and forced to surrender themselves for imprisonment. In Central Greece, the opposition leader, Odysseas Androutsos, was imprisoned and murdered shortly thereafter.

Ibrahim's invasion of the Peloponnese and the risk of complete defeat led to an atmosphere of compromise. For their part, the Egyptians hoped to profit from the situation by offering amnesty. With Missolonghi under siege, the Third National Assembly began functioning in Epidaurus. News of Missolonghi's fall led to a suspension of the assembly until September, and to a request that Britain play a mediatory role in the hope that a compromise might be reached with the Ottomans. D. Ypsilantis's reaction to this resolution resulted in him being stripped of his political rights, creating a new source of tension. Renewed conflict was avoided thanks to the intervention of British citizens Hamilton, George and Cochran, and when the Third National Assembly began functioning again in Ermioni on 19 March 1827, a compromise had been reached. Ypsilantis's political rights were restored, George assumed leadership of land troops and Cochran led the fleet. As compensation for this British control over land and naval troops, the third National Assembly elected I. Kapodistrias, former minister of the tsar, governor of Greece. The political Constitution of Greece was also approved, which clearly enumerated the responsibilities of the executive, legislative and judicial branches. Until Kapodistrias's arrival, the country was governed by a three-member vice-governmental commission.

International context

The diplomatic context for the War of Independence was initially quite unfavourable to Greek efforts. Ypsilantis's invasion of Moldavia came at a time when uprisings were contesting the political status quo in Naples, Piedmont and even Spain. Inevitably, the uprising in the Danubian Principalities was perceived as another attempt to overthrow the Restoration and was treated as such by members of the Holy Alliance who convened in Laibach (modern day Ljubljana). At a time in which each attempt to challenge a legitimate ruler was considered condemnable by supporters of the status quo, the fact that this instance involved Christian populations fighting against Muslims hardly mattered. The major question that arose among stake-holding forces was whether the dissolution of the Ottoman Empire was desirable, and what its consequences would be.

The tsar immediately condemned Ypsilantis and gave his consent for the Ottoman invasion of the Danubian region, causing a major diplomatic and military setback for the War of Independence. The hanging of Patriarch Gregory V and the subsequent massacres of Christian populations undoubtedly worsened diplomatic relations between the Porte and Russia, and the latter withdrew its ambassador from Constantinople. During the Holy Alliance's next summit in Verona, which lasted from October to December 1822, the Holy Alliance did not alter its stance; the delegation sent by the rebels with high expectations was not accepted by the other participating powers.

Yet at the same time, the advent of philhellenism and the galvanising of rebellious philhellene committees played a catalytic role in how the governments of the Great Powers treated the Greeks. An admiration for ancient Greece facilitated support of the Greeks' struggle for freedom, regardless of political orientation. Philhellenic clubs were founded in many major European cities and substantial efforts were made to support the warring Greeks both militarily and economically; efforts were also made to place pressure on countries to change their stance on the struggle. Hundreds of young individuals rushed to Greece, offering their lives for the cause. Lord Byron was undoubtedly the most famous among them. The fact that an equally notable number of philhellenes were disappointed by their experience of the war—as the Greeks did not offer them what they hoped to gain, or perhaps because the behaviour they encountered in Greece was not what they had expected from the descendants of ancient Greece—is of little significance.

As philhellenism progressively shaped European public opinion in favour of Greece, Britain—not a member of the Holy Alliance—changed the balance of international diplomacy. George Canning, Britain's secretary of foreign affairs from August 1822 onwards, was mainly responsible for this change, which was first evident with the ban prohibiting British ships from transporting food and supplies to fortresses besieged by the Greeks. In other words, Britain took a neutral stance towards the warring parties, thus implicitly recognising the

Greeks. In March 1823, Britain's stance became clearer after Canning's declaration of British neutrality, while earlier he had announced that a prerequisite for good relations between the Porte and Britain was the fulfilment of the former's obligations to its Christian subjects. Obviously, this British attitude, favourable towards the Greeks, reinforced Anglophile spirit in Greece and enabled the signing of two loans with trade banks in the City of London. Thus the gradual shift in the Great Powers' attitudes towards the Greek situation drew their representatives closer to matters of Greek domestic policy.

Britain, more concerned than any other country about the weakening of the Ottoman Empire (as it was afraid of a challenge to its supremacy in the Eastern Mediterranean and the possible ascent of Russian power in the Middle East), gradually realised that such a development would not necessarily come at a political cost as long as it could keep the new state in check. In this respect, British policies varied—at least initially—from the Austrian approach, which refused to tolerate an extension of Russian influence into the Balkans. In other words, the major problem in Greece was precisely the Greek struggle's identification with Russian interests, despite Alexander I's repeated assurances that his country had no involvement in the war, and his refusal to support it, as he fully identified with Austrian policies.

Britain's position encouraged the tsar to change tactics as he feared that his repeated identification with Austrian views would have unwanted results. Thus in early 1824 he decided to send a memorandum to the other Great Powers in which he proposed the creation of three principalities—Eastern Greece, Western Greece and the Peloponnese—which would be tax tributaries subject to the sultan. Conferences with the Great Powers followed, yielding no results. Around the same time, the Egyptians arrived in the Peloponnese, and defeat seemed imminent for the Greek struggle. At that very moment, the Third National Assembly accepted a resolution on the basis of which 'The Greek nation willingly places its sacred repository of freedom, national independence and political being under the sole protection of Great Britain.' Although Canning replied that it was not possible for Britain to accept the proposal, this Greek manoeuvre put the Great Powers back in the game.

Alexander I's death in late 1825 and the ascent of Nicholas I to the Russian throne, who was much more hostile towards the Ottoman Empire than his predecessor, changed the international balance of power once again in favour of the Greeks. On 23 March/4 April 1825, the two powers, Britain and Russia, signed the Protocol of St Petersburg, the first step towards international diplomatic recognition of the Greeks' right to political independence.

According to the protocol, barring any objections from the Ottoman Empire, Greece would become a tax tributary state subject to the sultan's control, though it would now be administered by rulers the Greeks themselves would choose, enjoying freedom of thought and trade. The two powers would regulate the borders, and along with the remaining powers they would ensure a joint solution between the warring sides. If the Ottoman Empire refused to accept the proposed solution, the two forces would attempt to impose the reforms suggested by the protocol themselves.

Seeing itself as capable of quashing the latest efforts of the Greek resistance, the Ottoman Empire had no reason to accept the solution, and it refused to accept the terms in the protocol. So did Austria and Prussia. For France, however, these arrangements offered opportunities that were impossible to ignore. Having been left on the side-lines during the redrawing of European borders, it saw the Ottoman Empire's collapse as a chance for a new say in the Great Powers' diplomatic balance. Thus, seeking a more dynamic presence in international diplomacy, France accepted the terms of the protocol. On 24 June/6 July 1827, the three powers signed the Treaty of London, which essentially re-stated the Protocol of St. Petersburg. Shortly thereafter, in mid-August 1827 the three powers delivered notice to the Porte demanding acceptance of the treaty's terms within fifteen days.

The Ottomans did not accept the terms. Naval vessels belonging to these three powers present in the Mediterranean were then ordered to prevent the continuation of military operations. Ibrahim, who had gathered the Turkish–Egyptian fleet in the Bay of Navarino, refused to leave the Peloponnese without instructions from the sultan, and his troops began to loot the mainland. On the evening of 8 October 1827, the two fleets were driven to conflict, resulting in the complete destruction of the Turkish–Egyptian fleet. The Greek War had been won, just a few months after Canning's death.

Soon after, in April 1828, Russia declared war on the Ottoman Empire, provoking British anxieties as they saw their worst fears come true. The Ferronays plan, named after the French foreign minister, came to the rescue: France and Britain would not intervene with the Russian initiative in the Danubian regions, but would send troops to Greece in order to control the situation and counterbalance Russian aggression. The tsar agreed, realising that his troops would not be able to meet his expectations on the Ottoman front while warring with the Persians at the same time. The British also agreed, but they proved unwilling to intervene militarily in the Peloponnese, instead prioritising domestic concerns.

Thus on 7/19 July 1828 the London Protocol was signed, under which France would send an expeditionary force to the Peloponnese to chase out the Egyptians. On 9 August, the Treaty of Alexandria was signed, outlining the Egyptians' peaceful departure. These last two agreements were owed to Kapodistrias's actions; he sought Ibrahim's rapid withdrawal from the Peloponnese and also wanted to prevent the French from claiming the title of Greece's 'liberators' all to themselves.

Kapodistrias's military successes and achievements in terms of internal organisation and national pacification were such that he could argue for the existence of 'authorities capable of maintaining existing relations within Europe,' allowing him greater freedom to negotiate the conditions for Greece's independence. At the Poros Conference of September 1828, he put forward some very ambitious demands and spoke of borders ranging from the Gulf of Volos to Crete. After all, it was at the Poros Conference—during which the vice-ambassadors of the Great Powers suggested Greece's borders—that the Volos–Arta line would be drawn, including Evia along with the islands of the new Greek state, but not Crete. Thus the danger of circumscribing Greece to the Cyclades and the Peloponnese, as prescribed by the London Protocol of 1828, was avoided. Under the new London Protocol of 1829, the vice-ambassador's proposals were more or less accepted.

Further developments followed after Russia's victory over the Ottoman army and the Treaty of Adrianople, which was signed in September 1829. The Greek question had now been resolved according to the terms stated in the March 1825 Protocol. Meanwhile, Russia succeeded in gaining significant privileges in the Danubian Principalities. In order to counteract Russian influence in Greece, Britain proposed the independence of this fledgling state, and the proposal was accepted by the French and Russians. Thus, on 3 February 1830, the London Protocol recognised the Greek state's independence.

Kapodistrias

Elected governor of Greece by the Third National Assembly, I. Kapodistrias arrived in the country in early 1828. Despite the fact that his election was decided almost unanimously (even including British consent), it was not met without opposition. The appointment of British leaders to the Greek fleet and military counteracted these concerns to some extent, but they did not completely negate them. Kapodistrias, a former minister of the tsar who had retired and lived in Switzerland, identified with Russian policies. Consequently, his election as governor of the Greek state could not appear as anything but contrary to British interests in South Eastern Europe, as Britain sought full control over the Greek state. This initial distrust, which evolved into hostility over time, accompanied Kapodistrias throughout his tenure as governor.

The situation he was met with in Greece was not a pleasant one by any means. The Ottomans still held a large percentage of the rebellious regions and most of the main fortresses, while the general population had been completely devastated from many years of war. Indeed, the Ottomans still held most of Central Greece, which ran the risk of being excluded from the newly drawn borders of the Greek state for this very reason. Ibrahim found himself in direct and indirect control of a large portion of the Peloponnese thanks to the fortresses he controlled on its western shores; he also controlled a large part of the mainland thanks to soldiers he had placed in various fortified positions. Even the remaining territories were not controlled by the central government—whose role at this stage was rather symbolic—but were instead commanded by various local rulers, as robbery and piracy ran unchecked.

That Kapodistrias had served as minister of foreign affairs to the tsar was both an advantage and disadvantage in the first stage of his administration—both for him and for the Greek state itself. On the one hand, it was an advantage, as he possessed a thorough knowledge of European diplomacy and could speak with representatives of foreign powers in the same language. On the other hand, the fact that he had served as minister to the tsar made the other two powers, France and Britain, suspect him of harbouring loyalties to Russia. This suspicion was expressed mainly through the refusal or obstruction of financial support to his administration. As a result, Russia shouldered most of the burden of supporting Greece in the form of advances on future loans. A philhellene banker from Geneva, Jean-Gabriel Eynard, also supported Kapodistrias in his attempt to transform these plundered lands and pillaged populations into an independent state. Essentially, Kapodistrias's project offers us the opportunity to observe the establishment of a state without the use of external resources—an undertaking completely contrary in nature to the Bavarian example that would soon follow.

Upon arriving in Greece, Kapodistrias's first move was to consolidate his control of power. Thus in April 1828, the National Assembly convened again, where the 'Provisional Government of the State' was established. Kapodistrias assumed legislative and executive power, which he would exercise with the twenty-seven members of the advisory council known as the 'Panellinio'; the secretary general was to co-sign resolutions and correspondence with Kapodistrias. The self-dissolution of the National Assembly followed.

Kapodistrias proceeded to create a basic state apparatus, regulating the organisation and function of the council, and recommending the creation of a military, cabinet, and church committee. Shortly thereafter, he selected the council's first nine members, appointing Spyridon Trikoupis as general secretary. With the support of these institutions, Kapodistrias implemented massive legislative and political changes aimed at forming the elementary mechanisms of a state administration—mechanisms that could be supported by the Greek state's meagre finances. He actively initiated a campaign to eliminate banditry and piracy, achieving impressive victories, while he also reorganised the army and fleet, rendering them battle-ready.

The military's main objective was to drive the Ottomans out to the Arta–Volos line so that the region could be claimed by the Greek state. Kolokotronis, Ypsilantis and Church assumed leadership of the Greek counter-offensive in the Peloponnese and Eastern and Western Greece respectively. Andreas Miaoulis assumed leadership of the Aegean fleet. The army was quickly reorganised, incorporating irregular troops, and soon moved forward to regions it hoped to reclaim from the Ottomans, thus relieving villagers there from the burden of enforced support of these troops. Meanwhile, Kapodistrias took care to negotiate favourable terms with the captains of mainland Greece that had betrayed the revolution, thus facilitating the recapturing of territories in the area.

These Greek military initiatives proved highly successful, all the more so as additional troops joined the efforts. These successes were secured with the victory at the Battle of Petra in September 1829. After this battle, the Ottomans were forced to capitulate and were allowed to pass through the Strait of Petra so that they could come to the aid of the Ottoman army that had been ravaged by the Russians. They also released all Greek prisoners and withdrew their garrisons from all strongholds south of Lamia except for Athens and Karababa, opposite Chalcis. Meanwhile, the Greek fleet, supported by the fleets of the Great Powers, eliminated piracy in the Aegean. As for robbery, reorganisation of the army was the main precondition for its disappearance, as it absorbed all the bandits that had formerly ravaged the countryside.

Armed campaigns were also mounted in Crete and Chios, in the latter case funded by the Chiots themselves. Indeed, in Crete, despite Kapodistrias's proposals to the contrary, the war broke out again, and by late 1829 the Ottomans had been confined to their fortresses. But on all these occasions, advances, when they were made, were temporary. In any case, Kapodistrias did not believe it would have ever been possible to incorporate these regions into the Greek state.

The organisational achievements and success of the national army and fleet certainly weakened the power of notables and chieftains. An example of the discontent generated as a result was Spiros Trikoupis's resignation in early 1829 from his position of secretary general of the council; Kapodistrias then hastened to appoint him secretary of external affairs. Yet from mid-1829 onwards, opposition to Kapodistrias's policies became all the more intense. This forced him to partially abandon his policy of tolerance towards notable groups, and his efforts to integrate them into the political scene by including them in consultative bodies. Increasingly, he turned to relatives and trusted individuals, the majority from the Ionian Islands and Corfu. He also took special care to support agriculture, which in many cases had been neglected for years, thus gaining the support of the rural population.

But the situation worsened with the convening of the Fourth National Assembly in Argos in July 1829. Its representatives had essentially been selected by Kapodistrias, and their choices largely conformed with his plans. Up until this point, his political project and recommendations for future policies had been received with approval; indeed, the assembly's vote to pay damages to the islands of Hydra, Spetses and Psara had appeased the islanders. But from this point onwards, things took a turn for the worse, as many members of notable groups resigned or refused to take up the government posts they were offered, while others were excluded from participating by Kapodistrias himself.

The opposition Kapodistrias encountered to his attempts at subduing local political and military elites rapidly increased in the face of his inability to serve their various needs and requests and, more importantly, to impose authority. The pressures and criticism he was subjected to pushed him towards increasingly authoritarian forms of government and the persecution of his opponents. Following the July Revolution in France, his only remaining ally was Russia; all other powers more or less openly supported the opposition. He turned to his supporters in order to bring national politics back under his control, but in doing so justified the suspicions harboured by representatives from the Great Powers over his pro-Russian positions. In truth, he had no alternative.

Leopold of Belgium's appointment as king of Greece at the hands of the Great Powers also proved to be a temporary solution. To gain the throne, Leopold had aggressively sought the expansion of Greek borders beyond what the Great Powers were willing to accept, resulting in his resignation. The opposition accused Kapodistrias of being responsible for Leopold's resignation, arguing that he had misinformed the candidate for the throne so as to force his resignation.

The opposition's actions culminated with the capture of the Greek fleet by islanders from Hydra, led by a wartime hero, Miaoulis, and the burning of the *Hellas* frigate so that it would not fall into the hands of the Russians who had surrounded it. Soon after, Kapodistrias was murdered by members of the Mavromichalis family from Mani. Within a very short time, whatever project had been in place at that point collapsed, causing the country to fall into complete anarchy. Shortly thereafter, the Great Powers appointed Otto—not yet of age, and the second son of King Ludwig of Bavaria—as king of Greece.

Particularities

Attempts are often made to understand the War of Independence as a deterministic outcome of preceding transformations within the Ottoman state; that is to say, as a product of the economic, political and intellectual growth of Orthodox populations belonging to the Patriarchate of Constantinople. This growth is then linked with the 'decline' of the Ottoman Empire.

The War of Independence did not break out in a spontaneous or unannounced manner. It was the product of many years of preparation, and of specific goals, regardless of whether those goals were unrealised or unsuccessful compared with their motivators' intentions. The formation of the Philike Etaireia, and the manner in which it infiltrated or failed to infiltrate social groups in power that could catalyse the war, cannot be neglected in any attempt to understand the process.

Important merchants or high-ranking prelates did not participate in the Etaireia; nor did any of the great reformist or Phanariot scholars. None of the groups with economic, social and political authority over the Christian population took part in organising the war effort with the exception of some marginal and unimportant examples. The Ypsilantis family, Alexandros Mavrokordatos, even Alexandros Mavrokordatos the younger and Thodoris Negris did not represent the Phanariot aristocracy in power around the time the war began. To the contrary, they represented families that had lost their claims to power. Similarly, clergy participating in the Etaireia were of local importance, while scholars and important merchants were perhaps the most notable absentees.

If the War of Independence cannot be understood independently of transformations within the Ottoman Empire, then it must be understood as an eminently political event. Economistic arguments are unable to offer a satisfying explanation.

Disgruntled and displaced individuals within powerful social groups participated in organising the war effort, with the exception of the Peloponnesians and some island notables, who, as noted previously, were subject to other pressures. As for the chieftains, only those who had been marginalised seem to have participated. Thus, perhaps, we should adopt the concept of a 'marginal elite' that has often been used in the literature on revolutions in order to conceptualise a certain social phenomenon at the root of revolutionary movements.

In other words, the preparations for war did not connote massive participation or initiatives by social groups involved in the administration of Ottoman power. This is to be expected, as these groups had little reason to mobilise against a system that perpetuated their power and supported their interests. To the contrary, it was a small-scale initiative that created the conditions for a war against the Ottomans and sparked its outbreak. It thus follows that the war was almost immediately contained in the territories where Christian leaders had enabled the conditions for the common division of power with resident Muslims—that is, in the Peloponnese and on the islands—something that also explains the high rates at which these particular notable groups participated in the Etaireia. Elite Christian groups were certainly subject to strong pressures from Ottoman rulers in these same regions.

As it ultimately changed course and resulted in the recognition of a Greek nation, the War of Independence proved unable to satisfy those who pioneered it by virtue of its own trajectory. A war waged by notable groups seeking to emerge as the central authority of a nascent state had disastrous results, negating all the efforts to create the state, as no party or group was able to decisively impose itself on another. Thus, there arose the need for an external mediator.

In the end, the task of organising the Greek state was assigned to those who were removed from the struggle for power and those who had fought to obtain it. Either way, the Great Powers were truly responsible for the establishment of the Greek state, which served their pursuit of stability in the context of the Restoration. From the outset, they made it clear that they would not let the situation escape their control; the next step was to get the notables to stop fighting for what they believed was rightfully theirs. This struggle only ended with Otto's fall in 1862, or, by other accounts, in 1875 when the political scene came under the complete control of the political elite with the adoption of the parliamentary principle.

3

THE BAVARIANS IN GREECE

(1833–43)

The kingdom

Even before Otto was appointed king of Greece, the nation's political system had already been prescribed by the Great Powers. The London Protocol of 22 January/3 February 1830 essentially laid the groundwork for establishing absolute and hereditary monarchy in Greece. The Treaty of London on 25 April/7 May 1832 further aided this process, defining the powers of the regency council that was to govern the country until Otto came of age. In fact, the council's powers were unlimited, and it constituted an institutional expression of absolute monarchy. Ludwig I of Bavaria adhered to these prescriptions as he established a context for exercising power in Greece until his son came of age on 1 June 1835.

Reforms to the regency council's internal functions stipulated that decisions had to be taken by majority vote, though all documents would require the signature of all three members. With a decree of 23 September/5 October 1832, Ludwig appointed Josef Ludwig von Armansperg, Georg Ludwig von Maurer and Carl Wilhelm von Heideck as members of the regency council—persons distinguished if nothing else by their political or intellectual activities in Germany.

Naturally, these appointments were not welcomed by the domestic military and political leadership. This was of no consequence anyway, since they had no say in decisions made by the Great Powers, and by extension the decisions made by Ludwig of Bavaria. In the Fourth National Assembly, held in late July 1832, Otto's election was ratified, though the contents of the Treaty of London were not made public. The assembly was then immediately dissolved. But in the end, an alternative had finally emerged to the prevailing chaos in Greece, a chaos that was to no one's benefit.

Timetable 1833–43

1833	Otto arrives in Nafplion. Until he comes of age, the three-member regency council composed of Armansperg, Maurer and Heideck holds power.
1834	The Ottomans abandon the Acropolis. Kolokotronis and Plapoutas are tried and sentenced. Athens is named capital of the state.
1835	Otto comes of age and undertakes royal duties in conjunction with the chief Chancellor Armansperg. The State Council is established. Piraeus Municipality established. Archaeological Society established.
1836	Royal Palace established. Otto marries Amalia, daughter of the grand duke of Oldenburg.
1837	Otto returns to Greece, dismisses Armansperg and appoints Ignatius von Rudhart as president of the cabinet. University of Athens is founded. Rudhart resigns. Otto personally assumes the presidency of the Cabinet.
1838	25 March inaugurated as National Day.
1841	Revolt in Crete, which is quickly suppressed. Mavrokordatos government. Mavrokordatos resigns after two months and Otto resumes the presidency of the Cabinet.
1843	3 September movement. Metaxas government. Elections for the National Assembly. The First National Assembly begins on 8 November.

The manner with which the regency council sought to establish the political and administrative foundations for the Greek kingdom was rather predictable. Hugely suspicious of domestic political forces, it placed Bavarians (arriving in Greece especially for this purpose) in most of its key positions. In doing so, it hoped to fully control the state apparatus and distance Bavarians from party conflicts and antagonisms between the ambassadors to the Great Powers. As for the remaining positions that could not be filled by Bavarians, the regency council appealed mainly to individuals of Greek origin from regions not included within the Greek kingdom, who became known as *heterocthons*. They were the only ones able to meet the requirements of new state policies thanks to their qualifications. The introduction of a capable state administration required people capable of implementing it, and by definition these people could not be locals.

A subsequent series of legislative decisions determined the framework within which national political activity would occur; limits to press freedom were also established. The overall philosophy determining these measures was simple: the goal was to bring a European style of governance to Greece, and it was to be configured according to the Bavarian model, which in turn, in many cases, had assimilated the French legal and administrative system. The goal was none other than the prosperity of a state that subordinated the welfare of its subjects to its own goals. Those in power possessed the knowledge and technological means to achieve these aspirations; what remained was for the subjects to adapt to these new conditions.

The regency council's policies were far from unreasonable. Its members may have behaved in a paternalistic and often authoritarian manner, and one may attribute a 'pedagogical' attitude to their treatment of the Greeks, but this was neither strange nor novel for the time. The Greeks were still a long way off from Western civilisation and had to be taught how to assimilate into it. After all, the Bavarian goal was none other than to consolidate strong central authority, and, lacking local political and social support, they had to resort to coercion, the threat of violence and finally violence itself. The emphasis placed on the army—and transport of German mercenary troops on to Greek soil—indicates this same intention, which, in any case, was never hidden to begin with. The trial and conviction of Kolokotronis shortly after the Bavarians' arrival in Greece categorically shows their absolute refusal to allow anyone, even a hero of the war with great political influence, any grounds to challenge their authority. Thus it is no coincidence that the only ministry that Otto tried to keep under Bavarian control at all expense was the Defence Ministry, where Christian Von Schmaltz remained in charge from 1 June 1833 to 2 July 1841, with the exception of a fifteen-month interval when—naturally—another German, Wilhelm Le Suire, took charge from 11 March 1834 to 10 June 1835.

Apart from the regency council, the cabinet comprised the main instrument of central government under a decree of 3/15 April 1833. The seven secretaries of state, as the ministers were called, were all appointed by the regency council, and the head of the cabinet (who, despite his title, possessed the same powers as the others) was appointed by the king. Each secretary of state directly implemented the monarch's will and executed government decisions. He applied laws and decrees in his area of responsibility and proposed new laws to the cabinet accordingly. The cabinet was nothing more than a consultative and executive body, as the king was not beholden to accept its recommendations, even if they were adopted unanimously. Though the Bavarians allowed Greeks to participate in decision-making to a limited extent, they always had the final say on the policies to be implemented.

The regency council's decision to govern collectively proved to be a poor one. Decisions were made by majority rule, but all members had to undersign them, and Armansperg served in his role as head secretary without any particular powers. Very soon, disputes arose between members, which were nurtured by the ambassadors to the Great Powers who saw an opportunity to strengthen their own influence in the Greek kingdom's political landscape by way of influencing the regency council members themselves. Armansperg and the British ambassador emerged victorious from these disputes, but Ludwig ordered all other members of the regency council recalled back to Bavaria.

Otto's coming of age and his takeover of the state in 1835 confirmed the national government's authoritarian tendencies. Armansperg was not removed, and indeed was appointed chief secretary of state, a rank that effectively made him an intermediary between Otto and the cabinet. He remained in this position until the beginning of 1837, when he was dismissed. Another German, Ignatius Von Rudhart, took his place, assuming the title of secretary of the secretariat for the royal house and foreign affairs and the title of 'first among the servants of the state'. He was also appointed head of the cabinet and was granted participation in cases handled by the Privy Council.

Rudhart, understanding the discontent caused by the Bavarian government, tried to enhance the cabinet's role with the aim of making public administration more efficient. He also tried to limit Otto's interventions, as the king proved to be increasingly indecisive, and particularly suspicious. But he did not succeed; his proposals for the gradual elimination of foreigners from administrative positions in the Greek state and the progressive granting of these responsibilities to Greeks clashed with the monarch's political stubbornness and rigidity. He was finally discharged in December 1837, and Otto himself took up the position of chief of the cabinet. In cases when he was absent or indisposed, he would be replaced by the vice presidents of the Council of State.

The Council of State, a juridical and counselling body, was founded in 1835 as a higher advisory body 'in which and by which the king discusses the key affairs of the state with "pre-eminent men"'. Its founding came to compensate for the exclusively Bavarian management of power and embellish the absolute monarchy's reputation by incorporating the most prominent members of the political and military elite.

The council's role was extremely limited, but the inclusion of twenty powerful members from the national political oligarchy created a rallying force that would have consequences for the monarchy. It also created a framework for political negotiations. In his important and overlooked work on the monarchy,[1] P. Pipinelis highlights the importance of the State Council with regard to 'the organisation of anti-monarchic movements and the electoral rights of the people'.

Regardless of all this, after the abolition of the chief secretary position, the Privy Council became the autocracy's main instrument of power. It drew on the staff of the secretariat to the regency council and consisted exclusively of Bavarians. It was initially established for technical reasons related to the translation and forwarding of documents prepared in German and addressed to local administrative centres. Gradually, however, its activities broadened, and it took on widespread political and administrative powers that it exercised in secret. After Armansperg's discharge, the king himself took over its supervision.

These adjustments aimed to minimise the power of political elites without entirely excluding them from political bodies, and to mediate the resulting tensions, though these tendencies would gain a stronger foothold in the following period, namely after 1843. Otto was willing to cede a small share of power, especially at the local level, but always in such a manner that his power was not contested. This became evident in his management of the local administration, as we will see. In other words, on the whole Otto sought to restrict the activity of the so-called elite to a local level, maintaining full sovereignty on a state level himself.

Either way, the national capital, Athens, was the centre of political power and decision-making. It is no coincidence that Otto was only truly challenged twice, in 1843 and 1862—both instances in which the capital's guards mutinied. In all other instances, movements, uprisings or rebellions on a local scale were relatively easily suppressed by the state. We have no indication that Otto's government sought to develop mechanisms that could extend his range of influence over increasingly large portions of the populations, or in other words mechanisms that would allow for state diffusion into larger portions of the population or, put differently, into local communities. Throughout his reign, Otto adhered to the practices of governing through notable groups, mediating their differences with nearly religious devotion.

Thus Otto's policies did not in any way exclude political elites from the workings of the state; we must not forget that, shortly after arriving in Greece, most of the Germans who came with the regency council departed back for their homeland. With no other choice, Otto's regime turned to the Greeks, though it continued to prefer *heterocthons*. The latter group's basic need to build political foundations in order to survive within the new state made them more vulnerable to royal manipulation than native-born individuals that maintained their roots in local communities. Positions were also made available for most of the first-class fighters in the war effort. Though the Bavarian presence was significantly reduced in number, those who stayed behind occupied the highest positions and implemented state policy. Similarly, even in the army of 1839, when most German soldiers had returned to their country, most officers were still not Greek.

Despite limitations to their power and a curbing of their ambitions, local elites were included in the political/institutional context and sought to strengthen their political role under these conditions. The monarchy's role was never truly challenged during the nineteenth century, though it did face challenges from time to time. The experience of civil war was too recent, and the results of Otto's attempts at mediation, which led to the pacification of the country, too obvious for the Greek politicians to seek a break with the royal government. To this same end, Otto insisted on maintaining a strictly monarchical regime, within which he undertook the responsibility for all political action. He pointed out the following problem immediately after his arrival in Greece: a huge responsibility weighed heavily on the Greeks themselves, who had failed to capitalise on what the War of Independence had granted them. Since they themselves could not come up with the proper solutions, the only way out was the imposition—at any cost, mostly through the limitation of constitutional freedoms—of order by a group that had little to do with the place it had come to govern. It was this same orientation that constituted the regime's Achilles heel and limited its room for manoeuvring.

The regime's inflexibility was first demonstrated in the so-called Mavrokordatos incident. Otto, seeking to allay reactions against his regime, moved to grant Mavrokordatos a ministerial rank and appoint him head of the cabinet. France, which had taken the initiative to coordinate the Great Powers in an effort to save Greece from the difficult situation they saw it to be in, pressured him to do so. Mavrokordatos set certain terms for acceptance of the position, terms that highlighted points of friction between the Bavarians and the Greek political elites. Specifically, he asked for the expansion of the State Council's jurisdiction (especially with regard to taxation), the dissolution of the Privy Council, the autonomy of state ministers, at least in some of their capacities, for which they would have personal liability, the appointment of a

Greek defence minister and lastly the gradual removal of Bavarians from public office.

Regardless of the fact that Mavrokordatos's proposals were based on existing proposals for the improvement of Greek state administration that Guizot had filed previously with the other protecting powers, the extent of the actions of the political elite became immediately apparent without substantively challenging the legality of the status quo. Yet a challenge to the legality of the monarchy would lead to conflict with the Great Powers and upset a political balance surely preferable to the interminable, indecisive conflicts of the recent past. The claim to a constitution and the elimination of Bavarian public office positions were, doubtless and independent of the actual content of the claims, two points that seemed absolutely normal and moderate after the absolute monarchy's first failures, especially since these failures were attributed to the authoritarian style of governance at Bavarian hands, and the effects of excluding elites from direct management of power. The pressure for change intensified, as did opposition to the regime.

Otto's reluctance to furnish an answer to Mavrokordatos's request led the latter to present his views on the country's governance to the Ministerial Council. Mavrokordatos's reformist project, which has since become known as the plan to introduce a 'tempered' monarchy, would constitute a transitional stage towards a constitution. He himself, under the influence of past experience, harboured a deep suspicion of the country's capability to immediately adopt a constitutional system, despite being an avowed advocate of liberal ideas. For this reason, he deemed an intermediate stage of preparation necessary. Yet Otto's refusal of Mavrokordatos's terms led to the latter's resignation. This was an example of the monarch's lack of adaptability and foresight—both elements that characterised his reign—but also to some extent the inevitable consequence of the logic of absolute monarchy, since the acceptance of these reforms, full or in part, would automatically entail the overthrow of the political balance and therefore the entire system. The distribution of power thus remained unchanged under the control of Otto and his court. The only concession made to these pressures was the decision to abolish the Privy Council. In its place, the private office of the king was created, which essentially functioned in the same manner as the Privy Council and remained in place until Otto's ousting in 1862. At the same time, Otto assigned the highest position in the cabinet to the most senior minister in cases when he could not participate himself.

Whether or not Otto could have pursued different policies is debatable. Without a foothold in the land, and with an opposition seeking privileges it hoped to have gained after the War of Independence—privileges the Bavarians had deprived them of—the king's remaining option was to limit notable groups to positions that would match their ambitions, or more accurately their vanity, while preventing any actual exercise of power. Implementation of this approach, however, was based on certain economic and political conditions that the system in place was increasingly unable to offer as time passed. One such basic premise was the financial viability of the state, which, after 1836 and the depletion of the first loan instalment of 60 million francs, given to Greece with a guarantee from the Great Powers, quickly vanished and turned to a nightmare. Another condition was absolute control of the military, which was the sole guarantor of the incumbent government's survival. After 1837, Otto had to deal with the desperate state of public finances, which took a turn for the worse in 1842 when he was obliged under pressure from the Great Powers to enact spending cuts amounting to 850,000 drachmas—cuts mostly made by way of salary reductions and layoffs. His decision to grant 200,000 drachmas in the form of a personal sponsorship to cover the deficit does not seem to have improved the situation, which soon deteriorated when the government—yielding yet again to the pressures of the Great Powers for even greater austerity to service the loan they had guaranteed in 1833—was forced to reduce staff in all sectors. At this time, Guizot believed that through this process Greece would be able to solve one of its two major problems: state finance. But in fact it became increasingly clear that Otto's opponents had an easy task ahead.

Configuration of the institutional framework within which the country's political elite would act was established more or less in the first half of 1833. From this moment until 1843, modifications made were of minor importance; if nothing else, this was a sign that Bavarian decisions were satisfactory, at least from their own point of view. Indeed, mechanisms for integrating the political elite should be regarded as effective insofar as they did not discriminate and functioned on the principle of including each and every notable. This issue was dealt with very differently in Serbia, where Obrenovic and his notable supporters were opposed to other members of the elite, or later in Bulgaria, where local elites were excluded from the centre of power. This explains the less conflict-ridden formation of the Greek state when compared with the neighbouring Greek states before the dawn of the nineteenth century.

Though Otto's strategic choices regarding notable groups created the preconditions for coordinated reactions on their part, they also created the basis for a consensual approach to politics. As a seasoned Roumeliot chieftain put it in 1841:

> We're no longer of any use; you have to take up public office if you want to exert influence today. What use is it if someone was once a good freedom fighter? He needs to be the owner of property to cultivate it, and to play an administrative role in his local council. Only then will he be able to have allies and supporters, so that he can use them for his own benefit and counter his rivals.[2]

The Bavarian objective was to integrate the majority of the political and non-political elite into the political process and governing mechanisms and to minimise their power by granting exclusive legitimacy to the newly founded state. One cannot but recognise their success in this respect. At times, of course, there were exceptions to the rule of elite participation in the country's governance, exceptions linked both with Otto's stance towards the Great Powers and with his personal choices, but in substance this method worked, creating long-term conditions for the institutionalisation of political power and the establishment of a centralised state rid of separatist tendencies.

... of the peasants

Assembling the central government was a straightforward project in terms of its conceptualisation and bureaucratic execution. But this was not the case for the organisation of the administration on a local level.

In April 1833, the country was divided into ten regions and forty-seven provinces to which corresponding prefects and governors were appointed by the government. The powers delegated in both cases were rather limited. On the one hand, they constituted the direct representative bodies of the central government in the Greek countryside and were charged with executing the responsibilities of all ministries on a local scale, though they were beholden to the Ministry of Interior Affairs. On the other, it was clearly the intention of the Bavarians to avoid an excessive concentration of power in their hands, especially in the case of prefects. Evidence of this is found in the fact that even the administrative heads and secretaries of each region were appointed by the central government, while other regional officials such as the registrar, public treasurer, bishop, ranking army corps engineer and certainly the chief of the military unit presiding over the region's capital exerted simultaneous, if not superimposed power, thus encroaching on the prefect's power. Though the Bavarians thus avoided concentrating power in the hands of one person, it often rendered decisions difficult.

A few months later, in December 1833, the Bavarians proceeded to establish 750 municipalities, which incorporated the country's thousands of settlements. Three years later, in 1836, the number of municipalities would be limited to 250. The main reason for creating them, and the subsequent adjustment of their number, was to separate local leaders from their operational centres. Or, as Pericles Argyropoulos, a specialist on local governance in this era, notes: 'In wanting to create better municipalities than those already in existence, the government employed the creative methods of Medea, overturning every community relation ...'[3] Another expert, Georgios I. Angelopoulos, professor of legal administration at the University of Athens, put it more bluntly:

> It was necessary for the government to take on the required power, and all the more necessary, because the unity of the nation was endangered by those long pre-existing communities that were destined to develop the narrow mindset of prioritising the local, with no opportunities for it to easily develop and reach beyond the confined boundaries of municipalities and provinces. Thus there was the need for uniformity of legislature, unity of administration and submissions of local groups to the central administration, so that the nation would not fall into the wrong hands after liberation from the Turkish yoke: that is to say, that it would not break down into sections, leading to the creation of independent states, following the example of the ancients' states, which have irreversibly disappeared, forever.[4]

The first problem to arise with the application of municipal law was the determination of territorial boundaries, a significant issue insofar as final arrangements would define and limit the power of local rulers. In the case of Livadia, this issue would be a subject of constant debate and friction between city notables and elders of neighbouring areas and wealthy villages. It is safe to assume that the restriction of boundaries in the Livadia municipality also meant a restriction on the possible benefits derived by the city's notables from the system of tax farming, and, to a lesser extent, a shift in local electoral balances.

Mayors, who had personal responsibilities over primary education, policing and land security, among other things, were chosen—depending on the size of the municipality—by the king or the prefect from a list of three candidates chosen by the 'mayoral council'. The latter was made up of members of public councils and an equal number of citizens paying a higher tax rate. But the range of options for the king was often limited, and in fact this system allowed for the election of mayors preferred by local notable groups. This is why George Finlay wrote in 1850 that with these laws set by the regency council: 'A system of local oligarchies was introduced which prevails at present,' though he neglected to mention the fact that management of local power had been conducted by the same groups since the Ottoman period, something he himself would later admit.[5]

The election process within public councils as regulated by the Bavarians did not provide any guarantee of secrecy; nor did it appear that there was any such intention. Each ballot was accompanied by a serial number, ensuring that the votes were not more in number than those registered to the electoral roll. They were then given to the head of the mayoral council, who noted the voter's name on a list and cast the vote in the ballot box. The casting of the ballots was obviously done in plain view, and the voter was required to record the name, surname and profession of their chosen candidate on their ballot. In the event of illiteracy, an individual could ask someone else to fill out this information.[6] In a population where the majority was in fact illiterate, voting for municipal authorities was a controlled process. Or, as an observer put it at the time: 'We instilled divisions within our communities on account of the infernal municipal system and its open voting process.'[7]

Control of local politics was certainly the key to effective state governance. Resistance from local communities—which will be discussed below, specifically in the context of the 1836 uprising—persuaded the Bavarians to pursue a tougher approach to local elites. That very year, with Otto's departure to Germany in search of a wife, Armansperg took the initiative to impose a more centralised administration and settle accounts with local notables once and for all. As previously noted, the number of municipalities was reduced from 750 to 250, and local balances of power seemed to have been violently overturned once again. This measure was ostensibly justified on the basis of the weak economic potential of municipalities, but it was actually aimed at the immediate elimination of local oligarchies that created obstacles for the Bavarian regime and the promotion of those who would be loyal to it. Therefore, instead of promoting the great political families from each region, it supported the small landowners upon which the Bavarians sought to stabilise their government. In the end, the results of this effort were paltry, if not a complete failure: in the elections of 1841–2, the old notables reclaimed their seats, and in doing so emphasised that administration of the state was not possible in their absence.

In fact, the entire system of local governance was an extension of central power in miniature. This, after all, is what the Bavarians had sought to accomplish. The superimposed power relations that formed were designed to replace all individual networks of political and economic power with a wider one that held Otto as the single point of reference and legitimiser of power, regardless of their level. So, in turn, local elites were placed within the new state's institutional framework, leaving them limited room for manoeuvring. The government did not deny them their privileged positions locally—this was attempted in 1836 and failed—but these positions now had to pass through the administrative mechanisms of the state.

This is why the country's political elite competed above all else for control of local power, from where they derived all their political power; for the same reason, until the end of the nineteenth century, municipal elections (and not national elections) were those that most motivated the local population. So, even in 1880, when the question of parliamentary representation came up for the residents of Piraeus (which had by then become the country's major commercial and industrial centre), they answered that they were interested in only municipal, and not parliamentary representation. Citizens of Ermoupoli, the administrative centre of the Cycladic Islands, initially showed a similar indifference to participation in Parliament. Timoleon Philemon, acting as mayor of Athens, even attested that local party interests (and not broader political objectives) determined mayoral elections in the capital.

Taking all this into account, we must view available analyses of the functionality and actions of political parties in these years of autocracy (and the years that would follow) with great reservations. Though it is clear that what were called 'parties' in those years had little in common with modern political parties, the way they are treated in the scholarship leads to an understanding of them as national organisations. The function of clientelist relations in the time of absolute monarchy, as detailed by John A. Petropoulos in the 1960s, provides instrumental solutions for analyses on a local scale, but on a national level serves as nothing more than a distorted enhancement of the small-scale model. In any case, none of the conditions necessary for party functionality on a national level existed. It is telling that, in 1844, Piscatory, the French ambassador in Athens, began to measure the power of the three so-called parties at the National Assembly: the British, the French and the Russian parties. But he was soon forced to abandon this effort when he saw that his calculations led nowhere.

In 1841, when Piscatory was charged with the duty of travelling through Greece, reporting on the situation in the country and sending Guizot his impressions, the comments he made on political parties in Greece reflect a deep sense of confusion. For the national party, he stated, 'France can hope for more than this. It can endorse the National Party, which, to the contrary, does not have ambitions to fulfil a purpose or commitment toward Greece, but rather has the adequate institutions to establish and ensure the proper government and protection of individual interests.' He would add doubts about the existence of a British party—he claimed that Mavrokordatos did not seem to belong to the British party—and that the Russian party seemed to be the only one standing, comprised of certain noted families that had concerted their efforts in the time of Kapodistrias. He would later state with no reservations that there was no differentiation between parties in relation to national issues.[8]

Therefore, the term 'party' can only be used during this period in reference to a factional and geographic network of local oligarchies with a common political culture, from which politicians emerged—and not for an organised entity, even on a clientelist basis. Thus it is ultimately misleading to rename an element of social formation in local communities as an element of the political organisation of the Greek state. The existence of certain political figures, such as Mavrokordatos, Kolettis and Metaxas, who identified with the ambassadors of the Great Powers—from whom they gained political power—may help to form opinions on these foreign-national political parties, though said rallying around these figures shifted constantly depending on specific problems that needed to be addressed. This is more or less clear from the political choices made by members of Parliament in the 3 September National Assembly: the traditional British, French and Russian party distinctions disappeared and political parties were redefined based on ministers' positions on the issue of *heterocthons*.

This perspective, which emphasises local particularities as fundamental elements of rural communities, helps us more easily comprehend local attitudes towards the emergence of a new state; the creation of basic governing structures at Bavarian hands was never an action that remained without a reaction from peasants and local communities more generally. In fact, given the details available, it can be surmised this was a traumatic period that aimed to bring many significant changes over a short period of time. Even from the first year, in 1833, villages in Messinia, Arcadia and Laconia rebelled and refused to pay taxes, often violently countering visiting tax-collectors and officers. Again, in 1833, the same thing was seen in villages on Tinos, extending even to the island's capital. The following year, in 1834, further refusals to pay taxes were seen in Arcadia, Messinia and Limni, in Evia. The most extreme rebellion occurred in 1834 in Mani, where efforts to disarm residents and the destruction of notables' towers led to armed confrontation with the army. The conflicts between the Maniots and the government's army were particularly bloody and diminished the latter's prestige when they resulted in a Bavarian defeat. After this victory, the Maniots demanded exemption from taxation, special ecclesiastic and monastic status, and exemption from military service. The government's failure to impose its power resulted in the formation of a special arrangement in Mani that would survive throughout the nineteenth century.

In 1835, rebellions and refusals to pay taxes were observed in the region of Megalopolis, Messinia, Missolonghi and Methoni, while in 1836 the situation turned more difficult as the region of Aetolia-Acarnania spun away from central control. That same year, in the Peloponnese and especially in Iliada and Messinia, the situation was also out of control. These were the conditions under which the Bavarians sought to control their municipalities, and it soon became clear that they would only manage to secure short-term successes.

In 1838, Spetses and Hydra mutinied. Both islands were motivated by demands to avoid classification for conscription in the land army, hoping to serve only in the navy. The same year, Pylia rebelled, while the year after that yet another uprising occurred in Mani. Then, in 1840, Nisi and Pyrgos revolted after the government demanded they pay a usufruct tax.

This limited information, which represents only a portion of all the opposition from the local population to the imposition of state power, demonstrates that the Bavarian task was not a simple one by any means. As already noted, these uprisings and revolts occurred in the context of a traditional system of political values, in which these acts constituted an effort to restore order, or perhaps more correctly, justice. Traditional communities were unable to accept monetary, human or other losses that might threaten local equilibriums or go against what they regarded as fair.

Most of the uprisings and revolts seen after the Bavarians' arrival were related to tax payments. These disputes are not likely to have resulted from the imposition of a slightly larger tithe in comparison with the past, but rather from the way it was collected. Populations were often accustomed to community tax payments and shared family tax burdens collected with intra-community procedures. Despite their awareness of this system, the Bavarians did not seem to pay complete respect to it. Maurer was aware of the problem:

> When an auction was held for the lease of the tithe, the lowest bid had to be proportionate to at least the estate tax of the last year. If it did not reach this lower limit, the state immediately took on its exploitation. The auction took place in provincial capitals and involved specific communities, entire towns or the whole prefecture. This happened so that even the poorest communities or individuals could take part in the auction process ... In order for the state to exact the tithe tax

> from these tenants, but also in the cases where the state itself, as mentioned above, directly assumed responsibility for this, collection was conducted by appointed general registrars in each region, and provincial registrars in each province. This was done after Mavrokordatos's initiative, and proved not only flawed as a system but dangerous for the staff it utilised, as suggested by Mavrokordatos. The pressure exerted by these marshals on farmers and the former's various extortion tactics reached a point where complaints and protests were widespread. Later all admitted that this was the cause of the outbreak of riots on Tinos, and that Kolokotronis took advantage of this situation to organise his conspiracy.[9]

This state presence upset local equilibriums and led to a violent reaction from the population, which was usually suppressed with force. Community balances were upset as foreigners inserted themselves; these foreigners did not respect or even take these balances into account, but rather sought to exploit their positions for personal gain. Despite the fact that Mauer seemed to accept that this interface between state and rural community was flawed and caused tensions with the villagers, continued revolts in later years indicate that the rationale and policies of the new state could not be easily reconciled with rural traditions. It is worth mentioning that, shortly thereafter, these communities were no longer permitted to extract tax-farming fees themselves, probably because this process had strengthened local elites. This act, in turn, exposed them to manipulation by central authority.

Local community reactions to the central government's attempted impositions were the most painful and difficult side of the problem. Yet, seen from another angle, it could be argued that within a relatively short period of time—the 1830s—the government was able to impose its authority, to temper the unavoidable reactions, and finally establish itself as the sole source of political legitimacy.

The monopoly on legitimate violence

Understandably, the Bavarians never believed that they could rely on Greek military forces—which at the time were totally disorganised if not destroyed—to impose their rule. Haidek, one of the members of the regency council responsible for organising the nation's military forces, had extensive experience with Greece, as he had taken part in the War of Independence. He knew that the situation was a shambles:

> Yet if an observer with fair-minded imaginings steps on to the land of Greece at this time, how disenchanted he will become! In vain would he set his eyes on even the shadow of an organised army! Instead he will come across packs of armed men led

> by brutal leaders looting towns that had just been rebuilt from ruins, decimating entire provinces, setting villages alight, brazenly seizing livestock, ruthlessly tormenting innocent citizens, laying waste, extorting money, in short, sowing fear and terror throughout the land and forcing its unfortunate inhabitants to seek refuge with the Turks.[10]

Fully aware of the problem, the Bavarians had also decided how to cope with it.

The regency council had arrived in Greece accompanied by 3,500 German mercenaries, which proved to be a highly valuable tool for enforcing Bavarian control over the Greek population. One of the first measures put in place by the Bavarians was a decree entitled 'Declaring Irregular Troops', which required the demobilisation and disarmament of irregular troops recruited after 1 December 1831—an estimated 5,000 in total. Irregular troops recruited before that date could be included in the military forces being developed, but only under certain conditions. Those under thirty years old could join the infantry line, while those above that age were allowed to join the rifle ranks. The government then demanded complete disarmament of all Greeks and ruled that possession of a weapon required a firearms licence.

The Bavarians were a rank above the rest when it came to the army's internal organisation. Their pay was far higher than that of the Greeks, as they were hired by their own country; they also received a mandated bonus payment equal to their salary from the Greek government in times of war. This is but one example of how the Bavarians supervised and intervened in Greece. Bavarian officers also had the supreme authority over a military unit even if they had a lower rank in cases where Bavarian units collaborated with the Greek army. In practice, mixed units were created so as to control Greek sections of the army and prevent them from acting autonomously. It naturally followed that these regulations and the contempt with which native Greek soldiers were treated became a point of friction between Greek and German troops. Other frictions resulted from the Bavarian effort to discipline Greek units, a concept that was completely alien to the Greeks.

The gendarmerie, in turn, was set up to mitigate reactions from irregular troops. It amounted to 1,200 men but was initially treated with suspicion; a year after its founding, it shrank to only 400 men in number. A literacy requirement was mainly to blame for the difficulty in recruiting gendarmes, and the government soon had to become more flexible in its requirements for military service. This particular unit served as a complementary group of soldiers to the army and was beholden to its general rules of procedure; it was also the privileged and favourite group of the Bavarian regime. Its higher wages as compared with those of other soldiers were a basic condition for the loyalty its troops showed to the regime. In fact, the gendarmerie was the only group not involved in the events of 1843, and even acted to suppress them.

In September 1835, shortly after Otto's coming of age, the Phalanx was established in order to appease those who had fought in the war. The Phalanx was essentially an entity that allowed certain distinguished fighters in the War of Independence to be paid without actively participating in the country's military activities. This purely symbolic military body included 800 men. Officers in the Phalanx would later be deployed to combat banditry, though perhaps for this very reason, many of them actively participated in bandit groups and raids.

Bold efforts were also made to organise the navy. A naval base was established in Poros, where a unit of craftsmen, organised by Bavarians, created warehouses and repaired all existing vessels. The Bavarians had even greater ambitions, and by 1833 they had managed to manufacture a 43-ton gunboat, followed by another twelve gunboats and two yachts by 1835. Their aim was to suppress piracy, which still flared up periodically in the Aegean. This task was carried out successfully with the help, of course, of fleets belonging to the Great Powers.

Initially, military forces were staffed by German mercenaries and Greeks that had already served as regular or irregular troops. From 1837 onwards, recruitment of Germans came to an end as their upkeep cost was extremely high, and the mercenaries began to slowly return to their homeland. One year later, not a single German soldier would remain in Greece—officers excepted—and as a result efforts began to create a system that would allow Greek recruitment. From 1836 onwards, civil records were kept to facilitate the work of the military recruitment office. The inventory law, passed on 28 November 1837, provided for replacement of departing German soldiers with Greeks and specified the recruitment conditions for Otto's subjects. This system led to major abuses, staffing the army with men from the poorest strata of society, since the wealthy were able to pay to exempt themselves from duty, or pay someone else who would take their place. Furthermore, those at risk of being conscripted against their will made sure to register in municipalities where the census had already been completed. Information also suggests that self-amputation was widely practised. In January 1838, the details of duty for conscripted soldiers were laid out. Soon after, the rebellion on Hydra broke out, resulting from the islanders' refusal to serve the land army. The state also proved incapable of resolving the problem of mass desertions, despite having taken tough measures against deserters and even their families.

The army was clearly organised in such a manner so as to enforce Bavarian power over an armed population ready to dispute any attempt at imposing central power. There was no alternative, and Otto could not be convinced otherwise, even if Trikoupis wrote to him that 'A nation without a national army seems more like a conquered country than an independent nation.'[11] It is also not surprising that the resulting army had the exclusive goal of suppressing internal enemies and enforcing public order—as opposed to the purpose of fighting a foreign enemy. This is why the Bavarian subsidiary corps was headquartered in Athens and comprised the Athenian garrison along with other Greek army units. The army's strength was minimal, and its organisation such that any attempt at long-term and large-scale campaigns was unrealistic, thanks to a lack of supervisory and recruitment support. In other words, the Greek army was created to support central power and had no other ambitions, and was far from entertaining the idea of battling the Ottoman Empire.

This same army avoided incorporating key military chiefs from the War of Independence. It was the Bavarians' clear intention to restrict any possible influence the latter group could have on the army. It was also clear that the military organisation of the country as realised by the Bavarians assumed the figure of the monarch as its sole reference point. All appointments of officers, irrespective of the military corps they served in, depended solely on Otto's preferences. This was also the case with admittance or rejection from the Military Academy, the expulsion of students and the awarding of scholarships, where the royal prerogative applied its full force to form a corps of officers dedicated to the king.

The way the regency council organised and subsequently managed the army had a range of consequences: a great number of irregulars that were unable or unwilling to join the Bavarian army would pose an array of problems for the kingdom's efforts to maintain law and order. Some of these individuals, chiefly those originating from areas not incorporated into the Greek state, were forced to withdraw to territories of the Ottoman Empire and to join the Derbendcis, while others joined groups of bandits that then looted regions on both sides of the border.

Yet it would be unreasonable to argue that the phenomenon of banditry was caused exclusively by the system of military organisation imposed by the Bavarians. With few exceptions, when central power is unable to gain a foothold in a region, there is always the possibility it will be replaced by armed forces questioning its monopoly on legal force. Armed violence was a characteristic feature of rural societies, and just as it existed before the foundation of the Greek state, so it continued to exist after.

The first major wave of banditry took place in 1834 and 1835, concurrently with the uprisings of those same years. It was a natural effect of the first collective reaction to the regency council's regulations and a probable outlet for irregular troops who found themselves out of work after the new system of military organisation was imposed by the Bavarians. The regency council's first reaction was to send military forces to fight them, led by the Scottish philhellene Thomas Gordon. But this was a move that would bear weak results, forcing the Bavarians to find other ways of addressing the issue.

Roumeliot captains and irregulars were recruited to eliminate the bandits, as they were familiar with their tactics and knew how to locate their hideouts. This was a victory for the military elite, as it enabled them to re-enter the scene that they had been excluded from up until that point. In this way, the limits of the new authorities became clearly understood by all. Around the same time, Gordon submitted a series of proposals for dealing with banditry. Beyond the punitive approach, which had already proven ineffective, Gordon stressed the importance of creating municipalities so as to document all residents within their region and proposed the use of passports for monitoring movements of individuals within regions. He also suggested mandatory permanent residence for the nomadic farmers that often protected and nurtured bandits. For the central government, the problem stemmed from the inability to control the population and its movements, something that far exceeded the capacities and capabilities of the government and state apparatus.

The uprising in 1836 would further highlight the limits the state faced in its attempts to monopolise legitimate violence. For the first time, regular troops were not sent to chase the bandits, and henceforth, the former group's role was limited to protecting the regime and guarding the capital and the king. Suppression of uprisings was entrusted to the informal militia, that is, to the regional captains that formed their own ranks to fight bandits: men were inducted into these groups based on agreements between the captains and local mayors, but also between the captains and the men themselves. The presiding municipality bore the costs, while the bandits themselves entered and exited these groups constantly in an attempt to derive the most benefit from the situation. In this same process, military officers began to see the game of local power within reach.

The limits of the public policy Bavarians sought to implement were evident in their failure to monopolise the use of violence. As a result, they had to pursue milder policies and often had to negotiate with challengers to their power, and in more than a few cases win the latter over by offering something in return. The struggle for the enforcement of state legitimacy was assigned to third parties that were able to boast some order in their respective provinces. Otto's state, thus, was not any more effective than its Ottoman predecessors in controlling violence and certainly did not succeed in asserting itself over the Greek population with the decisiveness it would have liked. What it ended up doing, from the moment it recognised its failure, was integrating provincial military leaders into its own networks and negotiating for their allegiance, thereby returning to Ottoman-style policies.

The monopoly on spiritual violence

Upon arriving in Greece, the regency council rushed to address the ecclesiastical question—unresolved since the outbreak of the War of Independence—and the suspension of relations with the Ecumenical Patriarchate. G. Maurer, responsible for the regency council's religious matters, wrote: 'In any case, along with the political freedom of the Greek state, religious freedom must also follow.'

The Bavarians first sought to address the question of the Greek church's autonomy from the Patriarchate, acting with the greatest possible legitimacy and avoiding challenges at all costs. Yet it is doubtful whether they succeeded in this.

In March 1833, the regency council appointed a committee with the task of examining the status of the Greek church. The dominant figure of the committee, who undoubtedly determined its developments in the years to come, was T. Farmakidis, a major reformist scholar. The committee began its work in April 1833. Already from the first meeting, members were able to agree on the necessity of an autocephalous Greek Church. Reactions to the committee's final recommendations were relatively limited and would only intensify slightly with the arrival of the Russian attaché Katakazis, who used his relationship with the Patriarchate as a key instrument to pressure a government led by Catholics and Protestants, which therefore had to be particularly careful when handling issues involving Orthodox traditions, whatever form they took. The argument of the domestic opposition, which would remain the same for many years, was that this new charter cut the Greeks off from the spiritual roots of the orthodoxy, running the risk of rendering them Protestants or Catholics.

On 3 July, a meeting, which took place over twelve days in Nafplion, was convened to discuss the committee's positions. All the active bishops—no more than sixteen in number—were invited to the meeting, as were titular bishops from the Ottoman Empire. The bishops, twenty-two in total, gathered in Nafplion and accepted the proposals with only minor amendments. The committee then accepted them in turn. In the end, the re-drafted text was signed by all twenty-two individuals. Subsequently, another fourteen bishops signed the new statutory charter. The objection raised at the time was that most of the bishops originated from the Ottoman Empire, thus invalidating the session. Indeed, with the start of the war, many bishops had sought refuge in areas destined to become the Greek state, and therefore now found themselves in Greece without a diocese, and with their survival depending on Bavarian goodwill. Consequently, they would hardly react in a hostile way to the latter's wishes. But the problem was not so much canonical as it was political. These scattered and finally inconsequential objections notwithstanding, on 23 July 1833 the Statutory Charter of the Greek Church was published. The first article stated:

> The Orthodox Eastern Apostolic Church of the kingdom of Greece recognizes no other spiritual leader apart from the founder of the Christian faith, our Lord and Savior Jesus Christ. The King of Greece is its leader in administrative affairs, and it is autocephalous and independent of all other powers, safeguarding doctrinal unity from corruption, in accordance with what has always been expounded by all the Orthodox Eastern Churches.[12]

In this way, the question of the Greek Church's independence from the Ecumenical Patriarchate was solved smoothly and painlessly, at least for the time being. It would have been bizarre if any other solution was given, as it seems inconceivable for one to think that a state just finished with a war would leave a basic mechanism of controlling the populace in an opponent's control. Apart from that, what government seeking its own autonomy would accept supervision of the Patriarchate, within which the influences of Russian politics were very strong? In any case, neither the governments during the war nor Kapodistrias thought to offer up an alternative solution.

The autocephalous status of the Orthodox Greek Church was undoubtedly one facet of the ecclesiastical question that the Bavarians were forced to address promptly. Another had to do with the relations between church and state. For the Bavarians, control of the church, or more accurately the direct subordination of the church to state control, was crucial, precisely because the powerful core of the opposition resided within the church. In addition, it also offered an effective manner of legitimising their power over local populations.

As early as April 1833, right after the ecclesiastical committee had convened, a decree was published outlining the responsibilities of the various ministries. The responsibilities of the Secretariat of the Church included the power to convene a synod. Anyone unconvinced about the Bavarians' intentions now realised the status of the situation after reading this document. A very young Otto had also realised the need for these types of adjustments when he wrote to his father: 'the spiritual authority of this country's clergy could become dangerous for the secular ruler if the highest ranking clergy members rallied a group of supporters, since the clergy could then assemble the people on his side against the supreme leader ...'[13]

The regency council gave special emphasis to control over monks, who, as we will see, comprised the core of opposition resistance. At best, the latter group served to shelter and protect those persecuted by state power; at worst they harboured networks of opposition to government decisions that often maintained huge power at a local level. The large amount of property often owned by monasteries rendered them significantly influential over local populations and prominent allies of notable groups. Consequently, one of the regency council's first decisions was to significantly reduce the number of monasteries; it was decided that all monasteries with fewer than six monks would be closed and their assets transferred to the state. A total of 412 monasteries vanished, with the nation's 3,000 monks being forced to relocate to the remaining 148 monasteries. This number would be reduced even further in the following months. The number of women's convents was also significantly reduced, with the intent of eventually limiting them to three. Only Mani was exempted from these monastic reforms, mainly because of the severe opposition it provoked. In fact, Mani rebelled in 1834, protesting the closure of monasteries among other things. This in itself demonstrates the important place monks held in local communities, and how necessary it was to restrict and control their movements.

The Bavarians sought to deal with this issue quickly; the Holy Synod's first decision included limitations on the unrestricted movement of monks. Henceforth, for a monk to preach in the area, the bishop responsible for the region had to grant him permission. Yet these measures only increased monks' movements: those whose monasteries had been disbanded headed to the few remaining monasteries, which were entirely hostile to them, resulting in the fleeing and relocation of these monks in various villages and towns where they tried to survive in every which way. Meanwhile, an ecclesiastical fund was created from the proceeds of the closed monasteries with the aim of supporting the church and education. The number of monasteries eventually fell to eighty-two. A multitude of public notices followed that limited the privileges of monasteries and placed their activities under public control.

The organisation of dioceses seemed to follow the French model and adapted to the administrative partitioning of the country, creating yet another state authority alongside the position of the prefect. Provisional chairs were granted to the forty bishops active in Greece at the time. Over time, and due to natural hardships, they shrank to a total of ten. Yet state supervision went one step further: the synod decided to appoint a protosyncellus and an archdeacon to each region, the former as a consultant and the latter as secretary to the bishop, in such a way that corresponded to the consultants and secretaries appointed to prefects. Restrictions were also imposed on the issuance of ordinations. All these measures were taken in 1834, rendering the church a branch of the state apparatus, at least as far as its leaders were concerned. In this domain, the Bavarians had no reason for concern.

Over time, balances and political associations shifted, and beginning in 1837 Russian influence on the government grew significantly. This shift was not without consequences for the Holy Synod. As the latter changed members on an annual basis, it quickly passed into the hands of those opposed to the reforms of 1833. The new members owed their positions to a conservative movement that had rallied around an emblematic figure, Constantinos Economos, who had won over the support of G. Glarakis, minister of ecclesiastical affairs. These new members began to lobby for a reversal of the Statutory Charter of the Greek Church and for a closer relationship with the Patriarchate. In the same period, the religious hierarchy seemed to take on a much more interventionist role—using the pretext of its religious role, but acting as a secular power—seeking to control the populations under its yoke. In other words, the church of the kingdom of Greece assumed the role it was essentially destined for, one that it knew how to play well.

Intellectual discipline

The issue of education only came to the regency council's attention later, indicating it was certainly not one of its top priorities compared with other areas of state development. This is understandable given the prevailing chaos in Greece, which rendered it impossible for educational institutions to operate.

The groundwork for a functioning network of public schools was only established after the decree of 6 February 1834. In fact, primary education was an area of minimal interest to the Bavarians, since it had nothing to offer them—at least in the short term. As minister of education, C. Christopoulos would later identify the objectives of primary education:

> Of course primary schools do not only aim to teaching reading, writing, arithmetic, etc. Above all they should contribute to the moralization of the nation, and especially in the cases of needy children, substitute for their upbringing at home. But directions for education in elementary schools can only be administered appropriately by ensuring edification of teachers based on Christian virtues ... Along with the ideal priest and the ideal judge, the ideal elementary school teacher acts more effectively upon society than those more complex and expensive apparatuses, nearly rendering the use of any other governing body redundant.[14]

In other words, the moral education of the king's subjects rested on the three basic pillars of the state: education, the church and justice. Education for its own sake was not accepted. However, for political reasons—even more so because they were governing Greece—the Bavarians could not disregard the development of an educational system, even if this had to happen at the lowest possible cost. Therefore, in accordance with a decree initiated by Maurer, it was decided that primary schools were to be established in each municipality. Schooling would be compulsory for all children and last seven years. Administration of the schools would be undertaken by the municipalities.

In fact, the regency council harboured no illusions about how this project would function. In accordance with their capabilities, municipalities would have to create these schools 'bit by bit'. This became a serious problem as schools required resources, resources that many municipalities in the country could not allocate. In many—or in fact most—cases, basic education was already organised around the community priest, who in this manner had the opportunity to secure an additional income.

The lack of suitable teachers continued to be a key obstacle to the expansion of primary schools across the country. This is why the peer-tutoring method of education took hold, although in theory, most of those developing the young state's educational initiatives were opposed to it. This method minimised the number of teachers, thus reducing the cost of primary education. In 1834, a centre for training teachers was established. I. Kokkonis, who would become the first important educator of the Greek state, took over as its director in 1835.

The system of primary education created by the 1834 decree did not produce satisfactory results. In fact, it was nothing more than an exercise on paper. In rural communities, education offered by primary schools was a luxury and did not appear useful to children and their parents. It was no coincidence that the ministry blamed the delay in development of primary education on parents, who preferred to put their children to work in the fields instead of sending them to school. The schools that priests organised were much more convenient to these rural communities, and from 1834 onwards, two intersecting and overlapping parallel networks of primary education emerged. In 1855–6, 300 grammar schools enrolling over 10,000 students complemented the services offered by 495 peer-tutoring schools teaching 41,597 pupils. It should be noted here that these numbers are insignificant considering that all sources available point to a prevailing disorder in education during this period. A glaring example of the failures in primary education is evident from the extremely high rates of illiteracy that still characterised Greece in the late nineteenth century.

This was compounded by the municipalities' inability and unwillingness to meet their financial obligations, resulting in a progressive—and early—decline in elementary schooling. Those who had been employed by primary schools began to drop out, and those who had the chance to take up jobs with them avoided doing so. Even the number of students attending the training centre shrank gradually, as the prospects for finding a job were slim. Only in 1855 did the Greek state seek to address the problem, paying salaries in advance for these municipal teachers. In major cities, the low wages earned by teachers and professors drove them to find secondary jobs at private schools, which only further undermined the proper functioning of public education.

Primary schooling was the first step in the Bavarians' educational project. The second came two years later with the decree of 31 December 1836, which reformed secondary education, Greek school and high school. The Greek school, divided into three grades, functioned as a preparatory school for high school, which in turn had four grades. Each region was required to have a Greek school, and each province a high school. These reforms made secondary education a privilege for the very few, that is, for the residents of large urban centres, for no other reason than that it was unlikely that a child in a rural area would continue their education in the region's capital, even if they managed to finish primary school. Thus, in the 1855–6 academic year, as previously mentioned, there was a total of 41,597 pupils in primary schools. In the Greek schools, the pupils amounted to 4,224, of which only 441 graduated. The number of pupils in high school totalled 1,182, of which 102 received a diploma. In other words, the number of children who continued their studies after primary school was exceptionally small due to the many barriers that prevented their ascent into higher levels of education.

While practical progression from one tier of education to the next was extremely difficult, the institutional relationships between them were also unclear. Nowhere were the preconditions for going from elementary school to high school explicitly stated, apart from the fact that the pupil had to demonstrate knowledge of a primary education. As a result, the system for moving from the first to the second educational level was rather open. In secondary education, the situation was more clearly defined: the system was based on yearly exams, three in Greek school and four in high school, while from the outset the Bavarians had planned to diversify the schools among themselves and give them a practical focus. Yet once again, this plan would once falter due to a lack of sufficient human resources.

In 1837, the University of Athens was founded, with four departments: Theology, Medicine, Law and Philosophy. The university's ambitions, at least in the eyes of its founders and professors, far surpassed the capacity of the Greek state's administrative framework at the time. The establishment of Otto's University, as it was originally named, claimed the Enlightenment of the East as its main objective. This is confirmed by the numbers at our disposal. From 1855 to 1856, the years we have data for, of its 590 students, 215 were foreigners, without a doubt a noteworthy number.

But the university did not play the role for which it had originally been founded. Conclusive evidence for this can be found in the small number of scientists that trained there, evidence of which can be found in the corresponding number of degrees granted (or, more precisely, not granted). In any case, several years passed before the first students earned their diplomas. This could have resulted from an inadequate system, evidenced by the indifference of its professors, who usually sought other government positions—which they often occupied—but also a high cost of attendance, which made it difficult to facilitate educating low- or middle-income students. In truth, in the first years it functioned, the University of Athens was nothing more than a mechanism for integrating scholars into the Greek state.

This process was indeed inevitable, as Bavarian efforts at state consolidation would necessarily assimilate these scholars into the Greek state. This was achieved in many ways: they were employed in various positions, hired at the university, or, finally, lured by incentives if they adopted an attitude that was friendly to the establishment. These scholars were an extremely small group and their effect on communities in the Greek state—where the vast majority of the population was illiterate—was limited.

Scholars supporting the Bavarian state had formed as a group during the Ottoman period and generally experienced a decline in their status during this time. Most of these scholars were Phanariots, though some of them originated from the Ionian Islands; as C.T. Dimaras noted, they represented the 'end of a world', a world that occupied positions of power and had no ambitions to adopt a critical stance towards the Bavarian regime. This is understandable, to the extent that this declining group of scholars belonged to the upper levels of the social hierarchy in accordance with their fields of specialisation and could not challenge the foundations upon which its existence was based.

In the educational realm, the regency council pursued completely different policies from those of Kapodistrias. In place of the latter's spartan, utilitarian educational system, the Bavarians aimed to create an integrated and elaborate system, despite its initial reservations. This system certainly surpassed the needs and capabilities of the Greek state, and it would be too simplistic to argue in terms of the system's absolute success or failure. Surely, it was unable to embed itself in communities—or rather, this process took an extended period of time, highlighting the limits of the relationship between the state and the populations it sought to dominate. Primary education was most developed, as one would expect, in the most affluent and commercially developed regions of the nation. Secondary education concerned a limited population, delineating the educational system's limitations. In any case, the education of villagers was of little importance for state functionality in this first phase; the latter group only needed to be educated enough to tolerate state discipline. But for city-dwellers, education had the added goal and allure of providing a position in state administration. In other words, it was a system that had defined its goals and contributed to the process of incorporating the country's population into state mechanisms, though this mostly only held true for urban populations and the intellectual elite.

The Greek educational system, as configured by the Bavarians but also as it continued to function throughout the nineteenth century, was an open system; it did not rule anyone out *a priori*. In this respect, it might be contrasted with the educational systems of Slavic countries, which throughout the nineteenth century categorically refused to give their masses of peasants open access to education. This would be a major problem during the twentieth century.

The king's justice

Naturally, the juridical organisation of the Greek state was taken on by Maurer, a legal scholar himself and an advocate of Volksrecht—the creation of civil law on the basis of domestic habits and morals. Inevitably, he turned towards common law to create the corpus of Greek civil law, which would also incorporate elements of Byzantine-Roman law. So as to collect relevant information on the status of law in the countries he co-governed, he appealed to local authorities and asked them to reply to a questionnaire he sent them. He received many answers, but was not given a chance to proceed. In the summer of 1834, he was forced to leave Greece after the revocation of the mandate granted to him by Ludwig I.

A few months later, Minister of Justice G. Praidis commissioned a committee to draft a decree stipulating that civil law would be based on the *Hexabiblos*, the fourteenth-century work of Byzantine legal scholar Constantine Harmenopoulos, which had served as crucial legal help in the years of Ottoman sovereignty. It also stipulated that general customs would continue to be valid. The committee in turn proposed that the *Hexabiblos* be replaced by the laws of Byzantine emperors, since only the latter had legal power. The committee also proposed that general customs should not continue to be valid—as stated in the draft law—but rather that local customs should prevail, as these were more dominant. The proposal was finally written in the following way: 'The civil laws of the Byzantine emperors contained in the *Hexabiblos* of Constantine Armenopoulos shall apply until the Civil Code is published, whose preparation we have ordered. Customs, however, such as have been established by longstanding habit or judicial rulings, shall prevail wherever they used to apply.' This reform shaped civil law in Greece, as the committee drafting this civil code created by the regency council (which continued to exist until 1874) was never given the chance to complete its task. In fact, after the founding of the Greek state, the Ottoman system continued to apply, the only difference being that it was not administered by the church but instead by political authorities. But a smooth transition from one to the other was not to be taken for granted: in just one telling example, priests continued to draft contracts despite repeated government notices and threats to void contracts not drafted by certified notaries.

Along with the regulation of issues related to civil law, the Greek state adopted the Napoleonic commercial code, already in effect for trade within the Eastern Mediterranean.

Things were different in the realm of criminal law. The adoption of reforms in this area was an urgent subject. Public order was a shambles throughout the kingdom. The three temporary courts created by the regency council shortly after its arrival—in Nafplion, Missolonghi and Thebes—had this exact purpose: to address the plethora of criminal offences. Certain temporary reforms were introduced, both in order for these temporary courts to function and to punish offenses against national security. Given the volume of work at hand, Maurer published his criminal code very quickly, which he characterised without modesty as 'the best and simplest criminal code extant in the world at the time'. Implementation of the new criminal code, which was based on its Bavarian counterpart from 1813, began on 17 September 1835.

The new penal code outlined a range of offences against public order, as well as offences involving the use of force. Through this legislation, the state sought to safeguard and outline its monopoly on violence. By the beginning of 1835, the new system of courts had begun to function, and the temporary courts were suspended.

This new system allowed for the creation of ten courts, one in each prefecture of the country, and two appeal courts, one in Athens and the other in Nafplion. Commercial matters were handled by a unique commercial court created in Ermoupoli, as was only natural. A network of municipal courts was also established for the resolution of minor issues. By 1842, they had grown to a total of seventy-six. Finally the Areopagus, the Supreme Court, was founded in Athens. All these courts, with the possible exception of the local courts, were staffed by *heterocthons* from Constantinople, the Ionian Islands or cities in Western Europe, who had gone to university in the West. At the same time, Bavarians and also philhellenes, such as the Scot E. Masson, took up crucial positions in the legal system.

Beyond the court system, the Bavarian corps of engineers rushed to repair and fortify two castles in Nafplion and Chalcis which would later be used as prisons. Executioners for these temporary courts—brought in from elsewhere, as a local person would not agree to undertake such a task—also executed their first convicts. In Missolonghi, for example, on 8 May 1834, eight convicts were executed by guillotine in a single day. The zeal was such that the government rushed to ask local authorities to mitigate it. Yet these executions would continue for a long time, chiefly as a means of imposing state power.

The development of justice, particularly its penal dimension, occurred in such a way so as to support Bavarian state power, and it also served the needs of the moment. It could not have been otherwise. But in this very same period, the regency council found it impossible to impose its authority exclusively by legal and military means. Shortly thereafter, the Bavarians began negotiating with groups that questioned their power, and the use of amnesty became yet another weapon extensively used to address problems when violence and coercion did not yield results. Besides, these same methods strengthened the king's position and role, as it now encompassed all the attributes of state justice: prevention, persecution, repression, condemnation and, finally, granting of amnesty.

The establishment of mechanisms for justice did not lead to that which the Bavarians theoretically sought, which was the unification of a state legal apparatus. Despite prohibitions and condemnations, justice often continued to be administered by those who had administered it before the arrival of the Bavarians. The role of the church, priests and the political elite continued to be important for many years. Rural communities certainly preferred to resolve any disputes between their members without recourse to external parties. Lastly, traditions of vendetta and blood feuds would continue for decades to come as ways of resolving disputes among rural populations.

Great hopes, but few possibilities

The Bavarians arrived in Greece with many ambitions and every intention to realise them. Initially at least, all indications seemed to show they had the ability to do so. First, they had the economic strength provided by a loan of 60 million francs. Second, they had the ability to impose military power, and third, a political regime that allowed for decision-making without many concessions. The project they carried out was important in every respect, and in fact would lay the foundations for a state that surpassed traditional models of population governance. They were able to address all areas of state organisation on an institutional level, and irrespective of whether their reforms were finally effective, they established a precedent that would not be undone in the years to come.

The overarching logic for their choices can easily be traced to Bavarian and German perceptions of state organisation. The policies they adopted had the 'welfare of the state' as their main objective, and its implementation necessitated a series of regulatory provisions governing interpersonal relationships. Indeed, the government was faced not with individual people, but with a population, a complex reality, whose mechanisms of reproduction had to be controlled. This Bavarian perspective was evidenced in the frequent use of the originally German method of 'science of police' (*Polizeiwissenschaft*), and the administrative equivalent of mercantilism: the term 'police' as found in various Bavarian documents was less related to maintaining order and more linked to a combination of practices and regulations that could lead to the diffusion of the state's well-being through all levels of society.

This approach was expressed explicitly in the health sector, and especially in cities that were in the first areas in which general police regulations were adopted internationally. In the first case, referred to extensively in the next chapter, the whole of Bavarian policy aimed to protect its territories from disease epidemics, specifically the plague and much later cholera, which could affect general welfare, namely state health. Beyond that, disease was a problem that had to be addressed on a family level. Only the growth of urban centres, with all the resulting consequences in terms of poverty and sanitation, finally drove conditions to the point where local leaders or wealthy elites intervened by creating organisations, for the most part charitable. This approach would remain in effect until the early twentieth century, emphasising among other things the momentum of broader changes within the Greek state.

This logic of 'general policing' was especially present in cities. The royal decree of 3 April 1835, 'On Building Healthy Cities and Villages', which constituted the basis for city-planning until 1923 and was supplemented by subsequent decrees, is a classic example of this approach. The regulations that would define the configuration of entire cities, and the ways in which even minor issues were to be settled, were included in this decree. It aimed to regulate aspects of people's lives in such a way that their choices could lead to the welfare of the state, and imposed these regulations in an authoritarian, even pedagogical way.

Apart from trying to understand the underlying rationale of Bavarian policies, it is worth noting that the most important legacy they left behind was that they did not seek to exclude any category of Greek individual, even if the powers they granted were limited and supervised. By doing this, they created the conditions to institutionally assimilate political opposition, which would prove crucial in the long term for the development of Greek political activity. Simultaneously, making use of this rationale and these policies, the Bavarians formed a centralised state whose central power was never challenged.

Yet the resulting state apparatus they created far exceeded the Greek kingdom's capabilities in every respect, as the state's existence presupposed many more resources (both human and non-human) than were available. The attempts made to conduct a demographic and geographic survey were a telling example of this. The ambitious attempts were made upon the establishment of the Office of Public Finance, seeking to create a 'topographical and political/economic branch of jurisdiction', and finally to 'devise a complete census of the kingdom'. They were the first to meet a dead end as public finances faltered, but also because of a lack of individuals competent enough to execute the projects at hand. This included the Bavarian census effort, the creation of a land registry and the mapping of the country, but also the creation of a registry system. These failures in staffing and funding would lead to the downsizing and ultimate fall of the Bavarian regime. In any case, the country's elite never seemed willing to live with the crumbs of power granted to them by the Bavarians, and the weakening of the regime—mostly due to its inadequate control of the military—would provide them with an opportunity to overthrow it.

The practice of incorporating groups of political elites came to take the place of the hostility towards them that the Bavarians initially chose, as it proved impossible to control the political, economic and social situation through their own methods. Apart from the examples mentioned above, the attempted establishment of a bank and the eventual creation of the National Bank of Greece are also indicative. The first 'innocent' efforts to create an organisation that would support the nation's economy very quickly gave way to adjustments that would allow the economic elite to participate in the bank's activities, with resulting benefits for both sides. Intentions to create a bank that would finance the rural economy, similar to those characterising the National Bank at the time of its founding, were quickly abandoned when faced with the reality of the situation. Without the participation of groups in possession of capital, the National Bank's very existence was called into question.

In all these instances, the Bavarians were forced to retreat, compromise and ultimately accept a mode of governance similar to that which native populations had previously experienced. The state that the Bavarians eventually ended up forming had nothing to do with their original intentions, and the foundations of a national/governmental space would not be established for many years. A typical example of this can be seen in the economic realm. If the creation of a single currency area expresses national sovereignty more than anything else, then the Bavarian failure at such an effort very openly demonstrated the limits of their capabilities, the limitations to state sovereignty, and finally, the very nature of the state they built. The drachma may have been created, but until at least the 1870s it failed to become the national standard for transactions. Imported coins, often Ottoman, fulfilled this role while the drachma served chiefly as a scriptural currency (i.e. a currency that serves purely accounting purposes).

There could hardly be a break in continuity with the past based on the political voluntarism that initially characterised Bavarian policies.

4

KING OTTO AND THE GREEKS

(1844–62)

The kingdom of the Great Idea

The period following the Napoleonic Wars, during which the Greek state was founded, was marked by the Great Powers' desperate attempts to support the strategic balance emerging after the Restoration. In the context of the Concert of Europe, no state was able (or, in fact, willing) to attempt to obtain a strategic advantage. The main concern in the decades to come was maintenance of stability within the borders of larger Western European nations, a stability at risk from the French Revolution.

Greece was a creation of the Concert of Europe and one of a few small states born in those years—Belgium being another example—with the aim of reconciling its members' divergent views on the regional issues at hand without resorting to war. Insofar as the Concert of Europe functioned effectively, which was the case up until the Crimean War, all transnational problems were solved via negotiations with other members of the Concert. Other states were only allowed a limited say in matters concerning them, even if their interests were directly at stake.

In these years, the international system functioned according to two basic principles. The first was the Great Powers' joint responsibility for maintaining the territorial status quo established in 1815 and resolving problems arising in Europe; the second, regarding changes that needed to be made and solutions that had to be given, was a process of collective decision-making involving specific diplomatic practices. These principles were derived from the notion that the Great Powers had the exclusive right and obligation to preserve international order. Or, as the British ambassador to Otto during the Crimean War put it, 'The foreign powers have established the kingdom's independence and given Greece a King. This gives them the right to expect gratitude and respect of their interests.'[1]

Timetable 1844–62

1844	Andreas Metaxas government (3 September 1843–16 February 1844). Konstantinos Kanaris government (16 February 1844–30 March 1844). Constitution published on 18 March. Otto sworn in. Alexandros Mavrokordatos government (30 March 1844–6 August 1844). Elections. Kolettis government (6 August 1844–5 September 1847).
1847	Elections. Kolettis wins an absolute majority. Kolettis dies. Kitsos Tzavellas government (5 September 1847–8 March 1848).
1848	Georgios Koundouriotis government (8 March 1848–15 October 1848). Kanaris government (15 October 1848–12 December 1849).
1849	A. Kriezis government (12 December 1849–16 May 1856).
1850	Greek coastline blockaded by British fleet. Parker incident. Independence of the Greek Church from the Patriarchate recognised. Elections. A. Kriezis gains the majority.
1852	T. Kairis is sentenced.
1853	Crimean War. New elections, which A. Kriezis wins yet again.
1854	Riots in Epirus, Thessaly and Macedonia. Turkish–Greek diplomatic relations suspended. Blockade of Piraeus by British and French troops. Kanaris government (16 May 1854–17 July 1854) and Mavrokordatos government (17 July 1854–22 September 1855) (Ministry of the Occupation). Relations restored between Greece and the Ottoman Empire.
1855	D. Voulgaris government (22 September 1855–13 November 1857).
1856	End of the Crimean War. Treaty of Paris. The Great Powers guarantee territorial integrity of the Ottoman Empire. D. Voulgaris wins in the election.
1857	Anglo-French occupation army departs from Greece. Miaoulis government (13 November 1857–26 May 1862).
1859	Elections. Miaoulis triumphs.
1860	Publication of Constantine Paparrigopoulos's *History of the Greek Nation* begins.
1861	Elections. Renewed triumph of Miaoulis. Greece recognises Italy.
1862	Rebellion against Otto in Nafplion suppressed. Gennaios Kolokotronis government (26 May 1862–11 October 1862). Uprising in Athens overthrows Otto. D. Voulgaris caretaker government (11 October 1862–9 February 1863). Elections for the National Assembly. Proceedings begin for the Second National Assembly on 10 December.

Consequently, states exhibiting opportunistic political behaviour were a cause for unease and were treated with severity. Internal problems between the Great Powers were of the utmost gravity, or were at least treated as such by their leaders, to the extent that any action that risked leading to political tensions or military action was considered a breach of international peace and had to be combated accordingly.

With this in mind, it becomes much easier to understand Greece's military and diplomatic policies—and their ineffectiveness—during the period Otto was in power. However, we can also better grasp attitudes the Great Powers maintained in relation to Greece. Why should Greece spend large amounts on its military, especially when it was unable to make basic payments towards fulfilling its loan obligations, when its territorial claims were only to be fulfilled at the Great Powers' negotiation table? Similarly, why should Greece be interested in its diplomatic representation abroad, which only incurred additional costs without presenting any particular advantage? Conversely, for the same reasons, the Great Powers fought against any expenses related to the country's military organisation, and considered any attempts at fortifying its diplomatic staff unfounded. The presence of their attachés in the Greek court was sufficient; anything else was excessive and suggested a willingness to upset the international balance.

Otto's goals for the expansion of the Greek kingdom would only be realised if the Great Powers could be convinced that they were necessary—and naturally, that they would not disrupt the existing equilibrium. The country's foreign policy, identified with the king himself (let us not forget that until 1862 the Foreign Ministry was a Ministry of the Royal House), was nothing more than a declaration of the Greek 'problem', and a demonstration of the country's demands at the exact moment when it seemed the balance of the Concert of Europe was most fragile. These declarations were often expressed bluntly, as in the case of the dispatch of irregular troops and subsequent inciting of riots in territories belonging to the Ottoman Empire. Similar situations presented themselves in 1841, and again during the Crimean War. For the monarch, it seemed that the support of one of the Great Powers was enough to realise his goals. Yet this approach, which was the only option given the circumstances, was doomed to fail.

Consequently, the terms under which Otto sought to implement his irredentist policies were different from those described by most writers at the time. Otto's administrative decisions, which nearly excluded the British party from power, certainly won over a group of politicians that 'represented' most of the country's population, but they also gave him the opportunity to indirectly associate with whichever Great Power would in theory support Greek claims in the region. Indeed, the preference that Otto and Kolettis showed for France was product of a perception that saw France as the most convenient diplomatic partner, since its interests in the East were rather limited, but also as the power that, for the very same reasons, could provide the most services.

On the other hand, Russia could have qualified as the nation's main ally for the simple reason that both countries sought the dissolution of the Ottoman Empire—at least until the Slavs appeared on the scene. For this very reason, even A. Mavrokordatos, head of the so-called 'British' party, believed that Russia was the most capable of helping the Greek state achieve its goals. In a memorandum of his dated to around 1849, Mavrokordatos indicated the need for Greece to be prepared to benefit from every future opportunity in which Russia could be an ally to the Greek cause—primarily regarding the possibilities of a Russo-Turkish conflict or Slav revolution. Furthermore, Russia was a stable supporter of the model of absolute monarchy.

Britain, thanks to its support of Ottoman integrity, remained a threat to Greek aspirations. What Otto and his political advisors had not assessed correctly was the fact that none of the powers intended to create a rift in the Concert of Europe by dramatically changing strategic balances in favour of Greece or any other party—at least until the Crimean War.

From this perspective, it was a major error for Otto to believe he could benefit from the Turkish–Egyptian war of 1839, but also from the intensification of the Eastern Crisis in the years that followed up until 1841. His initial alliance with Mehmet Ali and the French had brought him into conflict with the other two Great Powers that sought to maintain the Ottoman Empire's integrity at the time. The only hope remaining for him after the issue was settled—namely by the concession of Crete, which had rebelled and rid itself of Egyptian sovereignty—proved to be in vain, as France soon changed its attitude as well.

Otto emerged even worse from the Crimean War. In a naïve assessment of the situation, he believed that he could reap benefits by uniting the whole of Europe in favour of maintaining the Ottoman Empire intact. Despite warnings from Greek ambassadors in Paris and London that France and Britain would intervene with force if necessary to prevent aggression against the Ottoman Empire, his actions after the outbreak of the Crimean War worsened Greece's relations with both countries and led to the occupation of Piraeus. It became clear that Otto had very little room to manoeuvre when exercising foreign policy—and, to be more precise, he could hardly have made a different choice. The international situation was prohibitive of greater flexibility and efficacy, and his decisions during the Crimean War would spell his demise, despite having temporarily won the support of a significant portion of his subjects.

Demonstrations of force such as the 1850 naval blockade commonly known as the Parker incident and the Anglo-French occupation in 1854 were only the tip of the iceberg of the pressure exercised by the Great Powers and had relatively little impact on the formation of state policies. The systematic, daily pressure on Otto's regime to fulfil its various obligations—most of all the regular repayment of its 60 million franc loan—had much more of an impact, influencing the process of state consolidation much more methodically and effectively. Indeed, the legal framework that allowed for the creation of the Greek state also offered, typically, the possibility to exercise these pressures. In the London Treaty of 25 April/7 May 1832, the Great Powers reserved the ability to intervene if they believed the Greek state had deviated from its prescribed path. To take but one typical example, the treaty referenced Greece's obligation to repay the 60 million franc loan the Great Powers had guaranteed in a timely fashion. Various authors have written about this specific regulation, as it contains the first traces of the institution for international financial control. Though it has been justly noted that it was never implemented, it was this exact clause that constituted the legal pretext for continued interventions by the Great Powers in Greece's internal politics.

From the moment the Greek government began pressing for the final instalment of the 60 million franc loan in order to address its troubled state finances, the Great Powers had found a sensitive spot in Greek foreign policy that they could use to pressure Otto to adapt to their imperatives, which of course differed according to each power's interests. Indeed, from 1837 onwards, when British influence in Greece had evaporated, the British government stopped at nothing to put the Greek government into a difficult position in hopes of forcing it to adapt to its own choices. As a result, difficulty repaying the 60 million franc loan up until 1843—and an inability to service it—emerged as the most effective weapon for forcing Otto to adapt to British policies—though it did not prove very successful in the end. What it did manage, without a doubt, was to weaken his position on the throne.

At the same time, as the French and Russians gained stronger positions, both countries began treating Greece more favourably, though depending on the situation and their individual goals they did not hesitate to exert pressure and put the Greek government in a difficult position. Russia, for example, could always play the exceptionally popular card of the autocephalous Greek Church, or exploit the successor to the throne's religious preferences in order to intimidate Otto's government.

As previously mentioned, Greece's suspension of loan payments, which came after the rebellion of 3 September, allowed the British to claim the right to intervene—more than once—in the kingdom's domestic affairs in order to ensure proper repayment of the debt the Greek state owed. The Greek political elite's ambiguity dramatically facilitated their task. Kolettis's death led the British to hope that they could finally regain their influence over Greece. But they were wrong: with the exception of Mavrokordatos's 'Ministry of the Occupation', the country's prime ministers were selected not on the basis of party affiliation (though it was customary to hear that ministries were staffed by members of the French and Russian parties) but on the basis of personal relationships with Otto and the extent to which one particular Great Power might aid and support his regime and ambitions with regard to the Ottoman Empire.

The intensifying tone of Greek diplomacy caused by the prospect of an impending Russo-Turkish war increased the pressure the French and British placed on Greece for the repayment of the loan. In response to criticisms of administrative mismanagement, the Greeks finally adopted an exemplary accounting system in 1852. The French and British occupation of Piraeus and the forced handover of the premiership to Mavrokordatos—the leading figure in a cabinet composed of French and British sympathisers—allowed for the possibility of a dynamic effort at reformulating Greece's reputation abroad, and all the projects that had not been implemented thus far were attempted over a very short time span. Discussions began, some of which led to legislation and its implementation, including construction of a bridge over the Strait of Euripus, construction of a railway line from Athens to Piraeus, gas-lighting of the capital, construction of a road network and the systematic extraction of emery from Naxos, marble from Paros, and more. A commercial treaty with the Ottoman Empire that had been pending for many years was also signed, as was an agreement between the two countries to combat banditry and limit criminal activity on territorial boundaries. It was no coincidence that the Ottoman Empire began its own series of reforms at this time, and the erratic attempts at institutional change seen in Greece during the same period must be seen as their counterpart. Both countries felt obliged, or were pressured, to be seen in a better light by the Europeans.

Mavrokordatos was forced to resign in 1855. D. Voulgaris replaced him as prime minister, a position he would retain until 1857. That year, after the end of the Crimean War, foreign troops withdrew from Greece on the condition that the Greek government would accept the creation of a tripartite financial committee that would investigate the 'Greek problem' and submit proposals to improve the economic situation and enable repayment of the 60 million franc debt. This committee, founded in 1857, submitted its proposals in 1859, and Greece accepted the recommendation that it pay 900,000 drachmas each year towards the loan. But in the end, it only paid one of the instalments.

After the Crimean war, Otto sought diplomatic footholds in both Italy and Serbia. But the benefits he had to offer in return ranged from the insignificant to the trivial, and the results of this mission proved minimal. In fact, Italian achievements had created a difficult benchmark of comparison for Otto's reign that did not escape anyone's attention. Meanwhile, the Great Powers came to an unambiguous conclusion: they needed direct control and supervision over Otto's Greece in order to ensure repayment of Greece's loan. To this end, they declared their intentions to set up a checkpoint at the country's customs beginning on 1 January 1863. Yet just two months before it was put into effect, Otto was overthrown. Unsurprisingly, the Great Powers' plans for customs control were set aside.

For the entire duration of Otto's reign, interventions by the Great Powers tended to limit policies that could be harmful to the balance of the region, thus rendering the Greek kingdom powerless to achieve its goals and vulnerable to external policies. Pressures caused by the loan owed to the Great Powers were one facet of these policies; the blockade of Piraeus in 1850 and its occupation in 1854 were another. Both of these examples highlight how Otto's actions were doomed from the start, but also the degree to which national politics was influenced by these interventions.

Constitutional corruption

The 3 September rebellion has been described in many different ways. In practical terms, it was nothing more than a military rebellion that had the direct and indirect support of select notables, chiefly from Athens, and the indirect support of almost all the political elite groups. In 'Past and Present',[2] a text written much later than the events of 3 September, Charilaos Trikoupis stated that 'in the revolution of September 3, the senior officers took the initiative, securing total loyalty of even the most disinterested'.[3] Unease over layoffs and the wage cuts implemented by the government to meet its financial obligations, the government's insistence on keeping Bavarians in positions of authority and a deteriorating economic situation led the situation to a breaking point. The inevitable reaction came from the army, which had the means to impose its leaders' views. Except for Athens, no other urban centre reacted, and all simply accepted the outcome of the rebellion. Despite everything that has been written to the contrary, no mass mobilisations took place except for a gathering of curious onlookers outside Otto's palace: 'Soldiers, inhabitants of the Madrasah area, street loiterers, and a tiny number of citizens—we all shouted out demanding a constitution.'[4] The rebellion owed its success more to Otto's poor assessment of information about a potential uprising in the capital than its own effective organisation.

The rebellion granted a share of power to notable groups, and in this respect it can only be seen as a rebellion expressing the will of local oligarchies. Yet it is rather difficult to point to this moment as the beginning of liberal institutions in Greece, to the extent that processes at play were neither impersonal nor egalitarian. Additionally, the democratic views that dominated Greek political discourse were not a construct of liberal thought or certain constitutional political demands, but the product of the need to include certain elites in the political game. As mentioned earlier, Otto's decision to integrate leaders from the War of Independence into political institutions had reshaped the terms of the political debate, and the exclusion of certain groups was no longer possible. The struggle for power henceforth involved all versus all, and no group so strongly dominated others as to impose their will on them. And this was the case insofar as there were no central elites that could oppose local elites. In the end, the arbiter of this conflict could be none other than the king.

Given the prevailing situation in 1843, the nation's political oligarchy could only claim their share of power by adopting a representative institution and creating a constitutional charter delineating the monarch's powers. Both domestically and abroad, Otto's kingdom was still unquestionably viewed as the legitimate regime, and it was clear that faction leaders feared the possible consequences of a conflict that could force Otto to resign. His intermediary and arbitrative role had proved extremely useful in the past decade, and Kolettis, Metaxas and Mavrokordatos—the political leaders of the time—did not want to risk the possibility of civil war. In fact, the role of this royal power became clear during the interregnum period following Otto's fall, when the civil war that broke out left no doubt about the balancing role that the royal institution played, and would continue to play until the First World War. Thus the regime that came about after 3 September was nothing more than an oligarchic foundation for joint political sovereignty shared between Otto and the political elites. What was at stake here was a share in the distribution of state power. This same view was repeatedly espoused during the National Assembly's meetings, during which positions in government were seen as 'spoils of war' by more than one representative from the provinces.

The most representative view on this matter was expressed by Makrygiannis in the National Assembly, who, referring to *heterocthons* holding public positions in the absolute monarchy, said:

> So now, by their kindness, may they settle in our shared land, and look after their own affairs, but keep their hands out of the affairs of the country; they have worked all these years, now may the Greeks of the independence struggle work just as many. Only then they can get involved again, by their kindness—for I can't imagine, as a Greek freedom fighter, that just as I have been liberated from the tyranny of the Sultan, I have become a slave of the covetousness and deception of such persons. From now on they must cease from all meddling.[5]

This understanding of the state is a far cry from the Weberian bureaucratic, one that is reminiscent of an Ottoman past and of rights deriving from the possession of power.

With this shift in 1843, groups of native-born notables gained the right to jointly manage public funds. But in political terms, these changes were substantially less important than they are usually credited to be. The national political system did not change to a large degree; Otto continued to maintain power over decision-making and nearly complete control of the situation. While certain notables were able to take over positions from Bavarians and *heterocthons* involved in state administration, the former group's potential for intervention was limited by the extreme power still maintained by the king, who had every intention of wielding it, or ignoring or systematically violating a constitution that he had fashioned according to his wishes. This was all the more true after Kolettis's death in 1847. In fact, certain prime ministers—for the most part players in the War of Independence like K. Kanaris, G. Kountouriotis and A. Kriezis—did not even have the ability to choose their ministers. Essentially, these key figures of the war were incorporated into mechanisms of governance, becoming Otto's advocates. There is no greater irony in this development than the privileged position of Gennaios Kolokotronis, son of Theodoros, who was adjutant to Otto and his final prime minister. The 'domestication' of political oligarchies proved to be successful in every respect, despite the fact that the regime was unable to survive.

The political alliances by which Greece was governed after 1844 highlight the substance of this change. In fact, and regardless of how paradoxical it may seem, the 1843 rebellion actually enabled Otto to abolish existing parties and form his own, a feat he had not been able to manage previously. In this period, two parties (in the simplest sense of the term) were formed: the royalists and the opposition, the two separated by a particularly vague line.

This reality was reflected in the rebellious movements that sprang up at the time, which after 1843 were limited to reactions from regional leaders, most of them pre-existing chieftains who either sought to satisfy personal interests or acted out of their own dissatisfaction. The Mani revolt of 1845 fell into this category, as did the uprisings of 1847, particularly those led by Grivas in Acarnania and Kriezotis in Evia. So did those led by Roumeliot captains. In all these cases, and also in 1848, local elites reacted decisively to this challenge to their power from the central authorities and to claims for rights they believed derived from their place within these communities.

What changed most of all in the 1844 Constitution was the framework for exercising power. The Constitution was based on the French equivalent from 1830, which had established a constitutional monarchy. The king was not only supreme ruler; he was also the supreme and sovereign instrument of the state. His power was bound only by the limitations expressly included in the Constitution, while the same document recognised his person as sacred and inviolable. Unsurprisingly, the Constitution stated that justice stemmed from the king and that it was conferred in his name.

The king also was also granted executive power, which was exercised by his ministers, who were ultimately responsible for their own actions. The ministers were appointed and dismissed at the king's bidding. Legislative power was exercised jointly by the king, Parliament and Senate. Although there were provisions for government oversight by the legislative body, legislative initiative and the right to sanction laws belonged to the king. The latter further extended his powers and authority through his unlimited right to dissolve Parliament and appoint members to the Senate. There could be no fewer than eighty members of Parliament, elected every three years, while the twenty-seven members of the Senate were appointed for life by Otto. However, this number could be increased to a maximum of half of the total number of members in Parliament. The Senate was the primary body that served to satisfy the political and military elite's demands and aspirations. Indeed, at the National Assembly it was agreed that 'they [the senators] will be chosen from the men who served the Nation during the War'. The Constitution guaranteed individual freedoms—a concept rather alien to the political culture of Otto's period—introduced the confidentiality of formal letters and guaranteed the impartiality of the judiciary. At the same time, the Council of State was abolished, despite the fact that the 3 September rebellion had been legalised by it. Views on its fate were divided at the National Assembly, but in the end its critics prevailed, not least because its continued existence made little sense: up until then, prominent members of the political elite had made up the Council of State, but now that the 1844 Constitution had granted them positions in the Parliament or Senate, the existence of a third institution could only complicate matters.

The Constitution did not delineate the extent of suffrage; this was achieved later with the electoral law of 18 March 1844, passed by the National Assembly. The law stated that

> all Greeks born within the Kingdom or who join it by virtue of the fact that they own some property, whether chattel or real estate, the income-generating and taxable status of the citizen pursuant to legislation, over 25 years old, have the right to vote within the province where they hold civil resident status or carry out any profession or independent occupation.

Thus it only excluded domestic servants and apprentice craftsmen. As a result, universal male suffrage was adopted and so was the direct vote. This was completely unprecedented in comparison with international norms at the time, given that universal direct suffrage only existed in Switzerland.

At this point, a notable differentiation occurred between municipal and national elections. In the former case, the censitary system (i.e. where certain votes carried more weight, depending on a person's rank within the census) was kept in place, in stark contrast to the universal suffrage of parliamentary elections. Why was the Greek government not interested in coordinating the two systems? Whatever the answer, that these two systems were maintained points to the minimal attempts made at change in a realm at odds with the theoretically 'liberal' spirit of 1843. In fact, the system of municipal elections ensured the supremacy of the local oligarchy and the monarch's influence over politics—the same equilibrium established by the Constitution of 1844, so there would be no reason to tamper with it. Yet for national elections it was necessary to introduce a system that would satisfy the egalitarian ideology stemming from the War of Independence, since the claim for a constitution drew its legitimacy from the war.

Assessing the electoral process is no easy feat, since the population's rate of participation is unknown. In the elections of 1910, G. Dafnis estimates that the total number of voters did not exceed 10 per cent of the population. By 1952, the last elections without the participation of women, the figure rose to

23.21 per cent. Thus it is reasonable to assume that rates of participation were even lower during the nineteenth century. The elections of 1844—in which the number of voters per region did not surpass 2,000 to 2,500 individuals, excluding urban centres—confirm this.

These numbers must be understood in relative terms given the manner in which elections were conducted; this first period in which representative institutions were implemented was marked by the adulteration of electoral will via state bodies and enforcement mechanisms. Parliament itself supervised the elections, resulting in a system where the faction holding the majority was able to strengthen its position further, annulling rivals' votes. The government ruled on the legitimacy or illegitimacy of elections in accordance with its wishes, and Otto's. Save for the first election of 1844, all other elections were won by the governments that staged them. This happened not because the governing party won the electorate over by promising certain benefits, but because it used violent means to enforce the outcome it desired—both among the rural constituency and within Parliament itself, where election results were validated. Voters existed only to the extent that their physical presence was necessary to legitimise the process.

In practice, each government proposed its own candidates before the elections, known as the 'dedicated' group, as opposed to the opposition's candidates, who became known as the 'desperate'. According to testimony from the time, towards the end of his reign, Otto 'composed the Parliament in his office, compiling a list of members, which the institutions subsequently implemented in the so-called elections'.[6] In each region, the electoral process began from the moment that the royal candidate was nominated, and in cases when the latter's election proved difficult, the vote was postponed by the region's prefect. This could happen two or three times, resulting in elections that often lasted several weeks. Mayors also played a decisive role in electing the government's preferred candidates, since they were the ones to coordinate these practices on a local level. This is also the reason why, after Otto's fall in 1862, all mayors were dismissed, while some disappeared as soon as they were informed of the king's dethronement, fearing reprisals.

State-sponsored violence introduced yet another factor into the electoral process: bandits. Or, as George I later described the problem, 'The brigands which could be used by the government to upset Turkish interests were also used by the opposition to upset the government.'[7] This was a logical consequence of the electoral process. From the moment one candidate was supported by state power, the other had to make use of some other source of violence to ensure his political survival.

Predictably, I. Kolettis won the first elections after adoption of the Constitution. Lyons, Britain's ambassador to Greece, had already considered this likely to occur as early as 1835 in the event of Bavarian withdrawal from Greece, thanks to Roumeliot supporters that would be able to push the balance of violence in his favour. Kolettis's victory allowed him to establish a form of rule that Otto then inherited and pushed to its furthest consequences due to his own personal weaknesses.

During this period, Otto's government displayed an extreme rigidity that was completely incongruous with the general developments occurring in the country; only after the Crimean War and the occupation of Piraeus by British and French troops did the king's position change. Even then, Otto refused to proceed with any changes in political governance and continued to believe that he was in a position to completely control the nation's political scene, despite the fact that from 1859 onwards many ministers indicated to him that general unrest prevailed in the kingdom's capital and provinces.

By early 1859, overt opposition against Otto had begun to appear. Resentment developed for many reasons, one of which was Otto's obsession with controlling the process of governing the country himself and employing staff absolutely devoted to him. Around the same time, a new generation of political personae made an appearance, many of whom, such as Epameinondas Deligiorgis and Alexandros Koumoundouros, owed their prominence and place in Parliament to Otto. It was this generation that would seek to enact a number of reforms after the Crimean War, though it was not very successful in reacting effectively to the regime's failures—whether imagined or real. This new momentum was expressed with greater passion by groups of youths in Athens, especially students. In the name of liberalism, they confronted the government, and as a result of the Skiadika incident in 1859 they established a strong movement of opposition. Then the rebellion of Nafplion in February 1862, led by military officers confined for charges of conspiracy, and local political leaders was violently repressed. This only served to exacerbate tensions even further.

The political rallying of notable groups also had another cause. After the elections of 1859, Parliament—composed of government MPs—refused to vote in the king's favoured candidate, Dimitrios Kallifronas, as president, electing Thrasivoulos Zaimis in his place. This provoked a violent reaction from Otto, who dissolved Parliament with the aim of demonstrating his power in the next elections. To this end, he aimed to prevent the election of all sixty-two ministers that had voted against Kallifronas. Expressing their loyalty to Otto more than any other group, a significant number of mayors were elected in an exercise of extreme violence acted out by the government of Athanasios Miaoulis, such that the Parliament established was called the Parliament of Mayors. At the same time, Otto proceeded to appoint eighteen new senators, many of whom did not have the necessary qualifications, and began a campaign against the press, which was a fierce critic of the government at the time.

Otto's attempts to resolve the situation were eventually hindered by his own obstinacy, as well as the opposition to his rule. His refusal to implement basic reforms such as those suggested in 1861 by K. Kanaris—reforms the latter had demanded before he would accept the premiership—resulted in the establishment of a front that united all the political elites, those 'beholden to the nation's leading families', as one writer from the period put it, against him—except, of course, those participating directly in state governance. The system that had taken shape in 1844 had now reached its final consequences.

The regime change of 1862 was not much different from the rebellion of 1843; in both instances, the army had instigated the change. Yet Charilaos Trikoupis, in the text mentioned previously, identified one difference. While the high-ranking officers led the charge in 1843, 'In the October coup [of 1862], lower ranking officers played a leading role, conspiring against their superior officers.'[8] In 1862, the Vonitsa garrison, led by the renowned Theodorakis Grivas, rebelled on 4 October, followed by garrisons in Missolonghi and Patras. Benizelos Roufos played a key role in the latter case. It was only after the Athens garrison also revolted on 10 October that the movement to overthrow Otto was truly united. The War of Independence had finally reached the conclusion its protagonists had hoped for.

The profile of the state

Bavarian efforts to assemble the first mechanisms of government in Greece were ambitious in every respect and exceeded the small state's capabilities. Though the 60 million franc loan offered financial comfort in earlier years, the framework in place could not be maintained, and it shrank year by year until the decade of the 1860s. Research on the kingdom's public finances clearly substantiates this: during Otto's rule from 1833 to 1862, the ratio of public spending to gross domestic product, which is a way of expressing the size of a state, diminished.

Some peculiarities must be noted in the calculation of state size. First, the figures for the period from 1844 to 1862 are misleading to some extent, as the repayment of public debt was included in calculations of total government expenditure; this repayment was suspended after the 1843 rebellion. In addition, certain problems arise when drawing comparisons with other countries since it is impossible to subtract amortisation from total public expenditure. Finally, the size of the non-monetised sector of the economy, which was not included in GDP estimates, meant that comparisons with other countries—particularly those in Western Europe—were unrealistic. In the Greek case, this non-monetised sector was quite extensive, especially at the time of the founding of the Greek state, while it was much less significant in Western Europe. Therefore, it can reasonably be argued that calculations based on the available data lead to an overestimation of the size of the state.

4.1: *Greek State Public Spending 1833–62*
(Averages per decade, in drachmas)

Period	*Current Prices*	*Per capita in current prices*	*Constant prices*	*Per capita at constant prices*	*% GDP*
1833–42	19,056.694	24	31,008.679	40	19
1843–52	17,015.725	17	28,081.534	29	16
1853–62	23,695.809	22	33,893.280	32	14

Source: A. Antoniou, 'Greek State Public Spending (1830–1939)', unpublished paper, Historical Archive of the National Bank of Greece, Athens, 1999, pp. 47ff.

Taken as a whole, the period from 1833 to 1862 was balanced in budgetary terms, leaving behind a small overall surplus. In this respect, claims expressed regarding the 'orderliness' of Otto's government are justified to some extent, though they are still far from the truth. This was a different model of managing public expenditure—and public funds in general—in comparison with the subsequent period.

The breakdown of public expenditure during Otto's rule is not particularly surprising. The greatest amount of public expenditure in this period was devoted to military spending. During the first decade of Otto's administration, military spending made up 50 per cent of total public expenditure, a figure that gradually shrank, settling at 39.5 per cent between 1853 and 1862. All this, of course, for the upkeep of an army that was never destined to fight beyond its borders.

The second highest expense, at least for certain period of time, was the repayment of public debt. It made up 25.9 per cent of total public expenditure during the period of absolute monarchy, shrinking to 2.1 per cent after the suspension of payments from 1843 to 1852, and then settling at 9.1 per cent in the final decade of Otto's rule. This last increase was related to the servicing of internal loans.

Conversely, the smallest item in terms of relative importance in public expenditure was public works, which took up insignificant resources for the greater part of the period. It should be noted that a significant portion of costs for road construction, for example, or even construction of bridges and other public works, were covered by municipal budgets and not included in calculations of state spending. During the first decade, a series of projects was implemented by the Bavarian engineering corps and army geared towards the immediate establishment of state infrastructure, which were also not included in the public works budget. Not surprisingly, this aspect of Otto's policies was strongly criticised. It is telling that, during his entire reign, only 240 kilometres of road were built. For Otto, public works were considered an undesirable expense; when pressed by the British to explain why he had not submitted a budget to the Council of State as dictated by law, he replied that if he were to do so, 'there was a danger of diminished spending on the secretariat to the military, and that more public money could be squandered on building roads, bridges and ports'.[9]

Expenditure on education was also very low, though it increased over the span of Otto's reign from 2.9 per cent of total public expenditure in 1833–42 to 5.2 per cent from 1853 to 1862. It should also be emphasised that the king himself incurred extremely high expenses when compared with the limited money spent on education. This only serves to emphasise the abundant public resources available to be used at the king's discretion. Otto was repeatedly accused of living luxuriously, and the construction of the royal palace was a prime example of this. In retrospect, these accusations were not unfounded.

To better understand the composition of public finances in nineteenth-century Greece, it must be noted that from 1833 to 1842 only three types of expenditure—interest on public debt, military spending and the king's expenses—accounted for 82 per cent of public spending. The lack of differentiation in state activity and the central role the king maintained in this system was clear, as military spending at the time supported the strength and stability of the regime itself. Even the public debt was due to a loan taken out to finance this same mechanism that would allow him to govern unrestricted. In certain moments of financial difficulty, he was temporarily aided by his father Ludwig of Bavaria. In fact, it would not be an exaggeration to say that under Otto, for an extended period of time, the public finances of the Greek kingdom and finances of the royal court were one and the same. Lyons, the British ambassador, even accused Otto of managing public funds as if they were his personal accounts, taking out money that he would never return.

4.2: Adjusted Public Expenditure by Category, 1833–62

Period	*Public Expenditure*	*Public Debt*		*Military Expenditure (%)*	*Education (%)*
1833–42	19,054.693	4,934,017	25.9%	49.6	2.9
1843–52	13,219.194	275,922	2.1%	46.1	4.5
1853–62	20,158.061	1,826.055	9.1%	41.4	5.2
	Public Works %	*Staff Compensation (%)*		*King's Expenses (%)*	
1833–42	–	–		5.8	–
1843–52	0.6	38.1		7.2	–
1853–62	2.3	45.4		4.9	–

NB: The data used in the above table reflects a deduction of accounting—not implemented—payments of public debt. See previous table.
Source: K. Kostis, 'Public Finances', in K. Kostis and S. Petmezas (eds), *Η ανάπτυξη της ελληνικής οικονομίας κατά τον 19th αιώνα (1830–1914)*, Athens: 2006, p. 305.

Even the management of public accounting corresponded to this logic. It comes as no surprise that the absolute monarchy avoided publicising its financial accounts. Indeed, the accounting system set up by the Bavarians did not provide for disclosure or supervision of the budget or any accountability for public finances—with the exception of the proper functioning of state payments, which was overseen by the Court Council that had been founded in late September 1833. But in 1835 it was decided that 'the budget for each fiscal year shall be submitted to the Council of State for review, discussion and commentary. Similarly, the financial law accompanying the budget shall also be submitted for review and comment before enactment.' In 1836, the first budget was published publicly, including the accounting balances for 1833, 1834 and 1835. As one might expect, these statements were not published with the same consistency in the following years: indeed, budgets were only occasionally published, and only after pressure had been applied by foreign diplomatic missions in Athens—chiefly the British. It was only with the constitutional change of 1843 that Parliament would gain the right to vote on budgets, after which it began publishing them consistently in 1845.

One last remark concerning expenditure on wages for personnel: contrary to what has been written about the state-as-employer, the available figures reveal that expenditure on staff wages was not excessive. This expenditure increased regularly over time only due to the fact that fees related to the nation's military organisation were increasingly included in the same category. It should be noted that, even if the focus is widened to include the entire nineteenth century, the highest expenditure occurred during Otto's reign and declined in the years that followed. This holds true even when accounting for pensions and other social spending.

To summarise, the oft-supported argument that there was an oversized Greek state does not hold true for Otto's reign. By extension, the view that the Greek state was a state-employer is also not supported by facts. Certain categories of expenditure, such as those included in the broader categories of 'social costs' and 'pensions', might have been larger than would be expected; but it must be remembered that Otto's regime also provided honorary and other essential aid to those who fought in the War of Independence as a form of legitimising itself in the eyes of its subjects.

A 'drainage system'

From the outset, the nature of the tax system adopted by the Greek kingdom was without a doubt a continuation of Ottoman practices. As S. Petmezas writes, 'The Ottoman tax system was largely used as a template for the gradual establishment of a Greek system of public revenue.' Therefore, it should come as no surprise that certain regions of the country, such as Laconia, invoked Ottoman practices when requesting differential tax treatment. There were also significant differences in comparison with the system in place before the War of Independence—the abolition of both capital and emergency taxes, for example, which resulted in a significant reduction of the tax burden—though the manner with which it was organised and administered was similar. This was a natural consequence of the importance of agrarian production in the economy, among other things.

Taxes, strictly defined, offered the bulk of the state's regular income for the duration of Otto's rule. Their relative contribution diminished slightly over time, accounting for 90 per cent of public revenue in 1833 and 78 per cent in the year of Otto's dethronement. The composition of these taxes also followed a corresponding pattern. Initially, for the most part, around 65 per cent were direct taxes—necessarily including the state's usufruct right for tax-renting national lands—while indirect taxes, mainly customs duties, accounted for the remaining 35 per cent. Towards the final years of Otto's rule, these proportions varied, though they did not change dramatically.

Soon after their arrival in Greece, the Bavarians reinstated an in-kind tithe tax on all products. This meant taxation on gross production, which of course was much more burdensome for small-scale farmers than it was for large-scale producers. It also assigned the same tax burden to products with different costs of production such as oil, grapes and grains. In addition to these drawbacks, the tithe caused problems in the collection process: each municipality's tax revenues were leased to private contractors, and the latter acquired significant power over the farmers, who, among other things, had to request the contractors' permission to undertake any agricultural work. Additionally the manner in which the total product was estimated was largely arbitrary, while a problematic distinction was made between private properties (which paid 10 per cent of gross production) and state properties (which were obliged to submit 30 per cent and then eventually 25 per cent of gross production). Naturally, tax farmers preferred the latter arrangement. Finally, the cost of transporting these in-kind taxes from various municipalities to the nation's capital, where they were stored in public warehouses, was also significant.

The Bavarians were not in a position to adopt a different tax system; such an effort presupposed economic and social interventions beyond their capabilities, interventions out of reach given the time and place in which they found themselves. Indeed, budgetary predictions at the time proved particularly worrying for the small kingdom's future. Armansperg had estimated that the Greek state could only succeed in balancing its budget by 1843—ten years after the Bavarians had arrived in Greece. But—at least according to their declared intentions—they hoped to enact changes as quickly as possible, even more so after the initial experience of collecting tax revenue had proved unpleasant for both taxpayers and the government.

Yet they proved unable or unwilling to change the tithe system. This was only natural, since the fiscal reform they desired presumed a level of state organisation that was inconceivable given the situation in Greece at the time. For example, land registry work soon proved meaningless since the ownership status of property required clarifications and rules that would take years to formulate, and at great cost. Secondly, the system of tax farming allowed the

4.3: Taxation Rate in Greece, 1834–62, in Drachmas Per Capita as a Percentage of GDP

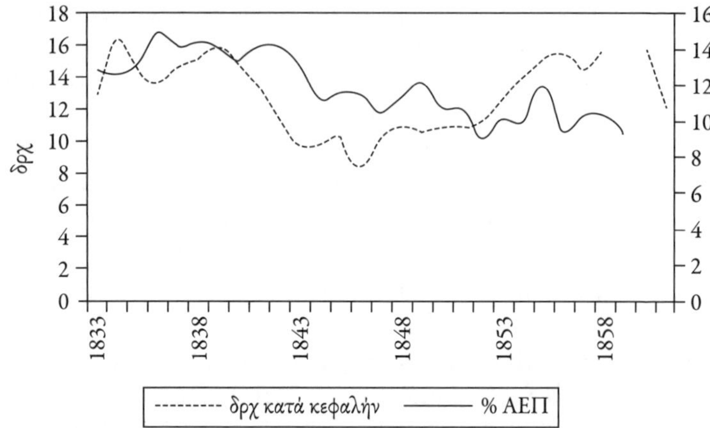

Source: Calculations based on information from G. Kostelenos, S. Petmezas et al., *Ακαθάριστο Εγχώριο Προϊόν 1830–1939*, ibid., and G. Dertilis, *Ατελέσφοροι ή τελεσφόροι. Φόροι και εξουσία στο Νεοελληνικό κράτος*, Athens: 1993.

regime to increase its influence over political elites, who often implemented the process and were certainly unwilling to give up a fundamental mechanism for influencing provincial populations without protest.

The tax burden at the time was particularly onerous, though it should be noted that the tax burden as percentage of Greek GDP did gradually decrease until the mid-1860s. The tax burden per capita, which may be more accurate in calculating the estimated tax burden on the Greek population, reached its lowest point in the 1840s—an extremely difficult decade for the Greek economy—and then rose steadily until Otto's fall. Rural populations were subject to the largest share of the tax burden.

One of the goals of Otto's regime—which it realised, to some extent—was to better organise the tithe tax and make it less burdensome for those collecting it. By 1839, for currants, the tithe was paid upon exportation to customs, in cash. Gradually, this system extended to other products such as silk and figs, while for certain other crops from vineyards, vegetable fields, gardens and orchards, the tithe was replaced by taxation per *stremma*.[10] Efforts were also made to improve the system of tax collection, to reduce the coercion of local cultivators and to minimise the extremely long delays involved in tax farmers submitting their taxes to the state.

The tax system during Otto's rule was based on particularly strict mechanisms of partitioning agricultural surplus. This is why A. Andreadis has described it as an 'ideal drainage system,' which was to be expected in a political system that treated its subjects with particular cruelty. In fact, adjustments made to this system revealed larger transformations taking place within the mechanisms for governing the population. The Bavarians' intention of overhauling the tax system was abandoned almost immediately, as the tax system was incorporated into the administrative mechanisms of the state itself. Though efforts were made to renew its image, few things changed substantively during Otto's reign. The resistance of tax farmers must have been significant, since local elites benefited from the system themselves. Besides, via mechanisms for delegating tax-revenue collection, Otto had gained another tool to harness these groups and integrate them into state institutions. It was only towards the end of Otto's rule that attempts would be made to reform this tax system and other sectors of public administration, though both processes never reached their conclusion.

The fight for land

In a rural country such as nineteenth-century Greece, land necessarily comprised the basic component of wealth and social power. Land was also a decisive factor in shaping national political and economic dynamics. Indeed, as the War of Independence broke out, the question of national lands was of paramount concern: that is, the land that before 1821 belonged in full or part to the Ottoman state, to Muslim charitable institutions, and to Muslim individuals. This land was now in territory belonging to Greece, or at the very least seeking to be a part of it.

There are no measurements to detail the extent of these national lands. The most reasonable estimates converge on an area of arable land ranging from between 4 and 4.5 million *stremmas*, while in total the land amounted to roughly 10 million *stremmas*. But any assessment can only be provisional, as there was never any attempt to document national land. In the words of a report published by the Council of State in 1865: 'The amount of occupied land is unknown, as is the number of individuals occupying it and their distribution throughout the land.' But this lack of clarity regarding its precise size should not lessen its significance as a catalyst for the establishment of landownership in Greece during the nineteenth century—and thus for the nation's social consolidation.

The first answer to the issue of national lands was given during the War of Independence: by 'right of war', all properties in this category became property of the Greek state, with the intention that they be distributed to cultivators, but also to any other Greek or foreign citizen wishing to use them. But things did not develop as anticipated, and many complications arose in the use of national land until its standardised distribution in 1871—complications that decisively influenced the development of Greek agriculture and political relations within the Greek kingdom.

As previously mentioned, disputes over national land did not only concern the land itself but the sum of all Ottoman properties. For this reason, the term 'national properties' often appeared, divided into two categories: 'alienable', mostly consisting of buildings, houses, windmills, oil mills and so on, and 'inalienable', including rural areas, cultivated land, pastures and even fallow land. During the war, the sale of 'alienable' properties was permitted and generally conducted to meet the economic needs of war, in contrast to the inalienable properties, whose sale was prohibited by the National Assembly. The latter properties were used as collateral for national loans during the war and even as a guarantee for issuance of paper money from the National Financial Bank founded by I. Kapodistrias. Furthermore, in many cases, large tracts of land became the property of captains and notables as a reward for their services, or else were simply occupied.

Exceptions to this system of national lands were noted in Eastern Central Greece and Evia. When the first Protocol of the London Conference was signed in January 1830, these lands were still held by the Ottomans and only fell into Greek hands under the Treaty of Constantinople of 1832. As a result, 'martial law' did not apply in these regions and the prevailing international conditions enabled Ottoman 'proprietors' to keep or sell their 'alienable' and 'inalienable' properties. The Greek government was given only those belonging to charitable institutions (*vakufia*), which were under the sultan's control. In contrast, lands belonging to 'family owned charitable institutions' (*vakifs*), which Muslim individuals had the right to usufruct, were recognised as the undisputed property of the Ottomans.

In the end, most if not all Muslim landowners preferred to sell their land to Christians in possession of the requisite capital. Consequently, the system of large property ended up surviving in these areas. Records of buyers' names exist for some areas in Attica, and it is reasonable to assume that *heterocthons* and foreigners were the main buyers, though locals also made their appearance: the duchess of Plaisance, George Finley the philhellene, Gropius, the

Austrian consul in Athens, K. Zografos, Prince Kantakouzinos, I. Soutsos, Theodorakis, a captain from Hydra, and A. Louriotis were some of the owners of capital who were able to benefit from the Ottoman withdrawal by purchasing significant portions of Attic land at cheap prices.

4.4: Estimates of the National Estates by Leading Contemporaries and Historians (in thousands of *stremmas*)

	Cultivated land	*"Arable" land*	*Vines, orchards, gardens*	*Forests & pastures*	*Total area*
Kapodistrias replies to Poros Conference	–	–	–	–	5,432
Dawkins' report to London (1831)	–	–	–	–	Between 19,050 and 25,400
Urquhart (1833)	–	9,398	53	8,890	18,340
Thiersch (1833)	2,340	–	65	–	–
Greek government report to Allied Powers (1835)	4,126	20,600	58	5,158	36,058
Strong (1842)	6,018	16,018	–	–	–
Allied Joint Financial Commission (1858)	–	–	–	–	11,000

Source: W.W. McGrew, *Land and revolution in Modern Greece, 1800–1881*, Kent State University, 1985, p. 239.

Clearly, the issue of national lands was particularly difficult to resolve. To a large, extent this was due to the difficulties in transitioning from Ottoman to Byzantine Roman law. This much was clear from the manner in which representatives of the Great Powers attempted to address the problem, especially when Greek courts had to deal with contested lands, and the process resulted in various protocols.

According to Ottoman law, land belonged to the state, though significant rights were also granted to land cultivators. Indeed, all Christian cultivators that had the right of absolute ownership (*tessarouf*) for land they cultivated before the war—a transferable and inheritable right—were recognised by the Greek state as full owners of the land. These individuals had to prove their claims with titles of ownership (*mulkname*) recognised by Ottoman law, or even with church decisions that certified transfers of properties and real estate (*huccet*). The right of absolute ownership was also recognised for cultivators that had first tilled and cultivated the land in question before 1821. This obligation to prove land ownership became burdensome not only for cultivators but also for the Greek state, which had to supply titles justifying claims to ownership of land.

Apart from the rights mentioned above, Ottoman law also recognised a number of other proprietary rights for cultivators. As a result, diverse and overlapping ownership rights emerged: rights of ownership, rights to use and occupation, rights to multi-year crops and the non-cultivatable portion of the soil, even the right to sources of mineral deposits, and finally proprietary third-party rights to land, as in the cases of *emphyteusis*. In many cases, powerful Ottoman families succeeded in guaranteeing their right to lands, coming into conflict with Christian farmers, some of whom possessed titles proving their rights, while others did not. In addition, a series of customary rights applied to the utilisation of the land, further complicating the situation. Examples include grazing and logging rights of communities in surrounding forests and pastures, or even extra-economic hierarchies of potential owners and buyers of land within communities such as the right of pre-emptive use, which was only abolished in 1856. Finally, the perennial connections that families of tenant farmers shared with the lands they worked presented problems to the establishment of property relations as specified under Byzantine Roman law.

These overlapping rights meant it was nearly impossible to acquire private property on a constitutional and legal level and acted as a deterrent against investing in land. The result was none other than a weak, and in some cases non-existent, market for land, constant disputes over the status of large areas of land, minimal financing of agriculture by banks, and high interest rates in rural areas. One of the Bavarian lawyers who had arrived with the regency council in Greece noted this problem:

> When one realises that in Greece there is no concept of a guarantee, since creditors have no security, the most basic pillar of national prosperity is lost. One can only smile with compassion as he hears how all things horrible will be abolished as soon as some foreigner quickly arrives—probably one from the French mortgage agency.

For these reasons, the same author argued that the concept of usury was non-existent in Greece, while lending based on the right of *antichrisis*, also known as the right of *prostichi*, was related to the lack of clear property rights.

This right stipulated that lenders were guaranteed preferential right to the goods produced by cultivators as a form of repayment; the loan was repaid from future production and at a predetermined price.

The rebels in the War of Independence first declared their position on national lands in the Peloponnesian Senate, which determined the distribution of lands belonging to the Ottomans before the outbreak of the war in the decree of Stemnitsa. These lands were to be used to meet the needs of military operations. The first assemblies in Western and Eastern mainland Greece made similar decisions. In other words, the local authorities established after the outbreak of the War of Independence sought to take over the rights of the Ottoman government and Muslim landowners. Soon after, the First National Assembly in Epidaurus enabled the sale of some of these national lands, provided that Parliament had given prior consent. The same assembly then adopted the Peloponnesian Senate's decision regarding villagers' payment of a three-tenths tax for production cultivated on national lands.

During the Second National Assembly of Astros in 1823, legislation was passed that allowed Parliament to decide on the sale of national lands according to the needs that arose. But this reform provoked opposition, and the legislation was altered, after which a new resolution was passed that only permitted the sale of 'alienable' properties (e.g. workshops, houses, mills, mosques, inns, oil mills). Sales of large-scale national properties were conducted in accordance with the law created on 16 June 1824, which allowed for the sale of a quarter of the 'alienable' properties in each province.

The government's economic destitution, especially during the period of the siege of Missolonghi, eventually led to a new property law in February 1826. Contrary to a resolution that had been passed in the Second National Assembly, it permitted the sale of all kinds of national property in order to raise money, which would be used to support the besieged. It has been argued that a large amount of national land was sold off under this law.

Meanwhile, leaders of the War of Independence attempted to use the national lands to attract and reward those who had participated in military campaigns. With the law of 7 May 1822, Parliament secured compensation for each soldier: a *stremma* of land for each month he had served. Further resolutions on 5 May 1827 and 29 July 1829 provided for the distribution of land to these fighters, while a resolution on 8 February 1832 gave the government the ability to grant national land not only to soldiers but also to widows and orphans, and even to others who had been subjected to suffering during the war. However, none of these legislative provisions were actually implemented.

Upon its arrival in Greece, the regency council hurried to create a system that would prevent any encroachment of national lands. To this end, a decree in 1833 proscribed the sale of any national land. But the state's financial needs soon led it to view these lands as a potential source of revenue and as an instrument to exercise social and economic policy. Another problem that had to be overcome was the mortgaging of national lands for loans during the War of Independence in 1824 and 1825, as their status then prevented any attempt at distributing them. This was true under Kapodistrias, when representatives of the Great Powers used their mortgaged status to prevent the governor from distributing national lands. In order to uphold this general principle prohibiting distribution without preventing the divestments necessary for the needs of the public treasury, the status defining national 'alienable' properties was broadened to include all types of land. As mentioned previously, the earlier definition included property such as windmills, inns, baths, houses and so on.

Thus it is fairly clear that the Greek state sought to achieve two objectives with these national lands. The first was the creation of a class of small-scale landowners. This would also serve to prevent the emergence of a group of large-scale landowners, which would only result in the local elites gaining further power, increasing their potential to undermine central power. Secondly, securing significant public revenue through the exploitation of national land was a fundamental goal for the Greek state. Beyond these basic objectives, the policies the Greek state sought to implement often concealed other aims. One of the aims of the endowment law discussed below was the mandatory settling of populations within a certain municipality—that is, control over and restriction of the mobility of rural populations. Indeed, for someone to benefit from the endowment law, they had to have been registered in the municipal registry belonging to the municipality of their choosing.

Ultimately, the mass expansion of agriculture—especially when labourers were involved—proved nearly impossible given the conditions prevailing in nineteenth-century Greece. The lack of capital in the first decades of the Greek state's existence, combined with an abundance of uncultivated land and a widely diffused population, meant that systems involving the exploitation of small-scale family agriculture were adopted instead. Ottoman lands were also purchased, in which cases the Chiflik system was adopted.[11] In other words, the cultivation of large estates through direct supervision was not generally practised in Greece. Small-scale family farming prevailed on small-, medium- and even large-sized properties.

The endowment law of 1835 and the associated executive order of 24 June 1843 limited the sale of national lands to forty *stremmas* of irrigated land, eighty *stremmas* of lowland but non-irrigated land and 120 *stremmas* of mountainous land per cultivator. This plan of land distribution failed miserably. Only 835 families were endowed with land in the first year of the law, at a time when the state predicted endowment to 15,000 families. Seventeen months after the law had been passed, only 66,506 candidates from fifty-nine of the 316 municipalities had applied for endowment. The main reason for the law's failure were the high land prices resulting from the Bavarian auction system, which caused values to skyrocket in comparison to what the land could offer. The bidder was also required to pay 1 per cent of the land's value as an instalment and 5 per cent interest until the total was paid back. For these reasons, the law's period of validity was extended and maintained until the final national lands were distributed in 1871. Over 176,000 *stremmas* of land were eventually distributed in this way.

In 1838, a law entitled 'Concession of National Lands to the Phalangists'[12] was adopted, which was followed by a further law entitled 'On Settling Crete' in 1848. In both cases, promissory notes issued on credit were not used by the owners themselves, but were instead sold at a price below their nominal value and then used by their new owners to purchase national properties or to repay other obligations. A law of 20 February 1848 granted one *stremma* of land to each cultivator for the purpose of building a house. In 1856, a law relating to the distribution of all the wild olive groves belonging to the state was voted on; the groves would be granted to anyone interested in cultivating the olive trees, with the provision that half of the olive groves acquired in this way would be left to the cultivator and the other half would be returned to the state after twelve years. According to one source, the laws issued during Otto's reign led to the distribution of 280,000 *stremmas* of land. However, according to another source, 700,000 *stremmas* had been distributed by 1870.

To some extent, it is surprising that an issue that was so central to the formation of the Greek state throughout the nineteenth century was not quickly resolved. It was a telling sign of the times that although no one explicitly disagreed with the abolition of the tithe and the distribution of national lands, all policy efforts in this direction failed. D. Psychogios has shown how there were more than a few individuals opposed to the distribution of lands or alteration of the taxation system in place, since both ran counter to their interests—though they did not explicitly state their positions. The powerful groups opposed to the distribution of land included tax farmers and those with rights to land, as they anticipated that their revenues would shrink in the process of land distribution. At the time, the usufruct tax was hardly insignificant: for cultivators of national land, it reached 15 per cent of gross production, no small sum. From a certain point onwards, payment of this tax determined the legal status of the land, whether or not the state possessed the necessary titles. Thus the law on the taxation of products in 1849 stipulated that 'the government continues to hold the right to legal possession of national lands and properties, provided it enjoyed the right to usufruct them up to 1843, unless it had lost such right by virtue of court ruling or its own decision to waive such right'. Contrary to what appeared to be a more logical approach—where taxes would be determined by land status—the opposite held true in the Greek case, as the type of land taxation determined its legal status. Even worse, at least for the cultivators, the tax farmers were the ones who played a decisive role in determining whether land was national property or not.

Likewise, owners of large tracts of land were opposed to the distribution of land, fearing that farmers on their estates would abandon them in order to cultivate their own land, further exacerbating the problems they faced as a result of a limited workforce. Regardless of whether they were right or wrong, they constituted a group with significant political power. Working in conjunction with public revenue farmers, they managed to delay the distribution of national lands.

By the end of Otto's reign, the lack of national land distribution and the continued implementation of the tithe tax had become major problems. These very same years ushered in the first attempts at tax reform, attempts associated with Alexandros Koumoundouros. The latter's approach to the issue was not dissimilar to the positions taken by a new generation of politicians that began to appear late in Otto's rule; these politicians had often gained positions thanks to the king himself but sought to free the Greek economy and society from the stagnation to which it had been condemned by Otto's regime—or so they believed.

The issue of national lands was resolved with two laws in 1871, introduced to Parliament by S. Sotiropoulos, minister of finance in the Koumoundouros government. The first law regulated the distribution and allocation of national lands, while the second provided a solution to *emphyteusis* already made on national lands. Based on this legislation, up until 1911, 357,217 documents of ownership were issued, corresponding to 2,650,000 *stremmas* with a total value of 90 million drachmas. Various laws and legislative decrees followed, which aimed at solving specific problems involved in the implementation of related legislation.

The distribution of national lands was ultimately a long-term process that took around forty years and had mixed results. First, the economic benefits for state coffers were much lower than expected, since by 1911 the government had only managed to collect 55 per cent of the total value of distributed lands. Secondly, it has been argued that the distribution had a negative effect on Greek land cultivation, since it contributed to the fragmentation of small farming plots. A. Sideris has argued that those who gained the most from this distribution were landowners and individuals unrelated to agriculture who took advantage of low land prices to buy vast tracts of land. A survey from the region of Amaliada partially confirms these observations. According to the survey, individuals with the same surname, which the author identifies as belonging to the same large family, bought neighbouring plots of land that were larger than those of the average province at the time. It was calculated that 16.8 per cent of a total of 310 families with 937 titles held 58.4 per cent of the total land. According to the study, these families represented the dominant families of the region. In practice, intermediaries also participated in this process of acquiring land, buying it for third parties or purchasing property from landowners or title traders in cases where owners of the land were unable to utilise it for one reason or another.

But the situation in Amaliada is not validated by research in other areas. In Argolis, for example, national lands were for the most part purchased by those cultivating them, while merchants or notables played a small role in the allocation of land distributed according to the system in place in 1871. Similar conclusions can be drawn from another survey conducted in the municipality of Myrtoundio in Ilia. Here, merchants and notables purchasing national lands represented a small percentage of the total, both in terms of their numbers and the size of land they purchased.

It has been argued that the distribution of national lands did not lead to egalitarian agrarian ownership, but rather that the primary goal of distribution was to disadvantage peasants so they would be forced to work as labourers on the lands of large-scale landowners. In other words, the law on the distribution of national lands was not aimed at preventing the concentration of land in the hands of political and economic elites. Yet as shown from the eventual outcome, distribution of land per se was not so important. A large amount of it was already in farmers' hands, a fact that was known to the legislators. Indeed, this is why many peasants never bothered to legalise their property titles.

The only region of Greece in which land ownership was concentrated in a small number of hands was the western Peloponnese, and this was certainly an exception linked to development of currant cultivation in the area. As described above, this did not represent a general trend but rather an exception to the rule that regarded small-scale property ownership and agriculture as sufficiently established. Indeed, even in the regions of the western Peloponnese, these large estates would be subdivided in the long term.

The distribution of national lands and estates, which occurred in a period when available land was increasingly occupied by an ever growing population, aimed to clarify property rights in such a way that they would principally support the development of currant cultivation, which was expanding rapidly. It is no surprise that the legislation on the distribution of national lands and estates was exploited more frequently in areas used for cultivating currants and other tradeable crops than it was in areas used to cultivate grain.

Ecclesiastical adjustments

The uprising on 3 September changed the relationship between the church and the state. For the Holy Synod, which viewed the insurrection favourably, the event represented an opportunity to extract itself from the restrictive stranglehold of the state, and it hastily proceeded to express and submit its views to the National Assembly. Unsurprisingly, the church also sought to limit royal intervention in the synod's activities, submitting a request according to which the synod would appoint a president only after a proposal made by its own members. It also asked for a revocation of all laws that ran contrary to ecclesiastical regulations, even seeking to limit state intervention in the church's internal affairs. Lastly, the synod requested that attempts be made to renew relations with the Patriarchate.

Other requests addressed to the National Assembly by the Holy Synod followed, including abolition of the royal commissioner's veto on its decisions. However, the new provisions included in the Constitution did not alter the system established in 1833. Trikoupis had come to the defence of the latter system, contesting the views of M. Schinas, rapporteur of the synod's proposals to the National Assembly and personal friend of Konstantinos Economou, maintaining that adoption of these requests would diminish the political establishment's power. In fact, the only difference in the Constitution of 1844 was that the Patriarchate was now explicitly mentioned; it did not change the status of the church.

The crucial moment for the Greek Church came soon thereafter, when talks commenced for its recognition by the Patriarchate. At the time, the ordination of new bishops was a major problem for the government. The number of bishops had declined, yet they proved impossible to replace since their unction required myrrh—a substance only the Patriarchate could provide. As a result, the bargaining power of the remaining bishops increased. Meanwhile, the opposition had put Otto in an uncomfortable position by insistently raising the issue of his own successor's religion, and he gladly accepted the unexpected opportunity which the Patriarchate offered the Greek state. Subsequent talks led to the drafting of the 'Synodal Tome', which declared the Greek Chuch autocephalous in relation to the Ecumenical Patriarchate. However, this declaration was accompanied by a series of preconditions that Otto was not willing to implement. In order to avoid conflicts, the government proceeded to draw up the Holy Synod, led by Neophytos, Bishop of Attica. According to prelates in order of ordination, the government was interpreting the Tome in a legally questionable way. Soon, however, Otto made use of his favourite tactic: procrastination.

Otto began moving towards a legislative solution to the problem only in January of 1852, just as the situation in the Eastern Mediterranean had begun to intensify. Meanwhile, in Greece, the Papoulakos revolt had many potentially negative implications for Otto's regime. As previously mentioned, this period was rife with both religious and political tensions. In order to avoid criticism of his religious policies, Otto chose to appoint Stavros Vlachos as minister of religious affairs, a man faithful to 'conservative' views on the church. Though Vlachos's proposals were completely in line with the Synodal Tome, the final law that was adopted was very different. Although there was no reference to the king's role in the most important articles, other articles provided opportunities for state involvement. The law also provided for the existence of a royal commissioner to the synod, who had to co-sign all decisions in order to render them valid. Other articles defined the internal and external affairs of the church, the former significantly more limited than the latter. Correspondence between the synod and foreign church authorities was still prohibited. From that moment onwards, the metropolitan of Athens was made president of the synod, while other bishops in the synod were appointed by the government. Members of the synod were required to give an oath of loyalty, which was referred to as an 'asseveration' to the king.

These reforms did not correspond to the demands of the Synodal Tome. Nevertheless, Otto succeeded in getting these reforms approved unanimously, demonstrating the great influence he held in both Parliament and Senate when he so desired, but also the reluctance of politicians to contradict the king when it came to ecclesiastical issues. In fact, no strong faction of politicians emerged to demand the church's emancipation from the state; any attempt to strengthen the church was treated with suspicion.

Another law was passed in the same period determining the creation of twenty-four dioceses across Greece: Athens was recognised as the metropolitan seat, while dioceses of the capitals in each prefecture and Corinth were named archdioceses. These choices were simply another example of Otto's efforts to take away with one hand what he gave with the other. The increase in the number of bishops enabled successive governments to handle internal conflicts between prelates with greater ease, especially since many dioceses were no longer economically powerful due to their size. During this time, prelates became civil servants: though only members of the synod had previously been remunerated, laws passed in 1852 provided remuneration for all bishops. The process of electing bishops was also established; three candidates would be proposed to the king, who would choose one of them. By passing these laws, Otto succeeded in maintaining crucial control over the church, avoiding tensions while also granting the church some freedom of movement.

These reforms were passed at the same time as a major religious revolt was taking place. Among other things, Christoforos Papoulakos's movement revealed the extraordinary power that religion and monasticism held over the lower social classes of the cities and countryside. Initiatives led by the Philorthodox Company and Kosmas Flamiatos played an equally important role. Indeed, this was the very reason why Otto had rushed to approve the aforementioned laws.

Christoforos Papoulakos, also known as Christos Panagiotopoulos, was a butcher by profession born in the region of Kalavryta in 1770. He became a monk and took up a position at the Megalou Spilaiou Monastery, later moving to a hermitage near his village. At the age of eighty, he began to preach with decidedly impressive results, his fame spreading rapidly. He preached beyond moral imperatives and was explicitly opposed to Otto and his government. He was apprehended for this reason and reprimanded by the metropolitan of Kalavryta, who also forbade him from any further preaching.

A few months later, ignoring the bishop's orders, Papoulakos commenced preaching again in the southern Peloponnese, rousing thousands of people, especially women. Yet his preaching was still bitterly critical of Otto, who finally signed a decree confining Papoulakos to a monastery. Papoulakos then sought refuge in Mani, where Gennaios Kolokotronis hunted him down in his capacity as head of the military corps. Eventually, the residents of Mani were able to deter Kolokotronis and distance him from the region. Meanwhile,

Papoulakos's followers in various towns and villages rose up against representatives of state power. Papoulakos was arrested for treason, and after his followers had begun to abandon him due to the hardships they were subjected to, he was imprisoned for two years and then exiled to a monastery on the island of Andros after being pardoned.

The Papoulakos movement demonstrates the influence of low-level members of the church over the Greek countryside. It also reveals the upper rank's limited ability to enforce its authority. Preachers that had been dispatched by the Holy Synod were received with indifference, as was Bishop Markarios of Assine's decision to excommunicate Papoulakos. According to the available sources, 2,000 armed individuals would accompany him on his journeys, thwarting any attempts to arrest him. It is possible that the Papoulakos movement was the last rural mobilisation against state power. From 1852 up until the beginning of the twentieth century, rural movements took other forms, and the Greek countryside began to find a new balance in relation to state power.

Great expectations

The founding of an independent Greek state satisfied all those who had forcefully and fervently supported the Greek struggle for independence; it also filled them with expectations. First came the philhellenes, who played an invaluable role in Greek state-making. Despite endless frustrations with the Greeks during the war, they never ceased believing that removing the 'Turkish despot' from the land constituted the proper and necessary condition by which Greeks would escape from the 'barbarism' they had been driven to by their despotic rulers. This came as no surprise, since this belief was nothing more than the natural result of widespread perceptions rooted in the Enlightenment itself. This view was inimitably expressed by an individual intimately familiar with the Greek situation at the time, F.H.C. Pouqueville:

> Today's Greeks, like all peoples, have their own physiognomy, and this physiognomy, unfortunately, draws its principal character from the servitude and the oppression into which they have been plunged! Everyone knows that the execrable tools of despotism can degrade peoples and individuals alike.[13]

Now, after the conclusion of the War of Independence, nothing prevented the Greeks from joining the chorus of civilised nations once more.

The protecting powers also harboured their own expectations. Upon 'securing' the country's independence, they took care to find a suitable ruler and provided the basic resources necessary to create elementary state infrastructure, something unprecedented at the time. They hoped that this new state could further the goal of international stability, located as it was in a highly sensitive geopolitical region.

The inhabitants of the new nation also had great expectations. After a decade of warfare, they felt the time had come to enjoy the fruits of their sacrifices. Although not everyone had the same expectations, security was undoubtedly the most important goal for the great majority of the kingdom's inhabitants who hoped to work the land and live from it. They also anticipated working the fields that had belonged to the Turkish oppressors just a few years earlier, which were now uncultivated and ownerless. The national assemblies held during the war had made it clear that this land would be shared among cultivators; all that remained was the process of distribution itself.

On the other hand, those who emerged as military and political leaders over the course of the struggle expected to maintain their power and even increase it in exchange for the assistance they provided. Others, who found themselves enclosed by the newly liberated territories—as their native lands had not been included in the new state—had no choice but to hope for relief from the new regime in order to survive. Quite a few others, represented most prominently by the islanders who had led the war effort, awaited reparations that would enable them to restore their pre-war prosperity—or so they thought.

Yet the initial conditions upon which these hopes were pinned seemed (and were) extremely adverse, offering very few immediate advantages. The territories granted to the Greek state were economically destitute. Indeed, though they may have been armed with information from sources about conditions prevailing in Greece, and though they may have left Germany brimming with optimism, the Bavarian founders of the Greek state must have come face to face with a disheartening reality when they came ashore at Nafplion. Whatever romanticism tinged their conception of this kingdom of villagers, it had certainly disappeared after the War of Independence and the civil war that ensued after the assassination of Kapodistrias. All the delicate balances that ensured survival of the population in the state it had assumed power over had been destroyed, productive activities had been disrupted and the social reciprocities that local communities relied on were completely uprooted. Wretchedness was a logical consequence of all this. Maurer writes:

> Wherever you might turn your gaze, naked rocks, dry brush, uncultivated fields. Roads or bridges were nowhere to be seen. People lived either in caves or little huts, sometimes made of dirt and other times of rocks simply placed one on top of the other. You not only looked upon deserted houses, but whole villages and towns. Athens, which numbered 3,000 houses before the struggle for liberation, now con-

> tained barely 300. The rest had devolved into indiscriminate piles of stones, and most remain like this to this day. The vegetation around Nafplion and other regions, as dense as it was, had now disappeared. The day we arrived, spotting the city from afar, many houses were still smoking. One did not dare to venture beyond Nafplion for the danger. The city was not even paved, but consisted of narrow streets through which vehicles could not pass. The main square, Platanos square, was filled with dirt and rubble from collapsed houses. To head to Arconauplia, one had to climb on foot, since the roads there were non-existent. This was also the case for Palamidi. The aqueduct bringing water from Argos was leaking in various places and the precious water collected in pools here and there. The moat around the walls had transformed into a marsh with awful fumes, yet people lived in there along with swine. The fortification works and the dockyard lay in rubble. And I won't even discuss the houses we lived in! ... yet they claimed they had prepared them specially for us.[14]

Bavarian politicians, bureaucrats and intellectuals arriving in Greece expected that the country would soon transform into a modern state as a result of their governance. They also recognised the possibilities for a career that would have been unthinkable had they remained in their own country. The masses of opportunists accompanying the regency council to Greece shared the same hopes. The nascent Greek state's unploughed terrain offered many hopes of a bountiful harvest for all who could bear the temporary difficulties.

Along with them, the Saint-Simonianists appeared with their expectations that the ex nihilo formation of the Greek state would enable the implementation of at least a few of their utopian plans. Their first concern involved the settlement of the rural countryside by German and mainly Swiss peasants, who would arrive to the ravaged land with livestock and agricultural expertise. Implementation of their plan, they believed, would breathe new life to Greek land cultivation.

Utopianism manifested itself not only with the Saint-Simonianists but also with various intellectuals arriving in Greece hoping to dedicate themselves to the revival of a glorious past: the Greek capital's transfer to Athens, a symbolic city for Western Europe, opened the floodgates for a race to identify with this past. The city's ancient ruins imbued the effort with prestige and indicated its direction. The Greek state was to be established based on this poorly definited ancient Greek heritage.

Initially, it seemed the potential for favourable developments existed. Only ten years after the Bavarian arrival in Greece, a foreign observer, F. Strong, wrote:

> So far from taking a gloomy view of the state of Greece, like many who believe her to be on the point of a general bankruptcy, it is his [the author's] opinion that there are few European states in a more prosperous condition; and that improvement in the revenue, the development of national wealth, the progress of education, the extension of agriculture and commerce, the increase of knowledge, the impartial administration of justice, and the reduction of expenditure, which have hitherto been so rapid, will be carried on in the future to a much greater extent even than hitherto, and give Greece, in a few years, an important and conspicuous rank in the scale of nations.[15]

Strong was undoubtedly a biased observer. The mere fact that he was the Bavarian ambassador in Athens is enough to arouse suspicions about his glowing depiction of King Otto. Moreover, only a year after the publication of his book, the Greek state went bankrupt, contradicting his praises, while the 3 September revolution then limited King Otto's powers—at least in theory. In any case, setting these exaggerations aside, the progress of the Greek state was not called into question, even by individuals such as Guizot who had reason to do so. For him in particular, the only problem in the country during the 1840s was the 'weakness and inaction of authority'. A few years later, in 1847, a French diplomat, Thouvenel, took a similar position:

There can be no doubt that Greece is progressing. Between 1838, when I came to Athens for the first time, and 1847, I would dare to say that a true material revolution took place in the country.

> Land resources were intelligently capitalised upon, while shipping grew to the point that today there are almost 4,000 ships, 1,200 of which are 300 tons or larger; the layout of cities such as Piraeus, Vostitsa, Patras, Galaxidi, and Kalamata has completely changed. In short, economic activity in Greece has only been hampered by its small population and limited resources. Everything that individuals could do has already been done.[16]

But comments of this type became increasingly rare. Ultimately, any progress made by Greece in these first years of its existence was not sufficient to meet the great expectations held by those directly and indirectly invested in the country—those hoping to make it a part of Europe and of the West. The pace of change was slow and restrained at best, or so observers thought, which is what counted in the end. The spirit of philhellenism had been exhausted, and what remained was the situation at hand, as perceived through the eyes of each observer.

In the 1850s, Greece participated in the International Exposition held in London. The British journalist who visited the Greek pavilion commented:

> Greece was a passing reminder at the international fair, as it is inconceivable to suppose that its natural and manufactured products are limited to just the few

> samples of marble, textiles and dried fruits that have been sent abroad ... It is likely that Greek manufacturing, having just been released from the bonds of slavery and the difficulties of turbulent social reorganisation, is afraid of showing its tiny scale, regarding which, however, there were many serious reasons for justification in the eyes of everyone. Because of excessive modesty it was impeded, it seems, from being represented as it should have been. Nevertheless, it was a sorry appearance.[17]

If just a few decades earlier the past was the primary supporting material for the creation of the Greek state, now, twenty years after its creation, it stood as a depressing benchmark. Everything seemed to be stacked against modern Greece. In the end, Greece's own inhabitants were its biggest critics, perhaps because they were most directly involved and because they harboured the greatest expectations of all parties involved in the Greek situation.

Casting the blame was an easy task. For Guizot—and everyone else—the problem was political: while Turkish despotism had been the obstacle to all Christian progress in the years of Ottoman rule, Otto's Bavarian despotism had led the country to a standstill. The establishment of the 1844 Constitution did not lead to any major improvements, as the king undermined its implementation and continued to rule in an authoritarian way. Instead of seeking to fulfil the goals prescribed at its founding, Greece pursued an alternative model, which was none other than the Ottoman reality from which it had been born. But the overthrow of the Bavarian king in 1862 opened new horizons and raised expectations once again. It was time for democracy.

These domestic political responsibilities went hand in hand with international responsibilities, which Greeks often used to justify themselves: from the outset, the kingdom's limited borders formed a constricting noose, preventing growth, and it seemed that only their expansion could grant the nation momentum to realise the project for which it was destined. This was one of the arguments used by Leopold of Saxonburg, the first candidate to the Greek throne, when he finally renounced the crown of the Greek kingdom; it was also exactly the same argument used by Greek diplomats every time they sought to annex territories belonging to the Ottoman Empire. This expansion of the Greek state would rectify, in part, the toxic conditions produced by the Great Powers when they created a lean, and thus unsustainable, kingdom.

Perhaps the most notable element of these 'great expectations' was the fact that the Greeks themselves had internalised and assimilated their failure to fulfil their destiny. In 1848, Alexandros Soutzos wrote: 'For how much longer will the Greek state, with its minute bodily stature and oversized head, provoke the world to laughter as a hunched and grotesque homunculus?'[18] There were of course also those who tried to see things with more moderation. One of these people was the first professor of political economy at the University of Athens, I.A. Soutsos, who wrote in 1860:

> When we think of Greece's wretched state in 1828, with no construction activity, cultivation, ships, livestock and so on, and when we consider what its people have done since the establishment of lawful order so as to restore the ruins that surrounded it, we must rightly marvel at the labours that have been made to improve the situation.[19]

These voices of moderation were seldom heard in a country intoxicated with grand ambitions and an unattainable past. Indeed, it should be noted that Soutsos penned the above opinion in a period when criticism of the Greek kingdom had reached its peak. Born amid expectations that it would soon be the country to bring Enlightenment and civilisation to the East, Greece had disappointed all those waiting for it to carry out the task. The *enfant terrible* of Greek politics in the nineteenth century, Epameinondas Deligiorgis, wrote at the time: 'A kingdom for thirty years now, Greece finds itself much below the expectations of the Greek people. Believe me, I write this to you with tears in my eyes.'[20]

The new state made numerous mistakes. Greece had failed in diplomatic and military terms, reaching a low point during the Crimean War when it became associated with Russia, further worsening its economic system and image. Greece had failed to become a civilised state, civilisation being synonymous with urban development, industry, trade, development of agriculture and economic growth more generally. In a country where the overthrow of the Ottomans was considered a necessary and sufficient condition for a return to civilisation, the realities of everyday life prevented any steps towards progress: Greece had proven itself incapable of keeping up with the 'civilised' countries.

5

THE GREEKS AMONG THEMSELVES

(1863–80)

The notables' triumphs

On 11 October 1862, the day after Otto's deposition, leading figures of the rebellion met at the university and formed a new revolutionary government headed by a three-member committee. Dimitris Voulgaris presided as president and was joined by Konstantinos Kanaris and Benizelos Roufos. However, it soon became clear that they were unable to create a viable political regime. This was largely due to the fact that even the temporary elimination of the royal mediating role between conflicting political groups led to situations of conflict, if not outright civil war. From the outset, the political opposition had become completely polarised, and this polarisation only increased over time, as did the violence these groups inflicted on one another. Once again, the state was a spoil of war waiting to be claimed. In the words of P. Koronaios:

> From the very first day of the Revolution, those who governed showed a divided heart. Their only thought was to secure the terrain, which would be to their personal benefit and to the detriment of the others. To this end they used the National Assembly on one hand, and, on the other, the lance.[1]

In itself, Otto's departure did not lead to widespread unrest, though some rallies held by citizens of Mani and Tripolite villagers in the Peloponnese had a limited impact on the new government. Then, General Theodoros Grivas's decision to march from Akarnania against Athens momentarily caused a major problem. The general had not been accounted for in the distribution of power among political leaders that had taken place in the capital, and he decided to take back what he believed he was owed by force. The panic his move instigated dissipated very quickly when Grivas, who had been granted the rank of field-marshal in an attempt to appease him, died during the march.

Meanwhile, the main concern for both the government in Athens and the Great Powers was the search for a new king. Britain, which had treated Otto—and by extension the Greek government—with hostility, changed its attitude towards the new government. It sought to curry its favour, fearing that Greece might take the opportunity to establish closer relations with Russia. Specifically, Britain was worried about the possibility of the new king being a descendant of the Russian imperial family, or even being sympathetic to the country of the tsar. The duke of Leuchtenberg was often mentioned as a suitable replacement, something that France was not necessarily against; as a result, the British government decided to revise the position it had held in relation to Greece up to that point. The British tactic proved effective and the revolutionary government rushed to take advantage of the situation, suggesting Alfred, second-born son of Queen Victoria, as a candidate for the Greek throne. In fact, everyone knew that Alfred's rise to the Greek throne was impossible. The international situation prohibited any members of the protecting powers' royal families from becoming king of Greece. Therefore, above all, it was a gesture of goodwill and acknowledgement towards the British. In the referendum that followed, Alfred gained the overwhelming majority of votes. This was a major success for the British, as it essentially weakened the remaining candidates—especially the duke of Leuchtenberg.

The new National Assembly, which emerged from the elections held on 24–7 November 1862, also endorsed the monarchy. Despite the fact that no powerful anti-monarchist movement existed in Greece, this declaration at the National Assembly was meant to reassure the Great Powers. Indeed, the presence of Henry Elliot, special envoy to Athens, who promised that the Ionian Islands would be granted to Greece, undoubtedly played a role in the National Assembly's decisions. But given Alfred's inability to become king, someone needed to be found in his place. Thus the Greek crown arrived on the 'auction block' of the European courts, and the Great Powers, led by Lord Palmerston, finally decided on the son of the heir to the throne of Denmark. George I was declared king of Greece in a resolution of 18 March 1863 at the Second National Assembly of Athens.

Timetable 1863–80

1863	Conflict between the Montagnard and Girondin factions at the National Assembly. The National Assembly assumes executive power through the presiding vice-president, A. Moraitinis (9 February 1863–13 February 1863). George is appointed king of Greece. Conflicts between the Montagnard and Girondin factions claim many victims. Governments of Zenobius Valvis (13 February 1863–27 March 1863), Diomedes Kyriakos (27 March 1863–29 April 1863) and Benizelos Rufos (29 April 1863–25 October 1863). D. Voulgaris government (25 October 1863–5 March 1864).
1864	K. Kanaris government (5 March 1864–16 April 1864). Treaty signed in London uniting Greece and the Ionian Islands. Z. Valvis government (16 April 1864–26 July 1864). K. Kanaris government (26 July 1864–9 February 1865). The new Constitution is ratified.
1865	Benizelos Rufos government (9 February 1865–2 March 1865). Koumoundouros government (2 March 1865–20 October 1865). Epameinondas Deligiorgis government (20 October 1865–3 November 1865). D. Voulgaris government (3 November 1865–6 November 1865). Koumoundouros government (6 November 1865–13 November 1865). Deligiorgis government (13 November 1865–28 November 1865). B. Rufos government (28 November 1865–9 June 1866).
1866	D. Voulgaris–E. Deligiorgis government (9 June 1866–18 December 1866). Uprising in Crete. A. Koumoundouros government (18 December 1866–20 December 1867).
1867	Treaty of Feslau. A. Moraitinis caretaker government (20 December 1867–25 January 1868). King George and Olga marry.
1868	D. Voulgaris government (25 January 1868–25 January 1869). Greek–Turkish diplomatic relations suspended.
1869	Paris Conference. The Cretan uprising comes to an end. Th. Zaimis government (25 January 1869–9 July 1870).
1870	The Independent Bulgarian Church is founded. Massacre in Dilessi. E. Deligiorgis government (9 July 1870–3 December 1870). A. Koumoundouros government (3 December 1870–28 October 1870).
1871	Th. Zaimis government (28 October 1870). D. Voulgaris and A. Koumoumdouros government (25 December 1871–8 July 1872).
1872	E. Deligiorgis government (8 July 1872–9 February 1874). The Patriarchate declares the Bulgarian schism.
1874	Voulgaris government (9 February 1874–27 April 1875).
1875	'Stilitika' episodes. George recognises the parliamentary principle. C. Trikoupis government (27 April 1875–15 November 1875). A. Koumoundouros government (15 November 1875–26 November 1876).
1876	Uprising in Herzegovina. Serbia and Montenegro declare war on the Ottoman Empire. E. Deligiorgis government (26 November 1876–1 December 1876). A. Koumoundouros government (1 December 1876–26 February 1877).

1877 E. Deligiorgis government (26 February 1877–19 May 1877). Russo-Turkish Wars. Greek military forces enter Epirus and Thessaly. A. Koumoundouros government (19 May 1877–26 May 1877). Universal government with K. Kanaris as prime minister (26 May 1877–2 September 1877). After Kanaris's death, the government remains leaderless.

1878 Revolution in Thessaly. A. Koumoundouros government (11 January 1878–21 October 1878). Treaty of San Stefano. Britain assumes administration of Cyprus. Congress of Berlin. C. Trikoupis and Th. Zaimis government (21 October 1878–26 October 1878). A. Koumoundouros government (26 October 1878–10 March 1880).

1880 C. Trikoupis government (10 March 1880–13 October 1880). Berlin summit. A. Koumoundouros government (13 October 1880–3 March 1882).

In fact, the new king's appointment did not solve any pressing problems, since the distribution of power resulting from the October rebellion did not lead to any sort of equilibrium. The opposition dividing the two factions of the National Assembly—the Montagnards and the Girondins, as they were called based on the French revolutionary example—intensified and finally resulted in armed conflict. Attempting a temporary solution, the National Assembly itself assumed executive power through its vice president A. Moraitinis, a choice that soon proved ineffective, resulting in another clash between the two groups, this time leading to many casualties. The successive governments of Benizelos Rufos, D. Voulgaris and K. Kanaris that were then assembled all proved unable to secure the necessary support to successfully govern the country. George I's arrival in Greece seemed to be the only solution to the country's political problems.

The committee appointed by the National Assembly, which was composed of K. Kanaris, Thrasivoulos Zaimis and D. Grivas, handed over the Greek crown to George I on 25 May 1863 in Copenhagen. George, then eighteen years old, was immediately declared of age in order to avoid the risks associated with a regency council being established. He arrived in Greece in October 1863.

At this difficult moment for Greece, a treaty declaring the union of the Ionian Islands was signed in London. This was the first step towards national unification. Shortly thereafter, following George's arrival in Greece, the National Assembly proceeded to legally certify this annexation of the Ionian Islands. Elections were held immediately on the islands and their representatives were sent to the Second National Assembly. Initially, they established themselves as an autonomous group, stating their intention to stay above party rivalries. On the other hand, the political opposition also delayed the drafting of the new constitution. George was forced to resort to blackmail in order to resolve the problem, threatening to depart if necessary steps were not taken immediately; the threat worked. Drafting of the constitution advanced rapidly, and the new document was ratified at the National Assembly and published in the government gazette. It came into effect on 17 November 1864.

Greece's new constitution, modelled on the Belgian constitution of 1831 and the Danish constitution of 1843, was extremely liberal and established a constitutional monarchy. In contrast to the constitution of 1843, power resided in the popular will rather than the monarchy. The king exercised executive power through his ministers and participated in the legislative branch by ratifying laws voted on in Parliament, yet he was excluded from the larger revisionist project. Popular sovereignty was expressed exclusively through Parliament, since the new constitution abolished the Senate, which had come to be viewed as a puppet for royal power. The judiciary remained independent, but the reforms of the previous constitution, under which justice stemmed from the king, were abolished. Democratic principles were further incorporated into the constitutional charter through a series of provisions that expanded civil rights, established the right of assembly and association, and provided universal suffrage. The latter was adopted in municipal elections with the introduction of article 105 of the constitution, thereby consolidating the electoral process at a national and local level. This change redefined the role mayors played in the nation's political landscape. The inclusion of the nation's entire male population in the municipal electorate significantly promoted the positions of mayors in party politics and led to the formation of a system in the late nineteenth century that became known as the 'mayorocracy'.

The adoption of universal suffrage, and more generally the ratification of a liberal constitution, was not met without opposition. But this eventually subsided, if for no other reason than because all the political groups involved in the process were satisfied. In fact, if, as already mentioned, notable groups managed to gain a share of power in the 1844 constitution, they managed to appropriate it in full with the changes made in 1864: above all else, 1864 was a triumph for the political oligarchy and the successful fulfilment of the War of Independence as its leaders had imagined it. The task that remained was to clarify the king's role within this new system of power, a process that was not completed until the adoption of the parliamentary principle in 1875.

Elections continued to be held according to patterns established during Otto's rule, and violence and fraud remained constant factors in the ballot-counting process. However, some of the measures taken in response, such as the adoption of a reform in the 1864 constitution that prohibited amnesty for the crime of robbery, did lead to improvements in the situation. Thus, a primary extra-institutional factor in the electoral and political process was weakened.

Another factor that improved the political process was linked to the changes in the electoral process itself. During Otto's rule, the electoral system was majoritarian and included many separate rounds of voting: if all members of Parliament were not elected after the first vote, then the vote was repeated for double the amount of candidates in relation to the required number of ministers. Candidates for this secondary vote were chosen by those that had consolidated a relative majority in the previous election, and the process was repeated until all ministers had been elected by an absolute majority. The extensive duration of the electoral process—which often lasted many weeks—and the use of ballots when the population was largely illiterate, meant that elections could easily be rigged.

Thus in 1865, the system of voting using lead beads, previously used on the Ionian Islands in order to limit British intervention in the electoral process, was adopted. To a large extent, the system ensured privacy and facilitated voting for illiterate individuals. It also encouraged partnerships between candidates, rendering violence and fraud unnecessary and even counterproductive. These partnerships occurred on the local level, often between conflicting factions, who nevertheless ensured the election of desired candidates in this manner. This was also a system that emphasised local conflicts, and to some extent it served to hinder party cohesiveness at a national level. But it also led to a more peaceful electoral process, as it forced opponents to collaborate with each other. It even included measures such as subtracting votes from a candidate if they exceeded the actual number of total voters. These new conditions in turn facilitated the establishment of local 'cartels' by notable groups.

Electoral legislation passed in 1877 provided for the active involvement of the judiciary in the electoral process—both via the drawing up of electoral registers and supervision of proper electoral conduct—and was an important component of the broader institutional changes of later years. The same legislation also limited the voting period to a single day, thus preventing multi-day elections.

While these actions addressed some of the chronic problems plaguing Greek politics, the makeup of political personnel remained unaltered. At least until 1910, and in reality until long after that, political life in Greece continued to be dominated by locally rooted political oligarchies.

The parliamentary principle

Initially, George I showed no desire to stay out of politics. The king's privilege of appointing governments according to his own preferences persisted until at least 1875, when the parliamentary principle was established during C. Trikoupis's government. Until that point, the king played a decisive regulatory role, and individual groups seeking power gathered around him—groups with limited respect for democratic rights and the processes that guaranteed them.

The constituent assembly was dissolved in November 1864 after a new electoral law was passed that determined how elections would be held. At the time, K. Kanaris was the leader of the government, but due to a dispute with the Minister of the Interior Alexandros Koumoundouros, who supported the government, Kanaris resigned immediately after the constitution was enacted, and the new Koumoundouros government carried out the first elections. According to all indications, they were conducted smoothly. All the leading names in Greek politics were elected to the new Parliament. But the situation was complicated, and pre-existing opposition continued to influence political life. The fragmentary nature of the leadership and the inability of political leaders to rally a significant number of ministers around their causes only guaranteed temporary survival for governments in power.

For the whole of 1865, one government succeeded the next, as rumours of uprisings and coups seeking to overthrow the democratic system circulated throughout the country. This governmental instability and all that resulted from it was attributed by some to the democratic system and the liberal institutions adopted in 1864. The argument that Greeks were not ready for such a system of government began to gain ground. The solution adopted in late 1865, was a government formed of allied groups led by A. Koumoudouros and D. Voulgaris with Benizelos Rufos as acting prime minister. This government remained in power until summer of 1866, when it was replaced by another government led by Prime Minister D. Voulgaris, joined this time by Epameinondas Deligiorgis and D. Christidis.

This constant alternation of leaders and governments could hardly enable the conditions necessary to tackle immediate problems, which were neither few nor insignificant. The situation became all the more difficult after the Cretan insurrection broke out. Faced on the one hand with the enthusiasm of the capital's residents and on the other with harsh criticism from the opposition, led by A. Koumoundouros, the government's tactics towards Crete were extremely unambitious, mainly because it sensed that Greece did not have much of a chance at succeeding in what it demanded. Though this attitude demonstrated a type of realism, it nevertheless failed to help the government survive the pressures it was under. The opposition succeeded in toppling the government in December 1866. In its place, a government was formed by A. Koumoundouros, in which C. Trikoupis became minister of foreign affairs. The new government addressed the Cretan affair much more aggressively, outfitting weapons, sending aid to Crete and exerting strong diplomatic force. Meanwhile, Greece and Serbia also signed the Treaty of Vöslau, the Greek state's first alliance treaty. George I, who was abroad at the time, was well aware of Greece's extremely limited capacity to intervene in the Cretan affair.

George I's return to Greece—after a voyage during which he had married the niece of the tsar, Grand Duchess Olga—did not change the prevailing situation, despite the opposition's harsh criticisms of the government's actions. Soon after, George, convinced that the situation in Crete would soon shift and that Greece stood no chance of success, recommended that Koumoundouros change his approach to the matter. This prompted Koumoundouros to submit his resignation. A caretaker government was established led by the president of the Supreme Court, A. Moraitinis, which refused to dissolve Parliament if it was defeated in the vote for the election of the president of Parliament. Moraitinis ultimately resigned. The subsequent government led by D. Voulgaris conducted extremely violent elections in which it annulled many opponents' votes, thus gaining a majority in Parliament.

The actions of the Voulgaris government were highly indicative of Greek politics at the time, which involved layoffs of political personnel, mass persecution of opponents, and finally the pursuit of Koumoudouros, who surrendered for trial after besieging the tower of Zarnata in Messinia. Koumoundouros was convicted but acquitted after an appeal, which led Voulgaris to dismiss all the judges participating in the trial. At the same time, Voulgaris's indecisive stance on Crete drove Greece to complete isolation and the suspension of diplomatic relations with the Ottoman Empire. The possibility of a Greek–Turkish war now seemed very likely, though it was clear that Greece was incapable of rising to the demands of a military confrontation. The situation was resolved thanks to Russia, which proposed convening a conference in Paris. Failure to give Greece a vote in the proceedings led it to abstain from attending, and it condemned this exclusion as a violation of international law. The Voulgaris government refused to accept the conference's decisions and resigned. George immediately called together a council of political leaders—to which Koumoundouros, who was then on trial, was not invited—which reached the conclusion that the only solution was to comply with the suggestions of the Great Powers.

A government led by Thrasivoulos Zaimis was then formed in which Theodoros Deliyannis accepted the position of minister of foreign affairs, and it finally accepted the terms of the Paris Conference.

Once the Cretan issue had been resolved, the Zaimis government proceeded to elections in which it gained a strong majority. Yet an incident in Dilessi upset international relations once again: a group of British visitors in the region of Marathon was kidnapped by bandits, and some of them were eventually murdered, resulting in an international outcry against Greece. In many Western European newspapers, proposals called for the occupation of Greece by a Western European army to restore order. Indeed, the basic cause for this incident originated in the country's system of government. Lord Clarendon, speaking with P. Vrailas-Armenis, ambassador to Greece in London immediately after the Dilessi massacre, put it bluntly: 'But of course, the highly democratic nature of the constitution hinders proper government of the land ... even in England, which is so advanced in terms of constitutional experience, no government would be possible if such a constitution prevailed.' Vrailas-Armenis hastened to agree with him: 'I myself publicly criticised the excessively democratic nature of the constitution when it was discussed, and foresaw the consequences ...'[2]

Following these developments, the Zaimis government was forced to resign, and the leader of the weakest party in Parliament, Epameinondas Deligiorgis, assumed the premiership. He remained in power until November 1870, when he was voted out of Parliament and then resigned. Successive changes in government followed. The impasse was obvious to all; the system in place was blatantly ineffective, and criticisms of the liberal regime mounted.

In essence, the period's political instability was nothing more than a component of the political opposition at the time, expressing a sum of trends that varied depending on the level of trust each government placed in Parliament, where there was no consistent majority. This helps explain these successive ministerial crises. They were nothing more than crises of adaptation, similar to those seen in the Third French Republic.

The actions of the Voulgaris government that assumed power in early 1874 stretched the political opposition to its limits, but it also supplied a definitive solution to the question of parliamentarism. Voulgaris himself supported the overthrow of liberal institutions, and was himself autocratic by nature. These characteristics became evident in their entirety during his term. Unconstitutional actions marked the tenure of the Voulgaris government: two ministers, one of which was his son-in-law, were indicted for simony, and attempts were made to limit the powers of Parliament through constitutional amendments that even foresaw the resurrection of the Senate. Finally, the government's attempt to bypass parliamentary legitimacy during the voting of the budget led to the so-called *stilitika*, a name derived from the column on which names of ministers who had disregarded parliamentary procedure were written. George then expelled the ministers who had disregarded parliamentary procedure. In this instance, the way in which other political leaders and groups rallied against the risk of changing the rules of the political game is highly revealing. If Voulgaris's intentions had been fully realised, he would have had a clear advantage over other political leaders who, in turn, would have run the risk of political extermination. Their united response prevented the possibility of constitutional amendment and ended Voulgaris's political career.

In this political climate, Trikoupis published 'Tis Ptaei?', an article in which he held the king responsible for the country's political situation, singling out his lack of respect for the terms of parliamentarism. What the parliamentary principle could mean in a Parliament with very fluid parliamentary groups is questionable; it is also debatable whether the parliamentary majority was taken into account before the granting of the mandate to a political leader through a vote for the election of president of Parliament. Despite what he wrote in the article, Trikoupis accepted the mandate to form a government from George I, though the parliamentary group he led was small. He proceeded to conduct blameless elections, which handed victory and the premiership to Koumoundouros.

This moment proved pivotal, as the Eastern Question was growing increasingly tense while the Russo-Turkish war of 1877 led to the Treaty of San Stefano and the creation of Greater Bulgaria. Regardless of whether or not the Treaty of Berlin then went on to limit Bulgaria's territorial expanse, Greek governments faced the problem and other developments in the region in an exceedingly confused manner. The country's political leadership was divided over Greece's participation in the war, as opinions on what action to take next differed dramatically among political leaders. As the crisis worsened, the solution found by the end of 1876 was the establishment of a 'universal government' led by Kanaris in which all the political leaders (Koumoundouros, Trikoupis, Zaimis, Deliyannis) would participate. This solution soon proved unsustainable, since there was a complete lack of communication between them. Kanaris's death then left the government leaderless, and Greece, just after the outbreak of the Thessaly uprising, without a government.

From the Great Idea to a Model Kingdom

The new generation of politicians that took over the reins of Greek politics after Otto's fall realised that they had to enact significant changes for the nation to achieve its goals. Trikoupis himself unambiguously asserted as much to Lord Russell:

> Beginning on 10 October, I spoke to him about our policies, which involve a departure from the pursuit of the 'Great Idea' through armed conflict and unrest, and rather seek the same ends through peace and setting a good example—policies which the king stated in his declaration, saying that he will make Greece a model free state in the East.

This was not simply a turn of phrase aimed at pacifying British hostility against Greece. Trikoupis did not deny that the pursuit of territorial expansion would continue—he simply stated that it would be pursued on different terms. Attempts to subdue uprisings and unrest had proved futile up until then and had tarnished Greece's reputation. It became clear that new approaches were necessary, approaches that necessitated alterations to the way the state itself functioned. To this end, Greek priorities changed, and the transition from Great Idea to Model Kingdom led to a complete rearrangement of state policies, though this rearrangement would take time to be implemented. The plans expressed by an undoubtedly farsighted politician such as Trikoupis and the reactions of relevant state mechanisms were separated by a great distance. This became very clear from the Cretan rebellion.

On 2 September 1866, the Cretan General Assembly declared Crete's union with Greece. Greece's official stance remained neutral, but for the first time Greek diplomacy acted with unprecedented vigour. The Serbs, Egyptians and Bulgarians accepted exploratory proposals for joint ventures initiated by the Greeks. This resulted in the country's first alliance treaty with Serbia, known as the Treaty of Vöslau, in 1867. This secret treaty provided for mutual 'defensive' war with the aim of liberating the Christian populations of Ottoman-occupied Europe and the islands. The treaty laid out Greek claims (Epirus and Thessaly) and Serbian ones (Bosnia and Herzegovina). There was a separate clause in the treaty for Crete, which was considered part of Greece. It is worth noting that the treaty also contained elements designed to win over other Balkan nations including Romania, Montenegro and Albania. Whichever of them decided to participate in the war would be free to unite with Greece or Serbia or create their own autonomous state. Eastern Christianity constituted a totality, and no foreign power would come to replace Ottoman sovereignty. Despite the fact that the treaty was soon annulled because of the assassination of the Serbian leader, Mihail, it demonstrated the Greek state's efforts to seek international support, something unprecedented up until that point. The treaty was also evidence of a shift from the perception, prevalent until the Crimean War, that the Greeks could expand through a 'second War of Independence'—or even from the idea of the empire as a system capable of rehabilitating Hellenism to its 'natural' and 'historical' limits. It was not a question of synthesising Greek and Slavic elements, but rather a question of collaboration between the two that other interested parties could participate in.

The alliance treaty with Serbia constituted one facet of the Greek state's activities. Another was related to military preparedness. The Greek state urgently needed to improve its military, since from 1843 onwards the Greek army and navy were in a state of profound disorganisation, and the situation had worsened dramatically after the regime change in 1862. Greece essentially found itself with no army or fleet to challenge the Ottoman Empire.

Consequently, governments in these years tried to rebuild the army and navy: provisions for conscription were revised to include previous exemptions from duty, the army grew in strength, large quantities of military supplies were purchased and for the first time an attempt was made to organise the army so that it could challenge other armies, and not just chase bandits and protect the political status quo. At the same time, three battleships were purchased and two more warships were ordered in the hope that their presence in the Aegean could upset the balance of power that heavily favoured the Ottomans.

Yet as Greece sought an ally for the first time in its modern history and attempted to create an army and navy out of nothing, the Cretan issue reached a tipping point. The Ottoman government delivered an ultimatum with terms that Greece was not in a position to accept, and the Ottoman ambassador left Athens. Greece was humiliated, though the Great Powers intervened to avoid a conflict with the Ottomans by convening the Paris Conference in which France, Britain and Russia participated, as did Prussia, Austria, Italy and even the Ottoman Empire. Greece was given only a consultative vote. In a show of protest, it did not take part; all it had left were its catastrophic public finances.

The Cretan issue exhibited the problems and weaknesses of the Greek state to their fullest extent. It also demonstrated the difficulty the government had in adapting to changes in the international arena. The drastic changes brought about by the Crimean War proved impossible for Greek political leaders to quickly integrate into the political system. The Concert of Europe had ceased to exist, or had certainly begun to function in a different manner. Small states developed capabilities that they had not previously possessed. Their fate would no longer rest in the hands of the Great Powers; they would rely on their own policies. Both the British–French victory in the Crimean War and the German victory in the Franco-Prussian War some years later demonstrated that only countries able to rely on a powerful army and a delicate array of diplomatic relationships could survive, let alone thrive. Of course, the nations that managed to excel militarily were none other than those with a broad economic and industrial foundation. Britain, and then Germany, indicated the way forwards for those who sought to succeed.

Greece continued to stumble in both its domestic and foreign policy. Though Greek politicians agreed on the necessity of change, the fact that they agreed did not clarify specific priorities, or necessarily lead to common ground. Nor, in the end, did it guarantee the state mechanisms necessary for the implementation of direly needed policies. Political instability alone, with its frequent changes of government, meant that it was nearly impossible to formulate coherent policy in any sector, including foreign policy. There was not even a consensus on the manner in which Greece could achieve its goal of territorial expansion. It has been argued that after George I's rise to the throne, Greece aligned itself with British policies, but this is debatable. If George himself was portrayed as a mouthpiece for British policy (which is untrue), this was certainly not the case for the nation's political leaders. Epameinondas Deligiorgis and Voulgaris were indeed devotees of a foreign policy oriented towards Britain and hoped to foster good relations with the Ottoman Empire. But the key figure of the political scene in those years, Koumoundouros, was clearly friendly towards Russia and continued to see St Petersburg as the key to solving Greece's problems. In other words, the solution to the Greek problem continued to be dependent, at least in the minds of the political leadership, on the choices and actions of a Great Power. Secondly, there were great divergences in the proposed solutions to Greece's problems; even the necessity of a well-organised army was called into question. It is therefore not surprising that, even at the end of the nineteenth century, propositions as extreme as abolishing the army could still be heard in opposition to those who demanded its full restructuring. The impending crisis of the Eastern Question soon turned the Greek state towards more rational choices.

Since 1858–60, the Bulgarians had openly indicated their dissatisfaction with the policies of the Ecumenical Patriarchate. Ten years later, in 1868, Bulgaria requested that the Porte create an archdiocese for them headed by a

Bulgarian archbishop. Though their proposal was rejected, they were emboldened by the support they were offered by Russia. In February 1870, the Bulgarian exarchate was founded, and two years later, the Porte granted the exarch the necessary *berat* to perform his duties. Greek protests and a session convened by the Ecumenical Patriarchate, in which the Bulgarian church was declared dissenting, made no difference.

The uprising of 1875 in Bosnia and Herzegovina, along with other uprisings in Serbia and Bulgaria the following year, massacres of the Bulgarian population, and the nascent Russo-Turkish war turned all attention to the Black Sea. The Russo-Turkish war provided an opportunity for Greece. Yet the way the Greek leaders handled the issue was completely ineffective and showed, if anything, the lack of a specific focus in Greek foreign policy: according to some, such as the Greek ambassador in Berlin, Rizos Rangavis, the Greek population needed to rebel, so that Greek involvement in the war would be justified in the eyes of the Great Powers. The second perspective called for an alliance treaty and mobilisation of Greek troops only when the Greek state would be ready to fight. The final result for a government with various political leaders but no common conception of the problem was indecision; in the end, Greece acted at the worst possible moment.

Once more, the Greek military found itself completely unprepared. The Greek state made few attempts to reinforce its military organisation until the eve of the Russo-Turkish war's declaration. Reminiscent of the Cretan affair in the 1860s, the Greek state rushed to purchase arms at the absolute last moment, altering the military's organisational structure. In 1878, it introduced universal conscription for the first time. Once more, all of these desperate efforts had inevitably devastating effects on public finances.

Under these circumstances, Greece invaded the Ottoman Empire at the exact moment the Ottomans had admitted defeat, signing a truce and liberating troops that would be allowed to move southwards. But such a manoeuvre proved unnecessary, as the invasion of Thessaly ended in tragedy on its own, and the Greek state was forced to immediately withdraw its army. Things could not have gone worse. Yet paradoxically, Greece would emerge victorious out of this crisis in the long term, as it would gain Thessaly and part of Epirus. But these benefits paled next to the emergence of a formidable opponent as a result of the Treaty of San Stefano: Bulgaria. Bismarck then took on a balancing and mediating role that rescued the situation for Greece and Serbia, since the treaty was never upheld and Greater Bulgaria's influence on the Aegean never came to be.

But from then on, things would never be the same. Greece was no longer the only Christian state in South Eastern Europe, patiently waiting to succeed the Ottoman Empire after its collapse. Regional balances changed radically, not only with the creation of Bulgaria, but also as Austria gained control of Bosnia and Herzegovina. The resulting pressure on Serbia directed international attention southwards again. The Macedonian question had become an unavoidable fact.

Distortions

The impressions formed of the Greek state by Greek and foreign observers were mostly based on personal experiences: they were partial, fragmented, largely impressionistic and certainly biased or at least shaped by personal perceptions and prejudices of how Greece should have been. Very often, these observers did not even bother to consult official statistical information, which was undoubtedly limited, but it certainly existed. Perhaps this was because, in doing so, they would have had to alter their mental picture of the country. This 'image' of Greece in the 1860s could be summarised in two words: a 'desert landscape', where 'desert' stood for nothing more than failure and lack of civilisation. This was exactly the opinion expressed in the beginning of the 1860s by P. Chalkiopoulos when he said: 'The land is as deserted, uninhabited, uncultivated, lacking in street planning and abandoned as in its native state.'

E. About, who played an important role in shaping France's perception of Greece in the nineteenth century, expressed a similar opinion. He did not hesitate to confirm, with characteristic confidence and arrogance, that 'the population has remained stagnant, and has not developed considerably in the past twenty-five years'. This was 'the most important of all other observations', which confirmed, more than anything else, the Greek state's failure to create necessary and sufficient conditions for development (in every sense of the term) of its population. Yet About had access to information that disproved his point. The same was true of the philhellene Finlay, who repeated About's findings, yet he was a permanent resident of the kingdom and was assuredly informed—or at least should have been informed—of the facts, since such information was regularly published in the government gazette.

But this was not the only problem. Since comparisons with ancient Greece inevitably coloured modern Greek reality, calculations of populations in regions within the Greek territories and comparisons with the population of the same regions in ancient times proved crushing for nineteenth-century

Greeks, and even more so for the Greek kingdom. Among others, the doctor A. Goudas collected estimates of classical Athens's population circulating at the time: 139,500 free inhabitants, with the same number of slaves and metics. In total, Attica contained over 700,000 inhabitants, not including Megarida, whose population was estimated at 143,000. In other words, the population of ancient Attica approached the overall population of the Greek kingdom in the 1830s. If the number of inhabitants in a nation was directly proportional to its successful governance, as many believed in the nineteenth century, then such comparisons between states established hierarchies between their systems of governance. The results of this were once more detrimental to the Greek state. I.A. Soutsos, a professor at the University of Athens, admitted as much when he wrote: 'An increase in population is hence rightly considered a measure of progress and prosperity within a nation.'

5.1: Population and Extent of Greece, 1828–79

Year	*Population*	*Average rate of yearly increase (per 1,000 residents)*	*Territory (in square kilometres)*	*Density (per square kilometres)*
1828	753,400	–	47,516	15.9
1839	839,236	8.2	47,516	17.7
1848	986,731	20.3	47,516	20.8
1853	1.035,527	9.7	47,516	21.8
1861	1.096,810	7.2	47,516	23.1
1870	1.457,894	11.7	50,211	29.0
1879	1.679,470	15.9	50,211	33.5

Source: M. Chouliarakis, *Γεωγραφική, διοικητική και πληθυσμιακή εξέλιξις της Ελλάδος, 1821–1971*, vol. I, part 1, Athens: 1973, p. XVIII; G. Siambos, *Δημογραφική εξέλιξις της νεωτέρας Ελλάδος (1821–1985)*, Athens: 1973, p. 24.

Despite the stagnation noted by observers at the time, the population of the Greek kingdom increased rapidly. From 1839 to 1848, for example, over nine years, a 20 per cent increase in population did not reflect stagnation by any means, or at least should have prevented About from claiming that the population had not grown sufficiently. Up until 1860, corresponding percentages increased less rapidly, though the general trend was one of sustained population growth. After 1860, the pace picked up again.

Greece's rapid rates of population growth were of course linked with the population's efforts to recover from hardships faced during the War of

Independence; they were also related to the fact that the young population used no methods of contraception. Yet again, the 'findings' of one of the advisors to the regency council 'that the crime of abortion is so widespread and happens so shamelessly, that one cannot encounter anything of the kind anywhere else. In Greece it is committed by married women against the fruit of marriage, so often that it is not considered a crime in peoples' minds' were not corroborated by the facts.

G. Siambos's estimates of the population's composition by age indicate that, from 1821 to 1860, the elderly population (that is, the population over sixty-five years of age) accounted for only 3.5 per cent of the total population. The young population (under fifteen years of age) in both 1840 and 1850 amounted to 43 per cent of the total population, while in 1828 it accounted for 38 per cent mainly due to a lack of births during the War of Independence, and possibly due to a higher infant mortality rate. E. Quinet also noticed this phenomenon during his visit to the Peloponnese in 1830: 'We must observe that at this time in Morea there are an inordinate number of children still breastfeeding. But there are hardly any children above this age. Either they died from hardship and hunger, or, as I heard, infertility hit women during the most terrible years of the war.'

Unfortunately, significant studies have yet to be conducted on the average age of marriage for Greek populations, a decisive factor in determining fertility. Yet it seems safe to conclude that another claim by About, according to which 'the Greeks marry young ... They marry on a whim and without a secure future', was inaccurate. In Ermoupoli, capital of the island of Syros, the typical wedding in the period from 1845 to 1853 involved women of a very young age: under twenty years old to be precise, though this age later increased. Meanwhile, men married at an average of twenty-seven years old. It was very rare for women to remain single, and more common for men to do so. This 'model' for weddings, often referred to as the Mediterranean model, did indeed lead to high fertility rates, though it applied to urban populations, which constituted a small percentage of the Greek population in the nineteenth century.

Another study based on the censuses of 1861, 1870 and 1879 reports that the average marriage age for women across all of Greece was around 23.5 years old, well above that of Ermoupoli. It also demonstrated that geographical variations were insignificant, and that very few individuals never married. The same study also suggested that the population's fertility rates remained high until at least the early twentieth century.

In both cases, available evidence suggests that women married at a young age, and few remained unmarried for life. This in turn translated into a population with a high fertility rate. This must be regarded as a natural consequence of the high infant mortality rates also prevalent in this same period. In any case, research at our disposal is hardly capable of leading us to definite conclusions with regard to a model for marriage in Greece.

Regardless of our inability to calculate average marriage age—a decisive factor in shaping birth and fertility rates—estimates indicate increasingly high rates of real population growth in certain periods. From 1839 to 1848, growth increased by over 2 per cent each year. This increase cannot be solely attributed to natural population movements, as previously demonstrated. Therefore, it can be assumed that a significant number of people moved to Greece from the Ottoman Empire and elsewhere during this period, a fact ignored in Findlay's observations on the Greek state's inability to attract Christian populations residing in the Ottoman Empire.

These population movements and the broader mobility of populations were constant factors throughout the period in question. In other words, large portions of the population had yet to acquire settled homes. Frederic Thiers described the prevailing situation in the following way:

> Thus, land that yielded only three to four times the seed generally remained untilled or was private property. Farmers moved towards the plains, where it was much more advantageous for their goods, and where one generally reaped eight to twenty-five times what one originally seeded. Such is the countryside of Amyclae, Pamisou, Marathon, the lakes of Kopaida and Achelous. Generally, the farming class that cultivates land it does not own is not very linked to that land. These people find themselves more exposed to discrimination by authorities and the wrongdoings of local leaders, while they are also the poorest, often with nothing more than a thatched hut to protect themselves from winter and a few bits of cloth to cover up their nakedness. For this reason they easily pack up and move from one place to the other, migrating to Thessaly or Asia minor, then coming back, depending on their fortune or chance. Men, women and children carry everything down to the last pot, even travelling with roosters or pigeons. When they can support the financial burden, they load up their mules and oxen with plows and mattresses, along with their wives and children.

This is confirmed by other accounts of the situation, which refer to an increase in population movements in 1842, when adverse conditions in the Greek economy pushed large numbers of peasants to relocate to the Ottoman Empire. Indeed, newspapers of the period estimated that, from the establishment of the Greek state until 1842, between 200,000 and 300,000 individuals abandoned the country and headed for the empire. Although these numbers are almost certainly an exaggeration—given that they aimed to tarnish the reputation of the Ottoman government—they do convey the fluid nature of the population movements during this period. In fact, this mobility seems to have been more prevalent in the opposite direction, involving individuals headed to the Greek state. It would be impossible to interpret the dramatic population increase in the period from 1839 to 1848 any differently.

This pronounced population mobility—supplemented by the phenomenon of temporary and seasonal migration, especially in the nineteenth century—was a variable that the Greek state could not ignore as it was a direct challenge to state power and its civilising goals; seasonally migrating livestock farmers were de facto considered evidence of backwardness. They were also a permanent source of danger, thought to be the main component of a system perpetuating banditry. Similarly, wandering vagrants tarnished the image of the Athenian capital and the other cities of the kingdom.

In general, mass or individual mobility was treated as evidence of lawlessness. As the Greek state created incentives to facilitate permanent settlement of displaced peoples, it took care to create a mechanism to control these movements, introducing passports for domestic travel issued by the police authorities in each municipality. It was then the obligation of each individual who reached a region other than the one in which they resided to present themselves at the community's town hall for a passport check and permit, without which a stay in another municipality was illegal. The rationale behind these domestic passports was expressed by Deliyannis in 1862:

> It is to be hoped that this law on internal passports will be abolished, and the passport requirement be lifted so that citizens will be able to move unhindered through the territory. This law implies a degree of suspicion on the part of the state towards the good intentions of its own people, and obliges them to remain stuck in their homes, and allows them to leave their place of residence for another part of the land only when the authority representing the state examines the case and is convinced that such movement of individuals does not comprise a threat. In short, it is a law that is repressive, and assumes that the normal situation is one where the citizens have immoral intentions and is accordingly suspicious of them, and it serves to aggravate the repressive actions of the police force beyond what is proper ...

The population's mobility, or even the rapid rate of natural population growth, led many observers to reach another conclusion: the population density per square kilometre was extremely low at the beginning of this period, and though it would more than double by the end of the period, it was still considered low compared with Western European averages. According to

Soutsos, this explained the country's economic problems, yet it also offered some solutions:

> Our country's small population is the reason why part of it still lies uncultivated and that national industry lacks even a minimum of necessary manpower. Wages are often extremely high, which not only causes great harm to the wage labourers who cultivate these lands, but also harms consumers due to the appreciation of these products, as well as industrial enterprises whose products are then sold abroad. This small population leads to another conclusion as well—the introduction and use of machines in our economy will be of great benefit, since the latter will help compensate for this much-felt lack of work hands.

That Greece was a very sparsely inhabited country also served to encourage many Europeans to relocate to the newly founded state. However, very few of these attempts proved successful—perhaps due to the lack of a solution to the problem of national lands—with the exception of a few Germans, remnants of the Bavarian army that accompanied Otto to Greece, who settled in Heraklion of Attica, creating their own settlement. This sparseness in population would largely determine population movements in the country as well as the differential demographic development among its regions.

5.2: Distribution (%) of the Population of Greece by Geographic Regions, 1839–79

	1828	*1839*	*1845*	*1861*	*1870*	*1879*
Central Greece	30.7	31.4	33.2	36.6	31.6	33.2
Peloponnese	55.4	54.0	52.6	51.9	44.3	44.3
Cyclades	12.6	13.3	12.9	10.8	8.5	8.0
Ionian	–	–	–	–	15.0	13.9
Thessaly	1.3	1.2	1.3	0.8	0.5	0.6
Total	100.0	100.0	100.0	100.0	100.0	100.0

Observations: Until the census of 1879, the province of Skopelos was included in the region of Thessaly.
Source: Based on information in G. Siambos, *Δημογραφική εξέλιξις της νεωτέρας Ελλάδος*, Athens: 1971, p. 40.

Population growth was not consistent throughout Greece: Eastern Central Greece, with the exception of the province of Livadia, saw an impressive increase in population—Psychogios calculated annual increases ranging from 2.1 to 2.9 per cent from 1839 to 1861—while Attica experienced the most growth. The naming of Athens as national capital led to an explosion in economic and construction activity in the region, thus attracting a significant number of immigrants.

With the exception of Syros, the islands experienced very weak demographic growth. In the Peloponnese, only the provinces of Patras and Kalamata experienced population growth comparable with that of Eastern Central Greece. Rural regions such as the Aegean Islands lost much of their populations to other regions of the kingdom.

5.3: Change (%) in the Population within the Greek Kingdom's Geographical Regions, 1828–1907

	1839/ 1828	1845/ 1839	1861/ 1845	1870/ 1861	1879/ 1870	1889/ 1879	1896/ 1889	1907/ 1896
Central Greece	12.1	23.2	25.7	15.0	20.8	20.3	13.4	18.3
Peloponnese	6.7	13.5	12.7	13.5	15.0	8.1	11.1	3.8
Cyclades	15.8	12.7	–4.8	5.1	8.9	–3.0	3.1	–3.7
Ionian islands	–	–	–	–	6.8	2.1	5.9	0.8
Thessaly	–	–	–	–	–	–	14.1	7.3
Total	9.4	16.5	14.3	32.9	15.2	30.3	11.3	8.1

Source: Based on information in G. Siambos, *Δημογραφική εξέλιξις*, p. 40.

A significant share of the population movements during this period must also be attributed to attempted takeovers of new lands. Existing testimonies confirm this, as does the fact that a large percentage of the population was highly mobile—a previously mentioned phenomenon. At the time, the population was at least two-thirds rural, and it was only natural that the freeing-up of land in flat regions would act as an incentive to relocate from the mountainous regions, though various obstacles certainly presented themselves in the process. Malaria, for example, plagued the flat regions for many years and was a huge obstacle for the permanent relocation of populations to the plains and the utilisation of this fertile land. This remained the case for many years.

In his demographic studies, V. Valaoras argued that until 1890 the net inflow or outflow of the Greek kingdom's population was zero, or close to it. But this should not be taken to mean an absence of migratory movements. On the contrary, as already mentioned, population movements existed, and often on a large scale. It is just that counterbalancing movements also existed that maintained a balance in the equilibrium of this migration. The strongest waves of immigration away from Greece manifested themselves in the middle of the nineteenth century. The Anglo-Turkish trade treaty of 1838, the Treaty of Paris in 1856 (which internationalised navigation on the Danube and the Black Sea), and the beginning of construction of the Suez Canal in 1858 all created conditions for the establishment of migratory movements in directions that had not been exploited to any great extent. Romania, Egypt and the Ottoman Empire became desired destinations for inhabitants of certain regions in the Greek kingdom such as Evritania, Kinouria and the Aegean Islands. Following their incorporation into the Greek state, this was also true for Cephalonia and Magnesia. In all these cases, the movements were temporary, another factor that ensured a balanced migratory equation.

The lack of clarity in the scholarship on population size is due to the weaknesses of the available statistics. Though the Bavarians had attempted to establish the necessary mechanisms for collecting statistical information and a registry, neither of the two would survive after the fall of Otto. Statistics only truly became a tool for the state in the twentieth century. Previously, they were simply an aid, in the most optimistic of assessments. This certainly informed the state's appearance at the time, as well as the way it exercised power and implemented policies. Up until the twentieth century, the small quantity and poor quality of information available was a result of both state weakness and the population's refusal to adapt to its government's standards.

Slow transformations

The economy necessarily played its part in the complete dismantling, or at least deterioration, of the Greek state's achievements, with observers noting nothing but stagnation, delay and failure. Here, too, these impressions played a decisive role in comparisons with the great expectations harboured for Greece and the role they hoped the country would play. A lack of statistical information and indifference in using it in cases when it existed certainly helped shape this impression.

Today, we have a well-researched understanding of the Greek economic situation in the nineteenth century. Information is still lacking, but not so much as to inhibit our understanding of general trends and key processes. The first observation that can be made is that the Greek economy transformed throughout the nineteenth century. The pace of this transformation was slow, but the change was certainly visible and anything but negligible. This can be seen in the composition of the economically active population. In 1861, the first year for which we have data, the primary sector employed roughly two-thirds of the economically active population (74 per cent). The corresponding figure for 1879 to 1881 dropped to 69.9 per cent. This reduction benefited both the secondary sector, which by 1879 to 1881 employed 11.8 per cent of the population, and the tertiary, which grew from 16 per cent in 1861 to 18.3 per cent in 1881.[3]

While Greece was still an agrarian nation in the early 1880s, forms of employment had begun to diversify. The landscape was now completely different from the country of farmers, shepherds, ship-owners and merchants that Otto encountered when he first landed in Nafplion. Urban activity, even if it was not very significant, could no longer be ignored. Nor could the existence of populations involved in manufacturing activities. The evolving distribution of GDP in sectors of economic activity tells a similar if not more detailed story. In the decade spanning from 1833 to 1842, that is, in the first decade of the Greek state's existence, more than 80 per cent of national GDP was produced in the primary sector. This should come as no surprise. The situation changed in the following years: in the decade spanning from 1873 to 1882, the contribution of primary sector production decreased by ten percentage points. Meanwhile, the secondary sector had increased its contribution seven times over. Though these changes do not indicate radical transformations, by the 1880s Greece had certainly diversified its economic base.

Thus it is clear from the above observations that the Greek economy grew at a low, though not insignificant, rate. Additionally, it should be noted that the growth rates of Greek GDP did not differ significantly from those of other European countries over the course of the nineteenth century; in fact, the opposite was true. According to the available data, the Greek economy began as the poorest among all of the Mediterranean economies. But in the period for which we have information, it managed to make up the gap, surpassing Portugal and converging with the other economies—with the exception of course of the United States, the fastest growing economy in the world.

The agrarian economy played a decisive role in these developments, supporting economic expansion, absorbing rapid population growth and nourishing rural populations. In fact, during the 1830s, the nation's rural economy was rapidly reconstituted as a growing population sought to occupy new lands formerly occupied by the Ottomans. In those years, cultivators enjoyed a favourable relationship with these lands. The vast majority of cultivation consisted of annual crops grown for purposes of consumption: mostly grains, which were a cornerstone of the population's diet. Livestock cultivation also played an important role and was seasonally migratory to a large extent. As for other crops, particularly perennial ones, it took considerable time for them to recover from the devastation wreaked by the War of Independence. Olive cultivation may have been an exception to this, as it played an important role, especially in certain areas.

5.4: Per Capita Gross Domestic Product at Constant Prices, 1834–1912
(In Latin Monetary Union Drachmas)

Year		*Base Year*		
		1860	*1887*	*1914*
		Average yearly increase %		
1833–4	104.20		124.50	169.90
1835–9	131.70	5.28	160.10	226.50
1840–4	113.90	–2.70	138.20	194.20
1845–9	100.10	–2.42	121.70	167.60
1850–4	110.90	2.16	133.60	192.20
1855–9	125.80	2.69	150.80	222.80
1860–4	141.10	2.43	166.40	226.20
1865–9	135.60	–0.78	157.30	211.70
1870–4	138.74	0.46	157.32	208.80
1875–9	141.54	0.40	159.92	207.84

Observation: 'Base years' are those for which the deflator was used to calculate true size.
Source: G. Kostelenos et al., *Ακαθάριστο Εγχώριο Προϊόν 1830–1939.*

But a crop that did not directly concern the diet of Greek populations soon took on a crucial role in the rural economy: it was the currant, chiefly destined for Britain, to be used in pastries. The first official information available on the cultivation of currants came from the Kapodistrias period: in 1830, its cultivation utilised 38,000 *stremmas* of coastal area stretching from Patras to Corinth, while annual production reached 19,000,000 Venetian litres. After the late 1830s, currant cultivation spread beyond its original limits to a larger swath of the Peloponnese, also reaching coastal areas of mainland Greece such as Missolonghi. Twenty years after the first available statistical information, in 1851, the total cultivated land covered 172,578 *stremmas* and produced 86,289,000 Venetian litres per year.

By 1870, currant cultivation surpassed 300,000 *stremmas* and a yearly production of 115,000,000 litres. From this period onwards, currant cultivation was expanded throughout the country. Adoption of the law distributing national lands greatly facilitated the usage of new territories for currant cultivation, a trend reinforced by lax lending practices, both from banks and other sources. Finally, the *phylloxera*[4] that affected French vineyards in 1878 granted Greece an extremely large market for currants—thanks to the demands of the French wine industry.

5.5: Real GDP Per Capita in International Dollars with 1990 Purchasing Power Parity

	Greece	*Portugal*	*Spain*	*Italy*	*USA*	*France*	*UK*	*Germany*
1850–4	752	946	1478	–	–	–	–	–
1860–4	957	824	1752	1427	–	–	–	–
1870–4	984	932	1922	1466	2537	1969	3384	2021
	Synthetic Index of Annual Change, Per Capita Real GDP %							
1852–72	1.34	-0.08	1.31	0.27	–	–	–	–
1872–92	1.04	0.81	0.92	0.39	1.59	1.13	0.86	1.25

Source: G. Kostelenos et al., *Εγχώριο Προϊόν 1830–1939.*

These developments help explain the emergence of industry in the Greek economy. Despite the objections frequently raised about the nature of Greek industrialisation—objections mostly based on rather uneven and unfair comparisons with Western Europe—it should be noted that industry made its appearance and was able to guide the transformation of the Greek economy. Plenty of factors determined the fate of the Greek economy in the 1860s, factors linked to the impetus provided by the development of the agrarian economy, in terms of both supply and demand and certainly in terms of raw materials.

This period of industrial development was not unrelated to the advent of a new era in Western European economies, particularly in industries of higher value added activities, and to the emergence of needs that could be filled, and eventually were met, by South Eastern Europe and the Eastern Mediterranean Basin. Indeed, the industrialisation of the Greek economy is not a phenomenon that can be exclusively explained endogenously and studied in isolation from international developments; rather, it was a process consistent with similar developments in the wider Eastern Mediterranean region (the Ottoman Empire and Mediterranean Europe). The establishment of small urban industrial pockets in ports or coastal zones supplying local and regional demands of cities and areas of industrial agriculture was linked to a revaluation of the international division of labour; industrial sectors with lower added value (hence less profitable and dynamic) shifted towards the economic periphery and its markets. This same pattern could be seen elsewhere, perhaps most noticeably in the mining sector, where international demand gave rise to extremely favourable conditions for development: legislation regulating extraction of materials from the earth (the first in 1861 and the second in 1867) led to impressive growth in this exclusively export-oriented sector. In 1875, the eighteen mining enterprises in the country, all founded between 1869 and 1873, constituted a paid-up capital of over 20 million drachmas, among which one company, the Lavrio Mining Company, accounted for 15 million, an impressive sum by Greek standards.

In both Greece and the broader Eastern Mediterranean region, during the period that began with the cotton crisis due to the American Civil War and ended with the Great Depression, industries that specialised in cotton textiles and other unrefined products moved closer to the areas that consumed the goods they produced—that is, to the poor urban and rural populations of South Eastern Europe. In other cases, such as the milling industry, the only change was pursuit of a higher percentage of profit on behalf of wheat importers. The progressive growth of urban populations created conditions for the profitable milling of imported grains. One could hardly expect anything otherwise, since Greece was lacking all the natural and human resources and capabilities that could reshape the Greek economy.

The characteristics of this first wave of national industrialisation from 1865 to 1870 and from 1885 to 1890 indicate its limited nature: it was concentrated in cities and ports—mostly oriented towards foreign trade and easily accessible raw materials and fuel; it focused on sectors producing basic consumer goods; and its development was limited by the domestic market, though the mining sector was a clear exception to this.

It is impossible to understand the process by which industrialisation came about in Greece would without accounting for domestic circumstances—the monetary expansion of the 1860s, for example, but also the generally more liberal monetary policy that was possible from that moment onwards due to a transition away from the convertibility of the drachma. In other words, if seen from the perspective of the financial sector, the development of the Greek economy was related to the abandonment—perhaps unintended—of the economic orthodoxy of convertible currency and the introduction of forced circulation, providing low-cost funding to the public sector. As part of this process, forces were unleashed that supported development of the Greek economy. But these same forces then became obstacles to further economic development, to the extent that the public sector proved competitive with the private sector in absorbing available capital.

While Greek industry developed, another sector of the Greek economy also experienced radical changes: shipping, one of the most important Greek economic activities of international scope. The development of Greek shipping was closely related to the exponential increase of grain exports from the Black Sea and Britain's gradual extrication from Eastern Mediterranean trade. It also benefited from the ban on commercial monopolies and commencement of international trade on the Danube and Black Sea. The rapid development of Greek enterprises associated with sea trade and transport was due to their successful integration into the broader European economy, and, in particular, the transportation of raw materials and industrial products from the Black Sea to Western Europe and vice versa.

Between 1830 and 1860, Greek shipping reinvented itself after the hardships of the War of Independence, growing at a breakneck pace thanks to technical expertise, available capital and pre-existing experience. Traditional Greek nautical centres sought to restore their former power, benefiting from Ermoupoli, by then the most important centre for construction and the financing of ships. In 1870, it was estimated that almost all the 2,500 seagoing ships owned by Greeks had been built at islands and ports of the Aegean and Ionian Seas. This first period came to be known as the Chiot phase, thanks to the major role played by Chiot entrepreneurs in commercial naval operations. It was an era of growth for entrepreneurial families, including the Rallis, Rodokanakis, Petrokokkinos and Skilitsis clans, who developed their activities on an international scale, combining commercial, credit and shipping activities. As noteworthy as these examples are, we must not forget that during this period Greek shipping moved forward according to a model that had taken shape before the War of Independence, a model fundamentally focused on the Greek state as the centre of its activity.

The international environment clearly had a decisive influence on the formation of the Greek economy. It could not have been any different, as the Greek economy was small and exposed to the effects of the international economy. Its development can only be understood through the constant influx of business capital. For example, as A. Fragkiadis has aptly shown, the national chronic trade deficit could not have been sustained without capital inflows. In fact, it is reasonable to assume that nineteenth-century Greece was a centre for important business networks headquartered in other countries that took every available opportunity to invest in Greece. Initially, Ermoupoli maintained a leading role as key mediator in the Eastern Mediterranean. Especially in the first decade after the formation of the Greek state, merchant trade grew at an incredible rate, and it could be argued that these profits alone were sufficient to cover a majority, if not all, of the trade deficit.

The process of financing the Greek shipping fleet's reconstruction after the War of Independence and the development of currant cultivation—both of which required large investments—can also be explained by the influx of foreign capital. The extent of this process inevitably leads to the question of Greeks living beyond the boundaries of the Greek state; a large portion of these important capital flows financing all economic activity in Greece seemed to stem from them.

In summary, it could be argued that the Greek economy of the nineteenth century managed to avoid the potential 'speed bumps' associated with extremely rapid demographic growth. It is also reasonable to assume that the system for protecting private property adopted by the Greek state created an environment favourable to economic activity, all the more so as the nineteenth century progressed. To be sure, the Greek economy was also able to take advantage of each opportunity granted by the international economy to strengthen its position, improving the Greek state's ranking in an international competition with other states of South Eastern Europe. That it was unable to improve its international ranking is perhaps more easily explained than many usually argue: more than any other factor, the small size of the national market was an extremely disadvantageous starting point.

Cities

Some broad but reliable estimates from the Kapodistrian period attest that no more than a total of 60,000 individuals—around 8 per cent of the population—resided in settlements of more than 5,000 residents. As provisional as these figures are, they provide a sense of Greece in 1828, a time in which the nation's total urban population was comparable to 1844. Over this period, no dramatic changes took place in comparison with the Kapodistrian period, and in fact overall changes were quite minimal. The total population living in settlements of more than 5,000 people amounted to 110,523 inhabitants, a number that corresponded to less than 8.5 per cent of the kingdom's total population that year. This is yet another indicator of the painful ways in which Greece changed in its first years of existence; it also points to the very clear continuities with the Ottoman system, since urban hierarchies had hardly changed.

Though Greek cities stubbornly refused to grow in the first decades of the kingdom's existence, it is worth noting that the sectors of urban planning and reconstruction developed significantly during both the Kapodistrian and Bavarian eras. In some cases, this work was purely symbolic, as in the demolition of the stone wall surrounding Athens, rendering it an 'open city'. In other cases, it was much more substantial. E. Manitakis, colonel of the Engineering Corps and director of public works for the Ministry of the Interior, declared in 1866 that ten new cities had been built and another twenty-three rebuilt. Efforts at constructing and reconstructing cities were modelled on Western European standards in an attempt at distancing them from their 'Ottoman past'. This project had only limited success, as it lacked both the economic and human resources that would ensure its proper implementation. In fact, any sort of urban momentum was lacking, as all efforts were focused exclusively on reconstruction of the capital.

Prevailing perceptions under Kapodistrias and Otto saw the city as a tool to civilise backward and barbarous rural populations. A classic example was the establishment of Sparta, undertaken at the request of residents in Monemvasia. It was intended to serve the purpose of supervising and civilising the people of Mani, in the same way that the city of Kalamata took on a similar role for the Messinian side of Mani.

A more continuous flow of information regarding the population of the nation's various settlements is available for the period after 1856. Again, the changes observed are not significant compared with the period immediately after the revolution; nor did major changes occur in 1861 or 1870. Rising urban population rates were almost exclusively due to the incorporation of the Ionian Islands, where processes of urbanisation had become more firmly rooted than in the rest of Greece. The census of 1879 even revealed a step backwards, as the rate of urbanisation decreased. This was due to inclusion of data from Thessaly, annexed in 1881, where urban development lagged in relation to the Greek kingdom at large.

Changes also occurred in this area. Yet to understand what these numbers represent, they need to be compared with their European counterparts. For all of Europe, excluding Russia, cities accounted for 18.9 per cent of the population in 1850. Greece lagged behind both in terms of absolute size and rate of urbanisation. The degree of urbanisation was of course not uniform throughout the continent: respective figures include 45 per cent for Britain, 34 per cent for Belgium, and 39 per cent for the Netherlands. But these were the exceptions. In 1850, Germany's urban population represented 15 per cent of the total population, while it was 20 per cent in Italy and 19.4 per cent in France. Spain found itself in a similar position to Greece with 18.5 per cent in

1850, while Portugal stood at 16 per cent. But the Balkan countries lagged behind Greece: for example, 11 per cent of Romania's population and 10 per cent of Serbia's lived in cities by 1850. In conclusion, though the degree of urbanisation expressed a degree of delay in the Greek economy compared with Western European countries, it also underlined its superiority in comparison to neighbouring potential competitors.

5.6: Settlements with More Than 5,000 Inhabitants in Greece, 1856–79

Year	*Number of cities*	*Total population*	*Average size*	*% of Greece's total population*
1856	11	129,095	11,736	11.77
1861	17	213,471	12,185	14.46
1870	19	222,926	11,733	15.29
1879	27	315,505	11,685	13.81

Observations: 1861 includes the Ionian Islands with data from the 1865 census, and 1879 includes data from Thessaly based on the census of 1881.
Source: Calculations based on publicly released statistics.

In quantitative terms, the changes involved in urbanisation were also related to changes in the urban sphere itself. New cities appeared, while others that had previously been relatively insignificant established themselves as important urban centres. Athens, for example, is typical of the latter category: the Bavarian decision to make the city many considered the 'cradle of European civilisation' the kingdom's capital not only had consequences for Athens but for Piraeus too: the latter transformed from a place with a few huts to a real city, and later became a huge harbour—the most important in Greece. The same decision condemned Nafplion, as well as Argos to some extent, to stagnation if not outright decline.

Yet over the course of the entire nineteenth century, Athens did not become an urban centre with particularly different characteristics. The fact that it was the national capital granted it a special place in the urban hierarchy, but its population was not disproportionate to the total national urban population. In 1856, it represented 23.3 per cent of the urban population, with this figure falling in 1861 to 21.2 per cent and to 19.9 per cent in 1870. In 1879, the figure remained virtually unchanged at 20 per cent.

In the realm of urban infrastructure, there were continuities between the Greek state and its Ottoman past. With a non-existent urban tradition as its starting point, the urban transformation would continue slowly and painfully until the 1880s. There was plenty of evidence of surviving Ottoman hierarchies, and as a result it was not surprising that two urban networks emerged, organised according to the geographical orientation of commercial activity: one was oriented westwards, and the other to the East. Few changes were made in the national transportation network. The Greek state still had a long ways to go before it could achieve a more consistent model for urban space and a hierarchical network of urban centres rooted in national government.

5.7: Distribution of Cities by Geographic Region, 1856–79

	1856		*1861*		*1870*		*1879*	
	Cities	*Pop.*	*Cities*	*Pop.*	*Cities*	*Pop.*	*Cities*	*Pop*
Peloponnese	4	39,627	6	53,746	7	57,691	9	84,232
Mainland/Evia	2	36,126	3	53,809	4	67,634	8	118,808
Mainland/Evia without Athens and Piraeus	–	–	1	6,059	2	12,161	6	34,379
Islands	5	53,342	4	44,628	4	42,854	4	39,600
The Ionian	–	–	4	61,288	4	54,747	4	54,133
Thessaly	–	–	–	–	–	–	2	18,732
TOTAL	11	129,095	17	213,471	19	222,926	27	315,505

From a healthy state to the discipline of health

The Bavarians' meticulous approach to creating an institutional framework for organising the Greek kingdom necessarily had to account for an extremely sensitive sector: public health. This sector provided all the care that the kingdom offered its subjects and served to demonstrate the nature and limits of state intervention.

In the 1830s, even in Western Europe, treating and eradicating disease was rarely a government priority. Nevertheless, advances were made in these same years, since health policy interventions managed to relegate major disease epidemics (such as the plague) to the past, significantly reducing population mortality rates.

From this perspective, diseases and their prevention were another element in the mosaic of circumstances that each country and society represented: they expressed the makeup of the population, but also the state's ability to impose its policies on it. An immediate outcome was the progressive classification of diseases as a particular type of social ill to be identified and isolated from society. Such a conception was an inherent element of Western state practices in the nineteenth century. Consequently, the Bavarians necessarily carved out their health policies based on the same ideas.

Configuration of the Greek public administration's organisational structure, and more specifically the responsibilities of the secretary of the interior, provided for the creation of a special department supervised by a medical consultant with the goal of organising a 'health service patrol', a term I have previously referred to, which must not be construed in its current meaning. Its duties could only be very general and advisory in nature, insofar as the existing infrastructure was rudimentary. Above all, protection against the plague was necessary, necessitating health outposts and quarantines.

This was no accident. The Greek kingdom was part of a region—the Eastern Mediterranean—in which the most threatening epidemic, the plague, continued to claim large numbers of victims and inhibit trade until the end of the nineteenth century. Controlling it and limiting its presence within state borders was an immediate priority. Among other things, this distanced the Greeks from the health and culture of the East. In other words, it was crucial because of the destruction potentially caused by an epidemic, but also because it demonstrated the difference between being a civilised or an uncivilised state. The urgency of the measures was also related to the Greek kingdom's integration into international shipping networks and to its communication with Western countries: open access for ships with Greek flags in the ports of Western European countries and Russia presupposed an effective Greek health policy, which would act as a guarantee to these respective countries that their ports of departure abided by certain protective health measures.

The Bavarians rapidly set about creating a network of public health services that gradually grew in strength: by the 1840s, health services had been established in twenty-six different territories within the kingdom, employing a significant number of staff. The best quarantines were found in Piraeus, the port of the capital and its only channel of international communication, as well as Ermoupoli, the most important economic centre in the country.

Judging from the results, it could be argued that health inspections were successful, since Greece suffered from the plague only once. This was in Poros in 1837, when despite—or perhaps due to—excessive brutality directed at the island's inhabitants, the epidemic was isolated and eventually controlled. Yet the extent to which these health protection measures decisively protected the population is open to question. Perhaps it was simply the case that Greece avoided suffering major epidemics during this period due to its small and dispersed population, in combination with a lack of large urban centres.

In addition, the population would often oppose the imposition of health measures, continually circumventing them. For example, in Poros there were many violations of health regulations in 1837—which is partly why an epidemic spread to the island—while in Mani residents reacted aggressively to any attempts at external control or limiting of communication with neighbouring areas. In Rumely, daily border crossings of settlers bordering the Ottoman territories rendered these health measures extremely unpopular, and clearly created conditions ripe for violating them. For this reason, the state administration often had to rely on nothing more than blind faith when implementing these regulations. Furthermore, rampant smuggling throughout the nineteenth century highlighted the weak links in these border controls. Finally, the ease with which the plague crossed the Greek border in the early twentieth century highlighted the difficulties in controlling a disease that was not transmitted from human to human.

Thus the Greek state gradually delineated its territory, classifying and ranking the region under its control, eventually creating basic mechanisms by which to supervise incoming populations. But this was an undoubtedly lengthy process, requiring both the consent and participation of these peoples. This problem would become apparent in its entirety in 1854 with the outbreak of the cholera epidemic in Piraeus.

In contrast to the prevailing view, the cholera epidemic of 1854 did not arrive from the East—it came from the West. It appeared for the first time in June 1854 among the French troops that had occupied Piraeus, and within three months it had taken the lives of one-fifth of the 6,000-man army corps. It then affected an occupying British regiment and claimed a number of victims among the city's population (ninety-nine in total). The delay in isolating Piraeus due to the fact that the military occupation could not be contained meant that the disease soon spread to the islands, including Aegina, Tinos, Syros, Mykonos and Paros. But the situation in Athens proved to be the worst.

In Athens, the epidemic began in October 1845, that is, after it had ended in Piraeus. For this reason, it was not thought to have originated from the occupying army, but rather from a vessel coming from the islands that landed its crew and cargo illegally on a beach near Attica in order to avoid a health inspection. Whether or not this was actually the case is of little consequence;

it is simply an example of how easy it was to evade health protection measures. The epidemic caused 1,500 deaths in the capital and spread to Fthiotida, Parnassida, Aitoloakarniania and the Peloponnese. It also appeared on the Ionian Islands, which were under British protection at the time.

Athens's experience with cholera may not have led to an extremely high number of casualties, but it was particularly traumatic and exposed issues that would soon play a key role in efforts to tackle poverty and disease. As the first cases of cholera manifested themselves, all the wealthy inhabitants of the city, or at least those who could afford the move financially, abandoned it. In a city with a population of more than 30,000 inhabitants, only around 20,000 remained, a figure that includes those who fell victim to cholera. Those who suffered most were the poorest and most deprived members of the population, and the harsh reality of poverty and disease reared its head. It was no coincidence that, just two years after the outbreak, the legal foundations were laid out for a city hospital that opened its doors in 1858.

The Greek state's limited ability to cope with disease epidemics and general health problems was made clear by the high levels of mortality prevailing throughout the nineteenth and early twentieth centuries. Estimates for mortality in Greece during the 1850s indicate a rate of 36.8 per thousand, which fell to 26.3 per thousand by the first decade of the twentieth century, in contrast to figures from other countries such as Britain (22.5 and 13.8), Russia (36.5 and 17.4) and France (23.8 and 17.4). In short, Greece's mortality rates were significantly higher than France's or Britain's, but similar to Russia's.

As expected, high mortality rates were much more pronounced at younger ages, as the graph on infant mortality below illustrates. The extremely high mortality rates for infants, toddlers and children largely determined overall mortality and underlined the limited effectiveness of health regulations at the time. Life expectancy was also very low, around twenty-nine years of age in the nineteenth century and thirty-five years in the early twentieth. About, in a rare instance of incisive commentary, wrote the following about the high child mortality rate:

> In the summer children die like flies. Those that survive usually have weak legs and an inflated stomach until thirteen–fourteen years of age. Parents take very little care of them and do not care for much else. They know that until thirteen years of age, their children's lives are nearly temporary. One day I asked a senior civil servant how many children he had. He counted on his fingers and responded: 'Eleven or twelve, I don't know. Seven have survived.'

The limited effectiveness of public health interventions did not mean that these efforts were lacking or misplaced. In the case of smallpox, for example, a

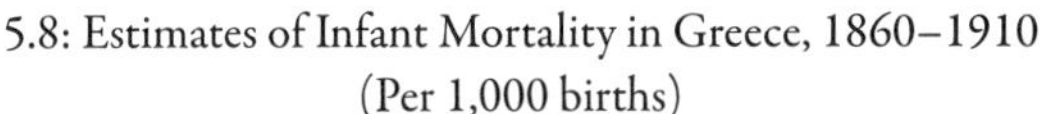

5.8: Estimates of Infant Mortality in Greece, 1860–1910
(Per 1,000 births)

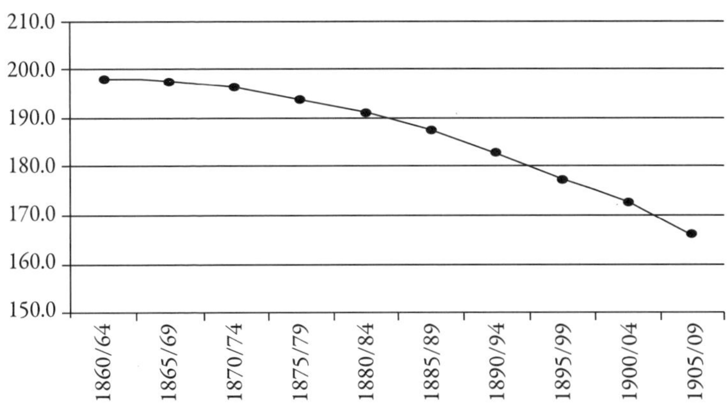

Source: V. Valaoras, *Δημογραφική ιστορία της συγχρόνου Ελλάδος (1860–1965)*, reprint, *Επιθεώρησις Οικονομικών και Πολιτικών Επιστημών*, Athens: 1960, p. 24.

disease that was often feared even more than the plague, the Bavarians sought to take preventative measures from the very outset. By royal decree in 1835, the Bavarian government required that everybody be vaccinated. No child that had not been vaccinated or infected would be allowed to attend a school or other educational institution, to practise any trade, and would certainly not be allowed to work in the public sector.

Whether these measures were effective is highly doubtful. In the following years, smallpox appeared, often in epidemics, some of which were caused by the mass arrivals of refugees in cities in the wake of various conflicts. Even in the early twentieth century, Konstantinos Savvas, professor at the University of Athens, noted that

> the disease, which, alas, has brought the greatest destruction on us, is smallpox. And even recently, people all over the country have fallen victim to smallpox epidemics. In the centre of Athens 2,312 people have been infected and 518 have died. ... One can judge how civilised a state is by the number of its people who die each year from smallpox.

It is also important to emphasise that the process by which a population assimilates scientific medical practices is very gradual. Taking this into account, the marked reluctance of inhabitants to vaccinate themselves and their children is not surprising; all the more so since it was widely believed that vaccination during an epidemic increased a healthy individual's chances of contracting the disease. In 1864, when smallpox had spread throughout the state and preventive (and then repressive) measures had failed, the government even appealed to the Holy Synod to bring the situation under control.

However, not even the Holy Synod's threats were enough to ensure the success of state goals. While in Western Europe smallpox disappeared as a threat to the population after the introduction of compulsory vaccination in the the 1850s and 1860s, Greece would have to wait a few decades more, until conditions granted the state more control over its populations, vaccination practices were accepted, and lastly, elementary practices in cleanliness and hygiene were introduced. Hence smallpox was only eradicated in Greece after implementation of a strict and systematic national vaccination programme in 1924, after which only sporadic and curable cases were recorded.

But things were very different in the nineteenth century. Even late in the century, it was common for the poorer urban classes to show a profound reluctance to vaccinate, while the founding of the quarantine in Athens as a place to isolate patients provoked terror and flight, since isolation was primarily intended to save the remaining inhabitants of the city and not the patients themselves. Even in the late nineteenth century, separation from relatives and restrictions on freedom were not commonly accepted practices for the Greek population.

Apart from the solutions offered by medicine, the reduction of disease was directly connected to improved hygiene conditions. Modern sewage and water systems, important mechanisms for preventing many diseases, appeared with great delay, even in Athens. It was only with the Marathon Dam, built in 1925, and the introduction of a water supply system in Athens and Piraeus, that incidences of typhoid fever and dysentery—both very common in the nineteenth century—significantly reduced. Living conditions, diet and personal hygiene also played an important role in reducing disease, though this is difficult to document.

Of paramount importance for questions of public health was the drying of marshes and the prevention and treatment of 'intermittent fevers', namely malaria, which for a long time was a main cause of disease in Greece. Upon its arrival in Greece, the Bavarian government began the process of draining the marsh of Kifisos, and later drained the swamps in Chalcis and Bersova, outside of Tripoli. However, it would appear these efforts were not particularly effective, and that Otto's regime was incapable of proceeding with large-scale projects in a sector with particularly high costs. Thus About had every right to claim that

> Greece is an unsalutary place. The fertile plains, steep rocks and smiling shores all hide a fever: it breathes poison into the scented orange groves. One could say that in this aging Eastern land, the air itself has decayed. Spring and autumn provoke fever throughout the country. Children die, adults suffer, and drainage of the marshes would require a few million, for the country to recover and a people to be saved. Thankfully the Greek race is so resilient that the fever only kills the small children ...

Twenty years after its creation, the Greek state was an unhealthy place, and there is no doubt what About meant in geographical and cultural terms: the little kingdom was a part of the 'aging East' and its prevailing air of decay. The robustness and health of the West was lacking. Greece had not yet managed to join the ranks of civilised nations and was still considered a dangerous place. And the reason was clearly political: though the marshes could be drained if the government provided the requisite funding, there was little political will to do so.

The draining of Kopaida—which was carried out for the purposes of cultivation—constituted the major project against malaria. Throughout the nineteenth century, the country's residential network continued to be defined by the existence or absence of these marshlands, while agricultural activities were oriented in a similar manner. Progress in this sector was very gradual, and yet again the problem of malaria would only be addressed during the interwar period with its large waterworks projects. In fact, the malaria problem would not be permanently resolved for the Greeks until after the Second World War with the large-scale use of insecticides.

Treatment of epidemic diseases demonstrated the limits of state policy in the health sector. Again, a lack of financial and human resources had a catalytic effect on the final result, rendering implementation of a disciplined health system wishful thinking for most of the nineteenth century. Nevertheless, an effort was made, and the intentions were good. Efforts were made to extend the presence of government health mechanisms throughout the country, which at the very least enabled the possibility of communication in the case of an epidemic. To this end, in 1833 the state appointed a doctor to each prefecture. Along with the prefect, judge, tax collector, metropolitan and ranking officer, the addition of a head doctor in each prefecture ensured that medicine joined these ranks as well. This practice of inserting doctors into provincial regions continued for a long time, though whether or not it was effective often became the subject of political debate.

The focus of the Greek public administration in the nineteenth century was on preventing the outbreak of major epidemics in urban centres. Public health did not concern individuals or groups, but rather the entire population. Health and diseases were problems that families needed to confront themselves—or with the help of charitable organisations. The state was concerned with its own health; references to health regulations indicated nothing more or less than the seclusion of infectious diseases beyond the kingdom's limits.

This same desire to protect state health manifested in the effort to draft an organised corps of doctors, composed of individuals who had studied in Western Europe. Indeed, all practising doctors would soon be required to provide documents proving their qualifications, in addition to a notice confirming that they practised their profession in their homeland. From this point onwards, a conflict emerged between scientific doctors and the empirical ones—phlebotomists, practical physicians, ophthalmologists, common doctors, practical surgeons, barbers, midwives, and so on—a conflict in which the former camp had the support of the state, which sought to impose a scientific and state-mandated health sector.[5] The latter had an advantage in numbers and direct contact with the general population. In essence, the problem was that a specific remedial model was being imposed on a population that could not recognise a direct benefit in it. This is one of the reasons why the mass of empirical doctors was able to survive for such a long time.

The confrontation between scientific and empirical doctors gained its most obvious institutional expression in 1843 with the founding of the Medical Committee, an advisory body under the auspices of the secretary of the interior, which had essentially taken on the organisation of health services in the Greek kingdom. Its first members were overwhelmingly foreign, and its president was the doctor consultant of the state, Carolus Vipmer, Otto's personal doctor. The Medical Committee, which managed to survive for a very long time—it was renamed the Supreme Health Council in 1922—was heavily involved in the preparation of legislation in the health sector. It also contributed to the establishment of a professional body of doctors. In a short period of time, it soon had to adopt more moderate views, as the overwhelming demand for doctors obliged it to judge empirical doctors less strictly than its members would have wanted. It also made sure to provide incentives to create preparatory schools that would furnish candidates with the knowledge required to practise their profession, at least until the Medical University of Athens could provide the necessary number of scientific doctors.

Here, too, it is possible to note a phenomenon manifest in other fields of state-formation: the state determined those who would exercise power in the health sector, establishing its own networks of power in that particular realm.

Because it was unable to satisfy the demand for care, it was also forced to accept many empirical doctors, who in theory were not supposed to benefit from state recognition—but from the moment a process of legalisation was enabled through public exams, these doctors were accepted as instruments of state power. The scattered information at our disposal shows that the overwhelming majority of the population would continue, at least until the interwar period, to resort to the services of empirical medicine, which operated outside these legal limits. The inability or indifference of the state to intervene in this realm was a contributing factor to this; another was the rural population's slow adjustment to these new conditions.

It is worth noting that efforts at improvement stalled for a long time under Bavarian rule. Some regulations and adjustments were indeed implemented, but there was a clear lack of any effort at changing the status quo. Perceptions on the precise role of the state in relation to public health did not seem to change, and the interwar period would have to arrive before the entire Greek public health system would change radically.

This lack of action was also apparent in the construction and standards of hospitals. In Western Europe, changes in the functions of hospitals occurred gradually, focusing on the transformation from a tool for containing the sick to a tool for disease treatment. Notably, in the Greek case, the hospital as an institution was only integrated into mechanisms for state health much later. One reason for this was the high cost of creating and maintaining a hospital.

As one might expect, the first hospital established in Greece was the military hospital; it is no surprise that the first nursing school was also created on the same site in 1861. This was to be expected not because it arose out of some tradition established during the course of the War of Independence, but because Bavarian troops arriving in Greece demanded such nursing support. The existence of an army without its own health service and hospital later became unthinkable.

The first attempt at creating a hospital in the Greek state dates back to 1842, when the Elpis Public Hospital of Athens was founded. A typical example of an institution that sought to provide charitable services to those inhabitants of Athens deprived of material goods and family, the hospital would be matched only in 1858, when the Astikliniki opened. The latter was not a hospital at all, but instead offered medical services to the poor in Athens both on-site and at home. It was founded as a result of the terrible experience of the 1854 cholera epidemic, which had mainly spread among the poorer populations of Athens and Piraeus and mostly afflicted those without the support of a family.

The founding of the Maternity Hospital in 1835 and the Opthalmiatric Hospital in 1843 did not alter the basic facts of the situation, since these institutions aimed to address specific problems from a purely philanthropic perspective and did not provide health services in the modern sense of the term. The Greek state was largely indifferent to the issue of organised healthcare until 1881, when the Evaggelismos Hospital opened its doors as a result of an initiative by Queen Olga. Its founding was undoubtedly a touchstone for national healthcare policy: a Christian-philanthropic approach and the need to support the lowest social classes gave way to an attempt to scientifically treat disease and patients. The reputation of these hospitals and the treatment of disease began to change, a development evidenced by the proliferation of medical facilities towards the end of the nineteenth century and dawn of the twentieth.

These changes presupposed individuals able to support and implement them. According to official statistics, in 1837 there were a total of eighty-five scientific doctors in the Greek kingdom. At the same time, 130 empirical doctors had been granted a permit to practise medicine by the government. Of these doctors, twenty-nine of them were based in Athens, of which about half were foreigners. There was only one doctor in Piraeus, while there were seven in Syros and five in Patras. This group was limited in size, and no matter how much social power its members held, it had very little potential to increase; all the more so in the middle of the nineteenth century, at a time when modern medicine's understanding of disease had not yet been imposed on an international scale. Medical services were urgently needed, and no one tried to ignore this fact. But it became clear that the university would prove barely capable of preparing the doctors that the country needed.

The standards at the university in its early years were extremely poor; it is doubtful whether students acquired any substantial practical experience in the School of Medicine. This changed after the founding of the Astikliniki and Opthalmiatric Hospitals, and the creation of a framework to support students. In these conditions, it is not surprising that the first graduate of medicine, A. Goudas, was awarded his degree in 1843, while for a long time the total number of graduates in Medicine per year could be counted on one hand. The pace only accelerated in 1860, resulting in a gradual increase in the number of scientific doctors, who then formed a critical mass and held great social influence that led to changes in the profession. Furthermore, in 1860 and much more so in the following years, this mass began to gradually renew itself: the old guard of the Medicine School gave way to all those, educated in

France and Germany, who sought to convey a new conception of health and the patient, and, by extension, of public health. Only then were the conditions ripe to transition from the quest for state health to the discipline of health.

If one had to give a symbolic date for this transition, at least as it was perceived, then it could be none other than the founding of the Ministry of Welfare in 1917, which was then renamed the Ministry of Health, Welfare and Care. These developments were accelerated by the influx of refugees arriving in urban centres and their miserable living conditions, leading to higher mortality rates throughout the Greek state—to take but one example, an epidemic of dengue fever in 1928 affected nearly 1.5 million people, among them Venizelos himself. The Greek government requested the assistance of the League of Nations, and after suggestions from a committee of foreign experts, the new framework for the Greek state's health policy was established.[6] It was a framework that dealt with issues of both hygiene and disease on an individual basis.

Uncertainty

The Crimean War was a turning point in international and political relations, with consequences for all European countries. Geopolitical rivalries turned increasingly tense. In this atmosphere, Otto was overthrown and the country's political elite assumed political power, completing the project they had been forced to leave in limbo since the founding of the Greek state. Around the same time, it became clear that major changes in the functionality of the Greek state would be required in order for it to hold its own in the international arena. Yet the national political situation in the period spanning from 1863 to 1880 would not allow for the realisation of those needs. Timid attempts at addressing the problems, together with reversals and delays, would characterise state policies in this period.

The great crisis of the Eastern Question in 1875–78 would have to dawn in order to convince even the biggest sceptics that Greece was far from achieving its goals, something that many had hoped would happen after Otto's monarchical regime had been overthrown. In fact, the opposite was true, and these goals only moved farther out of reach. Bulgaria's increasing power and influence was the most obvious proof of this. A different conception of state functionality was needed, a conception that rendered state mechanisms more effective, incorporating the entire population into them. The age of Charilaos Trikoupis had arrived.

6

THE FLIGHT FORWARD

(1881–97)

> Those, however, who, like us, believe that instability is imminent in the East—that shortly we shall see events inevitably draw us, too, into the fray, cannot begin to contemplate any change to the system. Rather it is imperative that our efforts focus on completing national military and naval preparations, in accordance with the country's means.[1]

Bipartisanship

Among other things, the Congress of Berlin suggested that Greece and the Ottoman Empire should come to an agreement regarding a redrawing of their borders. The congress suggested that the new border of the two territories be drawn at the Kalama and Penaeus Valleys. In case of a disagreement, it was proposed that the Great Powers would act as mediators to address the problem. Ultimately, it was no more than a proposal; adoption of its prescriptions depended on the goodwill of both parties involved.[2]

Greece, the country that stood to benefit from these new adjustments, had no objections to the proposal. But the Ottoman Empire—acting with the support of the Albanians, who had reacted to the Greek annexation of regions in Epirus—objected to many of the changes in the process of redrawing the border, causing delays. The situation was only resolved by a broader readjustment of diplomatic balances and the Austro-Hungarian Empire's realistic approach to the issue. Finally, the ambassadors of the Great Powers reached an agreement.[3] Although the border agreement reached by the second Convention of Constantinople in March 1881 was not what Greek politicians had hoped for, it also avoided the possibility of military conflict. Greece would be given Thessaly without the region of Elassona and the province of Arta in Epirus—a smaller landmass than the territories suggested during the Congress of Berlin.

In 1881, the arrival of Greek troops in these new territories led to a series of unexpected political developments. At least in theory, the integration of these territories should have been considered a triumph and personal vindication for Alexandros Koumoundouros, the country's prime minister at the time. But this was not the case, with the opposition, led by Trikoupis, harshly criticising the government, holding it responsible for not annexing all the land suggested during the Congress of Berlin. The opposition's tactics eventually proved effective, causing substantial damage to the political landscape.

Timetable 1881–97

1881	Alexandros Koumoundouros government (13 October 1880–3 March 1882). Convention of Constantinople. Annexation of Thessaly and part of Epirus.
1882	Trikoupis government (3 March 1882–19 April 1885).
1885	Elections; Theodoros Deliyannis government (19 April 1885–30 April 1886). Bulgarian occupation of Eastern Roumelia. 'Peace-War' period.
1886	Naval isolation of Piraeus. D. Valvis appointed caretaker prime minister of government (30 April 1886–9 May 1886). Trikoupis government (9 May 1886–24 October 1890).
1887	Elections; Trikoupis triumphs.
1890	Trikoupis defeated in elections. Theodoros Deliyannis government (24 October 1890–18 February 1892).
1892	Deliyannis removed from office. Konstantinos Konstantopoulos government (18 February 1892–10 June 1892). Elections. Trikoupis government (10 June 1892–3 May 1893).
1893	Trikoupis resigns. Sotiropoulos government (3 May 1893–30 October 1893). New Trikoupis government (30 October 1893–12 January 1895). Internal Macedonian Revolutionary Organisation (EMEO) founded in Thessaloniki.
1894	National Society is founded.
1895	Trikoupis's resignation. N. Deliyannis government (12 January 1895–31 May 1895). Elections in which Trikoupis is not elected to Parliament and withdraws from politics. Theodoros Deliyannis government (31 May 1895–18 April 1897).
1896	Trikoupis's death. Olympic games. A new rebellion in Crete.

1897 The Greek government attempts to occupy Crete. Greco-Turkish War. Defeat of the Greek army. Treaty of Constantinople. Crete becomes autonomous. Deliyannis's government falls. Successive governments led by D. Rallis (18 April 1897–21 September 1897) and Andreas Zaimis (21 September 1897–2 April 1899).

Despite Koumoundouros's hopes to the contrary, Trikoupis won a majority in Parliament in the elections of December 1881, as many of the MPs from recently annexed territories flocked to join the latter's party. This defeat and the criticism he was subjected to for mishandling Thessaly's annexation, combined with a bout of illness, led Koumoundouros to abandon politics. He died shortly thereafter in 1883. Theodoros Deliyannis assumed his party's leadership, and as a result, the two main parliamentary parties became fully consolidated, absorbing the other, smaller parliamentary groups.[4]

The emergence of Trikoupis and Deliyannis as party leaders launched an uncommonly long period of stability in Greek politics based on a two-party system. For G. Aspreas, Parliament in 1881

> presented the first party-based foundations for political principles from the perspective of the state, and despite the fact that these political expressions were subject to deterioration in the ensuing political conflict, they survived after an inconclusive battle for some years, taking root on terrain that was both conducive to their evolution into personal parties due to a lack of political education and prohibitive to the cultivation of a principled party system.[5]

The two parties were first assembled in the 1881 elections, took shape in the first session of the ninth term (1882) and were consolidated in the second session of the same term (1883). Newly appointed ministers entering Greek Parliament upon the annexation of the Ionian Islands and Thessaly—many of them former supporters of Deligiorgis—would prove to be many of the ministers in Trikoupis's party. For his part, Deliyannis managed to win over most of Koumoundouros's supporters, though his forceful insistence on maintaining party leadership and the emergence of new partisan dynamics led unsatisfied MPs to shift their allegiance in another direction.

Charilaos Trikoupis was a shining example of the Greek political oligarchy. Son of Spyridon Trikoupis and nephew of Alexandros Mavrokordatos, he possessed the necessary social capital to thrive in Greek politics—perhaps more so than any other politician. He had also pursued studies in France and had lived for many years in Paris and London, where he acted as secretary to the Greek embassy, headed by his father. He was thus able to acquire more than sufficient knowledge of international politics and diplomacy—which would be demonstrated for the first time during negotiations for the annexation of the Ionian Islands. His rival over the following fifteen years, Theodoros Deliyannis, was the descendant of another political family: he was nephew of Kanellos Deliyannis, a fighter in the War of Independence.

This bipartisan arrangement did not lead to the creation of modern political parties. Many years would have to pass for this system of parliamentary groups to give way to the organisation and hierarchy required by modern party organisations. Prospective MPs continued to be highly temperamental with regard to their party loyalty, which was largely determined by expected electoral results. In 1892, for example, before the elections that Trikoupis would win, of the 643 candidates declared throughout the nation, 316 were Trikoupists, just ninety-eight were Deliyannists, 181 were unaffiliated and forty-eight were supporters of the Konstantopoulos government.[6] The system of voting by lead bead was a catalyst for this, directly contributing to local factionalism and party instability. So, in the elections of 1902, only three regions—Attica, Corfu and Gortynia—had all candidates representing a single political party, while all other regions had candidates from multiple parties on the ballot.[7]

Local parties, or 'factions' as they are often referred to, continued to play an important role. In Patras, for example, two such groups were led by the Rufus and Kalamogdartis families respectively, both of which drew support from the region's notable families. The struggle for political dominance exclusively concerned the provinces where candidates were elected, and as C. Lyrintzis wrote, 'that which exists as a party on the national level is of little importance in the province of Achaia'.[8] He added that local factions identified more directly with national parties only towards the end of the century, and that the development and impact of the latter was ultimately determined by the actions and achievements of local forces. In any case, implementation of the parliamentary principle eventually led to the consolidation of two main party axes, the constant and often large-scale shift of MPs from one party to the other notwithstanding

The age of Bismarck

Trikoupis remained prime minister until 1885. During this time, he rapidly supported an important series of reforms in an attempt to render Greece capable of competing internationally. These reforms were exceedingly necessary, as rapid changes in international politics during the Bismarck era had an immediate impact on the Balkans. First, Italy and Germany soon joined the three powers (Austria, Russia and Britain) already involved in the Eastern Question. Secondly, the Congress of Berlin upset all pre-existing transnational relations by establishing the independence of Serbia and Romania and the founding of a semi-autonomous Bulgaria.[9] Inevitably, as the international system expanded and new countries emerged, the importance of the Eastern Mediterranean diminished. The country's diplomatic status shrank along with it towards the end of the nineteenth century—not that the remaining Balkan states were comparatively better off.[10] All of them, with the exception of the Ottoman Empire, which obviously found itself in a better position, were more or less in the same situation, and this certainly intensified the volatility and complexity of the Eastern Question.

Two possibilities emerged in terms of Greek foreign policy after the Congress of Berlin and the reforms the latter imposed on the Balkans. The first was to side with Turkey in order to confront the Slavic threat, biding its time until the country was ready to face the Ottoman Empire. The other would require a joint effort with the Slavs against the Ottomans. Until at least 1886, Russian influence and the Bulgarian annexation of Eastern Roumelia were also significant factors—especially since Russia gave continued assurances to Greece of its good intentions, gaining many Greek supporters as a result.

Yet the Congress of Berlin had also shown that Greece was running out of time. The annexation of Thessaly and a small piece of Epirus—a palliative for Greek expectations—opened new borders that were much more difficult to manage. Greece would have to readjust its entire approach if it still hoped for a chance to survive. In this context, Trikoupis was the foremost exponent of the need to implement new policies that could not be described exclusively in domestic or international terms, since they required a fundamental reformulation of the perception of the state's role and its position in an international context:

> If some believe that the situation in the East will remain calm for the next ten years, then the policies we are currently implementing are disastrous. If the next decade is peaceful, we should not spend as much on the army and navy as we do and will continue to do, which will surely end up being even more that what has already been recorded in the budget ... Whoever believes that we have a peaceful decade in store must believe that we can find the means in the Ministries of the Army and Navy to help elevate the nation's economy. But all who believe—like us—that there will be upheavals in the East, that there will be certain circumstances that will fatefully drive us to take action, should not in any way think of changing the system

> in place; instead, they must think of completing military and naval preparations in accordance with the nation's needs.[11]

From the moment he came into power, Trikoupis began this flight forward: in his first term, he sought to implement everything that had not been accomplished, or only timidly pursued, over the preceding two decades. His biggest concern was to strengthen Greece's position in the international competition for the legacy of the Ottoman Empire. This initiative of Trikoupist modernisation—and the reactions it caused—must be understood from this perspective. Everything had to be subordinated in the name of strengthening the state, and most important of all, reorganising the military. Without taking these priorities into account, it is impossible to understand Trikoupis's decisions and the subsequent reactions they provoked:

> These issues do not concern the distant future. Greece's politics cannot face questions such as these by pretending they are questions that concern a distant future. Each complication today could possibly expose us to difficulties that we cannot conceive of and should not hope to. This is why we disagree strongly with what has been said about the government: that it exploits war for its own benefit. To the contrary, the government's politics are peaceful. The government will do all in its power to extend the existing peace. The Greek government seeks to create closer relationships with its neighbouring states in every possible way.
>
> As a peace-seeking nation, Greece certainly hopes that peace will prevail; in this matter, Greece's role is not quite so important. As its development depends on others, it must support its military as much as possible, not only with regard to the kingdom's borders but also with regard to its rights and the rights of Hellenism. Greece's politics and the politics of any Greek government are opposed to any aggressive politics. We must take care in every way to develop our military power in keeping with the means at our disposal, and prepare so that each Greek may take up arms in a situation of need, trained in such a way that he will know to carry them, while limiting the burden that this training might impose on the state. To seek more than this would be akin to training the nation, akin to seeking the establishment of an army corresponding to the armies of small states such as Germany or Italy before each of them was unified—that is to say an army that attended to governmental rather than national aims. If we want soldiers for the establishment of the national army, all Greeks must be trained as the best possible soldiers, but not more trained than allowed by the economic means and the population of the state. These are the national policies we must aim for.[12]

Up until 1897, it was impossible to arrive at a general consensus in Greek politics on how the Greek state should expand. Trikoupis's expensive reform project had altered all political and social relationships, and was certainly not welcomed unanimously. His many opponents insisted that massive military expenditure was pointless, and that tactics such as revolts would enable Greece to achieve its goals:

> Personally, I was always of the opinion that we can only succeed in battle through the sudden occupation of neighbouring countries, and not through conscription. After occupying these countries we will gain strength from local resources, but also by conscripting certain men belonging to select age groups, thus conducting defensive war. Based on events that have already taken place, we can be sure that the Great Powers will retreat as they already did in the occupation of Eastern Roumelia.[13]

In 1889, Alexandros Rizos Rangavis expressed a similar view:

> The importance of a reasonable amount of military equipment on both land and sea must not be neglected. But we derive most of our strength from the fact that the stronger parties respect us. This has strengthened and supported us even when we were unarmed; for us, the most costly preparations are of but little importance.[14]

The great division between Trikoupist supporters and those aligning themselves with the opposite camp was maintained, as previously stated, at least until after the Greco-Turkish War of 1897. The conflict's unfavourable outcome for Greece demonstrated that the country could have no hopes for the future without radical reorganisation of the army and, more generally, a reorganisation of the state as suggested by Trikoupis.

The changes ushered in by Trikoupis were not only limited to the priority of military organisation. They also extended to a network of diplomatic alliances that had to be formed, though Trikoupis's political rivals also did not see them as indispensable. In fact, Koumoundouros repeatedly accused him of trying to reinstate foreign ambassadors' interventions in Greek politics. In other cases, he criticised him for his unilateralism, which is to say his orientation exclusively towards the British, and his hopes to make Greece the 'policeman of the East'. Trikoupis's responses to these remarks were clear: 'Greece cannot achieve anything for Hellenism without the help of Europe, but Europe offers assistance in defence of justice only to those that merit it. That is, to those that take initiative and are insistent in implementing it.'[15]

The need for Greek diplomatic representation was also not considered self-evident. On two occasions, from 1863 to 1867 and from 1873 to 1874, the Greek state closed its embassies abroad to save resources. In the latter case, according to Deligiorgis, the resulting funds were used for road works.[16] But Trikoupis's policies left no room for compromise, and no reason to choose between road works and diplomatic representation. Everything had to happen simultaneously. There is no doubt that diplomatic representation for Greece was necessary and required the appropriate individuals to staff it. Trikoupis was seeking to benefit from the new power relations forming both in Europe and the more immediate region. If, on the one hand, he developed close relations with Britain, on the other he was extremely wise to rely on France when reconfiguring the Greek state apparatus.[17] It should not be forgotten that financing for Trikoupis's policies was largely provided by French capital, while the rapid growth of currant exports to France created even closer ties between the two countries. In essence, the complexity of the international arena during these years gave Greece a large degree of freedom, but until the end of the nineteenth century, only Trikoupis had the experience, realism and knowledge to put it to use.

A modern army at minimal cost

Inevitably, this realignment of political relationships and clarification of state policies manifested itself most forcefully in the realm of military organisation. By 1878, army conscription had already been instituted, though this shift was less comprehensive than it first appeared; from the moment universal conscription was adopted, the Jewish community of Corfu made an agreement with the Greek state to pay a fee each year in exchange for exempting its children from mandatory service. Soon after, in 1881, following the annexation of Thessaly, Muslim populations were given a similar exemption.[18] Regardless of these exceptions, which essentially defined who was 'Greek'—and thus who would have to fight for their country and who would not—adoption of conscription was a radical change. But this change would only provide results if the entire state apparatus could be reorganised accordingly and if the social protests, of which there were many, were suppressed.

This much was clear from the repeated attempts to establish a properly organised military.[19] It took until 1880 for two such changes to be made, spurred mainly by the prospect of violent conflict with territories granted to Greece at the Congress of Berlin and the need to mobilise a powerful army, which in this case amounted to 40,000 men. But the bigger change came in 1882 with the introduction of yet another system of organisation, considered the best of its kind at the time. Under this new system, military forces in peacetime, which had amounted to 12,000 men in 1880, rose to 30,000. But the Greek state was not in a position to maintain such an army, and as a result the term of military service was reduced from two years to one for infantry troops, while the two-year minimum remained in place for artillery, cavalry, engineers and medics.

This reduction of mandatory military service stemmed from the Greek state's inability to sustain such a comparatively large number of active troops. For the same reason, even this reduced term proved unsustainable, and the army began to grant permits of leave to conscripts, especially in the summer months. As Trikoupis himself calculated, of a total army amounting to 28,000 men only 16,000 were available in normal conditions, of which an average of 24,000 were battle-ready.[20] He estimated that increasing the term of military service to three years—which many ministers had requested—would require an increase in military spending totalling 40 per cent of total annual expenditure, surpassing the economy's capacities.[21]

These solutions sought to create a well-trained army relative to available resources. This was first evidenced in its cost of upkeep, which was much lower than the costs incurred by other comparable armies. According to government calculations, in line with international standards, maintenance of such an army should have cost 24 million drachmas. The Greek state spent only 16 million.[22] For the Greek prime minister, this was a success in every sense, surpassing all expectations.[23] But Trikoupis only mentioned one side of the issue when he referred to national military organisation at reduced cost. These minimal expenses had another important effect on the effectiveness of the Greek army, and Trikoupis knew that Greece was the only state that had not modernised its arms. While competitors adopted new technologies such as smokeless gunpowder and the repeating action rifle, Greece was unable to make similar purchases.

Introduction of conscription and the reduction of mandatory military service revealed another aspect of the problem: the reluctance of Greeks to serve in the army. For Trikoupis, mandating a longer term of military service meant that it was not possible to recruit enough men. The Greeks, it seemed, were unwilling to fight for their homeland. In fact, in 1879, with the system of conscript replacement still in place, only a quarter of those required to serve presented themselves to fulfil their obligations: to be precise, 720 of 2,800 men. This confirmed the fear that, under the new system of conscription, with a two-year term, 'almost no conscript would come forward when called upon'.[24] The gendarmerie was plagued by the same problem, failing to reach the strength it should have done despite attempted increases in staff salaries with the aim of attracting new recruits.

All these changes presupposed the support of corresponding organisational modifications. In this respect, the Greeks were able to call upon the French army for aid. In 1882, the French military mission under Major Victor Vosseur was called upon to oversee Greek military training, developing its organisational plan and arranging for certain fortifications. The choice of France for this task was no accident.

Britain had no intention of assisting the development of another army in the Eastern Mediterranean, even if this army belonged to an ally, as the emergence of a powerful Greek army could cause the country problems in a strategically important region. For its part, Germany had undertaken the effort to reorganise the Ottoman army. Italy, the new power in the region, was not particularly powerful militarily, though it exerted pressure on areas claimed by Greece such as Epirus and Albania. France, a power with no particular claims to the area, was the only one left. Damaged from defeat in the Franco-Prussian war of 1870, it saw an opportunity to restore its tarnished reputation. Austrian involvement was out of the question.

The French mission remained in Greece until 1887. Many systematic additions to the Greek army's infrastructure were made upon its suggestion, including construction of barracks, warehouses for all kinds of materials, fortifications, and military roads. For the first time, the organisational foundations for a modern army were in place.

Yet these organisational problems could not be solved immediately, since it took time for the new practices to be assimilated. Difficulties in soldier mobilisation were acutely evident in 1878, when the absence of planning led to prevailing chaos.[25] The same problem manifested itself during the mobilisation in 1880. As the army's power increased significantly, recruitment proved to be a much harder task than Greek army officers had imagined, and military units were often assembled in a haphazard fashion.[26] During the mobilisation of 1885, this proved to be the case on a much larger scale, as no operational plan or military draft system had been established. Each unit leader prepared his own plan, and a five-day period of conflicts broke out that created significant tensions within Greek army ranks. During this same period of mobilisation, the Greek army's lack of organisational capacity was made blatantly clear by the 4,000 deaths caused by a lack of clothing, medicine and barracks for a total of 80,000 soldiers.[27] Trikoupis claimed that the conscription system would require at least ten years before it could begin to function effectively.

But ten years did prove to be enough, as the Greco-Turkish war of 1897 demonstrated.[28] In general, the Greek army's organisational problems were related to issues of recruitment, and disciplinary issues were also difficult to resolve because of officers' active participation in politics. Trikoupis tried to address the issue, but Deliyannis then repealed the relevant legislation, restoring the situation to its original state.[29] Subsequently, different solutions to the issue were attempted, especially once Prince Constantine and his court took on more and more power. As the argument at the time went, he was the only one not affected by the partisan passions of the era and thus could ensure total non-partisan administration of the army. This point of view would soon prove to be completely misguided.

A second element of the Greek army's organisational failure was related to a lack of capable middle- and lower-ranking officers—a feature that also marked Greek bureaucracy in general. This did not escape Trikoupis's attention, and he tried to address the problem. Thus, while the Cadet Military Academy was reorganised and its period of matriculation extended to five years, more emphasis was placed on other areas of military training. Academies for reserve officers and non-commissioned officers were established, along with a preparatory school for non-commissioned officers. Additionally, a logistical corps was founded, and military drills were introduced in schools for the first time.

An even greater effort was made in the navy, with very successful results. The navy was organised from the ground up, since it was in a state of complete disarray, and certain groups opposed to the reforms—mainly represented by the residents of Hydra—were so powerful that they stood in the way of every change. Trikoupis confronted the Hydra lobby, took care to create the Naval Academy for training navy officers and brought the French naval mission to Greece, which rendered the Greek fleet battle-ready by reconstituting its organisational structure and fortifying its equipment. Three warships, powerful for the standards of the time, were ordered: the Hydra, the Spetses and the Psara. Joined by nineteen new torpedo boats and four steamships, they completely changed the navy's capabilities, rendering it a peerless power in the Aegean.[30]

Thus, over the course of the 1880s, the Greek army set down a new path, comprising the key to succeeding with various national goals and the general project of state reorganisation. However, the changes that were enacted were not sufficient to render the army combat-ready; they simply set it on a new course, with results that would only be evident at a later date.

Roads, railways and ports

This reorganisation of the military comprised one stage of Trikoupis's reform efforts. The second, without which military restructuring would have been ineffective, concerned infrastructure. From the founding of the Greek state up until 1883, little more than 1,000 kilometres of roadway had been paved, 241 kilometres during Otto's rule and the remaining 880 kilometres from 1863 to 1883.[31] The experience of the 1878 revolts highlighted how important inter-regional infrastructure was for proper execution of military operations. To be precise, it demonstrated how much more difficult these operations became in the absence of such roadways. Transport of cavalry and artillery was practically impossible for much of the year, since the quality of the roads was terrible and the necessary bridges had not yet been built.[32] Their importance would be felt even more intensely some years later with the military mobilisation of 1885 and the blockading of the Greek coast in 1886 by the Great Powers, who sent their fleets from Souda to Piraeus, blocking the dispatch of the 1st Regiment to Volos.[33] Moreover, any effective recruitment making use of a new system of military organisation was pointless without the existence of a railway network that could carry mobilised soldiers to the borders at short notice.

Inevitably, transportation networks changed drastically during Trikoupis's tenure. Within a decade, from 1883 to 1892, 2,116 kilometres of road were built—a figure that rises to 2,600 kilometres if we include provincial and municipal roads constructed in the same period.[34] These public works continued after Trikoupis's period in power, and by the eve of the Balkan Wars Greece had a network of vehicular roads stretching 5,709 kilometres, a significant step towards the consolidation of national territory.[35]

Yet in countries such as Greece, vehicle-bearing roadways played a marginal role at best until the appearance of the automobile. This is the chief reason why Trikoupis invested most in the construction of a railway network. In addition to its economic importance, the project was prioritised for 'strategic reasons', as Parliament delicately put it. Though only one single railway line existed in 1882, stretching the 9 kilometres between Athens and Piraeus, the railway network grew progressively and by 1915 1,573 kilometres of tracks had been laid. The Greek state's declaration of bankruptcy in 1893 slowed the expansion of this network, though it never completely halted. The great project of constructing a railway from Piraeus to the northern borders, which held strategic importance for the Greek state, only began in 1904 and would be completed five years later in 1909.[36]

By the eve of the Balkan Wars, this transportation network was mainly used to cover the needs of various types of medium-haul transport; longer distances were still covered by boat. The network also supported state efforts at consolidation and control over the region. But this system still left out large tracts of Greek land and a significant portion of its population. It only began to reach

Map A: National Network of Roadways in 1892

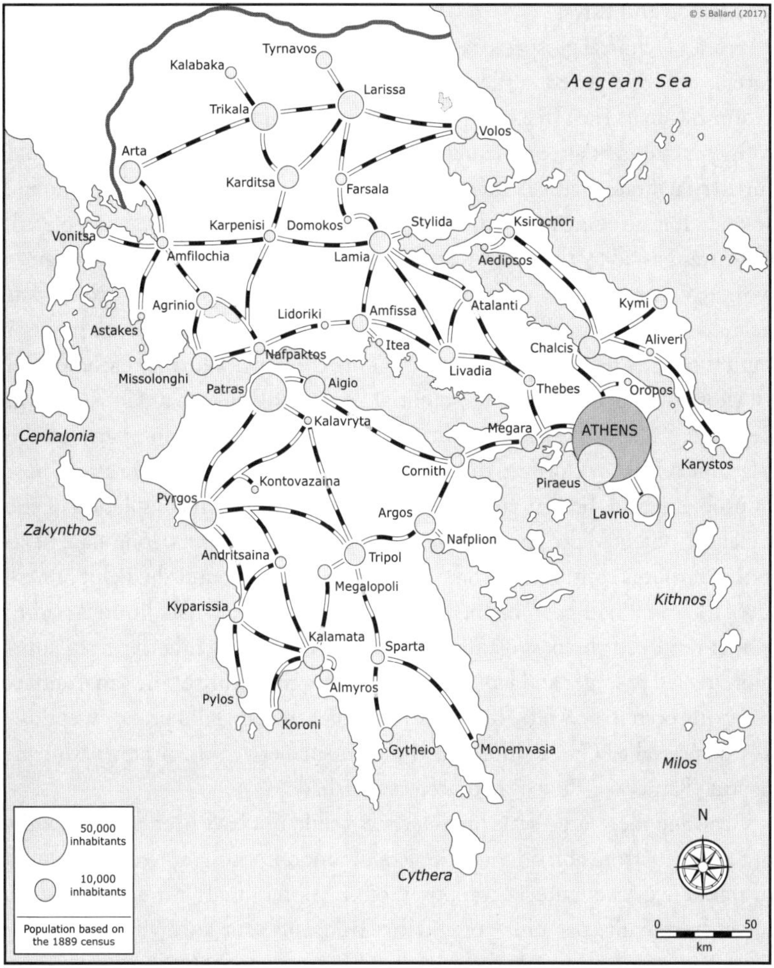

Source: M. Sinarellis, *Δρόμοι και λιμάνια στην Ελλάδα 1830–1880*, Athens: 1989, p. 104.

the rest of Greece's population after the large-scale road works of the interwar period were initiated, a project that was only truly completed after the war.

Along with this expansion of road and rail networks, the Greek state made significant progress in developing various ports. In the period from 1882 to 1900, twenty new ports were in a position to establish the infrastructure necessary to facilitate their integration into a larger shipping network extending beyond the five already developed ports—Piraeus, Kalamata, Katakolo, Ermoupoli and Patras.[37]

From a technical perspective, the most significant transportation infrastructure project completed in the nineteenth century was the construction of the Corinth Canal. The Greeks hoped the project would allow for a shorter route to Egypt, seeing it as complementary to the Suez Canal, and one that would further facilitate Greece's incorporation into major international economic arteries. It is no coincidence that the same year the Suez Canal was completed, a law was passed by the Zaimis government that would later serve as a framework to construct the Corinth Canal. But implementation of the project was delayed by twelve years and only began in the 1880s. The enthusiastic input of capital to the French company undertaking the project further emboldened all those who believed in the potential benefits of the canal. Construction began in 1881 with the founding of the International Company of the Maritime Canal of Corinth, though it was only completed in 1893 after a host of problems and the first company's bankruptcy. But even completion of the canal did not yield the results first expected by its supporters; long-haul navigational routes continued to take the extended way around the Peloponnese after the canal had been opened. This was due to the canal's limited width, which rendered the passage of large ships precarious, while trends in shipbuilding led to larger and larger vessels, making the future of the canal and its company even less certain. But construction of the canal did prove exceptionally beneficial to Greek shippers, who used smaller vessels. A new path connecting Patras and Piraeus had been established.[38]

Realising these large-scale public works would not have been possible without expertise from abroad. In 1878, Koumoundouros sought to create a corps of public works engineers composed of Greek nationals, though the effort never bore fruit; the more pragmatic Trikoupis sent an invitation to the French government in 1882, requesting engineers and technicians that could plan and assist with the construction of Greek public works. As a result, in 1883 the French Mission of Public Works was established in Greece and continued to function until 1895, although its powers were limited after 1892. For the duration of its stay, the mission played an important and decisive role in the construction of public works. Preparation, design, supervision and approval of all works was undertaken by these French engineers. Meanwhile, a corps of Greek engineers and technicians established itself, significantly influenced by a reorganisation of the Polytechnic University and more specifically the School of Industrial and Fine Arts after 1891.[39]

Armed begging and electoral reform

In 1885, at sixty-five years of age, Deliyannis succeeded Trikoupis as prime minister. He demonstrated a talent for organising opposition forces by mobilising and coordinating protests by various groups in Athens, but he soon caused problems in Parliament and demonstrated his incompetence in managing national politics as he rose to power. He presented his platform as a reversal of Trikoupis's policies. Thus Deliyannis united all those opposed to Trikoupis's reformist policies and those who believed that the violence of Trikoupis's reform effort was not justified.

In the realm of foreign policy, Deliyannis demonstrated even more incompetence. This became clear directly after his rise to power when, in a coup, Bulgaria annexed Eastern Roumelia: in September 1885, the Ottoman ruler of the Porte in Eastern Roumelia was expelled and the region was unified with Bulgaria under its new ruler, Alexander of Battenberg. The entire balance of power in the Balkans had been upset, though the events did not seem to provoke a reaction from the Great Powers or the Porte.

The Greek government reacted in the most fitful way: on the one hand, it demanded a return to the previous status quo and the dispatch of Turkish troops to Roumelia. On the other, Greece began military preparations so as to satisfy demands of the Tripartite Agreement and justify its prime minister's incendiary slogans. At the same moment, Serbia declared war on Bulgaria.

Bulgaria's crushing defeat of Serbia led to the Serbian government's de facto recognition of Eastern Roumelia's annexation. Despite finding itself isolated, Greece intensified its preparations for war, claiming a right to the Greek territorial border outlined by the Congress of Berlin in order to restore the balance of power in the Balkans. Certainly, Greece could not run the risk of invading territories belonging to the Ottoman Empire, all the more so now that Ottoman troops had taken up battle positions at the border. But it kept preparing its troops and claiming a right to 'restitution'. In reality, Deliyannis was simply trying to buy time, hoping that George would relieve him of his duties.

This period of 'armed begging', as it is mockingly called, came to an end with the blockading of Greek ports by fleets from Britain, France, Germany, Austria and Italy, and a demand for Greek disarmament. Deliyannis had no choice but to submit to their demands, yet he moved clumsily once more: in order to justify backing down from his great claims, he hurriedly published a letter from the French minister of foreign affairs Freyssinet indicating his need to immediately accept the Great Powers' demands. The latter, to show that they were not beholden to French policies, made additional demands and forced Deliyannis to resign, despite George's objections. At Trikoupis's suggestion, a caretaker government was assembled led by Prime Minister Dimitrios Valvis, formerly president of the Supreme Court.

Deliyannis submitted his candidacy for the presidency of Parliament but was soundly defeated by the Trikoupist candidate. The ministers that had formerly supported his government now offered their support to Trikoupis, who was soon reinstated as prime minister, governing for one year with the support of those who had defected from Deliyannis's party. Greece's humiliation was such, and the opposition's tones were so subdued, that Trikoupis rushed to take advantage. In 1886, he proposed two bills in Parliament with the aim of reforming the electoral process: namely broadening the electoral constituency from each province to each prefecture; using the number of registered voters as a basis for calculating the number of seats allotted to each voting district, instead of the legal population (the number of inhabitants according to the latest census); changing the manner of distributing the number of seats in each voting district by introducing proportional representation, in an effort to minimise disparities; and reducing the total number of ministers from 245 to 150.

Trikoupis's aim was to consolidate the parties and make ministers more beholden to their party leaders. He believed that by implementing this new system, and chiefly by enlarging voting districts, he could limit the contact politicians had with their voters and diminish the importance of party leaders. Weakening the relationship between ministers, party leaders and voters would, in his opinion, enhance the political nature of the vote as the process would become more impersonal. The opposition in turn voted against the bill on the basis that links between ministers and voters needed to be maintained. The ideological basis for this objection was that Parliament did not represent individuals—as Trikoupis argued—but rather principles and interests. The bills were passed and made national laws. The elections conducted in 1887 and 1890 were based on them, though the results in both cases were far from what the authors of the law had desired.[40] As a result, these reforms were abolished in 1890 by Deliyannis, and Trikoupis did not seek to reinstate them when he next assumed the premiership.

During this same period, Trikoupis sought to resolve the issue of military officer participation in elections. Until then, a large number of officers claimed the right to be elected to Parliament. Initially, these individuals were all part of the political elite—the elite born from the War of Independence—which held the reins of political and military power in the country.[41] But officer participation in the electoral process led to disorganisation within the army: not so much because of the fact that low-ranking officers gained political power they could use against their superiors, but because the electoral process led candidates to use the army as an instrument for electoral success, often before the electoral period began.[42] Indeed, according to the 1864 Constitution, officers were entitled to take a leave of office for five and a half months to prepare for elections. Up until then, it was common practice to calculate months of leave based on seniority. Clearly, Trikoupis was not in a position to change the constitution, but he proceeded to reform the legislation so that the duration of leave was no longer determined by seniority, while candidate officers were now also eligible. These changes proved to deter officers from seeking candidacy.

After successfully passing new electoral laws and stabilising the public finances—which had effectively collapsed during the crisis in Eastern Roumelia—Trikoupis proceeded to hold elections on 4 January 1887. As expected, they gave Trikoupis and his party a majority in Parliament once again.

National symbols, interests and demands

These changes in the electoral process constituted one facet of Trikoupis's policies in relation to the nation's political system. From another angle, he tried to render the monarchy a national institution that could unite all Greeks. To this end, he sought to cultivate its image by organising frequent public ceremonies and supporting it as much as possible. For the first time, the Greek state sought to shape its web of national symbols, seeking to cultivate the unity it needed to succeed in its goals.

If, on the one hand, Trikoupis sought to establish national unity, on the other he left no room for ambiguity regarding state administration of national issues. He decisively dismantled several 'national' associations that intervened in the implementation of Greek foreign policy.[43] Such organisations had been formed and gained strength in the wake of rebellions in Crete and Epirus-Thessaly, and one of them, titled 'National Defence', had become so powerful that it began intervening in the process of governmental decision-making. Their importance had grown from the moment that the Macedonian issue became a fundamental problem for both domestic and foreign policy. The annexation of Thessaly meant that Greece now shared a border with Macedonia, and it paid much more attention to the latter than ever before.[44] Meanwhile, the situation in Macedonia was extremely difficult and became more complicated by the day.

The Bulgarians and their armed forces pressed all the Slavic-speaking populations in mixed regions of Eastern Macedonia (that is, including both patriarchal and exarchist inhabitants) to join the Exarchate, as the Greeks despaired over the rapidly changing situation in the Balkans. At the same time, the situation in Western Macedonia had become crucial to Greek interests, further exacerbated by Bulgaria's annexation of Eastern Roumelia and the forceful campaigns mounted by armed Bulgarian forces in Eastern Macedonia. The Bulgarians won battle after battle as they expanded their network of influence in Macedonia. The situation became even more fraught when the Romanians tried to stake a series of claims related to the Vlach populations in Macedonian territory. Finally, Serbia's turn southwards under pressure from the dual monarchy and its vision of rehabilitating Greater Serbia multiplied the number of parties involved in the Macedonian situation.

For Trikoupis, the main concerns of Greek foreign policy had to be determined by a national centre—none other than the Greek government. The dissolution of national associations and societies solved the problem within the country, but a more difficult problem remained: relations with the Patriarchate. The latter, headed by Joachim III, set its own policies in an effort to determine the prevailing conditions of the era. Opposition between these two centres led to a confrontation between Trikoupis and Joachim III; this was also the case with ambassadors of the Greek state and local bishops and priests of the Patriarchate. This confrontation between the Greek state and the Patriarchate often concerned education policy. Up until then, public education had been the responsibility of the Patriarchate, but the Greek state now claimed it for its own purposes.[45] In the realm of international relations, it was clear that Trikoupis sought a period of peace, a prerequisite for the organisation of a state apparatus. For this reason, he also supported good relations with the Ottoman Empire. Joachim III, in contrast, was of the opinion that friendly relations had to be developed with Russia so that the Patriarchate could win over Bulgaria again. The Patriarchate's stance can be understood if we take into account the gradual weakening the institution experienced as the Bulgarians and Slavs slowly distanced themselves from its embrace. As the Ottoman state did not prevent this process—on the contrary, it validated it—Joachim III sought support that would enhance his influence over Orthodox populations. This appeal to Russia seemed to be the only solution, and this 'pro-Russian stance' a way out, as long as Russia's pan-Slavist plans did not render every hope of enforcing ecumenicity over the empire's Orthodox populations moot.[46] These two policies were incompatible and could not but lead to conflict. This resulted in Joachim III's resignation, and a new configuration of relationships between the Greek state and the Ecumenical Patriarchate—by now, the former was the more dominant voice. Besides, from the moment it was clear that Russian policies were incompatible with the Patriarchate's interests, the Patriarchate oriented its ecumenicity towards populations that continued to remain under its direct jurisdiction, gradually morphing into an instrument for implementing Greek ambitions.[47]

A political impasse

Trikoupis's reformist policies came at a considerable economic cost, and Greece had neither the abundant resources nor the capital to meet these demands. Thus, to finance his reforms, Trikoupis would turn to international loans. But in order to borrow internationally, Greece had to put its past debts in order, particularly those arising from the 60 million franc loan taken out in 1833, which it had stopped servicing in 1843. In 1878, with the Eastern Question at a critical juncture, Greece was obliged to negotiate an immediate compromise with its creditors. This had been avoided for the past thirty-five years, and now it had to be completed in a very short time, under rather unfavourable conditions.[48] Greece then benefited from the new opportunities offered by international capital markets, securing a series of loans until 1893, when it once again proved incapable of fulfilling its debt obligations.

The first foreign loan of 60 million francs, signed in 1879, forced convertibility of the drachma by settling all the Greek state's remaining outstanding payments. Successive loans followed with which attempts were made to create infrastructure, to establish the army and to address national crises. Servicing the loans became increasingly expensive over time: while 389,157,318 francs went towards interest and repayment, 121,700,000 went to the repayment of earlier loans and advancements, 100,000,000 went to the purchase of warships and other military goods, and various public works accounted for 120,000,000. Finally, the costs of issuing loans, brokerages and commissions added up to 25,000,000 francs.[49] It is telling that A. Simopoulos, minister of finance for many years under Trikoupis, claimed the following after the bankruptcy of 1893: 'If indeed one takes the approach of an unbiased historian, honestly studying our economic history independent of the effects our national politics have on our economic situation, they will have to admit that Greece defaulted in 1882.'[50]

Certainly, the Greek government did not limit itself to external borrowing. It also exhausted every possibility for raising borrowed capital in the domestic

6.1: Debt Servicing as a Percentage of Regular Income, 1833, 1912

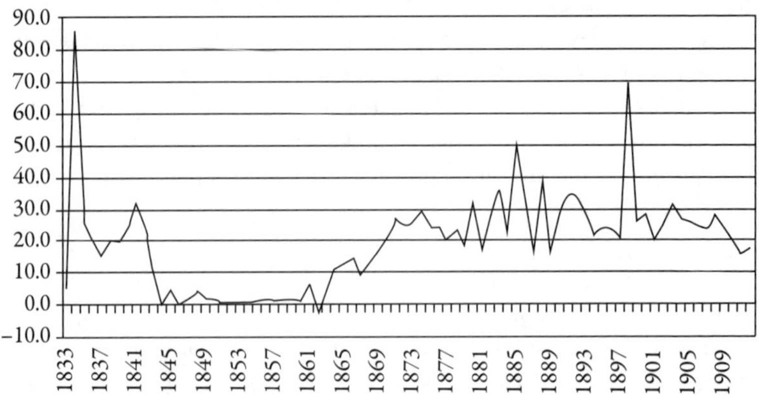

Source: See K. Kostis, 'Δημόσια οικονομικά,' K. Κωστής και Σ. Πετμεζάς, Η ανάπτυξη της ελληνικής οικονομίας.

market. As a result, the Greek state transformed into an entity competing with the private economy, resulting in reduced funding possibilities for the latter and an increase in interest rates. The cost of 'national integration' was immense; as immense as the ignorance in managing the problems that arose from foreign borrowing.[51]

6.2: Public Debt of Greece, 1869–93 (in drachmas)

	1869	*1875*	*1882*	*1887*	*1892*	*1893*
Public Debt	137,719,833	163,602,113	331,133,906	525,090,620	720,188,644	823,252,581
Public debt per capita	94.50	102.75	163.19	246.35	317.65	363.20

Source: D. Georgiadès, *La Grèce économique et financière en 1893*, Paris: 1893, p. 47.

In the elections of 14 October 1890, Trikoupis was defeated and the mandate to form a government was given to Deliyannis. The latter's first concern was to convince the embassies of the foreign powers that his belligerent reputation was false. Soon, however, he faced problems that he was incapable of managing due to positions he had taken previously and commitments he had made: the Cretan issue and Greece's public finances. The latter in particular had spiralled out of control, much more so now that the Greek state had difficulty borrowing from abroad. On 17 February 1892, George I declared that Deliyannis should resign, despite the fact that the latter had the support of Parliament. Deliyannis refused and George discharged him. The political situation escalated as Deliyannis requested a vote of confidence from Parliament, which he was immediately granted. He then began to protest to the royal court. In turn, many Trikoupist ministers organised demonstrations in favour of George I, further worsening the situation and—probably unintentionally—leading the king to become a supporter of Trikoupis's party. Yet when asked by the king to form a government, Trikoupis refused. On legal grounds, he challenged whether a royal decree had the right to remove a government voted in by the parliamentary principle.

Fifteen years after the adoption of the parliamentary principle, George I felt sufficiently dominant politically to take the initiative and become a reformer of the Greek political system. Criticisms of the parliamentary system had begun to intensify, and George found that he could use these sentiments to strengthen his power.

After Trikoupis refused to form a government, the mandate was given to Deliyannist minister Konstantopoulos in an effort to support the founding and reinforcement of a third party. Konstantopoulos was allied with a group of ministers that had left the Deliyannist party, including both Dimitrios Rallis and Konstantinos Karapanos. At this moment of acute economic crisis, the basic problem the new government had to confront was financial in nature. It proceeded to organise elections, held on 3 May 1892. Trikoupis won the majority of votes but was reluctant to form a government, leaving power in the hands of Konstantopoulos. He would only take control of the government shortly thereafter. In any case, the country's financial situation did not allow for much optimism: to avoid bankruptcy, the Greek state needed new loans from foreign creditors, who by now demanded the imposition of international supervision and control over the National Bank. Eventually, Trikoupis resigned.

Once again, George ignored the parliamentary principle and declined to grant a mandate to Deliyannis, which he was owed as leader of the main opposition party. Despite public opposition and an intensifying political climate, the king granted the government mandate to a small group led by Sotiropoulos and Rallis, the former assuming the premiership. The king's decision, which clearly sought to fragment the Deliyiannis-led opposition, was strongly criticised by Trikoupis. The government's fitful approach to servicing the public debt then led to its ousting by the Trikoupist majority, and Trikoupis assumed the premiership for the last time. But by then, the economic situation had deteriorated irreversibly. The confidence of international capital markets in Greece's ability to continue servicing its loans, greatly diminished since 1890, had disappeared.[52] What was clear was that Greece could not take out another international loan unless it accepted some sort of intervention in the management of its public debt.

Political resistance to these pursuits did not last long. In 1892, the harvest was good and Greece was able to fulfil its obligations, but the future still looked bleak. The tariff measures taken by the French state against currants were the *coup de grace*: while in May 1893 the price of the common currant was 21 shillings per hectolitre, in a few months it fell to 6 shillings. The consequences were immediate and led not only to reduced public revenues but also affected the currency exchange rate necessary to service the external loan. In late 1893, Trikoupis announced that Greece was unable to pay its debts. This spelled the end of his political career, since bankruptcy could reflect nothing else but the outcome of his own policy choices. Yet Greece itself was in an even worse situation. Though the Greek state had made some progress—about this there was no doubt—its reputation was now tarnished. Not only was the Greek state incapable of civilising itself; it had now proven unreliable in its financial promises. 'Greece is not a failed state like Turkey, Peru, Mexico, Honduras or other such unfortunate countries; Greece is the sole nation in the world to exist in a state of fraudulent bankruptcy.'[53]

The end of the tithe

By the late nineteenth century, the Greek economy was a shambles; along with the Greek state's bankruptcy, the currant crisis heavily affected urban populations and others involved in the currant trade. The new fiscal measures adopted by the Trikoupist government only worsened the situation and led to unrest in all major cities, fomenting the opposition. Indeed, according to I. Zografos, professor at the University of Athens, the national system of taxation as it had formed on the eve of the Balkan Wars was 'a facade of contradictions, injustice and inequality'.[54]

A large portion of the tax burden gradually shifted to urban populations, something which was to be expected since the urban population had become increasingly important for the Greek economy. An emphasis on indirect taxes could indeed support the assumption that the urban lower and middle classes were taxed progressively more as the end of the period in question approached.

Large incomes, in contrast, were only taxed incidentally. Definite conclusions cannot be drawn regarding the relative tax burden on the urban and rural strata as a whole.

The key moment for reorganising public revenues came in the 1880s—in 1885, to be exact, when revenues from state monopolies began to account for a larger portion of the state's regular revenues. This was preceded by the abolition of tithe taxation, which was replaced by taxation of labour animals.[55] In the process, a question reaching back to the founding of the Greek state was answered. Yet the repeal of tithe taxation and the introduction of a labour animal tax had the effect of exempting very low rural incomes (those who did not own animals for agricultural work). It also overly burdened small- and medium-scale farmers (and, in the case of Thessaly, crofters) who held the majority of labour animals, while it left large-scale landowners untaxed. Additionally, the way in which the labour animal tax worked rendered it gradually regressive.[56] Trikoupis, continuing his efforts to increase public revenues, and hoping to streamline the functioning of collection mechanisms, introduced a new protective tariff in 1884, though it was not successful from a fiscal point of view as tariff revenue soon fell. The state's urgent financial needs soon pushed the minister of finance to intervene, after which the tariff became exclusively fiscal.[57]

There was a clear overarching logic to these extremely rapid changes to the tax system. Trikoupis repeatedly made his case to parliament, which certainly fit within the larger network of political priorities he had set. The nation had to be quick about confronting its rivals in South Eastern Europe, and to this end these new taxes were unavoidable. Beyond serving their term of military service, Greek citizens also had to make an economic contribution so the country could prepare for the military conflicts that were to come. Going one step further, he stated that the policies of his government were the policies of those who 'showed that they believe in Greece by the way they vote in Parliament—that they believe Greece has the wherewithal of a nation destined to survive, that it wants to thrive and will thrive'.[58]

As the need to increase the tax burden was explicitly expressed in terms of national survival, Trikoupis also explained his reasons for choosing to tax consumption. In 1883, he issued a statement detailing that the government sought to avoid taxation on production (i.e. on the rural economy) since this was what in fact formed the basis of the Greek economy. He hoped that this would facilitate economic development, as it had in other countries, and that in a not too distant future the Greek economy would be in a position to

6.3: Tax Burden in Greece, 1833–1912, in Drachmas Per Capita and as a Percentage of GDP

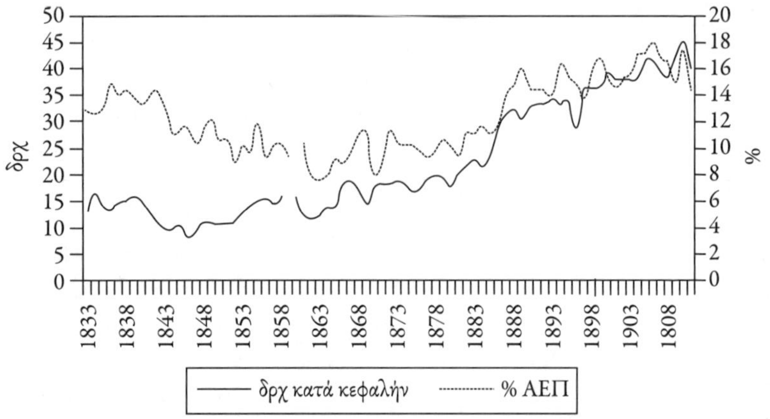

Source: Calculations based on data in G. Kostenelos and S. Petmezas, et al., 'Ακαθάριστο Εγχώριο Προϊόν 1830–1939', unpublished paper, and G. Dertilis, *Ατελέσφοροι ή τελεσφόροι. Φόροι και εξουσία στο Νεοελληνικό κράτος*, Athens: 1993.

decrease these taxes.[59] None of this happened, and the tax system became all the more burdensome for low- and middle-income groups. For its part, the opposition may have denounced Trikoupist fiscal policies, but when it assumed power it could hardly act any differently; the need to balance the public deficit and supply emergency expenses in periods of political crises did not leave any room for party-based differences in tax policy.

G. Dertilis has argued that the Greek state adopted discriminatory policies in favour of farmers and at the expense of urban populations from 1864 onwards. He claims this was related to the special influence that farmers acquired in the electoral process through the introduction of universal male suffrage, as they constituted the majority of voters. This view is not unfounded, but the extent to which public policy was influenced exclusively—or even decisively—by the electoral process is debatable.

A study of these fiscal policies demonstrates that the Greek state did aim to create favourable terms of taxation for farmers. Moreover, it should not be forgotten that the effort to relieve these farmers of an excessive tax burden was related to the negative effects the taxation could have on national development if it was maintained. And if the tax burden on farmers did decrease in comparative terms, as was the case in the nineteenth century, it is important to note that, in addition to state tax, farmers also had to pay municipal taxes, rent and debt amortisation, and other irregular sums owed to tax farmers.[60] The entire system of tax farming, as has been correctly noted, was a mechanism for income redistribution both at the expense of peasants and at the expense of the state—when tenants delayed in making their payments to the collectors.[61] Lastly, it should be emphasised that a reduced tax burden on rural populations was not unique to Greece. Thus it was not necessarily related to the parliamentary system of governance: in all other Balkan countries, most of which were not democratic, tax burdens on the rural population diminished significantly until 1910.[62]

Defeat

The crisis of the late nineteenth century led to the end of Trikoupis's political career. At a demonstration on 8 January 1895, Prince Constantine prohibited the chief of police from dispersing protestors, despite an order from the government to do so. Constantine's intervention led to an immediate reaction from Trikoupis, and then to the latter's resignation when George refused to support his cause. He immediately sought a vote of confidence in Parliament, which he gained, though he refrained from confronting the king any further. By this point, the crown had begun to attack both the major parties, if not to weaken the parliamentary system then at the very least to strengthen its own position.

George sought to hand over the government to Admiral M. Kanaris, son of Konstantinos Kanaris, a hero of the War of Independence. But the terms George set were not accepted, because they were considered a threat to political stability. The king had the intelligence to recognise the limits of political controversy. He suggested that N. Deliyannis, former Greek ambassador in Paris, assemble a caretaker government for which elections were held on 16 April 1896. The defeat of the Trikoupist party was overwhelming and Trikoupis himself failed to get elected, which led him to retire from politics. He died a few months later in Cannes. But it would be wrong to argue that the death of Trikoupis signalled the end of his reformist project. Greece had started down a path, along with other Balkan countries, from which it could not retreat.

T. Deliyannis thus returned to government without his major rival, Trikoupis. He first sought to compromise with the country's lenders, without arriving at any conclusion. Then, in the summer of 1896, as the first modern Olympic Games were held in Greece, a new uprising occurred in Crete. Violence broke out in Greece, and the mood was bellicose from the outset.

It was the National Society that played the key role in the developments leading to the Greco-Turkish War of 1897.[63] This society was a secret organisation founded in 1894 by a few young officers with the purpose of reorganising the military and supporting national claims.[64] It was based on the belief that the national political leadership at the time was incapable of completing the task of national integration:

> The Society, whose founding was provoked by the incumbent government's indifferent attitude with regard to the nation's military preparedness, derived great moral strength as notable believers of Hellenism writ large from every social class joined its ranks. They hoped for one thing above all—to correct the government's negligence without mixing itself up in internal affairs; to offer the government of the recently liberated nation of Greece the information necessary to correctly evaluate the unavoidable dangers posed to the nation; to more accurately calculate the strengths of Hellenism and to seriously consider how to thwart any dangers to it. This National Society was confident in achieving its aims since it represented elements of Hellenism that had no relationship with party conflicts, and in fact it hoped to become their unifying tissue.[65]

Soon, the National Society managed to gain substantial power and infiltrate every aspect of Greek politics. Spyridon Lambros—professor at the University of Athens and tutor to Constantine—was appointed its president. It was extremely critical of anyone who was opposed to belligerent policies, including the king himself.[66] Theodorus Deliyannis was not prepared to face such a problem.

The dispatch of Greek soldiers to Crete caught the Ottomans by surprise, but they reacted quickly and a broader military conflict ensued.[67] The front collapsed almost immediately, and the Greek army began a disorganised retreat.[68] Blame was cast in every direction, but mostly at the government, the king and Prince Constantine, leader of the Greek army. Newspapers even ran headlines calling George I a traitor, while all demanded that the prince step down from command of the army. Once again, Deliyannis was forced to resign, and he was replaced by Rallis. Meanwhile, George's intervention with Tsar Nicholas of Russia bore fruit, and just as the Ottomans were reaching Thermopylae, they agreed to sign an armistice.

After national bankruptcy, defeat in the Greco-Turkish War compounded the negative developments for Greece in the late nineteenth century. At this point, the country's reputation in the West could not have been any worse. It had come to be nothing more or less than a complicated piece in the Balkan puzzle and the Eastern Question—often a problematic piece, as it handled international complications badly. In the Western European imagination, it had joined the ranks of the Balkans. New competitors were emerging from South Eastern Europe after the Treaty of San Stefano shifted balances of power in the area. Thus the often malicious comments made by Greek scholars and politicians about Bulgarians—and even Slavs more generally—stopped making sense, since in a very short period of time they had managed to overturn the status quo and emerged as the dominant candidates in the race to succeed the Ottoman state. In contrast, Greece had fallen short. It could no longer see itself as the preferred—or even rightful—heir to the aging empire.

From a different perspective, dynamics in the wake of the crisis in the Eastern Question in 1878, which led to the Trikoupis era, radically changed the nature of the Greek state and led it to a new reality: the national state. The country entered an era of reforms aiming to strengthen its presence in the regional geopolitical situation. The international economic and political momentum had forced it in this direction, leaving no room for idleness if Greece hoped to stand its ground in this international competition. Yet these reforms presupposed an extreme mobilisation of human and financial resources and led to new societal balances. New institutions, new economic activities, significant resources flowing in from abroad—these were all stimuli and incentives for the transformations taking place in the social and economic realm.

Above all else, Trikoupis was the leader in this process of creating a national state. In other words, the urban transformation in Greece owed its existence to Trikoupis and to the need to strengthen Greece's geopolitical presence—not vice versa.

7

UNEXPECTED DEVELOPMENTS

(1898–1913)

> But what really happened after Greece's independence? The powerful—the chieftains, captains, notables and fighters for independence—they themselves, their children, their grandchildren, their sons, their protégés, their supporters, did they not share all the benefits among themselves? Land, positions, pensions, rights, power, influence, victory, the results of social opposition, privileges, titles and all the rest?
>
> But slowly, the reactions begin. The other classes—the oppressed ones—fight back to throw off the yoke ... the Peaceful Revolution will displace the dominant, corrupt oligarchy ...
>
> Acropolis, no. 6512, 28 May 1909

Political stagnation

As the Greco-Turkish War came to an end and the armistice was signed, negotiations for a peace treaty began in Constantinople. Greece was not present during this process. Its representation had been entrusted to the Great Powers. In the end, the treaty was not as bad for Greek interests as might have been expected, considering the outcome of the conflict. The Ottoman Empire's territorial claims were rejected by the Great Powers and only a small piece of land—an area of 200 square kilometres—was deducted from Greek territory in order to reach a border settlement agreeable to the Ottomans.

Things did not go as well for the Greek side in economic terms. Greece had to pay war reparations amounting to 100 million gold francs, a sum it would draw from a public loan to be issued with a guarantee from the Great Powers. The loan was accompanied by the financial supervision of the International Financial Commission, which aimed to ensure that the existing loans, which had remained unpaid since 1893, were serviced properly. The proposal to impose the commission was made by Germany and supported by Austria. The remaining powers—mainly Britain, which had initially been opposed to the proposal—were convinced by Russia, which sought to immediately resolve problems pending after the conflict. At the time, many voiced fears of possible complications that could have unforeseen consequences for the Greek royal family.

In theory, the most unexpected part of the peace treaty was the Great Powers' decision regarding Crete. Predicting the pressures the monarchy would be subjected to after the misfortunes of the Greco-Turkish War, Britain and Russia sought to support the crown by arguing for the resolution of the Cretan issue in a way that was favourable for Greece. But not wanting to provoke the Ottomans, they decided to place the island under the protection of the Great Powers and to appoint George I's second-born son (also named George) high commissioner. Germany and Austria made their positions clear without coming into conflict with the British or Russians, removing themselves from the joint undertaking. The other powers then obliged the Ottoman troops and fleet to withdraw from the island. The sultan's sovereignty was purely symbolic, represented only by the flag still flying at the fortress of Izzedin.

Timetable 1898–1913

1898	Attempted murder of George I. Law regarding the International Financial Commission. Prince George, second son of King George, sworn in as high commissioner in Crete. Alexandros Zaimis premiership (21 September 1897–2 April 1899).
1899	Elections in Crete. Elections in Greece; Georgios Theotokis's first term as prime minister (2 April 1899–12 November 1901). Cretan Constitution. First government of the Cretan nation.
1900	Law regarding general administration of the army. Law regarding founding of the National Fleet Fund.
1901	Cretan High Commissioner Prince George signs a decree expelling Eleftherios Venizelos from the Cretan government. The Gospel riots. Alexandros Zaimis premiership (12 November 1901–24 November 1902).
1902	Elections. Theodoros Deliyannis sworn in as prime minister again (24 November 1902–14June 1903).

1903 Successive premierships of Georgios Theotokis (14 June 1903–28 June 1903), Dimitris Rallis (28 June 1903–6 December 1903) and Georgios Theotokis again (6 December 1903–16 December 1904). Bulgarian bombing attacks in Thessaloniki. The Oresteia riots.

1904 Late in the year, Theodoros Deliyannis assumes premiership for the last time (16 November 1904–31 May 1905).

1905 Elections. Victory of Theodoros Deliyannis, who is murdered shortly thereafter. Rallis government (9 June 1905–8 December 1905). Fourth government led by Georgios Theotokis, who remains prime minister until 1909 (8 December 1905–7 July 1909).

1906 Elections won by Georgios Theotokis. Olympic Games (the 'Mesolympiad') in Athens.

1908 Crete declares its union with Greece.

1909 Goudis coup. Rallis premiership (7 July 1909–15 August 1909).

1910 Premierships of Kyriakoulis Mavromichalis (15 August 1909–18 January 1910) and Stefanos Dragoumis (18 January 1910–6 October 1910). Farmers' mobilisations in Thessaly. Elections and notable victories for supporters of the 'Restoration'. Eleftherios Venizelos forms a government and hastens to declare new elections, in which he wins with an overwhelming majority. He begins a huge reformist project.

1911 Revision of the Constitution. Italian occupation of the Dodecanese.

1912 The Liberal Party. Greece and its allies (Bulgaria, Serbia and Montenegro) defeat the Ottoman Empire in the First Balkan War.

1913 Second Balkan War. Greece and Serbia defeat Bulgaria. In March, King George I is murdered in Thessaloniki and succeeded by Constantine I.

Though the Treaty of Constantinople resolved a range of issues resulting from the Greco-Turkish War, the Greek leadership still faced a host of problems. The most urgent was the forceful challenge to the throne, which a great majority of Greeks saw as responsible for their defeat. As Prince Constantine had been commander-in-chief for the duration of the battle, he bore responsibility for the unfavourable outcome. Though George I sought to improve the throne's standing, an assassination attempt in early 1898 on him and his daughter Maria did not help matters. He also sought to benefit from a strong dissatisfaction with parliamentary democracy, which he himself considered responsible for the problems in Greece. Indeed, during his time in Greece he repeatedly spoke out against the parliamentary system, though he never directly challenged it. This was not the case for Prince Constantine, who had already begun to assemble his own court and circle of those he trusted, mostly officers, who enjoyed preferential treatment in whatever sector of state administration they were employed. His goals were facilitated by the Georgios Theotokis government's adoption of a law entitled 'Regarding General Administration of the Army' in 1900, according to which Constantine was appointed governor general and inspector of the army. The law also limited the powers of the Ministry of Defence. Its passing was met with strong opposition, yet Theotokis, then in his first term as prime minister, believed that it protected the army from party interventions, which were considered responsible for the defeat of 1897. But as soon became clear, he had created a very powerful centre of resistance that would challenge the authority of each elected government, as will be discussed below. Constantine would not have to wait very long to take action.

Meanwhile, as the environment stabilised after the Greco-Turkish War, the pre-war political status quo returned. The only difference was that George I was now much quicker to ignore the parliamentary principle when he saw fit; he also used Alexandros Zaimis's small, royalist party to intervene in politics. But other dynamics soon shifted. In the February 1899 elections, the Trikoupist party, led by Theotokis for the first time, won the elections. Soon after, in 1905, Theodoros Deliyannis, the prime minister, was murdered by a gambler disgruntled by measures the government had taken against gambling halls. However, the Deliyannist party remained cohesive thanks to a decision by Dimitris Rallis and Konstantinos Mavromichalis to work together in order to keep it from escaping their control. Political party organisation in those years continued to be based on decentralised 'federations' of political notables—often very fluid, and with a pronounced local character. This is clear from the fact that, for example, in the elections of 1902 only three regions—Attica, Corfu and Gortynia—had candidates belonging to a single political party. In all other regions, ballots consisted of representatives assembled from various different parties. A witness from the era tells us:

> Politics is a personal, hereditary profession, to be practised as one fancies, namely in accordance with one's own interests, both personal and regional. As for one's beliefs: we hardly need mention them. In the elections already underway, most of the former opponents of the government then began to support it because of local interests, and vice versa. Changing one's party is quite common and does not cause the slightest surprise or criticism. In Parliament, a minister's vote is personal, not political—political principles and beliefs are wholly lacking.[1]

Attempts were made to improve the system's efficacy, but they were all oriented towards raising the moral standards of politics by combating clientelism. A broader electoral constituency was adopted once more in 1906 by Charilaos Trikoupis's successor, Georgios Theotokis. This tension expressed a perception in which local interests were opposed to the establishment of a more centrally oriented political system. During a debate regarding the re-establishment of the broader constituency, one of its opponents, Dimitris Gounaris, noted:

> What, then, is the most unpleasant consequence of the parliamentary system as applied to our country? The close relationship, as they say, between voters and candidates, such that the voter expects the candidate to represent a great number of important interests, thanks to which the voter can grant power to the candidate, electing them as an MP and sending them to Parliament. With this power vested by the voter, the elected representative appears before the government and claims to use that power, which the government derives directly from popular representation and indirectly from the people, to serve the voters' interests, something which, as they say, harms our land.
>
> But when we say land, we mean people, and when we say people, gentlemen, let us avoid idealisations. Let us bear in mind that a 'people' is nothing more than the individuals that comprise it. And when we say the 'needs of the people', we mean the needs of the individuals that comprise it. We should not imagine 'the people' as an entity above and separate from the individual. We should not conceive of the interests of the people as interests that should be prioritised and separate from the interests of individuals. The sum, the union, the harmonious connection of all peoples' interests whose individual development, growth and improvement constitute—and must constitute—the subject of our own project, as they represent the people's interests. Anything else is just phrases devoid of content, useful only for deceiving the most naïve of people.[2]

In this context, the result could be none other than political stagnation—or apparent stagnation—with relatively frequent changes in government, upheavals and conflicts over issues such as the translation of the Gospel or Aeschylus's *Oresteia* into demotic language, debates on the Macedonian and Cretan issues, and tensions over the agrarian question in Thessaly. Meanwhile, Parliament was in an abysmal state, largely due to obstruction from the opposition: this included endless debates on minor issues, abstention from duties in parliament so that quorum was impossible, and speeches lasting hours. G. Skliros, a pioneering socialist, described the prevailing situation of the period as follows:

> If there is something that all of us Greeks agree on, it is the poor state of our country. Young and old unanimously agree that the official state finds itself in a miserable condition; many, indeed, have begun to feel that our very society is suffering from a chronic and incurable disease. Up to here, there is an unprecedented consensus! But when it comes to attempts to explain this situation, we observe a confusion of opinions, a frightening disagreement. Most blame the governing system as the sole

> cause of this desperate situation; others the ambition and uselessness of our politicians; others corruption and others the crown; some blame our language and the educational system, while others blame corruption of the press. Still others criticise the lack of national spirit, etc., etc. ...[3]

The movement against the parliamentary system found fertile ground to develop, and some now began to openly announce their opposition.

Recovery and discontent

The situation was not as bad in the economic realm; the crisis of the late nineteenth century had been overcome and all indexes indicated constant improvement. After stagnating for the last twenty years of the nineteenth century, national GDP surged upwards in the early twentieth century. After reaching an annual average of 254.03 drachmas per capita from 1885–9 in 1914 prices, the average from 1890–4 decreased to 230.43 drachmas. In the next five years, 1895–9, it increased slightly to 242.17. The figure then rose even more until it reached the highest levels of the period in 1910–11: 282.28 drachmas per capita. It is important to note that these figures do not include incomes derived from foreign assets or activities, incomes that played (and continue to play) an outsize role in the Greek economy. Certainly, the Greeks who lived through the Balkan Wars were richer than their predecessors. Indeed, in these years the Greek economy was growing rapidly, even in comparison to highly developed countries of similar size.

Thus, from the end of the nineteenth century onwards, the economy entered a phase of growth. The currant crisis was gradually overcome, and with the establishment in 1905 of the Privileged Society for the Protection, Production and Trafficking of Currants—founded with Greek and French capital—currant surpluses found an industrial outlet and market rates of the product showed signs of stabilising, if not rising. At the same time, large industrial units were established and the shipping sector developed. Profits made through these activities and the salaries of staff involved brought great benefits to the Greek economy. Additionally, mass migration to the United States offered new hopes to the poorest of the rural populations, especially those in mountainous regions that had suffered from the currant crisis; this migration was also an important asset to the Greek government's balance of payments. In fact, in this period transoceanic migration tempered prevailing rates of rapid, natural population growth and served as a solution for very high levels of underemployment, particularly in the countryside.

7.1: Relation of Indirect to Direct Taxes, 1879–1991

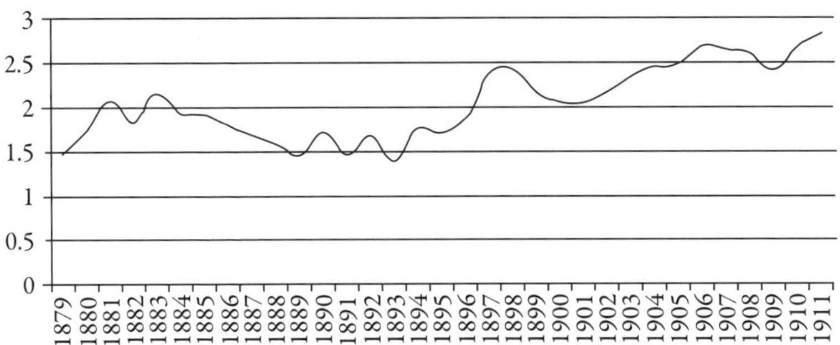

Source: Calculations based on data from the Ministry of Finance, *Έσοδα και Έξοδα του κράτους κατά τας οικονομικάς χρήσεις από του 1863 έως του 1915*, Athens: 1915, table no. 1.

Hence it was only natural for a banking system to emerge, which quickly became modernised and accumulated a significant number of deposits. In the same period, Greek banks gradually spread throughout the Eastern Mediterranean; a massive inflow of foreign capital soon followed. This was particularly true in the Ottoman Empire and Egypt, where significant Greek (and more generally Orthodox) populations had established themselves. What differentiated the Greeks from their Ottoman neighbours was the manner in which Greek capitalists and entrepreneurs were capable of equal participation with respect to their foreign partners in resulting institutional arrangements.

On the one hand, the fiscal discipline imposed by the International Financial Commission may have hampered efforts to finance military reorganisation—to the degree that this was even possible without access to international markets—and limited the sovereign rights of the Greek state. On the other hand, it led to a more rational approach to public spending. Indeed, the state of public finances exceeded forecasts of even the most optimistic observers. This was even acknowledged by the commission when it stated that its predictions for Greek public revenues had been incorrect—predictions it had relied upon when drawing up plans for servicing Greek public debt. While it estimated that this revenue would amount to 85.5 million drachmas in 1898 and 95.5 million in 1901, public revenues in 1898 amounted to almost 105 million drachmas. In 1901, according to the official assessment of the Ministry of Finance, they reached 115 million.

7.2: Total Taxes as a Percentage (%) of GDP, 1879–1911

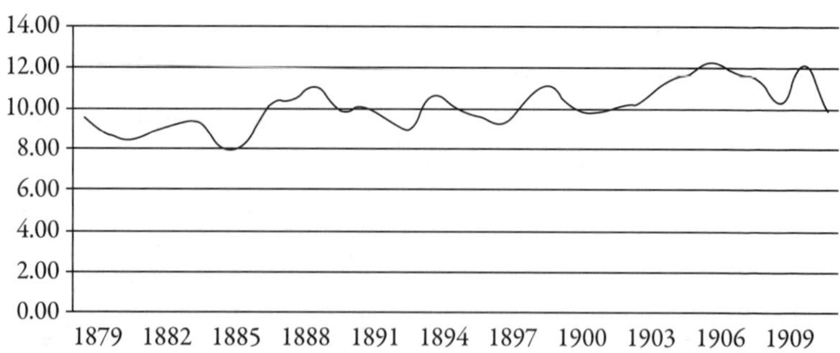

Source: Calculations based on data from the Ministry of Finance, *Έσοδα και Έξοδα του κράτους κατά τας οικονομικάς χρήσεις από του 1863 έως του 1915*, Athens: 1915, table no. 1 and G. Kostelenos's calculations of GDP.

The fact that Greece's economy experienced a robust period of growth—relatively speaking—was not the main subject of public debate. Instead, in public discourse, a sense of self-pity prevailed in relation to the national economy and especially public finances. In their annual reports on the state of the Greek economy, British diplomats indicated that pessimistic predictions accompanying reports on the Greek state's economic prospects might be attributed to the attempt at establishing a climate friendly for imposing new taxes and securing a new international loan. Any looser fiscal policies, which would allow revenue increases in other ways, conflicted with commitments made to the commission and were unthinkable. Though state finances were not as gloomy as the minister of finance made it seem, they were not exactly flourishing and capable of supporting substantial costs related to the reorganisation of an army and fleet—the government's first priority. This held more or less true for the governments that came to power in the wake of the military coup in 1909.

Though the economy did grow in general terms, many were still dissatisfied. And they had their reasons. The higher tax burden imposed after 1893 depended on a constant increase in indirect taxation at the expense of direct taxation—that is, increased taxation on lower incomes while higher income groups remained untaxed. Thus the press's constant criticism of excessive taxation on working-class and largely urban populations was not unfounded. In addition, the Greek state's strongly anti-inflationary policy, mandated by the commission, may have led to the 'national triumph' of the drachma's return to parity with gold, but it also led to limited liquidity and high interest rates.

Apart from this, Greece was also severely affected by the agrarian crisis of the late nineteenth century. The cultivators and the weakest members of society were the hardest hit: those who had come from the inland in search of a self-sufficient income, offering themselves for seasonal work cultivating tradable crops and generally accruing related incomes with the expansion of agricultural activities. It is precisely these populations that, pressured by reductions in supplementary sources of revenue, necessarily turned to intensified exploitation of available resources, and many ended up migrating. But dominant groups of merchants and landowners also found themselves weakened by the crisis, many of whom were directly affected and forced to suspend economic activity. As these groups found it impossible to address the problem, they exerted less influence politically. Soon, new groups arrived from the banking sector with the capital and the ability to address the problem, reaping the respective economic and political benefits in the process. The era of dealing with problems on a local level had come and gone; from now on, problems had to be dealt with on an international scale. Greece's 'belle époque' was not necessarily pleasant for all, and this fomented negative attitudes towards the 'plutocratic oligarchy' that emerged as the leaders of the national economy.

New urban hierarchies

The economic recovery also manifested itself in the renewed relocation of populations towards the nation's urban centres, a process occurring at the same time as external migration. Available statistics indicate that between the censuses of 1879 (which include data from Thessaly, incorporated into Greece in 1881) and 1889, the urban population of the country—that is, the population living in settlements of more than 5,000 inhabitants—increased from 13.81 per cent to 21.6 per cent of the total population. The currant crisis was most likely to blame for subsequent stagnation in this rate of relocation to urban centres, and this process only picked back up again in the early twentieth century—and even then only minimally, when urban residents amounted to 23.75 per cent of the total population.

These figures are only useful when put in context. In comparison to the 23.75 per cent of Greeks living in urban settlements in 1907, it is important to juxtapose the 40.8 per cent of the urban population in Europe (not including Russia) in 1910. Nation by nation, the urban population in 1910—always understood as the population living in settlements with more than 5,000 residents—amounted to 75 per cent in Britain, 57 per cent in Belgium, 53 per cent in the Netherlands, 40 per cent in Germany and Italy, and 38 per cent in France and Spain. On the other hand, Greece continued to surpass the percentage of urban populations in countries such as Portugal (16 per cent), Romania (16 per cent) and Serbia (10 per cent), the latter figure remaining notably stagnant between 1850 and 1910. Additionally, it should be mentioned that urban centres in Greece in 1907 had an average size of 15,961 inhabitants, while in Europe the average size was 21,200 inhabitants. In fact, the average size of Greek cities in 1907 was smaller than the average size of European cities an entire century earlier.

7.3: Settlements with More Than 5,000 Inhabitants in Greece, 1879–1907

Year	*Number of cities*	*Total population*	*Average size*	*% of Greece's total population*
1879	27	315,505	11,685	13.81
1889	35	473,231	13,521	21.6
1896	38	520,963	13,710	21.78
1907	39	622,496	15,961	23.75

NB: After their integration in 1861, the Ionian Islands were included in the census of 1865, and after Thessaly's integration in 1879 it was included in the 1881 census.

7.4: Distribution of Cities per Geographical Region, 1889–1907

	1889		*1896*		*1907*	
	Cities	*Population*	*Cities*	*Population*	*Cities*	*Population*
Peloponnese	12	121,545	14	141,797	15	149,404
Mainland Evia	8	186,720	11	216,577	10	302,560
Mainland Evia without Athens or Piraeus	6	45,142	9	56,872	8	67,099
The Islands	4	41,791	2	24,036	3	28,727
Ionian	5	64,556	5	63,243	4	55,526
Thessaly	6	58,619	6	75,310	7	88,279
Total	35	473,231	38	520,963	39	624,496

The geographic distribution of urban concentrations throughout the nation indicates that the former network of urban centres—if we can speak of such a thing—vanished in the 1870s, giving way to a new network. Cities on the islands declined, as did the old Peloponnesian cities, giving way to new settlements whose emergence was tied to the trade in crops. Ionian cities went through a period of stagnation, if not decline, while the cities in Thessaly—especially Volos—developed impressively; Volos grew from an unimportant settlement into a significant urban centre. In contrast to the resulting downturn on the Ionian Islands, Thessaly's integration into the Greek state was beneficial to the development of its cities. Here, national transportation projects played a decisive role. Volos benefited from construction of the Thessalian railways in the early 1880s, and became a harbour for exports linking Thessaly with Piraeus. Only in 1908—when the railway linking Athens and the northern borders was completed, securing Larissa's connectivity to the national capital by rail—did Volos's significance diminish.

Greece was still an agrarian nation, but by the early twentieth century it had established a strong urban momentum, developing urban hierarchies that were non-existent fifty years earlier. In other words, we can make the case for a coherent and hierarchical urban space that had begun to take root in the 1880s and had formed by the eve of the Balkan Wars. This process of formation began from the moment that basic pathways for domestic transportation—and, by extension, the means by which the capital could better control the provinces—existed. In these years, it was no longer necessary (though it remained important) for a settlement to be located by a port in order to ensure its development into a city. In this same period, relationships and dependencies between cities were recast, thanks, as always, to the development of transportation networks and infrastructure projects, and particularly the development of ports. Indeed, until the early twentieth century, a major city like Kalamata was obliged to resort to the markets of Athens and Piraeus for the foreign goods needed by its population, and to Ermoupoli for industrial products. Conversely, it sent its exports through Patras. This situation changed, as previously noted, in the late nineteenth century and especially in the early twentieth, when Kalamata finally built a port capable of meeting its commercial needs. Around the same time, in 1901, general access was granted to the railway line linking Kalamata and Miloi, granting the former direct access to remote sections of the Peloponnese and Athens itself. Up until then, the capital was only reachable by sea. The standards by which cities functioned had changed dramatically, and radically different networks formed to connect them.

Map B: The Greek Railway Network, 1912

Source: L. Papagiannakis, *Οι ελληνικοί σιδηρόδρομοι (1882–1910). Γεωπολιτικές, οικονομικές και κοινωνικές διαστάσεις*, Athens: 1982, p. 151.

Isolation

The improvement in economic terms was not accompanied by analogous successes in Greece's national claims. In this regard, it found itself in a difficult situation. Greece was extremely isolated, both on a Balkan and international level. As an observer at the time stated:

> Better big dreams—even if they are utopian—than a meagre reality. This is the sad psychology of nations that once had a great history and traditions. We are faced with despondency, which necessarily leads this nation to a utopian, false understanding of reality, and therefore to false, pernicious political tactics. Such were the tactics of Hellenism, and we can see the inevitably disastrous results clearly today. Reality avenges us terribly. Not a single friend! Only enemies! Because Hellenism denied everybody the right to existence?[4]

The potential for alliances in South Eastern Europe was limited as long as tensions prevailed in relationships with neighbouring countries. First, though it initially welcomed the possibility of a closer relationship with Greece, the Ottoman Empire soon changed its stance when Greek activities in Macedonia rendered such an approach impossible. Its relations with Bulgaria also deteriorated steadily to the point that the two countries found themselves competing for the same territory, while Serbia's appeal to Russia in 1903 complicated any cooperation with Belgrade. In addition, Greece's refusal to accept predetermined zones of influence in Macedonia at the very moment Serbia redoubled its demands rendered any agreement impossible. Finally, its brief dalliance with Romania at the turn of the century ultimately ended in an interruption in diplomatic relations between the two countries.

Greece's relations with the Great Powers were also at an extremely low point. By then, Russia had committed to supporting the Slavic states and could not play a supporting role for Greece; Germany became the protecting power of the Ottoman Empire, while France and Britain sought to further strengthen their positions in Bulgaria and Serbia. Italy's attempts to create an empire clearly posed a threat to Greek aims, while the Dual Monarchy, which initially welcomed Greece's political influence in the Balkans, changed its stance in 1906, seeking to win over the Ottoman Empire and Bulgaria.

The situation in Macedonia took an ugly turn for the Greek side after the country's defeat in 1897, which gave the Bulgarians a significant advantage: they were now capable of intervening in the Macedonian region unchallenged. In a short period of time, the entire so-called buffer zone that included the northern limits of Greek territorial claims—Monastiri, Stromnitsa and Meleniko—passed into the hands of the Comitatus, as the management committee for the Macedonian Revolutionary Organisation became known. Mass murders of 'grecomans', officers of the Greek faction, further weakened the Greek presence in the area. At the same time, the Comitatus began to demand autonomy for Macedonia and Trace, changing its name in 1902 to the Secret Macedonian–Adrianople Revolutionary Organisation (EMEO).

Hence it is no coincidence that Greece's territorial claims were treated with condescension, if not pity and contempt. Humiliation followed. In 1908, when Austria moved to annex Bosnia and Herzegovina—as Bulgaria simultaneously declared its full independence—the Cretans saw an opportunity to claim their union with Greece. The Ottoman administration's response was instantaneous; its troops began to gather at the border. In a memorandum to the Greek government, the Ottoman ambassador in Athens demanded a statement from Greece permanently rejecting union with Crete. The Greek government's response when faced with this new incursion was rather predictable. The prime minister rushed to seek assistance from the Great Powers, admitting to the French ambassador that the Greek army would be unable to resist the Ottoman army for more than a day. At the same time, the head of the Ottoman army declared his intentions to sip a celebratory coffee in Athens. The government in Athens and the Greek state in general seemed pitiful in the eyes of Greeks and foreigners alike.

Trikoupis's vindication

The impression one might form of the Greek state at the eve of the Balkan Wars based on testimonies of people from the era differs significantly from the picture that emerges when relying on other types of evidence. The country found itself in a process of transformation rooted in the 1880s and in the policies of Charilaos Trikoupis, a process that can only be understood when contextualised over a longer time period.

First, the size of the state altered. The situation had already changed the moment Otto abandoned Greece, and during the Trikoupist period the state grew impressively. This increase in state size was linked with conditions resulting from the Eastern Question—and it could not have been any different. As was the case with all countries in periods of war (or likelihood of war), public spending rose, though the end of the war did not lead to a return to pre-war levels. It is worth noting that, during the Crimean War, for the first time in many years public spending rose and surpassed the level of 20 million drachmas. As the dispute over Crete worsened in the 1860s, spending reached 50 million drachmas, while the crisis of the Eastern Question soon catapulted this figure to 100 million drachmas. In the 'Peace-War' period following Bulgaria's annexation of Eastern Roumelia, expenditure exceeded 120 million drachmas, soon levelling out at over 100 million.[5] In other words, expansion of the state was related to the conditions of crisis that Greece experienced at regular intervals—and with its efforts to cope with them.

7.5: Public Expenditure of the Greek State, 1862–1912

Period	*At current prices*	*Per capita in current prices*	*Constant prices*	*Per capita in constant prices*	*% GDP*
1863–72	36,810,516	26	45,752,925	33	16
1873–82	62,876,456	37	73,888,850	44	20
1883–92	117,754,283	55	135,921,559	63	25
1893–1902	126,634,697	52	129,393,364	53	23
1903–12	139,048,500	53	150,602,742	57	20

Source: K. Kostis, 'Δημόσια οικονομικά', K. Kostis and S. Petmezas (eds), *Η ανάπτυξη της ελληνικής οικονομίας τον 19th αιώνα*, Athens: 2006, p. 294.

Long-term shifts in the scale of public finances were directly related to processes of state-building. The static framework of public finances during the Ottoman period gave way—timidly at first, and then all the more decidedly—to a phase of expansion and radical reorganisation of the state, which sought to withstand challenges from Balkan rivals. This shift manifested itself most fully during the Trikoupis period.

As mentioned previously, this process was by no means unprecedented on an international level. It must also be clarified that the recognised importance of military spending as a source of state growth does not mean that the total increase in expenditure should be attributed to the army or navy. The organisation of a modern army and conscription necessarily presupposed a relatively robust civil registry, increasing administrative expenses. Indeed, expenses related to the civil registry established to support recruitment efforts in the 1860s were not included in overall figures for military spending. Similarly, the development of transportation networks was basically motivated by the need to enlist and transport troops to the borders in the shortest amount of time. Without these networks, a modern army was meaningless.

The state apparatus began to improve in qualitative terms as well. Public works took on an increasingly central role, as did public education, even in the period following the bankruptcy of 1893. On the other hand, the public debt swelled uncontrollably, and military spending remained a major burden. Finally, expenses related to the royal court and compensation for its staff were significantly lower than in the period of Otto's rule. Expansion of the state apparatus was driven by military expenditure, and for this very reason harsh criticisms were made of a state that had spent huge sums on an army still incapable of fighting.

7.6: Adjusted Public Spending by Category (%), 1863–1912

Period	*Public debt*	*Military expenditure*	*Education*	*Public works*	*Staff compensation*	*Expenses of the royal court*
1863–72	14.7	39.5	4.2	1.0	35.9	3.0
1873–82	19.7	46.4	3.0	0.7	26.6	1.8
1883–92	36.5	29.1	3.0	5.8	21.7	1.1
1893–1902	30.4	36.8	5.3	5.0	24.6	1.2
1903–12	28.4	37.3	4.9	4.0	24.6	1.0

Source: K. Kostis, 'Δημόσια οικονομικά', K. Kostis and S. Petmezas (eds.), x.), *xH ανάπτυξη της ελληνικής οικονομίας τον 19th αιώνα*, Athens: 2006, pp. 304–5.

But the state of the nation's military organisation was not as poor as it might seem. Among other things, as a result of the defeat in 1897, the necessity of a strong army and fleet was no longer disputed. Yet attempts to rebuild the army after its defeat in 1897 led to an impasse, mainly due to internal opposition and conflicts within the armed forces. As a result, even by 1906, the army was in deplorable shape: of its 18,000 soldiers, 3,000 were posted to the gendarmerie, 5,000 served as forest rangers, customs guards, police, prison guards and staffed other transitional positions, while the rest were scattered throughout Greece, often posted to small settlements. Such circumstances rendered any military training exercises impossible, and it is said that when the capital's garrison had to be mobilised it was so useless that a navy unit had to come to the rescue.

This situation changed dramatically with Theotokis's fourth term, which began in late 1905. His first concern was the signing of a 20 million drachma loan, guaranteed by the National Defence Fund. As a result of the loan, the time needed to prepare and implement the army's new organisational configuration shrank from five to three years. This configuration provided for a total of 60,000 men, well-trained officers and modern equipment. Thus this newly formed organisational model and its executive staff could begin to function. Seventeen new laws were created in the next three years that completely changed the very nature of the army; the result was a well-equipped army exclusively intended to combat the nation's external enemies. Use of the army for other purposes such as ensuring public safety was forbidden. Large-scale military training exercises were initiated with the participation of two reserve units, repeating rifles and artillery were purchased, while officers and health professionals were trained for wartime operations and the use of large mixed weaponry units. Construction also began for the railway line connecting Athens and the northern border, a necessary prerequisite for effective mobilisation in conditions of war. It is no coincidence that the line went into service just before the Balkan Wars.

In Macedonia, the situation had begun to change to the Greeks' benefit. The Porte's efforts at reform aimed to calm the situation, but they did not produce the expected results, and in 1904 the EMEO sparked the Ilinden uprising, which was harshly suppressed by the Ottoman army. If, on the one hand, this harshness rendered Europe increasingly aware of EMEO activities, on the other it made the Greek government realise that it would need to resort to violence in order to confront Bulgarian claims to Macedonia. It was clear that the proliferation of Greek schools was not enough. Reservations and resistance from the Theotokis government soon buckled, and subsequently, the appointment of new bishops to crucial dioceses and the formation of a dense network of Greek consulates in Macedonia ensued. This all laid the foundations for the gradual establishment of an effective support mechanism for Greek interests in the region. In the meantime, support from armed leaders dissatisfied with the EMEO's positions further strengthened Greece's claims. Progressively, armed Greek units began to dispute Bulgarian supremacy in Macedonia. Though it only managed to secure small victories at first, by 1905 the Greek presence had grown more pronounced and active, and in some cases even took on extreme forms. This shift irritated both the Western powers and the Porte, and the latter began to systematically pursue Greek forces. The Greek forces, much like the Bulgarian units in the area, faced problems of coordination and support. In the meantime, internal conflicts prevented both sides from developing a more organised approach, but it was clear that the Bulgarians no longer had the advantage.

1909

The Greek state's efforts at military reorganisation and its successes in Macedonia were not reflected in the political realm. The careless manner in which the opposition pounced on every effort at state reform wounded national pride.

The situation was aggravated by the Young Turks movement, especially after it embraced a more nationalist identity. Huge expenditure on military reorganisation did not seem to be yielding a result—which even the prime minister of Greece himself admitted to the French ambassador—while the national political leadership seemed to seek power for its own sake, content to busy itself with the trivial party politics of the process. Within the army, Prince Constantine adopted a 'clan-based' approach that reinforced his own supporters.

But major difficulties also emerged in other sectors. After its military defeat, the state seemed unable to fulfil its basic functions. A report submitted to Parliament on 26 May 1899 included 1,209 complaints against police officers, 125,241 denunciations against Greek citizens (though no procedures for trials had been initiated as a result), 1,843 indicted persons, 5,188 convicted persons, 12,850 fugitives and 88,901 pending interrogations—just in the month of May. In the end, the only solution found to address the pitiful state of the law was rather simple and effective: the state permitted all wrongdoers who were not wanted outlaws to leave the country.

The Military League, led by Colonel Zorbas, was soon established in response to this situation. The army revolted in Goudi on 15 August 1909 and a series of demands were made in the form of an ultimatum to the government. First among them was reorganisation of the army. Prime Minister Dimitrios Rallis was forced to resign and Kyriakoulis Mavromichalis took his place. The latter had support of the league, and sought to direct government policies using extra-institutional means. With no clear political goals, and facing a political situation that had developed to its detriment, the Military League soon began to deteriorate, turning into an organisation that solely aimed to serve its own members' needs. Any efforts at discipline vanished. Political parties criticised the league harshly for this, and the situation only worsened after navy officers also revolted, seeking to satisfy their own individual claims. An invitation was then made to Eleftherios Venizelos from Crete. At the time, Venizelos was a local political leader who had welcomed the Goudi revolt in an announcement made in the *Chania Herald* newspaper. In the past, he had also not clashed with George, high commissioner of Crete.

Venizelos came to Athens but refused to assume leadership of the league. Instead, he proposed to the league's leadership that a government led by Stefanos Dragoumis be established, and that a Double Revisionary Parliament be convened in place of a Constituent Assembly, which many members of the government had called for. The Parliament and George I agreed to the convening of the Double Revisionary Parliament, and the relevant law was passed. On 20 March 1910, the Military League announced its dissolution. It has been argued that the uprising of 1909 represented Greece's bourgeois transformation; in fact, it was noteworthy in that it facilitated Venizelos's rise to power, something that played a major role in Greece's significant achievements over the coming decade.

Elections were held on 8 August 1910 and the Revisionary Parliament convened for the first time on 28 September 1910. Despite the dispersion of political forces—mainly because of the many independent MPs that had been elected—the established parties, cohesively represented across most of the country, managed to secure a comfortable majority, winning 211 out of 362 seats. The so-called supporters of 'change' secured 122. Despite this, results of the election were considered a triumph for the movement in favour of 'rectification' that had been amorphous until then. But in practice, these electoral results did not offer enough support for the government and Stefanos Dragoumis resigned after failing to secure a vote of confidence in Parliament. George I then invited Venizelos to govern, who had been elected with the support of his friends as deputy MP of Attica-Boeotia, though he had not personally declared candidacy and was abroad during the election period. Venizelos formed a government and secured a vote of confidence from Parliament. But since the support he had in Parliament at the time was not enough to fully support his government, he dissolved Parliament with the approval of the crown and carried out new elections. This act would have extremely divisive consequences for the future.

The issue in this particular case was that sovereign bodies such as the Revisionary Parliament were not to be dissolved by royal decree; they themselves determined their longevity. Thus, the action of Venizelos and the King was a forced takeover. Opposition parties did not dare to react vocally, at least immediately, perhaps because they too had agreed to convene the Revisionary Parliament in a manner that was not consistent with the Constitution. Elections were called for 28 November 1910 in which Venizelos participated as leader of the newly founded Liberal Party. The opposition, for the most part, decided it would abstain from the elections in protest. This proved to be a crucial mistake, and the result was a triumph for Venizelos who was now backed by a majority of MPs in Parliament: the Liberals held 307 of 362 seats.

The Constitution of 1911 was based on the Constitution of 1864. Changes introduced by the Revisionary Parliament included: introducing parliamentary committees for the assessment of bills, which simplified the process of voting on them; prohibiting military officers from pursuing political careers and members of parliament from working in the private sector; and the safeguarding of judicial power. The Council of State was re-established as an administrative court, tenure was established for civil servants, primary education became free and mandatory, and freedom of press and right of association were protected. Essentially, the new Constitution improved the way the constitutional monarchy functioned, thus making the system more effective.

The new Constitution came into effect on 1 June 1912, and shortly thereafter Parliament was dissolved so that new elections could take place. Despite their expectations of an easy electoral victory, the established parties suffered another major defeat as the Liberals secured 80 per cent of the seats in the new Parliament. This development consolidated a new bipartisan system that gradually replaced the oligarchic bipartisan system of the late nineteenth century. This new bipartisanship would serve as the foundation of the National Schism in the period that began after 1915. The process of transitioning from one system to the other seems to indicate that Theotokis's party, succeeding Trikoupis's, constituted the core of the anti-Venizelist faction, while, conversely, a large percentage of Deliyannist politicians allied with the Liberals—at least until 1915.

Education and the intellectuals

In 1907, 66.3 per cent of the total population of the Greek state was illiterate, and the rate of illiteracy was even higher among the female population. Yet in comparison with the nineteenth century, significant advances had been made: in 1870, 82.2 per cent of the entire population was illiterate, while in 1879 this figure had fallen to 80.67 per cent. The difference between these two censuses was significant, though Greece did indeed continue to lag far behind in literacy rankings when compared with Western European countries.

As one commentator remarked in 1878:

> Thus, though the most special care and attention was given to the establishment of institutions of higher education (universities), for which the government was responsible to care and cater to, primary education—left in the hands of the public

> sector—was neglected to such an extent that in some districts of the capital passers-by might hear words the likes of 'Chi-bin, Si-skon, Panta-mir,' all remnants of Pericles's time. Approximately five kilometres from Athens, among the ruins from the temple of Demeter, if you don't know that bread is called 'bouk' and water 'ouiye,' you risk dying of hunger and thirst.[6]

However, as previously mentioned, advances in education were indeed made. It seems that Otto's fall was a catalyst for these changes, as the number of schools and students enrolled increased dramatically. The same applied for university students, whose enrolments multiplied exponentially over a very short period of time; the adoption of a democratic system resulted in the democratisation of education.

The major problem in the Greek educational system was not so much quantitative; rather, it was a matter of orientation and organisation. Classes were held haphazardly, each teacher taught as they pleased, and books, and even more so any other educational material, were scarce. Attempts to systematise and organise the educational system were made again after 1878: peer-learning processes were abolished, attempts were made to standardise teaching at a national level and lastly, in 1882, an attempt was made to systematise the preparation and selection of books taught in schools. Here, too, the national government made its appearance.

As the results demonstrated, all of these measures were unable to bring about major changes in Greek education, which became the object of disagreements between party factions over the aim and purpose of education. Restrictions were also constantly imposed by the Greek state's financial troubles. The issue became all the more acute due to the fact that education constituted the Greek state's basic instrument in its attempts to exert influence over regions of Macedonia and Hellenise the population; the establishment of schools in these regions was accompanied by complementary educational programmes aimed at developing a Greek consciousness. In addition to the Greek state, these activities were also supported by private organisations such as the Association for the Dissemination of Greek Letters, founded in 1869 with the aim of establishing schools and dispatching teachers to Macedonia. From 1882 onwards, the Greek state intervened more aggressively in this area, sending a representative to the association's meetings and supervising its financial expenses. In 1887, the Commission for the Reinforcement of Church and Education was founded under the direct supervision of the government. This momentum clearly had practical consequences for domestic educational policy, as it increasingly established a national education system and consolidated academic disciplines. Yet it also led to an obsession with classical education in educational practice and a distancing from the vernacular, as classical Greek was what defined the 'Greekness' of populations—or so they thought. Only in 1895 was the modern Greek language fully introduced in elementary schools.

In the realm of higher education, it has been argued that Greece was drastically out of step with the changes taking place in Western Europe. The national university's first directive limited teaching of the sciences to a minimum, and for this reason it was argued that the institution took a 'scholastic' approach to higher education. Throughout the nineteenth century, changes implemented in this domain were insignificant; it is telling that the first graduates of the natural sciences only appeared in 1865. And it was only in 1905 that the mathematics and science departments of Athens University became independent and founded their own schools.

The problems in the education system clearly reflected the limited capabilities of the Greek state and the lack of importance attached to education in Greece at that time. At the lower levels, education was often of little use to the population. On the other hand, only the middle and upper social strata were able to pursue a university education, as K. Lappas has shown, and these groups always had the option of pursuing their studies abroad. Indeed, a significant number of Greek students attended the universities of Western Europe, where they studied or supplemented their previous studies. At the end of the nineteenth and early twentieth century, a critical mass gradually formed from this group, and intellectuals started to play an increasingly prominent and influential role in the Greek state.

This class of intellectuals only began to emerge in the 1880s. These were years in which scholars gradually transformed into intellectuals seeking to intervene in social issues, demanding to have their own say. K. Dimaras identifies this movement—albeit in his own terms—when he writes that, under the influence of poet Kostis Palamas:

> We see the figure of the 'writer' emerge; literature ceases to be part-time employment, and takes centre stage in the writer's own life. This is something new. If we take the most prolific figures of the previous era, at the time when Roidis was involuntarily a writer, if we take Rangavis, Orfanidis, and Antoniadis, they all have one profession and exhibit their love for literature in their own writing. This indeed explains the incredible abundance of poets of the Romantic School. We are no longer dealing with amateurs here: the writer surely has a second job in order to make a living, but his social status is firmly a function of his literary profession. Thus the ranks of 'those who write' thin out while groups of writers accumulate, who are ten to twenty years younger than Palamas and Drosinis.[7]

By now, scholars were in a position to form their own networks, journals, and communities. They were no longer satisfied by the competitions organised under supervision of the university, and peers—rather than authorities—began to judge one another. The language question, which was a political issue above all else, came to play a central role in the critical attitudes these groups adopted towards state policies. In the end, intellectuals expressing their views on the nation's political and social conditions were undoubtedly influenced by the dispute over demotic language. A. Liakos has summarised this issue, explaining that 'the relative autonomy and centrality of language in the formation of the Greek nation meant that both discussions regarding the latter's very nature—conducted before the Revolution—and subsequent key discussions on the redefinition of national ideology (the demotic movement) were language-oriented'.[8]

An examination of the language question immediately after the founding of the Greek state certainly confirms that conflicting views existed, but it would be difficult to pinpoint major tensions or even create the social profiles of those who were for and against the issue. There was one language for more well-off social groups and another for the less well-off, something that was considered self-evident. Yet the language that prevailed throughout the period was *katharevousa*, insofar as it was used in schools, public administration and newspapers. It was a natural choice, to the extent that the Greek state could not abandon its relationship to antiquity—its basic mechanism of legitimacy in relation to Western Europe. The lack of major clashes is evidenced by the fact that Dionysios Solomos's *Hymn to Liberty* was established in 1865 as the national anthem. Meanwhile, the scholarly realm began to adopt more conservative positions, which in the context of the language question expressed themselves as a tendency towards archaism.

However, beginning in the 1880s, the situation changed. The scholarly realm began to gain wider influence and, as already mentioned, scholars were increasingly able to operate as an autonomous group. The demotic movement was an expression of these scholars' efforts to articulate their demands, demands related to wider changes in society. Both for Ioannis Psycharis and for other intellectuals who shared these views, the Greek state's malaise could only be attributed to the absence of adequate education. In turn, this absence could be attributed to the inadequacy of the linguistic corpus in use. Thus a strong demotic movement gradually formed that criticised the government's shortcomings and redefined the national project, introducing the people themselves as a fundamental variable in the equation. It is important to note that the arguments in favour of demotic language and education were essentially nationalistic arguments. If in France intellectuals used the Dreyfus affair as an opportunity to express themselves as a group, in Greece they were most occupied with succeeding in their national aims. This certainly determined the nature of this intellectual group.

Changes observed in the realm of historiography converge along the same lines. The first dean and professor of history at the University of Athens, K. Schinas, gave the following address to King Otto:

> In its heroic period, Greece was fragmented into numerous principalities; at its peak glory, it was divided into autonomous cities and small regions; it was then subjected to the Macedonian yoke, maintaining only a pitiful semblance of its former autonomy; finally, under Lucius Mummius, it was conquered by the Romans and was transferred as an inheritance of sorts to the Byzantine emperors, the successors to the Roman throne, who kept it under their rule; 400 years ago, it succumbed to that most absolute and intolerable reign of slavery. Thus, YOUR MAJESTY, Greece was never an independent and indivisible state. Originally it consisted of small states, hostile to one another. After that a small province of three successive great monarchies existed, of which the Byzantine was the only one with a consistent language and faith.[9]

In 1845, when Paparrigopoulos was criticised for publishing a translation in which the history of Byzantium was absent, he was similarly able to argue:

> It is true that the history of the Eastern Orthodox Empire is summarily outlined. Yet it is not true that this is the middle phase of our ancestral history. The middle phase of Greek history was the middle phase of *Greek* history ... essentially distinct, indeed, from Byzantine history. Thus it is this middle phase of Greek history that must be taught in our schools, and not the Byzantine.[10]

In other words, in his mind, Byzantium had not become a Greek empire; the Greek nation simply had a history parallel to that of its rulers.

In 1853, Paparrigopoulos published the first edition of his *History*. In the introduction, he defined precisely what he meant by the history of the Greek state: 'This book narrates all that occurred to the Greek nation from ancient times until today, all that is worthy of being preserved in the memory of people.' He took care to clarify that 'the Greek nation applies to all people who spoke the Greek language as their own.'[11] He then proceeded to a periodisation, dividing the history of the Greek nation into five periods: the novelty of this periodisation was that, from 476 BC to AD 1453, the Greeks regained their own freedom and their own kings, while Constantinople served as their capital:

> The Greek nation has existed for many thousands of years now. In this time it experienced both prosperous and unfavourable years. In order to distinguish these various events, we must divide this history into five parts.

> In the first part, we shall narrate what happened from the ancient times until 145 BC. This is the most illustrious period in the history of the Greek nation, because then our ancestors were not only free, but managed to emerge as the most important nation on earth thanks to their intelligence, virtue and education.
>
> In the second, we cover all that took place between 145 BC and 476 AD. This was when Greece was under the foreign Roman yoke.
>
> The third section consists of all the events between 476 AD and 1453 AD. In this period, the Greek nation was liberated again, with its own independent kings in the capital of Constantinople.
>
> The fourth section consists of all that took place from 1453 to 1821, when the Greek nation was once again subjugated by foreigners, this time by the Ottoman Turks.
>
> In the fifth, we recount all that transpired from 1821 until today, in which certain Greek regions obtained their freedom, establishing the kingdom of Greece, with Athens as its capital.[12]

In this manner, a framework for studying Greek history took shape, in which the Greek nation was attributed with particular properties that would characterise its existence. Thus in the preface to the second edition of his history, Paparrigopoulos writes:

> Ancient Greece, which did not manage to establish itself as a state, nor to extend the autonomous existence of its various individual cities, did not vanish from the pages of history as a result. After the untimely death of its own political inheritors, it successively adopted the work of Alexander the Great, of Christianity, and of Constantine the Great, morphing each time in accordance with the needs and circumstances of each new historical order, while always more or less preserving its essential spirit, playing a crucial role in the world for a long period of time. Indeed, this consecutive, tripartite series of revivals for the Greek nation constitute its highly distinctive feature in the history of mankind.[13]

Paparrigopoulos's book is not difficult to read and understand: he argued that it was addressed to children—in an instructive style. In some places, its political aims were more than clear. Thus, for example, when he referred to assimilation of the Slavic populations that had begun to enter Greece in the sixth century, he writes: 'this, indeed, will happen also in the northernmost regions of Greece, where some Slavic tribes retained their languages until recently, since they were more numerous than those that headed southwards.'[14]

On the other hand, up until the late nineteenth century, the main purpose of teaching history, at least at primary level, was character formation and the creation of ethical citizens; the objectives of national education were not as established as they later came to be. Moreover, history was not an independent course, and it was only taught to children attending schools in regional capitals. In these schools, the instruction of general Greek history emphasised the virtues and vices of historical figures, and the causes of the rise and decline of nations. It was meant to 'inspire in students the love of virtue and hatred of evil, respect for the status quo, patriotism and social virtues.'[15] It tended towards Christianity in terms of the values it sought to impose, both with regard to its overall conception of history and the educational system more generally.

The texts used to teach history were not written by Greek authors; nor were they crafted to serve the national goals of youth education. Most were translations of foreign texts. Only after 1882 was there a dramatic change in the approach to teaching history in schools, and especially after books began being subjected to inspection from 1907 onwards. The teaching of general history was abolished and replaced by the study of national history, which was based on a model that classified history into three periods (ancient, medieval and modern). This three-part model for the *History of the Greek Nation*, established by Paparrigopoulos in 1853, was only introduced in school instruction after 1880.

These changes need to be understood in terms of the period in which they were made. History, which initially played an instructive role in the Greek educational system, with the aim of creating virtuous subjects, took on a much more important role for the Greek state after a certain point. The Treaty of San Stefano and the creation of Bulgaria, which fought under more favourable conditions than the Greek kingdom for the annexation of Macedonian territories, changed the situation at the time and the way in which history was employed in its service. On the one hand, history was used as an instrument in the Greek state's claims, claims that required empirical documentation—something only the 'science' of history could offer. On the other, its role in the educational system was reformulated in an effort to develop nationally active subjects: the educational system could not ignore the Greek characteristics of the regions the Greek state sought to claim, much more so now that this model of education exerted considerable influence through the Greek schools that were founded in large numbers in these disputed territories. History was not an intellectual exercise, but a weapon in promoting the idea of the continuity of the Greek nation.

Rectifying efforts

The elections held between 1910 and 1912 led to radical changes in the Greek political system and to the ways in which political parties were organised. In the elections of 8 August 1910, socialist and agrarian MPs were elected to Parliament, together with many other new faces and new ideas. This renewal of political personnel was supported by—and led to—the first conscious attempt to create a structured party apparatus. To some extent, the Liberal Party, which continued to be identified primarily with particular people (rather than an ideology), had an advantage over the other parties in this process in that it possessed an effective organisational apparatus.

Independent of these changes following the Balkan Wars, Venizelos's rise to power accelerated the efforts to reorganise the Greek state in relation to the period's most urgent debates. The economy proved to be one of his key priorities. After assuming leadership of the government, Venizelos implemented a law on 4 May 1910 that had originally been introduced by the Dragoumis government. It allowed for the creation of a Ministry of Agriculture, Trade and Industry. The ministry became operational on 1 January 1911 and was soon renamed the Ministry of National Economy.

In 1914, Venizelos proceeded to establish the Ministry of Transport and Communications, which was also responsible for public works, demonstrating his intention to intervene in the realm of large-scale public works. The latter were sorely needed, especially in the Greek state's new territories. He assembled a multitude of talented young economists, engineers and agronomists, most of whom had studied abroad and enthusiastically supported his government's project. Many of these individuals were also directly involved in implementing the project, occupying various positions in the state apparatus.

Despite the numerous laws that were passed, especially in Venizelos's first term, the measures that were adopted were not particularly successful as the outbreak of war meant that people and resources would be absorbed by the war effort rather than the construction of public works. The financing of this war effort would become the chief concern of the Venizelist government up until November 1920.

In the military sector, the initiatives undertaken by the Theotokis government constituted the precondition for the Liberals' efforts to improve the army: constant training on every type of terrain, artillery exercises with live ammunition, and a new organisational framework implemented by the French mission invited to Greece under the leadership of General Joseph-Paul Eydoux. Despite its critics, the Greek army was well prepared at the eve of the Balkan Wars. Similarly, the Greek fleet was peerless in the Aegean, and this proved to be a real asset for Venizelos during the negotiations with the other Balkan countries over joint military action against the Ottoman Empire.

Greece's success in the Balkan Wars would have been unthinkable without the Balkan alliance—into which the nations of South Eastern Europe, willing or not, were thrust by the blackmail tactics of the Young Turks, together with the threat of Great Power intervention in these territories. The annexation of Bosnia–Herzegovina in 1908 by the Dual Monarchy and the Italian occupation of the Dodecanese in 1911 demonstrated that the threat was real. Even in Macedonia, it seemed that rivals had begun to converge. The decision of the Young Turks' governing committee to repress any dissidents forced Greek and Bulgarian armed troops to cooperate, at a time when both governments sought to increase their armed presence in Macedonia.

The Serbian–Bulgarian Treaty, signed under pressure from Russia, which wanted to limit Austria's presence in the Balkans, was a preamble for greater levels of cooperation in the Balkan region. Greek–Bulgarian talks followed, along with the signing of a treaty that facilitated alliances between Balkan nations, despite the fact that corresponding agreements between Greece, Montenegro and Serbia did not yield any immediate results. What was important was that, for the first time, the Balkan nations were able to establish a network of mutual support. This was the only way they would be able to defeat the Ottomans and oppose any attempt at Great Power intervention. Similarly, Bulgaria's defeat in the Second Balkan War would have been inconceivable without the Greek alliance with Serbia and the Ottoman Empire.

Greece's successes in the Balkan Wars were further enabled by the excellent state of its public finances. Along with the remainder from the advance of 40 million drachmas in 1910 and the loan of 110 million drachmas in 1911, the surpluses of 1910 and 1911 resulted in an abundance of cash for the Greek state just before the outbreak of the Balkan Wars. This is also why Greece managed to cope with the problems of financing the war effort without considerable difficulties, doing so without imposing new taxes. And it should be emphasised that it was an effort of colossal proportions: 280,000 men were mobilised to fight in a war that lasted nearly fifteen months, in a country whose army did not surpass 80,000 troops—a number equivalent to the total prisoners of war that would have to be fed and housed. Thus the 16 million pounds sterling that the Greek government would have to borrow in order to meet obligations related to the Balkan Wars was a reasonable sum given the magnitude of the war effort. But by Greek standards, this was a huge amount of money, and it was no coincidence that shortly after the Balkan Wars Greece experienced acute financial problems, especially in the second half of 1914 and early 1915, when the time came to settle accounts for past military expenditures and address current ones.

Beginning in 1897, over the course of fifteen years, Greece had managed something that no one could have imagined at the beginning of the twentieth century. The nation had achieved important successes during the Balkan Wars. Greece had clearly proved able to make the most of favourable diplomatic, economic and military circumstances in order to achieve its objectives. This would have been unthinkable without a well-organised military and a flourishing public and private economy to support its war aims. In other words, the Greek state proved able to mobilise human and other resources to successfully realise its irredentist foreign policy, without sacrificing internal social cohesion or political stability. In fact, over a short period the country capitalised on the cumulative growth it had experienced since the establishment of the Greek state. Without this growth, the results of the Balkan Wars would have been quite different.

8

A NEW GREECE

(1914–23)

Collective memory

Greece is perhaps the only country in Europe that does not celebrate the end of the First World War; the November holiday marked on the calendars of all Western countries does not exist on its national calendar. When discussing this period, Greeks are not in the habit of referring to it as the 'Great War'. Monuments for the conflict's fallen do exist, but for the most part they are not exclusive to this war; the names of victims in the Great War are included on tombstones along with names of casualties from other wars. This seems paradoxical since, precisely with the end of the war and its peace treaties, the Greek state appeared to have achieved the goal it had set when it had been created eighty years earlier: a 'Greater Greece'. Greece's participation in the First World War brought the country territorial benefits that would have been unthinkable just a few years earlier, and the dreams of Greek irredentism seemed to have been realised.

Though there are many reasons for the prevailing Greek attitude towards the First World War, they can be briefly summarised as follows. For Greece, the war did not begin in 1914 and end in 1918. The Great War was simply a continuation of the Balkan Wars and an introduction to the Asia Minor campaign (and the Ukrainian campaign in 1919)—another step in the process of national integration. For Greece, in other words, the war began in 1912 and ended in

1922; the First World War was merely an intermediary period surrounded by ten years of continuous war, which ended—despite gains conferred on Greece by the peace treaties at the war's end—with the country in ruins.

Yet there are also other reasons that must be taken into account in order to better understand the Greeks' refusal to view the First World War as a separate event of major importance in their national history. These reasons are tied to a national, and traumatic, collective memory.

Timetable 1914–23

1914	Outbreak of First World War. First clashes between Constantine and Venizelos, the latter prime minister at the time.
1915	Venizelos resigns, seeking to provoke elections. Dimitris Gounaris government (25 February 1915–10 August 1915). The Liberal Party wins the elections and a government led by Venizelos is formed (10 August 1915–24 September 1915). Due to conflicts over Greece's participation in the war, Venizelos resigns again. Alexandros Zaimis government (24 September 1915–25 October 1915). Stefanos Skouloudis government (25 October 1915–9 June 1916). The Liberals abstain from elections and the Royalists win by a large margin.
1916	The National Defence movement is created by Venizelists. Alexandros Zaimis government (9 June 1916–3 September 1916). Nikolas Kalogeropoulos government (3 September 1916–27 September 1916). Revolutionary government formed by Venizelos in September (19 September 1916–27 June 1917) is recognised by the Entente. Athens government of Spiridon Lambros (27 September 1916–21 April 1917). On 11 November, the government in Thessaloniki declares war on Germany and Austro-Hungary.
1917	Alexandros Zaimis government (21 April 1917–14 June 1917). The allies force Constantine to resign and flee Greece. The second born-son of Constantine, Alexandros, succeeds him. Venizelos returns to Greece and forms a government (14 June 1917–4 November 1920). The Parliament existing before the elections of 31 March 1915 (Parliament of Lazarus) is reinstated.
1920	Alexandros dies of septicaemia. In the elections of 1 November 1920, the anti-Venizelists triumph. Venizelos leaves Greece. Dimitris Rallis government (4 November 1920–24 January 1921). A referendum follows, after which Constantine returns to Greece.
1921	Nikolas Kalogeropoulos government (24 January 1921–8 April 1921). Dimitris Gounaris government (26 March 1921–3 May 1922).
1922	Nikolaos Stratos government (3 May 1922–9 May 1922). Petros Protopapadakis government (9 May 1922–28 August 1922). The Asia Minor front collapses in August. Destruction of Smyrna. Nikolas Triandafilakos government (28 August 1922–16 September 1922). In September, a military

rebellion led by Nikolaos Plastiras. Sotirios Krokidas government (17 September 1922–14 November 1922). Constantine resigns to be replaced by his son George II and abandons Greece once more. Six leaders of the anti-Venizelist faction are tried and executed as responsible for the Asia Minor catastrophe (Trial of the Six). Stylianos Gonatas government (14 November 1922–11 February 1924).

1923 Anti-Venizelist parties abstain from elections and the Venizelists triumph. George II is forced to leave Greece. Admiral Koundouriotis assumes the regency.

The Balkan Wars, which doubled the population of the Greek state, were waged at a time of national concord and unity—or so it seemed. With the war's end and Constantine's succession to the Greek throne after the assassination of his father George I, intense political tensions emerged over Greece's participation in the First World War. Whereas the new pro-German king had adopted a stance of neutrality, a decision that was favourable to the Germans, Venizelos had strongly supported Greece's participation in the war on the Entente's side. With the outbreak of war, conservatives now had the opportunity to take the political initiative they had lost a few years previously with the rise to power of Venizelos and the reformers. Constantine, on the other hand, saw the same situation as an opportunity to strengthen the political basis for his throne and his personal position. To achieve these goals, he increasingly adopted an authoritarian style of governance—which he and the political environment had tended towards since the late nineteenth century. Thus an anti-war stance in a conflict that—at least initially—seemed to be unrelated to Greece served to strengthen the faction that supported him, while the opposing camp suffered the inevitable damage associated with the pursuit of participation in war and the deprivations of wartime.

The National Schism

The conditions for a political crisis and an acute social confrontation would soon emerge. In February 1915, Constantine and Venizelos's disagreement over Greece's participation in the war led to Venizelos's resignation. In the elections of May 1915, the Liberals gained a large majority, and in August Venizelos formed a new government that proved short-lived: the general military mobilisation and the arrival of the British and French in Thessaloniki led to a new conflict with the king, after which Venizelos was again forced to resign. From this moment onwards, Parliament became nothing more than an

Map C: The Balkan Peninsula, 1913

instrument for monarchical rule. The Liberals' decision to abstain from the elections of December 1915 only encouraged this trend. As each of the two factions claimed to be the true representatives of Greece's national interests, designating the other as traitorous, Greece's position in relation to the war, let alone its participation in it, had become a extremely painful affair.

Tensions between the two camps intensified again in 1916. In May of the same year, the government surrendered the fortress of Roupel, on the border of Bulgaria, to German and Bulgarian troops. The Entente's forceful reaction obliged the royalist government to halt the process of mass military mobilisation. This in turn enabled the direct and rapid formation of the Panhellenic Reserve Association, the first mass political organisation in Greece, an organisation with ties to fascist and especially proto-fascist movements in other countries. With the informal characteristics of a militia group, but also the consolidated structure of a mass political organisation, these reservists, which mostly came from the nation's lower middle classes, were used by the anti-Venizelist faction to supress its political opponents. The civil war, euphemistically referred to as the 'National Schism', had manifested itself fully, and the ease with which soldiers passed from military mobilisation to political organisation highlighted the fluidity of the boundaries between the two. The experience of the two Balkan Wars undoubtedly played a catalytic role in organising these groups of reservists and helps explain the ease with which they resorted to violence, even against their own compatriots: the Venizelists were merely enemies, much like the Bulgarians or Turks. The fact that these opponents were unarmed citizens was of little importance. Extermination of non-combatants that did not support the winning side, regardless of nationality, in the context of ethnic cleansing, had already begun during the Balkan Wars. It could even be argued that the lack of a distinction between non-combatants and soldiers first made its appearance in the Balkan Wars and not in the First World War. The war continued for Greece in this period; but this time, the enemy was internal.

Yet the conflict had not yet reached its climax. In August 1916, a portion of Western Macedonia and all of Eastern Macedonia had been occupied by the Bulgarians, an incursion tolerated by the government. Greece was able to save face, portraying the event as a strategic move by the royalist government. Meanwhile, the Bulgarian government immediately began implementing a plan for ethnic cleansing in these territories, with many thousands of people being killed in the two years of the Bulgarian occupation. The Venizelist reaction was swift: in the same month, the National Defence uprising took place in Thessaloniki, enabling Greek military units composed of volunteers to participate in operations on the Macedonian front.

In the following month, Venizelos abandoned Athens, took on leadership of the National Defence movement, and formed a provisional government in Thessaloniki. Shortly afterwards, in November 1916, the royalists repelled an Anglo-French invasion in Athens and Piraeus and began mass-scale violent persecutions of the Venizelists, claiming many victims. In these circumstances, all Greeks—or rather all citizens of the Greek kingdom—had to align themselves with one faction or the other; they could not do otherwise. This was even the case for the socialists, whose anti-war stance pushed them towards anti-Venizelist views. This was also the case for the church, and in particular its senior ranks, which actively supported the king.

In turn, the allies established a military blockade to isolate the territory of Old Greece. Deaths resulted, whether directly inflicted or indirectly caused by hunger, and in May 1917 Constantine was forced to leave the country. A month later, Venizelos formed a government in Athens, the Allied military blockade ended, and the Parliament that had been elected in 1915 was convened. The Venizelists proved just as resourceful as their predecessors when it came to persecuting their opponents and did not treat the institutions in place with any more respect. Attempts to set up a battle-ready army in anything but favourable conditions led to reactions ranging from passive resistance to mass desertion and revolt. Executions were the immediate next step.

From this point onwards, both sides would find various pretexts—emotional and otherwise—for their unprincipled, revanchist attitudes. The contrast between these two 'worlds' marked Greek politics up until the confrontation between nationalists and communists that first manifested itself during the German occupation, and even more so after 1945. The animosity underlying this confrontation was evident from the fact that, just a few years after signing the Treaty of Sevres—the treaty with which Greece satisfied almost all its territorial ambitions—Venizelos was the target of an assassination attempt at the Gare de Lyon train station in Paris. The attempt failed, but by then there was little chance of compromise. While Greece had torturously but successfully managed to address the issue of institutionalising political opposition from 1875 onwards and had consolidated a constitutional-parliamentary system, now, within a very short period, it found itself on the path of questioning every institutional limitation to the pursuit of political power. The king's role transformed from mediatory to interventionist, contributing to this process. Unsurprisingly, as soon as news of the attempt on Venizelos's life reached Athens, the Venizelists retaliated. One of their victims was Ion Dragoumis, a leading figure in the anti-Venizelist faction.

The national political sphere continued to move in the direction of further confrontation. A Venizelist defeat in the elections of 1 November 1920 led to Constantine's restoration as king and a new wave of persecutions against the Venizelists. The country's international position deteriorated as allies took advantage of this shift, revoking their commitments to the Greek state. In this context, the advisor to the prime minster, A. Kampanis, recommended 'the founding of Greek Fascist Battalions that might apply Lynch's law against the small and reactionary minority', the Liberals.[1] The use of violence and coercion had now become a normal part of politics. All this transpired at a time when Greece was caught up in its exploits in Asia Minor—a campaign whose legitimacy was questioned by the anti-Venizelists.

Emancipation of the army

The collapse of the front in Asia Minor in 1922 led to a military coup. According to G. Mavrogordatos, the coup not only spelled a triumph for the military and consolidated Venizelist hegemony over the opposition; it also cemented the beginnings of the military's gradual emancipation from the political leadership of the party. Meanwhile, important differences began to emerge within these factions themselves over the nature of the regime in place.

With the anti-Venizelists completely disorganised and Constantine abandoning the country once again, the Venizelists were able to assume a dominant political position and made use of military courts to suppress their opponents. The execution of six figures (including the nation's prime minister, Gounaris) after the Asia Minor campaign in response to their alleged responsibility for the defeat suffered in the Greco-Turkish War can only be understood in the framework of legitimising violence as a means to regulate the political opposition. The preceding trial was purely a formality. Appeasing the political wrath of the population—an argument that was often used to justify punishment for high treason—may also have played a role. But this would not have been possible without the situation created by the National Schism, in which violence had become a necessary component of political practice. And yet again, even after the campaign in Asia Minor had come to a close, the end of war did not spell an end to the conflict.

This became clear after the military coup of 1923, in which the anti-Venizelists sought to benefit from the new regime's internal divisions: national politics were always on the verge of civil war, and the disagreements assumed the form of an organised military conflict. The coup's failure then resulted in the primacy of extreme Venizelists and the imposition of the Republic. Next, the Venizelists moved to purge the state apparatus of any anti-Venizelists.

While the National Schism continued to define the Greek political scene, the groups in power did not seem to feel any more comfortable in the international context brought about by the interwar period. Greece's newly drawn borders rendered it more vulnerable from the north, chiefly in relation to Bulgaria, which challenged the arrangements made by the Treaties of Peace. Serbia, in turn, pushed for an outlet on to the Aegean. Relations between the two allies of the Balkan Wars were not at their best during the interwar period. Moreover, the Italians, having already extended into the Dodecanese, seemed intent on further expansion: the Italian bombardment and occupation of Corfu in 1923 persuaded even the most optimistic minds of Mussolini's true aspirations for Italy. The League of Nations' inaction on this issue only resulted in further insecurity among Greek leaders. This hostile climate was further stoked by the Greek army's invasion of Bulgaria in 1925 due to a border incident, which showed just how delicate the balance of power was in the Balkans. The only positive development at the time seemed to be the warming relationship between Greece and Turkey, which resulted in a treaty of friendship between both countries.

Overall, the conclusion of these military campaigns ushered in a time in which the army played an increasingly regulatory role in Greek politics. With the battle lines drawn between Venizelist and anti-Venizelist camps, officers would often take the initiative, going beyond the prescriptions for managing political crises determined by faction leaders. Frequently, these very same leaders would accept the military's regulatory role in politics, encouraging it or even instigating it. Ultimately, whoever controlled the army would henceforth play a decisive role in determining which faction would maintain power. This was demonstrated by successive military coups during the interwar period; by the two dictatorships in the same period (from 1924 to 1925 under General Theodoros Pangalos, and in 1936 under King George II and Metaxas); and, finally, by the anxious attempts political factions made throughout the 1930s to give the army an instrumental role so as to secure their own power.

Economic Collapse

As previously mentioned, the Greek state was able to participate in the Balkan Wars at a prosperous moment in its state finances. Budgets from 1910 and

1911 left behind a large surplus, and a loan of 110 million drachmas in 1911 allowed the Minister of Finance Lambros Koromilas to allocate 75 million drachmas for use in case of war. Yet if these sums helped Greece face the Balkan Wars without financial difficulty, they did not lead to—nor could they possibly lead to—fiscal sufficiency capable of meeting the enormous costs of both the war effort and the administrative incorporation of the new territories.

By 1913, officially documented expenses for military operations amounted to 411,485,000 drachmas, in addition to another 280 million drachmas of collateral costs. Meanwhile, according to the Minister of Finance Alexandros Diomedes, the nation's public debt had risen by 755 million drachmas. These were dizzying figures given the state of Greek finances at the time, especially given the reluctance that successive Liberal governments displayed in imposing new taxes. Indeed, immediately after assuming power, Venizelos rushed to abolish the income tax that had been adopted in 1909. One solution remained: the National Bank, which made capital available to the government for the duration of these military operations in the form of advances or temporary loans.

But as the wars drew to a close, these pending debts had to be settled. To this end, the Greek government signed off on the first portion of its largest loan yet, a loan of 500 million francs, on 2 February 1914. The loan's favourable terms left no doubt with regard to the prevailing expectations in Western Europe about the future of the Greek state. It also demonstrated the competence of the head of the National Bank, Ioannis Valaoritis, who handled the negotiations. But this did not solve Greece's financial problems. In 1914, the budget amassed a deficit of 170 million drachmas, while Diomedes estimated the immediate needs to be covered (that had not been included in the budget) at over 300 million drachmas. Thus, issuance of the second portion of the 500 million franc loan proved impossible even before the outbreak of the First World War, and as a result, the Greek government turned to the National Bank once more.

These difficulties could not be solved by continuous borrowing. Even payments of regular salaries and civil service pensions were not being made on time, giving the opposition grounds for criticism of the government. The situation further deteriorated in the second half of 1914 and early 1915 when basic military needs, including the supply of food for soldiers, were only fulfilled thanks to advances from the National Bank. Venizelos's resignation from the premiership in February 1915 came just as the Greek state's financial failures reached a critical stage. In the period that followed, the state of public finances would only worsen further.

Venizelos's return to power came about under particularly adverse economic conditions. Inflation was rampant, and deep divisions within the state had dealt major blows to public revenue, which also suffered from the difficulties that long-term political instability had created for national economic activity. The acute political tensions meant it was difficult to reach a consensus on increasing the tax burden at a time when Greece's official participation in the First World War had caused a huge surge in public spending, which was impossible to offset with domestic resources.

It became clear that Greece would only be able to meet the needs of the Entente's war effort with Allied support. To this end, in 1918, Greece reached an agreement with the governments of France, Great Britain and the United States that made 850 million drachmas available to the Greek government in credit (as the amount was not immediately available as cash). Based on this credit and a broad interpretation of domestic monetary policy, a corresponding amount of banknotes were issued, which were then used to finance the war effort.

This credit was presented as a cover for monetary circulation, and consequently, subsequent inflationary pressures were regarded as a temporary phenomenon. Another contributing factor was the maintenance of the drachma's exchange rate on a par, and often even beyond parity, with other major currencies of the era: the sterling pound, the French franc and the dollar. Greece would also finance the war effort by using printing machines to issue massive amounts of paper money. Legal and monetary gimmicks, as well as the international economic and political situation, temporarily allowed the Venizelos government to conceal the problem and boast of a healthy economy, but it would soon be forced to face reality.

The sudden end of the First World War quickly upset the wartime balance of the economy. The drachma, which since 1910 had been seen as one of the most stable currencies in the war, now faced significant pressures. The National Bank's foreign currency reserves began to deplete rapidly. Credit made available by allies could not provide a counterweight to this momentum. Meanwhile, the country's financial needs showed no signs of diminishing. To the contrary, the nascent conflict in Asia Minor was to significantly exacerbate Greece's fiscal problems, gradually exhausting the nation's economy.

By the summer of 1919, the government's efforts to maintain a stable exchange rate for the drachma had failed. At that point, the Greek drachma began a downward spiral that had a negative impact on the state budget for servicing public debt and providing military supplies. The currency's devaluation only came to an end in 1923—and only temporarily, even then. Despite all the enthusiasm over the country's territorial expansion at the other end of the Aegean, the Greek economy had reached its limits. In September 1919, the Greek state sought to issue another internal loan of 300 million drachmas. The initiative faltered, indicating that the economy's strength did not match the political optimism at the time. Just one month later, Minister of Finance M. Negroponte wrote a letter to Venizelos on the issue of financing expenses for the campaign and the occupation of Asia Minor, ruling out the possibility of signing another external loan. Floating debt, a solution that had not been employed extensively until then, was employed, but this in turn could only cover a small part of the deficit.

In order to cover the costs of both the Asia Minor campaign and the participation of Greek expeditionary forces in the Ukraine campaign, the Venizelos government sought to establish new sources of credit with the Allies. Venizelos was still very much in political favour, and his efforts were met with some success; France and Britain offered Greece new credit amounting to 100 million francs. As before, this credit could not be liquidated, but it could support an increase in monetary circulation. This amount was insignificant when compared with the needs arising from the extension of the Smyrna occupation, and the role it was called to play was rather one of psychological support. But the Allies were no longer willing—and no longer in a position—to offer additional support to the Greek state. From May 1920 onwards, financing of the public deficit would be accomplished by issuing paper money.

The Greek government did seek out other ways to increase its revenues. In 1918, heavy taxes were imposed for the first time, while in 1919 a total overhaul of the Greek tax system was attempted with the introduction of a 'net income tax' that was modelled on the French income tax of 1914. This system proved to be a resounding failure. Once again, the Greek state would attempt to increase its revenues by resorting to significant increases in indirect taxes.

The return of the anti-Venizelists—and especially of Constantine—to power led the Allies to renege on their promise, prohibiting the liquidation of credit previously granted to the Greek state. Greece attempted to secure economic aid, focusing mostly on Britain, but even its requests for a loan would be doomed to failure. The economic crisis of 1920–1 then led to a sharp drop in the prices for agricultural commodities, exacerbating the situation. Having exhausted all the means at its disposal, the Greek government resorted to a desperate measure: it partitioned its hard currency in two, declaring half an emergency loan, while the other half continued to circulate at half of its nominal value. Defeat in the Greco-Turkish war was now accompanied by economic defeat.

Social confrontations

The National Schism undoubtedly shaped the broader context of Greek politics from 1915 onwards. Individual political and social conflicts were often lumped within it. The labour movement, for example, became increasingly prominent in Greece after the end of the war. Such a reaction was perhaps to be expected. It was hardly possible for the Greek economy to support such a long-lasting war effort, especially now that the conflict had extended past the end of the First World War.

As suggested above, during the Great War public expenditures were largely covered by increasing the amount of money in circulation, and much less so by increasing taxes. Given the Greek state's inability to resort to borrowing in domestic and international markets, this practice continued through the years of the war in Asia Minor. Eventually, however, a lack of alternatives ultimately forced the government to impose harsh taxes in order to finance its military operations.

Inflation, which rose rapidly from 1914 onwards, necessarily affected low- and middle-income groups, something that was expressed in the reduction of average real income per capita. These same groups had suffered the greatest hardship during the wartime blockade of Old Greece by the Allies, and they had also been affected more generally by the disruption of international trade, a crucial survival mechanism in a country as grain-deficient as Greece was at the time. The fact that the war would continue in Greece for another three years, requiring conscription and renewed financial sacrifices from the population, could only worsen the situation these groups found themselves in, leading to further opposition and confrontation.

Certain groups in Greece were in a far better financial situation than the majority of the population; these groups belonged mostly to the trade and shipping sectors and were able to reap extraordinary profits from the war. Additionally, scandals linked to the country's food-supply and more specifically to the Ministry of Provisioning further tarnished the government's image and caused severe tension.

Until 1919, the government was able to present an embellished portrait of the national economic reality, aided in this pursuit by allied financial solidarity. But from this year onwards, the economy spiralled out of control, the drachma's rapid devaluation serving as a prime example of this process. The campaign in Asia Minor exhausted the capabilities and resources of the Greek kingdom together with the strength of its population.

Two examples serve to highlight this. The first is the number of draft evaders and deserters: according to estimates available on conscription, in 1921 in Old Greece, Crete and the Archipelagic region, out of a total 342,000 individuals obligated to serve, 143,000 were evaders. Estimates on the number of draft-evaders and deserters in the whole country (including Asia Minor) exceeded 300,000. The second concerns immigration: in 1918 and 1919, the number of migrants shrank to an insignificant number relative to Greek norms, while the number of repatriated subjects grew. But the situation soon changed again, since in 1920 and 1921 the number of migrants grew impressively and the number of repatriated subjects shrank. While the crisis of 1920–1 may have played an important role in reversing this trend, so did the prolonged duration of the war and an increase in army conscripts destined for Asia Minor. Moreover, the huge number of deserters had collateral consequences: outbreaks of banditry and crime proliferated throughout Greece, causing a wave of persecution and repression.

In addition, the urban population had begun mobilising aggressively in pursuit of workers' rights. Disruption of foreign trade during the war had created an artificial protectionism that seemed to have helped strengthen Greek industry and the working classes. The war had also fomented a radical spirit and boosted trade unionisation of workers, leading to the founding of the General Confederation of Greek Workers in 1918. The confederation was established with the toleration, if not open support of, the Venizelist government, which hoped to gain a leading role in managing the labour movement and use it to the nation's benefit in international claims. This view was not far removed from the assumption that the 'labour problem' could be addressed through a scientific approach led by the state bureaucracy. Soon, however, the Venizelists would lose control of the situation as the socialists prevailed in the confederation, pushing it towards more radical policies.

As the First World War came to an end, a wave of mass strikes erupted throughout Greece, and in 1919 the first general political strike was held. The strikers demanded that leading figures from the socialist faction of the General Confederation of Greek Workers return from exile. The strikes continued, more or less in step with the country's deteriorating economic situation for the duration of the Asia Minor campaign. Independent of the economic demands made, they were also shaped by employees' opposition to policies aimed at the imposition of labour discipline.

Yet if up until 1918 workers' mobilisations were driven directly by demands set out by the workers themselves, this soon changed. The Socialist Workers' Party was established in November 1918; upon joining the Third International in 1920, it added the designation 'communist' to its title. Though it had little direct influence in Greek politics, it was to become a politicising factor in the labour movement. Regardless of the limited degree of influence communists had on Greek political life, they had decisive influence on the way in which the state created policies for dealing with the labour movement as a politically dangerous and socially subversive entity.

In his first term as prime minister from 1910 to 1915, Venizelos saw to the adoption of worker-friendly measures. This surprised onlookers, mostly because there had been little popular demand for him to do so, but also because the nation's working classes were still of minor importance politically. However, from 1918 onwards, the government's attitude hardened and workers' protests were often subject to violent repression. This difference demonstrated a declared change in the bourgeois state's attitude towards workers' demands. Henceforth, state policies moved away from a detached sense of protecting the weakest classes and towards social confrontation and violent suppression: the working class was now considered a potential threat to social order and a possible enemy of the state. The way in which strikers were treated during the general strike of 1923 and an assembly on May Day in 1924 is proof of this.

Ethnic conflicts

The arrival of large numbers of refugees further intensified the situation. Although most of the refugees, around one million in number, had arrived in Greece after the campaign in Asia Minor, a substantial portion—150,000—had arrived in the country during the First World War in order to avoid the Ottoman Empire's mass persecutions during its attempts to 'Turkify' its population. Most of the refugees that had arrived before 1922 had the financial means to find housing in urban centres, though they were anything but welcomed. Persecutions were already evident in 1916, when during the *Noemvriana*[2] clashes conscripts singled out refugees identifying with the Venizelist faction. Additionally, a number of refugees were killed by armed anti-Venizelists for being agents of the British and French. Conversely, gangs of refugees in Thessaloniki were especially violent towards the city's Muslim residents, throwing them out of their homes so that they themselves could settle in them. This resulted in the displacement of 15,000 Muslim residents (including the sister and cousin of Mustafa Kemal Atatürk) in just over two years. Muslims experienced similar treatment during the biggest wave of refugee arrivals directly after the Asia Minor campaign, until the exchange of populations decisively settled the 'issue'.

Impoverished and bereft, refugees arriving in Greece after the Asia Minor campaign immediately depressed indicators of hygiene and housing, dramatically worsening the country's economic situation. International organisations could offer very little assistance, and initially the Greek state sought to resettle the refugees using its own resources. This was a huge burden on public finances, further exacerbating the Greek state's financial woes and its need to appeal for relief from international capital markets.

The process of assimilating the refugees into society remained incomplete until the Second World War. As G. Mavrogordatos points out, what came about was a process of political and social diversification on the basis of an ethnicity, which essentially challenged the 'Greekness' of these refugees. In this context, it was probably no coincidence that the people of Asia Minor did not easily secure the protection of the Greek state from regular and irregular Turkish troops in August 1922; in the words often attributed to Aristeidis Stergiadis, high commissioner of Greece in Smyrna: 'Better that they stay here and be slain by Atatürk, because if they go to Athens they will overthrow everything.'[3]

Refugees arriving in urban centres reshaped the political, social and economic dynamics of the cities. The vast majority of refugees identified with the Venizelist faction and settled in the outskirts of large urban centres, leading to the creation of large settlements composed entirely of refugees. These centres of poverty and suffering were considered a potential danger to the bourgeois regime and were often treated accordingly. Refugees also constituted an increasingly important factor in the developing labour market. Very often, they were seen as a threat to local jobs, while in Thessaloniki fierce competition emerged between refugees and Jewish residents for dominance of the city's economy. As conscripts were discharged from the army who were also looking for employment—at the same time as the adoption of immigration quotas in the United States excluded migration as a way out—the situation was potentially explosive. Under these circumstances, those who sought to take advantage were none other than the Greek politicians, who exacerbated the local tensions to further their own interests. Speaking of the 'old veterans', the 'privileged class of reservists in Greece', and the need for their privileged reintegration into Greek life, an anti-royalist minister said in 1924 that

> This privileged class was not created by social conflicts or by the daily struggle of social classes. It is the privileged class created by the long-standing struggle of the Greek race, a class that spelled out its inalienable rights with blood spilled abundantly by the children of the Greek nation.[4]

As was only natural, the tensions between the local population and the refugees often resulted in violence. Refugees were often used as strike-breakers. In some extreme cases, such as the 1924 creation of the short-lived National Democratic Party, armed refugees coached by G. Kondylis, minister of internal affairs, were used as an instrument to break strikes and intimidate workers. In another instance, a political organisation called the National Union of Greece (founded by refugee merchants) attacked Thessaloniki's Jewish quarter, burning the shops and homes of residents—this at the height of an anti-Semitic campaign drummed up by an important city newspaper. Anti-Semitism lurked in the city up until the early 1930s, when the situation began to improve. The anti-Venizelists' rise to power—which was supported by Jews from Thessaloniki—likely played a role in this.

The adverse conditions prevailing in urban centres also determined state policies. For the first time, the Greek state was forced to intervene in many sectors that it had previously defined as beyond its sphere of interest. The fact that it sought to adopt a comprehensive approach to industrial policy as early as the 1920s was a telling example of this. But the urgent need to employ urban populations, and above all refugees, determined other priorities. This became much more evident in the agrarian sector.

Agrarian reform

For the entire interwar period, Greece was by all accounts an agrarian country. Most of its population lived from and in the countryside. This was all the more true for the Greek state's new territories, where infrastructure was clearly in a worse condition than in Old Greece and would require urgent intervention in order to be properly integrated into the Greek economy.

These differences manifested themselves more clearly through the status of land ownership in each of these areas. In Old Greece, where small-scale property ownership had been established very early on, the agrarian question was of little importance. Large-scale land tenure prevailed in very few areas, and only in Thessaly—annexed by the Greek state in 1881—did the existence of large estates constitute a social and political problem. Annexation of the new territories after the Balkan Wars changed the situation, since large landholdings and severe social tensions prevailed in these regions. This was confirmed by the fact that, directly after their integration into the Greek state, there was widespread looting of estates in these territories, while violence against landowners and their representatives became all the more common. Problems resulting from the distribution of estates were linked with the ethnic heterogeneity of the populations residing in these lands, and especially with the notable presence of Muslims.

For the first time, the revised Constitution of 1911 provided the possibility of expropriating private property in the national interest, leading to hopes that the issue of distributing large estates would be solved in this manner. The Balkan Wars delayed any resolution of this problem. In order to win over rural populations, but also to weaken large-scale landowners (most of whom belonged to the anti-Venizelist faction), the provisional government of Thessaloniki passed a law in 1917 according to which large landholdings were to be distributed to cultivators. But this law was never applied, or at least was never applied on a large scale, as an anti-Venizelist return to power led to a change in legislation.

This situation changed yet again with the Asia Minor campaign. In 1923, the explosive social situation and mass arrivals of refugees led the government to adopt radical laws on land distribution. This process was facilitated by the departure of several hundred thousand Muslims from Macedonia during the population exchange, whose estates then became the property of the Greek state. Thus, in a short period of time, Greece became a country of small-scale property ownership. Meanwhile, estate owners were unable to profit from expected reparations as inflation rendered them worthless. In other words, the Asia Minor campaign had two indirect consequences: it led to the consolidation of a system of small-scale property ownership and the destruction of a social group that had previously been highly influential politically.

Thus the large estates of Old Greece fell into the hands of those who cultivated them, while refugee farmers established themselves in the new territories. In both cases, the redistribution of estates led to a complete reversal in local balances of indebtedness, since very few farmers were able to use the land that now belonged to them completely on their own. The resulting instability in these regions took an increasing toll on rural families, who often ended up in debt. On the other hand, the same situation forced the Greek state to pursue more interventionist policies in the rural economy, policies that were only fully implemented beginning in 1927, continuing a trend that had begun on a small scale as early as the 1910s.

In the same period, the population exchange between Greece and Turkey changed the composition of the Greek countryside. As mentioned above, refugees increasingly established themselves in the estates of Northern Greece, taking the place of Muslims who had moved to Anatolia under the Treaty of Lausanne. Though the ethnic makeup of Northern Greece had been a constant headache for the Greek state up until 1922, the arrival of the refugees endowed the region with a remarkable degree of ethnic homogeneity. Western Thrace proved to be an exception to this, where the significant minority of Muslims and the nearby Bulgarian border led the Greek state to militarise and isolate the region.

The settlement of these refugees led to friction within the local population; the unexpected arrival of populations with completely different cultural practices from local residents resulted in tensions and conflicts. For the majority of native Northern Greeks, these incoming refugees deprived them of the lands that they had hoped to gain after the Muslim exodus. Consequently, tensions were more apparent in ethnically heterogeneous villages—that is, villages inhabited by both native populations and refugees. There were also tensions among minority populations (Slavophone Macedonians, Muslims, Albanians) that manifested themselves during the Second World War and the Civil War.

Violence in politics (yet again)

One of the Greek state's main goals during the nineteenth century was the institutionalisation of political power. This was an objective that had finally been achieved, such that from 1875 onwards the parliamentary system of government and national politics in general functioned relatively smoothly. Though the 1909 coup that brought Venizelos to power may have laid the foundations for military intervention during the interwar period, the nature and benefits of the political system were not brought into question. But this changed as a result of the First World War, which radically altered the political dynamics of the pre-war period. There are many reasons for this. First, by the time of the First World War, there were few similarities between Greece and Old Greece. Greece's territory and population had doubled, and a far greater proportion of people of other ethnicities and cultures now lived in the country. In addition, in economic and social terms, interwar Greece found itself in much a poorer situation than Greece in 1910.

Secondly, via the National Schism, the First World War had created the conditions for a civil war. This polarisation left no Greek on the side-lines and legitimised the use of violence. This process was facilitated as the army reinforced its social position and prestige thanks to its achievements, but also thanks to the militarisation of society and economy after a long period of war. For many, the army was the only institution capable of providing solutions to the problems of interwar Greece.

Intense social turmoil facilitated this process and rendered the use of violence a legitimate tool for resolving political and social opposition, a process that manifested itself in the form of military coups, the repression of social protest and the imposition of a new national order characterised by an increasingly anti-parliamentary conception of politics. It was no coincidence that many Greek politicians from across the political spectrum—including Venizelos—were admirers of the Italian fascist regime and hoped to reproduce it in Greece. Threats to the nation, which mainly originated from Bulgaria in this period, evolved alongside and laid the foundations for domestic repression on a widespread scale. In reality, Greece emerged from the First World War only to participate in several other conflicts, many of them lasting up until 1974.

9

PARLIAMENT AND DICTATORSHIP

(1924–40)

Democracy

The 'Revolution' of 1922 was able to prevent the impending dismantling, if not collapse, of the basic state apparatus immediately following the Greek defeat in the Greco-Turkish War. A revealing example of this was the rise of banditry, even in the outskirts of Athens. By implementing a range of repressive measures, the 'Revolution' managed to impose order and rebuild the army so that Greece possessed the necessary strength to resist Turkish demands during the Lausanne negotiations. The resulting Lausanne Treaty of August 1923 finally clarified the respective territories of Turkey and Greece: except for Asia Minor, which had been lost in battle, Eastern Thrace, Imbros and Tenedos were returned to Turkey. A few months earlier, the treaty for a compulsory population exchange between Greece and Turkey had been signed, which was also ratified under the Treaty of Lausanne. A rational approach guided both sides to sign the treaty, despite the fact that many in Greece resented granting Eastern Thrace to Turkey and preferred a more aggressive approach to Turkish demands.

In addition to executing six anti-Venizelist leaders, the Revolution of 1922 also dealt with the strikes of 1923 in an exceptionally cruel manner. It also proceeded to dissolve the General Confederation of Greek Workers. In this way, it made its resolve clear to both higher-level political elites and workers.

The Revolution then moved to block reconstitution of the army, executing a large number of deserters. The Italian occupation of Corfu, under the pretence of an Italian officer's murder in Albania during the settling of the Greek–Albanian border, had created what appeared to be a highly intractable problem. But despite Greek diplomatic failures, the problem was ultimately resolved. In any case, it was clear from early on that Italy was to play a basic role in the relations between Balkan states.

Timetable 1924–40

1924 Nikolaos Plastiras submits the 'Mandate of the Revolution' to the Fourth Constituent Assembly. Venizelos returns to Greece and forms a government (11 January 1924–6 February 1924). Georgios Kafandaris government (6 February 1924–12 March 1924). Alexandros Papanastasiou government (12 March 1924–24 July 1924). Greece is proclaimed a republic by a resolution in the Fourth Constituent Assembly. This proclamation is ratified by a referendum. Themistoklis Sofoulis government (24 July 1924–7 October 1924). Andreas Michalakopoulos government (7 October 1924–26 June 1925). Panagis Tsaldaris assumes leadership of the People's Party.

1925 Theodoros Pangalos forms a new government by way of a coup (25 June 1925–19 July 1926), which soon becomes a dictatorship.

1926 Athanasios Eftachsias is named prime minister (19 July 1926–23 August 1926) and Theodoros Pangalos is named president of the Republic. The Pangalos dictatorship is overthrown. Georgios Kondylis government (23 August 1926–4 December 1926). Parliamentary elections. Universal government formed with participation by Venizelists and anti-Venizelists, headed by Alexandros Zaimis. (4 December 1926–4 July 1928).

1927 Venizelos returns to Greece and settles in Chania. The Constitution of the Republic is voted on. Cashiered officers are once again incorporated in the army. The People's Party is excluded from government.

1928 Monetary stabilisation is attained. Georgios Kafandaris, finance minister of the ecumenical government, is forced to resign by Venizelos. The Liberal Party is reconstituted. Venizelos government (4 July 1928–26 May 1932). The Liberals triumph in parliamentary elections.

1929 Elections for the Senate. Alexandros Zaimis is named president of the Republic.

1930 The Treaty of Ankara: differences resulting from the Greek–Turkish population exchange resolved.

1931 Greece is forced to abandon the gold standard.

1932 Venizelos fails to secure new foreign loans. Greece suspends servicing of its foreign-held debt. Devaluation of the drachma. Restrictive measures enacted in foreign trade. Alexandros Papanastasiou government (26 May 1932–5 June

1932). Eleftherios Venizelos government (5 June 1932–3 November 1932). Parliamentary elections. The Liberals and People's parties share equal power. The latter recognises the Republic. Tsaldaris government, achieved with vote of tolerance from the Liberals (3 November 1932–16 January 1933).

1933 The Tsaldaris government is voted out. Last Venizelos government (16 January 1933–6 March 1933). Parliamentary elections. An equal number of votes, but a majority of anti-Venizelists in Parliament. The Plastiras movement. Alexandros Othonaios government (6 March 1933–10 March 1933). Tsaldaris government (10 March 1933–10 October 1935). Attempt on Venizelos's life. After a repeated election in Thessaloniki, the Venizelists triumph and begin preparations for armed confrontation.

1934 Re-election of Alexandros Zaimis as president of the Republic.

1935 A Venizelist uprising is suppressed. Venizelos leaves Greece for good. Persecution of the Republicans. Elections for the Fifth National Assembly. The Venizelists abstain. The Tsaldaris–Kondylis coalition prevails. The Tsaldaris government is upset by a coup aimed at restoration and establishment of the Kondylis dictatorship (10 October 1935–30 November 1935). A rigged referendum results in George II's return. Venizelos conditionally recognises the restoration. Konstantinos Demertzis government (30 November 1935–12 April 1936).

1936 Elections for the Third Revisionary Parliament. Venizelists and anti-Venizelists share equal power. The Liberal Party definitively recognises the restoration. A treaty between the Communists and Sofoulis is made, but never implemented. Death of Venizelos. Ioannis Metaxas government with a vote of tolerance from all parties (13 April 1936–29 January 1941). Tsaldaris's death. Attempts at a collaborationist government between the Venizelists/anti-Venizelists end in an agreement. Imposition of a dictatorship by George II and Metaxas.

1938 Uprising against the dictatorship in Chania suppressed.

1940 Italian invasion of Greece.

Yet once its urgent political problems had been resolved, the 'Revolution' of 1922 had to settle on a political orientation. The result was widely seen as Venizelist, thanks to its leader, Nikolaos Plastiras, who had always been loyal to Venizelos, and thanks to the execution of the Six, which became a symbol of anti-Venizelist unity. It was also thanks to the many Venizelists that held important positions for the period he was in power. What occurred at this point were the first attempts to emancipate the army from the political sphere. Indeed, one of the military's goals in this period was to form an autonomous political entity, regardless of whether or not this finally materialised.

It would be an exaggeration to argue that the military did not play an important role in politics before this point. The uprisings in 1843, 1862, and especially 1909 are all proof of this, though in the first two cases, the coups should be attributed to the political elite's general opposition to the regime in place and are not necessarily comparable with the army's actions after 1909. The interventionism of the Greek army during the interwar period was not and should not be considered unrelated to the ban prohibiting military professionals from participating in politics, a ban first imposed by Theotokis and then reinforced in the 1911 Constitution.

Thus military officers were left with the option of 'autonomous' action, which the preceding period of war had facilitated in two ways. First, the army had emerged as the dominant national institution as it had brought Greece closer to realising its irredentist dreams. If it had ultimately failed in Asia Minor, this was due (at least partly) to the treachery of politicians. The argument of 'betrayal' that was prevalent in many countries after the First World War found its counterpart in Greece. Secondly, as mentioned in the previous chapter, the period of war had opened the floodgates for extra-institutional resolutions to political problems, and the military was certainly the force in the best position to take on such a role.

After a ten-year period of war, there were many in the country whose interests would be compromised by a return to peacetime. The total number of military officers had increased significantly, including Military Academy graduates, lower-ranking officers promoted in wartime, and finally reservist officers who had been appointed for life. Yet, by this time, the opportunities for promotion had become increasingly limited. In the end, advancing one's own career advancement came down to being in the right military camp at the right time.

For this reason, the 1922 Revolution's efforts to win over royalist officers by offering ranks and promotions immediately elicited opposition from other officers, most of whom were Venizelists under the leadership of Generals Georgios Gargalidis and Panagiotis Leonardopoulos. Ioannis Metaxas also sought to take advantage of the situation, with the aim of assuming exclusive leadership of the anti-Venizelist faction after the execution of the Six. The uprising's failure—it was ill-prepared and badly implemented—strengthened those seeking to weaken the powers of the crown and further reinforced the military's role in politics. It also indicated the approach the 'Revolution' would have to adopt, frustrating its plans for political or party autonomy: from that moment onwards, and for the entire interwar period, the military was unable to escape from the Venizelist/anti-Venizelist opposition that determined the politics of the interwar period.

In late 1923, the 'Revolution' organised elections in the hope of convening the National Assembly. The anti-Venizelists, disorganised and leaderless, decided not to take part. The Liberal Party emerged triumphant with 250 of a total of 392 MPs. Parties such as Alexandros Papanastasiou's Democratic Union and the Party of Liberal Democrats, both of which supported the Republic, gained a total of 120 MPs.

The Liberals' triumph enabled Venizelos's return to Greece from France, where he had fled after the elections of 1920. He immediately took up the role of prime minister, only to realise very quickly that his era of supremacy had come to an end. Old supporters and colleagues, both military and political, placed pressure on him to immediately declare the state a Republic. He himself argued that a referendum had to be held in order to secure the greatest possible consensus on this change of regime. But this consensus required Venizelist concessions, and it was clear that such concessions would threaten the interests of powerful actors—including the military. Finally, realising he could not control the political situation, Venizelos resigned and was replaced by Georgios Kafandaris. The latter's fate was no better; in less than two months, he was also forced to resign under pressure from the military.

The next prime minister was the most radical of Venizelos's successors, Alexandros Papanastasiou, leader of the Democratic Union Party. Having secured the confidence of Parliament in addition to the support of a large share of the army, he passed the resolution that would declare Greece a republic. The resolution was endorsed by a referendum, and Admiral Pavlos Koundouriotis was elected president of the Republic. Yet the anti-Venizelists immediately challenged the result of the referendum. The only exception to this was Metaxas, who, upon recognising the result of the referendum, was granted amnesty for his participation in the 1923 uprising and returned to Greece. Meanwhile, Venizelos stated his intention to abandon politics yet again, causing the Liberals to split into smaller individual groups.

Papanastasiou belonged to the category of Venizelists that supported the Republic; indeed, he had been persecuted for his views by anti-Venizelists in 1921. On the other hand, perhaps more than anyone else, he had accelerated the army's politicisation with the aim of furthering his political career. During the National Assembly, he did not hesitate to accept army officers' right to participate in the formulation of government policy. He would pay for these choices dearly shortly thereafter; beholden to military factions, he was unable to refuse the demands they stipulated in exchange for their support.

The true nature of the democratic system established at this point was revealed by one of the first measures imposed by the Papanastasiou government, specifically by the Minister of Legal Order General Theodoros Pangalos: the decree 'On the Validation of a Democratic System' on 23 April 1924. The decree established a court to be appointed by the minister of defence that would deal with political offences against the state. This was a bad start for both the Republic and for Papanastasiou, who behaved in an autocratic way right from its very beginnings. But it did not save the leader of the Democratic Union, who resigned, fearing that he might otherwise lose his position in the military. He was succeeded first by Themistoklis Sofoulis and then Andreas Michalakopoulos, though both would share the same fate as their predecessor.

This situation called for a radical solution. General Theodoros Pangalos tried exactly that on 25 June 1925 and was initially very successful. The Pangalos coup was met with relief by many, and Papanastasiou supported the general in Parliament in the hope that he would cloak his actions in a parliamentary disguise, and that he could influence him to vote for the Constitution of the Republic. The boundaries between democracy and dictatorship had begun to blur.

But Pangalos had no intention of being ordered around by someone else. He soon resorted to more authoritarian measures, collaborating with both royalists and anti-royalists to gain support within the political system. He finally announced his candidacy for presidency of the Republic and, naturally, was elected. In a very short time, his actions led Greece to a state of international isolation and an economy on the verge of collapse. In August 1926, he was overthrown by the Democratic Battalions that had ushered him to power. They were crushed in turn by Georgios Kondylis, a prime example of the 'opportunist officer' figure often seen in the interwar period.

In the period between 1924 and 1926, the army had become a tool that all politicians sought to control. But this same tool often escaped their grasp and turned against them. As Serafim Maximos, a senior member of the Communist Party, put it at the time: parliament and dictatorship were simply alternative means of exercising power.

Another Greece

Lingering on these political tensions runs the risk of missing another element of the era's political problems, an element equally important for understanding them, namely that interwar Greece was completely different from the Greece that had existed before the Balkan Wars. The country's population and territory had doubled: based on the 1907 census, the last one conducted before the Balkan Wars, Greece was made up of 2,631,952 inhabitants and its territory amounted to 63,211 square kilometres. The 1920 census, conversely, counted a population of 5,531,474 inhabitants and a territorial expanse of 149,150 square kilometres. Finally, the census of 1928 recorded 6,204,684 inhabitants and a territorial expanse slightly smaller than the previous census: 129,281 square kilometres.

This impressive growth immediately raised questions related to the administrative integration of the new territories and the institutional assimilation of their populations. For two main reasons, these were questions that did not have straightforward answers. First, the Greek state's bureaucratic capabilities were rather limited in comparison with the task they faced. Wartime had not facilitated or even allowed for the assimilation of populations into the national administrative system. For most of the wartime period, even in areas not directly involved in military operations, populations from the new territories were treated as conquered subjects, and the state bureaucracy—largely located in Old Greece—behaved accordingly. This can be explained by the fact that officials sent to administer the new territories had often fallen out of favour, or had stood no chance of promotion in their former positions. On the other hand, any examination of this process must also account for the particular circumstances within these new territories, and more specifically, their ethnic composition.

Throughout the 1920s, the Greek state would be called on to address the issue of ethnic and other minorities for the first time. Until the Balkan Wars, the only minority worth mentioning was the Catholic population of the Cyclades, which was in no position to influence state policy. After the Balkan Wars, the number of minorities increased. Although they did not represent a quantitatively significant portion of the overall population—especially after the compulsory population exchange between Greece and Turkey—their political interests would play an important role in state policy. For one thing, the positions held by some of these groups held in the border territories of the Greek state led to rival territorial claims from other countries. This in turn explains the manner with which the governments of the time tackled the problem.

On a local level, the Muslims of Western Thrace, who had been excluded from the compulsory population exchange, were the largest minority. This group included the Pomaks, a distinct, Bulgarian-speaking group residing in the Rhodope Mountains. Yet most of the Muslims in Thrace were *palaiomuslims* who had been opposed to Atatürk's regime. As a result, at least initially, they found themselves cut off from the Turkish Republic and did not pose a threat to Greek interests. Only after the Greek–Turkish rapprochement of 1930 were the leaders of this minority expelled, after which the Muslim populations would begin to identify more conventionally with Turkey. In any case, their identity was not a problem in the interwar period—it only became one after the Second World War when relations between Greece and Turkey took a turn for the worse.

The Jews of Thessaloniki were another minority that played a notable role in the interwar years. There had certainly been Jews in Old Greece as well, and some of their communities—such as the one in Corfu—were significant. But none of them were as influential as the community in Thessaloniki. Before the Balkan Wars, the Jewish community made up the majority of the city's population, but by the 1920s and 1930s this no longer applied. In the new political framework resulting from the Greek state's annexation of Thessaloniki, the economic power of the Jewish community declined. As refugees arrived, proving themselves strong competitors for control of the city's commerce, the Jews of Thessaloniki chose political isolation. It is no coincidence that the Zionist movement found extremely fertile ground to develop in this same population. But in the meantime, the situation had changed, and the isolationist tactics chosen by the Jewish community would result in significant population losses and render them easy targets for refugees and Venizelists with anti-Semitic views.

But it was the Slavophone Macedonian minority that played a particularly important role in the interwar years, maintaining a significant presence in certain areas of Northern Greece. Some of them, especially those who lived in Eastern and Central Macedonia, migrated after the treaty for the voluntary exchange of Greek and Bulgarian populations. Yet in Western Macedonia, especially in the region of Florina, there were established Slavophone Macedonian populations. Before the annexation of Macedonia, a portion of the Slavophone Macedonian population known as Grecomans—Greek-speaking Macedonians—had already been incorporated into Greek and patriarchal networks. The rest, those that in interwar censuses identified as Slavophone Macedonian, were Exarchists, even though in those years Bulgaria and Yugoslavia each claimed them as their own for various reasons. It was precisely these populations that were a sensitive issue in foreign and domestic Greek politics, and they were subject to strong Hellenising pressures, especially during the Metaxas dictatorship.

In the interwar years, minorities such as the Albanian and Muslim Chams of Thesprotia, the Vlachs of Pindus, and the Armenians accompanying refugee populations on their exodus from Turkey (though the majority of the latter group eventually left Greece to settle in other countries) would play an increasingly prominent role in Greek politics. The most critical element of these minority populations, regardless of their total size proportional to the overall population and their consequences for the Greek state's foreign policy, was the degree to which they affected election results. For the most part, these minority populations backed the anti-Venizelists, probably in response to the mostly Venizelist refugees that often competed for their economic interests. Indeed, Venizelist attitudes worsened the political isolation of minority groups, one example being the organisation of electoral associations in ways that prevented Jews and Muslims from influencing electoral results in their areas, without completely depriving them of political representation. Additionally, the deliberate settling of refugee populations in areas previously dominated by the Slavophone Macedonians, with the aim of 'Hellenising' entire provinces, created tensions that often led to violence.

Refugees

As mentioned previously, the problems related to the management of these minority populations increased after the compulsory exchange of populations between Greece and Turkey. The census of 1928, the only one that offers reliable information in this regard, tallied 1,221,849 refugees, corresponding to about 20 per cent of the total national population. This is a considerable figure, even if we take into account that more than 500,000 Muslims and 92,000 Bulgarians left Greece in the period that followed. According to the same census, 151,892 refugees had arrived in Greece before the Asia Minor disaster, with the remaining 1,069,957 arriving after it. It should, however, be emphasised that a significant number of refugees—some accounts point to 200,000—arrived in Greece only to abandon it and seek their fortunes elsewhere. In yet other cases, they first sought to live in other countries and only later decided to settle in Greece. We must also not ignore the fact that of all the refugees, about half (636,954) originated in Asia Minor, 256,635 in Eastern Thrace, 182,169 in Pontus and the rest from other regions such as Bulgaria (49,027), the Caucasus (47,091) or Istanbul (38,458). In other words, this was by no means a homogeneous population; on the contrary, there were intense cultural differences among the refugees. This was even true of populations originating from the same regions, as in the case of Asia Minor, where there were enormous differences between individuals from the coasts and from Cappadocia. The sudden settlement of such a large number of people in Greece inevitably caused major upheavals on both a local and national scale.

The most drastic changes came about in rural areas, as most of the refugees settled in Macedonia and Western Thrace. In the former case, they filled the void left by Muslim farmers after the population exchange, while they were also used to upset balances in areas where local populations consisted of minorities considered a threat to the Greek state. The geographic distribution of refugee populations was extremely uneven: in Macedonia, they represented 45.1 per cent of the population, in Western Thrace 35.5 per cent, in Central Greece 19.2 per cent—the vast majority settling in Athens—and 18.4 per cent of the population on the Aegean Islands.

Related problems were not limited to the countryside, though this is where the most radical consequences could be seen. Thus problems also emerged in the cities, which were rapidly developing in the same period. In 1907, in Old Greece, individuals living in settlements with more than 5,000 residents accounted for 23.9 per cent of the overall population. In 1920, the corresponding figure was 26.6 per cent, increasing to 33.7 per cent in 1928. It should be noted that this was not a smooth process. At least half of the total number of refugees settled in Athens, Thessaloniki and other major Greek cities, creating pronounced social pressures and tensions. Most of these urban refugees found shelter in settlements established on the outskirts of cities, where they sought to survive and reproduce the conditions of their homeland. Isolating refugees to the outskirts of urban centres was in fact an aim of state policy, as it made them easier to control. Their presence was seen as a possible threat to the social status quo, and their isolation had the advantage of leaving the political balance in major cities such as Athens untouched. Yet regardless of where they settled, these mass arrivals exacerbated the problems in the country's infrastructure. It also put a major strain on public health policy.

The biggest problems emerged in the two largest Greek cities: Athens and Thessaloniki. In 1907, the population of the urban centre of Athens rose to 250,000 inhabitants. By 1920, this number surpassed 450,000, while the 1928 census recorded 802,000 inhabitants. By 1940, the number exceeded 1.1 million. These were considerable increases, even more so when given the rate at which they occurred. Thessaloniki changed on a different scale, but its growth was nevertheless impressive. In 1920, 176,000 inhabitants lived in its urban centre; eight years later, this number reached 244,000. The growth then slowed, totalling 254,000 inhabitants according to the census of 1940. In both cases, the relative increases in size were less important than the speed at which this change occurred and its consequences for the national economy.

The mobilisation of working-class populations—and the state's repression of the labour movement—combined with pre-existing impoverished urban populations, led to a new, completely unprecedented reality for the nation's urban populations. The threat of social revolt was very real and was urged on to some extent by the Greek Communist Party, which claimed to be the exclusive representative of the Greek working class. The same party also adopted the policies of the Communist International and promoted the autonomy of Macedonia and Thrace, echoing Bulgarian claims. As such, many viewed the Communist Party as both a threat to the bourgeois regime and to the nation itself. In response, with the Statutory Law of 1929, Venizelos created a legal framework that allowed for the persecution of anyone who sought to overthrow social order or encourage any part the Greek state to secede. This measure was used to persecute communists and members of the Slavophone Macedonian minority during the Metaxas dictatorship.

In reality, the Greek Communist Party was only able to rally a small minority of workers during the interwar period, mostly tobacco workers, and it failed to gain a strong following among the Slavophone Macedonian populations. But the influence it held over tobacco workers, who were the most active of the workers—and who always resisted efforts to modernise their industry, which was far from competitive internationally—enabled the party to make its presence felt in Greek politics. In May 1936, for example, the tobacco workers' strike in Thessaloniki evolved into a rebellion, and for some time the government lost control of the city. George II and Metaxas would later use another demonstration by tobacco workers in Thessaloniki as the pretext to impose the dictatorship.

Thus the contrast between the new territories and Old Greece was aggravated by the settlement of refugee populations. Above all else, the social and economic infrastructure in the new territories was greatly inferior to that in Old Greece, regardless of which indicators we use to measure it. Perhaps the starkest examples were the indicators of natural population movement, which were consistently higher in all regions of the new territories, indicating the existence of populations with different demographic behaviour. Beyond this, the degree of urbanisation in the Greek state's new territories was much lower than it was in the territories of the Greek state before the Balkan Wars. The rural population was also larger. This contrast between Old Greece and the new territories that marked the entire interwar period was founded on different economic realities. Another political divide in the country's population rested on this same fault line: the former were more royalist, and the latter, more Venizelist. One particular anti-Venizelist stance during the First World War was a logical consequence of this: Constantine had been willing to give up the new territories in order to prevent Old Greece's participation in military campaigns.

Refugee arrivals amplified these differences and led to increased tensions. As previously mentioned, the refugees were not given a warm welcome by local populations, much more so in areas where refugees would be competing with locals for land and employment. Their 'Greekness' was often challenged—their different cultures of origin and sometimes their inability to speak Greek made it easy to distinguish them as a separate group—and as a result refugee populations were subject to cruel exploitation. Their political affiliations, strongly Venizelist even before the Asia Minor disaster, contributed to this process, rendering them targets of the anti-Venizelists. Yet most of the refugees would continue to support Venizelism regardless, affecting the results of elections to a significant degree. Indeed, when a small percentage of refugees abandoned the Venizelist camp in 1933, it reshaped the political balance and eventually led to an anti-Venizelist victory.

By the outbreak of the Balkan Wars, the Greek nation had managed to solve two important issues in the process of becoming a modern state. First, it had achieved a high degree of national homogeneity. Secondly, it had managed to integrate politics into an institutional framework. In the interwar period, both of these issues had to be considered and addressed anew, under decidedly unfavourable political and economic circumstances. Populations in the new territories found themselves excluded from state mechanisms, while their ethnic and cultural differences meant they found it difficult to assimilate into the local population. This would only exacerbate the divisive conflicts of this wartime period.

Difficult years

The following ten years of war offered Greece considerable gains in territory and population. However, overall, the country was left much poorer and in a much less favourable international position. The interval between the Asia Minor disaster and Venizelos's return to power in 1928 did not offer much of a chance to improve the country's position in either regard. Rather, it aggravated the situation. Though the political instability of the period alone would have been sufficient to explain this turn, there were also other, equally important factors.

9.1: Gross Domestic Product Per Capita in Constant Prices, 1912–38 (in 1914 Drachmas)

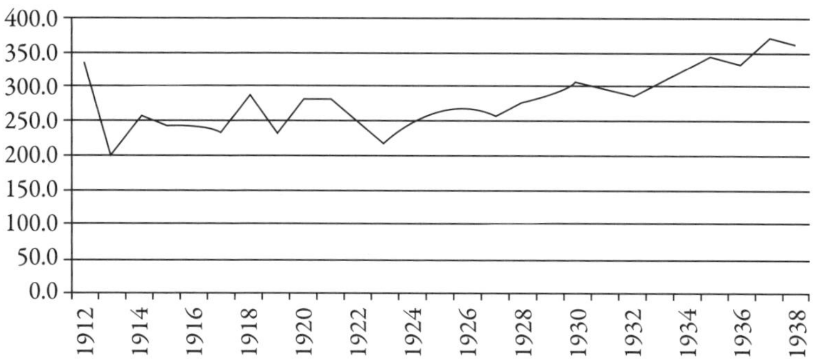

Source: G. Kostelenos, S. Petmezas et al., *Ακαθάριστο Εγχώριο Προϊόν 1830–1939.*

It is often argued that the refugee arrivals were the *deus ex machina* that led Greece to industrialisation and economic growth, a position based on the naïve argument that refugees were a cheap source of labour for industry. It has also been argued that refugees ushered in a new type of entrepreneurship to the country, together with large amounts of capital. During the interwar years, this view was held by very few individuals, most of them being refugees themselves. Others were fully aware of the significant problem posed by the refugee populations. Only after the Second World War, when the refugee/native-born opposition lost its importance, was the positive role of refugees in the Greek economy unanimously accepted. Until then, there were many doubts about the sustainability of the Greek economy.

It is worth noting that the arrival of refugees led to a dramatic deterioration in the Greek economic situation, since the country had to import significant quantities of goods in order to meet the emergency needs of these new populations. Once immigration to the United States was no longer a viable option, the pressures further increased as this route had previously reduced internal pressures on the population and served to supply significant benefits in income for the country's population, especially the poorest classes—an important factor in Greece's external trade balance. Thus despite the 12,000,000 franc loan granted to Greece on humanitarian grounds by the Refugee Settlement Commission under supervision of the League of Nations—to be spent on rehabilitating refugees—it proved difficult to balance the nation's public finances, curb inflation and halt devaluation of the drachma.

Meanwhile, beyond the specific needs related to the refugee situation, the general needs of the Greek economy had also increased. Large public works projects had been sorely needed in Old Greece since the beginning of the twentieth century. In the new territories, where infrastructure lagged hopelessly behind in relation to the rest of the nation, these needs were even more urgent.

The economic situation was particularly bad in rural areas, not only because Greece was still an agrarian country but because the rural economy was an impediment to any effort at economic development. As the years of the great crisis demonstrated, Greece was not even capable of ensuring the basic upkeep of its population, much less the provisioning of the state. Famine during the war had shown that—like many other European countries—Greece had to ensure grain self-sufficiency in order to avoid similar risks in the future. Moreover, the radical nature of land reform had overthrown pre-existing balances established in much of the agrarian Greek economy without offering possibilities for a new equilibrium. The chief result of this change was the increasing indebtedness of rural households, which rose dramatically between 1929 and 1931 when harvests were poor and prices fell. In these conditions, the future of national industry—which was largely dependent on the domestic market—seemed bleak. Although a new tariff in 1924, which would only be fully applied from 1926 onwards, established a protective framework crucial to the development of industrial units, it was not enough to absorb the underemployed populations in urban centres, especially those who had gathered in peripheral settlements. In the minds of politicians at the time, these populations were a threat to the bourgeois regime—real or imagined. The issue of national industrial development remained largely unsolved, despite the fact that manufacturing in the interwar period had grown to unprecedented levels, mostly because it seemed to be the only sector able to provide jobs for the unemployed and increase overall incomes.

The nation's military defeat and economic slump had purely negative consequences for its international standing. In international politics, Greece had tried to adopt a strategy that would allow it to keep up with its traditional allies, Britain and France. But both these countries had no reason to make commitments to Greece. France found Serbia to be its most valuable ally in the area, while Britain did not desire the commitments that Greece was demanding at the time. Understandably, the Greek state became a strong supporter of interventions by international organisations—which began to appear at this time—as well as the status quo established by the Treaties of Peace. Greece's foreign policy choices could not have been any different.

Weakened by defeat in the Greco-Turkish War, Greece was in urgent need of the economic resources necessary to solve its internal economic problems, and most of all, rehabilitating its refugees. At the same time, a reduction in military spending was impossible, as Greece was now faced with a significantly stronger Serbian presence and Bulgaria's revisionist aims.

The situation deteriorated in 1924 when Greece and Bulgaria signed the Politis–Kalfov Protocol, which stipulated that Greece would accept a League of Nations intervention to protect the 'Bulgarians' of Macedonia, while Bulgaria would protect the Greek minority living within its territories. Serbia immediately intervened, demanding that a new protocol was drafted recognising that the Slavophone populations of Macedonia were Serbian. Greece appealed to the League of Nations and managed to annul the protocol, an action preceded by the denouncement of the Greek–Serbian alliance treaty signed in 1913, which occurred when Greece refused to sign a new protocol favourable to the Serbs. Henceforth, relations between Greece and the two nations deteriorated considerably. Serbia claimed more and more concessions related to the use of Thessaloniki's free zone and the railway linking Thessaloniki with its territories. At the same time, the Bulgarians began to pursue more aggressive policies, resulting in an increasing number of border incidents.

The Pangalos dictatorship showed great recklessness in dealing with both of these regional neighbours. It made a show of force against Bulgaria even after a peace treaty had significantly reduced Bulgaria's military power, invading its territory following a border incident that resulted in the death of a Greek officer. Greece's actions were eventually condemned by the League of Nations. With Serbia, which was more powerful, Pangalos was much more submissive, offering significant concessions with the use of the Thessaloniki free zone, the Axios River railway line and recognition of Slavophones in Macedonia as Serbian in exchange for the signing of a new Greek–Serbian alliance treaty.

The 'Great Four Years'

In November 1926, the Kondylis government organised elections. They were the first to make use of ballots and were conducted flawlessly. Under pressure from an extremely unfavourable diplomatic and economic situation and the need to take on foreign loans to complete the process of refugee settlement, an ecumenical government was formed with Alexandros Zaimis assuming the presidency. The Liberals, the People's Party and Metaxas's Freethinkers' Party participated in it.

This new government's main task was to ratify a Constitution that provided for both a Parliament and a Senate. Equally important was the task of establishing monetary stability, a prerequisite for Greece's reintegration into international capital markets. The ecumenical government was also quick to denounce agreements between Pangalos and Serbia, attempting a new start for the country's foreign policy.

As the ecumenical government went about completing this task, the first frictions began to appear. The People's Party, having managed to partially reinstate their officers in the army, was the first to withdraw their support. From Crete, Venizelos began to criticise the government's choices, targeting their economic policies above all else. Papanastasiou then withdrew from the government because of a disagreement over plans for road construction that were supported by Metaxas. At the same time, the government's efforts to improve the nation's international relations led nowhere, with the exception of a non-aggression and arbitration pact with Romania. Yet in the same period, Greece had also made notable attempts to approach Italy, forcing other Balkan states to take a less aggressive stance with the former.

The criticisms levelled by Venizelos finally forced the government to resign, and the leader of the Liberals assumed the premiership. The 'dirty work' had been done by two successive coalition governments; now he himself could benefit. In the elections held in 1928, Venizelos gained an overwhelming majority in Parliament. With characteristic eagerness, in these so-called 'Great Four Years' Venizelos tried to address all the problems that had arisen after the war had ended.

In foreign policy, Venizelos began to collaborate closely with Italy and signed a treaty of friendship, simultaneously convincing Britain and France that this new partnership would not be detrimental to their interests. This pact with Italy also led to an improvement in Greece's relations with Yugoslavia.

However, Venizelos's most spectacular acts of foreign policy concerned Greek–Turkish relations. He managed to settle the problems that arisen over the ownership of the various Greek and Turkish estates resulting from the population exchange to Greece's detriment, despite the fact that the assets of Greek populations were—or at least were presented as being—far superior to those of the Turks. As a result, he managed to secure a treaty of friendship with Turkey, which was signed in 1930. Three years later, a new Greek–

Turkish pact guaranteed the nations' shared borders, a precondition to a defence alliance in the future.

In addition to these successes in foreign policy, or rather thanks to them, Venizelos attempted to implement an ambitious program of internal reconstruction during these four years, leaving no sector of the public sphere untouched. Especially in economic terms, the period from 1928 to 1932 is certainly the first in which the Greek state consistently applied policies of economic development. The reforms and measures taken during these years were unprecedented, despite the fact that difficulties encountered due to the economic crisis ultimately proved insurmountable. Yet this was undoubtedly one of the most fertile and ambitious periods in the economic history of the Greek state. It was also the first time a government had invested its political future in the economy. What was at stake was a wholly new conception of the state and its aims. Venizelos himself wrote that one of his main goals was to create 'a modern state that would secure the conditions by which it will continually increase its revenues, the latter distributed more justly so that all the more classes within the population will be given the means to live with greater ease and prosperity'.[1]

Optimism for the future of the Greek economy increased even further after Venizelos's first diplomatic successes at The Hague Conference of 1929, where an agreement was reached for a reduction in Greek public debt repayments. Thus, at this conference, organised to negotiate reparations, Greece managed to become a key beneficiary of Eastern reparations (that is, reparations payed by the states succeeding the Austro-Hungarian Empire and Bulgaria) and reaped more than 75 per cent of the total instead of the 12.7 per cent that had been allotted to it at the Spa Conference in 1920. After the conference had ended, Venizelos, having already refused to implement the agreement for settling the Greek debts to the French that Kafandaris had signed, managed to transform Greece's hitherto negative trade balance (between obligations to its allies in war debts and reparations revenues) into a surplus. The success was all Venizelos's doing.

This favourable turn in reparation payments was crucial politically and psychologically, but also economically. A stable currency could only be maintained to the extent that the country was capable of external borrowing until the large-scale productive works planned by previous governments—now being implemented by the Venizelos government—had been completed. Despite the naivety of this line of reasoning, which became evident only after some of these works were completed, these changes in reparation payments led to a significant reduction in pressure on the nation's international transactions.

The main goal of Venizelos's economic policies—and the policies of any other national government during the interwar period—was to increase productivity in the rural economy. The Greek agrarian economy fell short in every respect when compared with neighbouring countries, except possibly Albania, and all ambitions for the country's economic development necessarily demanded on an increase in its productivity. Thus it is no surprise that Venizelos immediately focused his attention in that direction. Public works in the plains of Thessaloniki, Serres and Drama constituted the cornerstone of these policies, and expectations of benefits upon their completion were extremely high. Completion of these works would create nearly 3 million *stremmas* of land for agricultural use, and Greece hoped that this would minimise, if not solve, the grain deficit that constituted a key element of its overall trade deficit. Many also expected that solving this issue would improve living conditions for the populations settled in Northern Greece—mostly refugees—the majority of whom lived in conditions barely sufficient for survival.

Thus, in addition to these large-scale works, the Venizelos government sought to improve the situation in rural Greece. In this period, scientific approaches to cultivation began to appear, and the state began to assert its presence in even the most distant settlements. Yet conditions during these years were largely unfavourable. Three of the four years of the Venizelos government's term coincided with extremely poor harvests; as a result, some populations, especially in the mountainous regions, faced the spectre of famine. The situation deteriorated in 1929 when prices for agricultural products—especially wheat—dropped sharply, reducing rural incomes even further. To address this problem, the government suspended taxation on agricultural production and legal sanctions on the sector in 1929. It also established the largest mechanism it could conceive for concentrating wheat, already institutionalised since 1927 with the founding of the Central Committee for Wheat Concentration. Though this mechanism did not succeed in keeping prices at their original levels, it did manage to limit their depreciation. Similar interventions were also made for tobacco, Greece's most important export product: older and current harvests that had not been bought due to the economic crisis were purchased by the state. An interventionist state had made its presence felt, even if it did so timidly, pressured by necessity.

The Agricultural Bank that was created in late 1929 would serve as an important instrument in this ever-increasing intervention in the economy, and it is no coincidence that the creation of a solid banking institution offering exclusively rural credit was among the first priorities of Venizelos's government; he had included it in campaign statements preceding the election of 1928. Shortly thereafter, he was able to realise these promises, making the Agricultural Bank the strongest institution in the country in terms of available capital. Beyond the abundant capital it possessed, when it opened its doors in 1930, the Agricultural Bank played an increasingly important role as the conduit for managing financial flows to and from the Greek countryside, an all-powerful tool by any government's standards. Not only did the Agricultural Bank have a monopoly on all types of lending towards the agricultural sector; it also assumed the task of collecting refugee debts and took on trading capacities for certain agricultural products, as well as supplying farmers with the goods necessary for cultivation, such as fertiliser.

The Venizelos government's agricultural policy was undoubtedly the most visible manifestation of its economic policy. Yet he was also responsible for a number of achievements in other areas of the economy. An extremely ambitious road construction programme, for example, the first of its kind since Trikoupis's era, changed relations between cities and the countryside. In Venizelos's four years, 1,950 kilometres of new roads were made available to the economy. For the first time, the state attempted to reach even the smallest and most isolated settlements. Along with these new roads, major building projects were launched in various ports. The effort to build schools also absorbed considerable resources and constituted the most important effort at

9.2: Ratio of Public Expenditure to GDP, 1912–38 (%)[2]

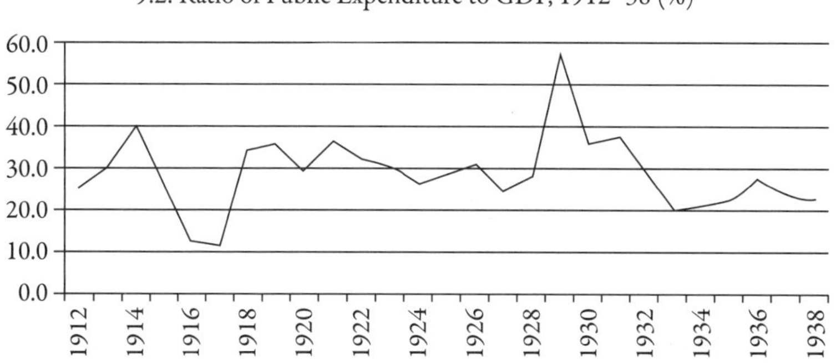

Source: The author's own calculations based on data from G. Kostelenou et al., and *Στατιστικής επετηρίδος της Ελλάδος 1939*.

creating public buildings since the founding of the Greek state. These initiatives were accompanied by far-reaching educational reforms, the main aim of which was to move a large number of students (40 per cent nationwide) from traditional high schools to technical and vocational schools.

Crisis

These policies relied on the maintenance of a fiscal equilibrium, no easy feat given that most of this four-year period coincided with the Great Depression. Nevertheless, the Liberal Party boasted that the administration's four years had left behind a significant surplus without increasing the tax burden. Venizelos's diplomatic policies certainly played an important role in this: they sought to build friendly relations with neighbours and thus helped reduce excessively high military expenditure.

Yet in a time of decreasing average incomes, fixed taxation policies necessarily resulted in a higher tax burden, which was one of the heaviest—if not the heaviest—in Europe. Though the government began to implement some tax relief, the measures did not suffice to solve the problems at hand.

A further downturn of the recession had certainly been averted by the larger- and smaller-scale public works in Greece, works that enabled the Greek economy to cope with the crisis. But the biggest difficulties arose from the huge demands posed by servicing public debt, which ensured that a disproportionately large portion of the national budget would be used for debt payments. For example, servicing of public debt in 1927–8 took up 25.6 per cent of public revenue. In the following year, this figure ballooned to 40.7 per cent, while in the last of Venizelos's four years the figure settled at 35 per cent. These variations were largely due to the amortisation schedules for government loans. To a lesser extent, increased lending also played a role. These figures left little room for flexibility in the government's budget.

Issues with implementing the Liberals' political agenda resulting from the economic crisis inevitably affected national politics, leading to a rise in political tensions. Venizelos's solution to this problem was opposed by other party leaders who were in favour of the Republic and took issue with their own exclusion from the government, harshly criticising him. Admiral Koundouriotis's resignation from the presidency of the Republic in 1929 exacerbated these tensions, as Venizelos suggested Alexandros Zaimis should take up the post—someone he considered to be more obedient—rather than Georgios Kafandaris, the more popular candidate. A series of public scandals then provoked even more criticism of the incumbent government.

Given this situation, Venizelos sought to form an ecumenical government that would be able to share the political cost of the crisis with the other parties. But this plan failed and led to an intense confrontation in Parliament with the leader of the People's Party, Tsaldaris, over policies implemented by anti-Venizelists a decade earlier.

Thus, if Venizelos was to stay in power, he clearly needed to make use of other tactics. The first was the suspension of national debt servicing on 1 May 1932. Then, on 26 April 1932, the government abandoned the gold standard and the value of the drachma began to fluctuate freely. Strict measures for limitations on currency followed that would affect the Greek economy for many decades, and a comprehensive balance sheet for the nation's international trade was implemented for the first time. These developments quickly mortgaged the ambitious economic policies implemented over Venizelos's four years in power. The Greek economy, like all national economies, would turn inwards and seek to develop by exploiting its domestic resources. A liberal approach to the economy now seemed outdated, and more centralised forms of economic management made their appearance as the state took on a leading role. By 1933, the Greek economy had recovered impressively the crisis, and the ensuing period of relative economic stability would last until the end of the interwar period. But this recovery did not solve the nation's economic woes, and towards the end of the interwar period all attempts converged on the search for and adoption of a new model for growth.

Venizelos's second step in this new context was to submit his resignation, and Alexandros Papanastasiou formed a new government. But very soon after, Venizelos brought down the government, fearing that Papanastasiou would be increasingly influential and prove to be a threat. He became increasingly confrontational with the anti-Venizelists, brandishing the threat of a return to monarchy. However, the results of the elections on 25 February 1932 only served to prove how much his power had weakened. The Liberals secured ninety-eight seats, the People's Party ninety-five, Kafandaris and the Progressives fifteen, and the Communists ten. Shortly thereafter, the People's Party was sworn in, led by Panagis Tsaldaris. The Military League, founded by Venizelist officers to defend the democratic system, was dissolved, and Venizelos submitted his vote of tolerance to the government led by the People's Party.

Dictatorship

The Liberals' tolerance of the People's Party did not last long. The Liberals soon found that Minister of Military Affairs Georgios Kondylis, a former

Venizelist who had joined the opposition camp, had begun to shift the balance of power among army officers in favour of the anti-Venizelists. As the possibility of assembling an autonomous government from existing parties seemed remote, the pro-republican camp had no choice but electoral collaboration. The change to a majority-rule electoral system delivered the parliamentary majority to an anti-Venizelist coalition despite the fact that the National League, founded by Venizelists, received more votes. General Plastiras—leader of the 1922 rebellion and considered one of the parties responsible for the execution of the Six—attempted a coup to stop the People's Party from assuming power, but this ultimately failed. Tensions between the two camps grew and in June 1933 a new attempt was made on Venizelos's life, an attempt that government officers seemed to have been involved in.

In this tense situation, it was only a matter of time before one of the parties would make a major mistake—and with an ill-organised coup on 1 March 1935, the Venizelists did just that. Georgios Kondylis rushed to benefit from the situation, purging the army of Venizelist officers, while Venizelos himself was once more forced to withdraw overseas. At this point, it was a simple matter to restore the monarchy. In the elections held on 9 February 1935, from which the Liberals abstained, the People's Party won an overwhelming 65 per cent of the vote, thus gaining tremendous power in Parliament. But Tsaldaris was not in a position to capitalise on the result, at least not to the benefit of parliamentarism. Thus Kondylis took the opportunity to play his own hand: military officers forced the government to resign and Parliament to vote on abolishing the Republic. MPs from the People's Party abstained from the vote and a referendum followed, the fraudulent nature of which was evident from the fact that the monarchy received 97 per cent of the votes. At the same time, purges were carried out in every sector of public life, especially in the army.

George II then returned to Greece. In order to give some semblance of legitimacy to his regime, he stripped Kondylis of his power and proceeded to call elections. The results of the election confirmed the deep political divisions in the country, and the Communist Party, with only fifteen seats in Parliament, found itself regulating the situation. Both parties turned towards the Communists, but any collaboration with the Communists proved impossible, causing severe tensions. Themistoklis Sofoulis, leader of the Liberals, described the situation prevailing in the country:

> In the surrounding atmosphere, all of us, without realising it, are subjected to a large dose of hypocrisy. We profess Communism to be the highest danger in order

> to hide the danger that we ourselves create, we the so-called protectors and supporters of the bourgeois regime. Our hate, our infamies, and our cynicism have amplified the division of the nation and provoked a danger, a danger that drags the nation towards complete destruction and total decomposition—this is the immediate, visible and palpable danger. A contempt towards all moral values and concepts has broken the foundations of the social order. Not much work remains for those who seek to upset the social order themselves.

The governments led by the People's Party also upset the foreign policy achievements that Venizelos had forged on the basis of bilateral agreements. The idea that Greece should not meddle in conflicts between the Great Powers—and that it should only participate in matters of regional security—was abandoned. In its place rose collective conditions for guaranteeing borders established by the peace treaties with the participation of Turkey, Romania, Yugoslavia and Greece. The treaty was signed in 1934, but after being placed under pressure by Venizelos, the People's Party government coalition declared that the Balkan agreement concerned the guarantee of borders against threats originating exclusively from Balkan countries. As a result, Yugoslavia turned to Bulgaria and Turkey for support, as it feared Italian action.

After the 1936 elections, a caretaker government under the leadership of Konstantinos Demertzis, professor at the University of Athens, took charge until the two sides could reach a solution. But Demertzis died soon after taking office. Around the same time, various other figures that could have played an arbitrating role also passed away, including K. Kondylis, Venizelos and Tsaldaris. Metaxas, minister of military affairs for the Demertzis government, imposed a dictatorship on 4 August 1936, with the support of George II, on the pretext of restoring social order at a time when there were violent clashes between workers' movements and the police and the army. In reality, it seems more likely that Metaxas was aiming to ward off a coup attempt by royalist officers: this fear was substantiated when the agreement reached between Venizelists and anti-Venizelists to re-integrate cashiered troops into the army sparked opposition from royalist officers, who had no intention of submitting to the consequences of this agreement.

To the surprise of his opponents and the two factions, Metaxas was able to establish a particularly cohesive model of governance. Though he was more or less dependent on the king in the first years of his dictatorship, from 1938 onwards it was clear that he had fully assumed political power. Though he tried to introduce fascist elements into his regime—creating a National Youth Organisation and referring to a 'Third Greek Civilisation'—he did not seek to build a state in the fascist mould. In fact, the only other element it shared with a fascist regime was its persecution of Communists.

Meanwhile, Metaxas began implementing policies aimed at increasing his popularity. These included a law on social security, which Venizelos had not implemented due to the economic crisis, and he immediately imposed new regulations on agricultural debts, forgiving a large portion of them. Metaxas also made the first (ineffectual) attempts at systematically exploiting the country's raw materials, establishing large-scale industrial infrastructure. The conditions under which this happened were extremely unfavourable, but it was hard to imagine that Greece could have done much better at that time, given that it had defaulted on its debts. Lastly, through the system of bilateral agreements, the Greek economy found itself increasingly dependent on Germany, which became the main market for Greek tobacco and other raw materials.

Internationally, the Metaxas regime increasingly turned to Britain in the realm of foreign policy, which had the consequence of exposing Greece to Italian and German pressure. However, in practice, there was no alternative. This was not only determined by George II's allegiance to Britain, but also the fact that smaller states had little room to manoeuver due to the diplomatic arrangements in place after 1936. Greece now found itself dependent on Britain, the Mediterranean's dominant naval power, something that the dictator himself openly admitted. Around this time, Metaxas also sought to strengthen relations with Turkey. In 1938, a supplementary treaty to the Greek–Turkish pact was signed, guaranteeing each party's neutrality in the case of third-party aggression against the other. Shortly after, in 1939, Greece entered into security agreements with France and Britain, just as Turkey signed the tripartite Anglo-French–Turkish Treaty of 1939.

But all this did little to prevent Greece's involvement in the war. By the summer of 1940, continued Italian provocations hinted at the developments that were to follow. Mussolini believed that Greece would be easy prey, despite the assurances of Field Marshal Pietro Badoglio, his chief of General Staff, that Italian forces in Albania—under Italian occupation—were not sufficient for such an operation. On 28 October 1940, Metaxas rejected an Italian ultimatum declaring the Italian army's invasion on to Greek soil in pursuit of strategic positions.

Parliament and dictatorship

In the interwar years, the Greek state showed all the symptoms characteristic of the prevailing European situation: first, a progressive decline of liberalism and the strengthening of anti-parliamentarist views and attitudes, exhibited even by leaders of the liberal faction, including Venizelos himself. Second was the assimilation of violence into national politics. A long period of war had shaped mind-sets in such a way that violent solutions were viewed as a legitimate way to solve political conflicts. Finally, the annexation of the new territories created a huge problem for national integration, as the state had tremendous difficulty incorporating these new areas and populations. Thanks to these factors, the process of consolidating a modern state encountered insurmountable difficulties.

One basic reason for this was that Greece had emerged in a poor position from the First World War, certainly poorer than pre-war Old Greece. The refugee situation also created demands that could hardly be satisfied given the country's economic conditions. Similarly, agricultural reform reconfigured long-established social relationships and set urgent priorities to ensure the survival of the rural populations. New governmental mechanisms established to address these problems needed time to bear results, as well as resources that did not exist. The 1930s underlined the huge difficulties and adversity that the Greek state was faced with as it sought to provide support for its population—in an international context that was becoming ever more threatening.

The inability of Greece's political leaders to supply parliamentary solutions to the above problems exacerbated authoritarian tendencies, while the emergence of external enemies of every sort provided the necessary pretext for authoritarian governance. The Metaxas dictatorship was the culmination of this entire process, which has been described as 'fatigued parliamentarism'. Beyond this, the Metaxas dictatorship introduced policies that would characterise the country for many decades to come.

10

WARS

(1941–9)

Italy

Italy had made extensive preparations for its offensive against Greece. As early as the summer of 1940, the Italian press railed against the country, with the tensions culminating in the events of 15 August 1940 when an Italian submarine, concealing its identity, sank a Greek warship in the port of Tinos. The Metaxas government faced these challenges with composure, though it could have hardly done otherwise if it wished to avoid conflict, which in any case appeared increasingly inevitable. Mussolini's Italy was in need of a military success for both domestic and foreign reasons. While Germany, its main ally, was triumphing on various fronts, Italy had only managed to take control of Albania, while its campaign in Africa had stalled after initial successes.

At a meeting on 15 October 1940, the decision was made to initiate military action against Greece. According to H.A. Richter, this process of deliberation and the subsequent decision was characterised by amateur militarism on the part of Mussolini and Galeazzo Ciano, while the other officers involved were boundlessly opportunistic, servile and careerist and demonstrated a complete lack of courage to speak up over the risks of initiating war between Greece and Italy without a properly prepared Italian army. It was simply taken for granted that Greece could not resist the vastly superior Italian forces.

Indeed, the Greek army was inferior to the Italian forces in every respect. Greece possessed significantly fewer aircraft, ships, tanks and even transport vehicles than Italy, while Greece's anti-aircraft defence systems were not prepared for the prospect of war with a European power. The explanation was rather simple: the entire national defensive infrastructure was configured in expectation of an attack from Bulgaria, the preeminent revanchist power in the interwar Balkans. For this very reason, significant fortifications had been built during the Metaxas dictatorship along the Greek–Bulgarian border. No such preparations existed on the Albanian border. In other words, the Greek army was organised and prepared for a Balkan war, both in terms of which opponents it was ready to deal with, and in terms of what type of military campaign it could participate in. Moreover, the Greek forces that could be directly marshalled to the Albanian front amounted to a total of 35,000 men. Though the Greek government had taken some care to be prepared for an Italian offensive, it had avoided general army mobilisation both because of its cost and the possibility that it might provoke an Italian attack. That very same moment, the Italians were prepared to deploy twice as many men to the front.

Regardless of the predictions of the war's outcome, by rejecting the Italian ultimatum of 28 October 1940, Metaxas managed to present himself as a figure of national unity; the response from all political factions to the call to defend Greece was enthusiastic and immediate. He was transformed into a national leader, albeit for a limited time. Even the Communist Party initially sided with the dictatorship in its battle against Italy.

It came as a huge surprise to all when it seemed that Italian military power had been overestimated. Initially, available Greek military units succeeded in their attempts to curb the Italian attack, falling into strategic positions. Both topography and bad weather contributed to Italy's inability to quickly achieve its goals. In the meantime, the Greek army had completed its process of mobilisation and gained its full strength, altering the dynamics in the balance between the forces and, by extension, the conflict. By mid-November, the Greek army had managed to repel the Italians back to the lines where they had initially invaded Greek territory, and began a counterattack. Greek successes came one after another, and soon the Greek army began to enter Albanian territories. These successes occurred against undeniably superior Italian forces including the navy and even air force, where Italian failures were completely disproportionate to their superior power. Gradually, however, the progress made by Greek troops in Albanian territory began to slow. Huge issues related to supply chains on extremely difficult mountainous terrain, a harsh winter and the strategic choices of the general chief of staff, Lieutenant General Alexandros Papagos—the same man who had engineered the monarchy's return in 1935—resulted in a front in which neither opponent was able to score a decisive victory. In March 1941, the two-week long Italian Spring Offensive was rebuffed by the Greeks, leading both armies to a halt and ultimately to a dead end.

The Greek army's successes had two key consequences for the nation's population. The first was extremely high morale, strong anti-Italian sentiment and the belief that anything was possible; as a result, there were calls for the Greek army to advance further and crush the Italian forces decisively. For this reason, from very early on, the apparent inability of the Greek armed forces to score a heavy blow against the Italians was associated with betrayals by senior officers and the country's political leadership. Secondly, as G. Margaritis has successfully shown, the Albanian front acquainted many Greek soldiers with the experience of war in the mountains, fought in small units, but also with violence and death. These experiences would prove decisive for Greek guerrilla forces and political developments in the future.

Meanwhile, the national political situation shifted. Metaxas died in late January 1941, exposing the regime in all its nakedness, as none of his successors possessed the skills to replace him. Despite this, George II demonstrated his unwillingness to distance himself from the dictatorial regime, appointing Alexandros Koryzis, who was the governor of the National Bank of Greece and, for a time, minister of social welfare, as prime minister. Yet Koryzis proved to be an ineffective leader who was unable to address the problems of the time. The most significant change in the situation came with Hitler's decision to attack Greece, a decision he had already taken in January 1940.

Timetable 1940–9

1940	Torpedoing of the light cruiser *Elli* by an Italian submarine near Tinos (August). Italian attack on Greece (October). Italian invasion of Pindus rebuffed (November). Gjirokastër is occupied (December).
1941	The Greek counterattack reaches its zenith (January). Alexandros Koryzis government (29 January 1941–18 April 1941). A British expeditionary force disembarks in Greece (March). The Emmanuel Tsouderos government (21 April 1941–14 April 1944) moves to Crete and then abandons Greece. The Germans occupy Athens (April). Giorgios Tsolakoglou-led collaborationist government in Athens (29 April 1941–2 December 1942).
1942	Famine. Konstantinos Logothetopoulos collaborationist government in Athens (12 February 1942–4 July 1943).
1943	In March, mass strikes and demonstrations in Athens. ELAS progressively creates a 'Liberated Greece'. Ioannis Rallis collaborationist government in Athens

(7 April 1943–12 October 1944). Creation of security battalions. In July, joint headquarters for resistance organisations (ELAS, EDES, EKKA) established under British guardianship. In September, clashes between ELAS and EDES.

1944 In February, a ceasefire agreement between ELAS and EDES. Political Committee of National Liberation (PEEA). President Evripidis Bakirtzis (10 March 1944–18 April 1944). In the Middle East, Sophocles Venizelos government (14 April 1944–26 April 1944). Alexandros Svolos appointed president of the PEEA (18 April 1944–2 April 1944). George Papandreou government (26 April 1944–3 January 1945). Conference of Lebanon (May). Caserta Agreement (September). On 18 October 1944 a government of National Unity is formed in Greece. 'Dekemvriana' clashes.

1945 Nikolaos Plastiras government (3 January 1945–8 April 1945). Treaty of Varkiza. Petros Voulgaris government (8 April 1945–17 October 1945), Archbishop Damaskinos government (17 October 1945–1 November 1945), Panagiotis Kanellopoulos government (1 November 1945–22 November 1945), Themistoklis Sofoulis government (22 November 1945–April 1946).

1946 Elections (31 March 1946). People's Party triumphs. Panagiotis Poulitsas caretaker government (4 April 1946–18 April 1946), Konstantinos Tsaldaris governments (18 February 1946–24 January 1947). A September 1946 referendum leads to the return of George II.

1947 Death of George II (1 April 1947). Paul is appointed king of Greece. Dimitris Maximos government (24 January 1947–29 August 1947), Konstantinos Tsaldaris government (29 August 1947–7 September 1947), Themistoklis Sofoulis government (7 September 1947–24 June 1949).

1949 Alexandros Diomedes government (30 June 1949–6 January 1950).

Germany

The Italians' failure to defeat Greece resulted in Britain's increasing interest in maintaining a more stable presence in the country. After the Italian attack, they rushed to dispatch a small force to Crete in order to prevent a similar manoeuvre by Italians there, though they did this without providing for the necessary defensive infrastructure. Up until that time, although Metaxas had requested assistance from the British—who had guaranteed Greek territorial integrity—he stopped short of closer collaboration to avoid provoking a reaction from Germany. But it proved impossible for the Germans not to interfere, to the extent that potential establishment of British military bases in Greece would threaten the Wehrmacht's supply of Romanian oil reserves at the very same moment it was preparing to begin operation Barbarossa against the Soviet Union.

Greece was clearly in no position to simultaneously cope with two powerful nations on its own. In case of a German attack, British assistance would be indispensable, even if few believed that the British would be able to offer the country significant support without substantially weakening their position in North Africa. Even the British themselves believed that their support of the Greek struggle was primarily political in nature, with the military playing a minor role. But there were significant differences between the Greeks and British when it came to organisation of the defence effort. The British believed that the Greek army needed to retreat, abandoning its position in Albania in order to defend a smaller line of defence stretching from Olympus to Aliakmonas. It was a reasonable proposal, but one that did not take into account the political implications. The Greek army was not willing to leave its Albanian positions; in other words, it was not willing to surrender a war it believed it had won. Furthermore, Lieutenant General Papagos was unwilling to abandon any piece of Greek territory without a fight, including the fortresses on the Greek–Bulgarian border, which he had established and maintained at great cost.

On 1 March 1941, Bulgaria joined the Axis forces, as Germany entered its territory that very same day. Yugoslavia, in turn, was considering a similar choice, which was only averted after a coup staged against the nation's regent, Prince Paul. Under these conditions, Britain finally decided to send an expeditionary corps of troops to Greece, which would remain on the Olympus–Aliakmonas line, supported by three Greek reserve divisions. In other words, the decisions made by Papagos remained in force, and Greece would only fight against Germany for the sake of preserving its honour, as the lieutenant general himself admitted.

The German invasion began on 6 April when German troops attacked Greek forces and fortifications in Eastern Macedonia and Thrace. The fortresses were surrendered quickly since Greek forces were outflanked from the west, much in the same manner as the Maginot line was in France. Additionally, the Yugoslavs were not able to resist for long, meaning that German forces also began entering Greece from Western Macedonia. On 9 April, the German army occupied Thessaloniki. The next day, at the instructions of General Command, the commander of forces in Eastern Macedonia signed a protocol of capitulation. The army in the forts across the Greek–Bulgarian border put down its arms.

On 12 April, German forces attacked the British on the Aliakmonas line, and as they had not yet fully organised their defensive formation, the British began to withdraw to the south. But Papagos gave no command to retreat from the Albanian front, and by the time he did it was too late, as the necessary manoeuvres were not feasible, and an organised retreat impossible. The Greek army in Albania began to slowly disintegrate as disloyalty spread and desertions multiplied. Commanders on the Albanian front began to consider the possibility of surrendering, even without the government's consent, while the British units fought their last battles as they retreated. In late April, they managed to withdraw to Crete and then Egypt, suffering significant losses.

At the same time, the situation in Athens had taken a drastic turn, worsening even more when the commanders of the three military corps in Epirus decided to send an ultimatum to the government, asking for permission in the next twelve hours to sign an armistice with the Germans. They were met with opposition from George II, who did not want to anger the British, though Papagos stated that he had no objections to such a manoeuvre. As a result, Prime Minister Koryzis committed suicide, and a ceasefire agreement was signed with the Germans upon the initiative of General Giorgios Tsolakoglou, an action that supported the assumption of treason. As the German troops marched towards Athens, the state showed signs of complete disorganisation.

Given the situation, it would be reasonable to have expected George II to seek the creation of a government in which all parties would participate. But he did nothing of the kind and pinned his hopes on Konstantinos Kotzias, an officer of the 4 August dictatorship who maintained friendly relations with Germany. When Kotzias was unable to find willing partners to form a government, he turned towards General Mazarakis and finally to Emmanouil Tsouderos, a liberal and former head of the Bank of Greece. Tsouderos was chosen both for his close relations to London and his Cretan origins, a fact that would facilitate the establishment of the new government on the island, where the population did not support the king. The new government would leave for Crete the moment Papagos submitted his resignation. Tsolakoglou, unable to do otherwise, signed a surrender agreement with the defeated Italians.

The next step in the complete conquest of Greece was Crete, where Greek and British soldiers had gathered, though they did not possess the weaponry necessary to face the Germans. Attempts to conquer the island lasted about ten days, despite the fierce resistance from the army and island residents: German losses surpassed 8,000 troops, more than had perished in the campaigns to occupy Yugoslavia and the rest of Greece. Civilian participation in defence against the Germans was considered a violation of international wartime law by Germany, resulting in reprisals carried out on hundreds of victims and the elimination of entire villages.

George II and the Greek government left the island for Alexandria. But they would not stay for long, as London was soon named the official seat of the government; only three military ministries would remain in Alexandria. In the tense climate that had been created in Greece, after the alleged 'treason' of the generals and capitulation to Italy, the king's flight with the government—and the Bank of Greece's gold—was seen as abandonment and significantly weakened the legitimacy of the exiled political leadership, which now had to rely on Britain for its political and material survival.

Occupation

Greece was divided into three zones after its occupation by Axis troops. The Germans took control of Athens, Thessaloniki, Crete, certain islands in the Aegean and Macedonia (up to the Aliakmonas–Strimonas line). Combined with the Yugoslavian territories, this Greek region comprised the South Eastern German Territorial Administration. The zone occupied by Italy included areas west of Aliakmonas, the Ionian Islands, the Cyclades and a small portion of Eastern Crete. After Italy's surrender in 1943, these areas fell back under German jurisdiction. Finally, Eastern Macedonia and Thrace were placed under Bulgarian control, thus satisfying the country's ambitions for a foothold on the Aegean, something it had not achieved in either the Balkan Wars or the First World War.

Despite this fragmentation of Greek lands, the Germans sought to present Greece to the outside world as a single state entity, which they called the Hellenic State. General Tsolakoglou, who had signed the capitulation agreement, became the first collaborationist prime minister, thus validating voices criticising him for treason. In order to strengthen his position, he turned against the Metaxas regime, declared Greece a republic and tried to win over the support of certain select politicians. But for the most part these political figures kept to the side-lines and waited. In November 1942, Tsolakoglou was replaced by Konstantinos Logothetopoulos, and in April 1943 the final collaborationist government was formed under the leadership of Ioannis Rallis, former minister in the People's Party. This shift was no surprise: it demonstrated the ways in which the former political leadership sought to react to challenges to its authority and its very existence, which intensified at the very moment that Germany's defeat in the war was clear to all.

The Greek government's ability to intervene in various Greek territories varied but was generally limited, even though diplomats representing Italy and Germany in Greece had defended the need for a Greek government that could govern the nation. The various conflicts from which the Greeks sought to benefit—between diplomats and military officers, between Italians and Germans—could only lead to a complete weakening of the Greek administrative mechanisms, though this weakening was not consistent across regions. In Old Greece, and mainly in the Peloponnese, where the state had the deepest roots and traditions, administrative mechanisms survived. In the new territories, military defeat was followed by state collapse as the majority of civil servants, descendants of Old Greece, abandoned their positions and fled to the south.

A similar experience could be noted in more remote territories, and particularly in mountainous areas. Essentially, the Germans and Italians were not interested in—or were not able to control—these mountainous territories where guerrilla resistance forces would develop, and these regions gradually escaped state control. Meanwhile, in the territories that had come under Bulgarian control, collaborationist governments had no way of dealing with the policies of ethnic cleansing and resettlement that were implemented. In September 1941, in fact, an insurrection provoked by communist incitement was suppressed violently by the Bulgarians. Several hundred were executed, while tens of thousands were forced to flee their homes.

Similarly, collaborationist governments were unable to deal with the new economic problems resulting from the nation's conquest. The complete Allied naval blockade was enough to explain the grain shortage that appeared in the early autumn of 1941—and this in a country that was only able to satisfy 65 per cent of its total wheat consumption before the war began. This shortage was exacerbated all the more because of the divisions imposed by occupying forces, which cut off communication between different parts of the country. Production itself must also be considered, which fell by 15 to 30 per cent depending on the commodity, due to wartime circumstances and the destruction of infrastructure caused to some extent during the British retreat. In order to fully understand the problem, it is important to emphasise that it was also objectively impossible to supply urban centres. If one adds to this local cultivators' refusals to deliver their products to state mechanisms for collecting grain—in any case rendered ineffective by occupying forces—then one can fully understand the famine that struck all major cities, and mainly Athens, from August 1941 until early 1943.

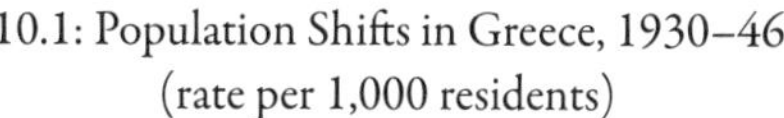

10.1: Population Shifts in Greece, 1930–46
(rate per 1,000 residents)

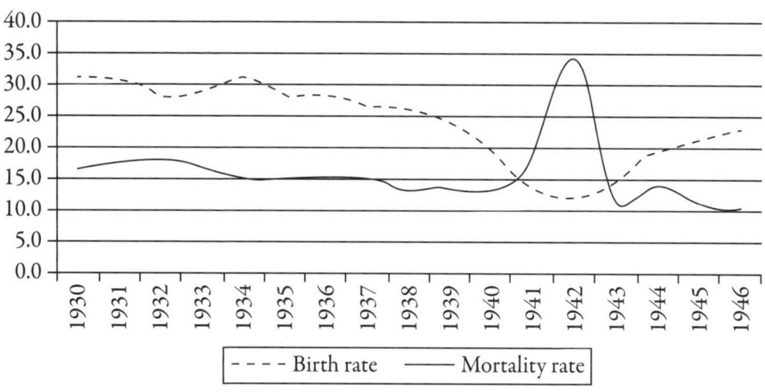

Source: Research group, *Η επιβίωσις του ελληνικού λαού*: Α: Τα δεδομένα, Athens: 1947, pp. 72–4.

This problem of food supply was the subject of difficult negotiations between the exiled government and the occupying forces. It remained partially unsolved until the end of 1942; then, a decisive solution was agreed upon in 1943 as the US government took on the cost of supplying food for Greece, and the Swedish Red Cross organised the process of transferring and distributing these essential goods. Estimates of deaths due to famine vary, since the majority of victims were from marginalised populations that found themselves in cities without the support of a family. This included soldiers unable to return to their homelands and other people who were simply in the wrong place at the wrong time. This explains the evidence of mass graves and numerous records of anonymous deaths. Many of the victims were from lower-income groups, most of them unskilled workers, though some were also certainly skilled workers. Although their standards of living had already been low, they dwindled so drastically during the famine that they became inadequate for survival. Thus, while the average individual in a working family consumed 2,300 calories per day in 1939 (an amount considered sufficient for survival), between November 1941 and March 1942 this shrank to 930 calories per day, rising again to 1,700 calories per day between January and April 1943—the latter amount still barely sufficient for survival.

It is estimated that around 300,000 people lost their lives in the famine during the occupation, a figure that includes childbirths lost as a result.

Though it may be a slight overestimation, this figure is by no means negligible for a population of 7,500,000. If we add deaths caused by the war and other occupation violence, the number of victims during the entire period of occupation may amount to around 500,000; in other words, 7 per cent of the entire population, one of the highest ratios in Europe. This number included the vast majority of Greek Jews, most of whom had been sent to concentration camps. Jewish populations' fatality rates ranged between 80 and 90 per cent of the total population, while the Jewish population of Thessaloniki was completely wiped out.

In this context, the collaborationist government proved unable to react and state mechanisms were unreliable in fulfilling their basic duties. Reciprocal and collective forms of addressing problems eventually appeared and grew in strength, ensuring the population's survival to some extent. The general dissolution of state mechanisms, the indifference of Italian forces—which controlled most of the country until 1943—in maintaining law and order, and the gendarmerie's ambiguous relationship with the occupying forces all led to a huge resurgence in banditry and the development of a parallel economy in which individuals of all sorts and ages participated.

10.2: Monetary Indicators, 1941–4

Date	*Monetary Circulation*	*Gold sovereign value index*	*Cost of living indicator*
April 1941	1.0	1.0	1.0
December 1942	15.7	127.7	156.5
December 1943	135.5	1.319.2	1.572.7
October 1944	8,276,320.0	1,633,540,989.0	2,305,948,911.0

Source: W.O. Candilis, *The economy of Greece, 1944–66: Efforts of Stability and Development*, New York: 1968, p. 17.

The national economy also progressively unravelled, the road networks established more or less successfully by the state were paralysed, and national average income shrank dramatically: scholars argued that it plunged to 30 per cent of pre-war levels. Certainly, the consequences of this were not felt equally across all population groups and regions; cities, mountainous areas and grain-deficient regions suffered the most. Moreover, while the occupying forces initially had an interest in keeping the domestic industrial sector operational—enabling fulfilment of large orders, the use of construction companies for public works, and the mining of materials that could be exported to Germany—from 1943 all these activities ceased as inflation began to take on dizzying proportions and the resistance began to mobilise.

The inflation problem was a distinct example of the Greek economy's progressive disorganisation, and of the manner in which it was plundered by occupying forces; Greece was forced to cover the costs incurred by the occupying army forces, which nearly surpassed the total amount of its national GDP. The Hellenic State was also forced to pay a large loan to Germany, which it would not have been able to fulfil even under normal circumstances. The state of extreme poverty in which most of the population lived soon led to significant state-hiring in the collaborationist government; this in itself served as a way to address penury and hunger in cities, but also as a way to gain local support for collaborationist government policies.

The occupation governments had only one way to fulfil the resulting demands: they turned to currency-printing machines. This resulted in an abandonment of the drachma standard for commodity prices, and producers of goods soon turned to a barter system. When the German administration tried to contain the situation in 1943, introducing gold sovereigns into the market, the sovereign then became the main means of exchange and measure of value.

Resistances

On the one hand, the occupation of Greece by Axis troops created a new institutional framework, which proved ineffective for most of the country; on the other, it disrupted the old one, basically marginalising political realities and collaborations that had existed up until that point. At this point, the battle for power took on different forms, giving new and largely unprecedented opportunities to previously marginal groups and individuals. It also, at least initially, left aside all those who had no reason to demand anything different from the existing political situation. Chris Woodhouse, head of the British military mission in Greece, summarised the situation in the following way:

> Naturally, those who sought to change things after the war acted much sooner than those who preferred a return to the same situation. It was this longing, and not an unbridled desire to defeat the enemy, that led these first leaders (but not their followers, yet) into the arena. All other organizations were more conservative and did not necessarily support George II because he was the King, but supported the established system because it was established ... They believed that the Greek

> nation's problems had been put on hold for the duration of the Occupation. They realized that they had a patriotic duty only much later than their opponents.[1]

Heroic actions led by resistance forces made their appearance very early—in fact, as early as the autumn of 1941. But the most important of these, politically and psychologically, was the destruction of the Nazi National Socialist Patriotic Organisation building in September 1942. It has been argued that this act led to the failure to establish any sort of domestic National Socialist Party. In this same early phase, guerrilla resistance groups first appeared in Macedonia, though they were fiercely repressed by the Germans; an early uprising against the Bulgarian occupation in Thrace led to several hundred fatalities. Finally, portions of various ethnic groups including the Chams, Vlachs and Slavophone Macedonians—some of which had suffered state repression in the interwar period—sought to take advantage of these new conditions by collaborating with the Germans and Italians.

In the same period, that is, in the autumn of 1941, the National Liberation Front (EAM) was established, initiated by the Communist Party. The latter had appealed to all the political parties in the country, inviting them to participate in a very modest platform prioritising national independence, assembly of an EAM-led interim government immediately after liberation and lastly, the right of the Greek people to freely decide its own future form of government 'by any means necessary'. Reactions from the political elite ranged from indifferent—the Liberals repeated their slogan of 'patience and prudence'—to negative, in the case of the People's Party. As a result, EAM only collaborated with three politically insignificant socialist-leaning groups, which justified usage of the term 'front'. But in this way, the nation's pre-war political leadership found themselves excluded from the political arena as it was being formed during the occupation at the very moment that EAM proved itself capable of rallying a large portion of the national population.

EAM's first efforts focused on organising urban populations, and most of the working class. These efforts were not always successful, especially at first when it insisted on political positions that had little to do with the realities of the moment. But it managed to adapt to circumstances, benefiting from them politically and establishing various organisations with which it eventually succeeded in uniting different groups within the population. This was especially the case in the remote suburbs of Athens and Thessaloniki, where the majority suffered from starvation and the state was least present. These organisations then played a key role in the first major confrontation with occupation authorities that arose from the attempt to conscript civilians: intense strikes and demonstrations led to the cancellation of civil conscriptions, and the relevant records held at the Ministry of Labour were destroyed.

In the long term, the most critical moment in EAM's development was its decision to establish the National People's Liberation Army (ELAS) in January 1942, which in a relatively short amount of time succeeded in imposing its authority over a large percentage of the Greek countryside. To ensure its survival, ELAS gradually established its own apparatus in the countryside, taking the place of a dissolving state apparatus. It imposed order and security, harshly persecuting bandits, thus inserting itself into the moral economy of the rural population. Despite the fact that organised military action would only come later—in December 1942—it became an unparalleled power in relation to all other forms of organised resistance.

In the autumn of 1941, the National Republican Greek League (EDES) was founded by Komninos Piromaglou and retired Venizelist Colonel Napoleon Zervas. EDES's founding declaration set out strong anti-royalist positions and stated its aim as being to establish a Greek republic. In this regard, EAM's platform was clearly more moderate. In any case, armed action was not initiated by EDES immediately, and Zervas continually put off such initiatives. But in July 1942 he left Athens, pressed by (and with substantial economic support) from the British, heading to his native Epirus where he would set up the organisation's first armed corps. Finally, the third organisation that would play a role in the resistance was the National and Social Liberation Group (EKKA), created by Georgios Kartalis and Dimitris Psarros, both of whom were in favour of the republican system. Apart from these three major organisations, a host of other smaller organisations with limited influence also emerged.

For the Allies, the importance of these resistance groups became clear in mid-1942, where they supplied necessary support to operations undertaken in North Africa. The major problem they stumbled into was political: the British government, notably Winston Churchill, supported the Greek king, while the three resistance organisations were anti-monarchist. Of the three, EAM was treated with greater scepticism by the allies due to its affiliations with the Communist Party; EDES was chosen as a means of counterbalancing them. In exchange for significant financial compensation, and in order to survive pressure exerted by ELAS, Zervas agreed to fall in line with the positions that the British and the exiled government held regarding EAM.

After December 1942, EAM/ELAS territorial holdings expanded steadily. A more cohesive administration progressively replaced the group's previously fragmentary authority, and by the eve of the German retreat it controlled a very large portion of the Greek countryside. In March 1943, ELAS even took control of two towns, Naoussa in Western Macedonia and Karditsa in Thessaly, maintaining control of the latter for several months. In the mountainous regions of Pindus, which proved inaccessible for occupation forces, EAM proceeded to create basic state infrastructure, and in March 1944 it even organised national elections. The Italians—and after their surrender, the Germans—were increasingly limited to cities, seeking in every which way to control the communities on major transportation routes. But after mid-1943, the Germans, reacting to ELAS advances, began a sweeping process of harsh reprisals, claiming many victims.

The efforts made by EAM to homogenise power were not unrelated to the efforts it made to control ELAS, which it did by adopting a regular army structure led by a political commissioner, an arch-captain (Aris Velouchiotis, representative of the guerrilla resistance forces), and a commander-in-chief. Stefanos Sarafis, who became a cashiered Venizelist officer after the 1935 movement, was appointed as commander-in-chief. This had the effect of making the organisation accessible to other officers and strengthened it more generally. Both coercive practices and the tangible prospect of the war's end played a decisive role in these efforts. On the one hand, the difficulties of communication in Greece at the time—not limited to those caused by the enemy occupation—gave local resistance groups and the Greek Communist Party (KKE) a large degree of autonomy, something that often had a positive effect on their overall efforts. Yet in certain instances, this had negative consequences, as local ambitions frequently played a more important role than EAM's broader political choices.

Extension of EAM power resulted in increased tensions between other resistance groups, the government and state/occupying forces. ELAS first targeted gendarmerie stations and police departments, and as a result many gendarmes joined their ranks, while the rest withdrew to urban centres. Frictions began in December 1942 and manifested themselves all the more so after February 1943. Violent clashes followed with resistance groups, many of which were disbanded in the process. In May and June 1943, EKKA was dissolved by ELAS, and its leader, Psarros, was murdered. At the same moment, EAM and EDES were openly in conflict. From this point onwards, the balance of the situation changed: British support turned increasingly to EDES, while Italy's capitulation greatly enhanced the ELAS's power in Central Greece. In fact, in September 1943, ELAS managed to seize equipment belonging an entire Italian division, significantly strengthening itself in the process.

In these conditions, the British faced a great dilemma. ELAS was incomparably more powerful than EDES, making exclusion of the former from plans for Allied support inconceivable. Though solutions limiting ELAS's autonomy were proposed, they proved unsuccessful. Acting on a suggestion made by EAM, the Allies then established a Joint General Headquarters that reported to General Headquarters in the Middle East, and in July 1943 the three major organisations signed an agreement for military cooperation. But this solution, which incorporated ELAS into a broader, internationalised institutional framework, did not prevent conflicts between the organisations themselves, nor the progressive escalation of violence perpetrated by Germans.

By the winter of 1943–4, at which point the prospect of German defeat was inevitable, the traditional political leadership began to face the prospect of open confrontation with EAM. The military leadership—which had kept to the margins up until this point—took action, seeking to nominate a successor and rival to EAM after the German retreat. But these efforts were either broken up or nipped in the bud by ELAS. With similar intentions but very different political foundations, the political government established in Athens led by Rallis introduced security battalions for the first time. The rationale behind creating these military units was clear: the most important element was not the occupying force, but the domestic enemy. This was in exactly the same period that Germany had begun to emphasise its role as Europe's protector against communism; as a result, the collaborationist government converged with both the broader declarations of the Nazis and a change in opinions observed throughout Greece. There was much concern, and even more resentment, about the increasing power of EAM.

Initially, a plan was drawn up to establish four security battalions, but as German forces in Greece proved insufficient to control resistance organisations, this number grew to include various armed coalitions forming across the nation that varied widely with respect to their staffing, organisation and relationship to the Germans and the Greek government. Although there was initially very little willingness to join these battalions, their strength gradually increased markedly, all the more so after the Italian capitulation, and the battalions established themselves with remarkable success in certain regions. In many cases, they were led by cashiered Venizelist officers, who saw in them the opportunity for a new career. But their increasing identification with anti-monarchist views eventually devolved into nationalism, manifested variedly in different cases. In any case, by the end of the occupation, the great dilemmas of the National Schism had lost their meaning. The battle against communism took priority, constituting the common denominator for a series of highly diverse groups.

In 1943, ELAS's efforts to create more resistance organisations—chiefly undertaken by its officers—strengthened the security battalions and further increased polarisation. Dissolution of these groups led many of their members to join the security battalions, as was the case with EKKA, whose members joined the security battalions in Patras after Psarros's death, or with the Greek army in the Peloponnese. The conception that EAM was not only the first but the only true resistance organisation led to the Manichean treatment of not only collaborators and alleged collaborators with occupying forces as well as other resistance organisations but even groups that were simply unwilling to work with it. Furthermore, the repressive policies pursued by the Germans—including the hunting down of resistance fighters and other harsh reprisals—had opposing results, as the threatened village populations sought refuge with resistance forces, while other villages agreed to collaborate with the security battalions. Over time, opportunities for achieving a compromise shrank dramatically. To be sure, in all their various forms, the security battalions reflected and incorporated a large portion of the population, and in regions of the Peloponnese and Eastern Macedonia, they established a true counter-movement to EAM. Attrition of resistance forces towards the end of the occupation—a process which H. Fleischer has commented on—was evident from every angle; now, it would be succeeded by the battle for power in a country on the verge of liberation.

As this moment approached, violence had become an elementary component of Greek society. In October 1943, EAM, significantly reinforced by Italian equipment that had fallen into its hands after the Italian capitulation, entered into widespread conflict with EDES and simultaneously dissolved the Panhellenic Liberation Organisation in Macedonia, which had been created with British assistance. The Germans temporarily intervened, carrying out reprisals and in many cases supporting EDES positions, subsequently carrying out fierce retaliations for attacks against them. In early 1944, fighting began once again between ELAS and EDES, and did not cease until the British intervened, after which an agreement signed between the three major organisations led to the creation of different zones of influence. The British then conclusively cut off their supply chain to ELAS, while in March 1944 EAM proceeded to create the Political Committee for National Liberation (PEEA) led by Alexandros Svolos, a professor at the University of Athens. In areas under its control, the PEEA held elections for the establishment of a National Council, and local self-government and mechanisms of welfare and justice led to impressive growth in these regions. In this manner, EAM (and, in fact, the Communist Party) established a form of political rule that could compete not only with the collaborationist government but, more importantly, with the exiled government. And their power was far from negligible: as early as the autumn of 1943, they had begun devising a military campaign to occupy Athens after the German departure.

Our understanding of the social effects of the political opposition during the occupation is rather limited. A typical example of this can be seen in the estimates of EAM's strength, which range from 200,000 to 2,000,000 individuals. Similarly vague estimates have been given for other organisations such as ELAS, and in fact, it is doubtful whether even the organisations themselves knew their own numbers. Identifying the social foundations of these various groups and organisations is an even more difficult task. It has been argued that *noikokiraioi* (i.e. small- and medium-scale landowners) were EAM's main source of support, but there is no serious evidence to confirm this. Another source argues that EAM derived most of its strength from groups such as public servants, office workers, traders, shopkeepers and urban professionals. Yet other sources highlight the superior educational level of workers who were members of EAM.

Christophe Woodhouse, in turn, identified the loyalty of rural populations to one faction or another in the following way: if they lived on one side of the mountain, they sided with the communists, and if they were from the other side they sided with the non-communists. If they lived in the lowlands, they sided with security battalions and collaborators of the occupation authorities. According to Woodhouse, there were no social factors involved in a population's loyalty to one faction or the other; it came down to political and geographical circumstance. Similarly, based on extensive empirical research with comparative figures from other instances of civil war, Stathis Kalivas has argued that the greater control an armed group possessed over a region, the more a local population collaborated collectively with it. These findings mainly applied to the countryside, while in cities, social factors seemed more likely to determine loyalty to resistance groups, as lower-income groups and youths joined EAM at higher rates.

Initially, veterans of the Albanian War played an important role in staffing ELAS ranks. But they lessened in importance as younger-age groups, particularly from rural populations, gained a larger role. As a consequence, EAM found it difficult to develop and maintain power in Athens, but it also found huge opportunities to grow in rural areas. Yet at the same time, there was an extremely strong reaction in rural areas to EAM's pursuit of total power. In Macedonia and Thrace, as already mentioned, significant anti-communist groups emerged that ELAS was unable to neutralise. The former found their footing as opponents of the enemy occupation that had directly threatened their survival and were supported by the local rural communities from which they originated. As the war neared its end, these groups gradually transformed into a dynamic, collective rival of the left. Communism's affiliation with the Slavic threat gave all these groups an ideological sheen, and they operated in regions where pre-war state mechanisms had collapsed and the menace of Bulgaria was tangible; they successfully fended off communist pressures with the help of the British. Elsewhere, in the Peloponnese, where state infrastructure had much deeper roots and had not been dismantled, EAM found it difficult to establish itself, and was met with strong opposition, expressed by the extensive prevalence of security battalions.

The Middle East

While these resistance organisations fought with the Axis powers and among themselves in the Greek mountains, other conflicts in Alexandria and Cairo proved just as decisive for Greece's future. In Egypt, where a large Greek population existed, an attempt was made to organise an army that would participate in the African campaign alongside Allied troops. By doing so, the Greek government hoped to gain a better seat at the negotiation table after the war. The backbone of this army was composed of officers and soldiers arriving from occupied Greece, reserve troops from various expatriate communities and ships from the Greek fleet that had withdrawn to the Middle East.

Yet this attempt at consolidating an army quickly became entangled in the political divisions of the interwar period, which had re-emerged in Egypt. British custodianship of the Greek government only aggravated these divisions and tensions between different factions. For his part, George II showed no inclination to abandon his dictatorial past, and he was joined by Emmanouil Tsouderos, who sought to maintain his position as prime minister of the exiled government in every possible way. Unconditional British support enabled George II and Tsouderos to handle issues of constitutional legality or illegality as they so wished. Then, in February 1942, George decided to annul the decree of 1936, which had suspended constitutional freedoms. Though this was purely symbolic, it did pave the way for other politicians to participate in the government. First among them was former professor at the University of Athens Panagiotis Kanellopoulos, who assumed the responsibilities of defence minister and vice president.

Within the prevailing climate of suspicion, the task of organising a well-trained army from the forces gathered in Egypt was no easy feat. Organised groups of royalist officers hoping to prevent Venizelists or leftists (such as the Antifascist Military Organisation, or ASO) from joining the army appeared. In theory, the army's role after the war's end would be decisive in determining who could claim and eventually administer power. This much was confirmed by events in the interwar period, and the fluidity of the situation in Egypt left all options open.

As early as 1941, soldiers had refused to obey orders from officers with ties to the 4 August dictatorship—and under wartime conditions this reaction was not treated with sympathy by the British, who provided for the Greek government and army. Indeed, the situation was charged with tension from the outset, though when Kanellopoulos took charge as defence minister, a Greek brigade was allowed to take part in the battle for El Alamein. But the Greek army's participation in Allied operations was short-lived as the lack of discipline prevailing in Greek units prevented them from participating in other campaigns. In February 1943, royalist officers submitted their resignations in order to demand the removal of Venizelist officers from key positions. This provoked an immediate reaction from the ASO, which imprisoned the officers concerned. British intervention led to a complete dissolution of these units, and the transfer of many of these officers and soldiers to military camps. George II thus found himself forced to reshuffle his cabinet once more, promise to form a representative government at the war's end, and to hold elections for a Constituent Assembly. But even these measures were not enough to calm tensions.

In August 1943, delegations representing the three resistance organisations and various political leaders arrived in Cairo. British insistence that George II return to Greece immediately after the end of the war and before a referendum was held did not make negotiations any easier; and this was despite the fact that all the representatives from Greece agreed with each other that George II should not return, while the cabinet had unanimously signed an agreement with the same purpose. The delegations were forced to return to Greece empty-handed.

EAM's growing influence in Greece forced both the British and the exiled government to alter its course. One option was to strengthen EDES; another was to attempt and reinstate pre-war political conditions; a third was to attempt to integrate EAM into a comprehensive model of political negotiation. Yet again, Tsouderos called representatives of political parties to Cairo—along with representatives from the Political Committee of National Liberation (PEEA), which had been founded in the meantime—in order to form a consensus government and place the resistance organisations under joint command. As the moment of liberation approached, these emerging power dynamics would play a decisive role in defining both the form of government to be established in Greece and who would govern the country.

But just before these representatives arrived in Egypt, without consulting EAM, a committee of army officers belonging to the Communist Party—influenced by the establishment of PEEA—demanded that Tsouderos create a republican form of government. They acted independently, a fact that led to the prime minister's resignation. Other members of his government soon followed suit. The British then intervened again, placing the Greek army and fleet under armed surveillance. In the meantime, Sophocles Venizelos, son of Eleftherios, assumed the premiership, while military units loyal to the government reoccupied ships that had mutinied. Military forces in the Middle East were dissolved, the majority of troops confined to concentration camps. Only small units loyal to the king remained intact. Once Sophocles Venizelos had completed this task, he was considered useless. He was replaced by George Papandreou, a rather conservative politician previously distinguished for the educational reforms he had led as a member of the Venizelos government from 1928 to 1932. He arrived in Cairo expressly to assume the premiership.

At the request of Papandreou—prime minister but also sole member of the government—a meeting was held in May 1944 between representatives of EAM, EDES, EKKA and other political parties in a remote village of Lebanon. EAM representatives agreed to co-sign an agreement for the restoration of discipline in the army and for the unification of guerrilla groups under a single administration. These concessions were made so as to create a government with national unity that would represent the country in the allied struggle and facilitate Greece's liberation. Had the result been different, EAM would have found itself isolated, which would have potentially led it to break off on its own, since all of its officers that did not belong to the Communist Party—and some communist officers themselves—were against open confrontation with the British. From another perspective, the Lebanon Conference led to the rallying of anti-EAM groups and parties and to the foundations of an anti-EAM camp that grew stronger and stronger over time regardless of internal differences.

The leftist leadership in the mountains did not accept the terms of the Lebanon agreement, claiming that their representatives at the conference made more concessions than they should have done. It demanded new reforms of the regime in place, public denunciation of the security battalions, a reversal of death sentences handed to its supporters after the April rebellion and a more significant presence in the ministerial council. Soon after, as relations between Papandreou and EAM worsened, the latter asked that the prime minister be replaced. This reaction from the Communist Party—since it was its members who were chiefly affected by the political concessions made by EAM representatives in Lebanon—led to a clash with the PEEA, which was much more moderate; it also nearly led to the breakup of EAM, which was only prevented by sustained attempts at compromise.

These contradictions in EAM policies are not difficult to account for. On the one hand, the supremacy it maintained in Greece led it to hope that the German departure would lead to its dominance. On the other hand, its efforts to impose power ran the risk of leading to conflict with the British, representatives of the Allied forces, at a moment when they had no contact with the Soviets so as to make their intentions known. The only solution could be compromise, and so the EAM presented itself as faithful to the Allied cause and national unity, buying time. The decision to reach some sort of compromise seems to have been linked with a Soviet military mission's visit to ELAS headquarters; though the Soviet mission was not entitled to give advice, it did contribute to EAM curbing its hard-line stance. Finally, it agreed to participate unconditionally in the government of national unity. In doing so, EAM and the Communist Party—which assumed an increasingly active role—became embroiled in a political game in which its position would be de facto disadvantaged.

In September 1944, the government of national unity was transferred to Caserta in Italy, where an agreement was reached under which ELAS and EDES forces were placed under the command of General Ronald Scobie, commander of the British force that was to disembark in Greece. The security battalions were to be considered enemy forces, while the administration of Attica was assigned to General P. Spiliotopoulos. In this instance too, EAM retreated, as the only other alternative would be to clash with the British.

Around the same time, German troops had begun their withdrawal from Greece, and violent clashes occurred between ELAS and security battalions.

Bloody battles took place, claiming thousands of victims in areas where ELAS was met with the greatest resistance from hostile groups. This was the case in Kalamata, Meligala, Gargalianoi, in Pyrgos of the Peloponnese and in Kilkis, Macedonia. Further bloodshed was sparked when, in the name of the government of national unity, ELAS purged any centres of possible resistance so as to strengthen its own position. By this point, it controlled not only the countryside, which had few advantages to offer by then, but urban centres too. After an intervention by Kanellopoulos, a representative of the government and of the British, these conflicts ceased. Meanwhile, in Northern Greece, Bulgaria's shift of alliances renewed the latter's hopes of retaining Macedonian and Thracian territories. The Bulgarian troops eventually withdrew, but only after intense Allied pressure.

Liberation

In early October 1944, before either the national government or the British army reached Greece, ELAS was in control of the entire country with the exception of Epirus, which was under EDES control. Despite this, ELAS forces stationed in Attica made no move to enter Athens after the German departure. Thus EAM respected the agreements it had signed. Regardless of this, reserve ELAS forces effectively controlled the capital and held a majority of working-class neighbourhoods under their control. At the same time, security battalion troops were disarmed by representatives of the national government and sent to various army camps, while the gendarmerie waited on the government to decide its fate, which initially looked none too promising. In the meantime, EAM militia groups had taken over its policing duties. Finally, members of the collaborationist governments and other German collaborators had been arrested and were detained in prisons awaiting trial. So, on 18 October 1944 when the government of national unity entered a liberated Athens, the mood may have been enthusiastic, but uncertainties and fears for the future prevailed. Who would govern the nation, and how they would do so?

Around the same time, the agreement between Britain and the Soviet Union for control of the Balkans took its final form. Churchill met with Stalin in Moscow on 9 October 1944, and the so-called 'percentages agreement' was implemented under which South East Europe was divided into spheres of influence. The Soviets also gave their consent for British troops to be sent in a mission to Greece after the German departure. Of course, the

British had no intention of relinquishing control over Greece, especially now that the Red Army's presence in the Balkan nations had radically changed the pre-war balance of power.

Back in Greece, the government of national unity faced an extremely difficult situation rife with political and social tensions and conflicts, despite efforts made to keep them in check. The economy had been devastated. As they retreated, the Germans had destroyed a large amount of infrastructure: problems of food supply for the population—at least in cities—were widespread and could only be resolved with the help of Allied aid. The state apparatus had collapsed, the pace of industry had slowed due to the destruction and scarcity of raw materials, while order and security could only be ensured by armed resistance groups. In the countryside, this devastation was equally visible, as large portions of villages had been destroyed and crops lay abandoned, flocks exterminated. Inflation ran unimaginably high, and the economy was in a state of complete disintegration.

Along with these huge economic and social problems, the political question persisted: how to transfer power from EAM to the national government. Disarmament of ELAS and other armed groups was a crucial goal, along with establishment of a regular army and reconstruction of mechanisms for ensuring the nation's domestic safety. These problems were not easy to address, least of all for a government incorporating individuals from across the entire political spectrum. The Liberals, whose participation in the government was rather symbolic compared with their pre-war presence, had no intention of facilitating Papandreou's project. The People's Party, or at least part of it, was in favour of the king's return, while everyone who had collaborated one way or another with the Germans sought ways to avoid indictment (though they often found support from the older political parties). EAM distrusted any initiatives made by the British and the prime minister, fearing that a coup would enforce George II's return and impose a new dictatorship. For their part, the British prepared for conflict: they believed that the Communist Party would soon act in the dispute for power, and saw this as the only chance to settle the score once and for all.

With this in mind, the British took care to fortify units such as the gendarmerie that could prove useful to them in case of conflict. On the other hand, they also sought to protect the security battalions and other groups that had collaborated with the Germans. They also hastened to transport the mountain brigade to Greece, the only surviving unit of the regular Greek army, which was valued both for its experience in battle and its loyalty to the king. The probability of conflict between the two camps hinged on very delicate balances, and it became evident that neither Papandreou nor the leaders of the Communist Party—and especially not General Scobie—possessed the skills necessary to maintain these balances, even if they had wished to.

The critical moment in this tension was the planned demobilisation of armed forces on 10 December 1944, which presented an opportunity for EAM opponents and the British to disrupt ELAS's military superiority. Naturally, the latter tried to maintain its power, or at least prevent itself from entering a disadvantageous situation. Another crucial question was whether or not the mountain brigade should be broken up. Mutual suspicion exacerbated difficulties in communication, and on 24 November 1944 an announcement provoked a storm of reactions, naming the fourteen administrators of the national guard battalions created to facilitate disarmament of resistance groups and reconstruction of the national army and gendarmerie, which had proven itself completely unreliable. Eight of these administrators were former security battalion officers. Although Papandreou rushed to correct the situation, suspicions mounted and negotiations for disarmament dragged on without any mutually accepted solution.

On 1 December, General Scobie gave instructions for the dissolution of all armed groups and made another clearly anti-EAM proclamation. Whether he had a right to intervene in this manner is still the subject of academic debate today. The same day, the cabinet—without the participation of EAM ministers—voted to dissolve civilian militia groups controlled by EAM and replace them with national guard battalions. EAM hurriedly withdrew its ministers from the Papandreou government and decided to hold a rally on 3 December, the tensions in Athens running high. On the eve of the rally, the cabinet issued a new decision to dissolve all armed groups with the exception of the mountain brigade, while EAM proceeded to reconstitute ELAS's Central Committee. This move demonstrated how the group had completely distanced itself from the agreements in force up until then, which stipulated that ELAS was under government command. All roads now led to conflict.

Despite a ban prohibiting it, the rally was held on 3 December and was attended by an impressive number of people. But during the march, demonstrators were shot—by the police, according to all indications—and twenty to thirty people were killed. From this moment onwards, the period known as the *Dekemvriana* began, which constituted one of the episodes in the Greek Civil War. The prevailing climate was memorably described by an important Greek intellectual, Giorgos Theotokas, who was also a witness to these events:

> Public opinion is split in two, perhaps irreversibly. Those under the influence of the KKE are as fanatical as ever, in a state of near-cultish secrecy, ready for anything that their leaders may ask them, ready for each dare, act of heroism or sacrifice ... On the other side, the side of the majority, a strong spirit of intolerance prevails. The great anti-Communist mass has forgotten all the differences that divided it until yesterday and asks for only one thing: to fight against the KKE with any and all means necessary, even the harshest ones. But it does not have the ideological fervor of its opponents. It is cool, reserved, tight lipped and brimming with grudges and resentments that have been gathering in its ranks these past weeks. If this prevails, and it is free to do as it pleases (that is, if it is not bound by external factors), it will be relentless. We've reached the same situation as the catholic majority of France on the Night of Saint Barthelemy itself. That's where we've reached.[2]

The clashes continued for a month. As was to be expected, lacking significant forces, capable military leadership and heavy weaponry in Athens, EAM was defeated. It failed to rally any international support in the process, even from the Soviet Union. At the same time, the main ELAS forces dissolved resistance groups in other parts of the country, including EDES in Epirus, though this did not lead to an increase in their own power. In contrast, British strength grew continually, and after a first difficult fortnight they were able to begin a counterattack and dissolve ELAS forces in Athens. In the process, they were assisted by the gendarmerie and police, by a large number of security battalion troops whom they armed once again to strengthen their forces, but also by paramilitary forces such as Organisation X, which had collaborated with the Germans and sought to clean up its past history by fighting the communists. The *Dekemvriana* developed fatefully for EAM, to some extent due to the communist leadership's lack of restraint and voluntarism, but also to a lack of political sensitivity that could have otherwise enabled them to capitalise on situations and reach some sort of rational compromise.

On 5 January 1945, EAM forces chose to evacuate Athens, acknowledging defeat. They took a substantial number of hostages, many of whom were executed. This was a major political mistake, which its opponents would point out at every turn thereafter. Not only did many conservative supporters desert EAM; once the British had spread the news, these executions also tarnished the group's international reputation. Meanwhile, its members in remote neighbourhoods of the city were subject to their opponents' violent reactions, and many thousands of them were sent to the army camps of the Middle East where they would join prisoners from the Greek army rebellion in 1944.

The general situation also shifted: Papandreou resigned, having completely lost control of the situation, and Archbishop Damaskinos assumed the regent's duties despite objections raised by George II. In this manner, a problem was solved, which, if it had been addressed earlier, probably could have led to a smooth transition to a democratic system. The new government, under the leadership of General Plastiras—who returned hurriedly to Greece from France where he had stayed throughout the war—now had to face economic and social issues requiring urgent solutions, but also a political problem whose solution had been suspended by EAM's defeat in Athens.

The Varkiza period

On 11 January 1945, British and ELAS forces signed a truce under which the latter was obliged to concede many positions it had held in Southern Greece and Thessaloniki up until then. In early February in Varkiza, negotiations began between the Plastiras government and EAM that led to the Treaty of Varkiza. The treaty stipulated that all EAM armed groups were to demobilise immediately and relinquish territories under ELAS control, martial law was lifted, constitutional freedoms were restored throughout the country, a national army with universal conscription was re-established and amnesty for 'political crimes' was granted. The treaty also provided for a referendum to be held on the future system of government, elections to convene a Constituent Assembly, and the punishment of any individual that had collaborated with the occupying forces.

It may be surprising that EAM—whose forces continued to dominate throughout Greece even after its defeat in Athens—surrendered to the demands of the British and Greek government, who were both incapable of extending their military operations beyond the region of Attica. But the success or failure of the compromise—in other words, whether it could lead to what was theoretically desired, which was to restore order and peace—depended on one key factor: the state's ability to enforce it. Given the circumstances, this proved impossible. The result was nothing more than a complete reversal of the political balances existing at the time the agreement was signed. On the one hand, ELAS was forced to surrender its arms—or at least a share of them, since it would soon become clear that a large number of weapons were never handed over—and dissolve. On the other hand, a variety of rival groups were now able to move freely across the country, imposing their own authority.

Mass persecutions of tens of thousands of EAM members followed. In the countryside, armed parastatal groups pursued members of the EAM portion of the left in an attempt to obliterate their political presence. At this point, the central government was extremely weak, or at the least unwilling to intervene. According to data provided by EAM, in the period spanning between the Treaty of Varkiza and elections on 3 March 1946, 1,289 murders (953 conducted by terrorists, 250 by members of the national guard, eighty-two by gendarmes and four by the British), 6,671 injuries, 31,632 incidences of torture, 84,931 arrests, 18,767 instances of looting and destruction, 677 destroyed offices, 509 attempted murders and 165 rapes were recorded. Though these figures may seem exaggerated, they undoubtedly highlight the atmosphere of terror prevailing for the left in post-war Greece. At the same time, the number of occupation collaborators in custody awaiting trial was remarkably small: in September 1945, of 2,773 legally convicted individuals, only 279 were former collaborators; of 15,006 detainees, only 2,312 faced charges of collaborationism. Many EAM supporters under attack found themselves isolated in the mountains and progressively established their own armed groups, seeking to survive their opponents' prosecution.

In this context, those who had collaborated with the Germans found an opportunity to purse their former persecutors under very favourable circumstances. Governments succeeded one another rapidly, as not a single one was in a position to tackle these problems, or even ensure the basic functions of public administration. Political polarisation reached its limits as the centre and right joined together against the left, which was believed to collectively represent the communist danger. This in itself was another way in which groups removed from power during the occupation sought to regain it again, and in this manner many collaborators escaped conviction, or were convicted but soon released to join the task force of the political system opposing the left and seeking to prevent any effort at liberalising the political system. Opportunities also arose for radical confrontation with various minority groups: the Chams in Epirus, who had collaborated to some extent with the Italians, were forced—first by EDES, then by the national guard battalions—to abandon their villages and seek refuge in Albania. The Slavophone Macedonians, many of whom had initially collaborated with the occupation authorities, and, subsequently, when Bulgarian defeat was in plain sight, had joined the Macedonian National Liberation Front (which collaborated with EAM), were forced to take refuge in Yugoslavian Macedonia until the beginning of the last stage of the Civil War.

EAM leadership faced these issues poorly, and soon the small socialist groups that participated in it—which had already distanced themselves to some extent during the *Dekemvriana*—took separate positions and broke off.

The Communist Party continued to maintain an ambiguous stance, condemning both those that sought more armed confrontation and those seeking full integration into the bourgeois political playing field. It also excommunicated ELAS's military leader, Aris Velouchiotis, who refused to give up arms, and then committed suicide upon being persecuted. Just before that, Nikos Zachariadis, general secretary of the Communist Party, had returned from Dachau, Germany, where he had been imprisoned for the entire occupation. But despite the fact that many were encouraged by Zachariadis's arrival—he was considered an inspiring figure and true interpreter of Stalinist practices and theories—the Communist Party did not change its positions. Only at the Seventh Congress held in October 1945 was 'massive popular self-defence' first referred to, though it was still not specifically defined.

As this persecution of the left continued, an effort was also made to rebuild the economy and reorganise state mechanisms. Neither was an easy process, and all efforts faltered due to the government's inability to implement coherent policies, as one government succeeded the next. In the end, reorganisation of the state apparatus simply meant purging EAM members from its ranks; the gendarmerie, police force and army were staffed by members of the right, many of whom had collaborated with the occupation government. In fact, the state that took shape immediately after the Second World War very quickly took on an anti-communist bent, placing emphasis on the persecution of communists, and thus allowing for the elimination of pre-war differences on every level.

In this tense climate of proliferating, uncontrolled state and parastatal violence, it was decided that elections would be held on 31 March 1946. The left committed the fatal mistake—which it would later admit—of abstaining from the elections, thus condemning its supporters to be easily identified and persecuted (since their election booklet remained unstamped) and dooming the fate of the party itself. On the republican side, the Liberal Party decided to take part, led by Themistoklis Sofoulis, who was prime minister at the time despite the fact that ministers were driven to resign, and many others protested until the last minute about the conditions under which the elections were conducted, since they were often prevented from touring their constituencies. Other candidates on the ballot included members of the Agrarian Party, two local unions from Crete, the monarchist right, and the National Political Union led by Sophocles Venizelos, Panagiotis Kanellopoulos and George Papandreou (which had avoided taking a position on the issue of the monarchy). Apart from the Communist Party, former members of the government itself also boycotted the elections, including Georgios Kafantaris, Georgios Kartalis and Ioannis Sofianopoulos. The latter had been the Greek government's representative at the time the Treaty of Varkiza was signed.

Various efforts have been made to calculate the power of the EAM faction based on rates of voter absenteeism. The majority, and the more reliable of these estimates, converge on a figure of around 25 per cent of all the abstaining parties, that is, including centrist parties. In any case, this was of little significance, because as Mavrogordatos has argued, the elections of 1946 and the referendums that followed in the same year were the last chance to secure an institutional solution to the national political problem in Greece—a solution that was rejected by the left. If all political parties had participated, given that the electoral system was proportional, the monarchist right faction would have been unable to obtain the strong majority it secured in the end, and a coalition government would have been the only choice.

Elections were held under violent conditions and in comparison with the circumstances prevailing at the end of the war, international relations had begun to shift rapidly. The reality of the Cold War was setting in. Already, in March 1946, a few days before elections were to be held, Churchill's words in Fulton had determined the Cold War's symbolic beginning. The left's decision not to take part in elections led to a direct confrontation with the right, which was represented predominantly by the monarchist People's Party and considered this gesture as validation that George II should return to Greece. Under these circumstances, despite the presence of foreign observers, the results were more or less to be expected. The monarchic right won 65 per cent of the valid ballots and 67 per cent of the seats. The National Political Union was left with 19 per cent of the vote and seats, while the republicans took in 16 per cent of the vote and 14 per cent of the seats.

The struggle in the mountains

On 31 March 1946, the same day elections took place, a leftist armed group attacked the gendarmerie station in Litochoro, a small town in the foothills of Mt. Olympus. Zachariadis refused to condemn the incident, and did not accept the results of the election. Confusion reigned in the leftist camp and EAM's momentum, already affected by the *Dekemvriana* and doubly so after Varkiza, now dwindled completely. The Communist Party found it difficult to take a position on the domestic peace effort or the question of overthrowing the political regime in place, thus giving its opponents every opportunity to fight it and to continue persecuting its supporters. Formation of a right-wing government under the leadership of K. Tsaldaris did harden the state's attitude in this direction, though not as much as one would have expected.

Attacks mounted by guerrilla groups against dispatched gendarmerie units, the national guard and right-wing groups, mainly in Northern Greece, occurred all the more frequently. In the summer of 1946, military units were even attacked. Though the Communist Party continued to move freely in Athens, this was far from the case in the countryside. Only in June 1946 did the government take the first steps at suppression, introducing the death sentence for offences related to the leftist armed struggle.

On 1 September 1946, a referendum—initially planned for 1948—was held on the political regime in place. The right's victory in the elections had accelerated the process, while the British did not appear willing to keep their promises to the centrists. Of a total of 1,900,000 registered voters, 1,660,000 voted, of which 68.4 per cent voted in favour of the king's return. Serious doubts were expressed over the credibility of the referendum, but in the end the centrist forces accepted the result. The Communist Party, as expected, refused to acknowledge the results. Directly after this, armed guerrilla campaigns multiplied, and in October 1946 the General Headquarters of the Guerrillas would be established. Shortly thereafter, at the end of the year, the Democratic Army was created, unifying hitherto scattered groups of existing guerrillas. These developments were accompanied by very effective attacks on various townships.

In March 1947, in his speech to Congress, President Truman argued for the necessity of supporting Greece and Turkey so as to prevent them from falling into communist hands. The British were no longer in a position to support the Greeks, and they handed the baton to the Americans, dramatically altering the context of the Civil War. Greece was now the privileged recipient of American economic and military support, and an important piece on the Cold War chessboard. The US presence in Greece led to changes in the political landscape. Seeking to avoid the criticism they were subjected to for supporting a right-wing government, the Americans would finally impose a coalition government led by Prime Minister K. Sofoulis, an aging liberal. It was this government's task to successfully end the Civil War.

Soon things intensified even more. After a failed attempt to find a way to grant amnesty and free many of the prisoners, the government adopted much tougher measures, including the mass arrests of leftists and the creation of three concentration camps. The first, on Makronisos Island, was made to house leftists serving in the army. The second, in Trikeri, was for citizens arrested in territories that underwent purging. The third was Gyaros Island, built for convicted leftists. The scale of these camps can be grasped by noting that from 1947 to 1950, 30,000 individuals passed through the Makronisos camp, most of whom were forced to sign declarations of repentance under extreme pressure.

On the military front, the government's dominance was not as straightforward an endeavour as one would expect, especially if we take into account the fact that the Democratic Army was mainly limited to Northern Greece. In fact, in 1947, guerrilla forces achieved many significant victories. At the end of the year, the provisional democratic government was formed, led by Prime Minister Markos Vafeiadis. Soon after, the government issued Emergency Law 509/1947, banning the Communist Party and all organisations under its control, providing for harsh penalties (including the death penalty) for those who sought to overthrow the state and/or secede from part of the territory. The possibilities for compromise had been exhausted.

On the other hand, the Democratic Army's chances for victory were extremely limited: it was supplied by routes through bordering countries, and was in a poor state compared with the power of the national army. The vast majority of the Democratic Army was composed of young and very young soldiers, while a substantial number of women also joined its ranks, their participation increasing over time, a sign of the army's inability to replace its losses. Moreover, a large portion of them had been recruited compulsorily. The Democratic Army's status diminished even more after the national army evacuated rural areas to eliminate potential strongholds for rebel support. By 1947, it had become nearly impossible for them to recruit soldiers from urban populations.

Even in international terms, the battle became progressively more burdensome for the communists as Tito distanced himself from Moscow and sought to garner support from the West. At the same time, the provisional democratic government did not succeed in being recognised by any country, not even the Soviet Union. In fact, it did not have any territory to call its own, lacking this basic prerequisite for state legitimacy. By late 1947, the Communist Party's internal contradictions manifested themselves fully with the clash between Vafeiadis (who advocated the tactics of rebel warfare in order to wear out the opponent) and Zachariadis, general secretary of the Communist Party, who sought to transform the guerrilla warfare into a larger military confrontation. Zachariadis prevailed, with Vafeiadis losing his rank and position as a result.

In the meantime, the national army had succeeded in completely reorganising, significantly increasing its strength and outfitting itself with equipment necessary for handling campaigns against the guerrillas. Beginning in late 1948, operations to clear the Peloponnese of hostile troops began, which would be completed successfully in the summer of 1949. At the beginning of the year, Alexandros Papagos was appointed commander-in-chief, assuming wide-ranging responsibilities. He managed to protect the army from political intervention, which up until then had been very frequent. In the meantime, the Communist Party insisted that victory was still possible for the Democratic Army and renewed calls for its interwar slogan demanding the 'need to restore the Macedonian people'. Zachariadis's move—which dragged members of the Communist Party and fighters of the Democratic Army into a thorny issue—can be explained by the significant participation of Slavophone Macedonian troops in Democratic Army ranks and the latter's dependence on the countries of the Iron Curtain for replenishing its troops. One other such fatal political mistake was the transfer of children from areas under its control to territories belonging to these popular democracies, a move that was given much coverage in government propaganda.

All of these were nothing more than fitful actions, and on 1 May 1949 the government's army began operations to clear Central Greece and Thessaly, where it crushed its opponents forces. At this point, the Democratic Army's sole hopes were pinned on its forces in the Grammos and Vitsi Mountains of Northern Greece. At that very moment, Tito chose to close off the borders and interrupt relations with the Greek Communist Party. The Democratic Army's room to manoeuvre tightened. The final attacks by government forces began on 2 August 1949 and ended that same month with the complete defeat of the Democratic Army, whose remnants fled to Albania. In this manner, a completely meaningless war had come to an end.

There were many more victims in this last phase of the Civil War in comparison with the Balkan Wars, the Asia Minor campaign and even with the war in 1940–1. In the Balkan Wars, 300 officers and 7,900 soldiers perished. In the Asia Minor campaign, 1,270 and 36,000 respectively; in the Second World War, 740 officers and 14,400 soldiers lost their lives. According to the official data from the army chiefs of staff, from 1946 to 1949, losses in the national army totalled 651 officers and 7,789 soldiers, while those missing in action respectively tallied 186 and 5,260. Overall, the number reached approximately 14,000 individuals. Fatalities in the Democratic Army have been estimated at 38,421, a number that has since been debated and revised to 25,000. In any case, this number of deaths surpasses the total victims from all other wars. If to these we add all the losses experienced from 1943 onwards—products of internal conflicts—the overall figure is exceedingly high. Furthermore, this figure does not account for the violence experienced by people at the time: estimates for victims of guerrilla violence, those who were forced to leave their villages and settle in the outskirts of cities, have exceeded 700,000 individuals, while arrests, deportations and concentration camps may not have led to death, but were certainly permanently scarring experiences. Additionally, several thousand people were forced to flee to Iron Curtain countries after the communist defeat, while one can trace the roots of Slavophone Macedonian migration from Northern Greece to the United States, Australia and Canada to this same Civil War period. It is no coincidence that even today the event that was the Civil War has not been completely overcome, at least as a landmark of political participation.

New standards, unchanged realities

While the Civil War raged on in Greece, the country's economy had to be rebuilt. In contrast with what might be expected, and contrary to most scholarship on the period, the economy performed impressively. All economic indicators returned to pre-war levels, in step with indicators from most other Western European countries. The path towards rebuilding Greece's economy was certainly much tougher in comparison with other Western European economies, since the devastation experienced in Greece during the occupation was far more severe, and the very process of reconstruction had to occur in conditions of war.

First of all, transportation infrastructure had been completely destroyed: by the end of the war, the national railway network was in a shambles, and many locomotives and train cars had completely disappeared; 90 per cent of large bridges and 50 per cent of smaller ones had been detonated, while the same held true for tunnels and various mountain throughways. Automobiles of all types had been confiscated by the occupation authorities, and at the end of the war only 14 per cent of the pre-war numbers remained. The merchant fleet had been reduced to just 35 per cent of its pre-war capacity, while all harbours had been destroyed both during Allied bombing and the German departure. The nation's few airports were in the same condition. Finally, it has been argued that 25 per cent of the nation's real estate capital had been destroyed during or immediately after the occupation.

The speed with which infrastructure was rebuilt, even in conditions of Civil War, would have been impossible to comprehend without Allied (and shortly thereafter American) aid, which initially ensured the supply of food to the population, and then invested very large sums in the reconstruction of the economy. It has been estimated that the amounts allocated by American assistance during this period far surpassed the total amount of foreign loans that Greece had taken on in its entire history up until that point.

10.3: Industrial Production in Western Europe, 1947–51 (1938=100)

	1947	*1949*	*1951*	*% increase 1951/1947*
Turkey	153	162	163	7
Sweden	142	157	172	21
Ireland	120	154	176	46
Denmark	119	143	160	35
Norway	115	135	153	33
UK	110	129	145	32
Belgium	106	122	143	33
France	99	122	138	39
Holland	94	127	147	56
Italy	93	109	143	54
Greece	69	90	130	88
Austria	55	114	148	269
Germany (federation)	34	72	106	312
All countries participating in the Marshall Plan	87	112	135	55
All countries participating in the Marshall Plan except Germany	105	130	145	37

Source: B. Eichengreen, *The European Economy since 1945: Coordinated Capitalism and Beyond*, Princeton, NJ: 2007, p. 57.

Gradually, agricultural production returned to pre-war levels, despite the fact that it was precisely these predominantly rural areas that had suffered most from the Civil War's conflicts. By 1947, agricultural production had reached 85.2 per cent of 1938 production levels. Industrial production followed a similar trajectory: by 1948, it had reached 73 per cent of industrial production in 1938, and by 1950 it had surpassed 110 per cent.

However, the Greek economy's main problem continued to be a monetary one. After the end of the war, the government tried to address this by introducing a new drachma in place of the old one, the value of which had since evaporated. But every effort to maintain a stable currency faltered due to the Greek state's inability to restructure its tax system and increase revenues in general. Of course, anything to the contrary would have been strange, since state mechanisms were virtually non-existent. Thus the only way that remained to finance public spending was to increase the currency in circulation, and the state resorted to this in order to pay off its obligations. Besides, attempts to increase tax revenues would have been met with resistance from the groups that would have to pay the price. All this happened at a time when large amounts had to be spent on the restructuring the army, on the nation's safekeeping and eventually on the national army's participation in the Civil War.

Despite these advances, Greece was still a poor country in the 1940s; it was the poorest country among the nations of the OECD, an organisation that had recently been established to facilitate implementation of the Marshall Plan. Indeed, it is very possible that the redistribution of income rapidly deteriorated in the decade spanning from 1940 to 1949—though there are no studies to corroborate this.

Efforts at rebuilding the Greek economy, which did not vary tremendously from those of other OECD countries, were accompanied by a radicalisation of thought defining Greek economic developmental models, and especially the role that industry was to play. In the interwar period, Greek industry had not achieved much worth bragging about; at the time, industry was more of a political and social necessity than an economic one, as it sought to address problems arising from the influx of refugees and then the 1929–32 crisis. The changes brought about by the Second World War altered perceptions of the nation's industrial future, while transformations in the international economic system heralded by the main players in the anti-Axis alliance created an auspicious climate for countries like Greece that hoped to improve their position in the global economy after the war.

Thus after the war's end, many political figures and parties—from the right-wing all the way to the Communist Party—invoked the necessity of larger-scale industrialisation that would rely on the use of raw materials and national natural resources. Moreover, the US mission in Greece, which aimed to assist with the implementation of aid provided by the United States under the Marshall Plan, saw industrialisation as the only solution to the Greek financial problem. According to the Porter Report (the first document that revealed American policies in Greece), mineral reserves, metallurgical industries, and the processing of agricultural products constituted the main pillars that the Greek economy would need to base its developmental trajectory on.

The four-year plan from 1948 to 1952 reaffirmed this perspective, while international organisations that turned their attention to Greece in the late 1940s reached the same conclusion. The United Nations Relief and Rehabilitation Administration (UNRRA) believed that Greece urgently needed to create basic—as it referred to them—industries that would rely on exploiting the nation's mineral wealth, and it judged any neglect of this effort as a critical fault.

The consensus between leftist and conservative attitudes over the prospects of developing the country's industry was surface-deep. For the left, a national plan constituted the first step in activating a process of development in which the state led the way, supported by a backbone of heavy industry. Full utilisation of the nation's energy resources would facilitate the creation of energy-intensive metallurgical industries, which in turn would support the development of mechanical engineering. The model proposed by the left provided for the full vertical integration of production in order to satisfy the needs of the domestic market. Starting from the assumption that the lag in the Greek economy was mainly due to economic and political dependence on foreign powers, this view emphasised Greek industry's ability to develop based on the robust accumulation of internal capital. These same views sought to combat the extremely widespread interpretation of the lag in the Greek economy being the result of an inherent lack of funds. Economic and political independence was considered the end goal and fundamental precondition of this plan for economic development. This was to be accompanied by an increase in the population's living standards, which could only be achieved under these conditions. But it is obvious—and the left by no means concealed this—that implementation of this plan presupposed something more than economic and political independence: it required a change in the political system, and enforcement of 'popular democracy'.

For conservative-leaning intellectuals and the nation's remaining political forces, external resources—repairs, loans, free aid—played a central role in the country's industrialisation, which had to focus on added value by processing raw materials locally and then exporting semi-finished products. A fundamental part of this process was the need to absorb surplus labour forces, which had grown to an alarming size due to the insecurity and conditions of war prevailing in the countryside. The degree of state intervention in industrialisation varied according to where each individual found themselves on the political spectrum. In the least interventionist case, the state was held accountable for creating favourable conditions in the sectors of infrastructure, public administration and the institutional network at large so that private initiatives—Greek and foreign—could take on the necessary risks.

Regardless of all this, it was to be a painful future for all kinds of industrial development in Greece, whether in the first or second iteration. In 1949, the Americans began to doubt the feasibility of the plans they themselves had drawn up a year earlier. At the same time, the OECD had begun to object to (and even worse, reject) proposals for the creation of businesses in sectors such as oil refinery, steel and chemical products, which Greece had a direct stake in, stressing the need for cooperation and collaboration between other nations and members in order to avoid creating a surplus of productive power, and, in fact, in order to avoid fissures in the European economic hierarchy. Finally, the Korean War would lead the United States to revise its priorities and end assistance for economic reconstruction, shifting resources to strengthen its defensive alliance. It would be another fifteen years until the new model of development was actually implemented.

11

THE ANTI-COMMUNIST STATE

(1950–74)

From the centre to the right

As might be expected, the end of the Civil War did not lead to the direct resolution of the problems and conflicts that had arisen in the 1940s. The hatred, violence and interests that took shape during the war were reason enough to establish clear dividing lines between the winners and losers, even if we leave aside their political choices and social backgrounds. Consequently, a completely different political landscape from that of the pre-war period arose. An important aspect of this shift, for example, was the fact that some of the most important political leaders of the post-war period emerged in these exact years, even if their careers had begun before the war.

In this situation, it was only logical for the winners to take advantage of their privileged position to set up an anti-communist state with the aim of eliminating and excluding the defeated side. Beyond this, invocations of nationalism created conditions ripe for pursuing policies aimed at remedying the weaknesses characterising the pre-war Greek state, favouring the national—albeit authoritarian—integration of the entire population. In this context, a large percentage of the left was excluded from this 'equality' that Greek citizens enjoyed, or were at least constitutionally guaranteed. Certificates of social conviction became a necessary prerequisite for working in the public sector, studying at universities, acquiring a passport and many other everyday activities.

The role of the police force and gendarmerie—whose ranks had been restructured to include persons collaborating with the Germans during the occupation and of course excluded all EAM supporters—was to persecute the left. Its decisions alone were enough to send someone off to exile on a barren island. Moreover, any attempt by political leaders to smooth over political opposition soon stumbled on the reactions of powerful and organized anti-communist forces. After all, the Cold War was the ideal environment for continuing anti-communist practices, even in their most extreme iterations, and strengthening the foundations of a nationalist state, much more so when the Communist Party leadership began to foster these same tendencies. As he announced the ceasefire and accepted defeat, Nikos Zachariadis, general secretary of the Greek Communist Party, took care to add that from this point onwards communists were to have their 'weapons at the ready.' In the meantime, the few remaining guerrilla forces in Greece did not cease their activities, thus enabling their opponents to continue persecuting the left.

At the end of the Civil War, political forces in Greece showed signs of fragmentation that more fully manifested themselves in the elections held on 5 March 1950. The party in first place, the People's Party, received 18.8 per cent of the vote and sixty-two of the 250 seats in Parliament, followed by the Liberal Party led by Sophocles Venizelos with 17.2 per cent of votes and fifty-six seats. The National Progressive Centre Union (EPEK) took 16.4 per cent and forty-five seats. The left, which took the form of the Democratic Alignment Party, came in fifth with 9.7 per cent of the vote and sixteen seats, while George Papandreou's Democratic Socialist Party surpassed it with 10.7 per cent of the vote and thirty-five seats. A multitude of other parties followed, covering the entire political spectrum from the extreme right to left. The nation found itself facing the assembly of a new political landscape as traditional political forces gradually began to collapse.

Timetable 1950–74

1950	Ioannis Theotokis caretaker government (6 January 1950–23 March 1950). Plastiras and Tsouderos found EPEK. The first post-Civil War elections are held. Sophocles Venizelos government (23 March 1950–15 April 1950), Plastiras government (15 April 1950–21 August 1950). Sophocles Venizelos government (21 August 1950–27 October 1951). Greek–Yugoslavian relations reinstated.
1951	Senior General Papagos resigns. Suppression of army coup. Papagos founds 'Greek Rally'. Elections. Plastiras government (27 October 1951–11 October 1952). Greece joins NATO.

1952 The Constitution of 1952 comes into effect. Nikos Belogiannis and three other officers of the Greek Communist Party executed. Air force trial. Dimitris Kiousopoulos caretaker government (11 October 1952–19 November 1952). Women vote in elections for the first time. Alexandros Papagos governments (19 November 1952–4 October 1955).

1953 Plastiras dies. Hellenic–American agreement regarding military bases.

1954 Greece appeals for UN aid in the Cyprus dispute. The UN Political Commission refuses to discuss the dispute in a decision ratified by the General Assembly.

1955 Armed struggle in Cyprus begins. Papagos's death. Konstantinos Karamanlis government (6 October 1955–5 March 1958).

1958 Konstantinos Georgakopoulos caretaker government (5 March 1958–17 May 1958). Konstantinos Karamanlis caretaker government (17 May 1958–20 September 1961). EDA becomes the largest opposition party.

1961 Konstantinos Dovas caretaker government (20 September 1961–4 November 1961). Election results are seen as the product of force and fraud by the opposition. Konstantinos Karamanlis government (4 November 1961–17 June 1963). The 'Uncompromising Struggle'. EEC association agreement.

1963 Karamanlis submits a proposal to revise the Constitution. Murder in Thessaloniki of EDA minister Grigoris Lambrakis. Panagiotis Pipinelis government (17 June 1963–29 September 1963). Stylianos Mavromichalis caretaker government (29 September 1963–8 November 1963). George Papandreou government (8 November 1963–30 December 1963). Karamanlis exits the political scene. Ioannis Paraskevopoulos caretaker government (30 December 1963–18 February 1964).

1964 George Papandreou government (18 February 1964–15 July 1965). King Paul dies, succeeded by Constantine II. Crises in Cyprus—the Acheson Plan.

1965 Political and constitutional crisis. Constantine II forces Papandreou's resignation. Georgios Athanasiadou–Nova government (15 July 1965–20 August 1965). Ilias Tsirimokos government (20 August 1965–17 September 1965). Stefanos Stefanopoulos government (17 September 1965–22 December 1966).

1966 Ioannis Paraskevopoulos caretaker government (22 December 1966–3 April 1967).

1967 Panagiotis Kanellopoulos government (3 April 1967–21 April 1967). Dictatorship. Konstantinos Kollias government (21 April 1967–13 December 1967). Georgios Papadopoulos government (13 December 1967–8 October 1973).

1968 First Constitution of the dictatorship.

1973 Monarchy is abolished by constitutional act of the dictatorship. Second Constitution of the dictatorship. Spyros Markezinis government (8 October 1973–25 November 1973). Uprising at the Polytechnic University. Papadopoulos is replaced by Dimitris Ioannidis. Adamantios Androutsopoulos government (25 November 1973–23 July 1974).

1974 Coup and attempted murder of Archbishop Makarios in Cyprus. Turkish invasion of Cyprus. The dictatorship collapses. Konstantinos Karamanlis government of national unity (24 July 1974–21 November 1974).

Meanwhile, the centrist parties had cumulatively gathered around 135 seats, granting them a parliamentary majority and enabling them to assemble a government with Plastiras as prime minister. Plastiras had recently founded the National Progressive Centre Union, a party that played a key role in the reorganisation of the Greek party system through its attempts to take advantage of, if not shape, the centre-left, as has been suggested. Most of its staff had been recruited during the resistance period and it was no coincidence that it touted slogans of peace and change. In this manner, it tried to attract those that had participated in the resistance but found themselves on the losing side as the Civil War wore on.

But Plastiras's anti-monarchic past provoked opposition from the Royal Palace, which managed to prevent Sophocles Venizelos—perennially vulnerable to royal influence, all the more so as he stood to assume the premiership—from participating in the coalition government. The nationalists reacted in much the same way, and it is typical of the period that Panagiotis Kanellopoulos characterised the National Progressive Centre Union's participation in government as 'nationally unacceptable'. Following this royal intervention, a new government began to form with the support of right-wing parties and Venizelos as prime minister. But the Americans, who by now played an extremely important role in the nation's politics, reacted to this development. Their aim was to present Greece to the world as a country whose liberal institutions functioned seamlessly. To this end, the centrist parties served their purposes much better than a right-wing government with its dark past. Under US pressure, the Palace was forced to fold, and in the end Plastiras assembled a government in which both the Liberals and George Papandreou participated.

Plastiras's immediate goal was to defuse Civil War tensions, but he was met with vehement opposition from both the People's Party and his opponents from the centrist parties, Venizelos and Papandreou. Thus at the first available opportunity—which came about after his statements were denounced as Communist-friendly—Plastiras was forced to resign. Various governments alternated in power, the most durable of which, Venizelos's, lasted a year.

But political instability hardly desirable, least of all in conditions requiring continuity in economic and foreign policy. At precisely this moment, spurred on by economic factors and media organisations collaborating with the Americans, Alexandros Papagos's moment had arrived. Papagos, glowing with victory from the Civil War, seemed to be in a position to rally the anti-communist forces. He resigned from the army, claiming the Palace's aggressiveness towards him as a pretext. In doing so, he provoked the wrath of the king, who feared that Papagos's emergence would weaken his own capacity to intervene. Meanwhile, a group of officers supporting Papagos, some of whom belonged to the military organisation known as IDEA, moved to prepare to reinstate him to chief command. This movement was criticised by Papagos himself and collapsed, although the organisers were granted amnesty. This decision reduced the credibility of the Plastiras government, which was in power at the time, since it showed that at least some officers were in fact immune to the law.

In late June 1951, Papandreou resigned from the government and Sophocles Venizelos proceeded to organise new elections in which Papagos participated as leader of a new party called Greek Rally. In the elections of 9 September 1951, Greek Rally emerged victorious, though it did not have a majority in Parliament. A coalition government was then suggested, which Papagos did not accept, since he rightly anticipated that he could gain full power in a subsequent election under the majority system. Thus Plastiras formed a government with the aid of the Liberals that remained in power for about a year. During his tenure, the Constitution of 1952—a more conservative revision of the 1911 Constitution—was voted on. In April 1952, Law 2058, 'On Measures of Peace', was passed, which commuted all death sentences issued up until then into sentences of lifetime imprisonment. The same law allowed for the review of judicial decisions made during the Civil War, while the release of many prisoners and exiles—often implemented by issuing permits—was permitted. Thus from the 14,000 imprisoned individuals held in October 1951, only 5,500 remained by late 1952, while the total number of displaced persons also dropped dramatically. In no time at all, these measures provoked a severe reaction from Greek Rally and opposition from both the Americans and members of the incumbent government.

In the elections that immediately followed, Greek Rally triumphed, winning 49.2 per cent of the vote and thus occupying 247 of the 300 seats in Parliament. The era of centrist dominance had faded, and a twelve-year period of complete domination by the right wing began, secured by massive electoral support from populations in rural areas and complete control of the state apparatus. Something of the sort was bound to happen, not only due to the fragmentation of centrist forces but also because the Cold War seemed to be gaining momentum on the international horizon, leaving no room for compromise. Though the Americans had preferred centrist figures until then, they solidly backed Papagos, giving the country much-needed political stability.

The centrist parties had suffered a great deal under pressure from the right and left wings, and, in the end, from a weakness in defining a specific policy line. Given the prevailing conditions of the era, it was doubtful that they could have done much more. The sentencing to death and execution of Nikos Belogiannis and three other members of the Communist Party in 1952 while Plastiras was prime minister was a major blow to the latter's intentions to compromise. In the same manner, the calling to trial of twenty individuals on charges of espionage against the air force caused severe tensions, exacerbated all the more by the allegation that their confessions had been obtained via torture. The goal—evidence of communist infiltration in the air force—seemed to have been achieved, even if a few years later the convicted parties were granted amnesty. Meanwhile, during the same prime minister's term, the government was obliged to adopt an aggressively anti-inflationary stance, even in the midst of an international economic crisis, resulting in negative effects on the lowest income brackets. In contrast, the right was soon able to benefit from continuous and impressive economic growth. The centrist parties had ultimately failed to differentiate themselves from the right even in areas where such a thing would have been possible. Their subsequent contraction and collapse was inevitable.

Finally, all the governments of the period found themselves forced to address problems resulting from the dependencies that had emerged in relations with the United States, which continued to offer significant economic and military assistance to Greece. It was this relationship that ensured the country's security with regard to its northern neighbours. Participation of a Greek expeditionary force in the Korean War was a logical consequence of this relationship, as was Greece's membership of NATO (along with Turkey). In contrast to these close relations with the United States, Greece's relations with Britain deteriorated due to the Cyprus dispute. The Cypriots had launched major demonstrations for a union with Greece, and, if nothing else, managed to win over Greek public opinion, laying the groundwork for the Cypriot dispute to turn into a major challenge for Greek domestic policy. Initially, the Greek government was very cautious with the matter, as it did not want to enter into conflict with any of its allies or create problems in the Western alliance. But these years established the preconditions by which the Cypriot dispute would transform into an issue of international importance, something that finally occurred during the Papagos government.

The backdrop to the political scene

As previously mentioned, the Constitution of 1952 took a more conservative approach when compared with its 1911 version, though political and individual freedoms in the context of the liberal parliamentary system were not affected. Along with these constitutional reforms, a set of emergency measures continued to be in effect, inherited from the Civil War, which contradicted the basic principles of the new Constitution. The third resolution of Parliament, Law 509/1947 (which outlawed the Communist Party) and Law 375/1936 (regarding espionage) remained in effect and were used, as they contained provisions that could be adapted to various cases and serve the needs of the state that had emerged in the wake of the Civil War. Consequences resulting from incorporation of these measures into the country's constitutional project were adopted by both the right wing and a large swath of centrist parties, resulting in the formation of an extremely powerful political bloc organised around the so-called 'Para-Constitution'.

These reforms were eventually watered down: executions ceased in 1955, with N. Kardamilis as the last victim, while the use of displacement tactics would end in 1962 with the closing of the camp in Agios Efstratios. The last groups convicted of espionage were released in 1966. Under these conditions, the left was alone in raising the issue of legalising the Communist Party. It would have to wait until 1960—and the détente years of the Cold War—for Venizelos and Tsirimokos to appear and speak in favour of legalising the communists, though their suggestions were met with fierce criticism, even from the centrist parties.

Yet in 1962, the termination of the legal framework that had remained in place after the Civil War did not offer definitive solutions for the practice of emergency measures; nor did it reduce their use. The power of the 'Para-Constitution' and all that it amounted to in practice (such as the certificates of social conscience) remained in force until the dictatorship, despite the fact that the centrist faction gradually distanced itself from it. But the right continued to rally around these measures, through which it supported the post-Civil War anti-communist state and the interests it expressed. Development also began to play a major role, which will be discussed in more detail shortly.

A large part of these interests were represented by the country's armed forces, which, in the end, had shouldered the burden of the Civil War. In the period from 1949 to 1955, the army was personally controlled by Papagos, whether in his capacity as commander-in-chief or as prime minister. But from the moment that Papagos fell ill and was unable to adequately perform his duties, the crown sought to control the army as it gradually became less autonomous. It became a 'reserve' force for maintaining social order when parliamentary options had been exhausted, directly influenced by a network of power in which the crown believed it had priority. Political rallying around the crown from the end of the Second World War onwards played an important role in this process.

In other words, parliamentary governments under Karamanlis were in a position to intervene in the military, representing the anti-communist state—under the condition, of course, that the crown had no major objections. But from this point onwards, interventions were controlled; all the more so after 1963, when the Centre Union made the terrible mistake of granting the crown complete control over the army. Despite much scholarship to the contrary, it appears that IDEA had little influence and was neutralised from the mid-1950s onwards, by which point its members had reached the highest-ranking positions and controlled the army. Nearly all of them would be cashiered by the early 1960s.

IDEA was a secret military organisation founded in the Middle East by royalist officers during the occupation. Between 1949 and 1951, IDEA had turned to Papagos for support and managed to enlist a large number of officers who had begun their careers during the Civil War. By participating in this organisation, officers lacking high social status could hope for a better career, as IDEA played a decisive role in promotions. Then, in 1951, upon Papagos's announcement that he would resign from chief command, they decided to overthrow the government led by Venizelos and impose a dictatorship. But Papagos's reaction to this led them to retreat, without any notable consequences, as the Plastiras government formed shortly thereafter granted them amnesty. In fact, after Papagos's rise to power, cashiered officers were returned to active duty and even given key positions. Papagos's purging of the armed forces, in which many were fired, finally led to a situation in which IDEA controlled the army. This provoked strong criticism from the opposition. Yet at the very same time that IDEA members occupied these senior positions within the army, their organisation had begun to weaken.

The Union of Young Officers (EENA) differed from IDEA but nevertheless benefited from the protection the latter organisation enjoyed. It had been founded between 1956 and 1958 and was initially led by D. Ioannidis—the *éminence grise* of the dictatorship—and later by future dictator Georgios Papadopoulos. As its name betrayed, the organisation was composed of young officers, most of whom had not taken advantage of the Civil War in order to improve their career prospects. They began to develop their identity by cooperating with US intelligence agencies and the Greek Central Intelligence Agency, with Papadopoulos as a typical example. They held much more radical opinions than the average Greek officer, and their only goal was to maintain the post-Civil War state they had been shaped by and from which they derived their power. Scholar Evanthis Chatzivasileiou has pointed out the difference between members of IDEA and EENA: the former were pro-Western senior officers, the latter were pro-Nasser mid-ranking officers.

But the Greek army's relationship with the Americans was not limited to intelligence; it was much broader, and the two worked closely together. Indeed, these relationships had been forged during the Civil War, in which the Marshall Plan played a decisive role in the reorganisation and effectiveness of Greek armed forces. The fact that between 1950 and 1969 the United States trained 11,229 officers and 1,965 cadets on American soil under its military assistance programme to Greece is a particularly indicative example of US–Greek cooperation. That the Greek Civil War was more than anything else an integral part of the first phase of the Cold War set the tone for the reconstruction of the Greek army as the first instrument of confrontation with the enemy camp: for the Americans, Greece had been an important and necessary tool for curbing Soviet ambitions in the South since 1946, and its armed forces were the most vital component of this. Accordingly, the ideology and practices of the post-Civil War Greek state were directly affected, much more so after the country joined NATO. Only the Cyprus dispute would call these already established relationships into question, at great expense to Greece as we will see below.

The basic parameters defining the anti-Communist state necessarily included mechanisms for controlling the trade union movement. Since 1948, the General Confederation of Greek Workers (GSEE) had been under the direct and complete control of a group of right-wing trade unionists led by Fotis Makris. In fact, the GSEE did not represent much at all, since the most powerful unions functioned independently of it, and the Makris group's majority was guaranteed by processes that existed thanks to the tolerance, if not outright support, provided by state mechanisms. This entire system only survived thanks to the compulsory contributions payed by salaried workers that ended up in trade union coffers by way of funding from the Labour House. The Makris group's power was such that when attempts were made to remove him from GSEE leadership—in 1953–4 and again in 1958–9—the ministers who had taken the initiative were forced to resign.

Papagos

By 1952, following the electoral victory that enabled Papagos to assemble a government, the Greek political scene had completely adapted to Cold War conditions. On the one hand, the right wing, more powerful than ever, was to remain in power for eleven years or so, maintaining a solid electoral approval rate of roughly 45 to 50 per cent. Then came the centre—the various groups occupying the centrist space—characterised by their heterogeneity and overall inability to formulate an alternative political proposal to combat the right wing. Finally, at the other end of the political spectrum was the left, which managed to rally the losing side of the Civil War under the banner of the United Democratic Left (EDA), in which Communist Party leaders played an important role, even if they themselves were based abroad. In the 1952 elections, despite failing to gain any seats in Parliament, EDA managed to secure 9.5 per cent of the vote, slightly less than it had accumulated in the elections of 1951 (10.6 per cent) when it had first appeared on the ballot. Thus it maintained a more or less constant level of support.

Meanwhile, Papagos was able to unite the entire right wing, from the extremists to the centre-right. The latter group included George Papandreou, who was elected a Greek Rally MP—though he abandoned the party a few months later to become joint leader of the Liberals. This in itself is a sign of the fluidity of movement between centrist parties, a fluidity enhanced by Greek Rally's ability to overcome interwar divisions created by the National Schism. So, despite the fact that Papagos was a prominent proponent of anti-Venizelism and a faithful servant to the 4 August regime, Greek Rally managed to absorb supporters from the Venizelist faction, but also—more importantly—to disrupt the opposition between the new territories and Old Greece, overturning the interwar period's electoral geography. In other words, state integration continued in Greece, overcoming interwar divisions through the establishment of a post-Civil War regime of government and its main representative, the right. Meanwhile, supporters of the left continued to find themselves subject to ongoing deportations and imprisonment. In 1954, the spectre of execution returned with the shooting of N. Ploumpidis, who was in charge of the illegally organised Communist Party in Greece, and who was repudiated by the party shortly thereafter.

The main focus of the Greek Rally's three-year tenure was the economy. Markezinis, minister of coordination, benefited from the harsh stabilising programme that the Plastiras government had implemented and reaped the rewards, moving to significantly devalue the drachma against the dollar and inaugurating a noteworthy period of monetary stability for the Greek economy. This created a solid foundation for the economic growth that followed. Meanwhile, the Papagos government proceeded to open up to the outside world, searching for economic partners and hoping to attract foreign capital to the country. Lastly, under Minister of Public Works Konstantinos Karamanlis, a vast series of public works were set into motion along with a restructuring of the nation's economic infrastructure.

In the realm of international relations, the Greek Rally government was extremely consistent in maintaining close relations with the United States. In 1953, the Greek–American agreement 'On Military Facilities' was signed, confirming the establishment of US bases in Greece and greatly facilitating the American army's presence in the country. On the other hand, Greece—for the first time—expressed its official support for the Cypriots in an intervention at the United Nations in 1954. As it turned out, this action was extremely reckless, as it did not take into account other factors that would interfere, possibly resolving the problem unfavourably for Greek and Greek–Cypriot interests. In this manner, Greece's foreign policy actions ran counter to the interests of two of its allies, Britain and Turkey, and weakened relations with the Americans in the long term.

Relations immediately deteriorated with both Britain and Turkey. The outbreak of the Greek–Cypriot armed struggle against the British in 1955 only worsened the situation. The tripartite conference between Greece, Turkey and Britain in August 1955 bore no results, except for the fact that it recognised Turkey as a country that had the right to participate in solving the Cyprus dispute. This was not necessarily an obvious conclusion: in the Cyprus Convention that followed the Treaty of Berlin in 1878, the Ottoman Empire could have ceded administration of the island to the British, maintaining sovereignty, while simultaneously providing for Cyprus's return to the Ottoman Empire in case of British withdrawal. But with the Treaty of Lausanne in 1923, Turkey decisively gave up its sovereign rights to the island. A telling sign of this reversal in relations, which had been friendly since 1930, were the attacks by the local population against Greek Orthodox Christians in Constantinople and the Greek consulate of Smyrna in 1955.

Karamanlis

Papagos fell ill during the last few months of his premiership, and the search to find a successor began with two main candidates: Stefanos Stefanopoulos of the People's Party, and Panagiotis Kanellopoulos, both vice presidents in the government. But to everyone's great surprise, after Papagos's death, King Paul gave the mandate to form a government to the incumbent minister of public works, Konstantinos Karamanlis.

Originally from Macedonia, son of a teacher and a tobacco-grower, Karamanlis was part of a group of intellectuals and politicians that shared the ideology of radical liberalism; he had first been elected an MP with the People's Party in 1936. Then as minister of public works he became very popular, securing American confidence. Karamanlis's rise to power marked a transition to a different era of Greek politics in which new political figures emerged. Those that had dominated until then faded from the scene in one way or another. As Karamanlis assumed leadership of the government, he immediately sought to win over a share of centrist support and hastened to change the name of his party to the National Radical Union (ERE), thus seeking to distance himself from Papagos's Greek Rally. The ERE's founding declaration highlighted the need for new political models, ones that would resolve interwar problems and abolish the particularly divisive practices of that period. It projected itself as the 'Leadership of the New Generation'.

Karamanlis, hoping to legitimise and reinforce his authority—which at first was strongly contested—proceeded to hold elections on 19 February 1956, in which the nation's female population participated for the first time. The ERE won 47.38 per cent of the vote, while 48.15 per cent went to the Democratic Union, a strange platform in which former opponents of the Civil War, centrists, left-wing parties (the EDA included) and the People's Party all participated. Perhaps it is here more than anywhere else that the contrast was clear between traditional political parties and that of Karamanlis, as the latter sought to appear as the representative of the 'new' face of politics. At the same time, the collaboration of all the opposition parties, which helped the left avoid exclusion, was in itself impressive and indicated imminent, worrying polarisation, largely for those in control of power. Based on the rules of the electoral system in place, the ERE took 165 of the 300 seats in Parliament, while the Democratic Union took only 132.

The major problem that Karamanlis and his government faced from the outset was the Cyprus dispute. As previously mentioned, the conflict in Cyprus quickly turned into a major problem for domestic policy; it often restricted and limited the range of diplomatic options the Greek government had at its disposal. Governments of the period found themselves under constant pressure from their opponents, who went to great lengths to use this national issue to claim more power. Pressure was also exerted by various interest groups promoting the union of Cyprus and Greece. Both the opposition and these groups ignored many variables to the problem, especially Turkey's interest in Cyprus not uniting with Greece and Cypriot Turkish reactions in the event of such an occurrence. The choice of the 'Cretan' model—the militant assertion of freedom by Greek Cypriots, which in Greece translated into an aggressive stance towards the country's allies—did not facilitate the union of Cyprus with Greece and made any solution to an already difficult problem less likely.

In 1959, it seemed that the Cyprus dispute had been resolved with the signing of the Zurich and London agreements, which established an independent Cypriot state. Under this agreement, the Republic of Cyprus was established, with a Greek Cypriot president and a Turkish Cypriot vice president, both elected separately by their respective communities. The cabinet was composed of seven Greek Cypriots and three Turkish Cypriots, while a corresponding ratio determined the composition of the House of Representatives, whose members were elected separately by each community. In order to become laws, some bills (such as taxation bills) had to achieve an absolute majority in each community. Public services were staffed with the same proportion (7:3) of Greek Cypriots and Turkish Cypriots, with the exception of the army where the ratio would be 6:4 in favour of the former. In Cyprus's five largest cities, municipalities were established for each community. Greece, Britain and Turkey would constitute the guaranteeing powers, each of them with the right intervene in order to restore constitutional order if joint efforts failed. A military force composed of 950 Greeks and 650 Turks would be established on the island. Finally, Britain acquired a foothold in the form of sovereignty and military bases that accounted for 2.7 per cent of the island's surface.

On the Greek side, there were quite a few people who accused the Karamanlis government of treason, since the goal of union with Greece had not been achieved, while the Turkish minority gained rights that—as they argued—were disproportionate to their numerical presence and financial status. In fact, as correctly pointed out by F. Crouzet, the Greek government had a greater interest in quickly resolving the issue. The Karamanlis government's room for manoeuvring was extremely limited and the Cyprus dispute had worn out Greece's relations with its allies and led to heightened domestic tensions. For Greece, Cyprus was never such a priority so as to put its own safety at risk or weaken its relations with NATO. Thus a solution had to be found that all parties would consent to, especially the leader of the Greek

Cypriot side, Makarios, who proved a difficult and unpredictable partner. For the first time, Greek foreign policy seemed to be seeking American mediation, together with broader support: in June 1956, the Soviet foreign minister visited Greece for the first time, while in October 1956 Greece avoided supporting the Anglo-French intervention in Suez. Karamanlis paid an official visit to Yugoslavia in December of the same year. He also sought to control the actions of the National Organisation of Cypriot Fighters (EOKA) and their leader Georgios Grivas, without much success. In retrospect, the agreements in London and Zurich must be seen as the failures that laid the foundations for the island's division; but at the time they were signed, it is doubtful that Karamanlis could have done much more.

In the process of addressing the Cypriot dispute, the Karamanlis government oriented itself increasingly towards Europe. For Karamanlis and his minister of foreign affairs, Evangelos Averof, the process of European integration offered an opportunity for national economic and political development, as well as a chance to bolster security. Moreover, a turn towards the European Economic Community (EEC) allowed Greece to mitigate its strong dependence on the United States and NATO—something needed more urgently than ever before: since the early 1960s, Greece had started to play a less important role to the Americans, while Moscow courted Belgrade again, increasing insecurities in Athens. The imminent interruption of US economic assistance was yet another factor that led to a push in the European direction, and on 9 July 1961, after lengthy negotiations, Greece signed an Association Agreement with the EEC. Unsurprisingly, this turn towards Europe was the only common ground the Karamanlis government shared with the centrist opposition.

In the domestic realm, Karamanlis sought to make terms of imprisonment in camps and prisons more lenient for the left, although his ability to do so was very limited within the prevailing anti-communist environment. This environment deteriorated dramatically after the elections of 1958, in which—despite the defection of several of its key members—the ERE secured a comfortable majority in Parliament, while the EDA came in second place with 24.4 per cent of the vote and seventy-nine seats. The centrists took third place. With the creation of the EDA, the left had managed to win over many moderate groups that did not wish to identify with the nationalist right; this was a huge achievement, but it would soon become clear that the party itself was not in a position to handle the result. The emergence of two poles that aggravated political tensions and reproduced Civil War confrontations could hardly result in a smoother democratic process, and for the ERE, the rise to power of a party such as the EDA was unacceptable.

While the leftists took care to maintain a moderate tone as the official opposition party, their emergence as the second biggest party set processes in motion that led to the formation of a centrist group that had the potential to overtake the EDA's position. The creation of an alternative national party composed of centrist forces was a political necessity, but it posed many difficulties. For it to be created, the polarisation that had emerged in Greece had to be overcome. So, after many attempts and failures, in 1961 the Centre Union was created under the leadership of Papandreou and Venizelos (who would die shortly afterwards). The Centre Union brought together all the non-leftist politicians that had not been able or did not want to cooperate with the ERE, in addition to the various successors of the Liberal Party. For example, Stefanopoulos, who had begun his career with the People's Party, was then a candidate to succeed Papagos, and departed from the Greek Rally after Karamanlis assumed the premiership. In the same manner, a percentage of leftists, originally members of EAM, went on to join the Centre Union, led by Ilias Tsirimokos. These two examples are typical of the oppositions inherent in the Centre Union from its very beginnings, oppositions that rendered it particularly unstable.

In the elections of 1961, the ERE managed to secure an absolute majority for the third time, gaining 50.8 per cent of the vote and 176 seats. The Centre Union came second with 33.6 per cent, and the EDA third with 14.6 per cent. Papandreou and Venizelos, the centrist leaders, claimed the results were the product of fraud and violence, and the EDA followed their example. Indeed, during the elections held by the caretaker government at the time, there were irregularities and both violence and fraud had appeared widely. It is rather debatable whether the ERE would have not won the elections even under these circumstances, since the difference in votes between the first two parties was so great. However, as has been pointed out, without the vote of the military—which played a decisive role in determining the results—and the forced conversion of voters in rural areas to the EDA's detriment, it was possible that the ERE would not have secured a majority in Parliament. After all, this was the issue in question.

The situation was soon exacerbated when Papandreou declared an 'uncompromising battle' against the ERE and refused to recognise the government's legitimacy. Regardless of whether or not interventions took place in the elections, questioning the authenticity of the results was the only way for Centre Union leaders to ensure party unity. Two years of demonstrations followed, often on a mass scale, with participation from the centrist and leftist parties.

There were more than a few protesters injured by clashes with the police at these rallies, and in one case a student was even killed. In this environment, Papandreou took every opportunity he could to criticise the Karamanlis government and the Royal Palace. The murder of leftist MP Grigoris Lambrakis in Thessaloniki by members of a paramilitary organisation under the informal protection of the state finally led to an explosive situation. Papandreou hastened to personally accuse Karamanlis of instigating the murder, and though Karamanlis certainly had nothing to do with the Lambrakis assassination, these para-state mechanisms rooted in the Civil War had undoubtedly managed to establish themselves, often with the support (if not the participation) of Greek state officials.

Around the same time, relations between Karamanlis and the Royal Palace began to deteriorate. On 11 June 1963, the prime minister was forced to submit his resignation due to a disagreement with the crown over an upcoming trip the royal couple was to take to London. In fact, Karamanlis's resignation had more to do with the ever increasing frictions between the king and prime minister, which had intensified after Karamanlis's initiative in the first half of 1963 over constitutional reform favouring the executive branch. Meanwhile, Venizelos sought to establish a greater level of collaboration between the two major parties, leaving their leaders out of the process.

Economy and society, transformed

By 1950, almost all economic indicators had returned to their pre-war levels. But this was certainly not cause to be enthusiastic about the condition and performance of the Greek economy—and no one was under that illusion. Based on the 1951 census, 59.5 per cent of the economically active Greek population was employed in the primary sector, which only contributed 27.9 per cent to GDP—a sign of low productivity. It was therefore not surprising that Greece still remained one of the poorest European countries with a per capita annual income of around $143 in 1950, a figure that reached $429 in 1960. But this increase had no effect on Greece's position in European rankings. The only important difference over these ten years concerned production from the secondary sector, which for the first time surpassed the primary sector's production. Understandably, tackling poverty was the central concern of all public policies, regardless of political orientation.

Thus the 'capital fundamentalism' that characterised governments of the time was justified. Though at the end of the occupation gross investments of fixed capital at constant prices rose significantly from 1951 onwards as a result of US aid, thanks to stabilising policies put into effect that year, they plummeted and remained low for many years while unemployment remained at very high levels. Wages also remained low compared with pre-war levels, as increasing inflationary pressures caused by the Korean War led to a clear deterioration in salaried workers' positions. Moreover, though the average tax burden for the entire period in question was low, it must not be forgotten that most tax revenue was levied from indirect taxation and entailed a burden on the lower and predominantly urban classes.

More generally, monetary instability had turned all economic activity into a matter of gambling. This became obvious from the fact that although national GDP surpassed its pre-war levels, bank deposits still remained at insignificant levels compared with 1939. Gold, commodities and real estate were the main forms of savings, thus setting restrictive limits on the financing of investments from domestic resources. In the end, the balance of payments could only reach an equilibrium thanks to US aid. The drachma, significantly overvalued in 1951 in relation to the dollar, maintained an equivalence to the former due to the central bank's continuous interventions, which also intervened in the gold market in order to absorb some of the liquidity created by the public deficit. In order to address these problems, systematic efforts to stabilise the economy began from 1949 onwards and intensified even more so beginning in 1951 when Kartalis became minister of coordination. As a result, the economy's upward trajectory flagged, and all sectors, especially industrial ones, showed signs of stagnation.

11.1: Annual Percentage Change in Gross Fixed Capital Investments, 1950–73 (% in comparison with the previous year)

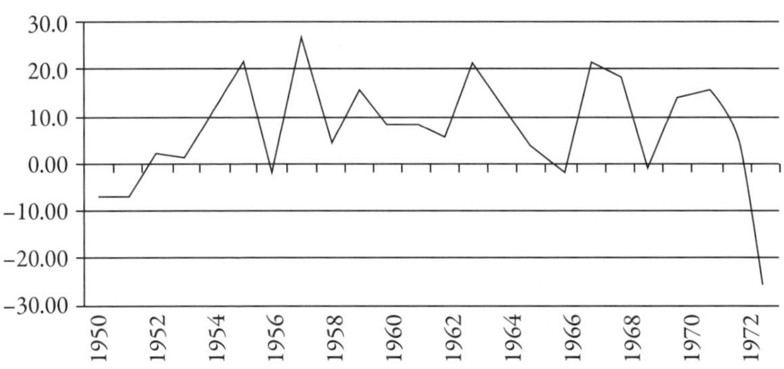

For a country as poor as Greece was in those years—a country that had experienced a recent Civil War—economic development was the foremost political necessity. The monetary stabilisation of 1953, which had been prepared by centrist governments and implemented by Greek Rally, constituted the first step towards boosting the Greek economy's potential for growth. The drachma was devalued by 50 per cent against the dollar (more than the actual exchange rate of the two currencies), and foreign trade restrictions were loosened. These measures allowed an increase in exports while limiting imports; dependence on financing imports from American aid was also minimised. Trade relations were also restored with nations of Eastern Europe, which absorbed Greece's less competitive agricultural products. An increase on nominal rates of interest on deposits later led to a dramatic increase in bank deposits and to the gradual emancipation of banks from the resources of the Bank of Greece.

After 1953, the macroeconomic situation began to support the achievement of the goals set by the government's economic policies; this would last until 1973. The stability of the exchange rate between drachma and dollar ensured an anti-inflationary discipline in monetary policy, while a constant effort was made to minimise the public deficit. More 'disciplined' labour relations allowed for a control of wage costs in such a manner that average salary increases did not exceed average increases in productivity. Further, the Greek banking system adopted a system of strict regulations and was required to finance the most important sectors to the development of the economy—industry, agriculture and export trade. Finally, the demarcation between private and public ownership became both clear and consistent, and no one questioned the orientation of Greece's exports towards the West's multilateral trading system. Henceforth, the Greek economy developed at blazing rates and did not halt until after the fall of the colonels' regime in 1974. Monetary stability was the basic pillar that enabled this feat.

The Greek economy's phenomenal growth—and the European economy more generally—was supported by other factors, as B. Eichengreen has shown: the country's low-level of industrial development facilitated rapid growth after a large number of workers moved from the primary to the secondary sector and its services. Secondly, the large gap separating it from developed economies allowed for rapid development and the introduction of technologies and organisational techniques from abroad. Lastly, the magnitude of damage inflicted during the war made for a very low baseline, which it was easy to improve upon.

The Greek economy's development was also supported by a climate conducive to attracting foreign capital. Article 112 of the 1952 Constitution pro-

11.2: Annual Percentage Change in Gross Domestic Product and Secondary Sector Production, 1950–74

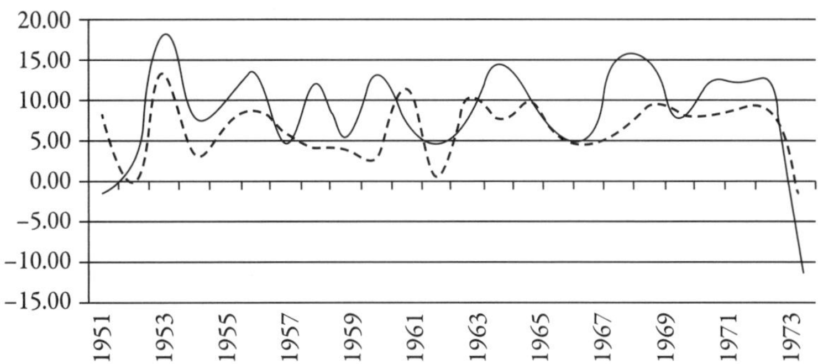

vided for a law that created governing regulations protecting foreign capital that entered the country. This law, Law 2687/1953, then established the inviolability of foreign capital (as opposed to domestic private property, which could be expropriated with due compensation). The same law specified the proportion of interest rates and profits that could be repatriated each year, while the Greek state offered significant tax benefits and guarantees for foreign capital, hoping to create beneficial conditions for keeping it in the country. Though by the end of the 1950s the benefits of these preferential arrangements were extremely limited, this legislation would be widely effective in the decades to come.

By the late 1950s, the first warning signs seemed to have appeared on the Greek economic horizon. After 1957, there was a slight slowdown in the national income growth rate, probably a result of cyclical fluctuations, while the next year the balance of payments showed signs of instability. The risk of upsetting all that had been achieved—at great social cost—appeared as a possibility once again. Lastly, the increase in imports due to rising incomes threatened to upset a balance that was impossible to stabilise using the agricultural products that made up a majority of Greek exports, thanks to their inherent low income elasticity. The shift in Greek trade towards Eastern European nations, the only ones that could absorb the low competitiveness of Greek agricultural products, was both economically and politically limited.

Towards the end of the 1950s, conditions were ripe for a change in the nation's model for development. The first step was to bring Greece closer to the process of European unification that began to be implemented in those years, with a focus on securing resources for public investment programmes. Greece's initial relationship with the European Free Trade Association (EFTA) soon led to an agreement of association with the European Economic Community, signed in 1961. Despite objections and the problems that arose during negotiations—largely because of Dutch opposition to supporting development in peripheral European countries—Greece was accepted thanks to French and German support. Both these nations had strategic reasons for linking Greece with the EEC. Thus, Greece managed to secure the necessary financing for a long-term plan to adjust tariffs to EEC standards, and promises of synchronisation with the EEC's newly formed common agricultural policies.

The second step concerned supporting industrial production in export-focused sectors. Thus an attempt was made to support all industries utilising domestic raw materials to create processed goods for export purposes. For example, in a short period of time, various metallurgical industries were developed, which began to contribute exponentially to GDP, increasing their contribution from 1 per cent of total exports in the period from 1961 to 1964 to 8.2 per cent from 1965 to 1969. At the same time, major infrastructure projects were supported, in addition to a number of other foreign investments that led to a rapid transformation of the Greek economy. Finally, the problem of unemployment was resolved thanks to newly accessible migratory routes to Germany, which was suffering from a labour shortage and undergoing a phase of explosive growth. Thus governments at the time were able to provide a direct solution to a potentially catastrophic problem, while the Greek economy again managed to cover its current account by utilising migrants' remittances.

Greece's turn towards the EEC had various effects on national political and economic life. Certainly, it meant an openness with Western Europe and a disengagement from the narrow horizons of the Balkans. Secondly, it meant gradual independence from US influence, and finally the imposition of a required model of modernisation that had significant consequences on national politics and economics—even if they would not be apparent during the 1960s thanks to the dictatorship, which put this new association on hold. On the other hand, the left opposed the model for development that had been adopted, insisting on a policy of replacing imports by expanding Greek economic relations with Eastern European countries. Today, it is clear that such an option would have made no sense for the Greek economy and would have only aggravated existing problems.

All these changes also affected the nation's social structure. People began moving away from the countryside, and the population (not including those who migrated abroad) began concentrating in urban centres—mainly Athens, and Thessaloniki to a lesser extent. New social groups formed, and the urban middle classes grew considerably in size. Greece was no longer a poor country, and the level of prosperity of its inhabitants improved significantly, even if this was due to models of development that were considered unorthodox (such as the great importance of housing in the development of the Greek economy). It is telling that, from 1950 to 1974, housing accounted for least one-third of total gross fixed capital investments, while manufacturing represented a much smaller portion.

The dictatorship did not change the growth trajectory of the Greek economy; it simply liberalised the overall institutional framework and rendered its financing mechanisms much looser in an attempt to quickly increase revenues (which it believed would strengthen the regime). But when the Bretton Woods system collapsed and the first oil crisis arrived, the monetary stability that had provided the basis for Greek economic development vanished.

The development model that was adopted in the post-war years had a major impact on the nation's regional development; Greece's economic development led to the creation of strong regional disparities, as the majority of development was concentrated along the Athens–Thessaloniki axis. Specifically, Athens experienced massive growth and acquired dimensions disproportionate to the national population. Beginning in the 1940s, the capital experienced an influx of migrants, and as a result the 1951 census listed 1,378,586 inhabitants. Ten years later, in the next census, that number reached 1,852,709, before climbing to 2,530,207 in 1971. These high rates of urban population growth were in striking contrast to the more gradual population growth rates in the rest of the country. While in 1951, the population in Athens represented 18.1 per cent of Greece's total population, twenty years later this figure had reached 29 per cent.

It is clear that such uneven development could only create a corresponding asymmetry in the national economy: Athens was not only an administrative centre but also the key economic pole of the country, whose growth led to the stagnation or decline of entire prefectures, especially of small cities and towns. The only exceptions to this—certain isolated incidents in the context of a more general trend—were those places that could rely on tourism to survive.

From Centre Union to coup

The new situation resulting from the agrarian exodus and transformations brought about by rapid economic growth directly affected the political balance of power established during the 1950s. The opportunities for social and economic growth, the demand for income redistribution and a political system that seemed to have overcome previous decades of inflexibility all led to a propensity for change, though this was not immediately apparent. Finally, the waning intensity of the Cold War discredited any legitimation of 'nationalism' as expressed by the right. Thus the elections that took place in 1963 not only proved that policies of the 'Uncompromising Struggle' adopted by the centrists had proven fruitful, but also revealed a new momentum in the political playing field.

The Centre Union came in first with 42.4 per cent of the vote, ERE followed with 39.4 per cent, and the EDA secured 14.3 per cent. With these results, the Centre Union would need EDA votes to form a government, though such a collaboration was de facto impossible, in the same way that a collaborative government between the centrists and the right was not an option. The king granted Papandreou the mandate to form the government, which received a vote of confidence with EDA support, thus provoking reactions from the nationalists. Papandreou announced that he would not accept the left's support, but took care to remain in power for fifty days, seeking to reinforce his electoral base. At the same time, in his effort to secure the favour of the crown and hold new elections, Papandreou had transferred considerable control of the military to the king. A large number of electoral provisions and generous campaign promises cleared the way for the next elections. On 30 December 1963, Papandreou resigned, and in the elections that followed his tactic proved worthwhile. The Centre Union received 52.7 per cent of the vote, the ERE 35.2 per cent. The left, which had supported the Centre Union in electoral regions where it did not expect to elect an MP, came in third with 11.8 per cent.

This Centre Union victory seemed to be a success for those hoping to avoid the polarisation that had resulted after the 1958 elections and from EDA's emergence as the chief opposition party. Yet in practice it provoked intense opposition from fanatical anti-communists and all those who feared that the scaffolding of interests left in the wake of the Civil War would collapse. The two dominant parties thus opposed each other in a confrontation that often seemed completely unregulated. In this context, military conspiracies began circulating, and in November 1964 an apparently forgotten mine exploded at a ceremony in Gorgopotamos, killing thirteen and wounding forty-five. The left was immediately accused of carrying out the act. Meanwhile, Andreas Papandreou, son of the prime minister, had rapidly gained in popularity thanks to his radical positions; he was accused of involvement with ASPIDA, an organisation within the army, and brought to trial.

The Centre Union certainly played a role in these increasingly unstable conditions, as it continued to be more of an opportunistic assemblage of candidates than an organised party. This problem was soon evident in successive conflicts between its members on various issues, conflicts that Papandreou proved unable to resolve. It is worth noting that when the Americans compared the Karamanlis and Papandreou governments, they argued that 'The Karamanlis government seemed more like a church where no one except the priest was allowed to speak, while the Papandreou government resembled a coffee house or a taverna.'[1] This was occurring at the same moment that relations with Turkey were deteriorating thanks to the Cypriot dispute, and by 1964, the two countries were on the verge of open conflict. The reason for this deterioration was the disastrous proposal of the Greek Cypriot side to revise the Constitution of the Cypriot Republic in order to limit the veto power of the Turkish Cypriot side. Before the latter had the chance to refuse, Ankara rejected the proposals. Armed clashes soon erupted between the two camps. The Greek Cypriots saw their chance to quash the Turkish Cypriot resistance, while the latter sought to implement a de facto split of the island into separate zones. It was clear that both sides were prepared for conflict. Beyond this, the very nature of the Cyprus dispute changed: from an issue concerning a British colony, and in fact, the Western alliance, Cyprus's independence and its system of governance turned into a battle between two opposing worlds. With this new line of reasoning, the United States became increasingly concerned, since the Soviet coalition stood to benefit from the situation on the island and strengthen its positions. Meanwhile, the conflict between Greece and Turkey weakened NATO's south-western wing.

In foreign policy terms, the Centre Union did not differ significantly from the ERE. It never raised the possibility of cutting ties with NATO, and in fact demanded more guarantees and assistance in protecting its northern borders. For the Centre Union, the challenge was to keep Greek–American relations balanced without ever raising the question of the nation's complete independence in foreign policy terms. But the Centre Union's insistence on negative positions in both the Treaties of Zurich and London regarding the Cyprus dispute created a particular dynamic on both a domestic and international level that necessarily affected Greece's relations with the United States and NATO. In the end, though, there was never really any question of separating from the Western alliance. Thus developments in the Cyprus dispute affected the Greek state's foreign policy, as its focus began to shift from the threat of socialist countries to the 'danger from the East'. Furthermore, developments in the Cyprus dispute had consequences for the economy, since Greece seemed to be the only country not to benefit from this downturn in international relations. It continued to spend disproportionate sums on military equipment, limiting the possibilities for these sums to be directed towards other sectors that were more vital to the economy.

In the realm of domestic policy, the Papandreou government's policies created a more lenient environment for leftist political activity: communists were released from prison, police measures were rescinded and trade union activity liberalised. But the results were none too impressive. Already from the beginnings of the 1960s, a strong union trade movement had developed around 115 organisations, which four years later had grown to 720 in number. This movement sought to claim control of the GSEE from the Makris group. In the ten years from 1964 to 1965, the Centre Union government tried to bring the confederation under its control, but it only managed a temporary court order based upon which the faction representing the Centre Union assumed leadership of the GSEE. A few months later, with political opposition in full swing, a new court decision led the former Makris leadership back to power again. These actions led to violent opposition from the right, while income redistribution measures enacted in favour of lower income groups incited a wave of right-wing protests amid claims that these measures would cause irreparable damage to the economy.

The Centre Union tried to bring more changes to the educational sector, liberalising its institutional framework. Tuition and exam fees were abolished, thereby facilitating access to education, the demotic language was adopted as equal with *katharevousa*, compulsory education was raised from a six- to nine-year minimum, two new universities were founded in Ioannina and Patras, and in secondary education the instruction of ancient texts was to be conducted from translations. The Pedagogical Institute was also founded, which had the responsibility of preparing curricula, updating textbooks and conducting pedagogical research. Though this educational reform was not excessive given the circumstances, it was met with great hostility from the right, particularly with respect to the issue of language. If in the interwar period demotic language expressed more or less liberal perceptions—it is worth remembering here that the dictatorship of 4 August had adopted demotic language in primary education—the Civil War had changed this, and the demotic was identified with the left. All attempts at language reform were rejected by the nationally minded right.

Thus it is obvious that though the quest for and subsequent seizure of power by the Centre Union may not have led to radical changes in the national political system—and in no way threatened its existence—it had rallied forces that progressively led to a democratising process that was opposed by other dominant groups. The Centre Union's tactic of advancing on two fronts was ultimately incomprehensible to the anti-communist state that essentially operated with the rationale of a single-front struggle against communism. The situation got worse after the EDA gained strength in the municipal elections of 1964 at the expense of the ERE, thus reinforcing right-wing fears of the 'communist danger'.

A tense environment prevailed as the Centre Union pursued policies that consolidated power by winning over groups that until then had been marginalised. The right saw this as a threat to the anti-communist state it had established. The period was marked by scandals and misguided efforts to refer Karamanlis and his peers to a special court for wrongdoings, which, even if they had been convicted, would have been commuted after a short time. But there were limits to the tolerance of the anti-communist state, and in July 1965, the young King Constantine II, succeeding his father Paul, refused Papandreou the right to personally take on the Ministry of Defence, using accusations made regarding his son Andreas's participation in the ASPIDA group as a pretext for the decision. Regardless of whether or not the king was right to deny the prime minister the office of minister of national defence, Papandreou's resignation, which followed, caused a huge political crisis and laid the groundwork for the imposition of a dictatorship—a dictatorship the king himself seemed to have been planning.

Initially, the king sought to fragment the Centre Union, assigning the premiership to another MP from the party. A small group of Centre Union politicians followed him, dissatisfied with other available choices: on the one hand, they resented the emergence of a strong left wing able to assume party leadership via Andreas Papandreou, and on the other they resisted the extreme positions the prime minister's son was taking. The first attempt at convening a viable government failed and led to new defections from the Centre Union. In September 1965, Stefanopoulos, supported by the ERE and other defecting MPs, managed to form a government that remained in power until the end of 1966. All the MPs that defected from the Centre Union then justified their own actions, arguing they had acted to stave off a coup. In fact, their 'apostasy', as the movement became known, was nothing more or less than common practice in the Greek political system, particularly by centrist politicians who sought to negotiate for a better position in the political hierarchy. What had escaped them, and what eventually led to their political failure, was the fact that the national political momentum had changed dramatically, and that confrontation with the right rendered such policies politically ineffective and immoral.

Apart from this, political developments and the king's attitude in particular led to a reversal in the monarchy's position within Greek politics. Until the early 1960s, the crown had enjoyed stability and acted as a unifying institution in the struggle against communism. As noted, for the first time since 1915, the monarchy was able to escape from the 'onerous legacy of the Schism to become a symbol of historical continuity for bourgeois democracy and a pole of resistance against "Slav rivals".'[2] After Paul's ascension to the throne, the monarchy had shown a resilience to both internal political conditions and the international situation, succeeding in preserving its prestige and position as an institution. This situation was upset after Karamanlis's forced resignation, and much more so after the events of 1965, where Constantine proved unable to assume a mediating role between different bourgeois factions. As a result, he became involved in these inter-party conflicts, weakening his own individual position and the institution of the monarchy itself. In the process, the king created the foundations for a new national schism and rendered the monarchy its new symbol. The issue was summed up in George Papandreou's rhetorical question: 'Who governs Greece? The king or the people?'[3]

Towards the end of 1966, the two major parties began to cooperate with each other, since it had become clear that the developing political crisis could well lead to an overthrow of the entire parliamentary system. Various solutions were sought, and finally in March 1967 the king gave the mandate to form a government to Panagiotis Kanellopoulos, who had assumed leadership of the ERE after Karamanlis's resignation and departure for France. That government never assumed power, as the military coup took place on 21 April.

Dictatorship

Much has been written about the origin of the military dictatorship, very little of which deserves to be taken seriously. Undoubtedly, Colonel Georgios Papadopoulos was the leader of the coup that resulted in the dictatorship. More than anybody else at the time, he represented the groups that had coalesced around the anti-communist sentiment that had built up during the Civil War—groups that then took advantage of the Cold War to dominate the political scene.

Papadopoulos, a member of 'Organization X' during the occupation, was one of the founders of EENA. His resume even included sabotage of a military unit in the region of Evros on the Greek–Turkish border, which he later tried to attribute to the communists. His role was well known to all, and his name had circulated in the halls of Parliament; he also had known associations with the American secret service. He implemented the coup as leader of a small group of officers known as the 'Little Junta'. The formal involvement of the US government in the process was never confirmed, although it seems that its representatives were informed about Papadopoulos's plans.

The 'Little Junta' coup succeeded in its mission right before an attempt by a similar campaign was to be made, prepared by the so called 'Big Junta', led by senior army officers and under royalist influence. The 'Little Junta' took the entire political spectrum by surprise; the government and political parties proved unprepared, especially after the coup turned against the right-wing government. Ministers and opposition leaders were arrested in their homes, and hundreds, if not thousands, of leftists were also arrested and sent to concentration camps and prisons. Almost no opposition was raised. It is telling that the issue of *Avgi*, the left's newspaper, which would have been published on 21 April 1967 (but never went to print), reassured its readers that there was no danger of a coup. The king, similarly caught by surprise, soon decided to collaborate with the dictatorship, hoping that he could thus subject it to his control. A few months later, in December 1967, he attempted his own terribly organised coup, hoping to overthrow Papadopoulos. But in the end, all he managed to do was to leave Greece, as the army was being purged and Papadopoulos's group further entrenched its power.

Immediately after the royalist coup attempt, Papadopoulos assumed the premiership and granted broad amnesty. He also sought to bring the state apparatus under his absolute control by moving to adopt a Constitution that could cloak his power with some semblance of legality and by removing anyone who sought to oppose his policies. He soon came into direct conflict with the Council of State, which refused to legitimise the illegal dismissals of judges.

But the greatest difficulties for the colonels' regime stemmed from the fact that it never managed to win international recognition and support. Even the United States, which was sympathetic to the regime, tried to keep a distance. Other governments were even more cautious, though they did not move to completely cut off their relations with the dictatorship. For their part, socialist countries recognised the regime from the outset. But this international isolation was expressed markedly when in December 1969 Greece withdrew from the European Council in order to avoid being expelled from it. Meanwhile, with regard to the Cyprus dispute, relations with the Cypriot president of the Republic, Archbishop Makarios, were terrible. Then, in late 1967, Papadopoulos made a fatal mistake: in order to avoid a military conflict with Turkey, he agreed to withdraw Greek troops from Cyprus, leaving the Greek Cypriot community essentially defenceless.

The international atmosphere and opposition from the Greek and international political scene confirmed that Papadopoulos had not managed to gain even a minimum of political legitimacy. Small-scale efforts against him soon took root, even if they had no particular political effect. The funeral of Nobel laureate poet Georgios Seferis in September 1971, which masses of people attended, was an indication of the minimal acceptance of the dictatorship. From another perspective, any group opposing the dictatorship was in no position to contest the colonels' power, while the colonels' economic policies sought and largely succeeded in winning over the general population and favour of the business world.

The key problems were to be found within the regime itself, as some of its officers supported a more authoritarian form of rule, while others were more in favour of moving towards a parliamentary model controlled by the army. Papadopoulos reacted, expelling regent Zoitakis and taking on the position himself. Shortly thereafter, following the suppression of a rebellion organised by royalist officers of the navy, Papadopoulos went on to abolish the monarchical regime and proclaimed a presidential democracy. He assumed the position of president himself, and moved towards adopting a new Constitution that would be the subject of a referendum and provide for a return to parliamentarism by 1974—under his supervision, no doubt. The referendum was held in July 1973, and the new Constitution was approved, as was expected, with 78.4 per cent of the vote.

Papadopoulos's actions were opposed by members of the junta and the army in general, as many soldiers and officers saw their positions compromised. Some officers of the dictatorship left the government. In October 1973, Papadopoulos gave the mandate to form a government to Spyros Markezinis, minister of coordination under Papagos, and then, after his departure from the Greek Rally, the leader of a small party. Markezinis was the sole politician who agreed to take on the responsibilities of governing under this new Constitution. The Markezinis government, in which members of the military no longer participated, endeavoured to approach the nation's politicians in an attempt to implement the new Constitution's model of supervised parliamentarism. The attempt failed, while the liberalisation of the regime allowed for the expression of mass opposition that finally led to the events of the Athens Polytechnic uprising in November 1973. It is unclear to this very day how many died; many were also wounded and a large number were arrested. After suppressing the Polytechnic uprising, Papadopoulos reintroduced martial law. The experiment of liberalisation under Markezinis had led to failure.

Papadopoulos's increasingly authoritarian stance did not save him or his regime. A week after the uprising had been suppressed, a new coup took place, led by the head of the military police, Ioannidis, among the regime's most ruthless individuals. A group of low-ranking officers rallied around him. The new regime appeared to be much more brutal than the previous one and was completely unprepared to address critical problems in both economic and foreign policy.

In the latter realm, the Ioannidis regime exacerbated already poor relations with Makarios, president of the Cypriot Republic, and in July 1974 he sought to overthrow him in a coup that he organised in Cyprus. A few days later, taking the initiative after the coup, he invaded the island, while the Greek army at the time was unprepared (at best) for a military conflict with Turkey. The dictatorial regime that ruled in the name of national interest suddenly found itself responsible for a national disaster it had created, and collapsed.

The state during the Cold War

The fall of the dictatorship undoubtedly defined the end of a discrete period in Greek history. As Y. Voulgaris has noted, the dictatorship was the 'epilogue for a system of power that dragged itself down and collapsed with it'. In order to determine the nature of this system, or rather this network of power, various terms and expressions have been used. A 'stunted democracy', or an 'incompletely legalized and somewhat formal, mutilated and supervised fragile democracy' are but two examples. All of them seek to emphasise the incompleteness or imperfection of a process, whether this process was moving towards some vague democratic ideal or towards the ideal of a Western-style state.

However, this interpretation—which often took the existence of a para-constitution as its point of origin—ignores the prevailing international circumstances during those years, circumstances decisively determined by the Cold War. This view must also recognise that similar characteristics can be attributed to other countries during the same period. Even the United States—a nation whose fundamentally democratic character has not been questioned to this day—could be characterised in those same years by elements identified with a 'limited democracy': the absence of political rights for a large part of the population (African Americans), and an intense anti-communist movement culminating in McCarthyism. Such elements ultimately constitute a kind of 'truncated democracy', though such a term does not seem to exist in the relevant scholarship. A similar argument could also be made for France, particularly during the period of its war with Algeria, and even more so for Italy. In all these cases, anti-communism was not only an element of ideological cohesion among Western countries but also a means of managing power to the benefit of established groups, that is to say the groups that took power after the Second World War. This was a global reality that would not change until the sweeping decade of the seventies.

Between 1950 and 1974, Greece was above all else a nation swept up in the Cold War, an anti-communist state, whose successful attempt at joining the Western alliance was a key component of its identity. Based on this, and the rhetoric of an anti-communist state, a new network of power established after the Civil War managed to control and effectively address the problems experienced by Greece in the interwar period. This was especially true of issues concerning the incapability to exercise centralised management of the national population, which first appeared during the interwar period as a result of rapid territorial and demographic expansion. The emergence of interwar opposition gave rise to both the Civil War and a repressive anti-communist state that recognised no unifying ideological project other than its own coherence. Indeed, the National Schism ceased to exist in the name of a national ideal: protection of the state from external and internal enemies. A portion of the population paid the price for this, as it was isolated from the benefits it stood to gain from distribution of power.

In this same period, the Greek state managed to minimise poverty in the national population, even if this meant emigration for a significant number of individuals. Addressing poverty was a fundamental aim of the anti-communist state and a founding component of its very existence: poverty and social inequality were seen as the root causes of social tensions, and the fight against them could only be waged by increasing average incomes. This logic was well suited to that of the Marshall Plan, which identified the development of consumer society as the most effective method of fighting communism. From this standpoint, the Greek society and economy transformed rapidly, faithfully following European standards, which Greece sought to incorporate institutionally through its agreement of association with the EEC.

The means by which the goals of the anti-communist state were planned and achieved were not overly complicated; available calculations indicate that, in the early 1960s, public employees only represented 7.8 per cent of the country's workforce, a proportion that did not change significantly until after the regime transition in 1974. This figure placed Greece well below the average for OECD countries. The ratio of public expenditure to GDP and wages of civil servants also reflected this. Both figures were low compared with those in other European countries, highlighting the fact that the size of the state from 1950 to 1974 was in every respect small and at no point grew exceptionally or notably. This was not unreasonable for a state that supported its public spending through tax revenue and, at least initially, foreign aid.

The one notable exception in the Greek state's fiscal behaviour had to do with defence spending, a sector that experienced rapid annual growth from 1962 to 1974—for which data is available—and that also placed Greece very high in international rankings of defence spending. But here it must be noted that the fastest rate of average annual increase in public spending was not defence (8.22 per cent) but health (8.47 per cent) and social services (8.52 per cent), followed by education (6.12 per cent).

11.3: Public Expenditure by Category as a Percentage of GDP, 1962–73

Period	*Administration*	*Defence*	*Justice*	*Health*	*Welfare*	*Education*
1962–3	3.82	3.73	0.70	1.80	5.38	1.61
1964–5	3.98	3.48	0.73	2.07	5.81	1.85
1966–7	4.07	4.02	0.70	2.14	6.66	1.95
1968–9	4.04	4.57	0.67	2.04	7.15	1.91
1970–1	4.01	4.48	0.59	2.11	6.86	1.88
1972–3	3.85	4.11	0.52	2.09	6.04	1.74

Source: G. Provopoulos, *Δημόσιες δαπάνες και οικονομική δραστηριότης. Η Ελληνική εμπειρία*, Athens: 1981, p. 68.

These figures demonstrate the priorities of the anti-communist state of the post-Civil War period. The army was the absolute priority, as it was an essential instrument in the competition with other eastern democracies and the Cold War in general. But it is also evident from the figures given above that in the fields of education, welfare and health great efforts were made to establish the basic foundations of a social state, even if in absolute terms expenses between the two categories can hardly be compared, since the costs of defence far exceeded the others.

Some of these developments were particularly impressive. In the educational sector, illiteracy decreased rapidly in comparison with the interwar period, even if Greece still lagged behind Western European countries: according to the 1928 census, 40.9 per cent of the population aged eight and above was illiterate. Based on the census of 1971, this figure had fallen to 13.9 per cent (though this census took into account the population of ten years and up). Women lagged behind men in this respect: while in 1928 one of every two were illiterate, in 1971 the ratio was still one to five. For men, the respective percentages were 23.4 per cent illiteracy in 1928 and 6.1 per cent in 1971.

Even if Greece lagged behind other EEC nations, this progress was nevertheless significant. Expansion of the national school network played a decisive role in these changes, as did the expanded capabilities of education, with an increasingly greater share of the population graduating from elementary to secondary education. According to one calculation in 1958, of every four students in primary school, one went on to secondary school; already by the early 1970s, seven out of ten ended up in secondary school. On the other hand, access to higher education was extremely limited, despite the efforts that were made: new universities were founded in many cities across the country (Ioannina and Patras, for example), and attempts were also made to increase opportunities for vocational education, especially during the dictatorship. Some indicative figures: in the 1959–60 academic year, 24,896 students attended Greek institutions of higher education, while in the 1973–4 academic year, this number surpassed 80,000 students. More than 24,000 students were enrolled in the University of Athens alone.

While the number of students increased as a whole, differences across gender lines, particularly noticeable in Europe at large, were relatively insignificant. In the 1960–1 academic year, women represented 25.4 per cent of the entire student population and were most present in certain departments or institutions such as the schools of philosophy and pedagogical academies. There were far fewer women at other institutions, such as the Athens Polytechnic University, accounting for only 12 per cent of students. Ten years later, in the 1970–1 academic year, women made up 32 per cent of the student population, indicating progress, though it was not enough to make up the difference separating Greece and other Western European countries, where this figure exceeded 40 per cent. But the most remarkable information is related to the students' social demographics. Again for the 1970–1 academic year, 27 per cent of students' parents originated from rural areas and

18 per cent were children of day labourers, percentages that indicate an open educational system.

These changes observed in the educational system were certainly related to the broader transformations the country experienced. During the period in question, the phenomenon of the countryside's emancipation—the end of the physical, intellectual and individual isolation of the Greek countryside—came about rapidly and was documented in the studies produced by foreign anthropologists and geographers visiting Greece in those years. Though it is true that this process would only come to its completion in the *Metapolitefsi* period, its momentum began in these years with the construction of a dense network of roads that sought to respond to the rapid growth of automobile use, the gradual introduction of the telephone and, finally, after the dictatorship, the spread of the television—a useful tool for propaganda, but also an extremely effective mechanism for corroding traditional society.

The Cold War environment thus facilitated the economic and social transformation of Greece, but it substantially complicated its political transformations. The moment, for example, when Western Europe experienced its social democratic spring, in Greece the dictatorship quickly overwhelmed whatever hopes the Centre Union had harboured until then.

12

IN EUROPE

(1974–2010)

> We were no longer the 'missing Balkan country', ignored by everybody, and became equals to the great countries of the West. If we are smart about it and don't push our luck—as we have done countless times under similar circumstances in the past—our new position will allow us to aspire towards continuing improvement and progress. Our people, who have suffered so much in the past, are now presented with the opportunity for a spectacular improvement in living standards.[1]

Transition

The collapse of the Greek dictatorship was a direct consequence of the Turkish invasion of Cyprus, and the entire system of political governance rooted in nationalism and the post-Civil War military establishment that went with it. The Greek army was totally unprepared to face the Turks, and the mobilisation commanded by the dictatorship ended in shambles, lacking both proper organisation and supplies. Having lost control of the situation, in a meeting held on the morning of 23 July 1974, the military leadership (with the exception of Dimitris Ioannidis, who chose not to react) decided to transfer power to the politicians. Another meeting followed, attended by the former prime ministers, which concluded with the formation of the national unity government led by Prime Minister Kanellopoulos—the last prime minister in power before the dictatorship was imposed. But after an intervention by Averof, a

National Radical Union (ERE) official and minister of foreign affairs under Karamanlis, the military officers ended up inviting Karamanlis from Paris, where he had been staying, in order to assume the premiership; Karamanlis agreed and returned to Greece. The transition from dictatorship to democracy was by no means an easy undertaking, all the more so now that the country found itself in a state of near-war.

Upon arriving in Greece, Karamanlis established a government of national unity, staffed mainly with centrist and right-wing politicians carefully picked with regard to the sensitive sectors they would be responsible for. The first task of this new government was to deal with the Cypriot dispute. Any thoughts of military confrontation with Turkey were abandoned, since the Greek army was not prepared to undertake such an operation. Diplomacy was the only solution left, though it would not offer Greece many options, since it had no means of pressuring the Turkish invasion. As was to be expected, the Greek–Turkish talks held in Geneva yielded no results. In fact, following the meeting, the Turkish army began new military operations and eventually took control of 40 per cent of the island. In these circumstances, the only thing left for Greece to do—even if it was only a form of protest—was to withdraw its military presence from NATO. Karamanlis did not hesitate to do so, despite objections made by his peers. In no time at all, another emblematic symbol of the post-Civil War system—Greece's integration into the North Atlantic Treaty—was abandoned. The Cyprus dispute became the main issue in Greek foreign policy.

Timetable 1974–2010

1974	Karamanlis returns from Paris and forms a government of national unity (24 July 1974–21 November 1974). Amnesty is granted and the Greek Communist Party is legalised. The Constitution of 1952 comes back into effect, with the exception of the provisions concerning the monarchy. In the November elections, New Democracy triumphs, led by Karamanlis (21 November 1974–28 November 1977). In a December referendum, 69.17 per cent vote in favour of the republic. Michalis Stasinopoulos is elected by Parliament as interim president of the republic.
1975	In June, the new Constitution of 1975 comes into effect. Konstantinos Tsatsos is elected president of the republic.
1977	New Democracy wins the elections again. Karamanlis government (28 November 1977–10 May 1980).
1979	Treaty of Accession signed by which Greece joins the European Economic Community.

1980 Karamanlis is elected president of the republic. Rallis assumes leadership of New Democracy and the premiership (10 May 1980–21 October 1981).

1981 Greece becomes the tenth member of the European Economic Community. PASOK wins by a large margin in the October elections. Andreas Papandreou is declared prime minister (21 October 1981–5 June 1985).

1983 The Agreement for Cooperation on Defence and Economy is signed with the United States, replacing the corresponding agreement from 1953.

1985 Karamanlis resigns from the presidency of the republic. Christos Sartzetakis is elected as new president. PASOK wins the elections. Andreas Papandreou government (5 June 1985–2 July 1989).

1986 Revision of the Constitution.

1989 Elections do not give any party a full majority. Finally, a coalition government between New Democracy and the left is formed, with Tzanis Tzanetakis as prime minister (2 July 1989–11 October 1989). Andreas Papandreou and his ministers are referred to a special court for economic wrongdoings. Ioannis Grivas caretaker government (11 October 1989–23 November 1989). In new elections, in November, no party has enough power to lead alone and an ecumenical government is formed with Xenofontas Zolotas acting as prime minister (23 November 1989–11 April 1990).

1990 In the elections of April, New Democracy wins 150 of the 300 seats in Parliament, nevertheless managing to form a government with Konstantinos Mitsotakis as prime minister. (11 April 1990–13 October 1993). Karamanlis is once again elected as president of the Republic.

1993 PASOK wins the elections and Andreas Papandreou forms a government (13 October 1993–22 January 1996).

1995 Kostis Stefanopoulos appointed president of the republic.

1996 Andreas Papandreou resigns from the premiership and as head of PASOK. Kostas Simitis is elected prime minister (22 January 1996–25 September 1996). Elections, and another win for PASOK. Simitis assumes the premiership (25 September 1996–13 April 2000).

2000 Stefanopoulos is elected president of the Republic again. In elections, PASOK wins again and Simitis forms the new government (13 April 2000–10 March 2004).

2004 New Democracy wins the elections; Kostas Karamanlis assumes the premiership (10 March 2004–19 September 2007). Greece successfully hosts the Olympic Games.

2007 New elections. New Democracy and Kostas Karamanlis triumph again (19 September 2007–6 October 2009).

2009 PASOK wins the elections. George Papandreou assumes premiership (6 October 2009–11 November 2011).

2010 Greece seeks external support mechanisms for its economy.

Yet beyond solving the Cyprus dispute at this critical stage, the Karamanlis government had to face the issue of restoring constitutional legitimacy. Two problems presented themselves: the first had to do with the transition from a dictatorial regime to parliamentary system while officers from the dictatorship still controlled key sectors of the state apparatus. The second had to do with the form of the government itself. Karamanlis proceeded with great skill, and eventually, as it turned out, with great effectiveness, despite the harsh if not unreasonable criticism levelled at him by the opposition.

Initially, the government avoided coming into direct conflict with the dictatorship. General Phaedon Gizikis remained head of state, a position he had assumed after the fall of Georgios Papadopoulos in 1973. Karamanlis's position with respect to the army was later vindicated, as it was unclear whether the military would have accepted subordination to a constitutional government. There were several reactions within the army itself, with rumours circulating furiously; it is telling that even in early 1975 an attempt at rebellion was made, though the government managed to neutralise it. Gradually, however, the government strengthened its position, relocating factions loyal to the dictatorship outside Athens and replacing officers thought to be loyal to Ioannidis. Around the same time, the Constitution of 1952 came back into effect, its fundamental provisions excluded, which remained suspended pending a referendum that would decide the future form of government. The incumbent government granted general amnesty, released all political prisoners and legalised the Greek Communist Party. Lastly, all those who had been stripped of their posts during the dictatorship were able to return to them.

After some time, the government's gradual return to strength allowed it to pursue stricter policies, clarifying that this general amnesty did not apply to the ringleaders of the coup, who were eventually tried and sentenced for rebellion and treason. Three were even sentenced to death, though these sentences were soon commuted to life imprisonment. Other trials were then held for officers of the dictatorship involved in cases of torture or the events of the Athens Polytechnic University uprising.

After Karamanlis had resolved these pressing issues, he was able to hold to elections, which took place in November 1974. In these elections, the party he had recently founded in the place of ERE, New Democracy, gained an overwhelming majority, winning 220 of the 300 seats in Parliament. The next step taken was to organise the referendum on the form of government, which took place in early December 1974 and led to an overwhelming majority (69.18 per cent) in favour of declaring the nation a republic. Thus, Greece turned an important page in a history characterised by post-Civil War and Cold War tensions. The neutral stance Karamanlis took with respect to the monarchy and the mitigation of sentences imposed on coup leaders allowed the Greek right to distance itself from the dictatorship without provoking wider fissures—though such fissures did come about in 1977 with the emergence of the National Camp (EP), a far-right party that gained 7 per cent of the vote in elections that same year. Yet Karamanlis's decision to step down from the New Democracy leadership averted any further complications. Supporters of the far right were incorporated into New Democracy, and efforts to create a separate party of their own failed. This in itself was one of the successes of the transition to the republican system of governance.

The factors that determined this smooth transition from dictatorship to democracy have been widely discussed elsewhere: first of all, in comparison with the Spanish or Portuguese regimes, the Greek dictatorship did not last very long and never gained mass popularity. Thus parliamentary democracy continued to exist as a recent reality and point of reference for most citizens. Meanwhile, party leaders that had played a major role in politics before 1967 never fully disappeared from the political scene. Furthermore, regardless of whether this was in fact the case, the dictatorship was presented as being grounded in a small group of officers and not as a movement based within the army's chain of command. This meant that the army was not necessarily considered collectively at fault for the national catastrophe resulting from the Cyprus invasion. Individual officers were blamed for this—the same officers that were later judged to have violated their oath. The army made no attempt to oppose this transition, all the more so since it occurred at a moment of national crisis during which the army was unable to play any role in furthering national interests. The monarchy had been essentially side-lined for the duration of the dictatorship, and it was unable to react or interfere with the transition process. Finally, though many had benefited from the dictatorship, on the whole it had not managed to integrate specific social groups or economic elites, which meant that there were no reactions from these groups. If, to these elements of a structural nature, we add the effective manner with which Karamanlis and his colleagues handled the transition, then it becomes easier to understand the exceedingly smooth transition to democracy that occurred in Greece—a much easier one than the corresponding processes occurring in Spain and Portugal over the same period.

The European vision

Karamanlis remained prime minister until he was succeeded by Rallis in 1980, who, unable to stand his ground against PASOK in the 1981 elections, was defeated. Meanwhile, Karamanlis, who scored yet another electoral victory in 1977 (albeit by a smaller percentage of overall votes), assumed the presidency of the republic, a move meant to stabilise the policies that had been adopted previously, specifically in the realm of foreign policy. PASOK, which emerged as the main opposition party in 1977 and was clearly on the path to winning the 1981 elections, challenged the entire spectrum of government policies, but above all the choices in foreign policy made by New Democracy—specifically regarding inclusion in the European Economic Community and participation in the political framework of NATO. Karamanlis sought to ensure that PASOK's rise to power would not upset these national choices, which he saw as fundamentally necessary.

Upon his return to Greece, Karamanlis set out to completely change the orientation of Greek foreign policy. His main objective was the nation's inclusion in the European Economic Community, something he considered necessary for the consolidation of democratic institutions. In other words, above all, Karamanlis and the New Democracy leadership saw political benefits from Greece's inclusion in the European Economic Community; the economic benefits played a secondary role. He himself described the importance of this choice in the following manner:

> I would like to stress that Greece does not seek this inclusion solely for economic reasons. It seeks inclusion primarily for political reasons, reasons that have to do with the stabilisation of democracy and the future of the nation ... By now it is clear that Greece's ascension to Europe will further external security and ensure consolidation of its own democratic system.[2]

The formal request for Greece's ascension to the EEC was filed in June 1975 and adopted one year later by the Council of Ministers. After laborious negotiations largely focused on issues of agricultural production—as Greece produced products similar to those of France and Italy—the Treaty of Accession was signed in May 1979. Beginning in 1981, Greece became the tenth member of the EEC. This was a decision that Karamanlis was stubbornly insistent on, and for which he was vindicated in every way, despite the strong opposition he faced on the issue from both PASOK and the left.

The first pillar of Karamanlis's foreign policy following the regime transition was integration into the EEC. The second concerned his efforts to escape from NATO's embrace. For this reason, he took great pains to approach both socialist and independent nations, mainly searching for support in addressing the Cypriot dispute and the general deterioration of Greek–Turkish relations. In essence, after 1974 Turkey had called into question the entire legal framework that had defined relations between the two countries following the Second World War: an agreement on 10 miles of Greek airspace, operational control within the context of NATO, and delimitation of the continental shelf. Under Karamanlis, the government chose to address Greek–Turkish issues through bilateral negotiations with Turkey; they were unable to reach a conclusion, since the interests of both countries were diametrically opposed. The only matter over which there was some consensus was the question of the continental shelf, which both parties agreed should be referred to the International Court of The Hague. But even in this instance, Turkey went back on its decision, forcing the Karamanlis government to continue bilateral negotiations and include the continental shelf as one of the many issues on the table for discussion. In 1980, the Rallis government eventually reached an agreement to reintroduce Greece into NATO's military ranks, calculating that the cost of not participating in the organisation far outweighed the benefits.

Reintegration into NATO did not directly influence the nation's new defensive doctrine, which was adopted again by the New Democracy governments that followed and focused not on the 'northern danger' but the 'threat from the East'. This shift, proposed in 1974 by Averof, minister of defence to Karamanlis already in 1974, did not disregard the communist threat—which would have been difficult in the years of the Cold War—but gave primary importance to the possibility of air force or naval conflict with Turkey in the Aegean. In fact, the country's entire military structure was rearranged in order to respond to the needs of this new defensive doctrine.

During these years, the renewal of Greek diplomatic and defensive policies went hand in hand with certain efforts the Greek state made to escape the ghosts of its past. This process was not necessarily easy, and objections were often voiced, which in turn led the government to back down or pursue more conservative options. Anti-communist feelings remained rhetorically important for New Democracy, and Karamanlis was not able to overcome this obstacle without endangering his political priorities. In fact, it is doubtful that he even wanted to try. One of the changes spearheaded by New Democracy leaders—which had real implications beyond its symbolic significance—was the adoption of demotic language, previously identified with the left, as the official language of the state. The compulsory minimum period for education was also raised from six to nine years of schooling. Overall, the policies implemented by Karamanlis and his successor Rallis sought to nurture a 'conservative liberal democracy ... a democratic system open to all powers, guaranteeing the rights of its citizens, and abolishing constraints of the post-Civil War period'.[3]

These priorities were on full display with the ratification of the 1975 Constitution. Beyond the government's transition to parliamentary democracy, the new Constitution, approved on 7 June 1975, provided that the state was responsible for taking on major economic and social responsibilities in order to ensure economic and social justice. At the same time, provisions were included for the protection of individual rights, and the state was obliged to ensure gender equality and environmental protection. Critically, the new Constitution also bestowed new powers on the president of the republic, aiming to make the position a counterweight to the power of each incumbent government. This was the reform that provoked reactions from the opposition. In the end, the Constitution was only voted for by New Democracy MPs, though it remained undisputed by the other parties (except for the clause concerning the president's powers, eliminated in the constitutional revision of 1986, although no president had made use of it in the intervening years). This lack of any reaction was understandable given the importance the parties were given under the new Constitution, which for the first time recognised them as key elements of the governing system. After 1974, the governing system was organised as a 'Democracy of Parties'.

The New Democracy government's greatest difficulties proved to be in the economic sector. In the later years of the dictatorship, the goal of monetary stability that had constituted the foundation for impressive economic growth in the 1960s seemed to lose its footing. The first oil crisis of 1973 aggravated inflationary tendencies in the Greek economy, while the impressive rates of economic growth that had previously been sustained began to dampen significantly (though they would remain positive overall). The nation's public finances also began to deteriorate significantly, as Greece increasingly turned to foreign loans in a bid to strengthen its army. The country's military expenditure, which was extremely high up until that point, continued to take up a high percentage of GDP; Greece had the second-largest military expenditure among NATO members after the United States. In general, the end of the dictatorship ushered in much looser macroeconomic policies when compared with the past, with the aim of redistributing incomes through wage increases and to foster development and employment in the new environment of the oil crisis. These policies were more or less maintained until 1990 with rather unsuccessful results, though it was possible to fully implement them thanks to low public debt following the regime change. It must be noted that it was during these years of New Democracy governance that the country experienced the most significant redistribution of income: the rate of absolute poverty was reduced from 23.5 per cent in 1974 to 8.8 per cent in 1981–2.

In these same years, the country's industrial sector experienced its first serious problems, as major manufacturing companies struggled to adapt to the new conditions caused by the oil crises and increased labour costs. Further, nationalisation of the second-biggest banking group in the country, the Commercial Bank, controlled by shipping magnate Stratis Andreadis, was a largely personally motivated move due to Andreadis's close relationship with the dictatorship. It also granted the Greek state full control over the banking system, as well as over a series of large businesses owned by the National Bank of Greece and the Commercial Bank. In this way, the Greek state came to directly control 60 per cent of the banking system. Through various administrative controls, it also determined the availability of most of the economy's banking resources to fund the economy. These nationalising policies drew scathing criticisms from entrepreneurs, but in fact reflected international tendencies in the same direction—albeit slightly delayed in Greece's case.

Generally, the predominant trend in the years directly after 1974 went on to characterise the entire period: while in political terms Greece participated in the process of globalisation, in economic terms it was unable or unwilling to do the same, seeking to maintain its achievements up until that point through various policies. Thus while in the political realm Greece succeeded in escaping the ghosts of its past, it found it impossible to achieve the same with the economy by adopting a new economic model.

Change

The election results on 18 October 1981 gave PASOK a parliamentary majority, exceeding the predictions of even the most optimistic party members. With its slogan of 'Change', PASOK, under the leadership of George Papandreou's son Andreas, was able to capitalise on anti-right-wing sentiments prevalent in Greek politics. PASOK presented an extremely inward-focused platform, which was as radical as it was vague, directed towards the 'non-privileged' Greek, in the words of Andreas Papandreou himself. Papandreou managed to draw a large percentage of votes from centrist parties—which were trounced in the elections and soon disappeared from the political spectrum—and from EAM leftists, who saw the potential to vindicate their own struggles in the promises of PASOK's radical slogans.

This development was aided by the fact that political parties in Greece—the Communist Party included—were supported by a diverse electoral base, without strong class divisions. Even if New Democracy was initially more popular with the upper classes and PASOK with the lower classes, the lack of a strictly socially determined vote made for an electoral result largely dependent on the political–ideological position of voters themselves based on the distinction between 'left' and 'right'. In order to benefit from this situation and attain its own goals, PASOK adopted positions that were chiefly focused on the complete contestation, if not political devaluation, of New Democracy policies—specifically the policies of Karamanlis, even though Karamanlis and his successor Rallis had refrained from such tactics themselves.

By the early 1980s, Greece had experienced significant transformations. Resulting expectations of social mobility emerged, which both PASOK's slogans and political policies were able to satisfy. This contrasted with New Democracy, which by this time seemed outdated with respect to both its rhetoric and the electorate it addressed. As a result, PASOK managed to impose its political hegemony and dominate Greece in the *Metapolitefsi* period.

In order to come into power, PASOK—which had been founded in late August 1974—essentially underwent a period of internal confrontation during which Papandreou eliminated all groups that could threaten his power within the party, thus monopolising all party decisions. He then went on to consolidate a mass-scale party, the first of the sort that managed to gain power in Greece. It reached 27,000 members in 1977, and then 110,000 in 1981. By 1984, it had doubled in size as many rushed to take advantage of its rise to power, joining its ranks. PASOK's organisational effectiveness, in combination with similar developments in other countries, gradually led New Democracy to organise itself similarly as a mass party. But this only occurred after the electoral defeat in 1981, and much more so after Mitsotakis's rise to leadership in 1984.

PASOK's victory in the 1981 elections immediately led to the party's attempt at controlling the state apparatus. One aspect of the process was the quantitative influx of its officials and supporters into the public sector, though this was surely not the most important one. More noteworthy was the complete change in relations between the party and the state apparatus. Up until then, the political party was no more than a minor component in a broader network of power based on the state and its mechanisms. Until 1981, New Democracy did not seek to change this arrangement, which was favourable to its own goals. But PASOK's rise to power completely changed this arrangement, as the party infiltrated the state and gained control of it in an attempt to satisfy its own demands and interests. For example, in the sector of public administration, the pre-existing practice of offering senior positions to functionaries of the ministry was abolished; political power was isolated from administrative responsibility. The position of general director of the ministries was eliminated and the role of special secretaries was introduced, staffed by interchangeable persons appointed by incumbent ministers. Among other things, this policy further limited the effectiveness of the public sector. This was further reinforced when in the mid-1980s a new evaluation scale was introduced, reducing the number of different ranking positions within the public sector, and rendering position and compensation independent from rank. Thus any type of incentive ceased to exist. On the one hand, these actions sought to renew the civil service hierarchy and resolve grievances—now, many more civil servants could serve in managerial positions. On the other, promotion in this hierarchy depended on decisions made by the relevant administrative council and on seniority, thus taking on a purely party-oriented character.

12.1: Public Sector Hires as % of Total Growth in Employment from 1975 to 2003 (in thousands)

	1975–81	*1982–9*	*1990–3*	*1994–2003*
1. Increase in civil servants	44.2	82.5	4.3	20.3
2. Increase in total employment	338.2	141.6	49.3	554.3
3. Relation of 1 to 2 in %	13.1	58.3	8.7	3.7

Source: T. Giannitsis, *Η Ελλάδα και το μέλλον. Πραγματισμός και ψευδαισθήσεις*, Athens: 2005, p. 159.

Meanwhile, massive political mobilisation in Greece after the regime change found an outlet in collective and unprecedented participation in social organisations, via PASOK's ascent to power and the party's own efforts to manipulate these organisations. The trade union movement was a classic example of this: existing practices by which trade union leadership supervised mass mobilisations gave way to collective organisational control and the predominance of collective processes. As a result, parties completely infiltrated this process, bringing with them the confrontational climate prevailing in the political realm. Very soon, these processes corrupted and completely weakened the role these organisations and the institutional framework were called on to play. In fact, there were no fixed rules on the emerging playing field. The latter was defined by a political culture successfully identified by Yiannis Voulgaris as determined by opponents of the right-wing state:

> This sheds light on the interrelations between new legitimising currents of various origins and historic foundations: values, memories, symbols of the EAM tradition, those defeated in the Civil War, the social strata that came out of the 1960s and abided by an anti-right wing culture which was not necessarily going to be expressed by PASOK, and youth radicalised over the course of the anti-dictatorship struggle. Within this amalgamation, elements of genuine social critique and populist stereotypes of the 'progressive-democratic' faction fused together.[4]

This exact political culture was exploited and cultivated by PASOK, something that Andreas Papandreou stated explicitly when he said that PASOK was the political expression of the vision of three generations: the generation of resistance, the generation of the radical movements in the 1960s and the generation of the Polytechnic uprising.

As a result of PASOK's rise to power, many laws rooted in the Civil War period were abolished. EAM's contribution to the national resistance was also recognised and honorary pensions were given to its surviving fighters. The process allowing political refugees to return home was finalised; until then, they could only obtain the right to return on a case-by-case basis. Perhaps Papandreou's most characteristic move on a symbolic level was the nomination of Vafeiadis—leader of the Democratic Army of Greece and first president of the 'Mountain Government' during the Civil War—as a candidate for the party in the 1989 and 1990 elections. Many thousands of people that had been repeatedly persecuted for their political choices finally felt vindicated, something that the traditional left had not been able to offer them.

In addition to these older leftists, PASOK was able to attract members of the urban low and middle classes and rural populations by offering them significant benefits. Policies redistributing income in favour of lower-income groups continued throughout the 1980s. But it would be unfair to linger on these benefits when assessing the importance of PASOK's legacy of social policy. The creation of the National Health System (ESY) redefined the terms of a very sensitive realm in social policy, despite the fact that the plans for it were not fully implemented and the system could not offer all that its creators hoped it would. Interests—and, by extension, opposition—in this sector were very strong. But in this context, health services were made available on a much more collective basis, and the subsequent creation of Health Centres enabled the system to spread—albeit imperfectly—to populations with no previous access.

PASOK also made major headway in the educational realm, beginning by renewing the relevant legislative framework. In higher education, a major change was seen in the universities' openness to new professors and subjects. Moreover, the PASOK government pushed through a complete overhaul of hitherto existing family law, voting in a new family code considered among the most progressive in Europe, ensuring full legal equality of the sexes.

By their very nature, PASOK policies came at a great economic cost, at a time when the Greek economy's growth potential had begun to dissipate. The second energy crisis in 1979 caught Greece completely unprepared to deal with the problems that followed, and the national economy went into a period of stagnant growth and high inflation rates. Excessive public borrowing aggravated the situation, and in 1985, faced with no other options, the government sought to implement a policy of economic stabilisation. Simitis, then minister of finance and soon to be prime minister, took on this responsibility. But the discontent caused by this new policy would lead Papandreou to change course, and to Simitis's resignation. From this point onwards, PASOK sought on the one hand to maintain its electoral base, permitting tax-free income from trade, the agricultural sector and liberal professions, while, on the other, spending heavily so as to meet the needs of public expenses. In a stagnating economy, these choices could not work for long, and they clearly inhibited any attempts at reform within the party, enabling a parasitism that drew resources from the informal economy only to be lent at steep rates back to the public sector.

The major difficulties faced by PASOK's economic policies were all the more glaring in the industrial sector. The process of de-industrialisation made its appearance in Greece as well, and many large industrial enterprises were placed under state control in an attempt to avert closure. Their compulsory financing through banks significantly burdened the latter until the Organisation for Business Reconstruction (OAE) was founded, which undertook the process of salvaging these industries with state funds. Maintaining the workforce at these companies—since this was what was really at stake—now became a direct burden to Greek taxpayers.

In the process, it became clear that during these years the Greek state had created an anti-competitive regulatory framework that facilitated the distribution of revenues to organised interest groups, which, in the long run, created the preconditions for corruption and abuse of power. The medical profession is probably the most prominent example of this.

12.2: Average Annual Rates of Change for Basic Economic Indicators from 1982 to 2004.

	1982–9	*1990–3*	*1994–6*	*1997–9*	*2000–4*
Growth in Greece's GDP	1.1	0.6	2.2	3.5	4.3
EE-15 GDP growth	2.6	1.3	2.2	2.7	1.8
Greek investments	0.5	0.8	3.3	9.5	7.8
EE-15 investments	3.5	–0.8	2.5	5.0	1.2
Budget deficit/GDP	–9.9	–13.1	–9.3	–2.8	–3.3
Inflation	18.2	17.6	9.3	4.2	3.3
Current account balance/GDP	–3.6	–3.5	–3.4	–4.6	–7.2
Unemployment	7.8	8.3	9.2	11.0	10.5
Social expenditures/GDP	19.3	21.9	22.4	24.3	27.0
Public debt/GDP	48.0	90.0	109.0	106.0	112.0
Real wages	1.2	–3.9	2.1	2.6	1.4

Source: T. Giannitsis, *Η Ελλάδα και το μέλλον. Πραγματισμός και ψευδαισθήσεις*, Athens: 2005, p. 82.

In the realm of foreign policy, PASOK abandoned its anti-Western rhetoric very soon after its ascent to power and sought, successfully, to redefine the terms of Greek participation in both NATO and the EEC. In the context of a plan for US military disengagement from the Eastern European region, US military bases were put on a schedule of withdrawal from Greek territory and finally closed, with the exception of those included in the NATO provisions. Theoretically, Papandreou's goal was to exercise an independent foreign policy, and for this reason he often provoked the discontent and anger of Western governments. In order to further this goal, he participated in the Initiative of the Six, which also included Sweden, Argentina, Mexico, India and Tanzania. He also refused to condemn the military coup of Wojciech Jaruzelski in Poland, objected to the installation of a European rocket system—an issue that the Western Europeans saw as a matter of life and death—and refused to condemn the Soviet Union for shooting down a South Korean airliner. But the benefits from these manoeuvres were minimal, especially with regard to Greek–Turkish relations, which remained the most sensitive area of Greek foreign policy. His hard-line rhetoric also yielded few results, especially after the decision to create the Turkish Cypriot state in 1983.

PASOK's momentum of 'change' began to show clear signs of fading after its victory in the 1985 elections, which it pulled off by forcing Karamanlis, president of the republic, to resign and—acting barely in the bounds of parliamentary legitimacy—electing Christos Sartzetakis in his place, a prosecutor in the Lambrakis case in the 1960s. Exploiting the anti-right wing reflexes of its voter base, PASOK once again secured a majority in Parliament. But as noted, by the 1985 elections it seemed that pre-existing dynamics of political and party confrontation had been exhausted; party leaderships only gradually came to realise that the society they were addressing had changed.

A year later, in 1986, PASOK proceeded to revise the Constitution with the basic aim of limiting the powers of the president of the republic. Papandreou maintained that these powers were a danger to executive power, and proceeded to remove them. In this manner, the prime minister became the 'dominant figure in national politics and the result was none other than the creation of a weaker Parliament, with powerless parliamentary groups and weak MPs, and no ability to veto in the political system of the *Metapolitefsi*'.[5]

Meanwhile, a second victory for PASOK and consolidation of political power led to growing political tension and a winner-take-all political culture. Coupled with the arrogance of PASOK politicians, this created an explosive mix of arbitrary power. This situation worsened, as mentioned previously, with Papandreou's decision in 1985 not to renew Karamanlis's term as president of the republic. That Mitsotakis—who had maintained a personal rivalry with Papandreou since the 1960s—was president of New Democracy only worsened the political climate even more. The repeated scandals that erupted towards the end of the second term of the PASOK governments, one of which the president of PASOK himself was accused of being involved in, had created an explosive situation by the eve of the 1989 elections.

Polarisations

Paradoxically, PASOK's decline, which New Democracy actively sought as a means to return to power, was not as intense as the latter had hoped in the 1989 elections. No party was able to gain a majority in Parliament; a basic reason for this was the change in the electoral system voted in by PASOK just before the elections, precisely so it could control the opposition party's rise to power. But driven by the risk that the offences of accused PASOK ministers might be allowed to lapse, the left and right collaborated—an event that was unprecedented in Greece—in a government whose main aim was to bring these PASOK politicians to justice in a special court. A New Democracy politician, Tzanis Tzanetakis, became prime minister.

Beyond taking on the process of referring these PASOK officials to court, the Tzanetakis government also supported a series of institutional changes for public transparency: procedures for parliamentary supervision of state contracts were reinforced, Parliament gained the right to select administrators of public enterprises and the independence of justice was promoted, while a number of laws used by the former government to manipulate justice were abolished. Lastly, in a symbolic move, the right- and left-wing coalition government proceeded to vote on the law for the 'Revocation of the Consequences of the Civil War', which recognised the rights of fighters in the Democratic Army of Greece and arranged for the destruction of the files that security forces kept on citizens.

Equally symbolic—because of abuses of the medium by past governments—but certainly essential was the abolishment of the state monopoly on television. On 20 November 1989, the first private television station started broadcasting. A multitude of stations were then founded, resulting in a chaotic mess of transmission signals that no government wanted to regulate, fearing confrontation with the powerful interests of the channel-owners. The failure to establish any regulatory structures was expressed as a victory for the channel-owners.

After Parliament voted to refer Andreas Papandreou and other ministers to trial, the Tzanetakis government was dissolved and new elections were held, which again failed to give any one of the parties a parliamentary majority. In the same period, the Greek economy deteriorated dramatically, and many feared the Greek state's imminent bankruptcy. In 1990, the public deficit amounted to an astronomical 15.9 per cent of GDP, while inflation for the same year reached 20.4 per cent. Massive amounts of capital flowed out of the country. The model for economic management adopted after the fall of the colonels' regime had now reached its limits and radical changes were necessary to avoid disastrous consequences for the Greek economy. The three parties saw the need to work together to address current problems, and to this end they formed an ecumenical government under the leadership of Xenophon Zolotas, an academic and former head of the Bank of Greece. In the end, the National Bank managed to prevent the collapse of the drachma, while the ecumenical government, as was to be expected, was unable to offer solutions to any problems: each minister sought to reap benefits for himself and for his party at the expense of the others. It comes as no surprise that an arbitrary decision related to the supply chain of a large Greek business—made without consulting the prime minister—ultimately led to the government's resignation and new elections.

Apart from its economic problems and political instability, the nation's position was even more unfavourable at an international level, especially after the collapse of the socialist regimes in Eastern Europe, many of which had served as Greece's allies since 1974. Thus after 1989, Bulgaria—which up until then had been a balancing force in Greek–Turkish relations—was weakened and not in a position to play its previous role. Furthermore, creation of the Former Yugoslav Republic of Macedonia (FYROM) led to a domestic war focusing on its naming and the various claims it demanded, forcing Greece to exhaust a significant amount of diplomatic capital.

The elections held in 1990 produced no winner for the third consecutive time. New Democracy managed to secure 150 seats in Parliament, and by winning over the sole MP of a small conservative party it gained the parliamentary majority needed to form a government. Mitsotakis's success was largely due to his attempt to overturn the conservative reputation of New Democracy and its identification with the pre-dictatorship right. He promoted liberalism as the fundamental ideological axis of the party and promoted politicians of this inclination. Yet in combination with the neoliberal awakening in Britain and the United States, these choices had a significant impact on Greek politics, and this new tendency was not always accepted, even within the ranks of New Democracy itself. At the same time, Mitsotakis took advantage of the situation to restore Karamanlis as president of the republic in the wake of the previous incumbent's failures.

The Mitsotakis government sought to adopt bold economic measures despite its tenuous parliamentary majority. It first sought to reduce the public deficit and control public debt, while it also looked to promote policies of structural change. In the same manner, it sought to make changes in public administration, streamlining the existing system. The position of the general director of the ministries was reintroduced, a new evaluation scale was created, positions were once more associated with rank, and the makeup of the relevant councils was altered, as was the recruitment process for public administration positions. All these changes provoked serious opposition from the trade unions, and the success of these reforms was ultimately limited. But for the first time, a serious effort was being made to turn the economy around. Meanwhile, in the realm of foreign policy, the tense political dispute over Macedonia became the main point of contestation for both major parties, leading the nation's foreign policy to a dead end. Large demonstrations were held in major cities in the name of claiming 'Greek rights', and under these conditions Mitsotakis's characteristic pragmatism did not fare well. A. Samaras, the young minister of foreign affairs at the time who had invested his political career in the Macedonian issue, left the party in the autumn of 1993 under rather hostile circumstances and went on to create his own party—though it was not particularly popular.

Around this time, judicial proceedings for the PASOK government scandals came to an end. Some ministers were found guilty and were imprisoned, one died during the process of the trial and Papandreou, who was already seriously ill, was eventually acquitted by three votes to two. These trials exacerbated an already polarised climate but also confirmed a marked socialist revival. This was clear from the elections that came after the fall of Mitsotakis's government, in which PASOK triumphed and once again returned to power.

But Papandreou was no longer the person he was in 1981. He was very ill, and seemed to be influenced by his entourage. Hospitalised and in serious condition in 1996, he was forced to resign from the premiership and died soon after. In the meantime, Greece had changed, as had the international environment. Existing socialist governments had collapsed, creating an international framework in which only one superpower remained, while instability prevailed in the Balkans. Furthermore, the Euroscepticism of the 1980s had been replaced by processes of economic and monetary unification and the forward march of rapid economic integration, in which Greece did not seem to be in a position to participate.

In Europe

But right at the moment that Greece seemed to be in the worst possible condition to keep up with developments in the Economic and Monetary Union, its position weakened in an unstable international setting, processes and initiatives fell into place that turned the situation around in a relatively short amount of time. Certainly, in the final two years of Papandreou's premiership (1994–6), the governments' shifting approach had become clear: typical examples included lifting the veto on the customs agreement between European Union and Turkey, which heralded a change in direction for Greek foreign policy, and even more importantly acceptance of the Maastricht Treaty obligations as guidelines for the Greek state's economic policies.

This shift should not be interpreted as the result of the decision of a 'ruling class', but rather as the product of consensus among a notable share of social groups that was then adopted by the two dominant parties—even if this consensus was not shared by the majority of party members themselves or their constituents. Elections from the period confirm this observation.

It was certainly clear that on both an international level and in the economic sector, the country found itself in a deadlock. Adoption of a new model was the only remaining option. The Maastricht Treaty facilitated political change, since achievement of financial targets set as the conditions for entering the EMU was accompanied by the prestige of European integration, eventually acquiring the status of a political orientation that became known as modernisation. It also spelled out the high cost of failure in this process for a country such as Greece.

During this period, the political scene underwent great changes. The coalition government between New Democracy and the Coalition of the Left and Progress (Synaspismos) confirmed the weakening of the right–anti-right opposition that had dominated until then, as the left turned increasingly to policies that differentiated it from PASOK. The fall of existing socialist regimes played a decisive role here, depriving the party of significant international support—both ideological and non-ideological in nature—and pushing it more and more towards stronger anti-European positions. On the other hand, New Democracy, having joined the movement for 'national reconciliation', sought to win over centrist voters and mostly succeeded. It also avoided adopting neoliberal positions, which in any case were not commonly supported by the Greek electorate. These changes were reflected in the social foundations of the parties, which varied significantly in the 1990s. PASOK drew most of its supporters from lower-income groups and the public sector, while naturally, the opposite held true for New Democracy.

As the millennium drew near, politics was increasingly treated with contempt, party loyalty at the polling booths decreased, and political cynicism grew stronger. Political parties gradually transformed into electoral-professional mechanisms dependent on the state and on mass media. In the process, ideological parameters that played an instrumental role in the elections of the 1980s weakened, and demand for effective governance finally emerged as the lead criterion for determining electoral outcome.

In this context, under rather contested conditions, PASOK chose Kostas Simitis as prime minister and then president of the party. Though he was one of PASOK's founding members, Simitis had a completely different personality from his predecessor, a personality also at odds with that nation's traditional political practices. A jurist who had studied in Germany, Simitis never managed to win over the sympathy of the Greeks, even when it came to those who had voted for him. But he turned out to be one of the most successful prime ministers in Greek history.

12.3: Employment and Educational Level of PASOK and New Democracy Voters 1993–2004
PASOK

					New Democracy			
	1993	*1996*	*2000*	*2004*	*1993*	*1996*	*2000*	*2004*
Total	46,8	41,5	43,8	40,5	39,3	38,1	42,7	45,4
Education								
Primary	51.9	46.5	45.9	45.1	37.2	36.2	42.8	44.8
Secondary	47.2	40.8	44.0	42.1	39.5	38.9	43.1	44.8
Higher	41.4	38.2	41.2	36.2	41.4	38.8	42.4	46.6
Profession								
Low-rank public sector	58.3	53.7	53.5	52.6	31.9	33.1	37.4	39.6
Low-rank private sector	51.1	43.2	47.4	42.6	32.7	32.3	36.9	40.2
High-rank public sector	48.8	46.1	46.2	41.7	35.5	33.4	36.3	42.9
High-rank private sector	37.1	35.1	41.4	35.0	39.6	37.3	41.0	46.7
Farmers	43.9	38.3	38.2	40.6	45.2	46.1	50.8	52.3
Traders, craftsmen	46.8	38.5	38.5	41.6	37.2	37.9	41.6	45.5
Self-employed	36.6	36.2	36.2	29.8	42.0	38.7	43.4	52.1
Unemployed	46.0	38.9	36.9	38.8	37.1	36.2	43.5	44.9
Students	36.7	37.0	41.9	43.6	45.1	40.3	44.1	37.8
Housewives	46.6	41.5	43.2	42.6	44.5	44.0	48.7	49.4
Pensioners (low-rank)	54.3	49.0	46.6	44.0	35.1	53.6	41.7	43.9
Pensioners (high-rank)	40.6	36.2	40.2	32.7	50.4	47.6	49.2	56.4

Source: I. Nikolakopoulos, 'Elections and Voters, 1974–2004: Old Cleavages and New Issues', in Featherstone, Kevin (ed.), *Politics and Policy in Greece: The Challenge of Modernisation*, London: Routledge, 2005.

During his eight-year premiership, Simitis succeeded in achieving the goals he had set out. In 2001, Greece managed to join the Eurozone despite the very serious economic problems it faced. Until the early 1990s, its macroeconomic policy had been characterised by a strong state presence in the economy and a system of administrative controls that created powerful disincentives for investment initiatives. Greece's decision to participate in the EMU led to a complete reversal of this system: public deficits shrank, while public debt as a percentage of GDP stabilised, albeit at an extremely high-level. With regard to revenue policies, there was a limitation of labour costs, though not so much so as to match the reduction of corresponding labour costs by trading partners. Here, the influx of migrants played its role, while unemployment remained at consistently high levels throughout the period. Certain advanced sectors such as finance and telecommunications were deregulated, and the state proceeded to privatise its shares in many businesses. This took great effort, but it paid off. The changes necessitated by Greece's integration into the Eurozone gave a great boost to the Greek economy, which for the first time in many years began to demonstrate higher growth rates than the European average. For Greece, with its long history of problematic foreign trade, integration into the Eurozone granted it new economic power, simultaneously creating an unquestionably favourable macroeconomic environment in which the Greek economy could develop.

Meanwhile, Greece also agreed to organise the 2004 Olympic Games. It was the first time that a small country was faced with such a complex organisational and technological project. Despite criticisms levelled at Greece during the preparations for the event, which largely represented pressures for the accommodation of specific interests, in the end Greece organised the Olympics with complete success. In the process, Greece, and in particular the overburdened city of Athens, was able to make leaps in improving its infrastructure, thus improving the lives of its inhabitants.

The Simitis government was also notably successful in foreign policy. Its move to establish friendly relations with Turkey proved effective, not so much regarding relations with the neighbouring country itself, but regarding improvement of Greece's position within the European Union. Greece ceased to be the country instigating problems in the relations between the EU and Turkey, thus highlighting the real problems between major European countries and the Turkish Republic that had previously hid behind the pretext of Greece's negative attitude towards Turkey. One result of these policy changes was Cyprus's successful integration into the European Union, which seemed as though it might facilitate a solution to the Cyprus dispute. More generally, a recalibration of Greek foreign policy to European standards considerably improved Greece's international position.

But Simitis's inability to win over the Greek population, his choice of advisors that became embroiled in scandals (despite his own integrity), and a redistribution of income detrimental to more vulnerable groups significantly weakened PASOK's position. In general, the Simitis governments sought to implement two important large-scale objectives: participation in the euro currency, and the Olympic Games. They achieved both, but measures that would have allowed for the diffusion of these benefits to larger social groups—especially those in need—were not successful. This trend was also evident in health and education, where despite significant spending in both areas, the situation did not improve. In fact, it worsened. This was a result of a failure to implement policies targeted at individuals that really needed support within larger groups rather than the groups themselves. In general, the Simitis governments may have achieved the broader goals they had set, but they failed to distribute these benefits across the social spectrum, especially to poorer groups, despite significant social expenditure. For example, though universities were built, the quality of university education decreased in all respects. In any case, in these years of economic convergence Greece benefited from an international environment of low interest rates in order to achieve major targets set by incumbent governments. It did not seek to create an alternative model for development from the one that was already in place, though this model was problematic in every respect. The final result was the establishment of a system that has been defined as profit-seeking, but also a stunning decline in savings: from 22 per cent of GDP in 1989, they shrank to 5–6 per cent in the mid-2000s, dropping even further in the following years. This was due to the role played by increasing private consumption, which was disproportionately high in comparison with European standards. In other words, over these years, Greece continued its attempts to minimise adaptations to the conditions of globalisation, which it participated in and benefited from through lavish public funding and private expenditure.

Furthermore, the Simitis governments were unable to use the broader momentum of change sweeping through Greece to facilitate the reforms the country needed. Instead, they handled a number of such issues awkwardly, often at significant political cost, and without any real reason or cause. The stock market's crash after 2000, which caused significant losses for lower- and middle-class income brackets, was greeted as a conspiracy favouring the powerful, while a conflict between church and state resulting from the issue with national identity cards also substantially damaged PASOK's reputation. Finally, attempts at pension reform in 2001 led to a conflict that ended the government's reformist attempts. It won the 2000 elections in a weakened state. This was a logical result of the fact that the entire effort at reform from 1996 onwards, identified with the term 'modernisation', never took root in the political system: instead, it was always seen as a tool for the accidentally efficient operation of the state. This was evident from the most critical sector of governance, the institutional one, where the constitutional reform of 2001 avoided radical changes and only promoted certain administrative reforms—and all this coming from a government that respected the rule of law and human rights more than any one of its predecessors since the founding of the Greek state.

By 2001, this modernising experiment had begun to lose momentum, and PASOK was abandoned even by its most traditional supporters: private and public sector employees. In early 2004, Simitis made the decision to hand over leadership of PASOK to Andreas Papandreou's' son George. Soon after, in elections, PASOK was defeated and New Democracy was restored to power under the leadership of Kostas Karamanlis, the nephew of Konstantinos Karamanlis. The nation's modernising experiment had ended, though its consequences would only be evident to their full extent after some delay.

The 'Greek disease'

The murder, in December 2008, of a fifteen-year-old student at the hands of a policeman in the Athenian neighbourhood of Exarchia was the catalyst for the outbreak—in the span of a few hours—of an unprecedented wave of protests in all of Greece's major cities, involving an overwhelmingly young demographic group. Major riots and destruction followed, chiefly in Athens but also in Thessaloniki. Greece was the first topic of all international news agencies, and, understandably, leaders of major countries in the European Union worried about the effects the Greek example could have on youth in their respective nations. The French government was forced to stop planned procedures for educational reform because of fears that the riots might spread there as well. People began to speak of the 'Greek disease'.

The riots, protests and destruction that occurred in Athens were indeed impressive in the eyes of the Western European observer for one basic reason: they happened in the very centre of the city, often right in front of Parliament, something unthinkable in any other Western European country. Corresponding riots that took place in Paris in November 2007 were certainly more violent, but were limited to the deprived northern outskirts of the city, taking on a different social significance in comparison with the Greek case.

Though it is worth noting that two factors—namely the geography of these December 2008 protests and police inaction over the same period—attracted considerable attention, to the extent that the French newspaper *Le Monde* wrote of a 'Greece with no government', both are of minor importance and can be easily justified. Specifically, police inaction was geared towards minimising the risk of another victim, which would render the government's position untenable. What is more interesting and worthy of study is related to the events themselves: What exactly were these protests expressing?

Naturally, many highly contradictory answers were given. The majority of the mass media seemed to justify the protests and respectively lambast police forces for all attempted uses of force. Perhaps this was because, in their own way, they were gaining—or so they thought—viewership or an audience, as they satisfied Greek parents worried about their children, but also about the state of youth in general. On the other hand, political parties, nearly all of them, did not dare act against the current. In Parliament, the minister of interior affairs even referred to the event as a murder while it was still under investigation. Very few attempted a more calm approach to the event, and those that did were often denounced.

No specific demands were made by the uprising. But without a doubt, its spirit of unrest can be summarised under the vague term of 'resistance', as was written on a large banner hung from the Acropolis by a group of youths. In return, the prime minister, seeking a solution, promised that discussions would begin to change the system of university entry examinations by the coming year, even though this demand had not been explicitly expressed. Simply, it was commonly accepted that the older generations were not treating the Greek youth appropriately, and the prime minister's advisors probably thought that some statement on the reform of entrance examinations could possibly show the government's sensitivity to a sector that—everyone admitted—was fraught with major problems and of course directly concerned a large number of the young population.

The vagueness characterising these youth movements' demands should instead be interpreted on the basis of their heterogeneity. From a certain point onwards, these protests were attended by high school students, university students, and other groups that had no clear relationship to either. The latter included so-called anarchic groups from the Exarchia neighbourhood, football hooligans and immigrants, among others. Obviously, these groups were very different from one another, and in the riots that followed, each group saw what it wanted to see according to its individual position. Some saw protest for a murdered teenager, some saw the possibility of violent political expression, others, finally, seized the opportunity for looting. Finally, attempts made by a faction of the left to impose its ideology on these protests failed completely, and thus the riots remained undetermined by fixed political or partisan content.

But it would be difficult to speak of the mass character of these demonstrations, at least in relation to the *Metapolitefsi*. A generous estimate points to 20,000 individuals, and this only for the first few days. They were characterised by their extremely violent nature, and this startled many Greeks. As much as they were familiar with violence in downtown Athens, it was the first time it was seen with such ubiquity and intensity. Around the city, many schools closed and a large number of university departments were occupied, mainly by leftist groups and anarchists.

In fact, via mobilisation of these younger age groups (note that those who exercised violence customarily are not included in this tally) the December unrest came to express a dissatisfaction and unease that was felt by the majority of the Greek population, a product of political practices leading to a dead-end and national political discourse lacking meaningful content. Without a doubt, there were reasons for this discontent that exclusively concerned the youth: this was the 'generation living on 700 euros a month', as the slogan went, with high rates of unemployment. But these were only symptoms of wider political and social problems.

The Karamanlis government had won the 2004 elections with promises of bringing morality back to national politics, invoking the rather ridiculous term of 'political culture' as a means to make their target more specific. The prime minister even went so far as to ask for 'modesty and humility' of his ministers at the beginning of their terms. PASOK was now marked by a series of scandals, and Karamanlis did not hesitate to call his predecessor, Simitis, the 'arch-priest of the plot'. Thus the scene was ripe for such discourses of catharsis, and for the creation of expectations of a 'moral' and proper government. New Democracy sought to benefit from this in every possible way.

But it was very soon evident that a change of government, a new prime minister and least of all a self-righteous attitude were not enough to change the political culture of a nation in which the concept of public interest was interpreted according to each minister or government official's whims. Soon after coming into power, New Democracy scandals began to succeed one another at an almost inconcievable rate. This happened at every realm of social activity—in the church, with the legal system, social security, and the ministry of culture—thus dispelling any false illusions regarding the 'ethics and proper administration' advocated by the government.

The prime minister more or less protected the ministers responsible for this, coming to the conclusion that all these events were the creation of a hateful opposition. Government failures began to appear at all levels of public life, culminating in the fires in the summer of 2007 in the Peloponnese that killed dozens of people, along with a form of economic management that employed various tricks to allay its main problems, and, in doing so, undermined the economy's potential. This proved devastating in the years to come.

It would be unfair to assign the New Democracy government full responsibility for the situation prevailing in Greece from 2004 onwards. In fact, this was the culmination of a situation that had already begun to form since 2001: that is to say, from the moment Greece joined the Eurozone. It fumbled with attempts at pension reform and did not proceed—or, more correctly, did not dare proceed—to adjust this error institutionally or otherwise, so as to address the very serious problems it faced. The latter were masked by the period's favourable economic trends, which would not continue indefinitely. The 2008 political opposition, which was the incumbent government up until 2004, clearly shared great responsibility for the prevailing situation, and as a result its reactions to all that was occurring were by no means convincing or compelling. The same was true for a large share of the left, which adopted a discourse during the unrest that justified any destruction that ensued, while another side of it kept a conservative stance, treating any movement not under its control with suspicion. Indeed, for the duration of the December 2008 unrest, all parties spoke in terms of political cost, completely ignoring the essential, underlying problems.

Thus the average Greek continued to face a political system trapped within itself and between inter-party balances, one that left no freedom for independent expression of diverse opinions. Similarly, all Greek state institutions and agencies manoeuvred solely on the basis of party choices and sensationalism, or for the interest of a closed circle of people. In this context, any initiative for something different always came at the expense of the person attempting it, which made it impossible for anyone to seek a solution to major problems. The most striking example of this dead-end political reality was the constitutional review of 2007–9, which only resulted in the review of article 57 of the Constitution, related to the professional activities of MPs, which had been adopted in the 2001 revision. This adjustment now allowed members to partake in the most lucrative activities associated with the liberal professions, with no obstacles, and with all the more effectiveness due to their parliamentary status. It is no surprise that all the parties in Parliament participated in the ratification, with the exception of PASOK, which had withdrawn from the vote.

Beyond the scandals indicating corruption at the highest political levels, everyday corruption also took place. This amounted to nothing more than mechanisms that allowed public servants and other employees to supplement their rather meagre incomes by offering more efficient services compared with those offered under normal conditions. From the issuing of drivers licences to the technical inspection of cars, hospitals and of course tax matters, pension contributions or permits for construction work, anywhere positions of power existed in relation to the citizen, parallel mechanisms allowed for the existence of significant 'parallel' incomes. But these were mechanisms without which everyday life for Greeks would become even more difficult, especially in sensitive sectors such as healthcare.

All this has led to a complete lack of faith in the Greek political system in the eyes of its citizens, even if all are involved to a greater or lesser extent, since they can do no differently when it comes to everyday practices of corruption. And this was certainly not due to the unrest, which at most expressed the accumulated discontent of a portion of the youth population, but rather focused on the political system's inability to solve the Greeks' basic problems. Today, the healthcare system is inadequate, and is a means of unlawful enrichment for many. Free healthcare is practically non-existent, since the incentives for state public health mechanisms in individual cases consist of under-the-table fees, and the few efforts made to improve the situation have buckled in front of the exceedingly powerful interests encountered. It is worth noting that private health expenditure in Greece is the highest in Europe, despite the fact that public health expenditure is also extremely high, even in comparison with countries that maintain exemplary systems of state-run healthcare. At the same time, the issues with funding the health system were so great that in early 2008 many began to talk of a default due to debts at public hospitals. The insurance system found itself in a very difficult position, and no one dared take radical measures to tackle the problem.

In education, the system developed in such a way that its standards were downgraded. Only those who were able to send their children to good private schools and then to Anglo-Saxon countries were able to secure them a good education. Moreover, the phrase 'free public education' was nothing more than a euphemism, since families paid a significant amount for supplementary tutoring and foreign-language instruction for their children. The Greek state is actually the first among OECD nations in terms of the ratio of number of university students compared with the general population. It thus follows that graduates of Greek higher education are unable to find jobs based on their qualifications and expectations, as the economy does not produce—and is unable to produce—a corresponding number of positions.

All this is evident and commonly accepted. Even so, any attempt at change faces the fierce reactions of the opposition in place each time, but also of groups affected by individual decisions. Eventually, every government bends when faced with this 'political cost'. In the meantime, maintaining existing mechanisms and their respective interests causes a huge economic and social burden, largely demonstrated through an increase in public debt. A basic cause of this, in addition to uncontrolled public spending, is found in the public revenue system itself, and more specifically in the tax system supported on the backs of salaried employees, enabling a huge space for the parallel economy. Although all this is widely known—as is the inability of tax-collecting mechanisms to fulfil their role—nobody has tried to seriously address the problem, while New Democracy destroyed the existing tax-collecting mechanisms. In this manner, the framework for a very unjust and unequal financial system came into being: certain groups such as the self-employed benefited greatly, while others, such as salaried employees and pensioners, paid the cost of state failure.

Finally, the notable development of the Greek economy over these past twenty years did not lead to improved indicators of poverty and social inequality. Indicators of relative poverty and social exclusion remain fixed at about 20 per cent from 1990 onwards, despite the fact that Greece has had one of the highest rates of poverty in the EU, regardless of whether these calculations consciously or unconsciously ignored the existence of many immigrants. Moreover, the unfortunate—in the best assessment—management of the immigration issue by state mechanisms shows both the failure of public administration as well as the lack of a political culture that would facilitate the assimilation of immigrants. It is now clear that a more coherent and equitable model of politics is needed if Greece hopes to escape from the sad state in which it finds itself.

Collapse

By December 2008, all the conditions were in place for the Greeks to be dissatisfied—some certainly more than others. The economic crisis had reared its head, and despite the fact that it had not yet become immediately apparent to the majority of the Greek population, it exercised an influence, mainly through the ominous daily predictions on the future of the Greek economy. Misinformation and the opposition's ruthless attempts to use governmental measures to their own benefit only intensified the situation. It was no coincidence that many older demographic groups applauded the demonstrations, regardless of whether or not they participated, while a percentage of them (not at all negligible, as shown by opinion polls) did not condemn vandalism of banks and public buildings. The prospect of new 'sacrifices' needed in order to address budget deficits, in combination with the large sums allegedly misappropriated by those accused of involvement in scandals, could easily lead people to adopt such a view. But things soon evolved in a worse manner than even the most pessimistic parties could have imagined.

Exactly one year after the December 2008 riots, Greece found itself facing another unpleasant surprise: after the October 2009 elections, the new government's estimates for the public deficit that year jumped to 12.7 per cent from the previous government's estimates of 6 per cent (but implicitly 8 per cent). Successive downgrades of Greek bonds by foreign rating agencies followed, which in turn accelerated an exodus of mostly foreign investors in Greek government debt. A bit late in the game, the new government tried to address the problem of rising borrowing costs by introducing a stability and growth pact. The pact was indeed approved by the European commission, but failed to quell the concern of markets as was soon evident from the high interest rates accompanying new issuances of public debt. It became progressively clearer that Greece would not be in a position to pay these high interest rates to refinance public debt for very long, but also that a possible default on behalf of the Greek government would not leave other members of the Eurozone unscathed. Continuing depreciation of the euro in relation to the dollar indicated that the Greek problem was not just Greek.

In the months that followed, the country's reputation abroad was tarnished all the more and the refrain of 'Greek disease' re-emerged in the international media, though it referred to a different situation. Once again, Greece was Europe's black sheep, and commentary in the international media ranged from derogatory to abusive. Despite assurances from the Greek government that it could face its problems on its own, time was not on its side. On 23 April 2010, the Greek prime minister submitted an official request for the activation of a Greek economic support mechanism by the International Monetary Fund and the European Union, a mechanism created after much procrastination only when it was understood that abandoning Greece could have unpredictable consequences for the European economies.

Resorting to this mechanism led to a series of tough measures determined by representatives of the IMF, the European Commission and the European Central Bank, and the Greek government was obliged to accept them. Other structural measures would soon follow. Paradoxically, reactions to these policies were rather mild, despite protests from trade unionists and the opposition, and often even members of the incumbent government. This was probably because it had become common knowledge that Greece was teetering on the precipice and could only be saved with the assistance of this support mechanism. But at the same time, polls showed a complete disillusionment with the Greek political system, something that was all the more exacerbated by revelations—though few in number—accompanying deliberations of Parliamentary Committees held for the investigation of scandals.

Once again, the Greek state was forced to adopt common sense measures—measures it should have implemented on its own initiative years ago—under pressure of foreign creditors, with the risk of the entire state framework collapsing. Unfortunately, even in these unpleasant circumstances, it became clear that the nation's politicians were unable to disengage from their old habits; this was demonstrated by how issues of running the pension system or liberalisation of transport were handled, but also from the attitude of the opposition, which refused to vote through the support mechanism in Parliament despite the responsibility it shared for the situation Greece found itself in. In other words, the political system was structured in such a way that it was designed to perpetuate party hegemony rather than solve problems at hand. All this led to practices that did little to inspire optimism in Greece's future, which was under guardianship of these international organisations, its negotiating power at an international level extremely reduced. Frustration was also provoked by a lack of elementary social solidarity as various social groups and interests sought to benefit from the circumstances, completely unconcerned with the state of the Greek economy and the status of other social groups. When we remind ourselves that the problems associated with Greek public debt will take many years to resolve, cause for optimism shrinks even more.

By 2010, Greece had achieved many of the goals set out at the founding of the Greek state, perhaps the most symbolic of all being participation in the Eurozone, that is, in the core of Europe. But what has been disregarded in the past fifteen years is that in conditions of globalisation, each country must constantly strive to improve its competitiveness in all sectors and maintain its position in an international hierarchy. But erosion of state mechanisms by party control meant that every effort at substantial reform was doomed to fail. The policies of New Democracy, which sought to consolidate power after a long absence from leading the national government—without particular misgivings about the cost of such policies—led the system to its limits. Only the high liquidity of the international economy in recent years and low interest rates were able to facilitate development under these conditions. This led to great fiscal and external imbalances, which exhibited themselves violently with the 2008 crisis. Greece found itself once again in conditions of near default, even if this was avoided at the last minute thanks to the support mechanism.

Thus, in less than two years Greece saw the entire economic and social model established after the 1974 regime change collapse: on the one hand, Greek society is now structured at the expense of younger generations and immigrants, who have played an outsize role in recent developments—to a much greater extent than any other European country. Servicing the extremely high public debt is naturally a burden on future generations, adding on one more intolerable weight. Meanwhile, tax evasion enables exploitation of salaried employees and pensioners by the self-employed, but also by all those who are able to use their positions to avoid taxation—a situation in which political and economic elites cooperate unreservedly, to their own benefit and at the expense of much of the population, indifferent to the costs of every kind that their thoughtlessness and complicity has for the country.

It is no coincidence that the economic model in place, one based on the parallel economy, has reached a breaking point, even though there is no alternative currently in sight. All this in a democracy characterised by equality, in which everyone has rights, though few seem to have responsibilities, and even fewer seek to meet them. The phrase a 'Democracy of Friends', which has been used in the past, seems very apt: it is just that such a democracy can only work up until a certain point, under favourable economic conditions. From the moment they stop being favourable, the conditions under which the system operates shift and one can expect that the system itself will change, causing polarising positions and social tensions.

Indeed, today, Greece finds itself at a critical juncture. Over the course of its history, it has managed to become a European country, something that was not necessarily to be taken for granted, and to attain a level of prosperity that would have been unexpected twenty years ago. Its participation in the European Union played a catalytic role in these developments, but Greece's political elite believed that the country's participation in the processes of

European integration alone would be enough to solve all problems, and that on autopilot, these processes would direct Greece to the promised land without reforms of any importance. It turns out that they were wrong, and the question from here on out is whether Greece will be able to maintain its achievements—a question with no obvious answer.

13

CRISIS

(2007–)

> As we were completing the so-called staff level agreement so it could be subsequently ratified by the Greek government, the Eurogroup, and parliaments in Greece and in our creditors' countries, and I had all the documents in front of me, I realised that this was the first time that the Greek state had a complete operational plan; a detailed and binding multi-year plan of policies with timelines and specific, fully budgeted programs. But it also came with a monitoring mechanism that would ensure that these commitments would turn into actions, with specific corresponding sanctions in case they did not: the refusal to disburse EU and IMF loan instalments, without which the country could not function.[1]

The problem

Responsibility for the public debt problem at the root of the crisis currently plaguing Greece cannot be attributed to a single political party or leader; the problem is more or less a key feature of the entire post-dictatorial political system, a system that sought to satisfy its ambitions for power through borrowing rather than resorting to measures that would have proven painful for its constituencies. A study of the national pension and healthcare system during these same years would suffice to convince even the most sceptical individual of the political practices of the period.

In all fairness, it must be acknowledged that certain efforts were made to curb such uncontrolled borrowing. During the second term of the Papandreou government (1993–6) and the Simitis government (1996–2004), public debt remained at high levels, but all signs indicated that it had been brought under control—or at least that efforts had been made to control it. Overall debt even decreased slightly over this period, while primary surpluses were recorded between 1994 and 2002. These trends would be completely reversed when New Democracy assumed power. To name but one example, from late 2003 to late 2009, national public debt increased from 94.1 per cent to 126.7 per cent of GDP—that is, by 32.6 percentage points. The economy's strong growth rates up until 2008 suggest that debt accumulation in absolute terms was far greater: from a total of 168 billion euros in late 2003, public debt had surpassed 298 billion euros by the end of 2009.

Regarding public finances, incumbent governments could have controlled the situation had they wished to do so—at least in theory. But in terms of the Greek economy's competitiveness, the situation was just as bad, while the possibility of adopting measures with immediately visible effects was very limited. The so-called structural reforms required time to pay off, and in 2008, Greece had run out of time. Between 2000 and 2009, the inflation differential between Greece and its partners had reached 10 per cent. Or, in other words, the prices of Greek goods increased by 10 per cent relative to the prices of its trading partners' goods. Consequently Greek goods and services became more expensive relative to those sold by the country's trade partners. Were Greece still in control of its own currency, this development would lead to a devaluation of the drachma. But in the Eurozone, especially since productivity of the Greek economy did not increase at a rate corresponding to the inflation differential, the only result was an increase in the deficit of Greece's external trade balance. The constant lack of competitiveness in the Greek economy had an extremely high and growing cost that could only be covered by borrowing.

Without a doubt, the Greek crisis was triggered from abroad—from the United States. The crisis that erupted there should have caught the attention of Greek politicians. Instead, New Democracy's finance minister argued that the Greek economy was protected from it. In the same vein, his successor declared: 'Those betting against Greece will lose yet again ... Greece has the will, the plan, and the determination not only to ensure a steady trajectory for its economy, but also to strengthen its competitive position.'

Yet all indicators pointed to a less than favourable situation for the Greek economy. In early 2008, spreads (that is, the price difference between Greek and German ten-year government bonds) for Greek bonds amounted to thirty-five basis points. At the end of the same year, the corresponding amount grew to 200 basis points, reaching 300 in early 2009. Only then, following the government's success in covering its borrowing needs, did these spreads decrease once more.

Though this development might have been reassuring for the Greek government, the International Monetary Fund was not convinced, and it warned Greece of the need to adopt a balanced stabilisation policy or face huge risks. Furthermore, once the previous year's general government budget reached 4 per cent of GDP, in April 2009, Greece was forced by the European Commission to join the Excessive Deficit Procedure.

In the autumn of 2009, Greece was led to elections precisely because tough measures were required to rein the economy back into a stable orbit. Unfortunately, in its quest for power, PASOK did not address the problem any more wisely than New Democracy had before it.

In the autumn of 2008, George Papandreou was elected prime minister, introducing his slogan, 'There's plenty of money!' which came to represent the prevailing carelessness of the time. He assumed power over a nation in the midst of economic collapse, and, according to all indications, a nation in which no one was aware of the full extent of the problem.

Thus it came as no surprise that the Papandreou government's first policy statements on 16 October 2009 did not even demonstrate a basic awareness of the problem, and in general, there was no conception of how to address it. This was inexcusable, since, as the opposition party, PASOK had been informed of the state of the economy by the Bank of Greece. Yet five days later, on 23 October 2009, PASOK's Minister of Finance Giorgios Papakonstantinou informed the European Commission that at the end of 2009 the budget deficit would reach 12.5 per cent of GDP instead of the 6 per cent that had been predicted by the New Democracy government.

The situation deteriorated on 27 October 2009 when the deadline passed for adoption of measures laid out by the Excessive Deficit Procedure that Greece had agreed to in April 2009. Introduction of the stability and growth programme, which was supposed to solve the problem in theory, was postponed until January 2010. As an immediate consequence, the Fitch credit rating agency downgraded Greece's credit rating from an A to an A-; but this was just the beginning.

As the situation evolved, three major questions emerged to be addressed by Greeks and foreigners in the coming months, questions that would determine the position of each party involved in the problem at hand. First, was Greece in a position to deal with its fiscal problems, and, in fact, to what extent did incumbent governments wish to address them? Second, how reliable were Greek statistics, and to what extent did they continue to underestimate the situation? Lastly, was the European Union in a position to help Greece—and did it want to do so?

From this point onwards, the Papandreou government began desperate efforts to reassure the Europeans by taking measures to balance the budget, while it simultaneously sought to appear faithful to the promises it had made to its constituency, from which it derived its mandate. But it was impossible for both to occur at the same time. Wavering on behalf of the Papandreou government, which emphasised a lack of understanding of the true magnitude of the problem, would only result in a waste of time and ultimately in an increased cost. It is indicative that the 2010 budget submitted to Parliament in late November 2009 provided for a planned reduction of the deficit to 9.1 per cent of GDP. This would be achieved by reducing expenditure to 7.8 per cent of GDP and increasing revenues by 23.6 per cent of GDP. The budget was accompanied by reductions in expenditure on culture, rural development, labour and social security. On the other hand, the budget provided for a 2.8 per cent increase in pensions in comparison with the previous year, in addition to increased spending on education, health, justice and public investment. The budget was voted in on Christmas Eve, but no one could have seriously believed that these measures would address the fiscal problem. As a result, Greece's credit rating was downgraded once more.

On 15 January 2010, the stability and growth programme was presented after some delay; its goal was to calm tensions and determine the policies the incumbent government would enact. But tensions only heightened—nor could it have happened any other way at the very moment when Greece had completely lost its credibility. Meanwhile, the measures proposed were still very mild compared with the true size of the problem that had to be addressed. Only in late January 2010, during his attendance at the World Economic Forum in Davos, did the prime minister finally recognise the seriousness of the situation.

In retrospect, these developments were only natural, to the extent that Greece was only one part of the problem. The other part, equally important, was the European Union, whose attitude towards the problem was no better than Greece's. The major issue here was the lack of guidelines for solidarity between states in cases such as the one at hand; each state was responsible for itself and its own debts. The problem became even more difficult as a significant number of Northern European countries began to see the Greek problem in ethical rather than political terms: Greece was facing problems now because it had not respected the rules of the Eurozone and had cheated its partners. From another view, the Greeks were lazy, and had borrowed in order to lead a life far beyond their means.

Under these circumstances, it was only natural that certain countries, including Germany, were opposed to any sort of aid package to the Greek state. In doing this, they were also playing by the rules, since conditions at the time did not allow for support of a state facing the problems that Greece was. On the other hand, there were countries like France, wary of the prospect that Greece could go bankrupt, since such an event could trigger widespread contagion and have detrimental effects for the remaining Southern European states, not to mention France, which had its own particular problems to solve at the time. Meanwhile, the US government, which with great effort and at great expense had managed to halt the collapse of the US banking system, intervened in Greece, fearful that the crisis could spread internationally. Along with all this, we must note the terrible difficulties that large European banks would face in case of Greek bankruptcy, since they had invested large sums in Greek public debt. These damages would be added to those already caused by their investments in toxic bonds, and as a result some of them would end up in a truly difficult situation.

The most that could be agreed on at first was a statement after the informal European Union summit convened on 11 February 2010: 'We fully support the efforts of the Greek government to do what is necessary, including additional measures which will ensure that the ambitious targets set in the Stability and Growth Programme for 2010 and the coming years are met.' That is to say, nothing at all.

Shortly thereafter, the council of EU Finance Ministers (ECOFIN) announced in their resolution that Greece constituted a risk to the proper functioning of the Eurozone, and expressed its displeasure at the poor quality of the country's fiscal data, which posed problems for Greece's credibility. The council demanded that Greece adopt significant measures that would have to be presented by 16 March 2010. These new measures were announced in Greece on 3 March, provoking intense reactions. The European Central Bank considered them an acceptable starting point and agreed to them, while also requiring corrective measures that would serve to address unemployment and economic growth in the medium term.

All indications demonstrated that the government sought to avoid a bailout plan that would be beyond its control in every possible way. This, after all, is the reason why it avoided adopting radical measures from the get-go, and committed to new measures again and again so as to secure implementation of the stability programme. A complete lack of communication between the Greek political forces in power made the situation even more unpleasant, and tactics employed by the government confirmed its inability to deal with the problems at hand. Most emblematic in this respect was the statement made by Finance Minister Papakonstantinou in late February 2010 that 'The government is trying to change the course of the Titanic, and that cannot just happen overnight.'

Statements of this sort demonstrated the government's indecisiveness, but the concrete issues at hand were what really predetermined the developments to come. In April and May 2010, Greece was required to pay 20 billion euros for the servicing of its public debt. Very few individuals believed that the country would be able to meet its obligations. The situation was aggravated by the high interest rates the Greek state was facing in capital markets, but most importantly, as was later proven, by a lack of awareness of the problem's magnitude on behalf of the Greek government and its partners. The country was in need of massive help—not in need of the 30 billion euros that the government thought could solve the problem.

Seen from another perspective, the problem worsened because of the attitudes taken by the other European countries. For them, it was unclear what would need to happen, and what effects the bankruptcy of a member state would have. Could a nation go bankrupt and stay in the Eurozone, or would Greece have to return to its own sovereign currency? Did an exit from the Eurozone also mean a withdrawal from the European Union? These were all unprecedented issues being raised for the first time, and the answer to them was anything but straightforward.

Both in Greece and in the European Union, the problem was purely political. But on a political level it was impossible to make a decision, largely because Greece was taking an evasive position, its own government unsure of how much it wanted outside help. In fact, it was certain that it wanted to avoid the latter, just as its partners were unwilling to finance it. Meanwhile, the legal issue of how such support would be given to Greece, if it was requested, was addressed: the aid would come from bilateral loans given by member states to Greece, and not in the form of a multilateral aid package from the EU, which was prohibited by governing treaties. Needless to say, everyone was still hoping to avoid this.

At the 23 March summit, France and Germany announced that they had found an intermediary solution. Though the Greek government had not asked for aid, the Eurozone member states were ready to grant bilateral loans to any member state if such an action was deemed necessary. This process could be initiated from the moment that the market alone could not provide sufficient financing. Meanwhile, member states of the Eurozone reached an agreement over the IMF's involvement in financing the country facing such problems.

Despite the fact that opinions converged on the necessity of supporting the Greek economy—and by extension, the economy of any Eurozone nation that faced such problems—no solutions were offered, and both Greek and foreign officials kept procrastinating. Everyone believed—or gave the impression they believed—that they could solve the problem through threatening declarations and wishful thinking, and in doing so they avoided addressing it with the gravity required by their position. Certainly, the markets were fully aware of the problems plaguing both Greece and the Eurozone, and this made any efforts at financing the Greek economy all the more difficult. This was most apparent in the widening spreads, which suggested an exponential increase in the markets' perception of the probability of a Greek default. The only political intervention worth mentioning in this period was the adoption of a major pension and healthcare reform in the summer of 2010, which in the long term could theoretically restore a fiscal balance. But it was already too late for that.

In early April 2010, the EU prepared a draft agreement for the loan to Greece, which would amount to 40 to 45 billion euros, of which the IMF would cover 10 to 15 billion. It would be a three-year loan at an interest rate of 2.8 per cent for the IMF portion and 4.85 to 5.0 per cent for the remainder of the loan. The Greek government continued to hesitate, and it seems that the final decision was made on 22 April 2010, after a phone call between the Greek finance minister and his American counterpart, Timothy Geithner.

On 23 April 2010, Papandreou, prime minister of Greece, announced his intention to request 'activation of the support mechanism created jointly with the European Union'. By now, the government had come to terms with reality—but still, no one could imagine what form it would soon take.

The components of the problem

The first and most important component of the Greek crisis, which is often forgotten, has to do with the fact that it was an inseparable part of the major international crisis that began in the United States in 2007 and then extended to the other developed countries. To neglect this fact, along with the fact that the crisis of 2007 was one of the biggest crises in modern economic history, is to avoid taking the substance of the problem into account. We also forget that though Greece was the first nation in the Eurozone affected by the crisis—as it was certainly the most vulnerable—other countries soon followed. Portugal, Ireland, Cyprus, even Spain and Italy expressed elements of crises rooted in their particular economic and political characteristics. That Greece continues to be in the midst of a crisis today should not make us blind to the fact that beyond the Greek situation, the crisis has not been resolved on an international level. In fact the global economy continues to follow a trajectory of de-globalisation, only intensifying with the passage of time, its conclusion unknown. The Greek situation is a part of this process.

The international dimension of the Greek problem is linked with Greece's participation in the Eurozone, a fact that prevents it from exercising autonomous national monetary policy—something that would facilitate a response to the crisis, as was the case in the early 1990s. Yet as has been shown again and again, the way the euro is structured is particularly problematic. In the process of creating a common European currency, key aspects of the Optimum Currency Area theory were ignored, including the need for a single, unified fiscal policy.

There is no doubt that the Eurozone is structured around the German economic reality. As a result, the remaining countries must adapt their policies to it, even if it is not in their direct interest to do so. Until 2009, this arrangement affected Southern nations that fell short of their productive capacity, resulting in large foreign trade deficits. Conversely, Northern countries experienced surpluses, which were only recycled to the Southern regions through lending, a process that inevitably posed certain limits on the borrowing capacity of deficit economies.

Yet the view that Greece's exit from the Eurozone would enable it to better face the crisis is nothing more or less than a naïve conception of reality, and in particular, of the process of globalisation. Greece's participation in the Eurozone and more generally in the European Union is not limited only to an economic dimension—and it is rather difficult in today's circumstances to imagine Greece's survival without participation in a large economic union; it has a political dimension too. The blow Greece would suffer after a withdrawal from the Eurozone would jeopardise the country's future for an undetermined and certainly very long time. The geopolitical problems that have arisen in the region—whether we look to the issue of refugees and immigration, or the explosive situation prevailing in the region—significantly strengthen the argument for Greece's necessary participation in the greater sum of the Eurozone.

In addition to the above, we must add Greece's productive weakness as an independent variable in this crisis. It has already been mentioned that, following the fall of the dictatorship, Greece was a pioneer in the democratising process (in and of itself a fundamental element of globalisation) though it sought in every which way to avoid the latter's consequences in economic terms. There was a great drop in the country's competitiveness, and a refusal to enact structural measures exacerbated the situation. The consequences of these choices were largely concealed thanks to Greece's ease in taking out loans, especially after its entry into the Eurozone, but the global crisis of 2007 revealed just how fragile the basis of the Greek economy was. It should be noted that Greece now must survive in an international environment in which it has to be globally competitive, as new powers enter the playing field, and the country can only truly exist by way of its participation in the European Union. The country's survival outside it would be an extremely risky venture, as already mentioned.

Greece's very low ranking in various competitiveness indexes serves to underline the above points. As much as one might have doubts about what the rankings really represent, it is indicative that Greece ranks poorly in all indexes calculated by international organisations, its position being inconsistent with its ranking based on per capita GDP alone. According to the 2015–16 Global Competitiveness Report compiled by the World Economic Forum, Greece ranks just eighty-first out of a total of 140 countries included in the index in terms of overall competitiveness. Its performance in more sub-specific sub-indexes is hardly better: it ranks eighty-first in terms of its institutions and thirty-fourth in infrastructure, while the ongoing crisis puts its macroeconomic environment at a deplorable 132nd place. Healthcare and primary education (forty-first) as well as higher education (forty-third) fare slightly better. The same cannot be said of goods-market efficiency (eighty-ninth), and less so of labour-market efficiency (116th). Financial markets rank particularly poorly (131st), largely thanks to the effects of the crisis on the Greek banking sector. By contrast, Greece surpasses the average in terms of technological readiness (thirty-sixth), while it ranks fifty-second on the basis of its market size. Finally, the country is ranked seventy-fourth in terms of business sophistication, and seventy-seventh in innovation. In the majority of cases, Greece's scores are far lower than those of its Eurozone partners.

All this would be surmountable if the country possessed an effective political system—that is, a different system from the one currently in place. Naturally, the course of the crisis would have been different if the key political forces in Greece had been able to find some common ground in managing the crisis. This was the case for all the other countries that found themselves weathering extremely unstable conditions, forced to resort to the support of a bailout. In other words, the Greek political system lacks the necessary institutional and collective capacities to impose the necessary policies, but also the discipline required to keep the country from going off the rails. The same held true for the policies that would need to be adopted in order to achieve economic growth. Three prime ministers refused to acknowledge the situation in the attempt to maintain their power, and in the end all three were forced to sign significant agreements with the country's creditors—despite all they had claimed up until then—so as to avoid complete ruin. If these problems had been dealt with in a different, more realistic manner, Greece would have borne a smaller overall cost. The most extreme example can be found in Alexis Tsipras: if he had signed the agreement that had been proposed to him upon his inauguration, Greece would have shouldered a much smaller burden than the 90 billion euros and the cost of capital controls levied after several months of meaningless blusters.

Perhaps it goes without saying that in these years of crisis, despite the fact that it voted for these reforms and fiscal adjustments, the Greek political system did not believe in their necessity for even a moment. It sought to avoid conflict with the various interest groups that preyed, and continue to prey, on state institutions and state-controlled enterprises. Incumbent governments and the Greek political system in general never came up with alternatives to the proposals submitted by creditors; even worse, despite ultimately accepting the terms of the memorandums once they had no other choice, the nation's entire political leadership avoided strictly implementing them in these very years of crisis. Greece paid a huge price for this, as it could no longer claim 'ownership' of the programmes, something often repeated by international organisations and considered critical for the success of these economic plans. In other words, these Greek governments sought to avoid 'ownership' of the memorandums that they had signed, thinking that this would salvage their political capital. This never happened.

Apart from the political system's overall flaws, the specific weaknesses of public administration have played a significant role in its failure to address the crisis. This will be further discussed below; here I only point to the inability of the civil service to support the Greek state during negotiations for the signing of the First Memorandum, and the inaccuracy of Greek statistical information.

Certainly, in political terms, the European Union bears a large share of responsibility for the outbreak of the Greek crisis. The European Commission declined to take on the role it had been assigned in monitoring the Greek economy, and the partisan solidarity of its President X. Almunia was such that he expressed no reaction when, on 30 September 2009, the incumbent New Democracy government sent data tables to Eurostat without the statistics for 2008 and 2009 so that the state of the economy would not be evident in the run up to the 4 October elections. Yet that very year, while the Greek state predicted it would require 40.5 billion euros in loans, it ended up borrowing the astounding sum of 105 billion.

Finally, nobody representing Greece, the EU or the IMF had a true sense of the magnitude of the problem. First of all, even in late 2009, PASOK insisted on disbursing a special 'solidarity allowance', which was obviously funded through additional debt. Furthermore, the Greek government believed that it could solve its problems by borrowing 40 billion euros—a figure that both the EU and IMF initially agreed on. In other words, many factors played a significant role in the creation of conditions that led to the crisis, and we can only understand the crisis in all its complexity if we take them all into account.

The First Memorandum

The negotiations between the Greek government and the Troika came to a close on 1 May 2010. It is rather doubtful if there were any negotiations at all. It is more likely that the Greek government was simply obliged to sign a document that it was not prepared to negotiate. The next day, the Council of Ministers accepted the agreement, and on the afternoon of that same day, the finance ministers of the Eurozone ratified it. On 3 May, the European Central Bank declared it would continue to accept Greek bonds as collateral for the provision of liquidity to Greek banks. On 6 May, the Memorandum was adopted by the Parliament and became law; two days later, the leaders of the Eurozone member states ratified the finance ministers' decisions. Finally, on Sunday, 9 May 2010, the Eurozone finance ministers agreed on the creation of the temporary European Financial Stability Facility, aimed at supporting Eurozone member states facing economic or fiscal stress due to emergency circumstances. This agreement constituted a significant departure from past Eurozone policies, and many believed that the foundations of common economic governance could be found at this point. In fact, there was still a long way to go.

Based on the agreement, a total of 110 billion euros would be made available to Greece, of which the IMF would provide 30 billion. The rest was made available through bilateral loans from the Eurozone member states. These would be paid out in instalments. Before each instalment, the Troika would monitor the timely implementation of the agreement, and consent to the disbursement of the corresponding funds to Greece. Interest rates varied: interest on the IMF loans was approximately 3.8 per cent, while Eurozone loans carried an interest of 4.5 to 5 per cent, which would rise to around 6 per cent over time. In other words, Greece was to pay dearly for its sins.

But beyond this, the terms of loan repayment were such that it would probably be impossible for Greece to fulfil them given the state of its economy. Repayment was scheduled to begin three years after each disbursement, in eight quarterly instalments over two years. Thus, for example, repayment of the May 2010 instalment was meant to begin in May 2013, and would have to be paid in full by May 2015.

The aims of the Memorandum were simple: first came the reduction of fiscal deficits, so that the country's debt would stop mounting. Second came a series of structural measures that would allow Greece to regain its competitiveness and address the imbalances in its external transactions. This was achieved through the so-called internal devaluation process that substituted currency devaluation—no longer possible due to Greece's participation in the Eurozone. The logic behind these choices was simple. Greece would experience a reduction in income, but would have the chance for a quick recovery. According to the drafters of the Memorandum, such a thing could happen in three years, that is, by mid-2013. Finally, the Memorandum sought to safeguard financial stability.

Thus the Memorandum was presented as the proposal for recovery of the Greek economy that no political party in the nation was in a position to offer. But its implementation required political behaviours and managerial capacities impossible to find in Greece. The situation worsened because the Greek economy was facing very serious problems, problems that required time to solve and were only aggravated by the Memorandum. In fact, the Memorandum maintained that these problems could be solved over a very short time.

Over the first year, the programme's results were not too shabby. On the most basic level, bankruptcy had been avoided. Secondly, the general budget deficit was reduced by an impressive 5.5 per cent of GDP, in line with the forecasts. But revision of the deficit from 13.6 per cent to 15.4 per cent rendered achievement of the 8.1 per cent deficit goal impossible. The deficit reduction also affected GDP, which fell for the third consecutive year by 4.5 per cent. Unemployment surpassed 12 per cent, average nominal wages fell by 5 per cent, and inflation remained high at 4.7 per cent thanks to an increase in indirect taxes. In contrast, the current account deficit showed few signs of improvement, dropping to 10.4 per cent in 2010, compared with 11 per cent the year before.

From the outset, fiscal adjustment prioritised tax hikes over expenditure reductions. However, experience suggests that lower public spending (and not a higher tax rate) is key to successful fiscal retrenchments. On the other hand, spending cuts and structural reforms posed the greatest challenge to the government, because of their impact on its electoral constituency. As a result, there was substantial reluctance to reduce expenses, and even greater reluctance in the implementation of major reforms.

More specifically, the structural interventions incorporated into the programme included comprehensive pension and healthcare reforms, privatisations, product- and labour-market liberalisation, the deregulation of 'closed professions' and the merger or closure of several public sector agencies. Inevitably, these were the measures that generated the strongest opposition. Tax hikes may be unpopular, but it is structural reforms that spark the most bitter conflicts, because they threaten the very existence of entire social groups. The opening up of a closed profession, for instance, challenges the very existence of the hitherto protected professionals.

As one might expect, the labour market offers some of the most characteristic examples of the kind of sweeping reforms pushed through by the Memorandum, from the early stages of its implementation. Hoping to cut labour costs and boost employment, the Troika doggedly sought to impose the priority of firm-level over sectoral agreements. Up until that point, Law 1876/90 based all collective bargaining on a sectoral level; enterprise agreements only came into play if they offered workers better terms. However, and herein lay the major challenge, this meant shifting the entire culture of collective negotiations from a model where enterprises were only indirectly involved, to one where they lay at the very heart of the bargaining process. This meant setting up and promoting enterprise (i.e. firm-level unions). This, in turn, threatened the primacy of existing sectoral (trade) unions, which served to segment the market into insiders and outsiders.

Implementation of the Memorandum was not only met with opposition from the most affected groups but also from the government itself, which sought in every which way to adapt its policies based on their political cost. In any case, during the first quarter of its implementation, the Memorandum's results were positive and the Troika's report highlighted the progress that had been made. This temporary euphoria continued, albeit at a declining rate, until the end of 2010. But in early 2011, the evaluation report compiled by the EU, the ECB and the IMF cited a shortfall in revenues and excessive spending outside the central government. The report went on to demand that new measures be taken for fiscal consolidation.

Meanwhile, of course, reactions from the opposition and the unions were bitter, which did not help foster a climate that might strengthen the economy. Even worse, during one of the ensuing rallies, protestors set fire to a bank, which resulted in the death of three people. In what was an increasingly confrontational atmosphere, there remained little room for feasible solutions. The government took a critical attitude against the very measures it adopted, fostering the impression that it could have chosen an alternative path but was not allowed to do so by the Troika. No attempts were made to explain the situation or to present an alternative—if, indeed, there was one to be found. An environment of fanaticism and oversimplification prevailed that proved fertile ground for the proliferation of demagogy and extremism on each side of the spectrum. Contributing to this oversimplification and fanning the flames of discord, the leader of the opposition, Samaras, shoulders much of the responsibility for this development. At one stage, he even declared that he could eliminate the entire public deficit within a year. These rather simplistic and extremely dangerous—as would be proven in retrospect—views were enshrined in the 'Zappeion I' and 'Zappeion II' programmes. These legitimized Syriza's simplistic rhetoric, and through the latter, the xenophobic, far-right party Golden Dawn. Greek politics was in a downward spiral egged on by the pursuit of power, and no one involved cared about the consequences of their actions.

It has been argued that the reforms included in the First Memorandum were unrealistic. Indeed, a reduction of the deficit by austerity measures amounting to some 18 per cent of GDP in three years was on its own a colossal reallocation of wealth that could hardly have been accomplished over such a short time. Besides, such transfers of resources are always met with violent social opposition. On the other hand, it became clear that no government, including PASOK, was in a position to implement even the most urgent measures: instead, they sought to protect groups of supporters, ignoring problems and creating the impression that the 'foreigners' were to blame for everything.

Furthermore, several of the predictions underpinning the Memorandum proved to be completely unrealistic. The primary surplus target of 6 per cent after 2014 was a striking example: few countries have ever achieved such a surplus, and Greece was unlikely to come anywhere near that mark. Forecasts of the expected recession were no better: between 2009 and 2012, Greece's GDP was expected to shrink by 7.5 per cent. When the final figure amounted to 23 per cent, little was left of the original calculations of the memorandum.

C. Iordanoglou has highlighted the fundamental assumptions underpinning the First Memorandum, none of which turned out to be realistic. Namely, first, that Greek public debt was sustainable; second, that Greece could regain access to capital markets in 2012; third, that the recession would be deepest in 2010 and continue through 2011, with the recovery beginning in 2012; the fourth and final point was also possibly the most crucial, and had to do with Greece's ability to fully implement the Memorandum's terms, and the extent to which this process would proceed as agreed upon.

These four assumptions that propped up the Memorandum had to do with the aforementioned perception that the problem in Greece was a problem of liquidity, which could be quickly addressed. That it was the first country to enter the process of a Memorandum made it easier for the Europeans to treat it as a special case, imposing terms with a rather moralistic undertone that would have most probably have been unworkable in any country for that matter.

The possibility of additional support for the Greek economy was first mentioned in the autumn of 2010, when interest rates on Greek bonds began to rise again. The developments to come confirmed these fears, especially since 2011 proved to be a year of major economic downturn. It became clear that the cost of this additional funding would be massive. As a result, the private sector would be called upon to shoulder some of the burden of debt consolidation, while privatisations would also have to be considered more thoroughly. This, at least, was the opinion expressed by Germany and German Chancellor Angela Merkel, who managed to convince the French President Nicolas Sarkozy, and by extension the rest of Europe.

The agreement reached on 21 July 2011 summarised these new developments. Greece would be offered a new loan of 109 billion euros at a low interest rate, while holders of Greek bonds would have to accept a 21 per cent haircut. Old bonds would be exchanged for new thirty-year bonds guaranteed by the EFSF. Greece undertook further commitments, as summarised by the adoption of the Medium Term Plan for 2011–15, which included additional fiscal retrenchment to the tune of 28 billion euros. Furthermore, privatisations were expected to yield another 50 billion euros to reduce public debt, as the 'voluntary' bond exchange was not sufficient to bring the debt to sustainable levels.

But the harsh reality of the situation would soon become clear. First came the conflict between the Greek government and the Troika, stemming from the efforts of the Greek finance minister, E. Venizelos, to renegotiate the 2011 deficit targets, which seemed untenable and required additional fiscal measures. The conflict ended in the Troika's withdrawal from negotiations, which triggered a U-turn on the Greek side.

On 26 October, the two parties reached a consensus and announced the New Loan Agreement. It was now recognised that Greece's debt was unsustainable. Privately owned bonds would have to face a significant haircut before being exchanged for new long-term bonds guaranteed by the EFSF. Aid to Greece would amount to 130 billion euros, which was to be added to the 45 billion remaining from the First Memorandum. Of this amount, 100 billion would be used to meet the Greek state's borrowing needs until 2014, while around forty billion would be allocated to recapitalise Greek banks, which had suffered losses as a result of the debt restructuring and faced rising shares of non-performing loans. Meanwhile, Greece would need to adhere to the terms of the Medium Term Plan that had already become a law, and continue on its path of reforms.

But political developments would soon determine what happened next. On 31 October, after an attack on the president of the republic a few days earlier at a commemorative parade in Thessaloniki, Prime Minister Papandreou announced his intention to call a referendum. This resulted in fierce opposition on both a national and international scale, and Papandreou was called to a meeting in Cannes with Sarkozy, the French president, and German Chancellor Angela Merkel, where he was asked to retract his proposal. Shortly thereafter he resigned, and on 11 November, a coalition government was formed led by New Democracy, including PASOK and Laos, led by former deputy of the European Central Bank Loukas Papadimos.[2] This government was assembled with a specific goal: to carry out the planned public debt restructuring known as the Private Sector Involvement (PSI) and pave the way for the Second Memorandum. These negotiations came to completion within the first two months of 2012.

In conclusion, the First Memorandum did indeed prevent Greece from going bankrupt, something that would have resulted in its expulsion from the Eurozone. But it proved inadequate to support the Greek economy. The huge amount of disinvestment that the Greek economy experienced is perhaps the most typical example of the blow it suffered—more so than the significant decrease in GDP. There are many reasons for this, and some have already been elaborated above. First of all, 60 per cent of budgetary adjustment was based on higher tax revenues, with lower expenditures accounting for the remaining 40 per cent. But experience suggests that reducing expenditures has a smaller contractionary effect on economic activity than increasing taxes. Secondly, there was clearly an inefficacy and delay in implementing measures. The combination of these two factors led to a much greater economic downturn than expected. Furthermore, this downturn was also caused by the effects of the fiscal adjustment, which were much larger than initially expected. This had to do with the well-known problem of fiscal multipliers, which meant that budgetary adjustments equalling one percentage point of GDP caused a greater economic contraction in Greece due to the closed nature of its economy in comparison with other countries. Later, the IMF would acknowledge its errors in calculating multipliers, but the price had already been paid.

The Second Memorandum

On 12 February 2012, Parliament voted through the Memorandum of Economic and Financial Policies (MEFP) and the Memorandum of Understanding on Specific Economic Policy Conditionality, both of which became Law 4046/2012. These measures sought to reverse the Greek economy's downward trend. Along with these reforms, the Memorandum created a new web of preconditions meant to finally 'resolve' the process of restructuring public debt that had been completed in early 2012.

After the Public Sector Involvement (PSI), the latter was reduced by approximately 106 billion euros held exclusively by private investors. The debt was reduced by another 31.9 billion euros in December 2012, amounting to a total reduction of 137.9 billion. However, benefits from this reduction of public debt were extremely limited for a number of reasons. First was the need to recapitalise Greek banks, which on its own required 42 billion euros in 2012 alone. Second was the need to borrow in order to buy back debt in December 2012; thirdly, because 16 billion euros of outstanding debt were held by Greek pension funds and other public sector bodies, thus constituting intra-governmental borrowing that could not lead to a genuine reduction in overall public debt. In fact, it became necessary for the country to borrow 4.5 billion euros from the EFSF to compensate pension funds for the loss of their assets, following the debt restructuring. It became necessary to borrow another 11.9 billion euros to cover the budget deficit in 2012, in addition to another 1.9 billion euros used to cover other government obligations. The overall net outcome was 51.2 billion euros.

The new Memorandum for the support of the Greek state provided for a new funding programme totalling 130 billion euros. If to this amount we also add the funds remaining from the first programme, then the figure for total aid now stood at a staggering 167 billion euros. At this point, the rationale was that Greece would be able to proceed to implementation of this new programme with no delay, and in doing so, halt its economy's downward spiral. As it turned out, things did not follow this course. On 11 April 2012, elections were announced for 6 May. But the result did not allow for the formation of a government, and elections were repeated on 17 June. Uncertainty had reached extreme levels, as revealed by the Economic Climate Index, which recorded its lowest rates of the period.

In June 2012, a coalition government was formed, halting the deterioration of most economic indexes. But the new programme had once again miscalculated its initial goals, and new, additional measures were required. Furthermore, in late December 2012 an IMF report noted the huge deviations in privatisation procedures, reorganisation of tax administration and control of public spending, accumulation of arrears, administration of justice, but also a series of other structural measures. At this point, a revision of the second Economic Adjustment Programme adopted by Greece in February of 2012 was inevitable.

Towards the end of 2012, the national political situation began to stabilise, and the economic situation followed suit. Despite the harsh conditions, the year's economic data proved to be better than one would expect: the budget deficit fell to just 5.8 per cent of GDP, the primary deficit was a mere 0.8 per cent, while debt was limited to 156.9 per cent. In any case, the improvements recorded in 2013 did not come as a surprise. For the first time, in this year, a small primary surplus was recorded, while a small surplus was also recorded in the current account. GDP continued to contract, albeit at a rate slower than originally predicted. As a result, Moody's upgraded Greece's rating in November 2013 for the first time since the outbreak of the crisis. Beyond these relatively positive developments, there were other, not-so favourable ones. Deflation set in, which suggested a response to the fall in demand, but also meant higher debt burdens for net debtors. Meanwhile, in these years, the banking system was subject to radical changes and underwent a process of extreme concentration.

In 2014, the situation developed in a similar manner to the previous year. It seemed one could hope that the Greek economy would finally put the era of memorandums behind it at the end of this year or the beginning of the next. The problems plaguing Greece remained extremely urgent, but at least the country could stand up on its feet. This, at least, is what all economic indicators pointed to—particularly GDP, which rose slightly for the first time during this period of crisis.

The political system resists

Many have argued that Syriza's rise to power represented the collapse of the political system established after the fall of the dictatorship in 1974. I do not see how such a view can be justified, especially since Syriza's rise to power constituted this political system's last attempt at survival, as Syriza enshrined and continues to enshrine the post-dictatorial conception of politics in its purest form.

Certainly, many significant changes took place in the political landscape during these years of crisis. As both Voulgaris and Ilias Nikolakopoulos have shown from a political perspective, it is possible to differentiate three phases of the crisis. In the first years of the crisis, that is to say 2008 and 2009, the government and the party that represented it, New Democracy, justified their inertia by invoking the theory of Greece's 'immunity' from the global crisis. The country was shielded from what was happening internationally, as its relations with the international environment were limited, and the Greek banks seeking to expand into South Eastern Europe had not invested in toxic assets. For its part, the main opposition party, as we saw, remained out of touch with reality and pursued the conventional Greek political strategy of cultivating expectations it would later be unable to support.

The 2009 elections led to the sound defeat of New Democracy, which recorded the lowest percentage of votes in its history at the polls. On the other hand, PASOK received a high number of votes, thus hiding the cracks in the system.

The second phase of the crisis began in 2010 and lasted until the beginning of 2011. The main aspect of this period, according to Voulgaris and Nikolakopoulos, was the realisation of the seriousness of the situation and the bankruptcy of the Greek state. This was a time of self-criticism and careless statements regarding post-dictatorial developments in Greece, as well as their complete denial. Within this environment, the rationale of a 'kleptocracy' gradually emerged, which formed the basis for a moralistic approach to the problem plaguing Greece. Both the radical left and radical right supported this rationale. The result was none other than an opportunity for Golden Dawn to emerge from obscurity.

Despite the reactions it provoked, the First Memorandum was not actually met with great resistance. Certainly, the austerity measures led to a migration of the electorate, especially away from PASOK, but in broad terms they did not lead to significant changes as recorded in the polls. Moreover, local elections in November 2010 did not point to any major changes: PASOK narrowly managed a victory with 36 per cent of the vote, while New Democracy took 33 per cent. Of the remaining parties, the Communist Party had seemed to benefit the most from public opinion.

The third phase of the crisis began in the spring of 2011 and came to a close with the double elections of 2012. By this point, the recession had caused major damage to Greek society and the economy, and the 'indignados' movement gradually began to manifest itself. Surely, it was unthinkable that the measures adopted—which by late 2013 amounted to 30 per cent of GDP—would not incite reaction and social tensions, even if these social tensions did not take the form of overt demonstrations and rallies. The prevailing rationale of political discourse had abandoned all contact with reality and began to refer to an 'occupation' the very same moment that anti-German sentiments gained more and more ground.

This was the same moment that the 'memorandum–anti-memorandum' opposition took hold, upsetting all pre-established equilibriums. During this phase, supporters of the drachma and sceptics of the Eurozone grew in number. New Democracy's adoption of anti-memorandum rhetoric may have seemed to its benefit, but in fact it legitimised a dichotomy within the political system founded on divisions that did not fall along party lines. Indeed, the economic crisis had led to a political crisis. Y. Voulgaris does a good job of describing what exactly this anti-memorandum camp represented:

> This anti-memorandum sentiment was a wave of protest steeped in a polarising, populist and nationalist rhetoric, and a divisively simple interpretation of the Greek problem, which for yet another time in our modern history reproduced the demagogically powerful but politically useless 'blaming of the other.' Here, the 'anti' camp produced neither concrete policies nor capable government, nor a realistic assessment of the disaster at hand.

Indeed, the 'memorandum–anti-memorandum' dilemma is a fictional one. The only dilemma Greece truly had to face was the preservation of its current system in the face of all the mandated reforms. In fact, the 'memorandum–anti-memorandum' opposition hid the interests affected by each of the attempts at changing the country's economic structure, and it sought to disguise a harsh reality in moral terms: there was no way that incomes and pensions would not be reduced. Incomes would shrink any which way the situation developed. The question was whether they could be reduced taking social inequalities into account instead of the power of interest groups, and whether it would be possible to create a framework of development that would allow the country to see its future optimistically.

Antonis Samaras bears full responsibility for legitimising the discourse of the anti-memorandum camp among wider sections of the general population with his slogan, 'Let's tear up the Memorandum'. He did finally manage to become prime minister, but he simultaneously enabled Alexis Tsipras and those around him to leap into the centre of the political scene, as they repeated those same phrases. Meanwhile, when in the name of supporting the Greek people it accepted the 'indignados' of Syntagma Square, Syriza, in turn, legitimised Golden Dawn.

Of all the changes observed in the Greek political system, it is crucial to understand how the left-wing–right-wing axis of electoral preference was sidelined and replaced with the memorandum–anti-memorandum opposition, in which economic and European issues were at stake. A second observation regarding the changes seen in the Greek political system during these years of crisis has to do with the fact that groups of citizens expressing leftist economic views and socially conservative views were not satisfied with their political representation. This was exploited by parties such as ANEL and Golden Dawn, both of which attracted supporters of social conservatism and state intervention. What is more, one should highlight the fact that a considerable number of voters until 2009 chose not to vote, at the same time that age became a key determinant in the voting process, surpassing all other influential factors up until that point.

Poll-wise, the great reversal took place in June of 2011 when PASOK's total vote decreased by eight percentage points, something that it would never recover from. The party was collapsing as its voters migrated towards the smaller anti-memorandum parties. In early November 2011, in an extremely tense atmosphere, the Papandreou government fell and was replaced by a coalition government led by Loukas Papademos, who had previously served as governor of the Bank of Greece and vice president of the European Central Bank. The coalition was formed by PASOK, New

Democracy and the far-right LAOS party, whose sole objective was to deal with a series of obligations to foreign creditors, of which the most important was the reduction of public debt in private hands. In return, Greece would receive another round of loan support.

Apart from the impact the crisis had on the political realm, it also sowed emotions that acted to inhibit mobilisation of the population. Contrary to the media-driven reports of 'gigantic' protests against the memorandums, the traumatic experience of the crisis arrested any forms of mobilisation. Even those who had not experienced the crisis traumatically and sought to mobilise only managed a weak turnout.

From the same perspective, since 2008, Greece experienced a great increase in suicides. Up until the late 1990s, Greece had the lowest suicide rate of the EU-15 countries. The rate then steadily increased and first passed the threshold of one suicide per day in 2008. In 2012, this figure ranged between two and three incidences per day.

In this adverse environment, the Samaras-led government that emerged victorious in the elections of 2012 showed, as mentioned above, that it was possible to stabilise the economy and lead it out of the memorandum cycle. In retrospect, it became clear that the sole criterion guiding the party's choices was its own political survival. So, after the 2014 elections for the EU Parliament, Samaras began to reshuffle the government with clear pre-election aims in mind; for this reason, he included a large number of officials belonging to the more populist wing of his party. Towards late 2014, it was clear that Syriza intended to use the upcoming vote on the new president of the republic to trigger a national election. The Samaras-led government proceeded with the process of electing the president. This effort failed, and resulted in preparations for new elections shortly before the conclusion of the Second Memorandum. The result was rather surprising, both because of the high percentage of votes for Syriza and the party's decision to cooperate with ANEL, a far-right party, to form a government. In fact, at the time of this writing, no political party in Greece had managed to articulate a position that transcended the rationale underpinning post-dictatorial politics in Greece, a rationale that was never anything more than the management of public finances in a consumption-oriented logic. Regardless of which parties were in power at that point, it was—and still is—perfectly clear that none of them was in a position to overcome this rationale, in which the conquest of political power was an end in and of itself. This tendency found its most extreme iteration in Syriza's rise to power.

'So much damage in such little time'[3]

In retrospect, it can be argued that Syriza came to the negotiating table with a very aggressive attitude and minimal experience of how these negotiations actually worked. Even worse, Syriza demanded to impose its own 'programme'—in fact, and according to all indications, this amounted to a list of objectives or intentions—in place of the memorandums. For Yanis Varoufakis, Syriza's first minister of finance, the government's 'mission' was

> replacement of the memorandum agreements which reproduce the crisis of debt and recession with a new Contract between Greece and Europe based on this 'therapeutic' sequence: first, a specific form of debt restructuring, then low primary surpluses (a maximum of 2% of GDP) and finally far reaching reforms (targeting large scale rent seeking).

All these, according to Varoufakis, constituted the elements of a fair agreement.

The means at Syriza's disposal—according, as always, to Varoufakis—were its willingness for concessions (in the form of privatisation) but also its readiness to break with negotiations if the Troika insisted on its 'failed' programme. For Varoufakis, such a rupture did not mean leaving the Eurozone. Instead, it meant three reactions to aggressive moves made by creditors: (1) postponement of payments to the IMF if lenders restricted liquidity of the state during negotiations; (2) delay of bond repayments held by the ECB as part of the SMP programme, if the ECB took steps that would force Greek banks to close; and (3) activating a parallel system of payments in euros if lenders delayed negotiations so as to leave Greece no choice but capitulation.

By all accounts, these were childish exercises on paper that did not account in the least for the consequences of these actions on the Greek economy and the way in which Greece's lenders would react. Syriza sought to radically change the 'rules of the game', in a move without precedent around the world. The government, in its ploys for attainment of a 'fair' solution to the Troika, was indifferent to the impact this would have on the residents of its country and its economy in general. That much is clear from its indifference to the potential consequences of countermeasures to the 'aggressive' actions of lenders, such as activation of a parallel system of payments to the euro—a move with completely unforeseeable results.

In writings and interviews, Varoufakis lists an inventory of faults—as he calls them—of the Syriza government that led to its defeat. Of all of them, it is worth mentioning the complete lack of disposition to negotiate, but also the belligerent imposition of the government's views through an underlying approach of unchecked moralising and manipulation that might have worked in university hall politics, but was rather ineffective in international negotiations. In fact, Syriza was most interested in its own political dominance, and not at all in the economy, which was nothing more than the means by which it could impose itself politically. This, in fact, was clear in speeches given by Prime Minister Tsipras.

The negotiations that resulted in the Third Memorandum, or, in other words, in Varoufakis's personal defeat, were inevitably followed by successive governmental capitulations, which he himself claims he is not responsible for. In the end, the government's weakness was exposed through the interruption in negotiations as soon as the banks closed. This was the view of Varoufakis, who essentially wanted to show that he had a plan, and that the unpleasant outcome was a result of not following it ... Essentially, in many more words, and not without embellishing the situation, he says what Deputy Prime Minister Yannis Dragasakis expressed in a phrase: 'We thought that if we threatened to exit, the Europeans would be scared.' Certainly, all the Greek negotiators were surprised to find that Wolfgang Schäuble, Germany's finance minister, was not only open to Greece leaving the Eurozone but even offered to help the process along himself, offering assistance so that this exit could happen in the smoothest and least painful way.[4] This was an element tied to the entire guiding philosophy of the negotiations that was hardly discussed, and in all its grandeur, it shows the naivety or stupidity—depending on how you see it—of negotiations under the Syriza and ANEL governments.

One of the more interesting aspects of Syriza's negotiation method was the deep conviction of its key players that they had justice on their side, and that this would be enough to impose their views. In an interview given upon assuming the position of finance minister, Euclid Tsakalotos noted that negotiations with the Troika had become more difficult 'because there were agendas that had nothing to do with the Greek economy. They had to do with the success or failure of the Syriza government, which would have set a bad precedent for some.'[5] The after-the-fact justification of the difficulty of negotiations at an EU level due to the presence of factors beyond the issue directly at hand—such as domestic political considerations—shows the incredible naivety (at best) with which the Tsipras government acted in these months.

What has not been mentioned up until this point, and is ostentatiously ignored in all of Varoufakis's writings, is the role that they expected Vladimir Putin and Russia to play in the success of Syriza's negotiation 'tactics'. It appears that the entire government expected Putin to support the Greek bluff, rendering the prospect of Greece's exit from the Eurozone truly credible, resulting in Europe's retreat and a writing off of Greek debt. Apart from this, the government seemed to be ready to leave the Eurozone in the very unlikely chance—as they saw it—in which their negotiation tactics failed, provided they had Russian support. Tsipras seems to have understood that any attempt at switching currencies without abundant currency reserves would end disastrously. He had asked Russia for a loan of 10 billion USD, but Putin instead most likely played Greece as a card in the Ukrainian situation, and of course refused to grant the loan. By all accounts, Tsipras became aware of his inability to secure loans from Russia on the night the referendum was held; this was the reason for his striking change in attitude regarding how he interpreted the 'No' vote, and his subsequent acceptance of all the Troika's demands. As for Syriza's leaders' stances on the drachma, Manos Matsaganis has successfully shown that two main groups were active in Syriza: the first was prepared to lead Greece to the drachma even without the support of Russian funds, while the other was not. In any case, nobody stated their position against an exit from the Eurozone.

On the whole, the government's tactics during negotiations achieved nothing except a pileup of errors, dramatically worsening Greece's economic and political situation. First of all, the aggression it adopted, all the more aggravated by the finance minister's conduct, distanced the nation from the sympathies of other powerful countries. This was chiefly true of France, which was inclined to support Greece because of its own interests, but did not wish to be identified with its aggressive tactics. Furthermore, the Syriza–ANEL-led government distanced Greece from the Southern European nations because of its aggression, and because of the problems these countries would face if Syriza's strategy proved effective. The situation worsened after efforts made by the Syriza government to establish close relationships with Russia, China and even Iran. Just at the moment when the crisis in Ukraine had reached its peak, Greece's stance led to its diplomatic isolation not only in relation to other European Union countries but also NATO itself. Finally, as the situation proved, in its naivety Syriza had overestimated Greece's importance to the Eurozone.

The government concluded its last evaluation of the Second Memorandum with adoption of the required measures in Parliament and began the process of negotiating a new agreement with its partners. So, the question remains: Why did the things that happened after seven months—under much worse conditions, and with the adoption of much more painful measures—not just happen from the very beginning? The answer to this question was supplied by Euclid Tsakalotos himself in an interview on TV, in which he admitted that the government resorted to a referendum so as to maintain party unity. It all amounted to an attempt by Tsipras and his followers to hold on to power, and they could only hold on to this power if they kept their party unified; the cost that this would have for the nation was of no importance to Syriza.

Despite whatever protests were still heard, signing of the Third Memorandum meant the end of the memorandum–anti-memorandum opposition. This was mostly thanks to the complete disenchantment with the anti-memorandum camp's prophets: after seven months in power, the only thing they had achieved was the country's international downfall and the signing of an agreement much worse than that which the country would have signed based on the situation in January 2015.

As Yiannis Voulgaris has rightly pointed out, the defeat of the anti-memorandum camp

> establishes that the only way to bring the country back to normal and back into international markets as an autonomous state is the way that all the other countries subject to memorandums had to pursue. They secured a minimum level of internal agreement, fulfilled the conditions of the loan agreement they had signed, and promoted wider reforms through their own initiative.

Perhaps this is now a chance for the Greek political system to realise that the country can only move forwards by taking advantage of its capabilities in its given international context, and certainly by no longer proclaiming itself a special case worthy of exceptional treatment.

It is in any case promising that the vast majority of Greeks are in favour of a future in the European Union. As Voulgaris aptly states once again:

> In this current crisis, the forces that tipped and tilted the scales in favor of rescuing the country proved ideologically, psychologically and socially strong enough. Because our modern national identity is interwoven with the idea of Europe. Because broader social groups composed of workers, the middle classes, and professionals, all understand almost instinctively that even their narrowest interests are intertwined with our participation in the European process. Because faced with the ghost of the drachma, the social majority seems to have realized yet again the European dimension of its material existence.

HISTORY'S SPOILED CHILDREN

IN LIEU OF AN EPILOGUE

The theme of this book is the transformation of a small province of the Ottoman Empire—a Muslim state—into a modern European state. This process was far from straightforward; indeed, the history of the other states comprising South Eastern Europe, or that which in the language of the region's inhabitants is referred to as the Balkans, is evidence of the upheavals that can occur in similar historical processes. In other words, historical processes are not deterministic; they do not always have a happy ending.

The problems arising during the process of the modern Greek state's formation could be equated to the corresponding problems in this period resulting from the West's efforts to impose its own political and cultural model on communities foreign if not decidedly hostile to it.[1] That the Greeks of the nineteenth and twentieth centuries were Christian and the Ottomans were Muslim is of little importance to the extent that both were confronted—or are being confronted—explicitly or implicitly as territories to be civilised and in no way treated as equal partners in the political project that has been rather poorly termed 'modernisation'. In any case, the Greeks' Christian identity never ceased to represent the Great Schism—particularly when compared with Western European conceptions, something not always appreciated and much less understood.

Yet such a comparison brings up a difference that cannot be ignored. This book is about Greece and the Greeks, and this decidedly national categorisation refers by association to the country that Western Europeans consider the foundation of their civilisation. This perspective offers an easy interpretation of the particular way in which the West happened to treat the populations that not only rebelled against the Ottoman Empire in the name of Christianity but invoked, by virtue of their name, a connection with a past in which Europe saw the roots of its own identity.

In fact, the question of what Greece actually represented and who the Greeks were before the creation of the Greek state was rather unclear. Consequently, the process by which both Greece and a Greek identity was established was not as straightforward as is often assumed. This is because, for the most part, we content ourselves with the study of processes by which a national consciousness is formed. Doubtless, these processes are completely necessary for us to be able to speak of the 'Greeks', but they are by no means unique or exclusive factors in the process by which Greece and the Greek identity was consolidated.

Greece was above all the product of travellers' imaginations but also of economic encounters and political oppositions. Indeed, by the mid-eighteenth century and later, this included oppositions between states in the context of the Eastern Question. In other words, it was the product of circumstances that gave birth to the Western European world, without actually belonging to it. Perhaps this can explain the way that Western Europeans often treat Greece as a baffling puzzle and account for the conflicting comments and observations Western Europeans make about the Greeks.

But beyond this, and to some extent as a consequence, Greece was also a product of the important transformations taking place in the Ottoman Empire during the seventeenth and eighteenth centuries. Here I am not only referring to the development of trade and the opening of the Eastern Mediterranean economy to the West, a subject about which much has been written; the process by which the Ottoman state reformulated itself in order to confront internal and external foes was equally important. This process led to forms of governance that allowed Greek-speaking Orthodox elites who had established themselves within patriarchal circles in Constantinople to create a new and unprecedented political and communicational network in South Eastern Europe; it also allowed them to nurture ambitions that would have been unthinkable previously. In a similar manner, though on a local scale, notables were in a position to be integrated into this network and benefit from it, just as they were able to gain political and economic benefits from the consequences that transformations in the Ottoman administration had for their homelands. In other words, the political, military and ecclesiastical elites wielded political and economic power on the eve of the War of Greek Independence, and they inevitably sought to monopolise it. From another perspective, every attempt at monopolising power came with significant risks, which could ultimately jeopardise the power that had been acquired.

It could be argued that the Greek War of Independence was an inevitable consequence of these changes. Its realisation required initiatives and an organisation in which those present and absent indicated the range of interests at stake. The War for Independence was waged by those who found themselves—or risked finding themselves—at the margins of power within the context of the Ottoman administration, but also by others displaced or simply far removed from power. These were groups that scholarship has termed the 'marginal elite'. But from the moment the war began, new factors emerged, rendering its outcome completely unforeseeable, a product of choices that did not have to do with the efforts of the Greeks fighting the war.

In fact, the founding of the Greek state was a product of both international and domestic processes that rearranged the place of Orthodox populations in the Ottoman Empire. Above all else, it was a struggle of Christians against Muslims, in which various groups of Orthodox leaders sought to lead the charge. But the way in which the war developed limited their ambitions and finally led to their destruction, while the geographic, and then the state dimensions of Greek freedom were limited to a small piece of the Southern Balkan Peninsula. It was no longer the Phanariots that had a say but the local notables, each of whom sought to claim power on behalf of the groups they belonged to, thus driving the war to the precipice of defeat. The Battle of Navarino, an 'untoward event' according to British diplomatic terminology at the time, was what finally led to the creation of the Greek state.

The new state necessarily had to survive by adjusting to the conditions that had created it. And these conditions were not only related to its small size—at least in relation to the hopes of the fighters in the war—or the international context and the imposition of a monarchy that came to Greece with the aim of civilising the population, but also to new social and political arrangements. So, if on the one hand, the institutional framework created by the Bavarians was by all accounts innovative and unprecedented for the region of the Eastern Mediterranean or South Eastern Europe in which it was to be implemented, on the other hand the techniques and mechanisms of political governance as well as the management of power could not simply be changed from one day to the next. This was all the more true given that the Bavarians had neither the human nor economic resources necessary to impose their choices.

Indeed, from various different perspectives, the Greek state that was born in 1833 constituted an extension of Ottoman reality. New institutions and the political discourse that accompanied them may have concealed this reality; so did efforts made by the state—in addition to scholars at the time, and scholars to this day—to de-Ottomanise the past. In fact, the continuities between these two historical periods can be discerned in whichever sector of political and social activity we examine. In terms of the management of political power, this was confirmed by the way in which the state treated its populations: under no circumstances did it seek—nor did it have the capability or ability—to gain full control over its territory and local communities. It contented itself with governing the population via the mediation of the local elites and by negotiating with them.

The particularity of the Greek case in comparison with the examples offered by neighbouring countries is most likely related to the way notable groups were managed: regardless of the political choices it made at the time, the Bavarian regime never excluded particular groups from the political playing field. This created a precedent that would remain in effect even after the fall of the autocracy. This was an important distinguishing element of Greek political life that differentiated it from the other countries of South Eastern Europe and also created the foundations for the democratic tradition that developed throughout the entire nineteenth century.

In this way, political elites were able to seek and claim an increasingly greater share of political power. Certainly, there was also another dimension to this phenomenon. In turn, notable groups were politically domesticated and assimilated, adapting to the rules of the political game. Progressively, a foundational characteristic of the modern state—pacification—took root within Greek territory. Beginning in 1875 with the adoption of the parliamentary principle, this process led to the institutionalisation of politics, since, in the end, it maximised the chances that the same groups would come to power. This development was an outcome of the efforts of a group of notables to contest the terms of the game: the so-called *Stilitika* incident that also took place in 1875 put an end to the careers of the main figures of this contestation, simultaneously determining the beginning of a new period in Greek political history.

From another perspective, 1875, or perhaps 1862 after King Otto's fall, constituted the conclusion—the end—of the War of Independence. The notable groups that brought the war to its end were then able to enjoy the benefits afforded by their efforts and to govern the state in accordance with their own preferences. It is no coincidence that, at this very same moment, political practices changed and the continued struggle to extend the Greek state's borders would from now on manifest itself differently, including the need to reform the way in which its populations were governed. The era of the heroes of the War of Independence and the Great Idea was gone forever. Greece now found itself in the period during which the 'Model Kingdom' was constructed.

Throughout the entire nineteenth century, Greece developed at a rapid pace, something largely unrecognised by observers at the time. As a result, the formation of the Greek state took place amid the constant criticisms and reproaches of both local and foreign commentators. Given the weight of the great expectations accompanying the state's creation, they expected much more tangible results from the process of Greece's return to civilisation. Yet despite the fact that heavy judgements were made of Greece, which were ultimately assimilated by the Greeks themselves, they did not obstruct the country from progressively converging towards the Western European realities that constituted the founding political goal of the creation of the Greek state. It is perhaps indicative of the political culture of the nation's dominant class that it never called the Western model of political and economic development into question—even in times of intense national introversion. Indeed, to the contrary, this model constituted the unique and exclusive example to be followed, regardless of its different interpretations.

But the intensity of this convergence with Western reality did not depend on the Greeks themselves. By the 1870s, Greece, integrated into a broader system of interstate relations, found itself forced to intensify its efforts in order to survive in an international environment that was becoming all the more competitive and complex. The period defined by Greek historiography as one of 'Trikoupist modernisation' was nothing more than a flight forwards, a road race with the other Balkan states, a race that focused primarily on military organisation, dragging along every other sector of the state in its wake. The parallel paths that all the Balkan states followed, the Ottoman Empire included, easily prove this observation in terms of the international dimension of the phenomenon.

This process was painful and complex, and its outcome was unexpected. Because, even if in 1897 Greece seemed to have confirmed the failure of both the philhellene dream and the modernising experiment attempted in the Trikoupist period, in a short span of time, only fifteen years later, it was vindicated in the Balkan Wars, and then glorified by the First World War. The Greek state began to transform into a regional power, and the ambitions of Greek irredentism had been satisfied. But this success did not last long. The devastation wreaked by the Greek–Turkish War came at the end of this long period of war, as did the beginnings of a civil war that grew out of the National

Schism of 1915. Greece's transformation into a modern state was accompanied by the growing pains of harsh policies and social opposition, both further intensified by the crisis of national unification.

So, though from 1875 onwards Greece managed to institutionalise politics and—with difficulty, no doubt—establish a parliamentary system that worked sufficiently well, by 1914 the previous situation had changed. King Constantine's clash with Eleftherios Venizelos over the question of Greece's participation in the First World War constituted the starting point of a long period of political and social confrontation. Under the cloak of the National Schism, social, ethnic and political opposition formed, in which violence played a primary role. Greece was certainly not the only European country in which violence was increasingly adopted in politics as a result of the First World War. However, it was one of the few countries in which the struggle between democracy and dictatorship proved to be inconclusive, resulting in successive political crises over the constitutional question and successive parliamentary and dictatorial regimes.

The Second World War did not resolve these problems. On the contrary, it intensified the situation. So, progressively, over the course of the occupation period, the royalist–Venizelist opposition was replaced by the communist–nationalist opposition, which led to the conclusion of the Civil War struggle with the defeat of the communists in 1949. The social dimensions of this process continue to be more or less unknown to us, while to a large degree we are unable to comprehend the political and economic factors of the conflict. Historians' political positioning on the issues related to the period in question is so marked and emotional approaches weigh so heavily that despite the large amount of scholarship available on these years, we still know only a minimal amount. The sure thing is that from 1945 onwards the communists had become isolated and lost their political and social momentum. In the end, they chose the route of military confrontation, from which they had no chance of emerging victorious. But the defeat was not only military: the left, no matter how much it failed to admit it, was dealt a huge political loss in these years from which it was unable to recover in the following years.

The collateral effects of the Civil War continued to weigh on the country until 1974. For the entirety of the period from 1949 to 1967, Greek parliamentarism was challenged—not only because the army and non-institutional forces more generally continued to play a significant role in the political playing field but also because the post-Civil War regime was the first to institute the exclusion of a large share of Greek citizens from national political life.

Despite the fact that the interwar period was characterised by the efforts of political factions to exclude each other from power—or at the very least by the extortive and often violent imposition of one faction's terms on the others—no single faction managed to dominate for a long period of time. The playing field was wide open; hence the instability of the political system and the successive *coups d'état*, constitutional upheavals, and alternating dictatorial and parliamentary periods. Yet the post-Civil War period escaped this model, entrenching the political and social exclusion of a portion of Greeks, creating traumatic and often catastrophic dynamics in the process. The system that was consolidated after the Civil War was not quite as exclusively Greek as has often been argued; rather, it represented Greece's version of the Cold War period. On the other hand, of course, it was from within these circumstances that the state eliminated the weaknesses of the interwar period. The cohesion and effectiveness of this state were indisputable.

At the same time, the political exclusion seen in those very same years was evidence of the deep contradictions in the functioning of the political system. How else could one describe the functioning of a parliamentary system with liberal principles that did not hesitate to resort to intensely repressive measures for a large share of its population? It was also deeply contradictory that an important portion of the population failed to benefit from Greece's economic development. It was also curious that another portion of the population was for the most part forced to emigrate abroad in order to survive. If, on the one hand, these occurrences do not seem problematic today, the experience that people had of them at the time was certainly traumatic.

Within the context of this exclusion, interests and alliances formed that were difficult to upend. This much became clear over the course of the period during which Konstantinos Karamanlis and George Papandreou governed the country. The coup of 21 April 1967 was certainly the consummation of this contradiction, which has its roots in 1914. On the one hand, it resulted in a tragedy—that of Cyprus—and on the other the failure of all the policies furthering the project of political exclusion in the name of the national interest.

After 1974, Greece passed into its European period without vacillations or doubts, though often with peculiarities. In a little over thirty years, it managed to undo the past, abolish exclusion, institutionalise democratic institutions and achieve impressive economic development. Its participation in the European Economic Community, and then in the European Union, certainly played a decisive role in these developments. At this point, the Greeks consider themselves Europeans, an assertion that could hardly have been made even in the early 1980s.

But it is not to be taken for granted that Greece's 'European achievements' will be maintained, because these very achievements provoked complacency in an era when the international system demanded a large degree of adaptability and flexibility in order for a country to maintain its place in the hierarchy. The result was that the country found itself in a dire economic position, deprived of a significant portion of its sovereign rights. Greece faces many problems stemming from the weakness or lack of will from its political elites, as well as its citizens, to bear the costs of their choices regarding participation in the processes of European integration, and to choose between a Western European-type state or the rather problematic 'democracy of friends' that has become entrenched at this point. Attainment of this 'European destiny' should in no way be considered a given. For the Greeks, from this moment onwards, it will be a continual challenge.

NOTES

1. THE EMPIRE TRANSFORMS, (1700–1821)

1. On the other hand, Athanasios Komninos Ypsilantis, a Phanariot himself, notes that the first Orthodox Christian subject of the Ottoman Empire to take up the position of ruler of Moldova was Dimitris Kantakouzinos in 1674. Thus he includes Mavrokordatos in a lineage that began with Kantakouzinos. See A. Komninos Ypsilantis, *Εκκλησιαστικών και πολιτικών των εις δώδεκα βιβλίον Η' Θ' και Ι' ήτοι τα μετά την άλωσιν (1453–1789)*, Constantinople: 1870, p. 781.
2. K. Koumas, *Ιστορία των ανθρωπίνων πράξεων*, vol. 4, Vienna: 1832, p. 535.
3. The church of Cyprus seems to constitute a particular case, as it was powerful before the mid-eighteenth century and it managed to remain independent in relation to the Patriarchate. See M. Michail, *Η εκκλησία της Κύπρου κατά την Οθωμανική περίοδο (1571–1878). Η σταδιακή συγκρότησή της σε θεσμό πολιτικής εξουσίας*, Nicosia: 2005, pp. 82 and 120.
4. K. Pitsakis, "Δίκαιο," Ιστορία των Ελλήνων, vol. 8: "Ο Ελληνισμός υπό ξένη κυριαρχία, 1453–1821," Domi, Athens, p. 201.
5. M. Giolias, *Ο Κοσμάς ο Αιτωλός και η εποχή του*, Athens: 1972, p. 412.
6. K. Koumas, *Ιστορία των ανθρωπίνων πράξεων*, vol. IB', p. 534.
7. G.G. Papadopoulos and G.P. Aggelopoulos, *Τα κατά τον αοίδιμον πρωταθλητήν του ιερού των Ελλήνων αγώνος τον Πατριάρχην Κωνσταντινουπόλεως Γρηγόριον τον Ε'*, vol. II, Athens, 1866, p. 517.
8. G. G. Papadopoulos and G. P. Aggelopoulos, *Τα κατά τον αοίδιμον...*, ibid., vol. I, Athens 1865, p. 230.
9. The term 'millet' maintained a different meaning for the first few centuries of Ottoman sovereignty, which later changed and in no way expressed the existence of religious communities with central power, the latter group led by religious leaders of doctrines or religions based in Constantinople. B. Braude, 'Community and Conflict in the Economy of the Ottoman Balkans, 1500–1650', doctoral thesis, Harvard University, Cambridge, MA, December 1977, specifically the third

chapter. See also: 'Foundation Myths of the Millet System', in B. Braude and B. Lewis (eds), *Christians and Jews in the Ottoman Empire*, vol. I, New York: Lynne Rienner, 1982, pp. 69–88.

10. M. Ikonomou, *Ιστορικά της ελληνικής παλιγγενεσίας ή ο ιερός των Ελλήνων αγών*, Athens 1873, pp. 26–7.
11. The term *ayan* emerged in the seventeenth century, but only began to acquire a specific meaning during the war of 1683–99, describing affluent members of provincial towns selected by residents to assume the role of intermediary between the local population and Porte officials regarding tax matters and military recruitment. Progressively, their place in provincial societies strengthened and they became a local aristocracy of large landowners. This transition was facilitated by lifelong tax farming titles, which progressively developed into personal incomes, while public property developed into quasi-individual property, i.e. estates. D. Sadat, 'Rumeli Ayanlari: The Eighteenth Century', *The Journal of Modern History*, 44, 3 (September 1972), pp. 346–63, R. Mantran (ed.), *Histoire de l'Empire ottoman*, ibid., pp. 323–8, C.K. Neumann, 'Political and diplomatic developments', in S. N. Faroqhi (ed.), *The Cambridge History of Turkey*, ibid., pp. 52ff., Y. Nagata, 'Ayans in Anatolia and the Balkans during the Eighteenth and Nineteenth Centuries: A Case Study of the Karaosmanoglu Family', in A. Anastasopoulos (ed.), *Provincial Elites in the Ottoman Empire*, Rethymno: 2005, pp. 247–68.
12. M. Perdikaris, "*Ρήγας ή κατά Ψευδοφιλελλήνων,*" *Επετηρίς του Μεσαιωνικού Αρχείου*, 11(1961), pp. 1–204.
13. Anonymous, *Ελληνική Νομαρχία ήτοι Λόγος περί Ελευθερίας*, ed. G. Valetas, 4th edition, Athens 1982.
14. N. Jorga, *Documente Greçesti Privatoarea la Istoria Romanilor*, vol. I, Bucharest: 1915, pp. 329–32, as mentioned by F. Iliou, *Ιστορίες του ελληνικού βιβλίου*, Heraklion 2005, pp. 23–4.
15. M. Giolia, *Ο Κοσμάς ο Αιτωλός και η εποχή του*, Athens 1972, p. 375.
16. A. Coray, *Memoire sur l'etat actuel de la civilization dans la Grece*, Paris: 1803, p. 50.
17. Ibid., p. 44.
18. K. Koumas, *Ιστορία...* ibid, pp. 599–600.

2. THE WAR OF INDEPENDENCE, (1821–32)

1. Fourth paragraph of the second chapter of the Political Constitution of Greece during the Third National Assembly of Troezen. *Τα ελληνικά συντάγματα, 1822–1975/86*, 2nd edn, Athens 1998, p. 135.
2. A. Daskalakis, *Οι τοπικοί οργανισμοί της επαναστάσεως του 1821...*, ibid., p. 102.

3. THE BAVARIANS IN GREECE, (1833–43)

1. T. N. Pipinelis, *Η μοναρχία εν Ελλάδι*, 1833–1843, Athens 1932.
2. I. Poulios, "Πολιτικά της Στερεάς Ελλάδος επί Οθωνος," *Επετηρίς Εταιρείας Στερεοελλαδικών Μελετών*, (1969–1970), p. 38.
3. P. Argyropoulos, *Δημοτική Διοίκησις εν Ελλάδι*, 1st edition, Athens 1843, ibid., p. 179.
4. G. I. Aggelopoulos, *Περί τοπικής διοικήσεως εν Ελλάδι εν συγκρίσει προς την εν Γαλλία και Αγγλία*, Athens 1879, pp. 18–19.
5. G. Finlay, 'Greece Again', *Blackwood's Edinburg* Magazine (1850), p. 535.
6. *Διάταγμα περί εκλογής των δημοτικών αρχών*, Nafplion 1834, pp. 12–13.
7. A. Chrysovergis, *Η Ελληνική Επανάστασις*, Ermoupolis, 1853, p. 53.
8. J. Poulos, 'La Grèce d'Othon vue en 1841 par l'homme d'Etat et diplomate Français Piscatory', *L'Hellénisme Contemporaine*, IX, 9–10 (1955), pp. 339–41.
9. G.L. Maurer, *Ο Ελληνικός Λαός, Δημόσιο, ιδιωτικό και εκκλησιαστικό δίκαιο από την έναρξη του Αγώνα για την Ανεξαρτησία ως την 31 Ιουλίου 1834, Αθήνα* 1976 [First German edition, Heidelberg 1835], pp. 592–3.
10. K. Vakalopoulos, *Τρία ανέκδοτα ιστορικά δοκίμια του Φιλικού Γεώργιου Λασσάνη*, Thessaloniki 1973, pp. 139–40.
11. A. Lambiris, "Ο Σπ. Τρικούπης εισηγείται στον Οθωνα την παραχώρηση Συντάγματος" (from an unpublished memorandum in 1835), *Μνήμων*, 6 (1976–7), p. 126.
12. C. A. Frazee, *Ορθόδοξος Εκκλησία κι ελληνική ανεξαρτησία (1821–1852)*, Athens 1987, p. 147.
13. C. A. Frazee, *Ορθόδοξος Εκκλησία…*, ibid., p. 143.
14. C. Christopoulos, *Γενική έκθεσις προς την Α.Μεγαλειότητα του Υπουργού των Εκκλησιαστικών και της Δημοσίας Εκπαιδεύσεως περί της καταστάσεως της δημοσίας εκπαιδεύσεως εν Ελλάδι κατά το λήξαν σχολικόν έτος 1855–1856, μετά στατιστικών σημειώσεων και παρατηρήσεων*, Athens 1857, p. 27.

4. KING OTTO AND THE GREEKS, (1844–62)

1. E. Driault and M. Lhéritier, *Histoire diplomatique de la Grèce de 1821 à nos jours*, vol. II: *Le Règne d'Othon: La Grande Idée (1830–1862)*, Paris: 1925, p. 405.
2. G. Tsokopoulos, "*Παρελθόν και Ενεστώς*," *Χαρίλαος Τρικούπης. Βιογραφία*, Athens 1896, p. 153.
3. G. Tsokopoulos, *Χαρίλαος Τρικούπης. Βιογραφία*, Athens 1896, p. 153.
4. As described by General Kalergis, leader of the movement, and reported by N. Dragoumis, *Ιστορικαί αναμνήσεις*, vol. II, Athens 1973, p. 71.
5. *Πρακτικά της εν Αθήναις της…*, ibid., p. 149.
6. T. Kolokotronis, *Αι τελευταίαι ημέρα…*, ibid., p. 7. As he himself relates, in cases where two candidates from the same province were descendants of families favoured by the king, then the electoral process remained free of state intervention.

7. E. Driault and M. Lhéritier, *Histoire diplomatique de la Grèce de 1821 à nos jours*, vol. III, p. 329.
8. G. Tsokopoulos, *Χαρίλαος Τρικούπης*, ibid., p. 153.
9. Athens Academy, Research Centre for the History of Modern Hellenism, *Επιτομές εγγράφων*, ibid., p. 481.
10. The *stremma* was the most widely used unit of measure for large areas of land at the time, varying slightly in equivalence from one region to another. It was standardised after 1836 to equal one-tenth of a hectare—1,000 square meters [translator's note].
11. I. A. Soutsos, *Πλουτολογία*, vol. I, Athens 1868, p. 228.
12. The Greek Phalanx was an honorary body that included captains from the War of Independence so as to justify a fee and honorary distinctions for the services they had offered. But since the maintenance costs of the Phalanx proved too burdensome for the overall budget, the state decided it was best to give each member of the Phalanx a creditory note with a value equal to five times their annual salary, a maximum of 8,400 drachmas, with which members could claim national lands of any kind.
13. Pouqueville's view in this passage, so often repeated later on, is referenced in D. Nikolaidis, *D'une Grèce à l'autre. Représentation des Grecs modernes par la France révolutionnaire*, Paris 1992, p. 43. On the same issue, namely reception of Greeks by the French, see also G. Tolias, *La médaille et la rouille. L'image de la Grèce moderne dans la presse littéraire parisienne (1794–1815)*, Athens 1997.
14. G.L. Maurer, *Ο Ελληνικός Λαός. Δημόσιο, ιδιωτικό και εκκλησιαστικό δίκαιο από την έναρξη του αγώνα για την ανεξαρτησία ως την 31 Ιουλίου 1834*, Athens 1976 [first German edition 1835] pp. 410–11. *Επιστημονική Επετηρίς της Φιλοσοφικής Σχολής του Πανεπιστημίου Θεσσαλονίκης* Η (1960) pp. 49–97.
15. F. Strong, *Greece as a Kingdom; Or, a Statistical, Description of that Country, from the Arrival of King Otto in 1833, down to the Present Time*, London 1842, p. ix.
16. M. Thouvenel, *La Grèce du Roi Othon*, Paris 1890, p. 130.
17. G. A. Anastasopoulos, *Ιστορία της ελληνικής βιομηχανίας 1840–1940*, vol. I, Athens 1947, pp. 108–9. See also the observations concerning Greece's participation in the International Exposition of Paris in 1867, S. Basch, *Le mirage grec...*, p. 139.
18. A. Soutsos, *Η Ελληνεγερσία*, Athens 1848, p. 20.
19. I. A. Soutsos, *Πλουτολογία*, vol. I, Athens 1868, p. 125.
20. Ep. Deligiorgis, *Πολιτικά ημερολόγια—πολιτικαί σημειώσεις—πολιτικαί επιστολαί*, part I 1859–1862, Athens 1896, p. 199.

5. THE GREEKS AMONG THEMSELVES, (1863–80)

1. P. Koronaios, '*Ελεγχος των δημοσιευθέντων εντός και εκτός της Ελλάδος εγγράφων περί των συμβάντων του Ιουνίου*, Athens 1863, p. 6.
2. For more on the massacre in Dilessi, see R. Jenkins, *The Dilessi Murders*, Plymouth:

1961, D. Dontas, *Greece and the Great Powers, 1863–1875*, Thessaloniki: 1966, p. 168.

3. The primary sector of the economy is the sector of an economy making direct use of natural resources or exploitation of natural resources. This includes agriculture, forestry, fishing and mining. In contrast, the secondary sector produces manufactured goods, and the tertiary sector provides services.
4. A small yellow insect that feeds on the roots and leaves of grape vines, girdling the roots and preventing the grape vine from growing.
5. Empirical doctors based their medical knowledge on inductive inferences, holding it to be reliable only if derived from a sufficient number of observations, and held no formal medical training or degrees.
6. G. D. Papakostas "Δημόσια υγεία," p. 393.

6. THE FLIGHT FORWARD, (1881–97)

1. A. Flerianou (ed.), *Χαρίλαος Τρικούπης. Η ζωή και το έργο του*, vol. I, Athens 1999, p. 378.
2. K. Ailianou, *Η Αυστρο-Ουγγαρία και η προσάρτηση της Θεσσαλίας και της Ηπείρου (1878–1881)*, Thessaloniki 1988, p. 54.
3. K. Ailianou, *Αυστρο-Ουγγαρία...* ibid., p. 151.
4. Hellenic Parliament, *Χαρίλαος Τρικούπης. Η ζωή και το έργο του*, ibid., vol. I, p. 607.
5. G. Aspreas, *Πολιτική ιστορία...*, vol. II, p. 134.
6. D. Pournaras, *Χαρίλαος Τρικούπης. Η ζωή και το έργο του*, vol II, Athens 1939, pp. 180–181
7. G. Aspreas, *Πολιτική ιστορία...*, ibid., vol. 3, p. 30.
8. C. Lirintzis, *τέλος των «τζακιών»»...*, pp. 96–97. For more on the importance of regional interests in Parliament see the observations of E. Deligiorgis, *Πολιτικά Ημερολόγια. Πολιτικαί Σημειώσεις. Πολιτικαί Επιστολαί*, p. 95.
9. N.B. Vlachos. *Το Μακεδονικόν ως φάσις του Ανατολικού ζητήματος, 1879–1908*, Athens 1935, pp. 5–6.
10. These observations are based on the work of J.D. Singer and M. Small, 'The Composition and Status Ordering of the International System: 1815–1940', *World Politics*, 18, 2 (January 1966), pp. 236–82, which analyses various countries' diplomatic status, chiefly focusing on their diplomatic representatives in other countries and their national capital. As formalistic as such an approach is, it can still be of use. To take but one finding, Greece's position in the hierarchy of diplomatic representation was much higher in the years following the establishment of the Greek state when compared with the years before the First World War.
11. A. Flerianou (ed), *Χαρίλαος Τρικούπης. Η ζωή και το έργο του*, vol. I, Athens 1999, p. 378.
12. A. Flerianou (ed.), *Χαρίλαος Τρικούπης. Η ζωή και το έργο του*, vol I, Athens 1999, p. 329.

13. A. Eftaksias, *Η Ελλάς εν χρεωκοπία*, Athens 1894, p. 42.
14. A. Rangavis, *Απομνημονεύματα*, vol. IV, Athens 1895, p. 552. In fact, one may find much more information on the same subject in the work of E. T. Soulogiannis & I. Botoropoulos (eds.) *Αλέξανδρου Ρίζου Ραγκαβή χειρόγραφος κώδιξ αρ. 35 από το αρχείο της οικογένειας Ραγκαβή*, Athens 1997, p. 155, which reproduces a large number of letters to Greek politicians and George I in relation to Greek foreign policy and the crisis of the Eastern Question during those same years.
15. A. Flerianos (ed.), *Χαρίλαος Τρικούπης. Η ζωή και το έργο του*, vol I, Athens 1999, p. 295.
16. E. Driault and M. Lhéritier, *Histoire diplomatique de la Grèce de 1821 à nos jours*, vol. III, p. 373.
17. For more on the realism in Trikoupis's foreign policy, see also the observations of E. Kofos, *Η Ελλάδα και το Ανατολικό ζήτημα 1875–1881*, pp. 90–91.
18. A. Anastassiadis, 'Comment réformer une institution traditionaliste? L'Eglise de Grèce et la sécularisation au temps de la formation de l'Etat national, 1852–1936: de l'inertie à la "rénovation conservatrice,"' doctoral dissertation, Institut d'Etudes Politiques, Paris 2006, p. 86. Similar exemptions and measures were adopted in 1912–13 with the annexation of Macedonia and Thrace. Even more so, with the Law 2400/23 June 1920, the exemption of conscription was institutionalised for religious minority groups in exchange for a fee that sometimes reached upwards of 3,000 drachmas. These exemptions were only removed when reforms to the system were made in 1927.
19. On these issues, see E. K. Stasinopoulos, *Ο στρατός της πρώτης εκατονταετίας. Ιστορική επισκόπησις της εξελίξεως του ελληνικού στρατού*, Athens 1935 and Γενικόν Επιτελείον Στρατού, Διεύθυνσις Ιστορίας Στρατού, *Ιστορία της οργανώσεως του Ελληνικού στρατού, 1821–1954*, Athens 1957.
20. A. Flerianos, (ed), ibid., vol I, p. 448
21. A. Flerianos, (ed), ibid., vol I, p. 313
22. According to statistics of the era, Greece spent the smallest amount per soldier and per capita in comparison with other European countries, but the largest proportionally to its budget. See P.A. Moraitinis, *La Grèce telle qu'elle est*, Paris 1877, pp. 247–8.
23. A. Flerianos, (ed), ibid., vol I, p. 448.
24. Excerpt from a speech made in Parliament by C. Trikoupis on 22/3/1880. A. Flerianos (ed), Charilaos Trikoupis, vol I, ibid., pp. 543–544.
25. K. Ischomachos, *Μελέτη επί της στρατιωτικής οργανώσεως της Ελλάδος*, Athens 1880, p. 122.
26. G. Aspreas, *Πολιτική ιστορία*, vol II, p. 120, D. Pournaras, *Χ. Τρικούπης*, vol I, pp. 234–235.
27. A. Flerianos, (ed), ibid., vol I, p. 458.
28. In the meantime, new changes had been made in the army's organisation. In 1887,

a law was passed that changed the army's organisational structure once again; another such change followed in 1893. Between 1887 and 1896, the army ranged from 28,684 to 26,362 men in size.

29. C. Vardas, "Ελλάδα στα τέλη του 19ου αιώνα," *Μνήμων*, 8(1980–82), p. 47.
30. D. Pournaras, *C. Trikoupis*, vol I, ibid., p. 275.
31. A. Andreadis, "Εθνικά δάνεια και ελληνική δημόσια οικονομία" A. Andreadis, *Εργα*, Athens, 1939, vol II, p. 385.
32. M. D. Seizanis, *Η πολιτική της Ελλάδος και η επανάστασις του 1873 εν Μακεδονία, Ηπείρω και Θεσσαλία*, Athens 1878, pp. 14–15.
33. L. Papagiannakis, *Οι ελληνικοί σιδηρόδρομοι (1882–1910)*,ibid., p. 127.
34. A. Andreadis, "Εθνικά δάνεια και ελληνική...," ibid.
35. S. Koronis, "Ελληνικοί σιδηρόδρομοι και σιδηροδρομική πολιτική," *Δελτίον του Υπουργείου Εθνικής Οικονομίας*, A/1, April 1914, p. 8.
36. L. Papagiannakis, *Οι ελληνικοί σιδηρόδρομοι (1882–1910). Γεωπολιτικές, οικονομικές και κοινωνικές διαστάσεις*, Athens 1982, p. 149.
37. M. Sinarellis, *Δρόμοι και λιμάνια στην Ελλάδα 1830–1880*, Athens 1989, p. 200.
38. E. Papagiannopoulou, *Η διώρυγα της Κορίνθου...*, ibid., p. 100 and B. Tsokopoulos, Μεγάλα τεχνικά έργα στην Ελλάδα, τέλη 19ου—αρχές 20ου αιώνα, Athens 1999, p. 69–71.
39. G. Antoniou, *Οι έλληνες μηχανικοί. Θεσμοί και ιδέες*, Athens 2006, B. Tsokopoulos, *Μεγάλα τεχνικά έργα...*, ibid., pp. 18–23.
40. See Hellenic Parliament, *Χαρίλαος Τρικούπης. Η ζωή και το έργο του*, vol I, pp. 179–180.
41. C. Vardas, "Πολιτευόμενοι αξιωματικοί στην Ελλάδα στα τέλη του 19ου αιώνα," Μνήμων, 8(1980–82), p. 60.
42. See also the related comments in C. Trikoupis's discussion of the above draft law in Parliament, Hellenic Parliament, *Χαρίλαος Τρικούπης. Η ζωή και το έργο του*, vol I, pp. 180–181.
43. D. Pournaras, *Χαρίλαος Τρικούπης. Η ζωή και το έργο του*, vol I, Athens 1939, p. 264.
44. For a good introduction to the subject, see S. Karavas, "Οι εθνογραφικές περιπέτειες του «ελληνισμού» (1876–1878)," *Τα Ιστορικά*, 36 (June 2002), pp. 23–74, June 2003, pp. 27–112.
45. C. Kardaras, *Ιωακείμ Γ'—Χαρ. Τρικούπης. Η αντιπαράθεση. Από την ανέκδοτη αλληλογραφία του Οικουμενικού Πατριάρχη (1878–1884)*, Athens 1998.
46. C. Kardaras, *Ιωακείμ Γ'—Χαρ. Τρικούπης...* ibid., S. Anagnostopoulos, *Μικρά Ασία, 19ος αι.—1919. Οι ελληνορθόδοξες κοινότητες. Από το Μιλλέτ των Ρωμιών στο ελληνικό έθνος*, Athens 1997, p. 419.
47. S. Anagnostopoulos, *Μικρά Ασία, 19ος αι.—1919...* ibid., p. 427.
48. A. Andreadis, *Ιστορία των Εθνικών δανείων, Μέρος Α': Τα δάνεια της Ανεξαρτησίας* (1824–1825)—Το δημόσιον χρέος επί της Βαυαρικής δυναστείας, Athens 1904.
49. For more detail, see D. Georgiadès, *La Grèce économique et financière en 1893*, Paris 1893, p. 62.

50. A. Simopoulos, *Αγόρευσις συζητουμένου εν τη Βουλή του προϋπολογισμού του 1894*, Athens 1894, p. 97.
51. The best history of public finances in this era has been written by I. Zografos, *Δημοσιονομικαί μελέται*, 2nd edition, vol. III, Athens 1925.
52. A. Fishlow, "Conditionality and Willingness to Pay: Some Parallels from the 1890s," B. Eichengreen & P. Lindert (eds.), *The International Debt Crisis in Historical Perspective*, Cambridge Mass. 1991, pp. 86–105.
53. L. Drucker, *Quelques documents concernant l'etat de banqueroute frauduleuse et les nouvelles tentatives d'escroquerie du gouvernement hellenique*, Leyde 1879, p. 13, also S. Basch, *Le mirage grec*..., ibid., p. 222.
54. I. Zografou, *Δημοσιονομικαί μελέται*, vol. II, 2nd edition, Athens 1925, p. 235.
55. M. Perakis, "Η αντικατάσταση της δεκάτης από το φόρο των αροτριώντων ζώων. Η πρώτη φορολογική αλλαγή του Χαρίλαου Τρικούπη," K. Aroni—Tischli & L. Tricha (eds.), *Ο Χαρίλαος Τρικούπης και η εποχή του. Πολιτικές επιδιώξεις και κοινωνικές συνθήκες*, Athens 2000, pp. 275–292.
56. G. Jeze and B. D. Georgandas, *Τα δημόσια οικονομικά και η ελληνική οικονομική νομορεσία*, vol III, Δημόσια 'Εσοδα, Athens 1915, p. 516.
57. G. Jeze and B. D. Georgandas, *Τα δημόσια οικονομικά και η ελληνική οικονομική νομορεσία*, ibid., p. 897.
58. A. Flerianos (ed.), *Χαρίλαος Τρικούπης*..., ibid., vol I, p. 369.
59. A. Flerianos (ed.), *Χαρίλαος Τρικούπης*..., ibid., vol I, p. 325.
60. S. Sotiropoulos, *Έκθεσις περί φορολογικού συστήματος*, Athens 1867, p. 18.
61. S. Petmezas, *Η ελληνική*..., ibid., pp. 82–86.
62. J. R. Lampe and M.R. Jackson, *Balkan Economic History, 1550–1950: From Imperial Borderlands to Developing Nations*, Bloomington 1982, p. 192, and S.K. Pavlowitch, *Ιστορία των Βαλκανίων, 1804–1945*, Thessaloniki 2005, p. 299.
63. N. Maronitis, *εθνικό ζήτημα στην Ελλάδα 1890–1910*, Athens 2009, p. 104.
64. G. Gianoulopoulos, *«Η ευγενής μας τύφλωσις...». Εξωτερική πολιτική και «εθνικά θέματα» από την ήττα του 1897 έως τη μικρασιατική καταστροφή*, Athens 1899, pp. 33–80.
65. [National Society], *'Εκθεσις των πεπραγμένων της Εθνικής Εταιρίας*, Athens 1897, p. 7.
66. [National Society], *Έκθεσις των πεπτραγμένων*..., ibid.
67. G. Gianoulopoulos, *««Η ευγενής μας τύφλωσις...»*..., pp. 131–170.
68. N. Maronitis, *Πολιτική εξουσία και εθνικό ζήτημα*..., ibid., p. 37.

7. UNEXPECTED DEVELOPMENTS, (1898–1913)

1. N. Kazazis, *Ο κοινοβουλευτισμός εν Ελλάδι*, Athens 1910, p. 53.
2. Cited by G. Mavrogordatos, *Μελέτες και κείμενα για την περίοδο 1909–1940*, Athens—Komotini 1982, pp. 79–80.

3. G. Skliros, "Το κοινωνικόν μας ζήτημα," *Εργα*, Introduction, commentary and editing by L. Alexios, Athens 1976, p. 81.
4. G. Skliros, "Το κοινωνικόν μας ζήτημα," *Εργα*, Introduction, commentary and editing L. Alexos, Athens 1976, p. 421.
5. The 'Peace-War' period lasted from the annexation of Eastern Roumelia by Bulgaria in September 1885 up until the intervention of Great Powers in April 1886 [translator's note].
6. M. D. Seizanis, *Η πολιτική κατάστασις της Ελλάδος και η Επανάστασις του 1878 εν Μακεδονία και Θεσσαλία*, Athens 1878, p. 11. The words 'bouk' and 'ouiye' are of Albanian origin [translator's note].
7. K.T. Dimaras *Ιστορία της νεοελληνικής λογοτεχνίας*, 7th edition, Athens 1985, p. 415.
8. A. Liakos, "Εξ ελληνικής εις την κοινήν ημών γλώσσαν," with A.F. Christidis, *Ιστορία της ελληνικής γλώσσας*, Thessaloniki 2001, p. 963.
9. Extract from the Dean's speech on the founding day of Otto's University, Athens 1837, pp. 1–2. Reproduced in K.T. Dimaras, Εν Αθήναις τη 3 Μαΐου 1837. Historical study, Athens, 1987.
10. Cited by K.T. Dimaras, *Κ. Παπαρρηγόπουλος*, ibid., p. 124.
11. K. Paparigopoulos, *Ιστορία του Ελληνικού Έθνους [Η πρώτη μορφή: 1853]*, ed. K. T. Dimaras, Athens 1970, p. 33.
12. K. Paparrigopoulos, *Ιστορία του Ελληνικού Έθνους [Η πρώτη μορφή: 1853]*, ed. K.T. Dimaras, Athens 1970, pp. 34–35.
13. K. Paparrigopoulos, *Προλεγόμενα*, ed. K.T. Dimaras, Athens 1970, p. 116.
14. K. Paparrigopoulos, *Προλεγόμενα*, ibid., pp. 104–105.
15. E. Abdelas, *Ιστορία και σχολείο*, Athens 1998, pp. 18–19.

8. A NEW GREECE, (1914–23)

1. As observed by G. T. Mavrogordatos, *Εθνικός διχασμός...*, ibid., p. 135.
2. This refers to a political dispute in December of 1916 that led to an armed confrontation in Athens between the royalist government of Greece and the forces of the Allies over the issue of Greece's neutrality during the First World War.
3. T. Kostopoulos, *Πόλεμος και εθνοκάθαρση...*, ibid., pp. 138–139 and A. Rigos, p. 257.
4. As observed by S. Marketos, *Πώς φίλησα τον Μουσολίνι! Τα πρώτα βήματα του ελληνικού φασισμού*, Vivliorama publishers, Athens 2006, p. 68.

9. PARLIAMENT AND DICTATORSHIP, (1924–40)

1. E. K. Venizelos, "Πώς θα λυθή το ελληνικόν πρόβλημα," *Εργασία*, 1/11.1.1930, p. 3.
2. The ratio of public expenditure to GDP is one way to express state size. Both this graph and data provided in previous chapters point to an increase in state size due to the wartime period, a trend that was more or less maintained in subsequent years. We must nevertheless bear in mind that the data used in this analysis also includes

public debt amortisation, and thus overestimates the size of the state. The drop evident after 1932 is to some extent an illusion, since after the bankruptcy of the Greek state, public debt repayments dropped significantly—by two-thirds—compared with the previous period.

10. WARS, (1941–9)

1. C.M. Woodhouse, *A Survey of Recent Greek Politics in Their International Setting*, London: Hutchinson, 1948.
2. G. Theotokas, *Τετράδια ημερολογίου 1939–1953*, Athens 2005, pp. 515–516. This statement was made on 5 December 1944.

11. THE ANTI-COMMUNIST STATE, (1950–74)

1. A. Papachelas, *Ο βιασμός της ελληνικής δημοκρατίας. Ο αμερικανικός παράγων, 1947–1967*, Athens 1997, p. 116.
2. K.E. Botsiou, "Η αρχή του τέλους της βασιλευομένης: Στέμμα και κρίση ηγεμονίας τη δεκαετία του 60," A. Rigos, S. Seferiadis, E. Hatzivasiliou (eds.) «Σύντομη» δεκαετία του 60, Athens 2008, p. 103.
3. Y. Voulgaris, *Η Ελλάδα της μεταπολίτευσης* 1974–1990. *Σταθερή δημοκρατία σημαδεμένη από τη μεταπολεμική ιστορία*, Athens 2001, p. 54.

12. IN EUROPE, (1974–2010)

1. G. I Rallis, '*Ωρες ευθύνης*, Athens 2010 [1983], p. 139.
2. 'Announcement of Greece's Proposal to Join the Nine EEC Member States', 12 June 1975, *Αρχείον Κωνσταντίνου Καραμανλή*, Vol VIII, p. 447.
3. Y. Voulgaris, *Η Ελλάδα της μεταπολίτευσης 1974–1990. Σταθερή δημοκρατία σημαδεμένη από τη μεταπολεμική ιστορία*, Athens 2001, pp. 39–41.
4. Y. Voulgaris, *Η Ελλάδα της μεταπολίτευσης 1974–1990*... ibid., p. 30.
5. This quotation is cited in X. I. Kontiadis, *Ελλειμματική δημοκρατία. Κράτος και κόμματα στη σύγχρονη Ελλάδα*, Athens 2009, p. 70.

13. CRISIS, (2007–)

1. G. Papakonstantinou, *Game Over. Η αλήθεια για την κρίση*, Athens 2016, pp. 74–175.
2. Bank of Greece, *Το Χρονικό της Μεγάλης Κρίσης*, ibid., p. 105.
3. A phrase borrowed from an interview given by Apostolos Doxiadis in *Ta Nea* in the September 12/13 2015 weekend edition.
4. *To Vima*, Sunday, 16 August 2015.
5. Euclid Tsakalotos, 'We Were Defeated by Negotiations', *Vima*, Sunday, 13 September 2015, p. A10.

HISTORY'S SPOILED CHILDREN: IN LIEU OF AN EPILOGUE

1. This comparison has already been made in international scholarship, though from the perspective of international relations. See G.J. Bass, *Freedom's Battle. The Origins of Humanitarian Intervention*, New York 2008. For Greece specifically, pp. 45–152.

BIBLIOGRAPHY

The bibliography presented below is of a purely introductory nature and aims to enable the English-speaking reader to make their first steps into modern Greek history. It is self-evident that it corresponds to the author's personal preferences.

Anastasopoulos, A. (ed.), *Provincial Elites in the Ottoman Empire*, Rethymno: University of Crete, 2005.

Anastasopoulos, A. and E. Kolovos (eds), *Ottoman Rule and the Balkans, 1760–1850: Conflict, Transformation, Adaptation*, Rethymno: University of Crete, 2007.

Anderson, M.S., *The Eastern Question 1774–1923: A Study in International Relations*, London: St Martin's Press, 1966.

Braude, B., 'Community and Conflict in the Economy of the Ottoman Balkans, 1500–1650', PhD dissertation, Harvard University, Cambridge, MA, 1977.

Candilis, W.O., *The Economy of Greece 1944–66: Efforts of Stability and Development*, New York: Praeger, 1968.

Clogg, R., *A Concise History of Greece*, 3rd edn, New York: Cambridge University Press, 2013.

——— (ed.), *Greece in the 1980s*, London: MacMillan 1983.

——— *Parties and Elections in Greece: The Search for Legitimacy*, London: Hurst, 1988.

Close, D.H., *Greece since 1945: Politics, Economy and Society*, New York: Longman, 2002.

——— (ed.), *The Greek Civil War, 1943–1950: Studies of Polarization*, New York: Routledge, 1993.

——— *The Origins of the Greek Civil War*, New York: Routledge, 1995.

Dakin D., *The Greek Struggle in Macedonia 1897–1913*, Institute of Balkan Studies, Thessaloniki 1993.

——— *The Unification of Greece, 1770–1923*, London: Ernest Benn, 1972.

Eldem, E., *French Trade in Istanbul in the Eighteenth Century*, Leiden: Brill, 1999.

Faroqhi, S.N. (ed.), *The Cambridge History of Turkey*, vol. 3, *The Later Ottoman Empire, 1603–1839*, New York: Cambridge University Press, 2006.

Featherstone, K. (ed.), *Politics and Policy in Greece: The Challenge of Modernization*, London: Routledge 2006.

Featherstone, K., D. Papadimitriou, A. Marmarelis and G. Niarchos, *The Last Ottomans. The Muslim Minority of Greece, 1940–1949*, London: Palgrave Macmillan, 2011.

Frangos G.F., 'The Philike Etaireia, 1814–1821: A Social and Historical Analysis', PhD Dissertation, Columbia University, 1971.

Gallant, T.W., *Modern Greece*, New York: Oxford University Press, 2001.

Hatzivassiliou, E., *Greece and the Cold War: Front-Line State, 1952–1967*, New York: Routledge, 2011.

Hionidou, V., *Famine and Death in Occupied Greece, 1941–1944*, Cambridge: Cambridge University Press, 2006.

Hirschon, R., *Heirs of the Catastrophe: The Social Life of Asia Minor Refugees in Piraeus*, New York: Berghahn Books 1998.

Holland, R.F. and D.W. Markides, *The British and the Hellenes: Struggles for Mastery in the Eastern Mediterranean 1850–1960*, Oxford: Oxford University Press, 2006.

Inalcik, H. and D. Quataert (eds), *An Economic and Social History of the Ottoman Empire, 1300–1914*, Cambridge: Cambridge University Press, 1994.

Kalyvas, St., *The Logic of Violence in Civil War*, New York: Cambridge University Press, 2006.

—— *Modern Greece: What Everyone Needs to Know*, New York: Oxford University Press, 2014.

Kalyvas, St., G. Pagoulatos and H. Tsoukas (eds), *From Stagnation to Forced Adjustment: Reforms in Greece 1974–2010*, London: Hurst, 2012.

Karamouzi, Eir., *Greece, the EEC and the Cold War, 1974–1979: The Second Enlargement*, Houndsmills, Basingstoke: Palgrave MacMillan, 2014.

Kitromilidis, P. (ed.), *Eleftherios Venizelos: The Trials of Statesmanship*, Edinburgh: Edinburgh University Press, 2006.

—— *Enlightenment and Revolution: The Making of Modern Greece*, Cambridge MA: Harvard University Press 2013.

Koliopoulos, I.S., *Greece and the British Connection 1935–1941*, Oxford: Clarendon Press, 1977.

—— *Brigands with a Cause: Brigandage and Irredentism in Modern Greece, 1821–1912*, Oxford: Clarendon Press 1987.

Koliopoulos, J.S. and Th. Veremis, *Modern Greece: A History since 1821*, Malden, MA: Wiley-Blackwell, 2010.

Konstantaras, D.J., *Infamy and Revolt: The Rise of the National Problem in Early Modern Greek Thought*, New York: Columbia University Press, 2006.

Kontogiorgi, E., *Population Exchange in Greek Macedonia: The Rural Settlement of Refugees 1922–1930*, New York: Oxford University Press, 2006.

Leon(taritis), G., *Greece and the Great Powers 1914–1917*, Thessaloniki: Institute of Balkan Studies, 1974.

Leontaritis, G., *Greece and the First World War: From Neutrality to Intervention 1917–1918*, New York: East European Monographs, 1990.

Llewellyn-Smith, M., *Ionian Vision: Greece in Asia Minor, 1919–1922*, Ann Arbor: University of Michigan Press 1998.

Mackridge, P., *Language and National Identity in Greece 1766–1976*, New York: Oxford University Press, 2009.

McGowan, B., *Economic Life in Ottoman Empire. Taxation, Trade and the Struggle for Land, 1600–1800*, Cambridge: Cambridge University Press, 1981.

McGrew, W., *Land and Revolution in Modern Greece, 1800–1881*, Kent, OH: Kent State University Press, 1985.

Mavrogordatos G. Th., *Stillborn Republic: Social coalitions and Party Strategies in Greece, 1922–1936*, Berkeley: University of California Press, 1983.

Mazower, M. (ed.), *After the War Was Over: Reconstructing the Family, Nation and State on Greece, 1943–1960*, Princeton: Princeton University Press 2000.

——— *Greece and the Inter-war Economic Crisis*, Oxford: Clarendon Press, 1991.

——— *Inside Hitler's Greece: The Experience of Occupation, 1941–1944*, New Haven: Yale University Press, 1993.

Papacosma, S.V., *The Military in Greek Politics: The 1909 Coup d'Etat*, Kent: Kent State University Press, 1977.

Pelagidis, T. and M. Mitsopoulos, *Understanding the Crisis in Greece*, New York: Palgrave Macmillan, 2011.

Pelt, M., *Tobacco, Arms and Politics. Greece and Germany from World Crisis to World War 1929–1941*, Copenhagen: Museum Tusculanum Press, University of Copenhagen, 1998.

——— *Tying Greece to the West: US–West German–Greek Relations 1949–1974*, Copenhagen: Museum Tusculanum Press, University of Copenhagen, 2006.

Pentzopoulos, D., *The Balkan Exchange of Minorities and Its Impact upon Greece*, Paris: Mouton et Co., 1961.

Petrakis, M., *The Metaxas Myth: Dictatorship and Propaganda in Greece*, London: I.B. Tauris, 2011.

Petropulos, J.A., *Politics and Statecraft in the Kingdom of Greece, 1833–1843*, Princeton: Princeton University Press, 1968.

Quataert, D., *The Ottoman Empire, 1700–1922*, New York: Cambridge University Press, 2000

Sotiropoulos, D., *Populism and Bureaucracy: The Case of Greece under PASOK, 1981–1989*, Notre Dame, IN: University of Notre Dame Press, 1996.

Tziovas, D., *The Nationalism of Demoticists and Its Impact on their Literary Theory (1888–1930): An Analysis based on Their Literary Criticism and Essays*, Amsterdam: Hakkert 1986

Woodhouse, C.M., *The Rise and Fall of the Greek Colonels*, London: Granada, 1982.

Veremis, Th., *The Military in Greek Politics: From Independence to Democracy*, New York: Black Rose Books 1997.

Voglis, P., *Becoming a Subject: Political Prisoners in the Greek Civil War*, New York: Berghahn Books, 2002.

INDEX

11 September Revolution (1922): 253–4, 269; political impact of, 267–8, 270, 288
3 September Rebellion (1843): 115–17, 269; political impact of, 117–18, 138
4 of August Regime (1936–41): 277, 289–91, 293–4; education policies of, 354; key figures of, 298, 311, 340

About, E.: 161–2
Abyssinia: Italian Invasion of (1935–6), 293
Aegean Sea: 29, 56, 160, 173, 243, 299
Aeschylus: *Oresteia*, 221
Agios Efstratios Camp: closure of, 337
Agrarian Party: members of, 320
Agricultural bank: creation of (1929), 285
Albania: 12, 26, 44, 157, 198, 268, 284, 297–8, 319; borders of, 294; Italian Occupation of (1939–43), 290, 293
Alexander of Battenberg: 203
Alexander I of Russia, Tsar: 53; death of (1825), 68
Algeria: War of Independence (1954–62), 360
Alfred: 148
Ali, Mehmet: 26, 56, 112; family of, 56
Almunia, X.: 407
Anabaptism Movement: 20
Anagnostaras: death of, 52
Andreadis, Stratis: 373
Androutsos, Odysseas: imprisonment and murder of, 66
Angelopoulos, Georgios I.: 86
Anglo-French-Turkish Treaty (1939): signing of, 290
Anglo-Turkish Trade Treaty (1838): 167–8
Anthrakitis, Methodius: 33
Antifascist Military Organisation (ASO): 311
Argentina: 378
von Armansperg, Josef Ludwig: 77, 80–1
armatoles: 61; concept of, 24; efforts to curtail power of, 25
Arta-Volos line: 71–2
Association for the Dissemination of Greek Letters: founding of (1869), 237
Astikliniki: opening of (1858), 185–6
Ataturk, Mustafa Kemal: 273; family of, 261
Athena (deity): 63

atheism: 31
Athens Polytechnic University: 359, 362
Athens Polytechnic Uprising (1973): 368; casualty figures of, 359
Athonias Academy: 33–4
Athos, Mount: 20–1, 41
Australia: 325
Austria: 161, 193, 203, 218
Austro-Hungarian Empire: 189–90, 283; annexation of Bosnia and Herzegovina (1908), 230, 244
ayans: 24, 26
Averof, Evangelos: 365–6; Greek Minister of Defence, 371; Greek Minister of Foreign Affairs, 344
Avgi: 357
Axis Occupation of Greece (1941–5), 299–304, 325–6; destruction of Nazi National Socialist Patriotic Organisation (1942), 304; resistance movement efforts during, 303–9

Badoglio, Field Marshal Pietro: 290
Balkan radicalism: 36
Balkan Wars (1912–13): 4, 200, 211, 222, 227, 233, 243–4, 247, 249, 251, 272–3, 277, 299, 427; belligerents of, 254–5; political impact of, 245, 324; Second Balkan War (1913), 203; Serbian-Bulgarian Treaty (1911), 244; territories annexed following, 262–3
Basarab, Constantin: 31, 38
Belgium: 175; Constitution of (1831), 151; urbanisation in, 175, 226
beratli: concept of, 28
Black Sea: 30, 160, 168, 173
Bosnia and Herzegovina: 157, 160–1; annexed by Austro-Hungarian Empire (1908), 230, 244; Herzegovina Uprising (1875–7), 160
Bretton Woods System: 351
Bulgaria: 193, 229, 242, 274, 281, 283, 294, 314; annexation of Eastern Roumelia, 203, 206; borders of, 251, 264, 297; government of, 251; Greek Invasion of (1925), 254; Independence of (1908), 230; Meleniko, 229; political influence of, 12, 156, 159–60, 187; refugee population of, 275

Cadet Military Academy: 199
Calvinism: 31
Canada: 325
Canning, George: 69; British Foreign Secretary, 67; declaration of British neutrality in Greek War of Independence (1823), 68
Cappadocia: 275
Catholicism: 31–2, 96, 273
Central Committee for Wheat Concentration: founding of (1927), 284
Cephalonians: 30
Chalkiopoulos, P.: 161
Chams (ethnic group): 304; collaboration with Italin forces, 319; role in Greek politics, 274–5
Chania Herald: 234
Chatzeres, Patriarch Samuel: 17, 20, 34
Chatzivasileiou, Evanthis: 339
Charalambis, Sotiris: 64
Chiflik (land system): 134
cholera: outbreaks of, 178–80
Christianity: 3, 16, 18–19, 23, 25–6, 34–5, 50, 58–9, 61, 75, 131–2, 145, 157–8, 161, 164, 186, 242, 423; excommunication, 17; Gospel, 221; Holy Communion, 17; noble groups, 22–3; Orthodox, 3, 11–12, 14, 16–17, 19, 21, 28, 30–7, 39–40, 43–8, 96, 206–7, 223, 341, 425

Chrstidis, D.: 153
Christopoulos, C.: 100
Churchill, Winston: 305, 321; meeting with Josef Stalin (1944), 314
Ciano, Galeazzo: 293
Clarendon, Lord: 155
Coalition of the Left and Progress (Synaspismos/): coalition administration with New Democracy, 383
Coalition of the Radical Left (Syriza): 410, 415; coalition with ANEL, 419–21; political impact of, 417–18
Cold War: 8–9, 321, 332, 335–6, 339, 352, 356, 359–61, 363, 371, 429; Iron Curtain, 324–5
Commercial Bank: 373
Commission for the Reinforcement of Church and Education: founding of (1887), 237
Communist Party of Greece (KKE): 277, 288, 294, 306, 309, 313, 320, 322, 324, 374, 416; banning of, 323; electoral performance of (1932), 287; members of, 272, 312, 316, 320–1, 332, 336; outlawing of (1947), 337; role in formation of EAM, 304; Seventh Congress (1945), 320
Concert of Europe: 2, 158–9; political impact of, 109
'Concession of National Lands to the Phalangists' (1838): 135
Congress of Berlin (1878): 189–90, 203; political impact of, 193; territories granted to Greece during, 196
Constantine I of Greece: 199, 213–14, 219, 234, 278, 428; accession of (1913), 249; escape from Greece (1917), 252; restoration of (1920), 253
Constantine II of Greece: refusal of Ministry of Defence control for George Papandreou (1965), 355
Convention of Constantinople (1881): provisions of, 190
Corfiots: 30; key figures of, 33, 49
Corinth Canal: 57; construction of, 202
Corydalleus, Theophilus: 31; students of, 31
Cosmas of Aetolia: 17, 33, 39
Council of State: 81–2, 124–5, 129, 357; abolition of, 119; founding of (1835), 80; members of, 80; re-establishment of (1911), 236
Court Council: 125
Cretan Revolt (1878): 200, 205
Cretan Revolt (1897–8): 213–14
Crimean War (1853–6): 2–3, 109–15, 146, 158, 230; belligerents of, 159; political impact of, 112, 121, 187
Crouzet, F.: 343
Cyprus: 336, 404, 429; coup d'état (1974), 359; Cyprus Dispute, 353–4, 358–9, 368, 371; Constitution of, 353; Greek, 341–3, 353; integration into EU, 385; Turkish, 343, 353, 378; Turkish Invasion of (1974), 359, 366, 369
Cyril V, Patriarch: 20

Dafnis, G.: 119
Damaskinos, Archbishop: 317–18
Danube, River: 168, 173
Danubian Principalities: 15, 39, 53, 66–7, 70; Phanariot presence in, 15–16
Deligiorgis, Epameinondas: 121, 191, 195; foreign policy of, 159
Deliyannis (noble family): 23, 57, 61, 64
Deliyannis, Anagnostis: 65

Deliyannis, Ioannis: execution of (1815), 23–4
Deliyannis, N.: caretaker administration of, 213
Deliyannis, Theodoros: 156, 165, 191, 198–9, 203, 214; administration of, 208; background of, 192; Greek Minister of Foreign Affairs, 155; resignation of, 203–4
Demertzis, Konstantinos: caretaker administration of, 289
Democratic Alignment Party: electoral performance of (1950), 332
Democratic Army: 323, 380; casualty figures of, 324–5; creation of (1946), 322; members of, 376; presence of Slavophone Macedonians in, 324
Democratic Socialist Party: electoral performance of (1950), 332
Democratic Union: electoral performance of (1923), 271; electoral performance of (1956), 342; members of, 271–2
Denmark: Constitution of (1843), 151; Copenhagen, 150
Diderot, Denis: *Encyclopaedia*, 43
Dikaios, G.: death of, 52
Dimaras, C.T.: 103
Dimaras, K.: 238
Diomedes, Alexandros: Greek Minister of Finance, 255
Double Revisionary Parliament: proposals for, 235
Doukas (clan): 14
Dragasakis, Yannis: 420
Dragoumis, Stefanos: 235
Dramali, Mahmud Pasha: military forces led by, 56

Eastern Greece (region): 72; creation of, 68
Eastern Question: 159, 187, 193, 207, 214–15, 230–1, 424; efforts to resolve, 3
Economic Climate Index: 414
Economos, Constantinos: 99
Economou, Antonios: mutiny led by, 55–6
Economou, Konstantinos: 138
Ecumenical Patriarchate: 17–19, 31, 33–7, 42, 96, 138–9, 159–60, 206–7; establishment of (1601), 12; incorporation of Ohrid and Ipek (1766–7), 16; Phanariot control over, 20
Egypt: 27, 298; Alexandria, 17, 299, 310; Cairo, 310–11; Suez Canal, 168, 202; Suez Crisis (1956), 344
Eldem, Edhem: 28
Elliot, Henry: Special Envoy to Athens, 148
Elpius Public Hospital of Athens: founding of (1842), 185
energy crisis (1979): impact of, 377
Engineering Corps: senior offices of, 175
Epirus Revolt (1878): 150, 200, 205
European Central Bank (ECB): 401, 407, 410, 419; personnel of, 394, 412, 417; Securities Markets Program (SMP), 419
European Commission: Excessive Deficit Procedure, 399; personnel of, 394
European Council: Greek withdrawal from (1969), 357–8
European Economic Community (EEC): 344, 360, 378, 429; Council of Ministers, 370; Greek accession to (1975), 370–1; members of, 350, 362, 370
European Enlightenment: 35, 146
European Free Trade Association (EFTA): 350

European Monetary Union (EMU): 383; member states of, 385
European Union (EU): 382, 393, 395, 400, 403, 410, 420, 422, 429; Finance Ministers (ECOFIN), 401; Maastricht Treaty (1982), 382–3; member states of, 385; Parliament, 418; poverty rates in, 392; Stability and Growth Programme (2010), 401; Summit (2010), 401
Eurostat: 407
Eurozone: 401–2, 407; European Financial Stability Facility (EFSF), 407, 411, 413–14; member states of, 384, 390, 393–4, 403; potential Greek exit from, 404–5, 420–1
Eurozone Crisis (2009–): second phase of, 415–16; third phase of, 416
Evaggelismos Hospital: 186
Eydoux, General Joseph-Paul: 243
Eynard, Jean-Gabriel: 71

Farmakidis, T.: role in development of Greek church, 96
Faroqhi, Suraiya: 25; observations of development in Muslim education, 39–40
fascism: 251, 265
Feraios, Rigas: 36
Filippidis, Daniel: 32
Finlay, George: 86–7, 130, 161
First Memorandum: 407, 411–12; implementation of, 409–10; negotiations for, 406; political impact of, 412–13; provisions of, 408
First World War (1914–18): 116, 247–8, 251, 255–6, 258–60, 264–5, 270, 278, 291, 299, 427–8; belligerents of, 256, 260; Treaty of Lausanne (1923), 267, 341
Flamiatos, Kosmas: 140
Former Yugoslav Republic of Macedonia (FYROM): 381
Fragkiadis, A.: 173
France: 27, 57, 71, 82, 155, 158, 161, 180, 187, 197, 210, 229, 256–7, 280, 356, 370, 402; Cannes, 412; Constitution of (1793), 63; Constitution of (1795), 63; Dreyfus Affair (1894–1906), 240; government of, 387; July Revolution (1830), 73; Maginot Line, 297; Marseille, 27; Paris, 37, 42, 62, 112, 154, 191, 252, 366, 387; Revolution (1789–99), 30, 35–6, 42–3, 109, 150; Third Republic (1870–1940), 155; trade activity in Levant, 27–9; urbanisation in, 175, 226; wine industry of, 171
Franco-Prussian War (1870–1): 159
Frangos, George: 52
Freethinkers' Party: 282
French Enlightenment: influence of, 43
French Mission of Public Works: establishment of (1883), 202; limitation of powers (1892), 202

Gargalidis, Georgios: 270
Gavroglou, K.: 35
Geithner, Timothy: US Secretary of Treasury, 403
General Confederation of Greek Workers (GSEE): 339; dissolving of (1923), 267; founding of (1918), 259; socialist faction of, 259
General Headquarters of the Guerrillas: establishment of (1946), 322
George: family of, 218; High Commissioner of Crete, 234
George I of Greece: 2, 120, 151, 156, 203, 209, 219, 235; accession of (1863), 150, 159; assassination of (1913), 249; family of, 154, 218–19

George II of Greece: 254, 290, 298–9, 310, 318; annulment of 1936 decree (1942), 310–11; proposed return of, 315; support for Metaxas regime, 289
Germany: 77, 187, 193, 229, 383, 401–2; Berlin, 160; Dachau, 320; efforts to reorganise Ottoman military, 198; government bonds, 398; urbanisation in, 175, 226
Giannoulis of Aetolia, Evgenios: role in development of School of Agrapha, 31
Girondins (political faction): 150
Gizikis, General Phaedon: administration of, 368
Glarakis, G.: Greek Minister of Ecclesiastical Affairs, 99
Glikis, Nikolaos: 17
Global Financial Crisis (2007–9): 392–3, 395–8, 403; US Subprime Mortgage Crisis (2007–10), 398, 403–4
globalisation: 373, 386; impact of, 394
Golden Dawn: 410; growth of, 416–17
Gordios, Anastasios: 46
Gordon, Thomas: military forces led by, 95
Goudas, A.: background of, 186; estimation of population level of Athens, 162
Goudi Coup (1909): 234–5, 270
Gounaris, Dimitris: 221
Great Depression: 286
Great Powers: 2, 46, 52, 57, 67, 69–70, 75, 78, 85, 89, 109–10, 131, 134, 145, 148, 154, 159–60, 189, 203, 217–18, 244, 289; attempted influence over Greek state, 80, 82–3, 101–6, 112–13, 189–90, 203, 229; blockading of Greek coast (1886), 200; internal disputes, 111, 114; naval forces of, 93
Greece: 1–7, 9–10, 34, 47, 53, 70, 78–9, 91–2, 99–101, 111, 113, 117–18, 134, 141–2, 145, 157, 160–2, 164, 172, 189, 193–5, 203, 207–8, 215, 241–2, 245, 247–8, 263–5, 270, 272–5, 280–1, 297, 310, 328, 331–2, 369, 399–400, 406, 423–4, 430; Acrocorinth, 65; Aegean Islands, 167–8; Aegina (island), 179; agricultural sector of, 169–71, 225; Aitoloakarniania, 180; Aliakmonas, 297, 299; Amaliada, 137; Ampelakia, 29; Anglo-French Invasion of (1916), 252; Anglo-French Occupation of (1854), 113, 121; Aracadia, 89; Argolis, 65; Argos, 73; Astros, 64, 133; Athens, 57, 72, 88, 94, 105, 114, 116, 126, 131, 139–40, 143–4, 147–8, 158, 162, 166–7, 175–6, 179–80, 182, 185, 200, 203, 227, 230, 233, 251–3, 261, 267, 276, 298–300, 304, 308–9, 314, 316, 322, 344, 350–1, 368, 385, 387; Attica, 164, 166, 179, 192, 220, 313; Chalcis, 72; Chios (island), 12, 23, 40, 72; cholera epidemic (1854), 179–80; civil service of, 375; Corfu, 73, 192, 220, 254, 268, 274; Corinth, 23, 140, 170; Crete, 56–7, 61, 70, 72, 112, 153–4, 157, 160, 205, 208, 213, 218, 230, 259, 282, 298–9, 320; Drama, 284; economy of, 164, 168–9, 171–4, 176, 208, 210–12, 222–4, 254–9, 276, 278–80, 287, 290, 302–3, 325–8, 340–1, 346–51, 372–3, 377, 380, 390, 393, 398–9, 403–5, 407–8, 411, 413, 415–16, 419–20; education system of, 100–3, 124, 391–2;

elections (1841–2), 87; electoral systems of, 151–2; Epidarus, 66, 133; Epirus, 25–6, 29, 55, 157, 160, 189, 193, 198, 314, 319; Ermioni, 66; Ermoupoli, 88, 173, 178; Evritania, 168; Fthiotida, 180; Gargalianoi, 314; GDP per capita, 123–4, 169, 380, 385–6, 399–400, 405, 408, 410–11, 413–15; Gorgopotamos, 352; Gortynia, 192, 220; Goudi, 234; government bonds, 398, 411; healthcare sector of, 405; higher education system of, 237–8, 405; Hydra (island), 30, 55–6, 60, 65–6, 73–4, 90, 93–4, 131, 199; Ileia, 23, 137; illiteracy rates in, 236, 362; industrial sector of, 373; Ioannina, 33, 52, 55, 362; Ionian Islands, 30, 52, 73, 103, 150, 191–2, 227; Jewish population of, 274, 302; judicial system of, 103–4; Kalamata, 167, 227, 314; Kalavryta, 23; Kaltezes, 61; Karababa, 72; Kidonies, 40; Kifisos, 182; Kinouria, 168; Kopaida, 183; Koroni, 55; Kos (island), 57; Kozani, 33; Laconia, 89; Lamia, 72; Larissa, 55; Litochoro, 321; Livadia, 23; Mani, 50, 74, 89–90, 98, 140, 147, 175, 179; Marathon, 155; Megalopolis, 90; Meligala, 314; Messina, 89–90; Methoni, 55, 90; military of, 197, 294–5, 365; Miloi, 227; mining industry of, 172; Ministry of Agriculture, Trade and Industry, 243; Ministry of Defence, 220; Ministry of Finance, 223; Ministry of Health, Welfare and Care, 187; Ministry of Interior Affairs, 85; Ministry of Labour, 305; Ministry of National Economy, 243; Ministry of Provisioning, 258; Ministry of Transport and Communications, 243; Missolonghi, 57, 66, 90, 104, 122, 133, 171; Monemvasia, 54; Morea, 24–5, 65; Muslim population of, 260; Mykonos (island), 179; Nafplion, 55, 65–6, 97, 104–5, 121, 142, 169, 176; national debt of, 287; national lands issues in, 129–30, 134–7; Navarino Bay, 69; Naxos, 114; Neokastro, 54; Nisi, 90; Olympus, 297, 321; Parnassida, 180; Paros (island), 114, 179; Patras, 23, 54–5, 61, 122, 167, 170, 186, 192, 202, 227, 362; Piraeus, 88, 112, 114, 178, 182, 185, 200, 202, 252; population growth of, 162–3, 175, 273; Poros, 178; Psara (island), 30, 55, 60, 73, 199; public debt of, 223, 255, 398, 401–2, 411, 413; public deficit of, 347, 393, 400, 408–10; public health issues in, 177–8, 182–5, 391; public works projects in, 284–6; Pyrgos, 90, 314; refugee population of, 275–6; Roumeli, 59, 65–6; Salona, 61; Serres, 284; Smyrna, 27, 40, 52, 261, 341; Souda, 200; Sparta, 175; Spetses (island), 30, 55, 60, 65–6, 73, 90, 199; Stemnitsa, 133; Strimonas, 299; Syros (island), 167, 179, 186; taxation system of, 126–9, 135–6, 210–13, 224, 257, 377, 392; Thebes, 104; Thessaloniki, 17, 30, 52, 249, 251–2, 260, 262–3, 276–7, 281, 284, 297, 299, 302, 304, 318, 346, 351, 412; Thessaly, 25, 55, 156, 160, 175, 190, 193, 196, 205, 211, 221, 225, 227, 262, 306, 387; Tinos (island), 89, 179; transportation network of, 199–202, 227; urbanisation in, 225–6; Volos, 30, 227; Vostitsa, 23

Greco-Turkish Population Exchange (1923): 273; impact on population demographics, 263–4
Greco-Turkish War (1897): 195, 214, 217, 229, 253, 258, 267, 281, 427; political impact of, 198–9, 218, 232; Treaty of Constantinople (1897), 219
Greek Central Intelligence Agency: 339
Greek Civil War (1946–9): 3–4, 6, 9, 264, 319, 322, 324, 331, 334–5, 338–40, 344, 346, 348, 352, 354, 356, 360–1, 366, 372, 376, 428; *Dekemvriana*, 316–17, 319–20; Greek national army participation during, 327; infrastructure reconstruction during, 326; political impact of, 332, 335, 428–9; population migration during, 325
Greek Constitution (1844): 118–19, 121, 151; political impact of, 145; provisions of, 118, 138
Greek Constitution (1864): 236; provisions of, 151–2, 205
Greek Constitution (1911): 270, 335; provisions of, 235–6, 263
Greek Constitution (1952): Article 12, 348–9; provisions of, 335, 337; voting on, 335
Greek Constitution (1973): 358–9
Greek Constitution (1975): ratification of, 372
Greek Constitution (2001): Article 57, 390–1
Greek Constitution (Epidaurus): approval of, 66; provisions of, 63
Greek disease: ideology of, 388; outbreak of, 387–8
Greek Enlightenment: 32, 37–8, 42, 45; key figures of, 36–7; key locations of, 51; limits of, 38
Greek Orthodox Church: 97–8, 138–9, 341; Holy Synod, 98–9, 138, 182; monasteries, 98–9; Secretariat of the Church, 98; 'Synodal Tome', 139
Greek Rally: 335–6, 340–2; as ERE, 342, 348; electoral success of (1951), 335; members of, 340
Greek War of Independence (1821–9): 4, 20, 25, 40, 43, 51, 62, 66–7, 74–5, 82, 84, 91, 93–4, 96, 116–17, 119, 122, 126, 130, 133–4, 141–2, 151, 162–3, 170, 173–4, 185, 204–5, 213, 424–7; Battle of Navarino (1827), 69; Battle of Petra (1829), 72; Battle of Phaliron (1827), 58–9; British neutrality in, 68; entry of Egyptian army into (1825), 56–7; Egyptian/Ottoman Occupation of Athens (1827), 57; Egyptian/Ottoman Occupation of Missolonghi (1826), 57; instigation of, 52–3; national lands issue during, 130; resistance force structure in, 57–8; role of naval fleets in, 30–1, 55–6; role of Philike Etaireia, 52; sale of religious texts prior to, 40–1; Siege of Corinth, 54–5; Siege of Ioannina, 54; Siege of the Acropolis, 59
Gregory V, Patriarch: 36, 42; hanging of, 67
Grivas, D.: 150
Grivas, Georgios: leader of EOKA, 344
Grivas, Theodorakis: rebellion led by (1862), 118, 122, 147–8, 269
Gropius: 130–1
Guizot: 84
Gyaros Island Concentration Camp: 323

Habsburg Empire: 11, 16; Bucharest,

41; Iasi, 41; Laibach, 67; Vienna, 40–1, 51
Hague Conference (1929): 283
Harmenopoulos, Constantine: *Hexabiblos*, 17, 104
von Heideck, Carl Wilhelm: 77
Hellenic Normarchy: 36
Hellenism: 195
heterocthons: 89, 117, 130–1
historiography: international, 9; Greek, 2, 9, 43
Hitler, Adolf: 295
Holy Alliance: Laibach Summit, 67; members of, 53, 67; Verona Summit, 67
Holy League: establishment of (1684), 11
Holy Roman Empire: Vienna, 11–12
Honduras: 210
humanism: religious, 33

Ilinden Uprising (1904): role of EMEO in, 233
Independent Greeks (ANEL): 417; coalition with Syriza, 419–21
India: 378
Initiative of the Six: participants in, 378
International Company of the Maritime Canal of Corinth: founding of (1881), 202
International Court of Justice: 371
International Exposition: Greek participation in, 144–5
International Financial Commission: 223; aims of, 218
International Monetary Fund (IMF): 393–4, 399, 403, 407–8, 410, 413–14, 419
Ioannidis, Dimitris: 359, 365; leader of EENA, 338
Ionian Sea: 173
Iordanoglou, C.: 411
Islam: 18, 23, 25, 129, 260, 275; conversion to, 39
Italy: 29, 158, 193, 203, 229, 306, 370; Bologna, 11; bombardment and occupation of Corfu (1923), 254, 268; Caserta, 313; Livorno, 40; Naples, 66; occupation of Dodecanese (1911), 244; Padua, 40; Rome, 33; Trieste, 30, 40; urban population of, 226; Venice, 30, 40; Verona, 67
Izzedin Fortress: 218

Jaruzelski, Wojciech: rise to power (1981), 378
Jesuits: 31
Joachim III: 206; resignation of, 207
Joannicius III, Patriarch: 20
Judaism: 12, 30, 261–2, 274–5, 302; anti-Semitism, 262, 274; Shoah, 302

Kafandaris, Georgios: 271, 283, 286; electoral performance of (1932), 287
Kalivas, Stathis: 309
Kallifronas, Dimitrios: 121; opposition to, 121–2
Kanaris, Admiral M.: family of, 213
Kanaris, Konstantinos: 117, 147, 150; death of, 156; family of, 213; suggested reforms of, 122
Kandakouzinos (clan): 14
Kanellopoulos, Panagiotis: 314, 320, 334, 342; administration of, 356, 365; role in government in exile, 311
Kantakouzenos, Prince: 31, 131
Kapodistrias, I.: 66, 70, 72, 89, 103, 134, 174–5; assassination of (1831), 142; background of, 70–1; founder of National Financial Bank, 130; Governor of Greece, 70; state apparatus developed by, 72–3

Karaiskakis, Georgios: 61; leader of Roumeliots, 59
Karamanlis, Konstantinos: 344, 346, 372, 379, 429; administration of, 342–3, 353, 368, 370; background of, 342; electoral victory of (1977), 370; family of, 387; foreign policy of, 370–1; founder of New Democracy, 368; Greek Minister of Public Works, 341; President of Greece, 370; resignation of, 356
Karamanlis, Kostas: administration of, 389; family of, 387; leader of New Democracy, 387
Karapanos, Konstantinos: 209
Kardamilis, N.: execution of (1955), 337
Karoifllis, I.: 31
Kartalis, Georgios: 321; co-founder of EKKA, 305; Greek Minister of Coordination, 347
Kastorianos, Manolakis: 11
Katakazis, Konstantin: 96
Katartzis, Dimitrios: 32, 34
Kitrmolidis, Paschalis: 20, 36
Kokkonis, I.: 100
Kolettis, Ioannis: 62, 89, 112, 116; death of (1847), 114, 117; electoral victory of (1844), 121
Koliopoulos, John: 6
Kollyvades Movement: 20
Kolokotronis (noble family): 57
Kolokotronis, Gennaios: family of, 117; head of military corps, 140
Kolokotronis, Panos: family of, 65
Kolokotronis, Theodoros: 56–7, 64; family of, 65, 117; vice president of executive branch of National Assembly, 64–5; trial of, 79
Kondylis, Georgis: 272, 288–9; administration of, 281; Greek Minister of Military Affairs, 287–8
Konstantas, Grigorios: 32
Korais, Adamantios: 35–7; background of, 36–7; lectures of, 42–3
Korean Air Lines Flight 007 (1983): 378
Korean War (1950–3): 329; Greek expeditionary force during, 336
Koromilas, Lambros: Greek Minister of Finance, 255
Koronaios, P.: 147
Koryzis, Alexandros: 295; suicide of (1941), 298
Kotzias, Konstantinos: 298
Koumas, Konstantinos: 12, 19, 45
Koumoundouros, Alexandros: 121, 154, 156, 159, 190, 195; administration of, 136, 154; Greek Minister of the Interior, 153; trial of, 154
Koundouriotis, Georgios: 65, 117; resignation of (1929), 286
Kriezis, A.: 117

Labour House: 339
Lambrakis, Grigoris: 346
Lambros, Spyridon: 214
Lavrio Mining Company: 172
Law 1876/90: provisions of, 409
Law 2058 ('On Measures of Peace') (1952): 335
Law 2987/1953: provisions of, 349
Law 375/1936: provisions of, 337
Law 4046/2012: 413
Law 509/1947: provisions of, 337
Le Monde: 388
Le Suire, Wilhelm: head of Greek Defence Ministry, 79
League of Nations: 187, 254, 281; Refugee Settlement Commission, 279
Lebanon: 312–13
Lebanon Conference (1944): key at-

tendees of, 312; political impact of, 312–13
Leonardopoulos, Panagiotis: 270
Leopold of Belgium: resignation of, 73–4
Leopold of Saxonburg: 145
Liakos, A.: 239
Liberal Party: 243, 282, 286; electoral performance of (1915), 249, 251; electoral performance of (1932), 287; electoral performance of (1950), 332; members of, 235, 340
liberalism: intellectual, 33
Livadia: 86
Lodos, Andreas: 65
Logothetopoulos, Konstantinos: 299
London Conference (1830): 130
London Protocol (1828): signing of, 70
London Protocol (1830): provisions of, 77; signing of, 130
London-Zurich Agreements (1959): 353
Lontos, Andreas: 64
Lontos, Sotiris: execution of (1812), 23
Louis XVI of France: execution of (1793), 36
Loukaris, Cyril: 31–2, 44
Ludwig I of Bavaria, King: 77–8; family of, 74, 77, 125
Lyons, Sir Edmund: British Ambassador to Greece, 121, 125

Macedonia: 25, 55, 161, 205–6, 229–30, 234, 237, 281, 299, 310, 342, 381; Bulgarian interests in, 230, 233, 251; Kilkis, 314; Monastiri, 229; Naoussa, 306; refugee population of, 276; Stromnitsa, 229; Western, 274, 297, 306; Yugoslavian, 319
Macedonia Revolutionary Organisation: Comitatus, 229–30
Macedonian Revolution (1878): 200
Mahmud II, Sultan: 43; offer issued to Mehmet Ali (1825), 56
Makarios III, Archbishop: 343–4, 358–9
Makarios of Assine, Bishop: 141
Makris, Fotis: control over GSEE, 339, 354
Makronisos Island Concentration Camp: 322–3
Makrygiannis, Yannis: 117
maktu: concept of, 21–2
malikane: concept of, 21
Malta: 30
Mani Revolt (1845): 118
Maniots: members of, 54
Manitakis, E.: 175
Marathon Dam: 182
Margaritis, G.: 295
Markezinis, Spyros: administration of, 358; Greek Minister of Coordination, 340–1, 358
Marshall Plan (1948): 327, 360; political impact of, 339
Maternity Hospital: founding of (1835), 186
Matsaganis, Manos: 421
von Maure, Georg Ludwig: 77
Maurer, G.: 90–1, 96, 142–3; expulsion from Greece (1834), 104; role in development of Greek judicial system, 103–5
Mavrogenis: 25
Mavrogordatos, G.: 253
Mavrokordatos, Alexandros: 11–12, 31, 52, 63, 74, 82–3, 89, 112, 114, 116, 191; family of, 15, 32, 62; Prince of Wallachia, 15; resignation of (1855), 65, 114
Mavrokordatos, Nikolaos: family of, 15, 32; *Filotheou Parerga*, 32

Mavromichalis (noble family): 61
Mavromichalis, Konstantinos: 220
Mavromichalis, Kyriakoulis: 234
Mavromichalis, Petrobey: 50, 62; leader of Maniots, 54; President of Greek Parliament, 64; President of executive branch of National Assembly, 64
Maximos, Serafim: 272
McCarthyism: 3, 360
Medical Committee: founding of (1843), 184; personnel of, 184; renamed Supreme Health Council (1922), 184
Medical University of Athens: 184
Medium Term Plan (2011–15): terms of, 411–12
Megalou Spilaiou Monastery: 140
Merkel, Angela: 411–12
Metapolitefsi: 1, 4, 363, 374, 389
Metaxas, Andreas: 89, 116, 254; vice president of executive branch of National Assembly, 64
Metaxas, Ioannis: 270–1, 282; death of (1941), 295; populist policies of, 290; regime of, 277, 289, 291, 293–4, 299
Mexico: 210, 378
Miaoulis, Andreas: administration of, 122; head of Aegean fleet, 72
Michalakopoulos, Andreas: leader of Democratic Union, 272
Mihail: assassination of, 158
Military League: dissolution of 235, 287; members of, 234
millet: concept of, 20
Ministerial Council: 83
Mitsotakis, Konstantinos: 379, 381; administration of, 381–2; leader of New Democracy, 374
Moisiodax, Iosipos: 32–3, 35
Moldavia: 12, 52; Ottoman control over, 15
Montagnards (political faction): 150
Montenegro: 157
Moody's: credit rating system of, 414
Moraitinis, A.: 154; Vice President of National Assembly of Athens, 150
Mussolini, Benito: 254, 290; regime of, 293
Mustafa, Grand Vizier Kara: 12

Napoleonic Wars (1803–15): 26, 31, 49, 109
National and Social Liberation Group (EKKA): 305, 308
National Assembly: 88, 117, 130, 138, 148; electoral law (1844), 119; executive branch of, 64; First (1821), 62–4, 133; Fourth (1829), 73, 78; parliamentary branch of, 64; Second (1823), 64, 133; self-dissolution of, 71–2; Third (1824), 66, 68, 70
National Assembly of Athens: 150–1, 271; Second (1863), 148, 150
National Bank of Greece: 209, 255, 348, 373, 399, 417; creation of, 108; foreign currency reserves of, 256; gold reserves of, 299; personnel of, 295, 380
National Camp (EP): 369
National Defence: 251–2
National Defence Fund: loans guaranteed by, 232
National Democratic Party: creation of (1924), 262
National Financial Bank: 130
National Health System (ESY): creation of, 376
National League: electoral performance of (1932), 288
National Liberation Front (EAM):

308–9, 313, 316–17, 319, 321; defeat of (1944), 317–18; formation of (1941), 304; influence of, 311–12; members of, 318–20, 345, 374; National People's Liberation Army (ELAS), 305–7, 309–10, 313–16, 320; organisation efforts of, 304–5, 309; representatives of, 312; supporters of, 319; territorial holdings of, 305–6
National Organisation of Cypriot Fighters (EOKA): 344; formation of (1955), 341; members of, 344
National Party: 88–9
National Political Union: electoral performance of (1946), 321; members of, 320
National Progressive Centre Union: 352–5, 363; attempts to control CSSEE, 354; electoral performance of (1963), 352; founding of (1961), 334, 345; granting of military control to crown (1963), 338; members of, 345–6
National Radical Union (ERE): 353, 355, 368; electoral performance of (1956), 342; electoral performance of (1958), 344; electoral performance of (1961), 345; formerly Greek Rally, 342; members of, 356, 365–6
National Republican Greek League (EDES): 306, 314, 319; founding of (1941), 305; representatives of, 312
National Schism (1910–22): 236, 251, 309, 340, 356, 428; collapse of, 360; political impact of, 254, 258, 264–5
National Society: founding of (1894), 214
National Union of Greece: founding of, 262
National Union of Youth Officers (EENA): 8
National Youth Organisation: creation of, 289–90
nationalism: 45, 252
Naval Academy: 199
Negris, Thodoris: 74; Ottoman Vice-Ambassador in Paris, 62
Negroponte, M.: Greek Minister of Finance, 257
Nenekos: 61
neoliberalism: 381
Neophytos (Bishop of Attica): 139
Netherlands: 27, 175; Hague, The, 371; urban population of, 226
New Democracy: 371–5, 379, 389–90, 392, 395, 398–9, 407, 415–18; coalition administration with PASOK and LAOS, 412; coalition administration with Synaspismos, 383; electoral performance of (1974), 368; electoral performance of (1990), 381; electoral performance of (2004), 387; electoral performance of (2009), 415; founding of (1974), 368; members of, 369, 380
New Loan Agreement (2011): 412
Nicodemus the Hagiorite: influence of, 42
Nikitas: leader of Peloponnesians, 59
Nikolakopoulos, Ilias: 415
Nikousios, Dragoman Panagiotis: 11–12; death of (1673), 12
Noemvriana: 260
North Atlantic Treaty Organization (NATO): 343–4, 353, 366, 371, 378, 421; members of, 336, 339, 372

Obrenovic of Serbia, Prince Mihajlo: 84
Office of Public Finance: 107

Oil Crisis (1973): economic impact of, 372–3
Olga, Queen: family of, 154; public health initiatives of, 186
'On Building Healthy Cities and Villages' (1835): provisions of, 107
'On Military Facilities' (1953): 341
'On Settling Crete' (1848): 135
'On the Validation of a Democratic System' (1924): 272
Opthalmiatric Hospital: founding of (1843), 186
Optimum Currency Area: 404
Organisation for Business Reconstruction (OAE): founding of, 377
Organisation for Economic Co-operation and Development (OECD): 327, 329, 392; public employment rates in, 361
Organisation X: 317; members of, 357
Orlov Revolts (1770–1): political significance of, 46
Osman, Topal: 24
Otto of Greece, King: 2, 5–7, 79, 81, 85, 87–8, 94, 96, 110–13, 115–18, 120, 122–3, 129, 139–40, 144–5, 148, 151–2, 166, 175, 182, 232; appointment of (1832), 74, 77–8; dissolving of Parliament (1859), 121–2; family of, 124; governing policies of, 80–2, 111, 113–14, 118, 120, 123–4, 135, 139–40; national land redistribution under, 134, 136; removed from power (1862), 75, 83–4, 115, 127–8, 147, 157, 168, 230, 237, 426
Ottoman Empire: 3, 5, 10–12, 14, 16–17, 19–20, 24, 26–7, 29, 32, 35–6, 42–5, 51, 53–4, 60–1, 67, 69, 74–5, 87, 94, 96–7, 104, 108, 129–31, 133, 154, 158, 164–5, 169, 174, 176–7, 189, 193–4, 206, 223, 229, 231, 243–4, 260, 341, 424–6; Alexandria, 17, 30; Antioch, 17; Christian population of, 164; collapse of (1923), 161; Constantinople, 12, 15–16, 18, 20–1, 24, 27, 30–1, 39, 41, 46, 48, 51, 54, 67, 217, 341, 424; Derbendcis, 94; Emlakika, 23; Imperial Council, 12, 14; Janissary Corps, 14; Jerusalem, 17; Karytainia, 23; land legislation of, 131–2; military forces of, 60, 198, 218; navy of, 15, 56, 60; opposition movements within, 44–6; Phanari, 23; Sublime Porte, 12, 15–16, 25–8, 49, 52, 54, 67, 159–60, 203, 233; Tanzimat, 43; taxation system of, 21–2; territory of, 12, 44, 55, 179, 217, 423; trading activity of, 28–30; Tripoli, 53–4, 58, 65, 147, 182; Wallachia, 53; Young Turks, 244

Palamas, Kostis: 238
Palmerston, Lord: 148
Pangalos, Theordoros: 254; coup led by (1925), 272; Greek Minister of Legal Order, 272
Panhellenic Liberation Organisation: dissolving of (1943), 308
Panhellenic Reserve Association: formation of, 251
Panhellenic Socialist Movement (PASOK): 370, 379, 382–3, 386, 389, 391, 399, 407, 410, 412, 416–18; coalition administration with LAOS and New Democracy, 412; educational policies of, 377; electoral performance of (1981), 373–6; electoral performance of (1985), 379; electoral performance of (2004), 387; electoral performance

of (2009), 415; founding of (1974), 374; members of, 379–80; supporters of, 383
Papaflessas: 62
Papadimos, Loukas: 412
Papadoupoulos, Georgios: 338–9, 358; background of, 357; leader of 21 April Coup (1967), 356; removed from power (1973), 368
Papagos, Lieutenant General Alexandros: 294–5, 297, 335, 337–8, 341–2; administration of, 336, 340, 358; death of, 342; military forces led by, 324; supporters of, 336
Papkonstantinou, Giorgios: Greek Minister of Finance, 399, 402
Papdemos, Loukas: 417
Papalexis (noble family): 23
Papanastasiou, Alexandros: administration of, 271–2, 287; leader of Democratic Union, 271
Papandreou, Andreas: 376, 378, 382; administration of, 382, 398, 400; electoral victory of (1981), 373–4; family of, 352, 373, 387; foreign policy of, 378; leader of PASOK, 373
Papandreou, George: administration of, 417; family of, 387
Papandreou, George (senior): 312–13, 320, 332, 345, 352, 429; family of, 352, 373; head of government in exile, 315–16; refused control of Ministry of Defence by Constantine II (1965), 355; resignation of (1944), 317–18
Paparrigopoulos, Constantine: 241; *History of the Greek Nation*, 240–2
Papas, A.: death of, 52
Papoulakos, Christoforos: 140; arrest and exile of, 141; background of, 140; preaching activity of, 140–1
Papoulakos Revolt (1852): 139
Papatsonidis (noble family): 23
Para-Constitution: 337
Parios, Athanasios: 33
Paris Conference (1856): 167–8; participants in, 158; terms of, 155
Parker Incident (1850): 113
Parliament of Greece: 63, 65, 89, 118–20, 126, 133, 136, 139, 152–3, 155–6, 209, 221, 234–5, 243, 249–50, 252, 282, 344, 368, 387–8, 394, 407, 421; dissolved (1859), 121–2
Parliament of Mayors: 122
Party of Liberal Democrats: electoral performance of (1923), 271
Paşa, Reşid Mehmed: 59
Pasha, Ali: 44, 54–5; defeat of, 55; family of, 26; territory controlled by, 25
Pasha, Ibrahim: family of, 56; military forces led by, 56–7, 61, 66, 69
Pasha, Köprülü Fazil Ahmed: 12
Pasha, Mahmud: 61
Pasha, Veli: family of, 26
Patiniotis, M.: 35
Patriarchal School: 33–4, 41–2
Paul of Greece, King: 297, 342; accession of, 356
Pazvantoğlu of Vidin, Osman: 44
Pedagogical Institute: founding of, 354
Peloponnese (region): 22–6, 50, 52–6, 58, 62–4, 69, 72, 75, 90, 147, 163, 170, 180, 227, 300, 324; creation of, 68; fires (2007), 390; land ownership in, 137–8
Peloponnesian Senate: 62, 64; abolition of (1823), 64; assembly of (1821), 61
People's Party: 282, 287, 289, 304, 334; electoral performance of (1935), 288; electoral performance of

(1946), 321; electoral performance of (1950), 332; members of, 287, 299, 341–2; support for return of George II, 315
Perdikaris, Michael: 23, 45; *Rigas, or against False Phihellenes*, 35
Peru: 210
Peter the Great: 15
Petropoulos, John A.: 88
Petmezas, S.: 126
Phalanx: establishment of (1835), 93
Phanariots: 14–15, 18, 31–3, 36, 46, 62, 103; concept of, 12; conception of government, 34; control over Ecumenical Patriarchate, 20; infrastructure developed by, 32; key families of, 48
Philemon, Timoleon: 88
Philike Etaireia: 25, 63, 74–5; founding of (1814), 47; Invisible Authority, 47–9, 51, 54, 62; members of, 47–50, 52; role in Greek War of Independence (1821–9), 52; social composition of, 51; weakening of, 52
Philorthodox Company: 140
Piromaglou, Komninos: co-founder of EDES, 305
Piscatory, Français: 88–9
Pitsakis, Konstantinos: 17
Plastiras, Nikolaos: 269, 318, 334, 336; administration of, 334, 340; resignation of, 334
Ploumpidis, N.: shooting of (1954), 340
Poland: 378
Political Committee for National Liberation (PEEA): creation of (1944), 308; elections held by, 309; representatives of, 312
Politis-Kalfov Protocol (1924): provisions of, 281
Polytechnic University: School of Industrial and Fine Arts, 202
Pomaks (minority group): 273
Popular Orthodox Rally (LAOS): 418; coalition administration with New Democracy and PASOK, 412
Poros Conference (1828): political impact of, 70
Porter Report: findings of, 327–8
Portugal: 169, 369, 404; urbanisation in, 176, 226
Pouqueville, F.H.C.: 141
Praidis, G.: Greek Minister of Justice, 104
Private Sector Involvement (PSI): 412–13
Privileged Society for the Protection, Production and Trafficking of Currants: establishment of (1905), 222
Privy Council: 80, 82; abolition of, 83; personnel of, 81
prostichi: concept of, 132–3
Protestantism: 31, 96
Protocol of St Petersburg (1825): signing of, 68–9
Provisional Government of National Defence: establishment of (1916), 251–2
Provisional Government of the State: establishment of (1828), 71
Prussia: 2, 158
Pruth River Campaign (1710–11): political impact of, 15
Psarros, Dimitris: co-founder of EKKA, 305; murder of (1943), 306, 308
Psycharis, Ioannis: 239
Psychogios, D.: 135, 166–7
Putin, Vladimir: 420–1

Quintet, E.: 163

Rallis, Dimitrios: 209, 220, 308, 374; administration of, 370–1; resignation of (1909), 234
Rangavis, Alexandros Rizos: 195; Greek Ambassador to Germany, 160
'Regarding General Administration of the Army' (1900): provisions of, 220
Regency Council: 104; members of, 77–8, 91–2, 96; 'Declaring Irregular Troops' (decree), 92; policies of, 79, 98; use of mercenary forces, 92
Regime of the Colonels (1967–74), 1, 8, 369; 21 April Coup (1967), 356–7, 429; collapse of (1974), 359, 365, 395, 415
Republic of Ireland: 404
Revisionary Parliament: first convened (1910), 235
'Revocation of the Consequences of the Civil War': 380
Richter, H.A.: 293
Romania: 157, 168, 193, 289; oil reserves of, 296; urbanisation in, 176, 226
Roumeliots: key figures of, 59, 84–5; supporters of, 121
Roupel (fortress): surrendered to German/Bulgarian forces (1916), 251
Von Rudhart, Ignatius: 80
Rufos, Benizelos: 122, 147, 150, 153
Russell, Lord: 157
Russian Empire (1721–1917): 16, 46–7, 49, 51, 57, 67–8, 88–9, 97, 112, 146, 148, 154, 158, 175, 178, 193, 218, 229; borders of, 52; Mariupol, 40; Odessa, 40, 47; St Petersburg, 159; urban population of, 225
Russian Federation: 420–1
Russo-Turkish War (1768–74): 25; political impact of, 43; Treaty of Küçük Kaynarca (1774), 16, 30
Russo-Turkish War (1828–9): Ferronays plan, 69; Treaty of Adrianople (1829), 70
Russo-Turkish War (1877–8): 160; Treaty of San Stefano (1878), 156, 160, 242

Sacred Bond of Greek Officers (IDEA): 8, 335; lack of influence, 338; members of, 339
Samaras, Antonis: 410, 417; Greek Minister of Foreign Affairs, 382
Sarafis, Stefanos: 306
Sarkozy, Nicolas: 411–12
Sartzetakis, Christos: 379
Savvas, Konstantinos: 181
Schäuble, Wolfgang: 420
Schinas, K.: 240
Schinas, M.: 138
School of Agrapha: development of, 31
School of Medicine: 186–7
Von Schmaltz, Christian: head of Greek Defence Ministry, 79
Scobie, General Ronald: resistance forces led by, 313
Second Memorandum (2012): 412, 414; evaluations of, 421–2; revision of, 414
Second World War (1939–45): 4, 6, 183, 244, 261, 264, 274, 279, 320, 324, 327, 338, 360, 371, 428; Allied naval blockade of Greece, 300; Axis Invasion of Greece (1940–1), 290, 293–8; belligerents of, 293–6, 305; concentration camps, 302, 320; Holocaust, 302; Italian Spring Offensive (1941): 295; Operation Barbarossa (1941), 296; resistance movement efforts during, 303–9
Secret Macedonian-Adrianople Revolutionary Organisation (EMEO):

formerly Comitatus, 230; role in Ilinden Uprising, 233
Seferis, Georgios: funeral of (1971), 358
Selim III, Sultan: 43
Senate of Greece: 151, 156, 282
Senate of Western Greece: abolition of (1823), 64
Serbia: 84, 154, 157–8, 160, 193, 203, 206, 244, 254, 280; Belgrade, 229; urbanisation in, 176, 226
Seven Years' War (1756–63): 30
Sideris, A.: 137
Siege of Vienna (1683): 11–12
Sigalas, Nikos: 39
Simitis, Kostas: administration of, 384–7, 398; background of, 383–4; foreign policy of, 385; reformist policies of, 386–7
Simopoulos, A.: Greek Minister of Finance, 207
Skiadika Incident (1859): 121
Skliros, G.: 221–2
Skoufas, Nikolaos: co-founder of Philike Etaireia, 47; death of, 52
Slavophone Macedonians (ethnic group): 264, 274–5, 277, 281, 304; collaboration with Italian forces, 319; migration of, 325; presence in Democratic Army, 324
smallpox: 180–1; eradication of, 182
Sobieski, King John: 11
Socialist Workers' Party: establishment of (1918), 260
Society of Observers of Man: 42–3
Sofianopoulos, Ioannis: 321
Sofoulis, K.: coalition administration of, 322
Sofoulis, Themistoklis: 288–9, 320; leader of Democratic Union, 272
Solomos, Dionysios: *Hymn to Liberty*, 239
Sotiropoulos, S.: Greek Finance Minister, 136; role in development of national land legislation, 136
South Eastern German Territorial Administration: 299
Soutsos, I.A.: 131, 146, 162, 165–6
Soutzos, Alexandros: 145–6; death of, 53
Soviet Union (USSR): 313–15, 317, 323, 353, 378; Moscow, 314, 323; Red Army, 315; sphere of influence, 339
Spa Conference (1920): repatriations issued by, 283
Spain: 30, 66, 369, 404; urbanisation in, 175, 226
Spilotopoulos, General P.: 313
Stamatis, Konstantinos: 32
Stalin. Josef: meeting with Winston Churchill (1944), 314
Statutory Charter of the Greek Church (1833): opposition to, 99; publication of, 97
Statutory Law (1929): 277
Stefanopoulos, Stefanos: 341–2, 345
Stergiadis, Aristeidis: 261
Stilitika Incident (1875): 426
Stourzas (clan): 14
Strong, F.: 143–4
Sultan, Beyhan: income of, 23
Summer Olympics (2004): 385–6
Supreme Court: personnel of, 154, 204
Supreme Court of Eastern Central Greece: abolition of (1823), 64
Supreme Health Council: formerly Medical Committee, 184
Svolos, Alexandros: 308–9
Sweden: 378
Swedish Red Cross: 301
Switzerland: 70, 119; Davos, 400; Geneva, 71, 366; Zurich, 344

Tanzania: 378
Theodorakis: 131
Theodoritos, Bishop Vresthenis: Vice-President of Greek Parliament, 64
Theophylact: *Interpretation of the Four Gospels*, 38
Theotokas, Giorgos: 316–17
Theotokis, Georgios: administration of, 220
Theotokis, Nikiforos: 33; *Elements of Physics* (1766–7), 34
Thiers, Frederic: 164
Third Memorandum: negotiations of, 420; signing of, 422
Third International (1919–43): members of, 260; policies of, 277
Third Reich (1933–45): 290, 293–4, 297, 299; Wehrmacht, 296
Thirty Years' War (1618–48): 31
Thrace: 230, 310; Bulgarian Occupation of, 304; Eastern, 267, 275; Muslim population of, 273; refugee population of, 275–6; Western, 273, 276
timariots: 26
Tito, Josip Broz: foreign policy of, 323–4
Treaty of Accession (1979): signing of, 370
Treaty of Alexandria (1828): provisions of, 70
Treaty of Berlin (1878): breaches of, 341; provisions of, 156
Treaty of Constantinople (1832): provisions of, 130
Treaty of Karlowitz (1699): 11–12
Treaty of London (1827): provisions of, 69
Treaty of London (1832): 78; provisions of, 69, 113
Treaty of Passarowitz (1718): provisions of, 28
Treaty of Sèvres (1920): signing of, 252
Treaty of Varkiza (1945): 318–19; signing of, 321
Treaty of Vöslau (1867): 154; provisions of, 157
Treaty of Westphalia (1648): 3
Trial of the Six (1922): 253
Trikeri Concentration Camp: 323
Trikoupis, Charilaos: 2, 5, 122, 156–7, 187, 191, 197–8, 203, 210, 215, 220, 230–1, 236; administration of, 153, 156, 192–4, 207, 209–10; background of, 191–2; electoral defeat of (1890), 208; electoral victory of (1887), 205; family of, 191; fiscal policies of, 212; Greek Minister of Foreign Affairs, 154; 'Past and Present', 115–16; reform policies of, 194–6, 199–200, 203–5, 211; resignation of, 209; 'Tis Ptaci?', 156
Trikoupis, Spiros: 94; resignation of (1829), 73
Trikoupis, Spyridon: family of, 191
Tripartite Agreement: 203
Troika: 419, 421; negotiations with Greek government, 407–8, 412; reports compiled by, 410
Truman, Harry S.: foreign policy of, 322
Tsakalof, Athanassios: 47; co-founder of Philike Etaireia, 47
Tsakalotos, Euclid: 422
Tsaldaris, K.: 322
Tsaldaris, Panagis: 287, 289; leader of People's Party, 287
Tsardom of Russia (1547–1721): 11, 34
Tsipras, Alexis: 406, 420; economic policies of, 421
Tsirimokos, Ilias: 345
Tsolakoglou, General Giorgios: 298; administration of, 299
Tsouderos, Emmanouil: 298, 310, 312

Turkey: 210, 254, 264, 267, 275, 282–3, 289–90, 336, 341, 353, 359, 382, 385; borders of, 357; Istanbul, 275; Karamania, 12; military of, 261; refugee population of, 275; territory of, 267
Turkish-Egyptian War (1839): 112
typhoid fever: 182
Tzanetakis, Tzanis: administration of, 380

Ukraine: War of Independence (1917–21), 247, 257
Union of Young Officers (EENA): founding of (*c.*1956–8), 338; members of, 338–9
United Democratic Left (EDA): 342, 345, 355; electoral performance of (1952), 340; electoral performance of (1958), 344; electoral performance of (1963), 352
United Kingdom (UK): 57, 67–9, 71, 158–9, 173, 175, 180, 193, 203, 218, 229, 256–7, 280, 290, 296, 341, 381, 425; City of London, 68; government of, 305; London, 112, 144, 150, 155, 191, 299, 344; urbanisation in, 175
United Nations (UN): 341; Relief and Rehabilitation Administration (UNRRA), 328
United States of America (USA): 3, 169, 222, 256, 261, 327, 329, 334, 344, 350, 357, 359, 372, 381, 398; Civil War (1861–5), 172; Congress, 322; government of, 301, 401; immigration to, 279, 325; military of, 341; Subprime Mortgage Crisis (2007–10), 398, 403–4
University of Athens: 146, 162, 238, 240, 362; faculty of, 86, 181, 210, 214, 289, 309, 311; founding of (1837), 102
Uprising (1836): political impact of, 95

Vafeiadis, Markos: 323–4; Mountain Government administration of, 323, 376
Vakalopoulos, Missolonghites A.: 61
Valaoras, V.: observations of growth of Greek population, 167
Valaoritis, Ioannis: Head of National Bank, 255
Valvis, Dimitrios: caretaker administration of, 204
Varoufakis, Yanis: Greek Minister of Finance, 419; writings of, 419–21
Velestinlis, Rigas: 32; secret society founded by, 47
Velouchiotis, Aris: 306; military leader of ELAS, 320
Venizelos, Eleftherios: 187, 234–6, 243, 249, 252–3, 257, 260, 265, 271, 277, 287, 289, 291, 345, 412, 428; administration of, 243, 249, 256, 278, 285, 338; agricultural policy of, 285; attempted assassination of (1920), 252; economic policies of, 283–5; electoral victory of (1928), 282; family of, 312; foreign policy of, 282–3
Venizelos, Sophocles: 334–5; family of, 312; leader of Liberal Party, 332; leader of National Political Union, 320
Victoria, Queen: 148
Vipmer, Carolus: President of Medical Committee, 184
Vlachavas, Efthimios: revolt led by, 26
Vlachos, Stavros: Greek Minister of Religious Affairs, 139
Vlachs (ethnic group): 38–40, 50, 304; role in Greek politics, 274–5

Volksrecht: concept of, 103–4
Voltaire: *Historical and Critical Essay on the Dissent of the Churches of Poland*, 33; influence of, 33; *Notes on Religious Tolerance*, 33
Vosseur, Major Victor: French military mission led by (1882), 197–8
Voulgaris, Dimitris: 114–15, 147, 150, 153; administration of, 154–6; foreign policy of, 159; opposition repression efforts of, 153, 155
Voulgaris, Evgenios: 33; teachings of, 33–4, 41–2
Youlgaris, Yiannis: 359, 376, 415–16, 422
Vrailas-Armenis, P.: Greek Ambassador to UK, 155

Wallachia: Ottoman control over, 15
Weber, Max: 1, 7
Western Greece (region): 62, 72; creation of, 68; provisional administration of, 61
Woodhouse, Chris: 303–4; identification of factional loyalties of rural population, 309
World Economic Forum (2010): attendees of, 400; Global Competitiveness Report (2015–16), 405

Xanthos, Emmanouil: 47; co-founder of Philike Etaireia, 47

Ypsilantis, Alexandros: 53, 59; family of, 49, 52, 62; invasion of Moldavia, 66–7; leader of Philike Etaireia, 50
Ypsilantis, Dimitris: 62, 72; family of, 52, 62; President of Greek Parliament, 63
Ypsilantis, Ioannis: 16
Ypsilantis, Konstantinos: family of, 49
Yugoslavia: 274, 289; Axis Invasion of (1941), 298; Greek relations with, 282

Zachariadis, Nikos: 321, 323–4; General Secretary of KKE, 320, 332
Zaimis, Alexandros: 220; administration of, 281–2
Zaimis, Andreas: 65, 156
Zaimis, Thrasivoulos: 121, 150; administration of, 155
Zakynthians: 30
Zappeion I Programme: 410
Zappeion II Programme: 410
Zervas, Colonel Napoleon: co-founder of EDES, 305
Zionism: 274
Zografos, I.: 210
Zografos, K.: 131
Zoitakis, Georgios: 358
Zolotas, Xenophon: 380
Zorbas, Colonel: leader of Military League, 234